# Transformational Coaching for Effective Leadership

The purpose of this book is to introduce the concept of transformational coaching and to educate professional business coaches or mangers-as-coaches in their organizations on the influential and relevant elements of *Transformational Coaching for Effective Leadership* designed for coaching individuals, teams, and businesses or applying such elements in any level of organization development intervention, either toward individuals, teams, groups, departments, or the organization itself.

Given the power and long-lasting influence of transformational coaching, it also could be beneficial to professionals in the _ elds of human resource development (HRD), workplace learning and performance (WLP), human performance enhancement (HPE), and, overall, in the domain of workforce education and development (WFED).

This book will start by reviewing the background and presence of transformational coaching in businesses and organizations, along with the general concepts, perceptions, and understanding of coaching. _ is book will examine the uses of transformational coaching in management and leadership development, human resource development for talent development and retention, and for developing managerial coaching skills and competencies. Additionally, this book will review the presence and use of transformational coaching concepts, theories, and practices, including transformational learning for human resources (HR) and HRD professionals to influence a workforce's attitude, behavior, and productivity.

Features

- Builds individuals' self-awareness, self-realization, and self-confidence
- Offers personal and professional development
- Teaches the concept of transformational learning and its use in transformational coaching
- Teaches rituals, skills, and strategies for individuals and teams to increase their productivity
- Offers an approach to building healthy and strong relationships with oneself and others
- Includes change management strategies for redirecting poor job performance
- Helps readers implement effective transformational coaching practices by offering many tools, such as forms, checklists, and worksheets

# Transformational Coaching for Effective Leadership

## Implementing Sustainable Change Through Shifting Paradigms

Behnam Bakhshandeh
William J. Rothwell
Sohel M. Imroz
with
Farhan Sadique

A PRODUCTIVITY PRESS BOOK

First published 2023
by Routledge
605 Third Avenue, New York, NY 10158

and by Routledge
4 Park Square, Milton Park, Abingdon, Oxon, OX14 4RN

*Routledge is an imprint of the Taylor & Francis Group, an informa business*



ISBN: 978-1-032-30238-6 (hbk)
ISBN: 978-1-032-30237-9 (pbk)
ISBN: 978-1-003-30407-4 (ebk)

DOI: 10.4324/9781003304074

Typeset in Garamond
by Apex CoVantage, LLC

**Behnam Bakhshandeh**

I love to dedicate this book of transformation to all individuals, teams, groups, businesses, and organizations who trusted me with their personal and professional development and growth through the last three decades. I am inspired by your commitment to your growth and to removing obstacles in the way of your development, personally and professionally. Your trust means the world to me.

**William J. Rothwell**

I dedicate this book to my wife *Marcelina*, our daughter *Candice*, our son *Froilan*, our grandsons *Aden* and *Gabriel*, and our granddaughters *Freya* and *Lina*.

**Sohel M. Imroz**

I would like to dedicate this book to my late father, Mdabu Waheed, who has always encouraged me and supported my work.

# Contents

## PART V DEVELOPING EMOTIONAL INTELLIGENCE, ASSERTIVENESS, RESILIENCE, AND POWER OF INQUIRY FOR SHIFTING PARADIGMS IN LEADERSHIP

# Preface

Welcome to the *Transformational Coaching for Effective Leadership: Implementing Sustainable Change Through Shifting Paradigms.*

The concept of coaching has grown to be highly popular. Many individuals find themselves in a position that needs a helping hand; in their personal lives as managers, they find themselves thrust into the positions of offering advice to their people at work. In today's professional coaching industry, there is a common understanding among the public that professional coaching is one process available for human development and enhanced learning that entails structured and intentional interactions using proven models, methodologies, and strategies with tools and techniques to bring individuals, teams, and organizations to their desired outcomes. Transformational coaching is one approach that assists individuals, teams, and organizations in inventing and implementing sustainable changes.

It is fascinating when you learn of your mental capacity to shift your thinking by shifting your paradigm. It is proven that *thinking* is one of the crucial elements that distinguishes a human from other species on the planet. It affords you the ability to shift this thinking paradigm and redirect your power and capacity to convey your minds to new commitments and interests in life.

In all human interactions there are always two sides to the connection. Also, relationships are built with people, and organizations are formed by individuals who form teams, groups, and departments. Without self-aware, self-managing, motivated, and competent individuals, either as employees or managers, no organization will survive the ineffectiveness that causes insufficient performance and low productivity, and that ultimately forces an organization to close or face a high turnover. Transformational coaching can be a valuable part of implementing sustainable changes through processes of organization development interventions in individuals, teams, departments, and organizations.

In this book, we offer the application of transformational coaching from the perspectives of philosophy, psychology, sociology, ontology, mindfulness, and management, which touches on elements of learning theories, human learning development, plus varieties of methods, tools, and techniques that support the transformational coaches in their undertaking of providing coaching for their participants in all levels of personal or professional interventions.

## The Purpose of the Book

This book offers comprehensive elements and methodologies, tools, and approaches to transformational coaching. While many approaches to coaching, in general, and transformational coaching, in particular, could assist a coach in facilitating coaching for improvement, the authors of this book favor a mixture of proven methodologies and informative, theoretical, and conceptual approaches to transformational coaching geared toward guiding and assisting participants identify the areas of ineffectiveness they need to improve in their personal and professional interactions, including relationships, performance, and productivity.

## The Target Audience for the Book

This book provides a comprehensive, detailed approach to implementing a transformational coaching effort for professional coaches who either a) work as internal coaches for organizations' human resources (HR) or human resource development (HRD) departments as internal change agents, or b) work as independent coaches and consultants providing their services as external change agents.

This book is written for those who seek to improve their self-awareness and increase the level of effectiveness in their relationships, performance, and productivity, in both personal and professional areas.

## The Organization of the Book

This book is pedagogically oriented, providing theories and methodologies, providing practices and tools, and guiding individuals and teams to increase their performance and productivity. Its content is meant for transformational coaches, high-performance coaches, managers-as-coaches, or professional life coaches.

Examined in more detail, the book consists of a **Preface** to summarize the book, **Acknowledgments** to thank contributors, an **Advance Organizer** to help readers assess which chapters they may wish to focus on, and a summary of the **Authors' Biosketches**.

The book is organized into six major parts. The first part sets the context and is titled **Presence of Transformational Coaching, Concept and History**. It comprises three chapters: Chapter 1, The World of Transformation; Chapter 2, Transformational Coaching Concept, History, Principles, and Use; and Chapter 3, Transformational Learning in Transformational Coaching.

The second part is called **Application of Transformational Coaching in Elements of OD**. It comprises three chapters: Chapter 4, Transformational Coaching and Organization Development; Chapter 5, Transformational Coaching and High Performance; and Chapter 6, Transformational Coaching and Talent Development.

The third part, **Transformational Coaching Theories, Methodologies, and Transformational Coaches.** It comprises four chapters: Chapter 7, Contributions to Implementation of Transformational Coaching; Chapter 8, Transformational Coaching Integration Model; Chapter 9, Transformational Coaching Methodologies; and Chapter 10, Transformational Coach.

The fourth part is called **Transformational Coaching Structure, Communication, and Effectiveness.** It comprises three chapters: Chapter 11, "Workable Structure for Transformational Coaching; Chapter 12, Effective Communication and Active Listening Caused by Transformational Coaching; and Chapter 13, Personal Effectiveness.

The fifth part is **Developing Emotional Intelligence, Assertiveness, Resilience, and Power of Inquiry for Shifting Paradigms in Leadership**. It comprises three chapters: Chapter 14, Emotional Intelligence Competencies and Effective Leadership Paradigm; Chapter 15, Developing Assertiveness and Resilience; and Chapter 16, Opening Powerful Inquiries.

The sixth and final part of the book is called **Assessment, Feedback, and Self-Evaluation**. It comprises three chapters: Chapter 17, Assessment and Feedback; Chapter 18, How to Use What You Learned; and Chapter 19, Transformational Coaches' Self-Reflection and Self-Evaluation through Self-Rating.

An **Appendix** reviews sources for education and implementations that will take readers to additional places that can broaden and deepen their understanding of transformational coaching.

# Acknowledgments


**Behnam Bakhshandeh**

I would like to express my gratitude to Dr. William J. Rothwell for his extensive knowledge of workforce education (WFED), organization development (OD), workplace learning and performance (WLP) and all related fields, and for his contributions to my academic and publication growth and advancement.

Also, thanks to Dr. Sohel Imroz for his partnership and willingness to play in the game of conveying knowledge and making a difference. I want to say thank you to my life partner, Cindy Gillen Klink, for her patience and support of my work for making a difference.

**William J. Rothwell**

I want to thank my wife *Marcelina* for her support. Thanks also go to our daughter, *Candice*, our son, *Froilan*, our grandsons, *Aden* and *Gabriel*, and our granddaughters, *Freya* and *Lina*.

**Sohel M. Imroz**

I sincerely acknowledge and appreciate my wife Bijoly's sacrifices throughout this journey. Without her, this project would have been impossible.

All authors like to express their special gratitude to Mr. Farhan Sadique for his chapter contribution to this book and his masterful work in compiling the Appendix of Resources at the end of this book.

**Behnam Bakhshandeh**
*Greenfield Township, Pennsylvania*
*November 2022*
**William J. Rothwell**
*State College, Pennsylvania*
*November 2022*
**Sohel M. Imroz**
*Port Orange, Florida*
*November 2022*
With . . .
**Farhan Sadique**
*State College, Pennsylvania*
*November 2022*

# Advance Organizer

Complete the following Organizer before you read the book. Use it as a diagnostic tool to help you assess what you most want to know about transformational coaching—and where you can find it in this book *fast*.

## The Organizer

### *Directions*

Read each item in the following Organizer. Spend about ten minutes on the Organizer. Be honest! Think of transformational coaching as you would like to practice it for yourself and to contribute to others' improvement in all aspects of life, personally and professionally. Then indicate what topics related to transformational coaching you would like to learn more about to develop yourself professionally. For each item in the center column, indicate ***Y* (for Yes)**, ***N/A* (for Not Applicable)**, or ***N* (for No)** in the left column in response to whether you would like to develop yourself. When you finish, score and interpret the results using the instructions appearing at the end of the Organizer. Then be prepared to share your responses with others you know to help you think about what you most want to learn about transformational coaching. To learn more about an item, refer to the number in the right column to find the chapter in which the subject is discussed.

| *I Would Like to Develop Myself To:* | | | | | |
|---|---|---|---|---|---|
| # | *Mark Your Answers* | | | *The Area of Knowledge, Understanding, and Development* | *Book Chapter in Which the Topic Is Covered* |
| | *Y* | *N/A* | *N* | | |
| 1 | | | | Understanding the concept transformational; what it is, how it works, and what is at work during the implementation of coaching. | One |
| 2 | | | | Transformational coaching and its place in organization development and change intervention, including the concept, history, core principles, and ethics of transformational coaching. | Two |
| 3 | | | | Principles and phases of transformative learning theory, plus its application in leadership development, including benefits and disadvantages. | Three |

(*Continued*)

| *I Would Like to Develop Myself To:* | | | | | |
|---|---|---|---|---|---|
| *#* | *Mark Your Answers* | | | *The Area of Knowledge, Understanding, and Development* | *Book Chapter in Which the Topic Is Covered* |
| | *Y* | *N/A* | *N* | | |
| 4 | | | | Relationship among transformational change and transformational coaching and organization development and application of transformational coaching in organization development. | Four |
| 5 | | | | Distinguishing among performance, high performance, and a high-performance workplace (HPW), and the role of transformational coaching in achieving high performance. | Five |
| 6 | | | | The role, use, and importance of transformational coaching for talent development. | Six |
| 7 | | | | Brief explanations and descriptions of some of the most used theories, practices, and approaches by coaches who practice transformational coaching. | Seven |
| 8 | | | | What is a coaching model? And what is the Transformational Coaching Integration Model? | Eight |
| 9 | | | | The purpose of transformational coaching and participants' expectations of transformational coaching, including what transformational coaches must offer. | Nine |
| 10 | | | | Mindset, principles, knowledge, skills, and competencies of transformational coaches, including their presence and agility. | Ten |
| 11 | | | | Transformational coaching structure and effectiveness in coaching engagement, rapport, and workability. | Eleven |
| 12 | | | | Barriers to transformational coaching, and role of inner chatter, effective communication, and active listening in transformational coaching effectiveness. | Twelve |
| 13 | | | | How we realize the way we relate to ourselves, to others, at work, and in the world we have created around us. | Thirteen |
| 14 | | | | Defining emotional intelligence, paradigms, paradigm shifts, and the role of emotional intelligence in paradigm shifts and effective leadership. | Fourteen |

| I Would Like to Develop Myself To: | | | | | |
|---|---|---|---|---|---|
| # | *Mark Your Answers* | | | *The Area of Knowledge, Understanding, and Development* | *Book Chapter in Which the Topic Is Covered* |
| | *Y* | *N/A* | *N* | | |
| 15 | | | | What is assertiveness and assertive behavior? Developing assertiveness and resilience through transformational coaching. | Fifteen |
| 16 | | | | Characteristics of empowering questions, how to ask empowering questions and turn inquiries to action plans. | Sixteen |
| 17 | | | | The importance of assessment and feedback in transformational coaching, including steps in how to carry them out. | Seventeen |
| 18 | | | | How can readers utilize what they learned, and where and with whom can they use what they learned? | Eighteen |
| 19 | | | | Transformational coaches' opportunity for self-reflection and self-evaluation through self-rating systems. | Nineteen |
| Total | | | | | |

## Scoring and Interpreting the Organizer

Give yourself *1 point for each Y* and a *0 for each N or N/A* listed in the Organizer. Total the points from the *Y* column and place the sum in the line opposite the word **Total**. Then interpret your score:

### SCORE

***16–14 points*** = Congratulations! This book is just what you need. Read the chapters you marked *Y*.

***13–11 points*** = You have great skills in transformational coaching already, but you also have areas where you could develop professionally. Read those chapters marked *Y*.

***10–8 points*** = You have skills in transformational coaching, but you could still benefit from building skills in selected areas.

***7–0 points*** = You believe you need little development in transformational coaching. Ask others—such as mentors—to see if they agree.

# About the Authors

**Behnam Bakhshandeh, PhD, MPS**

Behnam's formal education includes a PhD in workforce education and development (WFED) with a concentration on organization development (OD) and human resource development (HRD) from the Pennsylvania State University; a master's degree in professional studies in organization development and change (OD&C) from the Pennsylvania State University, World Campus; and a bachelor's degree in psychology from the University of Phoenix.

He is also the founder and president of Primeco Education, Inc. (www.PrimecoEducation.com), a coaching and consulting company working with individuals, teams, and organizations on their personal and professional development since 1993. He has authored and published four books in the personal and professional development industry. His last two books on the genre of OD are *High-Performance Coaching for Managers* (Routledge, Taylor & Francis Group, 2022) and *Organization Development Interventions* (Routledge, Taylor & Francis Group, 2021). The other two titles are *Anatomy of Upset; Restoring Harmony* (Primeco Education, 2015) and *Conspiracy for Greatness; Mastery of Love Within* (Primeco Education, 2009). Besides these books, he has designed and facilitated 17 coaching modules for individuals, couples, the public, teams, and organizations; nine audio/video workshops; 16 articles on personal and professional development topics; and 21 seminars and workshops.

He is an accomplished business manager known widely as a dynamic writer, speaker, personal and professional development coach, and trainer. He produces extraordinary results in record time by implementing his skills as a passionate, visionary leader. Behnam brings his broad experience and successful track record to each project, whether it involves personal development, implementing customer-focused programs, integrating technologies, redesigning operational core processes, or delivering strategic initiatives.

Before designing Primeco Education technology, Behnam led educational programs and later managed operations for a global education organization based in two major US cities. During those seven years, Behnam worked personally with tens of thousands of participants. In addition, he was accountable for expanding customer participation, training program leaders, increasing sales, and improving the finance department's efficiency and management of the overall operations for the staff and their team of over 400 volunteers, who served an annual client base of over 10,000.

Behnam designed the Primeco Education technology in 2001. Since then, he and his team members have helped countless businesses and individuals achieve their goals and transform their thinking. His proven methodology and approach are based on his extensive experience in business and human relations. Behnam enjoyed expanding into psychology as an addition to his already strong background in philosophy and ontology. He particularly enjoyed and was inspired by applicative inquiry, positive psychology, and the work of many psychologists who used the humanistic psychology approach for empowering and treating their patients. Behnam finds these two psychological approaches very similar to his own work, methodology, and approaches.

He can be reached by email at Behnam@PrimecoEducation.com and by phone at 760–518–9804. His office is at 27 N. Main Street Suite 202, Carbondale, PA 18407. See his website at www.primecoeducation.com, his videos on YouTube, and his wiki site at www.youtube.com/user/BehnamBakhshandeh/videos.

**William J. Rothwell, PhD, SPHR, SHRM-SCP, RODC, CPTD Fellow**

Dr. Rothwell is a distinguished professor at The Pennsylvania State University. He founded an online master of professional studies in organization development (OD) and change on Penn State's World Campus (see www.worldcampus.psu.edu/degrees-and-certificates/organization-development-change-masters/overview). He has also chaired over 108 PhD committees on OD and related topics in the Workforce Education and Development Program, Department of Learning and Performance Systems, College of Education, the University Park campus of Penn State. See https://ed.psu.edu/academics/departments/department-learning-and-performance-systems/workforce-education-and-development.

For nearly 15 years he worked as an internal consultant in government and then in a multinational company before he arrived as a tenured professor at Penn State in 1993. As an external consultant, his clients have included Motorola University China, Ford, General Motors, AARP, and many other organizations. He is best known for applying OD to succession planning and talent management, and his book *Effective Succession Planning*, 5th ed., has been a foundation for succession programs in Europe, Asia, Africa, Latin America, and the Middle East. He has visited China 83 times since 1993, Singapore 32 times, and every Asian country numerous times. Google Scholar metrics reveal that Dr. Rothwell's publications have been cited over 10,000 times to date and include over 154 books, 300 articles, 198 book chapters, and 2,107 presentations. In 2012, he earned the Distinguished Contribution to Workplace Learning and Performance Award by the American Society for Training and Development (now called the Association for Talent Development, or ATD). In 2004, he was given Penn State University's Graduate Faculty Teaching Award, a single award given annually to the best graduate faculty member on Penn State's 24 campuses. He was named a distinguished professor at Penn State University in 2022. Also, in 2022, he was given Penn State's Global Lifetime Achievement Award, a top university honor for working internationally and for embodying the best spirit of the university abroad. Additionally, he was named a Lifetime Achievement Award winner in 2022 by the Organization Development Network (see the award criteria here: www.odnetwork.org/page/LifetimeAchievement?).

Among Dr. Rothwell's recent books are *Rethinking Diversity, Equity and Inclusion: A Step-by-Step Guide to Facilitating Change* (Routledge, 2022); *Organization Development Interventions: Executing Effective Organizational Change* (Routledge, 2021); *Virtual Coaching to Improve Group Relationships: Process Consultation Reimagined* (Routledge, 2021); *Adult Learning Basics* (ATD Press, 2020); *Increasing Learning and Development's Impact Through Accreditation* (Palgrave, 2020);

*The Essential Human Resource (HR) Guide for Small Businesses and Startups* (Society for Human Resource Management, 2020); *Innovation Leadership* (Routledge, 2018); *Improving Human Performance*, 3rd ed. (Routledge, 2018); *Evaluating Organization Development: How to Ensure and Sustain the Successful Transformation* (CRC Press, 2017); *Marketing Organization Development Consulting: A How-To Guide for OD Consultants* (CRC Press, 2017); *Assessment and Diagnosis for Organization Development: Powerful Tools and Perspectives for the OD Practitioner* (CRC Press, 2017); *Organization Development in Practice* (ODNetwork, 2016); *Practicing Organization Development*, 4th ed. (Wiley, 2015); *Effective Succession Planning*, 5th ed. (AMACOM, 2015); *The Competency Toolkit*, 2 vols., 2nd ed. (HRD Press, 2015); *Beyond Training and Development*, 3rd ed. (HRD Press, 2015); *The Leader's Daily Role in Talent Management* (McGraw-Hill, 2015); and *Organization Development Fundamentals* (ATD, 2015).

Dr. Rothwell earned his PhD from the University of Illinois at Urbana-Champaign with a specialization in human resource development and organization development, his master of arts in business administration (MABA) with a specialization in human resource management at Sangamon State University (now called the University of Illinois at Springfield), his master of arts in English from the University of Illinois at Urbana-Champaign, and his bachelor of arts in English with high honors and department honors from Illinois State University. He was also awarded an honorary doctor of business administration (DBA) degree from the Alliance International University. He bears lifetime accreditation as a senior professional in human resources (SPRH) and accreditation as a Society for Human Resource Management Senior Certified Professional (SHRM-SCP). He is a certified professional in talent development fellow (CPTD Fellow) and a registered organization development consultant (RODC). Finally, he took ten graduate classes in insurance and earned the designation as a fellow of the Life Management Institute (FLMI) by the Life Office Management Association (LOMA).

He can be reached by email at WJRothwell@yahoo.com or by phone at 814–863–2581. He is at 310B Keller Building, University Park, PA 16803. See his website at www.rothwellandassociates.com, his videos on YouTube, and his wiki site at https://en.wikipedia.org/wiki/William_J._Rothwell.

**Sohel, M. Imroz, PhD**

Dr. Imroz is Assistant Professor of HR at the David O'Maley College of Business, Embry-Riddle Aeronautical University, in Daytona Beach, Florida. He received PhD in workforce education and development from Penn State University. Before his academic career, he had almost 20 years of professional experience in HR and IT. He is interested in two broad research areas: human resources/organization development (HR/OD) and IT service management (ITSM). In HR/OD, he has completed many projects and conducted research on leadership development, competency model, social network analysis, and team building. He is also interested in topics such as knowledge management, talent management and succession planning, employee engagement and retention, and data analytics in HR. In ITSM, his past projects include various ITIL processes (e.g., request fulfillment, incident, problem, change, and asset management), information security risk management, and professional online communities. Dr. Imroz also holds SHRM-SCP, SHRM Inclusive Workplace Culture Specialty, and ITIL certifications. His most recent book is *Organization Development Interventions: Executing Effective Organizational Change* (Routledge, 2021).

**Contributor:**

**Farhan Sadique, MPS**, is a PhD candidate and recognized student leader in the Learning and Performance System Department at Pennsylvania State University. Farhan served as an instructor and guest lecturer in various online courses for Penn State. In addition, he has years of working experience in management and training employees, where he successfully trained and supported multiple employees' career development. He has co-authored multiple peer-reviewed scholarly journal articles, book chapters, and newsletters; and presented in national and international conferences.

He is working on multiple projects, including an open-source innovation lab for organization development; a state-granted research program on evaluation capacity building of extension educators; transformational coaching methodologies; job satisfaction in stressful working environments for nurses, air-traffic controllers, flight safety trainers, and retail workforce development. Besides pursuing his PhD, he is also leading multiple student and professional organizations.

# PRESENCE OF TRANSFORMATIONAL COACHING, CONCEPT AND HISTORY

# I

This book introduces transformational coaching (TC) and educates professional business coaches or managers-as-coaches in their undertaking of the process of transformational coaching with individuals, teams, groups, at any level of an organization development (OD) intervention. Therefore, to begin, the primary purpose of Part I is to educate readers on the concept and history of transformation, transformational coaching, and transformational learning.

## Chapter 1. The World of Transformation

Chapter 1 covers the understanding of the concept transformational; what it is, how it works, and what is at work during the implementation of coaching.

## Chapter 2. Transformational Coaching Concept, History, Principles, and Use

Chapter 2 discusses transformational coaching and its place in organization development and change intervention, including the concept, history, core principles, and ethics of transformational coaching.

## Chapter 3. Transformational Learning in Transformational Coaching

Principles and phases of transformative learning theory, plus its application in leadership development, including benefits and disadvantages of it, are covered in Chapter 3.

DOI: 10.4324/9781003304074-1

# Chapter 1

# The World of Transformation

Behnam Bakhshandeh

## Overview

The purpose of this book is to introduce the concept of transformational coaching (TC) and to educate professional business coaches or mangers-as-coaches in their organizations on the influential and relevant elements of *Transformational Coaching for Effective Leadership* designed for coaching individuals, teams, businesses or applying such elements in any level of organization development (OD) intervention, whether focused on individuals, teams, departments, or the organization itself.

Given the power and long-lasting influence of transformational coaching, it also could be beneficial to professionals in human resource development (HRD), workplace learning and performance (WLP), human performance enhancement (HPE) and, overall, in the domain of workforce education and development (WFED) and human resource management (HRM).

In the last two or three decades, there has been fast growth of individuals, groups, and organizational coaching in industries and coaching as an effective instrument to increase productivity and talent retention and decrease employee turnover. Understanding the concept of coaching and transformational coaching, what it is, how it works, and what is at work during the implementation of coaching will assist executives and business owners to know how transformational coaching will help them and contribute to their professional growth.

This book will start by reviewing the background and presence of transformational coaching in organizations along with the general concepts of coaching. This book will examine the uses of transformational coaching in management and leadership development, human resource development for talent development and retention, and for developing managerial coaching skills and competencies. Additionally, this book will review the use of transformational coaching concepts, theories, and practices, including transformational learning for HR and HRD professionals to influence the attitude, behavior, and productivity of an organization's workforce.

To review transformational coaching and understand its models for affecting productivity and professional growth in all levels of management, business operations, individual and team performance and general productivity, we shall start from the general understanding of transformation and its presence in human culture.

DOI: 10.4324/9781003304074-2

**This chapter will cover these distinctions:**

- Definition of transformation
- Common metaphor for transformation
- Descriptions of personal transformation
- Essentials for personal transformation
- Different takes on transformation from:
- Philosophy
- Psychology
- Sociology
- Ontology
- Mindfulness
- Transformation and productivity

## Some Definitions and Descriptions for Transformation

To ensure understanding and provide clarity of the main terminology (transformation) in this book, we underline several definitions and distinctions of *transformation.*

### *Transformation*

According to *Merriam-Webster* (2020b), *transformation* can be defined in different categories, such as:

- The operation of changing (as by rotation or mapping) one configuration or expression into another under a mathematical rule *especially*: a change of variables or coordinates in which a function of new variables or coordinates is substituted for each original variable or coordinate
- The formula that affects a transformation

#### *Noun*

- A thorough or dramatic change in form or appearance
- A metamorphosis during the life cycle of an animal

#### *Physics*

- The induced or spontaneous change of one element into another by a nuclear process

*Cambridge English Dictionary* (2020) defines *transformation* as:

- A complete change in the appearance or character of something or someone, especially so that thing or person is improved (n.p.)

*Dictionary.com* (2022) defines *transformation* in several ways:

***Noun***

- The act or process of transforming
- The state of being transformed
- Change in form, appearance, nature, or character

***Theater***

- A seemingly miraculous change in the appearance of scenery or actors because of the audience

***Logic***

- Also called **transform**; one of a set of algebraic formulas used to express the relations between elements, sets, etc., that form parts of a system

***Mathematics***

- The act, process, or result of transforming or mapping
- Function

***Linguistics***

- Transformational rule
- The process by which deep structures are converted into surface structures using transformational rules

***Genetics***

- Transferring genetic material from one cell to another resulting in a genetic change in the recipient cell

### *A Scientific Definition for Transformation*

> The genetic alteration of a bacteria cell by the introduction of DNA from another cell or from a virus. Plasmids, which contain extrachromosomal DNA, are used to transform bacteria in recombinant DNA research.
>
> (Dictionary.com 2022)

## A Common Metaphor for Transformation

A common metaphor for transformation is that of a tiny, defenseless, not very attractive caterpillar evolving into a beautiful butterfly that flies around, and that we all enjoy observing (see Figure 1.1). This is an example of possibilities for any individuals to transform themselves

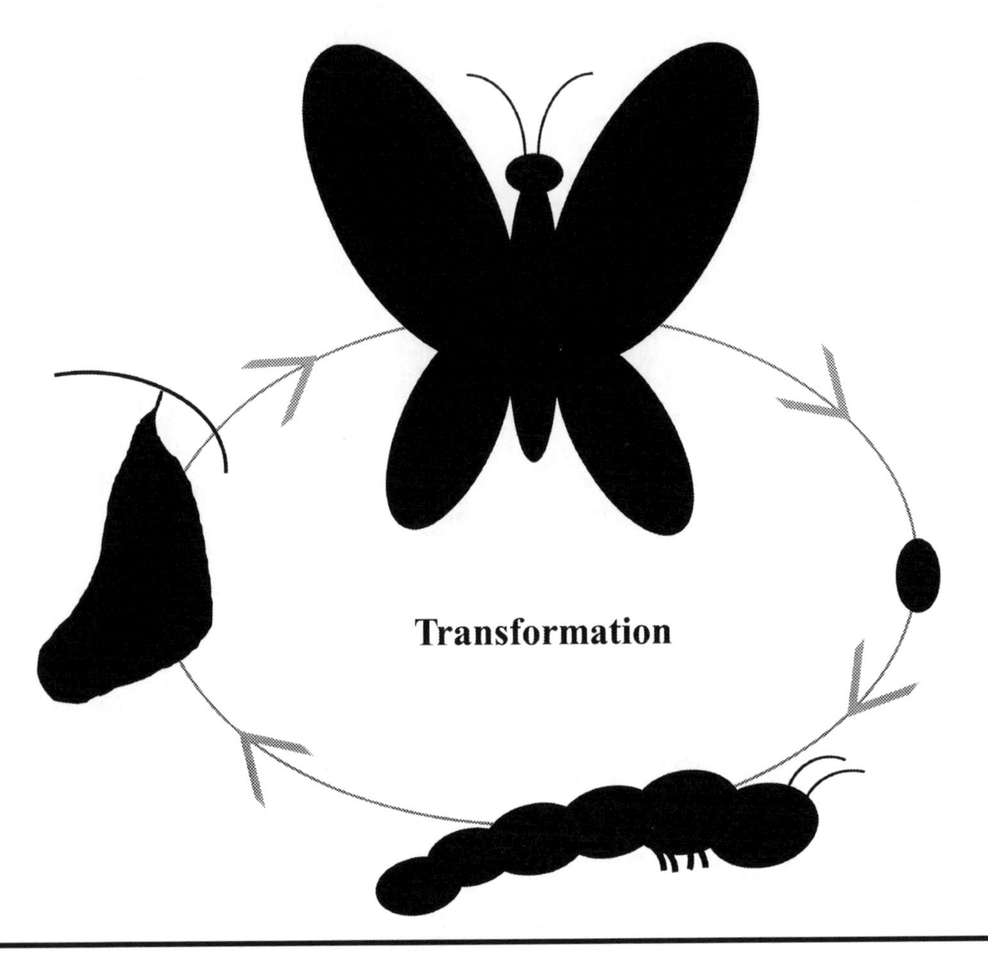


**Figure 1.1 Common Metaphor for Transformation. From an Egg to a Caterpillar, to a Cocoon and a Butterfly.**

*Source:* Author's Original Creation. Copyright 2022 by Behnam Bakhshandeh.

from who they are in any moment to something else they desire or wish to be. However, such transformation is impossible without the commitment, motivation, hard work, and vision for the outcome. Ralph Waldo Emerson once said, "The mind once stretched by a new idea never returns to its original dimensions" (PSCA 2022). The purpose of this book is to explain and educate the readers on how they can use transformational coaching for effective leadership and management to provide opportunities for mindset, behavior, and attitude transformation for workers.

This possibility for transformation brings us to another essential element of transformation among the workforce: the transformation theory in the adult transformative learning theory, which is generally credited to Jack Mezirow. According to Antipas (2019), Mezirow (2009) offers the following description for transformative learning: "Learning that transforms problematic frames of reference to make them more inclusive, discriminating, reflective, open, and emotionally able to change" (22). We will expand on the concept of transformational learning and its related elements in Chapter 3 of this book.

## Personal Transformation

The term *personal transformation* has been used by many coaching professionals or business and organization change consultants. It involves the personal effort to make major alterations into who individuals are for them to become the ideal people they desire to be. This personal transformation might include their looks, weight, hometown, acquiring new skills or profession, working on their relationships, or taking on life challenges such as finances or possible addictions (Bakhshandeh 2009).

"Personal transformation is a dynamic, uniquely individualized process of expanding consciousness whereby individuals become critically aware of old and new self-views and choose to integrate these views into a new self-definition" (Wade 1998, n.p.).

Given that teams, groups, businesses, and organizations are made up of individuals, the effort to provide transformational coaching will be directly relevant to individuals at the first level of transformation, which is personal transformation. However, as we are working on using TC for effective leadership, this book will focus on how personal transformation will cause an increase in performance and eventually increase in productivity. Managers-as-coaches or any other managers providing leadership can learn the elements of transformational coaching so they can become more effective in their managerial duties and leadership qualities, working with individuals, teams, and departments on their communication, teamwork, ethics, leadership, performance, and productivity.

## Essentials for Personal Transformation

For individuals interested in transforming themselves or any elements of their lives, either personally or professionally, in such areas as health, relationships, productivity, performance, careers, addictions, damaging behavior, or unproductive mindset, there are several central requirements to make such a transformation. This way, the personal transformation has a much higher chance to succeed (Bakhshandeh 2015; Bakhshandeh 2009). See Table 1.1.

In all relationships (personal and professional), individuals are forming teams (as a couple), groups (as a family), businesses (family business), and organizations. Personal transformation is the first step and the key factor to a change in the personal and professional aspects of their lives (2015, 2009).

## Different Takes on Transformation

In this part of Chapter 1, we look at meanings, definitions, descriptions, or applications of transformation, including personal transformation and the use of different scientific and educational disciplines, such as philosophy, psychology, sociology, ontology, and mindfulness.

You might wonder what these fields of study have to do with management and effectiveness in working with employees? We would have to reply, everything! However, suppose we can educate ourselves about what transformation is; what personal transformation is; and how people learn, experience, and apply it. In that case, we can implement our coaching approach in much deeper ways and create a long-lasting positive effect on our coaches or employees. As you go through this segment, you will notice how these fields are related to achieving personal and group transformation, even in businesses and organizations.

**Table 1.1 Essentials of Personal Transformation. Author's Original Creation.**

| *Essential for Personal Transformation* | | |
|---|---|---|
| # | *Area* | *Descriptions* |
| 1 | **Want to Change** | They must decide they are serious about the change and desire to change because they have seen the necessity of the change. |
| 2 | **Have a Vision** | They must have a solid vision of their transformation. What is the final picture, the outcome of such transformation? |
| 3 | **Request Support** | They must request and have their close circle of family and friends to support them and to keep them on the changing track. This support includes emotional, behavioral, or practical activities and can be extended to potential co-workers, supervisors, or managers in a professional setting. |
| 4 | **Have External Accountability** | They must have an external accountability partner. This partnership could have a personal coach or executive coach for personal issues or establishing a coaching and mentoring process with their managers-as-coaches for professional issues. |

*Source:* Copyright 2022 by Behnam Bakhshandeh.

## *Philosophy and Transformation*

Under any normal and expected circumstances, as individuals go through life, they get to know themselves as their bodies and their minds, thoughts, senses, emotions, feelings, and the elements of the life they live: their parents, siblings, relationships, and their histories, such as education, career, and their engagement with their communities and society. That is an expected process of someone's life. That knowledge is an ordinary state of being human (The Diamond Approach Online 2021).

The dictionary definitions of transformation do not fit the description or meaning of transformation in philosophy. Applying transformation in philosophy is not someone's change in their form or physical dimensions, but an alteration in what they are experiencing, the possibilities of change in their functioning and individuality, which is their identity from the viewpoint of philosophy (Welsh 2014). This concept of individual transformation can be used by management to raise awareness among their workforce to see possibilities of their altered mindset, which would affect their attitude and behavior.

Welsh (2014) draws a valuable distinction between the two variations of *self.*

> Philosophies such as Nietzsche's, Foucault's, and Merleau-Ponty's pull apart our easy ideas of the "self." When considering a standard idea of self-mastery, I am split between the self who must obey and the self who orders. After all, I am not who I want to be, so this current self needs to change her behavior.
>
> (496)

Anyone pursuing self-mastery who has the desire to become engaged in self-realization and self-mastery can tell you that frequently the *obeying self* is not always ready or willing to *follow* others' leads and orders (Welsh 2014). That is where the concept of personal transformation through personal development can see why and how they resist transformation, especially when it comes down upon them by their superiors or upper managers in businesses and organizations. But "transformation is profound, a fundamental change, altering the very nature of something" (Gass 2012, n.p.).

## *Transformation and Individual Experiences*

From the viewpoint of philosophy, when our body goes through a transformation process, either physically, mentally, or emotionally, we are experiencing something. These experiences are not like observing or hearing something, but they are experiences within you, some experience you feel internally, a subjective experience. These experiences include mind buzzing, a feeling of bodily discomfort, and some forms of mental or physical pain or sensation.

**Two Types of Subjective Experiences:**

1. Individuals are in touch with their inner experiences in different ways. Not everyone experiences the same thing when they are in touch within themselves. There is a whole world of individual experiences, such as visions, emotions, thoughts, notions, feelings, sensations, reactions, and so many other experiences. These mixed experiences would come from someone's subjective experience.
2. The other form of individual or subjective experience is controlled by our thoughts and emotions when we are in a dominating state of mind, such as reacting to someone or something. These are experiences linked to patterns similar to our past experiences or something in our history. These experiences can be generated from our upbringing, our culture or group, gender, race, sexual orientation, or even political affiliations. These experiences also defined our individual subjective experience, maybe in happiness, sadness, frustration, quietness, or reservation.

(The Diamond Approach Online 2021)

Figure 1.2 depicts how individuals going through a process of transformation (from the perspective of philosophy) are transforming their suffering to a mindset of freedom to be with themselves and accept who they are.

Figure 1.3 shows the differences between the theory of transformation and the practice of transformation. Someone who wants to go through a personal transformation to end their suffering and achieve their freedom to be with themselves, others, and life itself needs to link the theory to systematic practices that would guarantee the actual transformation.

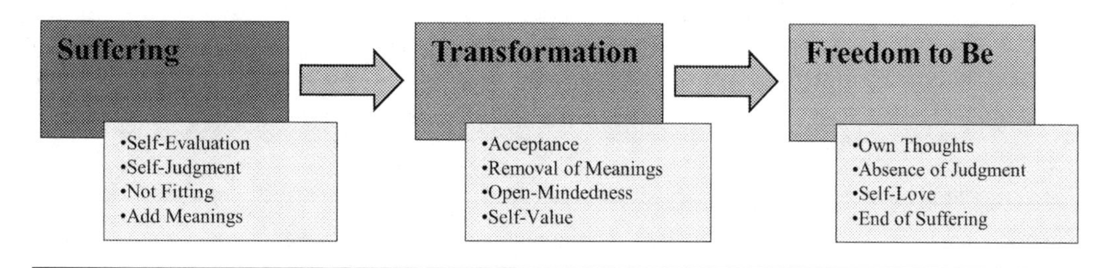


**Figure 1.2 From Suffering to Freedom to Be.**

*Source:* Author's Original Creation. Copyright 2022 by Behnam Bakhshandeh.

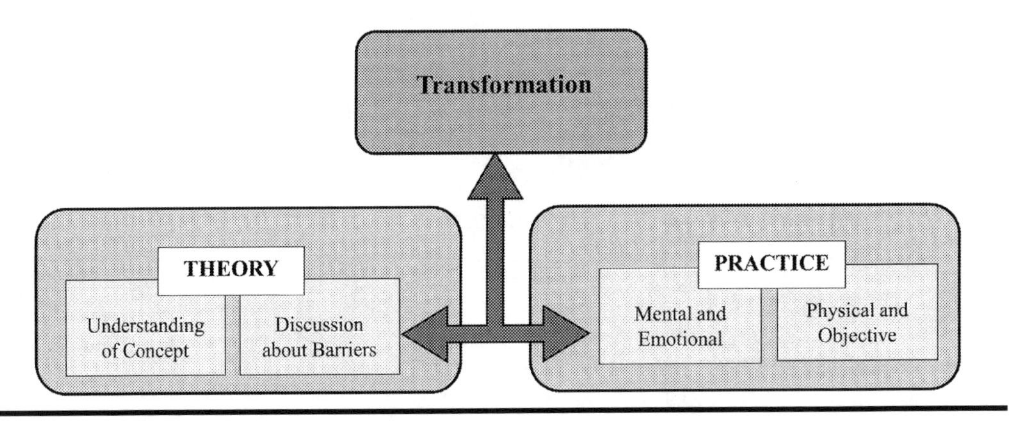


**Figure 1.3 The transformation from Theory to Practice.**

*Source:* Author's Original Creation. Copyright 2022 by Behnam Bakhshandeh.

## *Psychology and Transformation*

In a general understanding, psychology views transformation, or personal transformation, as individuals altering themselves into the people they want to be and living the lives they wish to live. Many people have reported various positive experiences and changes they are crediting to their transformation—mentally, emotionally, and physically. For example, some people want to achieve the feeling of contentment, fulfillment, and peace of mind, while some would reach to transformation for more self-esteem, self-confidence, or self-regulation. Through the field of psychology and at the branch of positive psychology, people find valuable and practical tools and practices for accessing the personal transformation they are looking for.

The positive psychology approach characterizes a psychological viewpoint of transformation transferred away from emphasizing an individual's pathology and dysfunction and more focused on the individual's positive attributes, strengths, and behaviors that promote more of their thriving. According to Lindley and Brooke (2021), by employing a positive psychology approach to achieving personal transformation, we can get our efforts to focus on enhancing the good characteristics of ourselves as a replacement for continuing to highlight what part of us needs to be fixed to become the best version of ourselves.

To become the best version of ourselves, we must literally cut off so many negative effects from our past lives past experiences and let go of many heavy weights we are carrying on our backs every day. We must cut off these negative experiences as much as possible for our transformation to occur and have a positive effect on our life experiences. "Traumatic experiences do not happen for a reason, but shifting your mindset to a growth mindset following adversity has worthwhile outcomes backed by positive psychology" (Lindley and Brooke 2021, n.p.).

### *Remove What Is Not You*

It has been said that people asked Michelangelo, the Italian master artist, genius inventor, and Renaissance sculptor, about his timeless beauty, the sculpture of *David*. "How do you carve the *David*"? He replied, "*David* was there; I just removed and cut off what was not *David*." Using transformational coaching, managers would bring out the best of their employees and give a chance for people to shine the best of themselves and thrive under positive and influential leadership. This story is another metaphor for transformation.

Another application of positive psychology through the application of transformation for altering life's biggest obstacles is what professional psychologists call benefit finding. In benefit finding, individuals facing hardship and difficulty identify the possible advantages or benefits that might arise from going through the difficult situation (Chiba et al. 2016). For example, based on a study conducted by Chiba et al. (2016) on 31 participants in Japan, "People dealing with mental illness were able to name numerous benefits from their experience including growth in relationships, personal growth, discovering values, better self-management, interest in mental health, and finding new roles in society" (142).

### *Redirecting Emotions and Feelings*

We cannot deny that people are relating to their emotions and feelings as a set of real events. According to Linley et al. (2011), in the domain of psychology, emotional representation is efficient in changing personal experiences of horror, fear, and helplessness and transferring them into an opportunity for some oppositional growth. For example, emotional expression can be displayed in different forms, such as applying art, playing music, or writing. It is a common psychological phenomenon whereby people are accustomed to displaying their moods from either bad or good experiences. However, we should not expect people to be happy all of the time. We should be expecting to recuperate from the hardships and difficulties we are experiencing in life (Bisawas-Dieber and Dean 2007).

Regarding the relationship between transformation and psychology and the impact of psychology on personal transformation, Garbarino (2011) mentioned,

> After many years of professional and personal struggle to know things about human nature, human behavior, and human development, I have come to the conclusion that there are not one but three principal paths to knowing: science and humanities, subjective human studies, and soul searching. A complete understanding of human life and the human condition requires all three.
>
> (65)

We collect our psychological memories from so many aspects of our minds, imaginations, and bodily or sensory facets. Figure 1.4 represents some of the elements of our collective memories. These memories directly affect how we relate to others and the world and another decision-making process. Decisions we are making about these memories and experiences directly affect the process of personal transformation (Bakhshandeh 2015).

For almost the last eight decades, the general public has developed a notion for psychology as a single topic—that of working with mental illnesses, in which the science of psychology has advanced well. In addition, the field of psychology knows a good deal about how human mind-related problems develop across someone's life span by genetics, biochemistry, and psychological triggers (Seligman 2002).

## *Sociology and Transformation*

Social change is a notion and theory that many people have taken for granted or are not aware of its impact on society and individuals. Yet, throughout the history of humanity and civilization, no

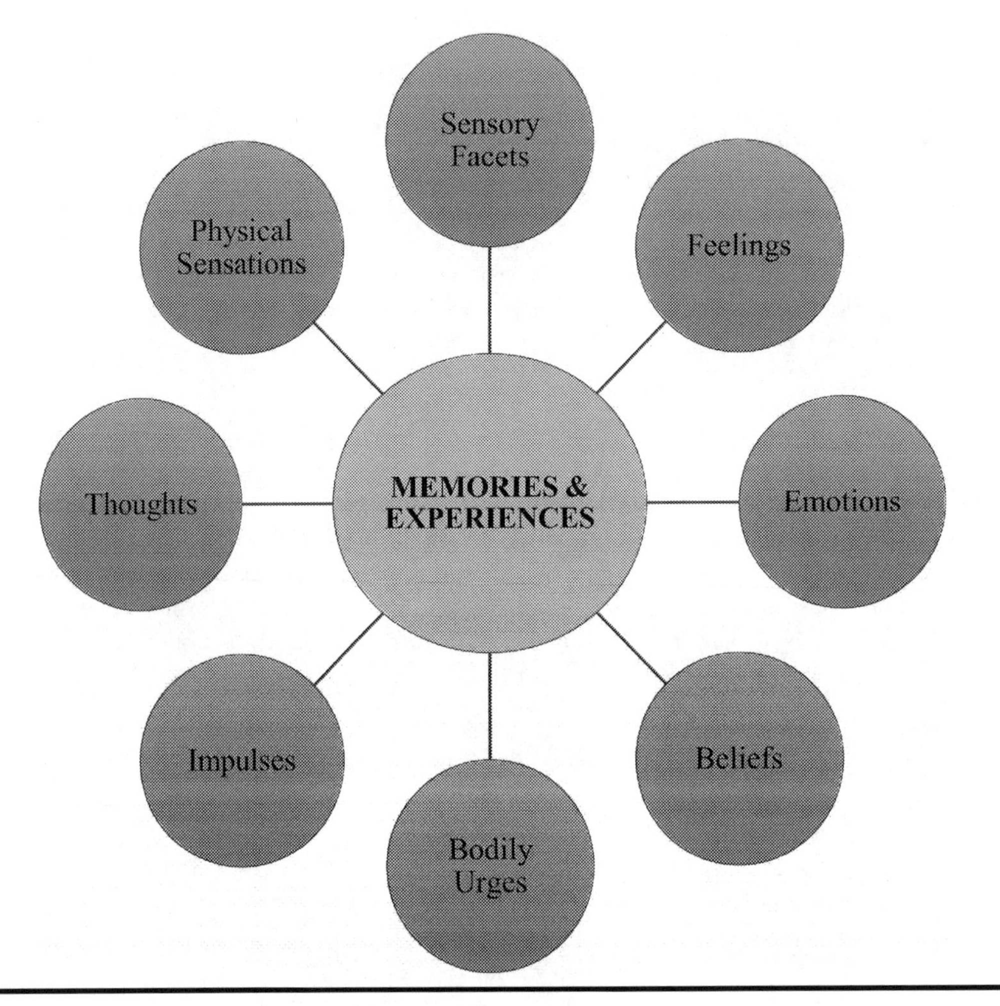


**Figure 1.4 Elements of Building Psychological Memories.**

*Source:* Adapted from Fisher et al. (2021); Bakhshandeh (2015).

society has ever continued to be the same for a long period of time. Change and society's transformation are always taking place.

"Social transformation refers to the process of change in institutionalized relationships, norms, values, and hierarchies over time" (Omondi 2018, n.p.). Social transformation is society's changes due to alterations along with massive changes in science, technology, economic expansion, or even war or political disruptions. Social transformation affects people's connections, communication, interactions, and elements of their lifestyle. Throughout social transformation, an individual goes from an attributed level to an accomplished level (Omondi 2018).

## *Transformation and Its Impact on Society*

Sociologists describe social change as variations or alterations in individuals' interactions and their relationships with others, transforming their cultural and social associations. These transformational changes take place over time, and mostly they have a profound and long-lasting outcome for society. To name a few, we can mention ending slavery, civil rights, desegregation of armed forces, women's voting rights, no discrimination in employment, and LGBTQ rights. Because of these social transformations, individuals have transformed, relationships have altered, organizations have improved, and cultural norms have changed (Dunfey 2019).

> Surrendering to an irresistible inner urging, one day, the caterpillar begins to shed its skin. Revealed within is the hard protective shell that becomes the creature's home, prison and womb for the change to come. This initiates one of nature's miracles—the transformation from an immobile chrysalis whose only defense is camouflage—to a breathtakingly beautiful, winged aviator we call "butterfly."
>
> (Gass 2012, p. 1)

As we mentioned in the preceding segments, the butterfly metaphor is one of the most used and classic models for describing a transformation. Transformation as a process, and personal transformation, in particular, is a profound undertaking because it is a fundamental individual, societal, or organizational change. It means altering or modifying the whole nature of someone or something. A true transformational change could be mutually individual or in groups or societies, and is both fundamental and viable. When someone or something goes through a transformation, they or it rarely go back to the precise shape or form before the transformation (Dunfey 2019).

Many factors influence how society will form and how hand to hand it creates the environment for individuals to develop their experience. Figure 1.5 displays some of the factors that dominate the format of a society.

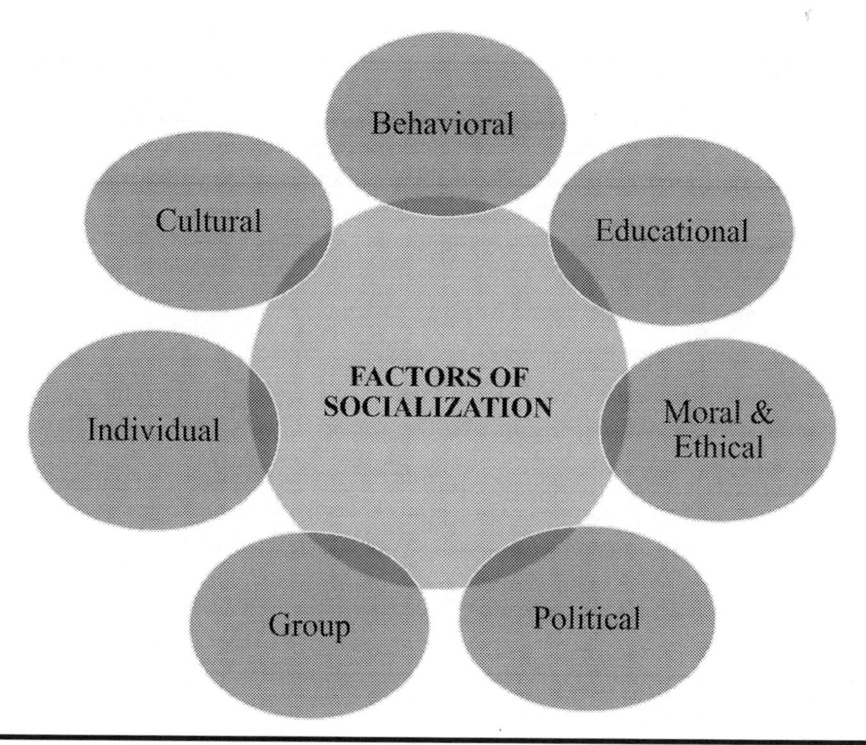


**Figure 1.5 Factors that Dominated Format of Society.**

*Source:* Adapted from Li et al. (2021).

## Ontology and Transformation

*Merriam-Webster* defines ontology as "A branch of metaphysics concerned with the nature and relations of being. Ontology deals with abstract entities. A particular theory about the nature of being or the kinds of things that have existence" (Merriam-Webster 2020a).

*Oxford University Dictionary* defines ontology as "A branch of philosophy that deals with the nature of existence" and "that shows the relationships between all the concepts and categories in a subject area" (Oxford University Dictionary 2020).

Wikipedia (2020) explains ontology as "the philosophical study of the nature of *being, becoming, existence*, or *reality*, as well as the basic categories of being and their relations." Customarily, ontology is recognized as part of philosophy and is identified as metaphysics, dealing with queries pertaining to "what entities exist or can be said to exist, and how such entities can be grouped, related within a hierarchy, and subdivided according to similarities and differences" (Wikipedia 2020).

In the analytic philosophy discipline, *Contemporary Ontology* primarily deals with queries about what things exist and what those things look, feel, and experience (Effingham 2013). Certain philosophers, particularly the Platonic School philosophers, argue for the point that all nouns, even conceptual nouns, describe the existence of individuals. But some philosophers argue for the point that nouns do not constantly describe individuals or entities. For example, using "mind" as an alternative for referring to an individual describes an assortment of "mental occasions" which was or is experienced by an individual (Effingham 2013).

### *Who We Are* Being *Impacting How and What We Are* Doing

We are human *beings*, but all we do is human *doing* most of the time. When we pay attention to how we are, we can see that regardless of our age, gender, nationality, race, culture, or upbringing, we are aware that when others have some upsetting situation or when they are happy, we can identify their state of being even if they are not speaking or explaining their situation. We can recognize resentment, regret, unhappiness, and other ways of being in others. But we can also identify someone interested, engaged, committed, communicative, result-oriented, and capable to lead.

In the book *Being and Nothingness*, Jean-Paul Sartre, the French philosopher and ontologist, explained this phenomenon. "There is no being which is not the being of a certain mode of being, none which cannot be apprehended through the mode of being which manifests being and veils it at the same time" (Sartre 1943, 24–25). They need not do anything, yet we can recognize those characteristics in them (Bakhshandeh 2009).

> State of being is what makes us all do what we do, or even feel what we feel. It makes us interested in what we do, and it allows us to relate to others or take ourselves away from them! It makes us succeed or fail, and it makes us love or hate ourselves and others!
>
> (22)

### Being *as a State of Mind*

I am sure you have said, or you have heard people addressing or describing themselves say, *I am committed*, or *I am a detail-oriented person*, or even *I am a happy person.* In all these simple examples, they have described their state of *Being* without acknowledging the direct recognition of

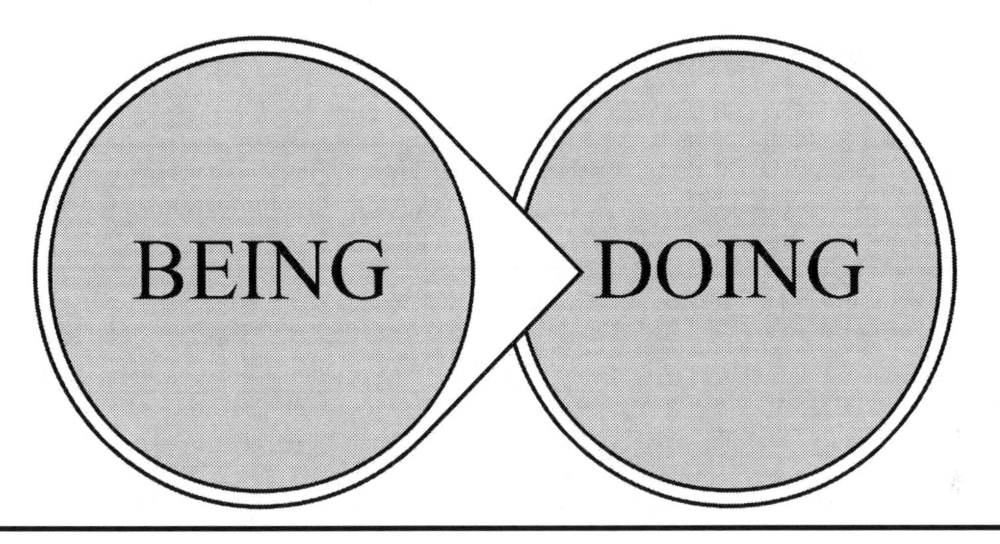


**Figure 1.6 Our Being Determine our Doing.**

*Source:* Author's Original Creation. Copyright 2022 by Behnam Bakhshandeh.

their state of *Mind*, but what they are describing is who they are *Being* with their certain mindset, while they are *Doing* whatever they are doing, at home or at work (Bakhshandeh 2009). When we declare, *I want to change*, or *I want to change something*, we are pointing at wishing to alter the nature of something, or ourselves; therefore, we start *Being* creative. This creativity might manifest itself in changed appearance, location, behavior and attitude, or habits. Therefore, we start being creative about the transformation we would like to see; we become creative, even if we don't know it! We think, plan, design, and even receive coaching (2009). "All creativity with that desire to have impact, and the ownership of that, desire everything. In that sense, conscious creativity, perhaps more than requires an admission of a particular state of mind" (Bain 2015, 2).

## *Knowing Where We Are Emotionally*

People experience their feelings and emotions differently; some individuals are more in tune with their feelings and emotions than others. According to professional psychologists, some individuals feel little emotion, while others are much in tune with their emotions, such as pain, tension, regrets or jealousy, and waves of anger. It is beneficial to know where we are with our emotions and what we are feeling while we are expressing such feelings. We shall know our experience with our bodies, hearts, feelings, minds, thoughts and images we allow in our mind and thoughts. These experiences allow us to know where we are emotionally (Van der Pol 2019).

The transformation of people's patterns in thoughts, mind, and actions are directly related to their emotions and what they feel to allow for the acceptance of transformation. Whether they are feeling something or not feeling, an effective and proper thing to do is to let the whole experience be the way they are or not! The access to an ontological transformation is to let the experience be; that experience will not change and stays with the individuals' minds, thoughts, and bodies. This is the way reality represents itself within us and displays itself, based on what we are experiencing as the reality at that moment, inside us (The Diamond Approach Online 2021).

### *Mindfulness and Transformation*

Another powerful element of people's personal transformation is to become mindful of their life and present. People cannot have an understanding and a deeper appreciation for their present experience when they are continually regretting or thinking about their experience or dreaming and planning for their future opportunities. The mindfulness process and practice illustrate and allow individuals to experience and learn of their experience in the present (Lindley 2021).

Some other benefits of mindfulness besides personal awareness are:

- Practicing mindfulness will give individuals a sense of connection to others (Aspy and Proeve 2017).
- Conducting a mindfulness meditation has shown improvements in individuals' self-evaluation, increased sense of physical self, and perceptiveness (Perridge et al. 2017).
- Practicing mindfulness is related to one's prosocial behavior and doing good deeds (Donald et al. 2019).
- Mindfulness meditation will decrease stress and increase mind and body well-being (Szekeres and Wertheim 2015).

#### *Having Purpose and Directions*

When people transform themselves into purposeful individuals, they are leading their lives more intentionally. They find more positive and uplifting meanings in their lives and for being alive. They regularly ponder on what they can provide for others and what they can contribute to the world around them, their community, their society, and the world (Bakhshandeh 2015).

People who practice purposefulness happen to be more inclined to succeed in what they do. They are passionate about goals and continue on their journey until they realize their objectives (Hill et al. 2016). People with purpose display their sincere commitment to particular life goals, personally or professionally. Their drive behind these goals is visible and present for people around them because they foster consistency in them. As Hill et al. (2016) mentioned, individuals committing to a certain purpose in their lives display more courage and build solid and positive characteristics to accomplish their objectives. Diener et al. (2012) added that purposeful people are happier and are satisfied with who they are and how they live their lives.

Figure 1.7 displays elements of mindfulness that help individuals go through their personal transformation and create relationships with others around them.

## Transformation and Productivity

Many people love to transform their procrastination to timeliness and discipline of time management. They keep talking about how much they don't like the way they fall behind their goals and want to be like people capable of constantly attaining their intentions and concentrating on their goals. Luckily, in this book and its chapters, we cover many theories, models, methods, and practical tools to apply the transformational coaching approach to transfer someone's mindset from procrastination to goal-oriented and time-managing individuals who perform at a higher level and produce more simultaneously than they have spent before.

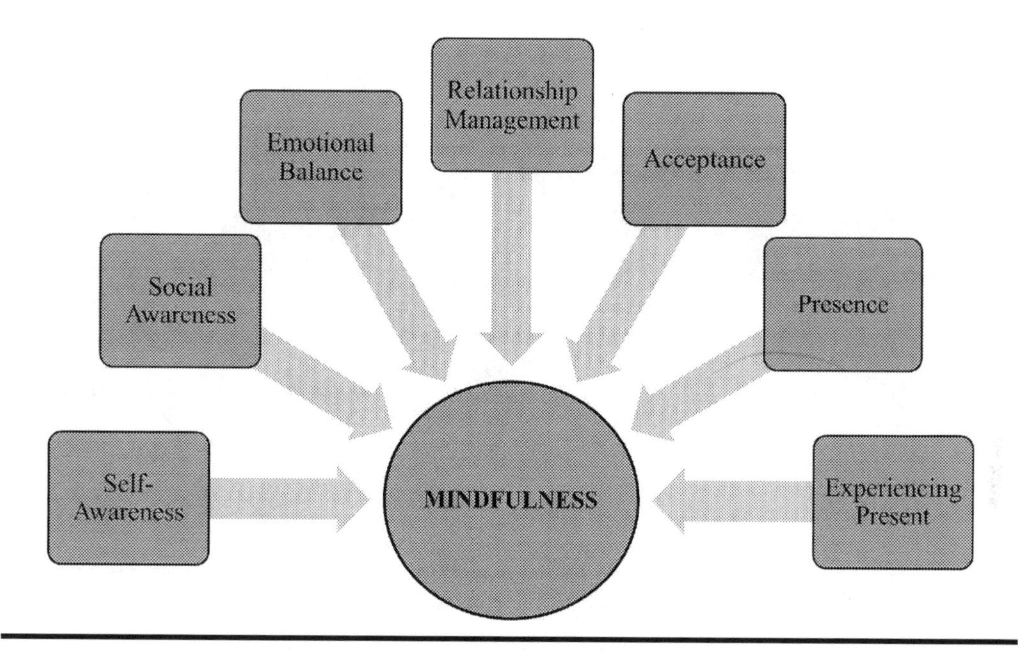


**Figure 1.7 Elements of Mindfulness for Assisting Creation of Individual Transformation.**

*Source:* Author's Original Creation. Copyright 2022 by Behnam Bakhshandeh.

A good indicator of an individual who is productive and constantly progresses in achieving their objectives is that they are practicing elements of personal transformation to realize their strengths and accept their weaknesses so they can understand the source of both and continue to work on improving their strengths and eliminating their weaknesses. As matter of fact, research has proven that people who recognize their strengths and use them to face life's challenges experience superior well-being and feel more personal satisfaction while accomplishing their goals (Linley et al. 2010).

One reason people are casual about their goals and continue procrastinating after attaining these goals is that they are unrelated to their future; they have no vision of how they want to live their lives and what they will accomplish in this lifetime.

By having self-continuity and understanding of who we are and what we would like to accomplish or by having a steady sense of individuality far into our future, we can control our present experiences, control our feelings, manage our emotional reactions, and make the best decisions that will support the future we are designing (Bakhshandeh 2009). This is the process of using transformational coaching for creating and living our future now, not someday, when it is not hard but easy to do! Looking into their future would increase their productivity proactively (Blouin et al. 2017). Without this powerful connection to the future, it would be hard to arrange new strategies, plan the actions, avoid stalling, have productive time, and experience positive well-being (2017).

During research conducted by Blouin et al. (2017), the researchers asked students to try vividly imagining their future, taking time to imagine, writing notes about that future, and going to that future to design what it would be when they got there. They self-improved in their future schoolwork, displayed more self-endurance and became more empathetic, and ultimately less

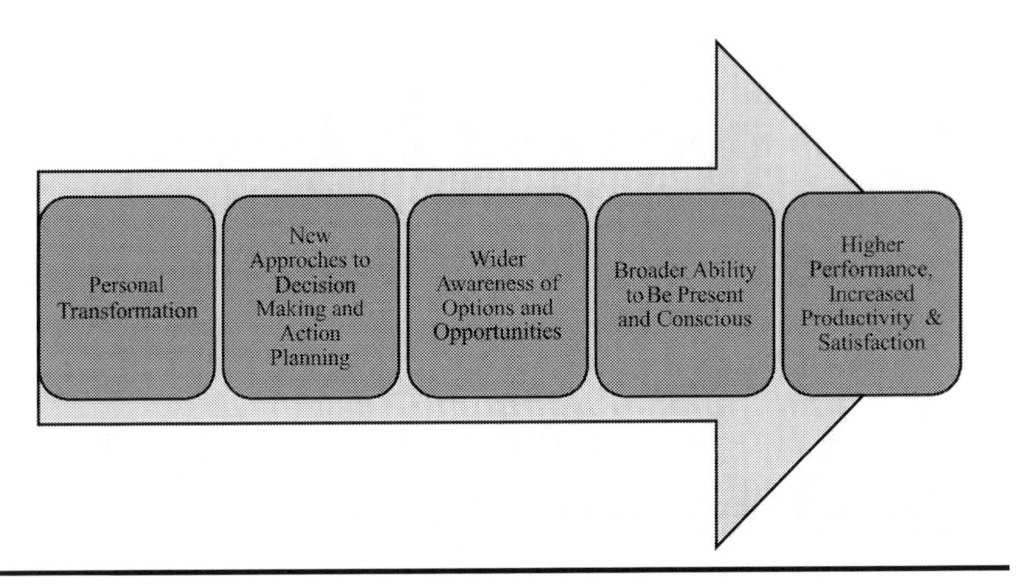


**Figure 1.8 Process of Opportunities and Abilities to Work on Personal Transformation.**

*Source:* Author's Original Creation. Copyright 2022 by Behnam Bakhshandeh.

procrastinating. This would be a great example of using powerful personal transformation elements to increase productivity.

The student participants were also taught mindfulness and how to capture their thoughts as simply thoughts, without adding or subtracting anything to them, and not relating their thoughts to necessary truths (Scent and Boes 2014). During such a process, students recognized that their procrastinations were merely an act of avoiding their undesirable thoughts and feelings and not necessarily avoiding the task itself. By the end, the students were determined to stop their procrastination by connecting to their motivations for accomplishing what they identified as their goals and using their values and principles to get there (2014).

Figure 1.8 shows us how paying attention and investing in personal transformation will produce much better and wider opportunities for individuals, teams, and organizations.

### *Something to Consider*

We need to emphasize this point: In no shape or form, do this book and its authors suggest that managers or a managers-as-coaches need to understand the impact and role of philosophy, psychology, ontology, sociology, mindfulness, and other body, mind, and spirit elements of personal growth and transformation. However, a little background and understanding of how these scientific fields influence your employee's mindset, behavior, and attitude are helpful to understand how to coach them to higher performance, better productivity, and more effective teamwork.

## Key Takeaways

The following are important distinctions and key takeaways from this chapter. These are elements of this chapter to remember and use while delivering transformational coaching for individuals, teams, groups, or organizations. As you are reading these key elements, you will notice the relevancy of these points to implementing transformational coaching and causing individual and group transformation, which will be discussed in other chapters of this book.

1. To utilize the principles of transformation in our lives, we shall start by understanding that intending to prevent undesirable thoughts and uncomfortable feelings is a normal human psychology.
2. Under any normal and expected circumstances, as individuals go through life, they get to know themselves as their body, mind, thoughts, senses, emotions, feelings, and the elements of the life they live.
3. Individuals are in touch with their inner experiences in different ways. Not everyone experiences the same things when they are in touch with themselves.
4. Our thoughts and emotions control the individual or subjective experience when we are in a dominating state of mind, such as reactions to someone or something.
5. Psychology views transformation as a process of individuals altering themselves into the person they want to be and living the life they wish to live.
6. The access to an ontological transformation is to let the experience be; that experience will not change and stays with the individuals' minds, thoughts, and bodies.
7. People cannot have understanding and a deeper appreciation for their present experience when they are continually regretting or thinking about their past experiences or dreaming and planning for their future opportunities.
8. When people transform themselves into purposeful individuals, they lead their lives more intentionally. They find more positive and uplifting meaning in their lives.
9. A good indicator of individuals who are productive and constantly progress in achieving their objectives is that they are practicing elements of personal transformation to realize their strengths and accept their weaknesses.

## Discussion Points and Coaching Questions

1. Do you clearly understand transformation and personal transformation?
2. What is your perception of personal transformation?
3. Are you in touch with your common thoughts, feelings, and emotions arising from those thoughts and feelings?
4. Have you recognized your strengths and weaknesses?
5. As a manager, are you in tune with your employees' overall feelings and emotions?
6. As a manager, are you in touch with the general sense of work environment and interpersonal relationships among your people?
7. As a manager, have you researched strengths and weaknesses among your teams or groups?
8. What would you do differently to recognize your own state of being related to your thoughts, feelings, and emotions?

## References

Antipas, Philippa, N. 2019. Core education. Transformation theory: A theory of adult learning. *CORE Blog*. http://blog.core-ed.org/blog/2019/05/transformation-theory-a-theory-of-adult-learning.html

Aspy, Denholm J., and Michael Proeve. 2017. "Mindfulness and loving-kindness meditation: Effects on connectedness to humanity and to the natural world." *Psychological Reports* 120, no. 1: 102–117.

Bain, Barnet. 2015. *The Book of Doing and Being. Rediscovering Creativity in Life, Love and Work.* New York, NY: Atria Paperback, an imprint of Simon & Schuster, Inc.

Bakhshandeh, Behnam. 2009. *Conspiracy for Greatness: Mastery of Love Within.* San Diego, CA: Primeco Education, Inc.

Bakhshandeh, Behnam. 2015. *Anatomy of Upset: Restoring Harmony.* Carbondale, PA: Primeco Education, Inc.

Bisawas-Dieber, Robert, and Ben Dean. 2007. *Positive Psychology Coaching. Putting the Science of Happiness to Work for Your Clients.* Hoboken, NJ: John Wiley & Sons, Inc.

Blouin, Eve-Marie C., and Timothy A. Pychyl. 2017 "A mental imagery intervention to increase future self-continuity and reduce procrastination." *Applied Psychology* 66, no. 2: 326–352.

Cambridge English Dictionary. 2020. Retrieved from https://dictionary.cambridge.org/us/dictionary/english/transformation

Chiba, Rie, Yuki Miyamoto, and Naoko Harada. 2016. "Psychological transformation by an intervention to facilitate benefit finding among people with chronic mental illness in Japan." *Perspectives in Psychiatric Care* 52, no. 2: 139–144.

Dictionary.com, LLC. 2022. Definitions. Transformation. Retrieved from www.dictionary.com/browse/transformation.

Diener, Ed, Frank Fujita, Louis Tay, and Robert Biswas-Diener. 2012. "Purpose, mood, and pleasure in predicting satisfaction judgments." *Social Indicators Research* 105, no. 3: 333–341.

Donald, James N., Baljinder K. Sahdra, Brooke Van Zanden, Jasper J. Duineveld, Paul WB Atkins, Sarah L. Marshall, and Joseph Ciarrochi. 2019. "Does your mindfulness benefit others? A systematic review and meta-analysis of the link between mindfulness and prosocial behaviour." *British Journal of Psychology* 110, no. 1: 101–125.

Dunfey, Theo, S. 2019. What is social change and why should we care? *Southern New Hampshire University.* Retrieved from www.snhu.edu/about-us/newsroom/social-sciences/what-is-social-change.

Effingham, Nikk. 2013. *An Introduction to Ontology.* Malden, MA: Polity Press.

Fisher, Wayne, W., Cathleen C. Piazza and Henry S. Roane. 2021. *Handbook of Applied Behavior Analysis* (2nd ed.). New York, NY: The Guilford Press.

Garbarino, James. 2011. *The Positive Psychology of Personal Transformation. Leveraging Resilience for Life Change.* New York, NY: Springer.

Gass, Robert. 2012. What is transformation? And how it advances social change? *Social Transformation Project,* stproject.org

Hill, Patrick L., Anthony L. Burrow, and Kendall Cotton Bronk. 2016. "Persevering with positivity and purpose: an examination of purpose commitment and positive affect as predictors of grit." *Journal of Happiness Studies* 17, no. 1: 257–269.

Li, Richard, Simon K. S. Cheunge, Chiaki Iwasaki, Lam-For Kwok, and Makoto Kageto (editors). 2021. Blended learning. re-thinking and re-defining the learning process. 14th International Conference, ICBL 2021. New York: Springer

Lindley, Brooke. 2021. "Personal transformation through positive psychology." *School of Positive Transformation.* Retrieved from https://schoolofpositivetransformation.com/personal-transformationthrough-positive-psychology/.

Linley, P. Alex, Aimee Felus, Raphael Gillett, and Stephen Joseph. 2011. "Emotional expression and growth following adversity: Emotional expression mediates subjective distress and is moderated by emotional intelligence." *Journal of Loss and Trauma* 16, no. 5: 387–401.

Linley, P. Alex, Karina M. Nielsen, Raphael Gillett, and Robert Biswas-Diener. 2010. "Using signature strengths in pursuit of goals: Effects on goal progress, need satisfaction, and well-being, and implications for coaching psychologists." *International Coaching Psychology Review* 5, no. 1: 6–15.

Merriam-Webster Online Dictionary. 2020a. www.merriam-webster.com/dictionary/ontology

Merriam-Webster Online Dictionary. 2020b. www.merriam-webster.com/dictionary/transformation

Mezirow, Jack. 2009. "Transformative Learning in Practice: Insights from Community, Workplace, and Higher Education.". In J. Mezirow and E. W. Taylor (Eds.), *Transformative Learning Theory* (pp. 18–31). San Francisco, CA: Jossey-Bass.

Omondi, Sharon. 2018, July. "What is social transformation?" Retrieved from www.worldatlas.com/articles/what-is-social-transformation.html

Oxford University Dictionary. 2020. "Ontology." Retrieved from www.oxfordlearnersdictionaries.com/us/definition/english/ontology?q=Ontology

Perridge, David, Kate Hefferon, Tim Lomas, and Itai Ivtzan. 2017. "I feel I can live every minute if I choose to": Participants' experience of a positive mindfulness programme." *Qualitative Research in Psychology* 14, no. 4: 482–504.

PSCA Website. 2022. Plan Sponsor Councill of America. Ralph Waldo Emerson Quates. Retrieved from: https://www.psca.org/news/blog/mind-once-stretched-new-idea-never-returns-its-original-dimensions-ralph-waldo-emerson#:~:text=Ralph%20Waldo%20Emerson-,%22The%20mind%2C%20once%20stretched%20by%20a%20new%20idea%2C%20never,original%20dimensions.%22%20Ralph%2Aruna have 0Waldo%20Emerson

Sartre, Jean-Paul. 1943. *Being and Nothingness: A Phenomenological Essay on Ontology.* Translated by Hazel E. Barnes. New York: Washington Express Press.

Scent, Camille L., and Susan R. Boes. 2014. "Acceptance and commitment training: A brief intervention to reduce procrastination among college students." *Journal of College Student Psychotherapy* 28, no. 2: 144–156.

Seligman, Martin, E., P. 2002. *Authentic Happiness. Using the New Positive Psychology to Realize Your Potential for Lasting Fulfillment.* New York, NY: Free Press.

Szekeres, Roberta A., and Eleanor H. Wertheim. 2015. "Evaluation of vipassana meditation. course effects on subjective stress, well-being, self-kindness and mindfulness in a community sample: post-course and 6-month outcomes." Stress *and Health* 31, no. 5: 373–381.

The Diamond Approach Online. 2021. Ridhwan foundation. https://online.diamondapproach.org/spiritual-transcendence-transformation/.

Vanderpol, Leon. 2019. *A Shift in Being. The Art and Practices of Deep Transformational Coaching.* Imaginal Light Publishing. Self-Publishing

Wade, G. H. 1998. "A concept analysis of personal transformation." *Journal of Advanced Nurses,* no. 4: 713–719.

Welsh, Talia. 2014. "Philosophy as self-transformation: shusterman's somaesthetics and dependent bodies." *The Journal of Speculative Philosophy* 28, no. 4: 489–504.

Wikipedia Online (2020). "Ontology." Retrieved from https://en.wikipedia.org/wiki/Ontology.

# Chapter 2

# Transformational Coaching Concept, History, Principles, and Use

Behnam Bakhshandeh

## Overview

In today's coaching industry, the word *transformation* has become a trendy term in discussions about business consulting, leadership development, and coaching approaches and models. However, when the terminology is used outside of its context and true meaning without restrictions, it often loses its true denotation and becomes a description of something different. A good example of such discrepancy is when the terminologies *transformation* and *change* are applied interchangeably (Van der Pol 2019; Bakhshandeh 2016).

The fact is that everyday people make personal and professional changes in their lives—the way they feel, the way they look, their actions, attitudes, behaviors, and ways of thinking—all the time. The individuals' changes occur deliberately and purposefully when they take a course of action to learn more about themselves and to grow, to self-regulate their emotions, or to learn how to communicate effectively to have a more productive life, better relationships. This deliberate decision attempts to change, and the more they grow and learn, the more they will change. But are they transformed?

All transformations are considered a change, but not all changes are considered a transformation (Van der Pol 2019; Bakhshandeh 2016; Berto and Plebani 2015). This misunderstanding is becoming apparent in the coaching industry. Some coaches claim that their coaching style and approach is "transformational coaching" with no evidence or backing of what they do and how they are doing it to cause any transformation. They simply use their own definitions and discretions of "transformation." Promising to conduct a coaching process to produce results such as an increase in production, growth, and development or some increased effectiveness is not necessarily a transformation in someone's life or business. These results are natural outcomes of any coaching, consulting, or training (2019; 2016; 2015).

DOI: 10.4324/9781003304074-3

**This chapter attempts to underline:**

- The definition of transformational coaching
- Some definitions used during coaching in organization development (OD) interventions
- Transformational change in OD
- The concept of transformational coaching
- Use of transformational coaching in change interventions
- History, core principles, and ethics of transformational coaching
- The bases and principles of coach, client, and participant collaboration
- Transactional coaching versus transformational coaching
- Four levels of inquiry and engagement
- Transformational coaches' strengths, skills, and competencies
- Core practical skills for processing transformational coaching
- How transformational coaching is distinct from life coaching

## What Is Transformational Coaching?

Transformational coaching concentrates on empowering and facilitating *self-actualization*. Its goal is to accomplish more than just "options-strategy-action" to accomplish intentions and goals or how to improve at something like a performance, act, job, or behavior. Transformational coaching digs much deeper into a person's psyche, concentrating on who that individual is *being*, and who that individual desires to *become*. Therefore, transformational coaching is an ontological approach to change because it is about *being* rather than *doing*, which this book will distinguish further in later chapters (Seale 2017; Seal 2011; Bakhshandeh 2009).

Usually, people become more open to transformation when they feel they have been genuinely understood, heard, and recognized for who they are and what they are offering. Paradoxically, when someone else suggests and tries to provide changing opportunity, most people resist and question the motive of the offering. Transformational coaching assists individuals in accessing and understanding who they are while witnessing the changing process and becoming present to the impact of their transformation. Transformation practically always entails a personal alteration in one's pattern of thinking and behavior (Lasley et al. 2015).

Transformational coaching has further developed into a comprehensive method of coaching, from a plain and simple "performance-focused" tool conventionally used as an approach by "humanistic" and "psychological" focus coaching to an approach in which the whole individuals' mindsets and behaviors are considered, versus an approach that just pays attention to their visible attitude and behavior (2017; 2011; 2009). "It is a reflective way of coaching that aims to explore the coachees' cognitive, emotional, sensory and relational patterns in order to create a complete understanding of their perspectives on the world" (Van der Pol 2019, 18). The individuals' personal awareness unlocks greater transformative shifts in their mindsets and views of the world around them (personally and professionally) and breaks down the negative outlines and patterns or opinions and beliefs about themselves and others around them that had held them back and influenced their relationships at home, at work, or in society. This breakthrough in the mindset impacts individual performance during individual, group, or organization-level OD interventions (2017; 2011; 2009).

## Transformational Coaching for Change

This chapter will introduce the concept of transformational coaching and its uses in change interventions management and leadership development, the influence of transformational coaching on productivity and employee attitudes, and the use of transformational coaching by workforce education professionals during OD interventions.

It is becoming clear for OD, human resource development (HRD), and workforce education and development (WFED) professionals that professional coaching, including transformational coaching, can be a powerful and effective vehicle to positively affect workforce education, self-awareness, and productivity. This book can bring forth the importance of the transformational coaching approach for educational and learning professionals to see the wisdom of learning more about transformational coaching, its approaches, and its methods so they can influence their employees' attitudes and behaviors, thus producing long-lasting results, regardless of their positions. The speed at which coaching is spreading through businesses and organizations is evidence of how important it is to know more about all types of coaching, understanding its dynamics and how to use it to empower the organization's vision and commitments. Given the directions that professional coaching is being used by organizations, the importance of using it is becoming more evident for OD, HRD, and WFED professional communities.

Before we get to where we can use transformational coaching in any change interventions, we are presenting a brief history of transformational coaching, its core principles, and its ethical standards.

## History and Background of Transformational Coaching

The concept of coaching is a relatively young approach, so there is not much recorded history about coaching. However, progressive coaching is developing its place among professionals in the fields of management, business, organization development, human resource development, and more.

Transformational coaching, per se, takes its origins from a variety of disciples and schools of thought. As we mentioned in Chapter 1, transformation can be linked to some old fields such as philosophy and ontology, and it also connects to newer fields such as psychology, sociology, and mindfulness. During the last four or five decades, transformational coaching has been used in management coaching and business growth for affecting a workforce's mindset, attitudes, and behavior to cause increasing productivity and enhance human performance. As Animas (2018) underlines, transformational coaching keeps valuable lessons and proven methodology of old-school coaching techniques and models while adding the wisdom of ages from relevant fields and adding newer and deeper insights and approaches. This powerful combination can only serve the participants to develop deeper interactions and become much more effective and impactful. Transformational coaching brings something extraordinary and powerful to the coaching relationship because it uses all the approaches to understand the human mind and actions from past learning opportunities and links them for participants to a more substantial degree (Lasley et al. 2015).

### *The Focus and Methodologies*

The transformational coaching approach focuses on empowering participants to shift and transform the way they think and feel, which directly affects the way they are experiencing events and incidents, and therefore transforming the way they act (Cox et al. 2010). This approach to coaching is only available through the experiences of developed professional transformational coaches with extensive experience and reputations in illustrating developments in philosophy (human mindset, choices, and experience), psychology (behavioral science and what humans do with their experience), and ontology (the nature of being). In addition, coaches' understanding of the human mind and mindfulness (where one's mind goes when experiencing) can guide participants to manage their mindsets and allow for alteration of their behavior. The transformation of one's mind will arise at the moment they could recognize the discrepancy between what they know to be real (in their mind as their perceived reality) and what is happening (the actual reality) with them and around them due to their existing mindset (Lasley et al. 2015; Bakhshandeh 2009).

## Central Principle

The central principle of transformational coaching concerns recognizing and utilizing someone's current mindset or perceived reality and then employing what it takes to facilitate a real change, a desired change that is sustainable. This transformation displays not only good intentions or temporarily improved behavior (Lasley et al. 2015; Bakhshandeh 2009). This implies that a transformational coach can work with individuals or groups on a much deeper and more rigorous level. The results of the transformational coaching approach can only materialize on a background of a solid trust between both ends; support by each end; and a safe, secure, confidential, and nonjudgmental environment (Cox et al. 2010).

The transformational coaches standing in the middle of possible change is one of the biggest elements of a successful transformational coach's undertaking. It takes courage from the coach's side to talk about challenging and altering individuals', employees', teams', or groups' mindsets, behavior, or just status quo. It takes a masterful mindset and stand to stay present and focus in unpleasant and challenging moments dealing with strangers and inviting them to change their entire mindsets about life or performance and productivity. The solid place to stand for a transformational coach is in their belief that this approach could be one of the greatest changes that could transpire for those individuals or groups; believing that the transformation process is not just altering some process but is changing someone's way of being, their view of themselves of others, and ultimately their view of the world around them (Bakhshandeh 2009).

## The Fundamentals and Notions

The fundamentals of transformational coaching are based on a holistic approach to human dignity and freedom; it is developed on the bases of principles of a partnership between (see Figure 2.1):

1. The nature of humans,
2. Freedom to be, and
3. The process of transformational coaching.

These fundamental beliefs are supported by creating a powerful background for the coaches' and participants' workable relationship by:

1. Establishing relationships based on trust, respect, and ground rules
2. Setting up channels for effective communication
3. Willingness to be open, vulnerable, and authentic
4. Welcoming intrusive coaching and inquiry

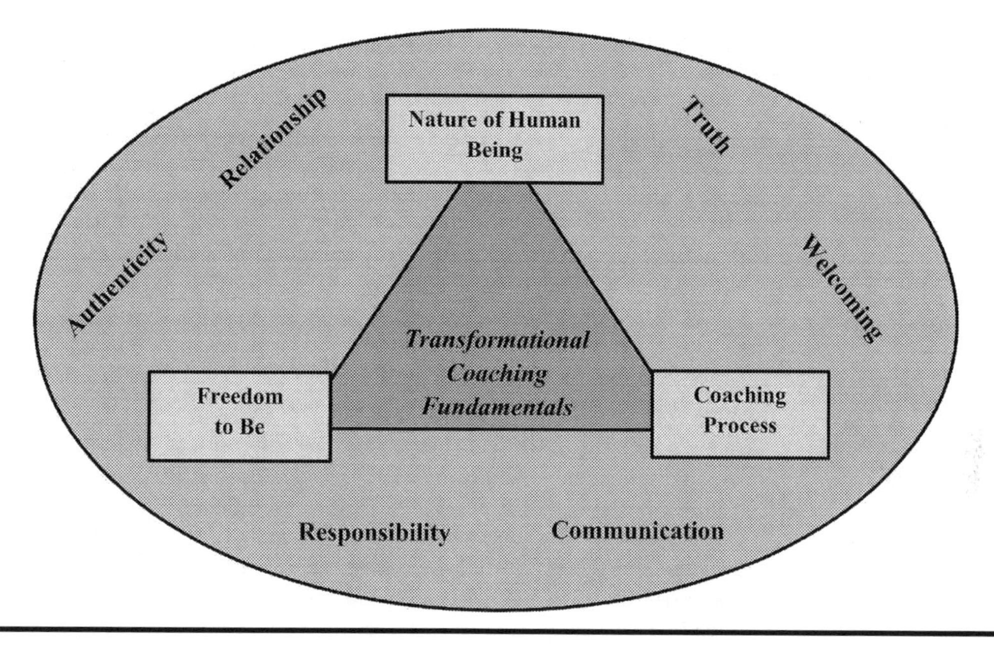


**Figure 2.1 The Fundamentals and Notions of Transformational Coaching.**

*Source:* Adapted from Lasley et al. (2015); Cox et al. (2010); Bakhshandeh (2009).

5. Taking personal responsibility
6. Telling the truth without blaming others

Our fundamental beliefs about participants and the coaching process infuse our facial expressions and body language and determine our personal energy while providing transformational coaching (Lasley et al. 2015, Cox et al. 2010; Bakhshandeh 2009).

## The Core Values and Principles

The core values of transformational coaching will assist coaches and participants in generating the receptacle for a powerful and productive relationship with minimum resistance. The coaches can share these core values with their participants or clients in advance to establish an authentic and trusting connection. Please see Table 2.1.

## The Foundation for Coach, Client, and Participants Collaboration

As we have underlined earlier, transformational coaching is established on core values that provide a range of supportive principles for leading both coach and participants to generate the most effective partnership.

### Who Is the Client?

In the context of coaching, the client could be the sponsor for the coaching project. The sponsor could be an organization or an organization's senior leadership, such as the president,

**Table 2.1 The Core Values of Transformational Coaching.**

| *Core Values and Principles of Transformational Coaching* | | | |
|---|---|---|---|
| # | *Values* | *Descriptions* | *At the Field* |
| 1 | **Practice Integrity** | The backbone of effective transformational coaching is the integrity in process, with the coach and the participants. | Without integrity, nothing will work. This powerful distinction influences every part of our day-to-day lives and what we are doing. To change our lives, we must start practicing integrity in all aspects of what we do, personally and professionally. The effectiveness of transformational coaching depends on the level of integrity that the coach and participants bring to the process. |
| 2 | **Being Whole** | There is nothing lacking with people; they are whole the way they are and concurrently develop a deeper experience of themselves and their lives. | Transformational coaching is not for fixing something with people, but for providing access for them to see their potential and practice their choices and own their state of being in the matter of their own lives. The world usually focuses on what's wrong with people or what needs to change or improve, which comes with assessments and perceptions of people's brokenness. Relating to people as whole moves the concept of broken to relatedness and respect, which would allow for establishing the foundation of partnership between the coach and participants. |
| 3 | **Honoring Diversity** | The transformational coaching process will go much deeper by honoring people's diversity of experience. | Transformational coaching is honoring people's diverse experiences, including their feelings and emotions about what they have gone through and what they experience during the process of coaching. The process allows for participants to embrace the breadth of their life experiences generated from their past, their family, their culture, and every other experience that might be in their way for transforming themselves and accessing deeper self-awareness. |
| 4 | **Responsibility** | We are free when we take responsibility for the way we have reacted to all upsetting events in our lives. | In the transformational coaching process, the coach invites participants to take responsibility for how they have reacted and responded to upsetting situations in their lives. Not as the creator of the upsetting situation, but as the ones who took the route they took. When we are responsible, we show our willingness to own every thought we have and own up to every action we take; good or bad, right or wrong, happy or sad, enough or not enough. |

| *Core Values and Principles of Transformational Coaching* | | | |
|---|---|---|---|
| # | *Values* | *Descriptions* | *At the Field* |
| 5 | **Accountability** | To get what we want in life, we must make promises and declare our intentions. | Our power and dignity are built on the background of our promises to ourselves and others. People do not clearly understand how much their actions impact the world around them. Any action, broken promise, and everything we say will influence our relationship with others. |
| 6 | **Creativity** | People are fundamental, creative, intelligent, and resourceful. | They are trusting that participants are creative, intelligent, and resourceful enough to find their ways through the transformation process. This place for a transformational coach to stand allows expansion of self-inquiry, curiosity, and emerging participation, connecting them to new insights, realizations, and actions. |
| 7 | **Authenticity** | Authenticity allows for complete self-expression and freedom to be with whoever is there to face. | What will lead people to become authentic is a combination of having the integrity and courage to own what they have done and who they have been in the face of life's upsetting situation, then become responsible for what we have done and face the reality of how we have done it. That is where people are giving up on learning about themselves when they think owning one's results admits guilt. It is becoming real, and that is powerful. |
| 8 | **Freedom of Expression** | People have complete freedom to respond and express themselves appropriately. | Coaches are freeing themselves from judgment by allowing participants to express themselves freely and share their experiences, circumstances, shortcomings, and even expectations. Coaches shall not take responsibility for how the participants feel and how they express themselves. By coaches accepting what participants' feelings are, they allow for natural transformation of such experience by the participants and allow for their experience of humility and honor by their coach. |
| 9 | **Having Choices** | People always have choices. They have a variety of choices in their wants and needs. | Participants can choose any actions, and anyway they want to approach their issues at work or in their personal lives. Coaches shall not interfere with the participants' choices of actions or reactions in any shape or form. The coaches' place is to remind participants about being responsible for possible consequences of their choices. The participants will be free when they own the outcome of their choices. |

(*Continued*)

**Table 2.1 (Continued)**

| *Core Values and Principles of Transformational Coaching* | | | |
|---|---|---|---|
| *#* | *Values* | *Descriptions* | *At the Field* |
| 10 | **Looking for Opportunities** | Looking for opportunities is a true expression of growth and development. | When participants are free of the restraints that their experience has on them, and when they understand the consequences of their choices and own the outcome of where they are, they may select opportunities for what is next for them. |
| 11 | **Be Open to Possibilities** | There are so many more possibilities for each person on any day of their lives. | The beauty of the transformational coaching process is in the mystery of the outcomes. Nobody can plan what might come out of this process, neither the coaches nor the participants can imagine in advance what might happen and what they might get out of the process. However, anything and everything is possible when people are open to transformation and do not resist change in their mindset and perception of reality. |

*Source:* The content of this table is from the book *Anatomy of Upset; Restoring Harmony* (Bakhshandeh 2015) and is used with express permission from Behnam Bakhshandeh and Primeco Education, Inc.

CEO, or COO. Sometimes, the client/sponsor also is the participant or one in a team or group. If there are clients/sponsors, they are the ones responsible for providing the logistics and paying the bill. Their involvement in the process of transformational coaching will be limited to their ideas of potential issues or their desired outcome for the coaching undertaking. The coach will be in touch regularly during the implementation of transformational coaching and provide a progress report, ask for feedback, or deliver feedback. Therefore the relationship between the coach and the sponsor is essential to the successful progress of transformational coaching.

### *Who Are the Participants?*

Participants could be an individual, a couple of individuals with some issues, a team, a group, a department, or the whole organization. The categories of potential participants for an OD intervention are presented in Table 2.3. Transformational coaching applies on an individual level, which would cause a personal transformation, and a team or organization level, which would cause a team, department, or organization transformation. Later on in this chapter, we have defined the levels of interventions and some definitions of related distinctions.

### *Who Is the Coach?*

The coach could be a professional transformational coach as an outsider coming in as a hired professional. Sometimes this coach has internal individual training to deliver transformational coaching and is part of the HR or HRD department.

Table 2.2 displays the foundation for collaboration between the coach, participants, and the client as the sponsor for the transformational coaching process.

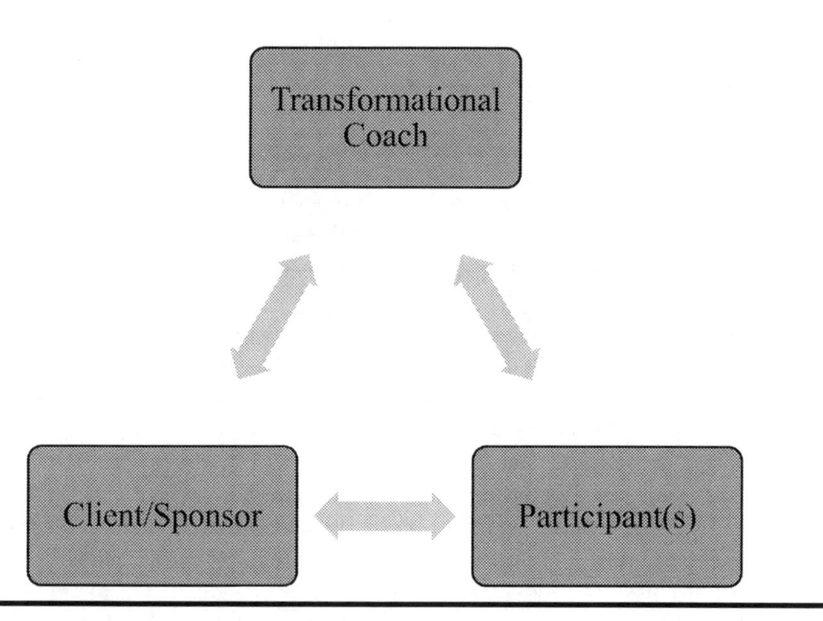


**Figure 2.2 Collaboration and Partnership Between Client/Sponsor, Coaches and Participant(s).**

*Source:* Author's Original Creation. Copyright 2022 by Behnam Bakhshandeh.

**Table 2.2 The Foundation of Coach, Client and Participant Collaboration. Author's Original Creation.**

| *The Foundation of Coach, Client and Participant(s) Collaboration* | | |
|---|---|---|
| # | *Principles* | *Descriptions* |
| 1 | **Established Coalition** | The first tier of the coaching coalition is between the coach and client/ sponsor to understand the issue(s) from the client's viewpoint. The second tier is the coach and participant(s) relationship. All three corners of this coalition (client, coach & participant) are vital in its success process of transformational coaching. |
| 2 | **Partnership in Approach** | The coach will be in partnership with the client for evaluating related issues and situations at hand. In this partnership, the client could learn from the coach's thinking processes and establish a trusting relationship with the coach to resolve the organization's issues and as a resource in organizations' or departments' strategic planning and designing collaborative work. |
| 3 | **Learning, Actions, & Practices** | A successful transformational coaching process depends on everyone's thinking, learning, planning actions, and implementing practices. The level of implementation and practices might differ from client to participant, but everyone needs to go through some learning and practices, even sometimes the coach. |
| 4 | **Active Engagement** | For best results of the transformational coaching outcomes, everyone (client, coach, and participants) needs to be actively engaged, be open and willing to be proactively involved when learning, and implement the change process. |

(*Continued*)

**Table 2.2 (Continued)**

| *The Foundation of Coach, Client and Participant(s) Collaboration* | | |
|---|---|---|
| *#* | *Principles* | *Descriptions* |
| 5 | **Critical Thinking** | Everyone involved in the transformational coaching process needs to learn and practice the critical thinking process and use it in their decision-making activities. Critical thinking is essential to conducting an effective inquiry. |
| 6 | **Application of Models & Methods** | The coach will use proven coaching models and tested methods to construct the coaching sessions and facilitate conversations and inquiries that will generate learning opportunities and produce results for the participant(s). |
| 7 | **Intended Outcomes & Pathway** | The coaches must be wary of the collective outcomes discussed by the clients and have their eyes on the progress at intervals. This way, the coach is paying attention to the pathway and progress of the coaching and how the process is positively affecting participants and the sponsor's needed outcomes. |
| 8 | **Goal Setting** | The coach will assist the participants in designing their individual, team, or departments' goals and setting up an action plan to achieve them. The goal-setting process is the platform that provides the coaching process its strategic attention. |
| 9 | **Being Present** | The transformational coach needs to be present, observe, and know where to participate at every process level. Coaches' ability to be present to themselves and their participants is correlated to their level of mindfulness, clarity, and certainty. |
| 10 | **Self-Awareness** | Coaches need to be self-aware of their own mindset, attitude, and behavior. This awareness will allow them to understand and have compassion for their participants' mindsets, attitudes, and behaviors. In addition, this awareness will allow for more effective interactions and interventions. |

*Source:* Copyright 2022 by Behnam Bakhshandeh.

## Potential Use of Transformational Coaching in OD Interventions

As indicated, this book looks at the use and impact of transformational coaching for the education and development of effective managers and their potential use during their change efforts in different levels of OD change intervention, especially individual, group, and organization levels.

OD professionals often specialize by the level of change. According to Rothwell et al. (2016), there are eight levels of organization change, which also define specialized professional OD practitioners involved with the change intervention (see Table 2.3).

## Some Definitions and Descriptions of OD Terminologies

It is essential to understand and provide clarity of the main OD terminologies in this book and to underline several definitions and distinctions:

**Table 2.3 Levels of Change Effort and Levels of OD Interventions.**

| *Levels of Change Effort and Levels of OD Interventions* | | |
|---|---|---|
| *Levels* | *Categories* | *Change Efforts* |
| First | Individual | Individual-Based Change Efforts. Need a change among individuals. |
| Second | Dyadic or Triadic | Dyadic and Triadic-Based Change Efforts. Need a change among two or three people. |
| Third | Team or Group | Team-Based Change Efforts. Need a change for the improvement of teams or groups. |
| Fourth | Department or Division | Departmental or Divisional Change Efforts. Need a change in a department or division within the organization. |
| Fifth | Organization | Organizational Change. Need a change in the organization. |
| Sixth | Industry or Community | Industry or Community-Based Change. Need for a major change or improvement in an industry or a community; also known as community development. |
| Seventh | National | National Change. Need for a nation's citizens to feel proud and positive about their country and to work cohesively for their nation's common goals. |
| Eighth | International or Global | International or Global Change. Need for a change on the international level among all nations. |

*Source:* Adapted from Rothwell et al. (2016).

## *Organization Development*

Many professional scholars and practitioners have several definitions and explanations for organization development (OD). In this segment, we display two such definitions:

Rothwell (2015) gives us a clear definition of organization development:

> OD is usually known to mean bottom-up change effort focused on improving employees' interpersonal relationships. OD usually involves internal or external consultants to facilitate the change process. These consultants apply the practical aspects of psychology, sociology, anthropology, and political science to organizational challenges.
>
> (9)

Cummings and Worley (2015) define OD as:

> Organization Development is a system-wide application and transfer of behavioral science knowledge to the planned development, improvement, and reinforcement of the strategies, structures, and processes that lead to organization effectiveness.
>
> (2)

## Change Intervention

This author would define change intervention as a systematic, nonlinear approach to educating, empowering, and directing an organization and its members to increase productivity, efficiency, and effectiveness while decreasing human resources (HR) issues and turnover, through the implementation of behavioral sciences such as psychology, ontology, and sociology (Bakhshandeh 2009). Change intervention provides space for organizations to transform their culture and management approaches. Implementing transformational coaching as an approach for organizational change could improve the organization's sustainability, modify its organizational structure in a positive way, and assist them in inventing a positive work environment to keep their staff and customers satisfied. OD and change intervention processes are vehicles for organizational transformation, building a whole new vision for the organization and its teams (Burke 2018; Rothwell et al. 2017; Rothwell et al. 2016).

## Individual Intervention

Individual intervention is the first level of organization development (OD) intervention and change effort. On this level of intervention, the focus is on improving the organization's tasks' execution and performance by engaging in individuals' skills development, self-awareness, and change in behaviors and attitudes to become more effective and productive, individually, in teams, with the organization's success in mind. This is the level on which transformational coaching would have the biggest impact. Individual-level intervention is one of the most used interventions by organizations, because individuals have the most influence and impact on making or breaking organizations. Some of the individual interventions are in recruiting new employees, training and developing of employees, replacement/displacement of employees, and providing coaching or mentoring for employees (Burke 2018; Rothwell 2015).

## Group and Team Intervention

Team building could be defined as a variety of activities implemented to improve relationships among team members and classify functions and responsibilities within the team, which most of the time encompasses cooperative tasks. Team building differs from team training, which is intended to develop and enhance the workforce's effectiveness and productivity more readily than interpersonal relationships among team members. According to Rothwell et al. (2021), team-building change intervention is one of the most popular types of organization development change intervention among organizations. Professional organization development practitioners and consultants consider the interpersonal relationships among team members to be a vital element of a team-building process that needs close attention, given that team cohesiveness and closeness are critical to the success of this level of change (Rothwell et al. 2017; Rothwell et al. 2016). According to Feldman (2018), team building is a collaborative process between organizations and individuals. It is almost a continuous process with no established ending. Feldman (2018) added: "Besides the work of finding the right people to join the team, there is the work of building relationships, engendering trust, and setting an agenda that is built on a mission, vision, core values, and a strategic plan" (87). This level is also very impactful for implementing transformational coaching. I don't think there is anyone out there who would deny that the well-being of organizations is directly linked to the performance and productivity of individuals and teams.

### *Organizational Intervention*

Organizational interventions are coordinated, and structured change effort programs resolve a problem in an organization, hence empowering an organization to achieve the goal for such desired change, either at an individual, team, or organization level. These intervention change approaches and activities are intended to improve an organization's functioning and enable many individuals, such as managers, supervisors, and team leaders to manage their departments and teams in a more effective way, such as sources by the organization culture including the organization's vision and mission statements and values. These organization interventions range from knowledge, skills, abilities (KAS), performance, process, motivation, technology, evaluations, career development, talent retention, and many more elements of organization development (Rothwell et al. 2021; Rothwell et al. 2016; Cummings and Worley 2015).

### *Change Agent*

According to many professional OD practitioners, the change agent oversees the change intervention process. This position could be a facilitator, coach, internal or external consultant, or trainer who will conduct the actual designed change intervention processes, such as workshops, seminars, activities, or training, to deliver the outcomes of the change intervention (Burke 2018; Rothwell et al. 2017; Rothwell et al. 2016). For this book, the change agent will be managers or a manager-as-coach responsible for developing their teams and departments.

## Transformational Change in OD

Even though we are all changing regularly, we are not transforming each time we are changing something about ourselves. Van der Pol (2019) defined transformation as "a thorough or dramatic change in form or character—a metamorphosis, of sorts" (5). Under normal circumstances, individuals rarely experience any real transformations. Most likely, any comprehensive or dramatic transformation phase could be counted on one hand. But these are occasions of *human transformation*, which would help to explain and define what transformational coaching is (Van der Pol 2019; Bakhshandeh 2009).

It would be appropriate to look into what the term transformation means in OD. As much as transformation is a challenging and relatively difficult undertaking, it is also possibly a rewarding endeavor for the organization and for its leaders. Transformation level change intervention holds the highest possibility of causing breakthrough results for an organization by causing a thoughtful and deep shift in a leader's worldview. Organization leaders would realize that the organization would not operate, function, or produce what the future world market demands. They would realize that their organization, including themselves, must undergo a major and radical change to shift their views, attitudes, and behaviors to meet the conditions and requirements for competing in a fast-changing marketplace and its fierce competition. It begins with the overt recognition that the status quo must change (Rothwell et al. 2016).

The initial challenge when conducting a transformational OD change intervention is that it is generally uncertain and unknown by the future's nature. It is apparent to the management team and to the OD practitioner that something needs to give, change, and transform; something else needs to get done, something very different from its present direction; however, it is not clear what needs to change (2016). Even though all OD professionals know that the first thing to do is the full organization diagnosis, no one will know completely what that entails going through such a diagnosis process. Therefore, in all three cases of a) the *future* state design and b) the procedures and processes to figure it out and, c) the implementation is often developing and emerging as the process occurs (2016).

Rothwell et al. (2016) underlined this phenomenon, stating that "Things are discovered along the way that could never have been known without first launching the journey. No plan stays in place for long. Through responding quickly to what shows up, clarity emerges" (65). Given this expected uncertainty, the transformational change process is nonlinear by nature, with the frequent course and directional corrections and modifications. These constraints are something that organization leaders are not comfortable with, especially middle management and employees who are waiting for directions and a clear plan of action (Rothwell et al. 2016; Cummings and Worley 2015).

## Transactional Coaching versus Transformational Coaching

To clarify and understand transformational coaching, this section highlights a major difference among transactional and transformational coaching approaches using the following fundamental premise.

### *Transactional Coaching*

Transactional coaching is standing on the assumption that an individual will discover what they want to know about themselves and move ahead in meaningful directions centered on their current *existing way of being.* Nothing should be investigated or shifted at an individuals' states of being for them to attain their desired outcomes in life (Cox et al. 2014). Transactional coaching can also be defined as a discussion (or transaction) among coaches and their coachees to define a goal or intentions. Here, the coaches' positions in the discussion will listen and raise questions to assist the coachees in obtaining clarity on their goals and intentions. After gaining such clarity, they can investigate new ideas, develop new perceptions, build new options, create new strategies, and develop an action plan that would forward their attention and goals (Egan 2013). "It is often conducted in a more systemized or process-driven way with change happening primarily through cognitive thinking and action—by 'thinking and doing differently.' Because of this, it can be perceived as a relatively impersonal approach" (Van der Pol 2019, 14).

One of the main differences of transactional coaching compared to transformational coaching is that in transactional coaching, there is a minimized need or requirement to dig into what transformational coaching calls the coaches' "internal operating system" (Cox et al. 2014). According to Egan (2013), the internal operating system is a multidimensional and complex mind system including many aspects of human mental processes such as beliefs, assumptions, mental models, meanings on life aspects, self-identity, and our conscious and unconscious states of mind. Van der Pol (2019) attempts to simplify the role of transactional coaching:

> To use a computer analogy, transactional coaching is focused on upgrades to our operating system that enable us to be more effective at what we are trying to achieve; it is not concerned with understanding the nature of the operating system itself or with any redesign of it.
>
> (15)

However, the concept of *self-awareness*, as the key element and heart of all coaching approaches, nonetheless is critical to transactional coaching and to transformational coaching and to any personal growth that transpires regardless of the issues or goal-driven stages. This idea will explain and define the concept of self-awareness in more detail in subsequent sections.

As the remaining fact, the process of transactional coaching will proceed with the coach or coachee not wanting to go deeper into potentially painful experiences and raw emotions or reconnoitering past trials that shape the coachee's existing experiences that affect potential future events. The transactional coaching approach will not look into profoundly kept beliefs and values, regardless of how limiting they could be in producing transformational results in one's mindset, attitude, and behaviors (Effingham 2013; Bakhshandeh 2009). "Transactional coaching remains on the surface of our human existence" (Van der Pol 2019, 15).

## *Transformational Coaching*

But transformational coaching stands on the assumption and principle that for uncovering what is needed to produce transformation, the coachees need to not only *expand their mindset but also to shift their way of being, which provides* the higher order of thoughts, new and empowering perceptions, and energizes their states of actions (Schmitt et al. 2016). Transformational coaching concentrates on empowering one's self-actualization. Transformational coaching goes beyond the "options-strategy-action" process, which assists the coachees in accomplishing their goals or providing clarity or making them improve something. In addition, it works with individuals to dive much deeper into their human psyche, concentrating on discovering who these individuals are being, who they desire to become, and getting what they want to accomplish in much more effective ways. This approach transforms the transformational to an ontological style of coaching, given it is working on *being* part of the individual instead of what they are *doing*. This awareness underscores a crucial distinction of the fundamental principles between the transformational and the transactional coaching methods (Seale 2017; Seale 2011; Bakhshandeh 2009). "The great transformational coaching question is, therefore, Who do you choose to be? and what makes this process transformational is learning and doing what it takes to grow into the embodiment of that choice in being" (Van der Pol 2019, 19).

To be clear, in a transformational coaching undertaking, coachees are still bringing their personal issues; their goals, objectives, ideas, and dreams to the table, as does the transactional coaching process; however, in transformational coaching, both coach and coachee are mindful that those mentioned interests function as the framework and context for a much deeper dive within themselves, not as the end game. It is a journey of self-realization and discovery to understand their *being* (Egan 2013; Bakhshandeh 2009). As Van der Pol (2019) stated, "The *becoming* process is the transformational path, and the end game is the embodiment of higher than realized levels of existence" (19).

For a better understanding of these two models and styles of coaching, see Table 2.4, a side-by-side comparison of transactional and transformational coaching.

**Table 2.4 Elements of Transactional Coaching versus Transformational Coaching.**

| *Type of Coaching* | *Transactional* | *Transformational* |
|---|---|---|
| **Focusing on** | *Do* Differently | *Be* Different |
| **Characteristics** | Pushes *Doing* | Drives *Being* |
| | Centers around issues | Finds one's essences |
| | Propels around results | Digs into one's dark and light sides |
| | It is action-oriented | Illustrates the individual's inner operational system |
| | Works on the surface | Works deeper than the surface |

*(Continued)*

**Table 2.4 (Continued)**

| *Type of Coaching* | *Transactional* | *Transformational* |
|---|---|---|
| **Intentions** | Discovers new ways to distinguish the issue | Explores new ways of being |
| | Thinks about your actions | Discovers ways to exemplify new ways of being |
| | Acts relative to an issue | Acts on resolving an issue based on the new way of being |
| **Assumption** | Individual's current way of being is adequate to create the preferred outcomes | Individual's new or shifted way of being creates the preferred outcomes |

*Sources:* Adapted from Van der Pol (2019); Bakhshandeh (2009).

## Four Levels of Inquiry and Engagement

According to Seale (2011), there are four levels of awareness that people are engaging with their experiences. Table 2.5 displays how these levels of engagement are linked to transactional and transformational coaching approaches and sourced by the state of *doing* and *being*:

**Table 2.5 Level of Participants' Inquiry Engagement in Transactional and Transformational Coaching.**

| *Levels of Participant's Inquiry Engagement in Transactional & Transformational Coaching* | | | |
|---|---|---|---|
| *Type of Coaching* | *Focus on* | *Levels* | *Examples of Typical Inquiries* |
| **Transactional** | **Doing** | Drama | • Something is wrong!<br>• Whose fault is this?<br>• Who is there to blame for this?<br>• This should not be this way.<br>• Can you believe this happened?<br>• Why does this always happen? |
| | | Situation | • How can we fix this?<br>• How fast can we fix it?<br>• How can we afford the fixing?<br>• How can we prevent it from happening?<br>• What needs to change here? |
| **Transformational** | **Being** | Choice | • Who do I choose to be in this situation?<br>• How do I relate to this situation?<br>• Nothing is wrong!<br>• I am responsible<br>• What is right?<br>• What is working here? |
| | | Opportunity | • What is the opportunity here?<br>• What do I want to happen?<br>• What is possible after this?<br>• What was the lesson learned here?<br>• What needs to alter and transform? |

*Sources:* Adapted from Bakhshandeh (2015) and Seale (2010).

## Transformational Coaches' Strengths, Skills, and Competencies

In terms of coaching others, coaches need to have confidence in their ability to see through the issues and have skills and competencies to keep the coachees focused on them, not just what appears to be an issue, but also the sources that caused it to show up in the coachees' lives or work environments. Regardless of the type of coaching, personal or professional, or integrating coaching with other methods of work, transformative coaching is about bringing vitality, zest, and creativity into individuals' lives and recognizing personal and professional potentials. The following are some of the key skills and competencies of a transformational coach by Bakhshandeh (2009, 2015).

### *Compassion*

Having and practicing compassion is one of the main elements of any successful coach to know that the coachees are where they are and what they are facing, knowing they are experiencing pain, suffering, or ineffectiveness. Make sure they get present to what happened in their lives and understand that it is insignificant compared to what is happening to their inner selves.

### *Patience*

Along with being compassionate, having patience with others is a helpful addition to empowering the coachees to go through spaces of self-awareness and self-realization without being pushed through it. They should know that not everyone works at the same speed of uncovering their personalities, behaviors, and attitudes.

### *Creating Safe Space*

Transformational coaches create and hold a safe environment that allows the coachees to feel safe and open up, using silence as a way for the coachees' greater self-examination and reflections.

### *Challenging*

The coaches will ask relevant questions that might be challenging and difficult for the coachees but provoke change through speaking about the unspoken. Skilled transformational coaches will not back down from uncomfortable situations with their coachees because they believe transformation will arise from being confronted and becoming uncomfortable.

### *Keen Listening*

Coaches should stand for their coachees' greatness and excellence without allowing pettiness to creep into listening to and viewing the situation. Coaches should make sure that the way they relate to their coachees does not become one of the thousands of reasons they come up with for why they cannot do or have what they want. A skilled coach is conscious and aware of what is being said and what remains unsaid and still lingers in the background and engages the coachee.

### *Deep Observation*

Coaches should closely observe and identify the coachees' core beliefs, interpretations, and thought process patterns that give existence to mindsets, behaviors, and attitudes with a direct effect on the quality of the coachees' life experiences at home or at work.

### Personal Responsibility

Coaches should also stand for the coachees to take responsibility for their choices. The source of suffering is often either to avoid making choices or not being committed to the choices they made. They should take a good, long look at themselves and what they don't want to be responsible for!

### Reality versus Interpretations

Coaches should point them toward what is real and what is made up. They should know when they are responsible for their actions and the totality of their lives; then the outcomes, circumstances, and conditions will not determine or affect the quality of their lives.

### Constructive Feedback

The coaches should give constructive feedback, reflect on what is being said, what is being observed, and what is being discovered, and share important information with the coachees from what the coaches have heard, seen, and felt in the session to open new possibilities for the coachees.

## Core Practical Skills for Processing the Transformational Coaching

To achieve the maximum benefits of transformational coaching, coaches need to move from a transactive mode and model involved mainly with their technical skills to a transformative model, primarily concentrating on shifting individuals' and group perspectives, interpretations, overall views of themselves and others, their values, principles, and a sense of purpose. Several core skills assist coaches in moving from being transactional coaches, dedicated to building skill and imparting coachees' knowledge, to becoming transformational coaches, concentrating on uncovering patterns and fluctuating coachees' perspectives (Bakhshandeh 2009; Cashman 2003). The following are three coaching processes required for such a shift in approaches to support their coaches.

### Building Awareness

For transformational coaches to help their coachees, they need to build awareness, which involves certain disciplines developed by the coaches to act as an expert and find approaches that will strengthen their coaching relationship with the coachees. Suppose the coaches are not aware of this key factor. There, they will impose their existing awareness onto the coachees versus developing the awareness of the coachees from the inside out. Building this vital awareness entails openness to assist the coachees in sorting out their own existing and present reality by themselves, for themselves, and imagine and develop alternative future possibilities for their lives (2009; 2003). Cashman (2003) underlined this important state of mind from the coach's part:

> To build awareness with people you coach, stay out of expert or fix-it mode questions to help people sort out their situation, be courageous enough to discuss the undiscussable, speak directly but with concern, help others explore their intentions, and uncover and align with what is meaningful and important to them.
>
> (11)

## *Building Commitment*

Having awareness is an important concept; however, awareness without an emotional engagement and a strong commitment results in entertaining an empty promise to ourselves and others. Many love to exercise, but when their hearts are not into it, they act as if they are forced to do it. Others affirm that their religious or spiritual lives are important to them, but they rarely reflect the tenets of their beliefs in their lives. They lie, cheat, and are hypocrites (Bakhshandeh 2009). Building awareness is a good start, but it's not enough to guide the coachees through their feelings and emotions to build a solid commitment and feel it. Unfortunately trauma is a fantastic teacher for people facing a lack of dedication to their expressed commitments. Lying in a hospital bed after a heart attack, giving into unhealthy eating habits, or not exercising can help them see the consequences of their behaviors against their commitments in no uncertain terms (2009; 2003).

Coaches must assist coachees in visualizing and foreseeing the potential positive and negative outcomes by displaying what they will possibly gain or lose. The cost of their actions compared with the payoff of their process, if they remain on their current path, will be helpful to develop a new commitment to alter their actions (2009; 2003). The transformation will commence when the coachees' emotions profoundly register because of convincing reasons to implement changes and stop the potentially detrimental behaviors. To build commitment with the coachees, the coaches must assist individuals in sorting out the consequences of their mindsets, actions, attitudes, and behaviors, which will allow the coaches' commitment to catalyze the coachees' commitment (2009; 2003).

## *Build Practices*

It is clear that there is no transformation at any level of coaching without designing and implementing practices. Coachees will develop a "new awareness" into their behavior, a new understanding that will replace their past understanding of themselves and situations.

People can learn of negative aspects of their lives at both personal or professional levels and commit themselves to noble and worthy goals to alter that behavior, but without designing and implementing new practices to put the new and empowering awareness to work, it will be like turning on a lamp and then immediately closing their eyes—nothing new, nothing transformed (Bakhshandeh 2009). As Cashman (2003) pointed out,

> Beginning practice makes the possible probable; advanced, enduring practice makes the possible real. Practices involve the consistent repetition of new behaviors that transform our lives. Exercise is a practice to build health. Meditation is a practice to unfold our spiritual life.
>
> (12)

Coachees' reflections on how their interpersonal interactions have affected their relationships develop their effectiveness with others in the home and at work. Not allowing fears or limiting views to interrupt their commitments and goals are examples of lifelong practices that help them to move forward when the distractive easier way or less painful and lazier way shows its ugly face and locks them and holds them back by limiting their belief systems (2009, 2003).

Transformational coaching illustrates the coachees' potential onto the possibilities of high personal and professional performance by building awareness, commitments, and new practices in living and leading. True accomplishment and success are achieved when we grow, change, or alter our behaviors and practices. As this author has always said, expecting to become a success without having a structure and plan to follow is like trying to build a high-rise without a well-planned, well-designed, and well-built solid foundation; the building is at the mercy of circumstances. Sooner or later, the building will collapse; it is not a question of **if**; it is a question of **when**! The fact is, in the physical universe, the only thing individuals can manage is what they are doing at this exact moment and follow through with their plan to the end; when they look back, they have built a future (Bakhshandeh 2009).

## How Transformational Coaching Is Distinct from Life Coaching

Traditional life coaching and transformational coaching share similar qualities, such as conducting an open questioning and concentrating on the coachee for answers; however, some significant differences also exist between them.

Traditional life coaches concentrate on the coachees' goals and objectives, working with the coachees collaboratively to discover possible ways to achieve such goals and objectives. The life coaches work with the coachees' blockers that would preclude successful progression and ultimately create a realistic and reasonable action plan to help the coachees reach their desired outcomes (Effingham 2013).

A transformational coach may well start with the goal-setting process and a perception of the ultimate outcome; however, the work and undertaking proceed differently. In extensive terms, in the transformational coaching approach, a coach explores and engages the coachees' view of self, others, and the world around them and their relationships to such perspectives. This approach could include looking at the current set of beliefs, assumptions, values, resentments, regrets, upsets, and the language used for expressing their views of such worlds around them, and the stories and drama formed in their lives and how these stories and interpretations affect their lives, personally and professionally (Bakhshandeh 2015; Effingham 2013; Bakhshandeh 2009).

## Key Takeaways

The followings are the main takeaways from this chapter:

1. The definition and distinctions of transformational coaching and personal transformation
2. Transformational coaching background, principles, values, and fundamentals
3. Transformational coaching as instrumental in the application of organization development interventions
4. The result of transformational coaching dependent on collaboration and partnership among the coach, the client or sponsor, and the participant(s)
5. The differences between transactional coaching and transformational coaching
6. Transformational coaches strengths, skills, and competencies
7. Core practical skills for processing transformational coaching

## Discussion Points and Coaching Questions

1. How confident are you in your ability to conduct a transformational coaching process? What do you think is missing to develop the ability?

2. Do you understand the differences between transactional coaching and transformational coaching?
3. How do you rate yourself from zero to ten, zero being the lowest and ten being the highest on your transformational coach's strengths, skills, and competencies?
4. What is your plan of action to develop yourself as a skillful and competent transformational coach?

## References


Animas. 2018. Center for coaching. Retrieved from www.animascoaching.com/blog/the-evolution-of-transformational-coaching-196/

Bakhshandeh, Behnam. 2009. *Conspiracy for Greatness; Mastery on Love Within*. San Diego, CA: Primeco Education, Inc.

Bakhshandeh, Behnam. 2015. *Anatomy of Upset: Restoring Harmony*. Carbondale, PA: Primeco Education, Inc.

Bakhshandeh, Behnam. 2016. *The Power of Belief; All Realities are Not Invented Equally!*. Carbondale, PA: Primeco Education, Inc. Retrieved from: http://media.wix.com/ugd/4afcde_ad36a7f8a3d74202afd-01966b83ffed7.pdf

Berto, Francesco, and Matteo Plebani. 2015. *Ontology and Metaontology: A contemporary guide*. London: Bloomsbury Publishing.

Burke, Warner. 2018. *Organization Change: Theory & Practices* (5th ed.). Los Angeles, CA: SAGE Publication, Ltd.

Cashman, K. 2003. "Transformational coaching build awareness and commitment." *Executive Excellence* 20, no. 1: 11–11.

Cox, Elaine, Tatiana Bachkirova, and David Clutterbuck (Editors). 2010. *The Complete Handbook of Coaching*. Los Angeles, CA: Sage Publications.

Cox, Elaine, Tatiana Bachkirova, and David Clutterbuck. 2014. "Theoretical traditions and coaching genres: Mapping the territory." *Advances in Developing Human Resources* 16, no. 2: 139–160.

Cummings, Thomas G., and Chistopher, G. Worley. 2015. *Organization Development & Change* (10th ed.). Stamford, CT: Cengage Learning.

Effingham, Nikk. 2013. *An Introduction to Ontology*. Malden, MA: Polity Press.

Egan, Toby. 2013. "Response to Nieminen et al.'s feature article on executive coaching and facilitated multisource feedback: Toward better understanding of a growing HRD practice." *Human Resource Development Quarterly* 24, no. 2: 177–183.

Feldman, Harriet, R. 2018. "Identifying, building, and sustaining your leadership team". *Journal of Professional Nursing* 34, no. 2: 87–91.

Lasley, Martha, Virginia Kellogg, Richard Michaels, and Sharon Brown. 2015. *Coaching for Transformation: Pathway to Ignite Personal & Social Change* (2nd ed.). New York: Discover Press.

Rothwell, William J. 2015. *Beyond Training & Development. Enhancing Human Performance Through a Measurable Focus on Business Impact* (3rd ed.). Amherst, MA: HRD Press, Inc.

Rothwell, William J., Sohel M. Imroz, and Behnam Bakhshandeh. 2021. *Organization Development Interventions, Executing Effective Organizational Change*. New York, NY: Routledge-Taylor and Francis.

Rothwell, William, J., Jacqueline M. Stavros and Roland L. Sullivan. 2016. *Practicing Organization Development: Leading Transformation and Change* (4th ed.). Hoboken, NJ: John Wiley & Sons, Inc.

Rothwell, William J., Angela L. M. Stopper, and Jennifer L. Myers. 2017. *Assessment and Diagnosis for Organization Development*. Boca Raton, FL: CRC Press. Taylor and Francis Group.

Schmitt, Antje, Deanne N. Den Hartog, and Frank D. Belschak. 2016. "Transformational leadership and proactive work behavior: A moderated mediation model including work engagement and job strain." *Journal of Occupational and Organizational Psychology* 89, no. 3: 588–610.

Seale, Alan. 2011. *Create a World That Works: Toles for Personal & Global Transformation*. San Francisco, CA: Weiser Books.

Seale, Alan. 2017. *Transformational Presence: How to Make a Difference in a Rapidly Changing World*. Topsfield, MA: The Center for Transformational Presence.

Van der Pol, Leon. 2019. *A Shift in Being: The Art and Practices of Deep Transformational Coaching*. Imaginal Light Publishing. Self-Publishing.

# Chapter 3

# Transformational Learning in Transformational Coaching

Sohel M. Imroz

## Overview

Jack Mezirow (1994) defined transformational learning as "constructivist, an orientation which holds that the way learners interpret and reinterpret their sense experience is, central to making meaning and hence learning" (222). Transformational learning causes a shift in an individual's perspective and involves a change in the way learners perceive things and acquire new information (Kolagani 2019). With business and workplace, transformational learning can bring a range of different benefits to employees who desire to succeed in their field. Transformational learning can be applied to workplace mentoring and coaching, social learning groups, personalized learning and development paths, micro-learning modules for self-study, scenario-based gamified learning solutions, and job shadowing (Boney 2018). Transformational learning can help individuals to be more critical, autonomous, and ultimately responsible.

**This chapter attempts to underline:**

- Jack Mezirow's transformative learning theory
- Phases of transformational learning
- Benefits and disadvantages of transformational learning
- Application of transformational learning in leadership development
- Transformational learning examples
- How to use transformational learning in transformational coaching
- Transformational learning practices

DOI: 10.4324/9781003304074-4

## Jack Mezirow's Transformative Learning Theory

The transformative learning theory (TLT) was first introduced by Jack Mezirow in 1978. It is based on the concept that personal experience is an integral part of the learning process (Mezirow 1978). The transformational learning process starts as learners get new information, evaluate the information through critical reflection based on their past ideas and understanding, and, as a result, shift their worldview. According to Valamis Group (2021), transformative learning theory involves four general principles. First, TLC has two basic focuses: instrumental learning and communicative learning (Mezirow 1997). Instrumental learning focuses on task-oriented problem solving and involves identifying and evaluating cause-and-effect relationships of events or situations (Valamis Group 2021). Communicative learning focuses on how individuals acquire communicative skills and learn how to express their needs, wishes, feelings, and emotions (Mezirow 1997). Second, learning in transformational theory involves a change in perspectives and meaning structures (Mezirow 1997). Perspectives structure can be described as the predispositions and assumptions that shape an individual's expectations, while meaning structure refers to the concepts, beliefs, judgments, and feelings of individuals that shape interpretation of information (Valamis Group 2021). Third, individuals can understand or change the meaning structure of a content, process, or premise using self-reflection, self-directed learning, and critical theory (Teaching & Education 2020). Last, transformational learning can involve individuals critiquing their assumptions, learning new schemes or structures, transforming perspectives, or elaborating meaning to existing plans or programs (Teaching & Education 2020).

The fundamental components of transformative learning theory that facilitate the learning and transformation of adults in the business environment are centrality of experience, critical reflection, and rational/reflective discourse (Taylor 1998). The following section briefly elaborates on these components.

- **Centrality of experience:** According to Mezirow (1995), the starting point and subject matter of transformational learning is the learners' experience. Taylor (1998) described experiences as socially constructed, therefore, they can be deconstructed and acted upon. Examples of learners' experiences may entail "what people do, what they believe in, what they can put up with, the way they react to certain situations, what they would be willing to suffer for, and moreover, their desires, perspective, dream, and faith" (Valamis Group 2021, para. Centrality of Experience). Learners' experience provides the gist of the second theme of transformational learning—critical reflection (Taylor 1998).
- **Critical reflection:** Individuals need to think critically about their experiences to transform their perspective or meaning (Valamis Group 2021). According to Mezirow (1990, 13), "by far the most significant learning experiences in adulthood involve critical [reflection]—reassessing the way we have posed problems and reassessing our own orientation to perceiving, knowing, believing, feeling and acting." Critical reflection involves critiquing the justifications and validity of the presuppositions and assumptions that are the foundation of our beliefs (Mezirow 1990). Critical reflection facilitates transformational learning by enhancing self-awareness and promoting a deeper level of self-understanding.
- **Rational/reflective discourse:** Mezirow (1990) stated that individuals need a rational or reflective discourse with others for a successful transformational process. Reflective discourse requires that individuals discuss their perspectives, assumptions, or experiences with others in a rational manner to pinpoint any biases, prejudices, or personal concerns (Mezirow 1995). Thus, reflective discourse helps individuals building consensus and arriving at the most sound judgment regarding an assumption, understanding, thought, or belief (Valamis Group 2021).

## Phases of Transformational Learning

Mezirow (1991) described ten phases of personal transformation: disorienting dilemma, self-examination of assumptions, critical assessment, recognition of shared experiences, exploration of new roles and actions, planning a course of action, acquisition of knowledge, trying new roles, building confidence, and reintegration (Brinson 2021). The following section briefly describes these phases (see Figure 3.1):

- **Disorienting dilemma:** A disorienting dilemma occurs when an event, a situation, or a life crisis causes individuals to call into question their existing values, understandings, assumptions, thoughts, or beliefs (Taylor 2000). Mezirow (1991) described disorienting dilemmas as acute internal or external personal crises. Events such as death, divorce, loss of employment, bankruptcy, and so on, are few examples. A transformational learning experience often begins with a disorienting dilemma. Although such a dilemma can be uncomfortable or challenging for learners, it is the catalyst of the transformational learning journey (Teaching & Education 2020).

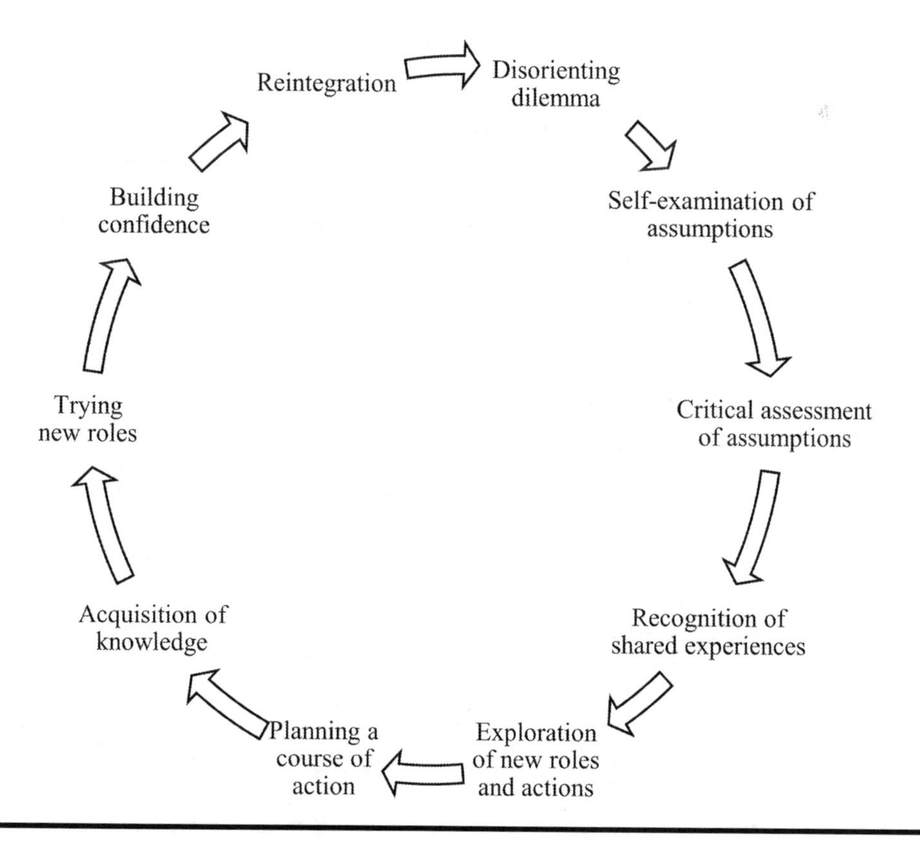


**Figure 3.1 Ten Phases of Transformational Learning.**

*Source:* Brinson (2021); Mezirow (1991).

- **Self-examination of assumptions:** After experiencing a disorienting dilemma, learners do a self-examination or self-reflection of their values, understandings, assumptions, thoughts, or beliefs—often based on their past experiences. The self-examination or self-reflection is often accompanied with a feeling of anger, fear, guilt, or shame (Roberts 2006). This phase helps the learners realize that their present perspective of the values, assumptions, and so on, may not be the only plausible one (Teaching & Education 2020). For learners, self-examination or self-reflection can lead to significant personal transformation (Mezirow 1997).
- **Critical assessment of assumptions:** In this phase of transformational learning, learners take a more comprehensive look at their values, understandings, assumptions, thoughts, or beliefs; review them critically; and check for their validity (Teaching & Education 2020). After a closer look, learners may realize that perhaps some of their past assumptions, thoughts, or beliefs were wrong. Therefore, they may become more open to new or alternative information, understandings, or thoughts. The openness creates a transformation of perspective. As the learners get to critically assess their assumptions and realize their true validity, the chances of them accepting new and alternative information and understanding increase (Kolagani 2019).
- **Recognition of shared experiences:** Shared experiences are a powerful learning tool because they bring learners together and enhance each learner's individual experience (Kramer 2022). Sharing an experience with others also makes the experience more enjoyable, memorable, and even intense. A shared experience is "seeing, hearing, or doing the same thing as someone else" (Kramer 2022, para. What are shared experiences?). The practice of sharing makes learners understand when others are in need and gives them a sense of responsibility. When learners share their experiences, it shows they care, and it facilitates the transformational learning process.
- **Exploration of new roles and actions:** In the next phase of transformational learning process, learners seek roles and actions compatible with their new or alternative assumptions, understandings, thoughts, or beliefs. They also create deeper relationships with other learners in completing tasks compatible with the new ideas and understandings (Valamis Group 2021; Brinson 2021).
- **Planning a course of action:** With an understanding of how their past assumptions, understandings, thoughts, or beliefs may have been wrong, and after having a perspective transformation, learners in this phase can plan a course of action toward the new insights, ideas, and understandings (Teaching & Education 2020). It is noteworthy that the course of action may not happen immediately, since learners may need to overcome "situational, emotional, and informational constraints that may require new learning experiences to move forward" (Mezirow 2012, 87).
- **Acquisition of knowledge:** The next phase in the transformational learning process for the learners is acquisition of knowledge, skills, and abilities to carry out their new course of action. Learners may have to learn new things, consider different points of view, and implement different behaviors to further enrich their learning. These may take extensive work and effort, but this is where the actual learning takes place and better results are achieved (Teaching & Education 2020).
- **Trying new roles:** In this phase of transformational learning, learners put their new knowledge, skills, and abilities to the test by actively applying them (Brinson 2021). This allows

learners to take advantage of experiential learning—getting hands-on, learning by doing, and reflecting on the experience (Teaching & Education 2020).

- **Building confidence:** As learners try new roles, gain new experiences, and make their own decisions, they should build greater self-awareness and self-efficacy—confidence and beliefs about their capabilities to produce desired levels of performance. Learners with substantial self-efficacy are more likely to "approach difficult tasks as challenges to be mastered rather than as threats to be avoided" (Bandura 1994, 71). As learners advance through the transformational learning phases, it is important for them to build confidence in their beliefs and understanding, and to continue to practice this transformational cycle (Teaching & Education 2020).
- **Reintegration:** In this last phase of the transformational learning process, learners get used to their new self and emerge back into their lives with fresh perspectives, ideas, understandings, and beliefs (Brinson 2021).

### *Summarizing Transformational Learning Phases*

Depending on the learner and situation, some of the aforementioned phases may be more dominant than others. Therefore, it is possible to summarize these ten phases into three core stages (Brinson 2021):

1. All transformations will start with dilemma or crisis. The dilemma or crisis spurs learners' realization that a transformation is needed.
2. Learners follow up the dilemma or crisis with reflection and examination of their perspectives, assumptions, values, and beliefs. Reflecting and examining can often lead the learners to challenge their existing perspectives. This core stage is about figuring out what transformation might look like.
3. The later stages of the transformation are about adopting and acting upon new perspectives. Learners discover what they need to learn and do to accomplish the new perspectives and make the transformation. Last, learners adopt new behaviors reflecting the transformation.

## Benefits and Disadvantages of Transformational Learning

Two of the greatest benefits of transformational learning are higher retention of learning and greater appreciation of knowledge (Harrington-Atkinson 2021). Upon completing the ten phases of transformational learning, learners remember the new information and apply it to new situations. Transformational learning also promotes higher levels of critical thinking skills (e.g., analyzing, evaluating, and creating) and personal development—when learners know more about themselves and their interests and work toward achieving them (Atieno 2018).

On the negative side, transformational learning may not be an appropriate option for all learning situations and would be ineffective for relationships, emotions, or feelings (Harrington-Atkinson 2021). According to Harrington-Atkinson (2021), the repeated questioning-reflection process could be detrimental for the emotional well-being of some learners causing them to question the truthfulness of even the most basic of thoughts.

## Application of Transformational Learning in Leadership Development

Leadership development is a set of activities that improves the skills, capabilities, and confidence of current and future leaders and prepares them to perform effectively in their roles (Gartner 2022). According to Gartner (2022), leadership development activities generally enable leaders to improve their skills and capabilities in the areas of decision making, project management, strategy, network building, team building and management, innovation, and coaching/developing others. Today's organizational leaders play an ever-increasing important role in creating a workplace environment and culture where employees feel valued and appreciated for being themselves and for their talent (Fisher-Yoshida et al. 2005). This sense of appreciation increases employee engagement and creativity (2005). A "sense of self and authentic connection to others" (2005, 562)—which includes caring, being there, listening, willingness to help, and ability to understand others—is the foundation of today's successful organizational leaders (2005).

Brown and Posner (2001) advocated using transformational learning concept and practices (e.g., critical self-reflection, meaning making, creating learning mindset, experimentation, etc.) in leadership development to reach the leaders at a personal and emotional level. According to Brown and Posner (2001, 279), "Transformational learning theory can be used to assess, strengthen, and create leadership development programs that develop transformational leaders." Fisher-Yoshida et al. (2005) shared these examples of transformational learning interventions to develop leadership capabilities:

- **Experiencing a multifaceted self:** The purpose of these interventions is for the leaders to better perceive and understand their abilities, traits, preferences, and personalities. Leadership development programs commonly use psychological tests (e.g., Myers–Briggs Type Indicator), tests for leadership type (e.g., Multifactor Leadership Questionnaire), 360-degree feedback, and so on, to carry out these interventions.
- **Creating learning partnerships:** Leadership development programs often create a partnership between two colleagues or between a mentor and a mentee in the same organization to share knowledge and expertise. These interventions help leaders develop meaningful interactions with others by creating a relationship mutually responsive and empathic (2005). To create an effective learning partnership, partners should set ground rules for working together, share personal insights, set mutually agreed goals and objectives, and jointly come up with action plans. Learning partnerships allow all partners to look at themselves through the viewpoint of the other, get a better understanding of their strengths and limitations, build confidence, and be encouraged and challenged in reaching their goals and objectives (2005).
- **Using arts to learn about self, others, and relationship:** Using arts is a powerful and creative way for building teams and improving group dynamics—how people in a group interact with each other. Popular arts-based team building activities are Chinese whispers drawing, blind drawing, left- or right-handed drawing, team Pictionary, team artworks, team murals, puzzle artwork, musical artworks, and so on (Ideal Art 2022). Leadership development programs using arts-based team building activities foster mutuality, help the leaders trust and honor each other, and build a sense of communal "we-ness" (Fisher-Yoshida et al. 2005, 563) essential for transformation.

## Transformational Learning Examples

Valamis Group (2021) has provided several examples of transformational learning in an organizational setting—job shadowing, scenario-based learning, cultural adaptation, career change, and co-working with different departments. Job shadowing is a useful means to learn more about a job of interest and involves following experienced professionals as they work (Doyle 2020). By observing the professionals for anywhere from a few hours to several weeks, learners can get a better understanding of their particular job and career (Doyle 2020). Scenario-based learning (SBL) is a popular "active learning" instructional strategy that uses real-life situations and provides a highly relevant learning experience to the learners (Pandey 2019). Cultural adaptation involves "reviewing and changing the structure of a program or practice to more appropriately fit the needs and preferences of a particular cultural group or community" (Samuels et al. 2009, 7). Helped by internet, more companies are conducting business globally and interacting with employees, customers, suppliers, and other service providers with various cultural backgrounds. Allowing employees to experience different cultures can expand their awareness and acceptance of diversity, and help them share empathy, compassion, and appreciation of equity and inclusion (Valamis Group 2021).

Experiencing a career change can have a drastic effect on individuals and alter their perspectives (Valamis Group 2021). A career is "individually perceived sequence of attitudes and behaviors associated with work-related experiences and activities over the span of the person's life" (Hall 2002, 12). Hall (2002) mentioned several important points about career. First, a career is a sequence of work-related activities and does not just imply someone's "fast" or "slow" advancement in their professional positions. Second, the success or failure of the career should be assessed by the person being considered, not by anyone else. Third, since the career comprises both behaviors and attitudes, there are two aspects of career—subjective and objective. Subjective career consists of changes in people's values, attitudes, and motivation as they grow older. Objective career consists of "the observable choices one makes and the activities one engages in, such as the acceptance or rejection of a job offer" (Hall 2002, 11).

As people advance in their career, they will obtain new knowledge, skills, and abilities; will have bigger responsibilities; and will perceive things differently, resulting in transformation. Working with colleagues and team members from other departments can help employees be more positive, reliable, flexible, willing to change, share information and resources, and respect their work style and habits. All these play important roles in personal and professional transformation toward being a valued team member.

## How to Use Transformational Learning in Transformational Coaching

Transformational learning principles and approaches may be suitable for transformational coaching for several reasons. First, learners can transform perspectives "from a right and wrong dichotomy to a palette of possibilities" (Fisher-Yoshida 2009, 150) by developing more self-awareness of their behaviors and by the impact of the behaviors on others. Second, learners can realize that the behaviors are created because of subconscious assumptions that also influence their actions and reactions to others (Brookfield 1987). Third, incorporating transformational learning may help learners develop an awareness of how well their operational assumptions are working for or against them (1987). Fisher-Yoshida (2009) described these steps of how to use transformational learning in transformational coaching.

- **Getting ready to begin:** This step can be described as needs assessment. Before commencing the coaching sessions, coaches understand the learners' current and desired states of thinking or self-awareness and their existing level of readiness to transform. To do this, the learners share their experiences, how they make meaning of the experiences, and how others may interpret and understand their experiences.
- **The coaching sessions commence:** When the coaching sessions start, coaches establish the foundation of how the sessions would be conducted, model their desired behaviors when interacting with the learners, and offer constructive and supportive feedback to the learners in a nondefensive and nonthreatening manner (Fisher-Yoshida 2009; Marsick et al. 2006). During the coaching sessions, coaches help the learners to better understand what they know by focusing on three levels of knowing—instrumental (based on concrete and observable data), socializing (based on the values and relationships), and self-authoring (based on the learners' own understanding) (Kegan et al. 2001). To help the learners with different levels of knowing, Fisher-Yoshida (2009) suggested that coaches use various tools such as Coordinated Management of Meaning (CMM), Daisy Model, and so on.
- **Preparing for the transfer:** To prepare the learners for transformation, coaches help them in clarifying what they actually know and what they need to know to make the transformation happen. Fisher-Yoshida (2009) found the LUUUUTT model, or storytelling model, useful because it allows the coaches to ask the learners questions and have them reflect, and even challenge, their own assumptions. As learners prepare for the transfer, they deepen and broaden their self-awareness and develop a deeper understanding of actions and reactions of their own and others.
- **Reaction to perspective shifts:** The coaching process is not always smooth or challenge-free. Learners often strongly hold on to their existing perspectives, beliefs, or habits, which can make the transformation difficult and time-consuming. The learners experience positive reaction to perspective shift when coaches help them distance themselves from negativity, change their emotional and mental inputs, manage expectations, and focus on impact and benefits of the shift (Lechter 2019).
- **Reflection:** Transformational learning may create resistance, discomfort, and emotional distress in learners, which may be alleviated by reflecting on the coaching process (Fisher-Yoshida 2009). Reflection helps turn experience into knowledge (Gilbert and Trudel 2001) and involves thought and exploration of a concept or an event (Gray 2007). Following each coaching session, Fisher-Yoshida (2009) recommended that coaches reflect on their own interactions, check their assumptions about what they know and understand about the learners, confirm what they expect from themselves and the learners, and challenge themselves to provide the learners with additional opportunities for discovery and transformation.

Different types of reflection may take place at different times and can benefit the coaches' reflective practice in different ways. Reflection-on-action means coaches think back on what learners did and review and inform how they can do something about it (Gilbert and Trudel 2001). It takes place after a coaching session has finished. Reflection-in-action means coaches think about what learners are doing while they are doing it (Schön 1983). It is likely to take place during a coaching session. Coaches need to be aware of the advantages and disadvantages of these two types of reflection (Scott 2019) for effective transformational coaching. Ghaye and Ghaye (1998) suggested that reflection should not be a description of what happened, instead, should provide a constructive critique of an issue. Reflection also needs to be fair, accurate, and honest (1998). Few useful tools for reflective conversation are critical incidents, storytelling, reflective metaphor, reflective dialogue, and reflective journal (Mitchell 2013).

## Transformational Learning Practices

There are numerous ways individuals can be taught, and there is no single correct way to apply transformative learning theory. However, Taylor (1998) emphasized three key points when applying transformative learning theory in practice. First, "ideal learning conditions promote a sense of safety, openness, and trust" (53). Second, "effective instructional methods support a learner-centered approach" and "promote student autonomy, participation and collaboration" (53). Third, "the importance of activities that encourage the exploration of alternative personal perspectives, problem-posing, and critical reflection" (54). To effectively carry out these key points, transformational coaches and learners must work together to deliver a quality transformational learning experience. A clear understanding of transformational coaches' and learners' roles and responsibilities is paramount for successful transformational learning. The following section describes a few critical roles and responsibilities of transformational coaches and learners.

### *The Roles of a Transformational Coach*

- One of the most critical roles and responsibilities of a transformational coach to foster an effective transformational learning is to assist the learners learn of their assumptions, interpretations, beliefs, habits of mind, or points of view and analyze them critically.
- Transformational coaches should assist the learners in how to recognize various frames of reference—a set of assumptions, conditions, or ideas that determine how something can be approached, perceived, or understood. In other words, coaches should encourage the learners to redefine and interpret problems from different perspectives. The goal of a coach should be to enable the learners to find the root cause(s) of a problem and uncover solutions that take the needs and feelings of everyone involved into consideration.
- Transformational coaches should provide the learners with opportunities to effectively participate in discourse that involves assessing values, understandings, assumptions, thoughts, or beliefs through critical examination of arguments, alternate points of view, and evidence. Coaches should encourage the learners to validate what they understand and make well-informed judgments based on their understanding.
- Transformational coaches should urge the learners be familiar with several useful methods to participate in discourse more effectively. Some useful methods are concept mapping (e.g., charts, flowcharts, timelines, etc.), consciousness raising (e.g., making people more aware of an issue), metaphor analysis (e.g., giving the learners a rich and insightful way to articulate an intricate and complex concept), life histories (e.g., individuals' personal experiences and their connections with past events), repertory grid technique (a method for eliciting what individuals think about a given topic), and participation in social action.

- Transformational coaches must encourage equal participation from the learners in discourse. To do this, the coach can require each group member take a turn in monitoring the direction of dialogue and ensure equal participation from all. When appropriate, coaches can also present controversial statements or readings from opposing viewpoints to encourage dialogue among the learners. However, the coaches must not interject their own ideas or viewpoints and avoid shaping the discussion.
- Setting objectives for the learners that include autonomous thinking is another important role of a transformational coach. Autonomous thinking or intellectual autonomy is a willingness and ability of the learners to think for themselves and make their own interpretations rather than acting on the purposes, beliefs, judgments, and feelings of others. The foundations of autonomous thinking often begin in our childhood and continue in our adulthood causing us reject ideas that don't fit into our existing belief and view. Transformational coaches can promote autonomous thinking by encouraging the learners be self-independent, having the learners take ownership of their learning, and facilitating peer-to-peer learning.
- Transformational coaches should promote discovery learning to the learners. Discovery learning can be done using various methods, for example, learning contracts, group projects, role play, case studies, and simulations. A learning contract identifies the learning objectives, resources, obstacles, solutions, deadlines, and measurements (Peterson 2019). These methods can facilitate transformational learning by helping the learners examine various concepts in their lives and by analyzing the justification of new information and knowledge.
- Transformational coaches should create and foster a learning environment that builds trust and care among learners focusing on diversity, equity, and inclusiveness. The coaches should behave like role models by demonstrating willingness to learn and change and be authentic.

## *The Roles of a Learner*

Through transformational learning, the learners achieve a change in their "perspective" by acquiring and constructing new knowledge about themselves or about the new values, understandings, assumptions, thoughts, or beliefs. The learners are an active participant having important roles in the learning environment and process. The roles and responsibilities of the learners in transformational coaching are described next.

- The learners must practice behaviors that include attention, civility, respect, and responsibility to help others learn. The learners should welcome diversity and inclusiveness in the learning environment and focus on peer collaboration.
- To critically reflect the perspectives and assumptions that underlie their intentions, values, beliefs, and feelings, the learners can use communicative learning approach and discourse analysis. A communicative learning approach is dictated by the learners' needs and is personalized according to their interests (Irmawati 2012). Discourse analysis looks beyond the literal meaning of language and focuses on interaction (Shaw and Bailey 2009).

- The most important role of the learners involves actively participating in discourse. Through discourse, the learners can analyze, evaluate, and validate what is being communicated to them. Active participation from all learners fosters collaborative learning by allowing them to critically examine evidence, arguments, and alternate points of view. The learners can actively participate by asking relevant questions for understanding and clarification, making valuable comments, sharing their own experiences and opinions, and by avoiding relying on the coach for learning.

## Key Takeaways

The following are the main takeaways from this chapter:

1. Transformational learning focuses on the idea that the learners can adjust their thinking and perspective based on new information. In this process of shifting their worldview, they evaluate their past ideas and understanding through critical reflection.
2. Three fundamental components of transformative learning theory that facilitate the learning and transformation of adults in the business environment are centrality of experience, critical reflection, and rational/reflective discourse.
3. Ten phases of personal transformation are disorienting dilemma, self-examination of assumptions, critical assessment, recognition of shared experiences, exploration of new roles and actions, planning a course of action, acquisition of knowledge, trying new roles, building confidence, and reintegration.
4. Experiencing a multifaceted self; creating learning partnerships; and using arts to learn about self, others, and relationships are examples of transformational learning interventions to develop transformational leadership capabilities.
5. Transformational learning framework is suitable for the coaching environment not only based on its principles but also because of its core components and facets: centrality of experience, critical reflection, and rational/reflective discourse.
6. A clear understanding of transformational coaches' and learners' roles and responsibilities is paramount for successful transformational learning.

## Discussion Points and Coaching Questions

1. Describe your most recent transformational coaching experience.
2. This chapter presents three fundamental principles of transformative learning theory—centrality of experience, critical reflection, and rational/reflective discourse. Which principle do you find most important in your transformational coaching experience? Please explain.
3. This chapter also presents ten phases of personal transformation. In your transformational coaching experience, which phase(s) did you find most challenging to overcome?
4. This chapter provides several examples of transformational learning interventions. What other interventions have you used for transformational learning?
5. Besides those listed in this chapter, what other roles and responsibilities of transformational coaches and learners would you recommend? Please explain.

## References

Atieno, Lydia. 2018. "The importance of personal development activities in schools." Retrieved from www.newtimes.co.rw/lifestyle/importance-personal-development-activities-schools

Bandura, Albert. 1994. Encyclopedia of human behavior. In V. S. Ramachandran (Ed.), *Self-efficacy* (Vol. 4, pp. 71–81). New York: Academic Press. (Reprinted in H. Friedman [Ed.], *Encyclopedia of mental health*. San Diego: Academic Press, 1998). Retrieved from www.uky.edu/~eushe2/Bandura/BanEncy.html

Boney, Erika. 2018. "Fostering a culture of transformative learning through informal learning experiences." Retrieved from https://elearningindustry.com/transformative-learning-informal-learning-experiences-fostering-culture

Brinson, Sam. 2021. "The 10 phases of Mezirow's transformational learning theory." Retrieved from www.diygenius.com/transformational-learning/

Brookfield, Stephen D. 1987. *Developing Critical Thinkers: Challenging Adults to Explore Alternative Ways of Thinking and Acting*. San Francisco, CA: Jossey-Bass.

Brown, Lillas M., and Posner, Barry Z. 2001. "Exploring the relationship between learning and leadership." *Leadership & Organization Development Journal* 22(5): 274–280. https://doi.org/10.1108/01437730110403204.

Doyle, Alison. 2020. "What is job shadowing? Definition & examples of job shadowing." Retrieved from www.thebalancecareers.com/what-is-job-shadowing-2062024

Fisher-Yoshida, Beth. 2009. Coaching to transform perspective. In J. Mezirow, E. W. Taylor, and Associates (Eds.), *Transformative Learning in Practice: Insights from Community, Workplace, and Higher Education* (1st ed., pp. 148–159). San Francisco, CA: Jossey-Bass.

Fisher-Yoshida, Beth, Geller, Kathy D., and Wasserman, Ilene C. 2005. *Transformative Learning in Human Resource Development: Successes in Scholarly Practitioner Applications–Conflict Management, Discursive Processes in Diversity and Leadership Development*. https://eric.ed.gov/?id=ED492441

Gartner. 2022. "Leadership development." Retrieved from www.gartner.com/en/human-resources/glossary/leadership-development

Ghaye, Anthony, and Ghaye, Kay. 1998. *Teaching and Learning through Critical Reflective Practice*. London: D. Fulton Publishers.

Gilbert, Wade, and Trudel, Pierre. 2001. Learning to coach through experience: Reflection in model youth sport coaches. *Journal of Teaching in Physical Education* 21(1): 16–34.

Gray, David. 2007. Facilitating management learning: Developing critical reflection through reflective tools. *Management Learning* 38(5): 495–517.

Hall, Douglas. 2002. *Careers In and Out of organizations*. Thousand Oaks, CA: Sage.

Harrington-Atkinson, Tracy. 2021. "Transformative learning." Retrieved from https://tracyharringtonatkinson.com/transformative-learning/

Ideal Art. 2022. "Art team building activity ideas." Retrieved from https://idealart.com.au/pages/art-team-building-activity-ideas

Irmawati, Noer Doddy. 2012. "Communicative approach: an alternative method used in improving students' academic reading achievement." Retrieved from https://files.eric.ed.gov/fulltext/EJ1079667.pdf

Kegan, Robert, Broderick, Maria, Drago-Severson, Eleanor, Helsing, Deborah, Popp, Nancy, and Portnow, Kathryn. 2001. *Toward a New Pluralism in ABE/ESOL Classrooms: Teaching to Multiple "Cultures of Mind."* Cambridge, MA: Harvard University Graduate School of Education.

Kolagani, Sushmitha. 2019. "Leveraging the power of transformative learning in eLearning." Retrieved from https://blog.commlabindia.com/elearning-design/transformational-learning-elearning

Kramer, Bryan. 2022. "The art of creating shared experiences." Retrieved from https://bryankramer.com/art-creating-shared-experiences/

Lechter, Sharon. 2019. "5 ways to change your perspective and be happier." Retrieved from https://sharonlechter.com/blog/2018/12/12/change-perspective/

Marsick, V., Sauquet, A., and Yorks, L. 2006. Learning through reflection. In M. Deutsch, P. T. Coleman, and E. Marcus (Eds.), *The handbook of conflict resolution: Theory and practice* (2nd ed., pp. 486–506). San Francisco, CA: Jossey-Bass.

Mezirow, Jack. 1978. "Perspective transformation." *Adult Education Quarterly* 28: 100–110.
Mezirow, Jack. 1990. *Fostering critical reflection in adulthood: A guide to transformative and emancipatory learning*. San Francisco, CA: Jossey-Bass.
Mezirow, Jack. 1991. *Transformative dimensions of adult learning*. San Francisco, CA: Jossey-Bass.
Mezirow, Jack. 1994. "Understanding transformation theory." *Adult Education Quarterly* 44(4): 222–232.
Mezirow, Jack. 1995. In defense of the lifeworld. In M. R. Welton (Ed.), *Transformation theory of adult learning* (pp. 39–70). New York: State University of New York Press.
Mezirow, Jack. 1997. "Transformative learning: Theory to practice." *New Directions for Adult and Continuing Education. No. 74*. Retrieved from www.ecolas.eu/eng/wp-content/uploads/2015/10/Mezirow-Transformative-Learning.pdf
Mezirow, Jack. 2012. Learning to think like an adult: Core concepts of transformation theory. In E. W. Taylor and P. Cranton (Eds.), *The Handbook of Transformative Learning: Theory, Research, and Practice* (1st ed., pp. 73–95). San Francisco, CA: Jossey-Bass.
Mitchell, Jeff. 2013. "Reflection as a coach development tool." Retrieved from https://coachgrowth.wordpress.com/2013/07/27/reflection-as-a-coach-development-tool/
Pandey, Asha. 2019. "A 5-step plan to create a captivating scenario-based corporate training." Retrieved from https://elearningindustry.com/scenario-based-learning-corporate-training-how-create
Peterson, Deb. 2019. "How to write a learning contract and realize your goals." Retrieved from www.thoughtco.com/how-to-write-a-learning-contract-31423
Roberts, Nella. 2006. "Disorienting dilemmas: Their effects on learners, impact on performance, and implications for adult educators." Retrieved from https://digitalcommons.fiu.edu/cgi/viewcontent.cgi?referer=&httpsredir=1&article =1249&context=sferc
Samuels, Judith, Schudrich, Wendy, and Altschul, Deborah. 2009. *Toolkit for Modifying Evidence-based Practice to Increase Cultural Competence*. Orangeburg, NY: Research Foundation for Mental Health. Retrieved from https://calmhsa.org/wp-content/uploads/2013/10/ToolkitEBP.pdf
Schön, Donald. 1983. *The Reflective Practitioner: How Professionals Think in Action*. London: Temple Smith.
Scott, Mark. 2019. "Thinking on your feet: how coaches can use reflection-in-action to develop their coaching craft." Retrieved from www.ukcoaching.org/getattachment/Resources/Topics/Research/Applied-Coaching-Research-Journal-April-2020-V-(1)/Thinking-on-Your-Feet-How-Coaches-Can-Use-Reflection-In-Action.pdf
Shaw, Sara E., and Bailey, Julia. 2009. "Discourse analysis: what is it and why is it relevant to family practice?" Retrieved from www.ncbi.nlm.nih.gov/pmc/articles/PMC2743732/
Taylor, Edward. 1998. *The Theory and Practice of Transformative Learning: A Critical Review* (Information Series No. 374). London: Center on Education and Training for Employment.
Taylor, Edward. 2000. "Fostering Mezirow's transformative learning theory in the adult education classroom: A critical review". *Canadian Journal for the Study of Adult Education* 14(2): 1–28. Retrieved from https://cjsae.library.dal.ca/index.php/cjsae/article/view/1929
Teaching and Education. 2020. "What is the transformative learning theory?" Retrieved from www.wgu.edu/blog/what-transformative-learning-theory2007.html#close
Valamis Group. 2021. "Transformative learning." Retrieved from www.valamis.com/hub/transformative-learning

# APPLICATION OF TRANSFORMATIONAL COACHING IN ELEMENTS OF OD

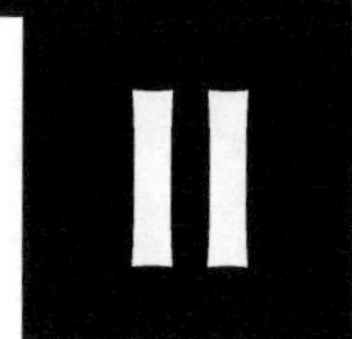


Transformational coaching applies to organizations and their workforces. An organizations' culture has an effect on how individuals and teams are coached and how they undergo transformation. Organization leaders who receive coaching can influence the organization if their mindset is transformed as well as the way they relate to people and their productivity, because individual transformation is often a pathway to organizational transformation. Part II focuses on the relevancy between transformational change and transformational coaching, and its application in process of organization development, high-performance, and talent development.

## Chapter 4. Transformational Coaching and Organization Development

Chapter 4 explores the relationship among transformational change and transformational coaching and organization development and application on transformational coaching in OD.

## Chapter 5. Transformational Coaching and High Performance

Topics discussed in Chapter 5 include distinguishing among performance, high performance, and a high-performance workplace (HPW), and the role of transformational coaching in achieving high performance.

## Chapter 6. Transformational Coaching and Talent Development

The role, use, and importance of transformational coaching for talent development is covered in Chapter 6.

DOI: 10.4324/9781003304074-5

# Chapter 4

# Transformational Coaching and Organization Development

William J. Rothwell

## Overview

Transformational coaching (TC) is carried out with employed people. That is important to know, since the corporate culture of an organization can influence how people are coached and how they undergo transformation. Leaders who receive coaching can affect the organization if they are transformed, and often individual transformation is essential to organizational transformation.

Organization development (OD) was defined in a previous chapter. But it is worth defining it again. OD is usually regarded as a top-management-supported effort to facilitate change in an organization by improving how people interact to achieve work results. Stated another way, OD applies democracy to the workplace by giving all workers—and that includes managers—say in decisions affecting them. An organization's management does not thrust change on unwilling people using a project management approach; rather, OD is based on the assumption that the best way to overcome resistance to change is to involve all those affected by it and give them a voice in decision making.

This chapter focuses on the relationship between TC and OD. It addresses such questions as these:

- What is transformational change?
- How does transformational change relate to transformational coaching?
- How does transformational change relate to OD?
- How does OD relate to transformational coaching?
- How is transformational coaching applied in OD?
- How is transformational coaching applied without OD?

The chapter concludes with a list of key takeaways from this chapter, discussion points and coaching questions, and references.

DOI: 10.4324/9781003304074-6

## What Is Transformational Change?

Transformation has become a popular buzzword in recent times. Managers toss around statements like "what we need is a fundamental transformation in our corporate culture." Others bemoan how long it takes to change corporate culture and yearn for low-cost strategies that can prompt radical change overnight.

There are *degrees or types of change*. First described in an award-winning article by Golembiewski et al. (1976), the authors posited that change can be categorized into three types:

- ***Alpha change*** "involves a variation in the level of some existential state, given a constantly calibrated measuring instrument related to a constant conceptual domain" (134).
- ***Beta change*** "involves a variation in the level of some existential state, complicated by the fact that some intervals of the measurement continuum associated with a constant conceptual domain have been recalibrated" (135).
- ***Gamma change*** "involves a redefinition or reconceptualization of some domain, a major change in the perspective or frame of reference within which phenomena are perceived and classified, in what is taken to be a relevant slide of reality" (135).

While authors Golembiewski, Billingsley, and Yeager were focused on classifying degrees of change in research and particularly in how to measure change in human systems, organizational researchers have long yearned for a way to classify degrees of organizational change. According to this scheme, gamma change is synonymous with transformational change.

A more recent way of thinking about types of change includes the distinctions between "calm water" and "white water rapids" change (Ranasinghe 2021). As Ranasinghe explains:

> Through the metaphor it says that planned changes come with the "Calm waters." However, emergent approach to change needs to be best fit with the "White Water Rapid." Organizations face change like a raft in an intense river and every time it has to handle with white-water rapids. (n.p.)

Most organizations in today's dynamic environment face "white water change" because major change looms as a constant issue. No sooner have managers handled a pandemic than the threat of a nuclear war looms on the horizon with no return to normalcy. *Black swan events*—seemingly trivial events that spiral out of control and grow to global proportions—have become more the norm than the exception.

Perhaps what is needed is a more robust scheme to describe categories of organizational and individual change (see Figure 4.1). Consider:

- ***Alpha change*** could mean the same as simple incremental change. In this scheme, the external environment does not undergo radical shifts. Neither do the people in the change effort: Staffing is stable. Change goals remain stable throughout the change project. Change could be represented as a straight line with a discernible beginning, middle, and end. By analogy, change is a simple staircase with a beginning point (the base of the stairs), midpoint (the middle point on the stairway), and an endpoint (top of the stairs).
- ***Beta change*** is a step or degree beyond simple incremental change. In this scheme, the people in the change effort remain stable. But the competitive environment shifts as the change effort is implemented. The change project goals remain stable. By analogy, change is

like an escalator. As the people work toward the change goals, the ground (the competitive conditions in the world outside the organization) is moving beneath them.

- ***Gamma change*** is a step beyond beta change. In this scheme, the people in the change effort and the competitive conditions are changing while the change process is underway. Yet change project goals remain stable throughout the change effort. By analogy, change is like an elevator. While the elevator begins on a ground floor and can move to the top of the elevator shaft, it can stop at any point along the way and people can enter or leave. The ground moves and the people change, but the change project continues.
- ***Delta change*** is a step beyond gamma change. The change effort has a definable beginning but the people and competitive conditions change during the change process. Likewise, there is no end point. Change moves like a spiral whereby changing competitive conditions and changing people can lead to changes in the change project goals even as the change project is underway.
- ***Epsilon change*** is a step beyond delta change. There is no starting point; there is no ending point to the change effort. During the change effort, the competitive conditions change, the people change, and the project goals change. Nothing is stable, and change is continuous. Change, by analogy, is like an Unidentified Flying Object: it can move in any direction and at any speed, changing course in ways that defy gravity and the laws of physics.

In this scheme, transformational change is akin to epsilon change. See Figure 4.1.

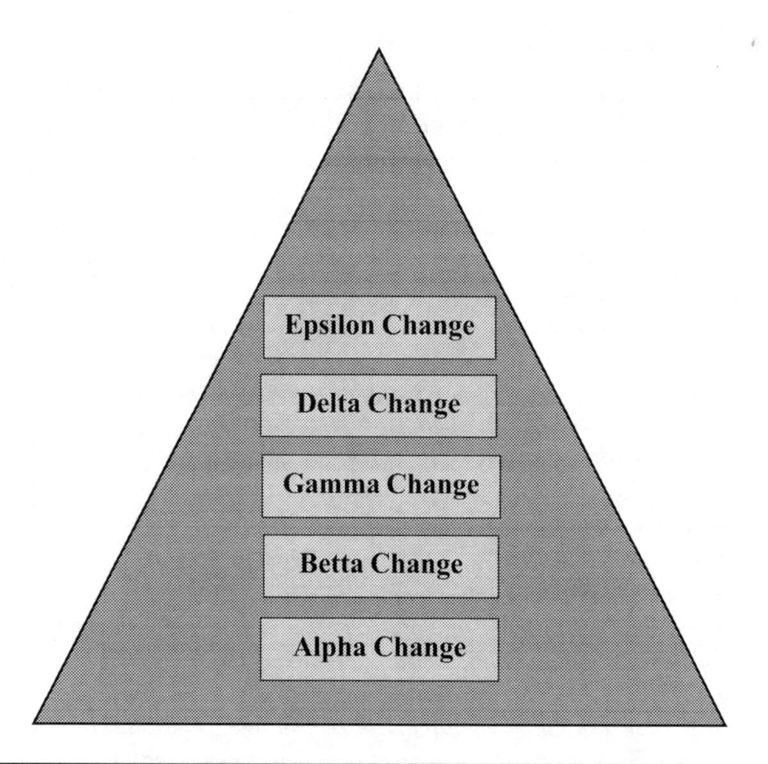


**Figure 4.1 Categories of Organizational and Individual Change.**

*Source:* Author's Original Creation. Copyright 2022 by William J. Rothwell.

## How Does Transformational Change Relate to Transformational Coaching?

If transformational change means a radical shift in perspective, then transformational coaching is geared to bringing about radical change in the individual and in the individual's perspective about his or her organizational and life context. In transformational coaching, people learn to see themselves and their life contexts differently than they did before the coaching experience. Their goals can change; their sense of their environment can change; and their sense of their close contacts can change. Transformational coaching thus brings about transformational change for individuals, teams, and organizations.

## How Does Transformational Change Relate to OD?

Organization development facilitates change at any level—whether alpha, beta, gamma, delta, or epsilon change.

Recall that OD is based on Kurt Lewin's Action Research Model or David Cooperrider's Appreciative Inquiry Model. Either model provides a roadmap for how to plan, implement, and evaluate a change effort using OD. They are actually similar. Their biggest difference centers on where they begin. The Action Research Model centers on solving an identified problem, while the Appreciative Inquiry Model centers on building on one or more strengths.

### *The Action Research Model*

While there are many published versions of the Action Research Model (ARM), one way to understand it is that the consultant from inside or outside the organization will (see Figure 4.2):

- ***Enter the scene***: The consultant is typically called into the organization to solve a problem. The end of this stage is a written proposal for consulting services to the client.
- ***Start up the change effort***: The consultant investigates the organization or the setting. The end of this stage is a negotiated contract.
- ***Assess what is happening and what should be happening by collecting information from stakeholders***: The consultant visits with many stakeholders, asking them what challenges face the organization and how important those challenges are.
- ***Feedback the data collected and help stakeholders in the organization to agree on***: the problem(s), solutions, action plans, and metrics, facilitating efforts by stakeholders to agree on problems, solutions, action plans, and metrics.
- ***Facilitate action planning***: The consultant works with the client to provide information gathered from stakeholders and then facilitates client efforts to devise a work plan to implement the solutions identified by the client.
- ***Facilitate the implementation of the action plan over time in an OD intervention***: The consultant works with the client during implementation of the action plan to facilitate information gathering and information sharing.
- ***Help the organization's members to adopt the change effort, making it part of the corporate culture***: The consultant encourages the client to lock the change into the corporate culture in a process variously called *adoption, institutionalization*, or *corporate culture change.*

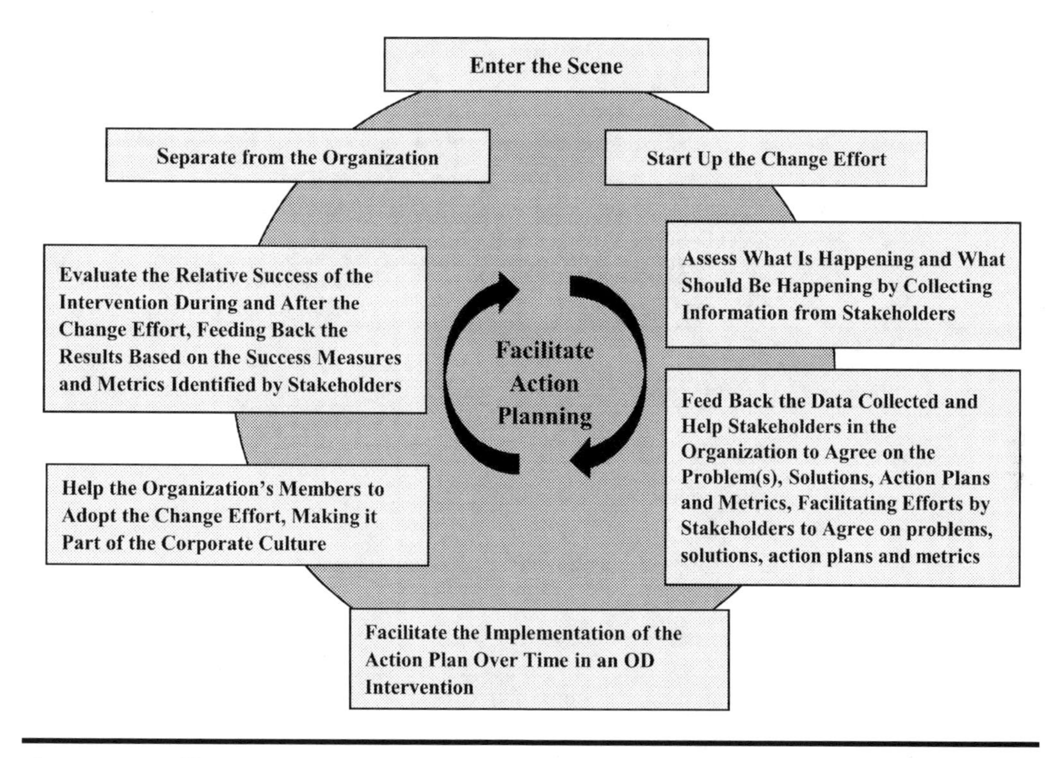


**Figure 4.2 Facilitate Action Planning from Action Research Model.**

*Source:* Author's Original Creation. Copyright 2022 by William J. Rothwell.

- ***Evaluate the relative success of the intervention during and after the change effort, feeding back the results based on the success measures and metrics identified by stakeholders*:** The consultant facilitates efforts by the organization's stakeholders to evaluate the benefits realized from the intervention.
- ***Separate from the organization*:** The consultant departs the client organization.

The model is illustrated in Figure 4.2.

Table 4.1 is a worksheet designed as a tool to direct the process of transformational coaching when using the action research model.

As you think about the preceding model, remember that:

- OD can be applied by anyone—managers and even workers—so long as those using it have had the proper training and know what to do and how to do it.
- OD most emphatically does not use the "medical model" of consulting in which an expert assumes there is an illness, a root cause that needs to be subjected to diagnosis, and that it is the consultant's job to recommend solutions; rather, OD seeks to facilitate members of the client organization to conduct their own diagnosis, reach their own conclusions about

**Table 4.1 A Worksheet to Guide Transformational Coaching Using the Action Research Model. Author's Original Creation.**

| *A Worksheet to Guide Transformational Coaching Using the Action Research Model* | | |
|---|---|---|
| *Directions:* Use this worksheet to guide a transformational coaching session using the Action Research Model (ARM) of organization development. For each step described under column 1, make notes for how you will conduct the session under column 2. | | |
| **Steps Using the Action Research Model Applied to Transformational Coaching** | | **Notes for How You Will Apply the ARM to a Specific Situation** |
| 1 | Enter the scene | |
| 2 | Start up the coaching effort | |
| 3 | Assess what is happening and what should be happening by collecting information from stakeholders | |
| 4 | Feedback the data collected and help stakeholders in the organization to agree on the problem(s), solutions, action plans and metrics, facilitating efforts by stakeholders to agree on problems, solutions, action plans and metrics | |
| 5 | Facilitate action planning | |
| 6 | Facilitate the implementation of the action plan over time in an OD intervention | |
| 7 | Help the organization's members to adopt the change effort, making it part of the corporate culture | |
| 8 | Evaluate the relative success of the intervention during and after the change effort, feeding back the results based on the success measures and metrics identified by stakeholders | |
| 9 | Separate from the coaching relationship | |



priorities and actions to be taken, and come up with their own success metrics. Alternatively, OD consultants may engage in dialogue with clients to help them unleash their own changed viewpoints and perspectives.

## The Appreciative Inquiry Model

There are important similarities between the ARM and the Appreciative Inquiry Model (AIM). While they may appear to be different at a casual glance, both models rely on facilitating change by the client rather than the consultant imposing unwanted change on unwilling people.

Several appreciative inquiry models have been published, but they are essentially the same. The OD consultant from inside or outside the organization will facilitate a process by which stakeholders will:

- ***Clarify the focal points guiding change in the organization*:** The consultant helps the organization's members to focus the change effort.
- ***Identify the important strengths of the organization*:** Facilitating the telling of stories about the organization, the consultant helps stakeholders identify what is going right in the organization.

- ***Agree on the organization's strengths*:** The consultant helps the stakeholders to agree on what is going right and what are the key strengths of the organization.
- ***Reflect on a vision of the future in which the organization's strengths are leveraged to maximum advantage*:** The consultant helps stakeholders to create a compelling vision or dream of the future in which the organization's strengths are maximized to best advantage.
- ***Devise an action plan to make the dream come true*:** The consultant helps the organization's members to devise an action plan to make the dream come true.
- ***Implement the action plan*:** The consultant facilitates the implementation of the change process by which to make the dream of a better future come true.
- ***Encourage adoption of the change as the action plan is implemented*:** The consultant should work with the stakeholders to ensure that the change is sustainable.
- ***Evaluate the action plan and the implementation results during and after they occur*:** During and after implementing the action plan, the consultant facilitates an evaluation process by which the client uses metrics of the client's design to evaluate the relative success of the change effort. Since appreciative inquiry seeks continuous improvement, positive language is used. For that reason, "evaluation" is often carried out as an "appraisal."
- ***Separate from the consultant, having made the change part of the organization's corporate culture*:** The consultant exits the scene.

The model is illustrated in Figure 4.3.

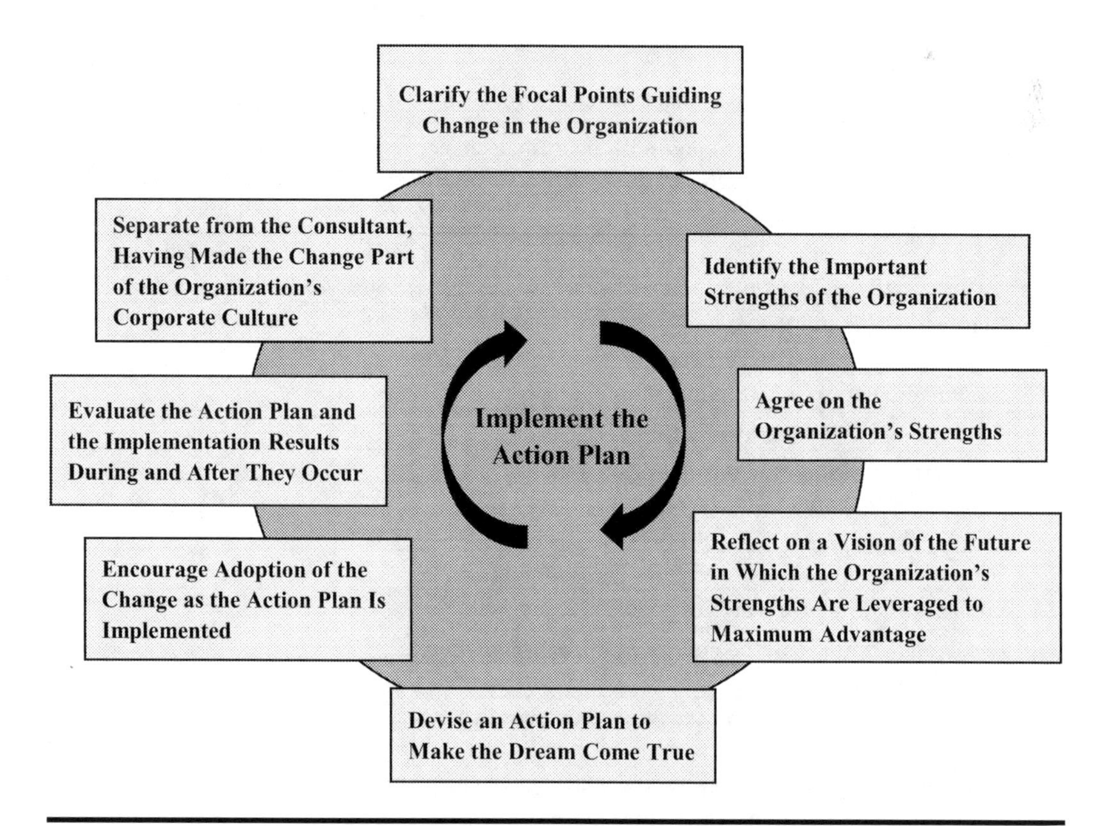


**Figure 4.3 Implement the Action Plan from the Appreciative Inquiry Model.**

*Source:* Author's Original Creation. Copyright 2022 by William J. Rothwell.

While many people want to combine the ARM and AIM to derive power by solving problems while simultaneously building strengths, that approach is generally not advisable. The reason: When problems are identified, people typically look for someone to blame. That so-called *blamestorming stage* is not compatible with efforts to identify strengths and leverage them to greatest advantage. It is best to keep efforts to identify dreams of a better future separate from efforts to discover and solve problems.

Table 4.2 is a worksheet designed as a tool to direct the process of transformational coaching when using the appreciative inquiry model.

## How Transformational Change Relates to OD

Organization development can be used to formulate and implement any change. That includes alpha, beta, gamma, delta, and epsilon change. It can also be used at any level—from individual to dyads (two people), triads (groups of three people), teams, work groups, organizational departments, organizations, and even communities, nations, and globally.

But a chorus of managers and other leaders have called for methods that can bring about radical (that is, transformational) change in brief periods of time. That can be done using a method like the *Whole Systems Transformational Change Conference* (WSTCC). First invented by Kathleen

**Table 4.2 A Worksheet to Guide Transformational Coaching Using the Appreciative Inquiry Model. Author's Original Creation.**

| *A Worksheet to Guide Transformational Coaching Using the Appreciative Inquiry Model* | | |
|---|---|---|
| *Directions*: Use this worksheet to guide a transformational coaching session using the Appreciative Inquiry Model (AIM) of organization development. For each step described under column 1, make notes for how you will conduct the session under column 2. | | |
| | **Steps Using the Appreciative Inquiry Model Applied to Transformational Coaching** | **Notes for How You Will Apply the AIM to a Specific Situation** |
| 1 | Clarify the focal points guiding change for the individual | |
| 2 | Identify the important strengths of the individual | |
| 3 | Agree on the individual's strengths | |
| 4 | Reflect on a vision of the future in which the individual's strengths are leveraged to maximum advantage | |
| 5 | Devise an action plan to make the dream come true | |
| 6 | Implement the action plan | |
| 7 | Encourage adoption of the change as the action plan is implemented | |
| 8 | Evaluate the action plan and the implementation results during and after they occur | |
| 9 | Separate from the consultant, having made the change part of the organization's corporate culture | |

*Source:* Copyright 2022 by William J. Rothwell.

Dannemiller in her work with Ford Motor Company in the 1980s, WSTCC, which operationalizes the Action Research Model on a large scale, is a means by which to bring about transformational change on an organizational scale. It can also be carried out using the Appreciative Inquiry Model, and (when it is) the event is called an *Appreciative Inquiry Summit*.

WSTCC is a radical approach in its own right because using it requires a major commitment from the organization's leaders. While there is more than one correct way to use the approach, a typical way is to shut down the organization during the event and plan for a conference of multiple days (usually four). While planning is carried out before the actual event to ensure that it can be implemented seamlessly without major logistical problems, a WSTCC might be carried out in a conference center with thousands of people in attendance. Using technology, the OD consultants can pose questions to large groups and have instant multi-voting projected on a screen in front of all participants. It is not unusual to position members of the organization at round tables where each table represents the organization in miniature.

By using the WSTCC or the Appreciative Inquiry Summit, the entire organization and its major external stakeholders can be involved in a corporate culture change effort in a relatively short time. Typically, there will be two leaders present at the conference. One leader represents the organization's senior team. (Often the CEO is on the stage in front of the entire organization.) A second leader represents the OD consulting team. (Often the OD consultant on stage is the OD consulting leader, but many facilitators are spread out in the audience.) Often there is a third group of helpers at a WSTCC or at an AI Summit. That group consists of members of a logistics team. The logistics team ensures that hotel space has been arranged for participants at the conference, that travel arrangements have been made when necessary, and that refreshments and after-hours socializing events have been well planned.

While the WSTCC and the AI Summit can be effective in bringing about transformational change in a short time, a major challenge is to ensure that the excitement and enthusiasm that results from a large-scale group event is carried back to workplace settings after those events. It is wise to establish standing committees or work groups to focus on implementing the action plans established during the large-scale event. Of course, technology can be used to create virtual groups to implement identified changes.

## How OD Relates to Transformational Coaching

Many coaching models have been published to describe the coaching process. One author has listed and delineated 12 coaching models (Sutton 2022). A coaching model guides coaches on how they should go about the coaching process. A model thus provides a roadmap to bring about the change process.

Perhaps the most famous coaching model is GROW, created by Sir John Whitmore (2017). GROW is an acronym that stands for

- ***Goal***: What is your destination, your vision of the ideal future?
- ***Reality***: What is your starting point?
- ***Options***: How can you reach your destination?
- ***Will***: What can you do?

Those four basic steps can guide a coaching effort. The coach helps the coachee set a goal or destination for a desired future, clarify the starting point, consider the range of possible actions to achieve the goal from the starting point, and fix on a clear action plan. Generally, coaching in this model is considered nondirective because the coach uses skillful questioning to draw out the coachee. The goal, starting point, range of action steps, and final action plan are decided by the coachee and not by the coach.

The Action Research Model and the Appreciative Inquiry Model provide alternatives to GROW, though they can be compatible, effective, step-by-step models by which to guide transformational coaching. Both ARM and AIM are foundational for organization development. But they can also guide transformational coaching for individuals and groups. That should come as no surprise, because any OD change effort—otherwise known as an OD intervention—should be based on one model.

## How Transformational Coaching Is Applied in OD

Transformational coaching can be a type of OD intervention (change effort)—like team building, survey-guided development, and many other OD interventions (Rothwell et al. 2021). When transformational coaching is carried out with an OD focus, then the coaching process is organized around the Action Research Model or the Appreciative Inquiry Model. Transformational coaching allows individuals to achieve personal or professional breakthroughs in their working and personal lives. Often transformational coaching is also combined with other OD interventions simultaneously to encourage radical change at the individual leadership level while the organization undergoes radical change.

## How Transformational Coaching Is Applied without OD

Can transformational coaching be applied without OD? The answer to that rhetorical question is "of course." When transformational coaching is applied without OD, it usually follows a project management model—such as the GROW model. That is neither "right" nor "wrong." It is simply an alternative approach to using transformational coaching.

## Key Takeaways

Important distinctions and major takeaways from this chapter are listed here. This chapter clarifies how organization development can carry out transformational coaching. What follows is a summary of the chapter's key points:

1. There are degrees of change. The highest level is epsilon change—which is synonymous with transformational change.
2. In transformational coaching, people learn to see themselves and their life contexts differently than they did before the coaching experience. Their goals can change; their sense of their environment can change; and their sense of their close contacts can change. Transformational coaching brings about transformational change for individuals, teams, and organizations.
3. Organization development facilitates change at any level—whether alpha, beta, gamma, delta, or epsilon change.
4. While many models can guide coaching, the key models foundational to organization development—Kurt Lewin's Action Research Model and David Cooperrider's Appreciative Inquiry Model—can be the foundation for transformational coaching interventions.

5. When OD models are used to guide transformational coaching, the change is more likely to be sustainable—and less likely to evoke resistance to change—than more directive approaches to change.

## List of Discussion Questions

1. How does transformational change for an organization relate to transformational change that results from the coaching of individuals?
2. How can transformational coaching be used as part of an organizational change effort?
3. What is the leader's role in transformational change?
4. What is the leader's role in transformational coaching?
5. How might the Action Research Model be a model to stimulate transformational change? Transformational coaching?
6. How might the Appreciative Inquiry Model be a model to stimulate transformational change? Transformational coaching?
7. What actions should a transformational coach take in working with a client?
8. How does the role of transformational coach compare to the role of OD consultant?

## References

Golembiewski, Robert, Billingsley, Keith, and Yeager, Samuel. 1976. "Measuring change and persistence in human affairs: types of change generated by OD designs." *The Journal of Applied Behavioral Science* 12: 133–157. Retrieved from https://doi.org/10.1177/002188637601200201

Ranasinghe, Thiloshi. 2021, July 10. "'Calm-waters' and the 'white water rapids' metaphors for change management." Retrieved from www.linkedin.com/pulse/calm-waters-white-water-rapids-metaphors-change-thiloshi-ranasinghe/

Rothwell, William J., Sohel M. Imroz, and Behnam Bakhshandeh (Eds.). 2021. *Organization Development (OD) Interventions: Executing Effective Organizational Change*. New York: Routledge.

Sutton, J. 2022, July 2. "12 Effective coaching models to help your clients grow." Retrieved from https://positivepsychology.com/coaching-models/

Whitmore, J. 2017. *Coaching for Performance: The Principles and Practice of Coaching and Leadership* (5th ed.). Boston, MA: Nicholas Brealey.

# Chapter 5

# Transformational Coaching and High Performance

William J. Rothwell

## Overview

Transformational coaching can result in individuals—and groups—that have been galvanized. One goal can be, and usually is, personal enrichment and fulfillment by encouraging people to be more mindful of who they are, what they can do, and how they can be. Another goal can be, and usually is, organizational enrichment by which the corporate culture is changed to support high performance and exceptional, even exemplary, productivity.

This chapter focuses on how transformational coaching can play an important role in individual and organizational productivity. It can lead to the creation of a *high performance workplace* (HPW), usually understood to mean a corporate culture where people want to perform to their peak in productivity and the organization's leaders have knocked down obstacles that make it difficult for people to achieve peak productivity. Efforts to create a high performance workplace are often associated with corporate culture change.

This chapter addresses several important questions:

- What is meant by the term *performance*?
- What is meant by the term *high performance*?
- What is a *high performance workplace* (HPW)?
- What role does transformational coaching play in achieving high performance?
- How does transformational coaching relate to performance management?
- How does transformational coaching relate to human performance enhancement (HPE) and human performance improvement (HPI)?

## Defining Performance

Managers often use the term *performance* in such a casual way that it implies the concept is easy to understand. But the term can actually be far more complex than is commonly understood.

DOI: 10.4324/9781003304074-7

## Performance Means Results

It is tempting to say that performance means results. Results refer to the outputs of work. Results are the final products of work activity. One way to think about that is to list all the job duties or work activities found on a job description and then, for each item, ask this question: *What is the final result of that activity?* The final results are the outputs.

## Performance Means Behaviors

But are results all there is to performance?

Consider: The behaviors demonstrated while workers are achieving results can rightfully be considered a component of job performance. Results amount to what is achieved. The behaviors demonstrated while achieving results amount to how the work is carried out and what is observable. It is possible to meet or even exceed the expectations for work results and still behave so badly as to be fired (Workopolis 2015). An example of that can be found with Wall Street bankers in 2008. To achieve high performance, the bankers broke the law. Their job results were outstanding. But the way they achieved them was simply illegal (Cohan 2015).

## Performance Can Mean Outcomes as Well as Outputs

*Outputs* are generally understood to mean the tangible results of performance. They can be tangible (example: a written report) or intangible (example: a satisfied customer).

But outcomes mean something different. Outcomes concern how different people perceive performance. Company managers, when working with their employees, may establish measurable work standards that identify the minimum and/or targeted results and behaviors that should be achieved to meet performance expectations. As a simple example, think of Key Performance Indicators (KPIs) that identify the most important performance targets that employees are to achieve. KPIs are usually negotiated between managers and workers.

But other stakeholders—such as customers, company suppliers, company distributors, and government regulators—may have very different views about what makes performance acceptable.

As a simple example, consider the job performance of medical doctors. A doctor may do everything right according to medical best practice, but the patient could still die. In a medical malpractice lawsuit, the viewpoints of many people will be considered when evaluating a medical doctor's job performance. Other doctors, and even world-class experts, may review the patient records and the course of medical treatment and conclude that the doctor acted properly. But that does not mean that the patient (if still alive) or the patient's family would agree.

Outcomes consider perspectives other than workers or their immediate organizational supervisors. They consider what the customer wants and what the customer values. Often that perspective differs from what managers want. Generally, managers place value on performance that is *efficient* (doing things right). But customers want what is *effective* (doing the right things).

## Performance May Include Alignment with Values and/or Ethical Requirements

Can performance be described properly by limiting its definition to results and behaviors alone? Perhaps not. Consider that performance may also require consideration of, and alignment with, values and ethical/legal standards. Work performance is thus not a uni-dimensional concept limited to one issue (such as results) but is a multidimensional concept that may include other issues—such as values and ethics.

*Values* refer to what is perceived to be important. Individuals have values; organizations have values. And there are different values. According to Walter Goodnow Everett (1922), values may be classified as (1) economic, (2) bodily, (3) recreational, (4) associational, (5) character, (6) aesthetic, (7) intellectual, and (8) religious values. That list is not exhaustive. Values may also center on politics, social issues, legal issues, cultural, moral, educational, scholastic, industrial, athletic, life, medical, language, technical, and emotional issues—to name a few (Min n.d.). Milton Rokeach (1973) identified 18 instrumental values and 18 terminal values. *Terminal values* are the ultimate desired end results sought from action; *instrumental values* are the means to the ends.

*Ethics* refer to what is perceived to be moral. Ethics also include what is legal versus illegal. But ethics go beyond legal requirements. It is possible to violate the spirit but not the letter of the law, and it is possible to violate the letter but not the spirit of the law. Likewise, ethical issues may go beyond legal issues to simple issues of right and wrong.

Consider Figure 5.1, which illustrates how performance may be conceptualized in three dimensions. There may be more dimensions, but this diagram clarifies that considerations of performance may require, at minimum, consideration of issues associated with results, behaviors, values, and ethics.

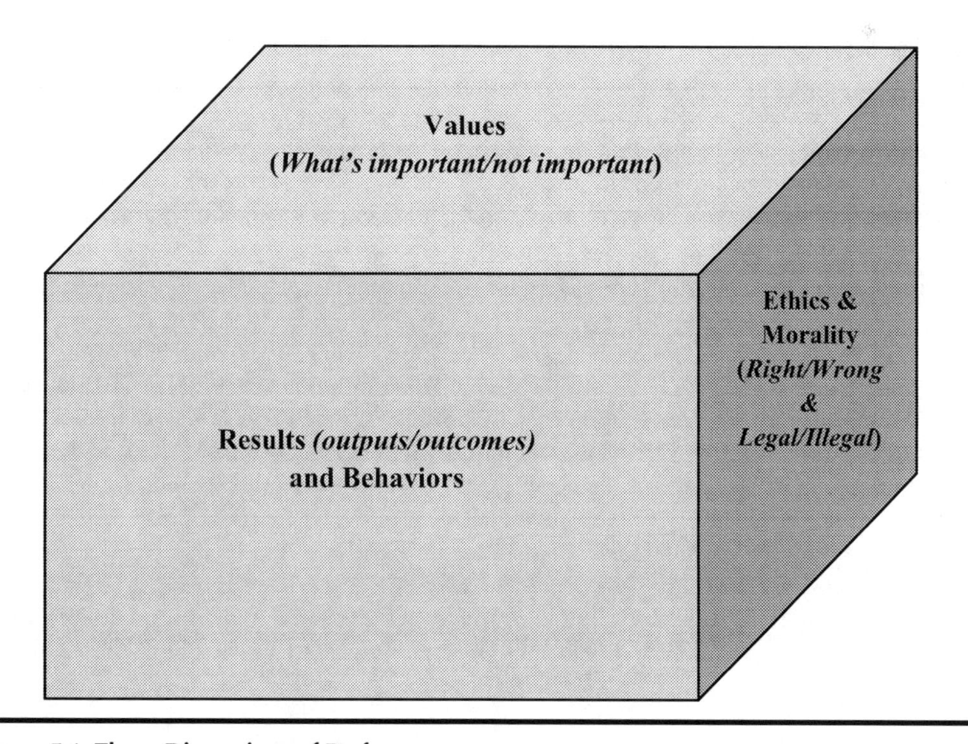


**Figure 5.1 Three Dimensions of Performance.**

*Source:* Author's Original Creation. Copyright 2022 by William J. Rothwell.

### Individual, Team, Organizational, and Other Performance Perspectives

Performance may be regarded according to the scope of work. That scope may include individual, team, organizational, and even larger perspectives such as industry, national, or global.

While organizational leaders often speak in terms of individual worker performance, what happens at higher levels in organizations affects performance at lower levels. Stated another way, what happens in the world affects national, industry, organizational, team, and individual performance. If the global economy is in depression, for example, the national economy likely will not be thriving, and workers may struggle to meet minimum performance expectations.

That view that factors beyond the control of the individual can affect individual job performance is well documented.

### Organizational Performance Includes a Balanced Scorecard

While some managers regard organizational performance as simple because it merely concerns making profits, there is growing awareness that organizational performance in business requires more than moneymaking. The Balanced Scorecard indicates that corporate leaders have thought beyond simple profit-and-loss thinking. For those who use the Balanced Scorecard, corporate performance must be graded in four dimensions: (1) financial, (2) market, (3) business operations, and (4) learning and growth.

### Performance Can Have a Cultural Dimension

Performance can also have a cultural dimension. In 1997 I was presenting a workshop on performance improvement in Beijing, China, to a group of top executives from a multinational company. On the fifth day of a five-day program, one executive raised his hand in the workshop and asked me to define again what was meant by the term *performance*. (I had defined the term in the first hour of the first day.) I patiently answered that "performance means the results of work and the behaviors carried out to achieve those results." The executive then said, "that is not how job performance is understood in China. In China, if your boss likes you, you are a good performer; if your boss does not like you, you are a bad performer." In response, I asked this question:

> Suppose you have two secretaries, and their jobs require them to do typing. One secretary is very nice and everyone loves her. But she cannot type. The other secretary is very irritable. Everyone who deals with her finds her the most difficult person they have ever dealt with. But this secretary can type 120 words per minute with no errors. If you are forced to tell me which of these two secretaries is the better performer, who would you say is best?

The executive shook his head and said,

> in China it would be the first one, but from what you have said, in America it is the second one. I suppose that is the difference between how performance is regarded in a developing economy and work in a developed economy.

## Defining High Performance

If the term *performance* is a multidimensional concept, then so too is the phrase *high performance*. High performance suggests there are different degrees of performance. But what are those degrees?

In the simplest sense, high performance would seem to suggest high productivity. The worker who achieves the greatest outputs with the least inputs would be regarded as a top performer. There is a label for the worker in any job category with the highest productivity. That worker is a called a *HiPer*. A HiPer differs from a HiPo (high potential), a HighPro (high professional), or a HiSoc (high social). A HiPer is simply the worker who gets the most productivity.

A *HiPo* has good productivity but is also regarded as promotion ready for one or more levels on the organization chart within the next few years. A *HiPro* is an in-house expert, the person to go to for expert advice on how to handle a specific work challenge. A *HiSoc* has the best relationships with various stakeholders of critical importance to the organization—such as key customers, key suppliers, key distributors, key labor union representatives, key government regulators, or others.

Those other labels—HiPo, HiPro, and HiSoc—suggest there are other ways to think about performance that go beyond mere productivity.

## Describing the High Performance Workplace (HPW)

The *High Performance Workplace* (HPW) is a work setting where workers can perform to their peak of productivity with minimal bureaucratic restrictions and optimal encouragement and support. The HPW is a type of corporate culture where people want to be productive, and the organization's management assumes an important role in knocking down barriers that stand in the way of worker productivity.

The HPW should not be confused with the High Involvement Workplace (HIW), High Engagement Workplace (HEW), the High Development Culture (HDC), or the High Creative Workplace (HCW). The *High Involvement Workplace* is a corporate culture that encourages and supports teamwork and worker involvement in decision making; the *High Engagement Workplace* is a corporate culture that encourages workers to be engaged; and, the *High Creative Workplace* drives out anything that will discourage workers from being creative and prompting them to find innovative solutions that can build organizational competitive advantage.

### *Ways to Identify Characteristics of the HPW*

Much research and writings over the years have focused on the HPW. Managers and academic researchers have been fascinated with the characteristics of a corporate culture that would lead to great competitive advantage. And many organizational problems are actually traceable to organizational policies and procedures—much more so than individual job performance problems. It cannot be disputed that a workplace that encourages peak performance is likely to attain a competitive advantage.

There are two major ways to identify the characteristics of the HPW for your organization. The first is the descriptive approach; the second is the prescriptive approach. The *descriptive approach* involves interviewing workers and managers, asking them a few important questions. The questions would include:

- How would you describe the characteristics of a High Performance Workplace, a work setting where people are eager to perform to the best of their ability?
- How does this organization compare to the characteristics you described of the HPW?
- What do you feel are the barriers to productivity imposed by this organization?
- What would managers in this organization have to do to knock down the barriers to performance that exist in this organization?

The *prescriptive approach* involves importing research-based descriptions of the HPW and then rating your own organization against them. One example is *The Road to High-Performance Workplaces* (U.S. Department of Labor/Office of the American Workplace 1994). That study was the basis of a questionnaire used to survey workers and managers in an organization to compare that organization to the 55 characteristics of a HPW corporate culture (see Dubois and Rothwell 1996a & 1996b). Once the survey results have been compiled, they can be fed back to senior leaders to facilitate the formulation of an action plan to bring the organization into alignment with the characteristics of a corporate culture that leads to the HPW.

More recent research on the HPW, conducted by consulting firm Gallup (Desimone 2019), has revealed that one factor sets the HPW apart from typical organizations: an emphasis on employee development. Gallup's research found that organizations investing strategically in employee development enjoyed 11 percent higher productivity and were two times more likely to retain workers than organizations not making those investments. Leaders must develop workers daily (Rothwell et al. 2015). Lack of adequate professional development is a leading cause of turnover, and nine of ten millennials (in particular) rate professional development as very important to them in their jobs (Desimone 2019). Managers bear the key responsibility for building a corporate culture that encourages productivity (Royal 2019).

A different research study by Zak (cited by Schneider 2018), who for eight years studied data on the brain chemistry of workers while they were at work, found eight characteristics of workplace culture that support peak productivity. Those are (Schneider 2018):

- Recognize people who demonstrate outstanding work
- Give workers challenges
- Delegate to workers
- Give workers the chance to do job-crafting
- Be transparent, sharing information openly
- Demonstrate care about people and relationships
- Invest in employee development
- Show authenticity in words and actions

Those characteristics describe not only a corporate culture—but they can also characterize what an effective leader does. They can be the targets or goals for change in transformational coaching. Consider using Tool 1 (see Table 5.1) at the outset of coaching to see how much the coachee would like to work on transformational improvements in those areas. Also consider using Tool 2 (see Table 5.2) to rate the corporate culture for its alignment with these factors.

## The Role Transformational Coaching Plays in Achieving High Performance

Transformational coaching is not the sole approach to achieve high performance for individuals or to build an HPW for organizations. But it is a powerful approach that can help in that respect. Transformational coaching lays the foundation for awakening the individual to new ideas about self and about work, and these help to shed light on new ways to perform. When many leaders participate in transformational coaching simultaneously and make progress on awakening themselves to new ways of thinking and of living, they are providing an important basis for creating a High Performance Workplace.

**Table 5.1 Tool 1: A Rating Instrument to Assess Goals for Transformational Coaching.**

| *Tool 1: A Rating Instrument to Assess Goals for Transformational Coaching* | | | | | | | |
|---|---|---|---|---|---|---|---|
| *Directions*: Use this instrument to rate areas you would like to work on in your coaching experience. When you finish it, give it to your coach and be prepared to explain your ratings and talk about what priorities should be set for goals to improve your life and work. For each item appearing in the left column, rate it in the center column using this scale: **0 = Not applicable; 1 = Need little or no work in this area; 2 = Need some work in this area; 3 = Need much work in this area; and 4 = Need very much work in this area.** In the right column, either the coach or coachee can take notes about the priority associated with that area and the results of any discussions between the coach and coachee about how to develop that area. | | | | | | | |
| **Goals for Transformational Coaching** | | **Rate How Much Work You Would Like to Devote to Improvements in the Area in Your Coaching Experience** | | | | | **Notes about Priorities and Ways to Develop the Goals through Coaching** |
| | | 0 | 1 | 2 | 3 | 4 | |
| 1 | Recognize people who demonstrate outstanding work | 0 | 1 | 2 | 3 | 4 | |
| 2 | Give workers challenges | 0 | 1 | 2 | 3 | 4 | |
| 3 | Delegate to workers | 0 | 1 | 2 | 3 | 4 | |
| 4 | Give workers the chance to do job-crafting | 0 | 1 | 2 | 3 | 4 | |
| 5 | Be transparent, sharing information openly | 0 | 1 | 2 | 3 | 4 | |
| 6 | Demonstrate that you care about people and relationships | 0 | 1 | 2 | 3 | 4 | |
| 7 | Invest in employee development | 0 | 1 | 2 | 3 | 4 | |
| 8 | Show authenticity in what you say and do | 0 | 1 | 2 | 3 | 4 | |
| 9 | Other (*Describe it here*): | 0 | 1 | 2 | 3 | 4 | |

*Sources:* Copyright 2022 by William J. Rothwell. The items in the left column are adapted from Schneider, Michael. 2018. "An 8-year Study Reveals the Key to a High-Performing Culture—and 8 Ways to Build It." *Inc.*

## How Transformational Coaching Relates to Performance Management

*Performance management* is a process by which the performance of organizations, divisions, departments, teams, and/or individuals is managed to meet or exceed planned targets.

Strategic planning helps an organization's leaders formulate organizational targets amid dynamic organizational conditions. The result of the process is a plan that establishes measurable targets. Strategic evaluation allows organizational leaders to compare results to goals.

Performance management at the individual level is usually associated with performance reviews carried out annually to compare an employee's results to the targets established at the beginning

**Table 5.2 Tool 2: A Rating Instrument to Assess Goals for Organizational Change.**

| *Tool 2: A Rating Instrument to Assess Goals for Organizational Change* | | | | | | | |
|---|---|---|---|---|---|---|---|
| *Directions*: Use this instrument to rate your organization on important areas linked with a corporate culture that encourages high productivity. When you finish this rating instrument, give it your coach and be prepared to explain your ratings and talk about what priorities should be set for goals to improve your organization's corporate culture. For each item appearing in the left column, rate it in the center column using this scale: **0 = Not applicable; 1 = Need little or no work in this area; 2 = Need some work in this area; 3 = Need much work in this area; and 4 = Need very much work in this area**. In the right column, note what actions you would recommend the organization's leaders should take to create a corporate culture that encourages high performance. | | | | | | | |
| **Characteristics of a High Performance Workplace** ***This organization. . .*** | | **Rate How Much Work You Believe Should Be Devoted to This Area to Improve the Corporate Culture** | | | | | **Notes About What Actions You Would Recommend the Organization's Leaders Take to Create a Corporate Culture That Encourages High Performance** |
| | | 0 | 1 | 2 | 3 | 4 | |
| 1 | Recognizes people who demonstrate outstanding work | 0 | 1 | 2 | 3 | 4 | |
| 2 | Gives workers challenges | 0 | 1 | 2 | 3 | 4 | |
| 3 | Delegates to workers | 0 | 1 | 2 | 3 | 4 | |
| 4 | Gives workers the chance to do job-crafting | 0 | 1 | 2 | 3 | 4 | |
| 5 | Is transparent, sharing information openly | 0 | 1 | 2 | 3 | 4 | |
| 6 | Demonstrates that the organization cares about people and relationships | 0 | 1 | 2 | 3 | 4 | |
| 7 | Invests in employee development | 0 | 1 | 2 | 3 | 4 | |
| 8 | Shows authenticity in what is said and done | 0 | 1 | 2 | 3 | 4 | |
| 9 | Other (*Describe it here*): | 0 | 1 | 2 | 3 | 4 | |

*Sources:* Copyright 2022 by William J. Rothwell. The items in the left column are adapted from Schneider, Michael. 2018. "An 8-year Study Reveals the Key to a High-Performing Culture—and 8 Ways to Build It." *Inc.*

of the performance review cycle. Many organizations today have a performance management system for workers at every level—from executive to manager to supervisor to hourly employee. Performance management for individuals clarifies what goals are to be achieved in the work they do. Efforts to plan and manage employee performance help to establish a logical link between what the employee does and what the organization needs to do to achieve its strategic goals.

The trend is to diminish or eliminate formal, annual performance reviews for individuals and carry out more frequent, but less formal, feedback sessions between managers and the employees who report to them (Doheny 2021). Given the dynamic nature of modern business organizations, feedback is best managed when immediate and specific (Hattie and Timperley 2007; Wisniewski et al. 2020). That feedback should also give due consideration to conditions outside of the control of workers that may affect their job results and behaviors. A good example of such conditions would be the Covid-19 pandemic of 2020 and 2021 that created unique challenges to managers and employees. Consider this conclusion based on a statistical study:

> Therefore, the COVID-19 pandemic effects felt by employees affected their general work performance, such that the more intensely they felt threatened by COVID-19 effects, such as cessation of activity at work, salary decreases, technical unemployment, changes in their lifestyle due to changes in interpersonal relationships imposed by isolation, physical distancing, or changing attitudes of people around them, the lower their work performance.
>
> (Popa et al. 2022)

Many other examples can be cited of how conditions outside of an employee's control can affect individual job performance—and organizational performance. As the pandemic raged, many workers resigned from one organization and moved to other organizations, which prompted much attention to the need to replace workers and train newcomers. The Great Resignation, the name given to a trend for workers to jump to other employers, created special challenges for employers in achieving organizational targets and created special challenges for the workers who did not resign but who were often asked to do more with fewer helpers.

Transformational coaching can help employee job performance by focusing attention on the sources of worker dissatisfaction that have given rise to the reasons for a record number of resignations. Workers seek meaning in what they do. Workers seek development. Workers want to serve customers they care about. Workers do not want to feel so much pressure in their work that they experience burnout.

## How Transformational Coaching Relates to Performance Enhancement and Improvement

*Performance improvement*—sometimes called *Human Performance Technology* (HPT) or *Human Performance Enhancement* (HPE)—is a method or approach by which to help individuals, teams, departments, divisions, and organizations achieve better results. Typically performance improvement is carried out in a systematic way.

HPI focuses on identifying and solving problems with human performance or taking advantage of opportunities for improving performance.

Performance improvement is based on several key assumptions, and they are worth summarizing:

- Human performance is complex.
- Organizations are more responsible for achieving results than individuals are. Since organizations are controlled and guided by management, management bears the chief responsibility for creating a work environment where people want to perform, can perform, are rewarded for performing, and are adequately equipped with the tools and other resources they need to perform.

According to performance improvement, training should always be the solution of last resort to solve problems with people because training is the most expensive solution. Typically, less-expensive solutions about performance problems center on providing more resources (time, money, and people), clarifying work goals, giving feedback to workers on what they should do to improve, offering new tools or equipment, providing clearly assigned responsibility, changing incentives or rewards, offering opportunities for practice, examining and trying to improve worker engagement, and much more.

Performance improvement is important because it focuses attention broadly on the causes of performance problems or where human performance can be improved. It is thus geared to increasing productivity and decreasing needless expenses. By doing that, it helps organizations to build an environment conducive to performance, and it matches the most appropriate solution to the underlying cause of a performance problem.

There are essentially two occasions when performance improvement can be used: (1) When other people request help; and (2) When other people do not request help. In the first situation, someone asks for help to solve a human performance problem. In the second occasion, nobody asks for help, but someone is looking for ways to improve performance.

## Applying Performance Improvement When Other People Request Help

A client—the person with the problem, who is usually a line manager—has a problem and asks for help in solving it. This situation is the most commonly encountered by most performance consultants—that is, those who apply performance improvement.

The problem that elicits the plea for assistance is called a *presenting problem*. It might be the real source of the trouble but may instead by a symptom (a consequence or result of) of another problem. To discover, those applying performance improvement should ask questions about it and should thereby engage in troubleshooting or performance analysis:

- Who has the problem?
- How many people are affected?
- Who are they exactly?
- What is the problem?
- What do you think caused it?
- What effects or consequences are you seeing because of it?
- What efforts have you made already to solve the problem, and what has happened because of that?
- When did the problem first seem to surface?

- When was it first noticed?
- How was it first noticed?
- By whom was it noticed?
- Where is the problem occurring?
- Is there a difference between geographical areas?
- Is only one area of the organization affected?
- How big is the problem in its scope?
- Why do you think that the problem exists?
- What is its cause?
- Why do you think so?
- How does the manager feel the problem should be solved?
- Why does the manager believe that proposed solution will attack the underlying cause of the problem?
- What makes him or her think it will succeed?
- How much is the problem costing the organization as measured by lost time, money, people, productivity, and other losses?
- How much will the organization gain by solving the problem?
- How much will it cost to plan, implement, and evaluate a solution?

These questions could also be posed to worker groups—and not just managers—who are experiencing one or more noticeable problems. If these questions are not asked, then the performance consultant may reach the wrong conclusions about

- Who is involved with the problem
- What the problem is
- When the problem became apparent
- Where the problem is affecting performance
- How the problem should be solved
- How much the problem is costing the organization in time, money, effort, and productivity

If these questions are not asked, managers may immediately make a logical leap to request a solution—such as training—when training is not at all appropriate. Consider the following dialogue:

*Manager:* My employees need training on writing.
*Consultant:* How do you know they need training? I wonder if we could backtrack a moment for my benefit so I get this clear. Tell me what is happening and what should be happening.

In this exchange of dialogue, the manager has jumped to the conclusion that training (a solution) is appropriate to solve a problem unknown to the performance consultant.

## Applying Performance Improvement When Nobody Requests Help

Managers and other decision makers do not always ask for help. They may not even go to a performance consultant.

In these more difficult cases, the performance improvement consultant should take initiative to visit key line managers. This amounts to prospecting for business. The performance improvement consultant should ask such questions as these:

- What are the biggest business problems you are facing in the organization—and in your area of responsibility?
- How are they affecting your business?
- What have you tried to do to solve the problems, and what happened because of your efforts?
- Who is affected by these problems, and how are they affected?
- When have you noticed these problems?
- Where have you noticed these problems?
- Why do you believe these problems exist?
- What is the root cause (or causes) of the business problem?
- How do you believe that the cause(s) of these performance problems should be addressed?
- Why do you think so?
- How much is the problem costing you?
- How would you estimate its effects on the organization?

Using the answers to these questions, the performance improvement consultant should be able to prepare a proposal to address the "business problems" as far as they are affected by humans.

### How Does Transformational Coaching Relate to Performance Improvement

Creative thinking is crucial to success in performance improvement. Performance coaching, by encouraging people to achieve breakthrough thinking in their way of living or working, can inspire insight and creative thinking. In this way, transformational coaching relates to performance improvement.

## Key Takeaways

1. Managers often use the term *performance* so it suggests that it is an easy concept to understand. But it can be far more complex than is commonly understood. Performance can mean results, behaviors, outcomes, and outputs. Performance may include alignment with values and/or ethical requirements.
2. The *High Performance Workplace* (HPW) is a work setting where workers can perform to their peak of productivity with minimal restrictions and optimal encouragement and support.
3. There are two major ways to identify the characteristics of the HPW for your organization: (1) The *descriptive approach* involves interviewing workers and managers, asking them a few important questions; (2) the *prescriptive approach* involves importing research-based descriptions of the HPW and then rating your own organization against them.
4. Transformational coaching is not the sole approach to achieve high performance for individuals or to build a transformational coaching culture for organizations. But it is a powerful approach that can help in that respect.

5. *Performance management* is a process by which the performance of organizations, divisions, departments, teams, and/or individuals is managed to meet or exceed planned targets.
6. *Performance improvement*—sometimes called *Human Performance Technology (HPT) or Human Performance Enhancement (HPE)*—is a method or approach by which to help individuals, teams, departments, divisions, and organizations achieve better results.
7. Performance coaching, by encouraging people to achieve breakthrough thinking in their way of living or working, can inspire insight and creative thinking. In this way, transformational coaching relates to performance improvement.

## Discussion Points and Coaching Questions

1. What is performance? Define the term in your own words.
2. Why is performance important?
3. What is the difference between individual and organizational performance?
4. There is a growing trend to eliminate annual individual job performance reviews. Why do you think that trend exists? What is taking its place?
5. What is a High Performance Workplace (HPW), and why might leaders want to establish a corporate culture that encourages peak productivity?
6. What is, or should be, the relationship between job performance and transformational coaching?
7. What is, or should be, the relationship between the HPW and transformational coaching?
8. What should leaders do to encourage high productivity?

## References

Cohan, William. 2015, September. "How wall streets bankers stayed out of jail." *The Atlantic*. Retrieved from: www.theatlantic.com/magazine/archive/2015/09/how-wall-streets-bankers-stayed-out-of-jail/399368/

Desimone, Rob. 2019, December 12. "What high-performance workplaces do differently." *Workplace*. Retrieved from: www.gallup.com/workplace/269405/high-performance-workplaces-differently.aspx

Doheny, Kathleen. 2021, January 12. "Annual performance reviews bow out." *SHRM*. Retrieved from: www.shrm.org/resourcesandtools/hr-topics/people-managers/pages/ditching-the-annual-performance-review-.aspx

Dubois, D., and William J. Rothwell. 1996a. *Developing the High Performance Workplace: Administrator's Handbook*. Amherst, MA: HRD Press.

Dubois, D., and William J. Rothwell. 1996b. *Developing the High Performance Workplace: Instrument*. Amherst, MA: HRD Press.

Everett, Walter Goodnow. 1922. *Moral Values: A Study of the Principles of Conduct*. London: Holt.

Hattie, John and Timperley, Helen. 2007. "The power of feedback." *Review of Educational Research* 77, no. 1: 81–112.

Min, Tong-Keun. n.d. "Philosophy of values: a study on the hierarchy of values." Retrieved from: www.bu.edu/wcp/Papers/Valu/ValuMin.htm#:~:text=Walter%20Goodnow%20Everett%20classified%20values,%2C%20(8)%20religious%20values.

Popa, Ion, Stefan, Simona, Olariu, Ana, Popa, Stefan, and Popa, Catalina. 2022, February. "Modelling the COVID-19 pandemic effects on employees' health and performance: a PLS-SEM mediation approach," *International Journal of Research in Public Health* 19, no. 3: 1865. doi: 10.3390/ijerph19031865

Rokeach, Milton. 1973. *The Nature of Human Values*. New York, NY: The Free Press.

Rothwell, William, Peter Chee and Jean Ooi. 2015. *The Leader's Daily Role in Talent Management: Maximizing Results, Engagement and Retention.* Singapore: McGraw-Hill Education Asia Collection.

Royal, Ken. 2019, September 14. "What engaged employees do differently." *Workplace.* Retrieved from: www.gallup.com/workplace/266822/engaged-employees-differently.aspx

Schneider, Michael. 2018. "An 8-year study reveals the key to a high-performing culture—and 8 ways to build it." Inc. Retrieved from: www.inc.com/michael-schneider/8-years-of-neuro-research-shows-you-how-to-increase-employee-productivity-by-50-percent-with-1-initiative.html

U.S. Department of Labor/Office of the American Workplace. 1994. Road to high-performance workplaces. ERIC ED380641. Retrieved from: https://files.eric.ed.gov/fulltext/ED380641.pdf

Wisniewski, Benedikt, Klaus Zierer and John Hattie. 2020. "The power of feedback revisited: A meta-analysis of educational feedback research." *Frontiers of Psychology.* doi. 10.3389/fpsyg.2019.03087

Workopolis. 2015, July 30. "The number one reason people are fired (Is the same as the reason they were hired." Retrieved from: https://careers.workopolis.com/advice/the-number-one-reason-people-are-fired-is-the-same-as-the-reason-they-were-hired/

# Chapter 6

# Transformational Coaching and Talent Development

William J. Rothwell

## Overview

This chapter focuses on the relationship between talent development and transformational coaching.

- What is meant by these terms?
- Why is the term *talent* so important?
- Who carries out transformational coaching and talent development?
- When and where is transformational coaching used in talent development?
- How is transformational coaching carried out so it contributes to talent development?

In summary, why is transformational coaching so important for talent development?

## What Is Meant by Transformational Coaching and Talent Development?

In previous chapters, it has been clarified that *transformational coaching* transcends traditional conceptualizations of "coaching." Transformational coaching speaks to dramatic, galvanizing personal and/or professional change.

*Talent development* refers to efforts to help individuals meet the minimum requirements to qualify for occupations or jobs, keep meeting the requirements for occupations or jobs over time as work requirements change, and prepare for future occupations or jobs at higher levels of responsibility or at higher levels of skills (Biech 2018; Caplan 2013; Galagan et al. 2019).

DOI: 10.4324/9781003304074-8

## Why Is the Term *Talent* So Important?

The term *talent* is important because the meaning of the phrase *talent development* can vary, depending on how the term *talent* is defined. Consider: Dictionary.com defines the word *talent* as follows:

1. *A special natural ability or aptitude*: for example, a talent for drawing.
2. *A capacity for achievement or success; ability*: for example, young people of talent.
3. *A talented person:* for example, the cast includes many of the theater's major talents.
4. *A group of persons with special ability*: for example, an exhibition of watercolors by the local talent.
5. *Movies and television*: for example, professional actors collectively, especially star performers.

In organizational settings, *talent* could mean these definitions—and more. Talent can refer to the unique abilities with which people are born or what abilities they cultivate through dedicated effort and practice. Is talent born or made? The answer is "either or both." People may inherit unique abilities from genetics, but those abilities are only useful when developed and the potential is realized. Dedicated effort and practice can also transform mediocre ability to something closer to inspired talent.

In many organizations today, there are dedicated efforts undertaken to identify *high potentials*. They are sometimes considered talent. Such people may consist of the top 10 percent of workers who are both good performers and have the potential for accepting greater responsibility. (A stricter definition of HiPo would limit the term to the top 1 percent of workers.) They are often the focus of leadership development programs or other efforts to ensure organizational continuity through succession planning, talent development, or related efforts.

Even in succession planning efforts, there are other ways to understand talent than high potentials only. For instance, *high professionals* are individuals best at doing one thing in organizational settings. A good example would be one engineer who is absolutely the best at performing one kind of technical task but is not so good at other tasks. A second example are *high performers*, individuals who are the most productive in a team, group, department, or division. Think of the top salesperson—the person who consistently gets the most sales. He or she may be a high performer but may not be a high potential or a high professional. A third example are people with the most social relationships and professional contacts.

Organizational leaders sometimes confuse these groups. They may think a person who gets the top results is a high potential. (Not necessarily.) And the person who is absolutely the in-house expert at just one thing—a high professional—has potential for promotion. (Not necessarily.)

Another way to think of it is that everyone has talent. Talent refers to a personal best, the one thing an individual can do better than others. It is akin to an *organizational core competency*, a strategic strength or the essence of what makes an organization competitive. It is the one thing that an organization does better than any other organization in its industry. While organizations have core competencies—and they are the essence of competitive advantage—so too do divisions, departments, work groups, teams, and individuals. The challenge is to discover those unique competitive strengths and leverage them—first to the individual's advantage, then to the organization's advantage, and finally to leave a legacy by helping other people, the community, and society.

How can each person's individual strengths be identified, developed, and leveraged to best advantage? Answering that question may be the essence of talent development. It is a difficult question, since individuals may not always know their strengths. Why? Simple: What you do better than anyone else comes so naturally to you that you take it for granted, mistakenly believing it is nothing special. If it comes that easily to you, it must come that easily to others. That is why it may take discussions with other people—peers, significant others, supervisors, mentors, and even those reporting to you—to discover individual strengths. Those discussions can occur within the context of transformational coaching.

## *Establishing Measurable Goals*

Goal confusion is common in many organizational efforts. It happens because, as a program is launched, managers may not agree among themselves on what results they want to see from that program.

There are several other reasons goal confusion can arise. First, top managers wear two hats—that is, they are asked to respond to talent program goals based on two conflicting agendas. Each top manager is part of the governing group for their organization. That is one role they play. But they are also the senior leader for their own area (division, department, or other work unit) of the organization. That is a second role they play. These two roles sometimes conflict, since the needs of one division, department, or function for a talent development program may not be the same as all the others. That conflict can lead to confusion in talent development program goals if not worked out and clarified.

What do we mean by talent development program goals? Goals are the reasons a talent development program exists. They are the results sought from the program. Those results should be measurable and should also align with the measurable strategic goals of the organization.

In many organizations today, one typical talent development program goal is to groom the next generation of leaders to address needs that stem from expected retirements. Baby boom retirements are affecting many organizations around the world—not just those in the United States or in the European Union. About one in every five senior executives is eligible to retire. Since there is a relationship between age and level on the organization chart—few CEOs are 21 years of age—many organizations face a challenge of many senior leaders at, or near, retirement age. Compounding the problem is that many organizations have downsized in recent years, which has (in turn) reduced the ranks of well-qualified, seasoned middle managers ready through their experience to be advanced to the senior executive ranks.

In some other parts of the world—such as Asia-Pacific—the challenge of pending retirements is intensified by explosive business growth. In too many cases, organizations are limited in their growth potential by not having enough well-qualified talent available internally to fuel their expansion requirements. That leads to much "poaching" or "hijacking" of talent externally. Many organizations compete for a few well-qualified applicants, which can lead to high turnover and bidding wars for salaries and wages in others.

Meeting needs resulting from expected business growth and retirements are by no means the only possible goals to be achieved. For instance, some organizations believe that other goals may also be important—such as improving the diversity of the workforce at all levels, increasing the retention of high potentials, and many other such reasons.

The goals of a talent development program may thus center on desired results. But they are not too useful unless made measurable. While it may help to say that a talent development program is necessary to meet needs stemming from executive retirements or from business growth, it is just not enough. *How many people* should be prepared over what time frame to meet the business needs? When *timebound, measurable criteria* are added to a reason for a talent development program, then it is transformed into a useful, measurable program goal.

## Questions to Consider in Establishing Measurable Talent Development Goals

Based on this chapter you may ask yourself these questions about talent development in your organization:

- What does the board of directors believe is the business need that leads to a talent development program? What measurable results are sought from the program?
- What does the CEO believe is the business need leading to a talent development program?
- What do the CEO's direct reports believe is the business need leading to a talent development program?
- How well are the answers to the first three questions agreed upon by all the groups? Do they share the same goals?
- Have the goals been made measurable? If so, what are the metrics? Are the metrics the same globally, or are there (or should there be) local differences?
- How much might talent development goals differ globally? Locally?
- Have the goals been made time-specific with results to be achieved along a specific, agreed upon timeline?

Use the worksheet in Table 6.1 to help organize thinking about ways to answer the preceding questions.

**Table 6.1 Questions to Consider in Establishing Measurable Talent Development Goals. Author's Original Creation.**

| *Questions to Consider in Establishing Measurable Talent Development Goals* | | |
|---|---|---|
| *Directions*: For each question appearing in the left column, provide answers in the right column. Circulate this worksheet to gather different perspectives of different organizational leaders to try to reach some level of agreement among them. | | |
| | **Questions** | **Answers** |
| 1 | What does the board of directors believe is the business need that leads to a talent development program? What measurable results are sought from the program? | |
| 2 | What does the CEO believe is the business need leading to a talent development program? | |
| 3 | What do the CEO's direct reports believe is the business need leading to a talent development program? | |
| 4 | How well are the answers to the first three questions agreed upon by all the groups? Do they share the same goals? | |
| 5 | Have the goals been made measurable? If so, what are the metrics? Are the metrics the same globally, or are there (or should there be) local differences? | |
| 6 | How much might talent development goals differ across national cultures? Locally? | |
| 7 | Have the goals been made time-specific with results to be achieved along a specific, agreed upon timeline? | |

*Source:* Copyright 2022 by William J. Rothwell.

## *Who Carries Out Transformational Coaching and Talent Development?*

Everyone can carry out transformational coaching or talent development—provided they have received proper training. While it is possible to facilitate either transformational coaching or talent development without training, it is more likely to happen if the coach or the talent developer has been trained in effective ways of coaching and developing people.

Different stakeholders play different roles in a talent development program. It is therefore important to clarify just what roles will be played by the board of directors (if a publicly traded company), the CEO, senior leaders other than the CEO, the human resources (HR) department, middle managers, front-line managers or supervisors, and even workers. The central question is "who should do what in a talent development program?" That can cause problems because, in an organization that has never had a talent development program, people may not automatically know what they should do and thus exactly how they should play their parts.

If roles are not clarified, then at the end of the year there can be much finger-pointing and blamestorming. HR leaders will blame the CEO, senior leaders, and managers for not doing what they were supposed to do to make the talent program successful. The CEO, senior leaders, and managers will blame HR for failing to single-handedly recruit, select, develop, reward, appraise, and retain the most talented people.

Finger-pointing does not get results.

A better approach is to clarify who should do what at the time of program launch.

## *How Are Roles Clarified?*

It is one thing to say that roles need to be clarified; it is another to do that. It is a fair question to ask "how is that done exactly?"

There are many ways to do it. But one approach is to call the leaders together for a management retreat. A facilitator introduces roles and then asks representatives of each key group—senior leaders and CEO, HR, and middle managers—to flipchart out what they should do in the organization's talent development program. Each role description reads like a list of work duties or responsibilities on a job description. After spending an hour doing that, each group is then asked to describe what role they believe they should play to all the other groups. Discussion is encouraged. By doing that, role conflicts and role confusion can be avoided.

There are other ways to clarify roles. Often the CEO and the board work together to clarify what they should do. Generally, the more involved the CEO is in the effort, the better it is.

And above all, the message must be sent that HR is not responsible for doing *everything*.

## *Questions to Consider in Establishing Talent Development Roles*

Consider:

- What should be the role of a board of directors in talent development?
- What should be the role of the CEO in TD?
- What should be the role of each senior executive in TD?
- What should be the role of the HR function or department in TD?
- What should the role of the learning and development function in TD?
- What should be the role of each operating manager in TD?

**Table 6.2 Questions to Consider in Establishing Talent Development Roles. Author's Original Creation.**

| *Questions to Consider in Establishing Talent Development Roles* | | |
|---|---|---|
| *Directions*: For each question appearing in the left column, provide answers in the right column. Circulate this worksheet to gather different perspectives of different organizational leaders to try to reach some level of agreement among them. | | |
| **Questions** | | **Answers** |
| 1 | What should be the role of a board of directors in talent development (TD)? | |
| 2 | What should be the role of the CEO in TD? | |
| 3 | What should be the role of each senior executive in TD? | |
| 4 | What should be the role of the HR function or department in TD? | |
| 5 | What should the role of the learning and development function in TD? | |
| 6 | What should be the role of each operating manager in TD? | |
| 7 | What should be the role of each front-line supervisor in TD? | |
| 8 | What should be the role of each individual in TD? | |

*Source:* Copyright 2022 by William J. Rothwell.

- What should be the role of each front-line supervisor in TD?
- What should be the role of each individual in TD?

Use the worksheet in Table 6.2 to organize your thinking, and that of other people, to answer the preceding questions.

## Establishing Accountabilities

*Accountability* is all about accepting responsibility for what has been agreed upon.

When managers are appointed to their positions, they accept responsibility for acting as a legal agent (representative) of the organization. What they do—and how they do it—reflects on the image of the organization. Job descriptions clarify what duties are associated with that position.

But job descriptions are notoriously incomplete.

Managers must attract, develop, and retain talented people for their organizations. If they try to shift that responsibility—to the HR department, for instance—then they are not accepting the full responsibility associated with their positions.

Accountability has a moral element to it. If managers accept the job, they also accept the responsibilities that go with it. If they fail to carry out those responsibilities, then they are not doing their jobs—and they are breaking the contract with their employer.

## *How Can Managers Be Held Accountable?*

While various organizations may establish different measurable goals for their talent development programs and while different stakeholders play different roles in such programs, each stakeholder must be held accountable for those goals and the stakeholder's respective roles.

There are many ways to hold people accountable. One way is to reward people for achieving their targets. A second way is to punish them if they do not achieve their targets.

There are also creative ways to hold different stakeholders accountable.

In some organizations, senior managers are told that they have measurable talent development targets to meet. If they are on an executive bonus plan, then they might be told that 80 percent of their annual bonus is contingent on meeting annual production targets and 20 percent depends on meeting measurable talent targets for their areas of responsibility. Another way is to make achievement of talent targets their Key Performance Indicators—such as KPIs for self-development and for staff development.

Another way to do it is to measure the percentage of Individual Development Plans completed, the turnover rate of High Potentials (HiPos), and the percentage of people successful upon their promotion. If managers fail to achieve their targets, their own future promotions may be jeopardized. As one example, the British Civil Service once had a rule that no manager could be promoted if he or she had not already developed a successor.

Creative approaches to accountability are only limited by the imagination. In one organization I am familiar with, the senior leaders hired an HR auditor. The auditor's role was similar to that of an internal auditor except that the HR auditor focused on each manager's performance in attracting, developing, and retaining talent. In that organization, the thinking was that managers had equal responsibility for financial and human resources and should therefore be audited.

## *Questions to Consider in Establishing Talent Development Accountabilities*

Consider:

- How should the board of directors be held accountable for carrying out its role in TD?
- How should the CEO be held accountable for carrying out his or her role in TD?
- How should each senior executive be held accountable for carrying out his or her role in TD?
- How should the HR function/department be held accountable for carrying out its role in TD?
- How should the learning and development function be held accountable for carrying out its role in TD?
- How should each operating manager be held accountable for carrying out his or her role in TD?
- How should each front-line supervisor be held accountable for carrying out his or her role in TD?
- How should each individual be held accountable for carrying out his or her role in TD?

Use the worksheet in Table 6.3 to organize your thinking, and that of other people, to answer the preceding questions.

# When and Where Is Transformational Coaching Used in Talent Development?

Transformational coaching (TC) is essential to effective talent development if TC is understood to mean a helping process that can lead to breakthroughs in new thinking, new mindsets, and even new identity for individuals (Rao 2013). To achieve strategic organizational goals, leaders must

**Table 6.3 Questions to Consider in Establishing Measurable Talent Development Accountabilities. Author's Original Creation.**

| *Questions to Consider in Establishing Measurable Talent Development Accountabilities* | | |
|---|---|---|
| *Directions*: For each question appearing in the left column, provide answers in the right column. Circulate this worksheet to gather different perspectives of different organizational leaders to try to reach some level of agreement among them. | | |
| **Questions** | | **Answers** |
| 1 | How should the board of directors be held accountable for carrying out its role in talent development (TD)? | |
| 2 | How should the CEO be held accountable for carrying out his or her role in TD? | |
| 3 | How should each senior executive be held accountable for carrying out his or her role in TD? | |
| 4 | How should the HR function/department be held accountable for carrying out its role in TD? | |
| 5 | How should the learning and development function be held accountable for carrying out its role in TD? | |
| 6 | How should each operating manager be held accountable for carrying out his or her role in TD? | |
| 7 | How should each front-line supervisor be held accountable for carrying out his or her role in TD? | |
| 8 | How should each individual be held accountable for carrying out his or her role in TD? | |



often think beyond the way things are done today. Changing corporate culture to achieve future strategic targets will require breakthrough thinking and breakthrough action.

Transformational coaching is thus an important component of any effort to achieve strategic talent development goals. That is essential to achieving organizational strategy goals (Ausmus 2021).

Transformational coaching should thus be planned for any leaders occupying key positions or for any key people in the organization. It should be planned from the beginning of the effort to pursue organizational strategy. And it should continue throughout the time horizon of the talent development effort linked to achieving organizational strategy.

There is no one right or wrong way to carry out transformational coaching. Likewise, there is no right or wrong way to carry out transformational coaching to contribute to talent development. Transformational coaching can be carried out with individuals and with entire groups of leaders. Transformational coaching can center on changing the whole person (or group) or else focus on specific goals directly related to the talent development structure the organization is using to achieve the organization's strategic planning targets. Even self-coaching is possible if leaders wish to reflect on, and meditate about, life-changing ways of performing their work or leading their lives.

## How Is Transformational Coaching Carried Out to Contribute to Talent Development?

Transformational coaching bears many similarities to other forms of coaching. Many models guide the coaching process. Perhaps the most famous is the GROW model, which was briefly mentioned in Chapter 4. GROW is an acronym that stands for

- **G**oal
- **R**eality
- **O**bstacles or **O**ptions
- **W**ay forward

There is debate about who first coined the term *GROW* and how it was coined. But the G stands for goal, and that refers to visualizing or visioning the desired end point or target for success. R stands for reality or clarifying present conditions. The O can stand for obstacles or options, meaning identifying what may stand between the goal and the present reality that may have to be addressed to make the dream come true. Options is another way of interpreting the O, and it means exploring various means to make the dream come true. W stands for the action plan to turn dream to reality by overcoming obstacles and using various options. The GROW model has been criticized as being less appropriate for developmental coaching than for targeted performance coaching, though some critics disagree with that view.

Research on coaching has identified common characteristics that can guide any form of coaching—including transformational coaching carried out to contribute to talent development (Carey et al. 2011). After examining 1,414 published titles related to coaching, authors Carey et al. concluded that the critical components of any coaching model consist of five key components:

- The coach-coachee relationship
- Problem identification and goal setting
- Problem solving
- Transformational process
- Mechanisms by which the model achieves outcomes

Each characteristic deserves elaboration as each applies to transformational coaching and talent development.

### *The Coach-Coachee Relationship*

In transformational coaching, the coach serves as questioner, using skillful questioning to stimulate life-changing paradigm shifts in how the coachee perceives self, work, life, and everything that is important. Socrates was perhaps the first transformational coach, since he posed questions that led his students to question their assumptions and rethink what was important.

Establishing effective rapport and building trust is essential to creating a coach-coachee relationship that will endure over some timespan. And it is rarely possible to bring about life-changing transformation in a few minutes, though it is possible to have one conversation that can change someone's life.

## Problem Identification and Goal Setting

Many coaching sessions focus on a problem. It may be a work-related issue; it may be a personal matter. But transformational coaching goes the step beyond that to focus on reframing how problems are conceptualized. Essential to the transformational coaching relationship is that the coach must be capable of stimulating the coachee to look past "in-the-box thinking" and to gain perspectives that would not have otherwise been gained if not for the coaching experience.

## Problem Solving

While traditional coaching centers on identifying and solving problems, it is possible to focus around strengths instead (McKie 2014). When so-called *appreciative coaching* (otherwise known as *strengths-based coaching*) is used, the coach and coachee explore what are the coachee's great strengths in life and work and then try to build on those to create new visions of what is possible for the future.

If traditional problem solving is used, then the coach directs the coachee to solving the problem rather than growing distracted by placing blame on others (or on oneself) or by blaming factors outside the individual's control. Focus on what can be controlled and what can be done rather than allow distractions to prevail.

## Transformational Process

To achieve transformation, individuals—or groups—must be guided by the coach to enhanced self-awareness, a reevaluation of perceptions, and a list of new perceptions. The coach helps the coachee see the future with optimism rather than pessimism and helps the coachee take responsibility for moving forward with confidence. The coach's most important role is to help the coachee commit to acting for change and accepting the responsibility for the future.

Taking responsibility is essential to talent development. It is impossible to develop oneself or leaders in an organization if they are unwilling to accept responsibility and show a willingness to act on solving problems or building strengths.

## Mechanisms by Which the Model Achieves Outcomes

The mechanisms are the steps taken to achieve results or outcomes. Any coaching experience is best managed with a model that guides the coach through the steps to take. The GROW model is one such roadmap to guide the coaching process. There can be others. Some models focus on what the coach should do; some models focus on the role of the coachee; and some try to encompass both players.

Structure or organization is important in any change effort. The structure provides the guidance so progress can be observed and noted.

Talent development, like coaching of any kind, must also be guided by a model. Link and align the organization's talent development strategy to the organization's strategic plan. Transformational coaching adds value by aligning the organizational strategy and talent development strategy to individual change.

## In Summary, Why Is Transformational Coaching Important for Talent Development?

Talent development is about developing the entire workforce of an organization. It can focus on one person at a time, or it can focus on building important competencies or capabilities for the organization to achieve its strategic goals. Transformational coaching is about achieving innovative breakthroughs, new ways of working and living (Barner and Ideus 2017). It is critically important to talent development to achieve organizational and individual goals. Transformational coaching is a way to bring about quantum leap change with people (Stanier 2016).

## Key Takeaways

1. Transformational coaching speaks to dramatic, galvanizing personal and/or professional change.
2. *Talent development* refers to efforts to help individuals meet the minimum requirements to qualify for occupations or jobs, keep meeting the requirements for occupations or jobs over time as work requirements change, and prepare for future occupations or jobs at higher levels of responsibility or at higher levels of skills.
3. The term *talent* is important because the meaning of the phrase "talent development" can vary, depending on how the term talent is defined.
4. Everyone can carry out transformational coaching or talent development—provided they have received proper training. While it is possible to facilitate either transformational coaching or talent development without training, it is more likely to happen if the coach or the talent developer has been trained in effective ways of coaching and developing people.
5. The goals of a talent development program may thus center on desired results. But they are not too useful unless made measurable.
6. Everyone has a role to play in talent development.
7. *Accountability* is all about accepting responsibility for what has been agreed upon.

## Discussion Points and Coaching Questions

1. How would you define *talent* in your own words?
2. How would you define *talent development* in your own words? How does it differ from *talent acquisition*, *talent engagement*, and *talent retention*?
3. What special knowledge, skills, attitudes, or other characteristics would be needed to carry out talent development? Transformational coaching?
4. What are the advantages and disadvantages of using transformational coaching as an approach to talent development?
5. Many talent development professionals are familiar with the 70–20–10 rule in which 70 percent of development should occur through on-the-job learning; 20 percent should occur through social media and social learning; and only 10 percent should occur through planned on-the-job, near-the-job, or off-the-job learning. How would you classify transformational coaching as part of the 70–20–10 rule? Why might that be important?

6. Could transformational coaching be carried out quickly, making it a method of microlearning? Why or why not?
7. How should transformational coaching be used as part of a strategic plan for learning?
8. How might transformational coaching approaches be different across national cultures?

## References

Ausmus, B. 2021. *The Transformational Leadership Compass: A Dynamic Coaching System for Creating Big Change.* Carson City, NV: Lioncrest Publishing.

Barner, R., and Ideus, K. 2017. *Working Deeply: Transforming Lives Through Transformational Coaching.* Bingley: Emerald Publishing.

Biech, E. 2018. *Starting a Talent Development Program.* Alexandria, VA. Association for Talent Development.

Caplan, J. 2013. *Strategic Talent Development: Develop and Engage All Your People for Business Success.* New York, NY: Kogan Page.

Carey, W., Philippon, D., and Cummings, G. 2011. "Coaching models for leadership development: An integrative review." *Journal of Leadership Studies* 5, no. 1: 51–69.

Galagan, P., Hirt, M., and Vital, C. 2019. *Capabilities for Talent Development: Shaping the Future of the Profession.* Alexandria, VA: Association for Talent Development.

McKie, Doug. 2014. "The effectiveness of strength-based executive coaching in enhancing full range leadership development: a controlled study." *Consulting Psychology Journal-Practice and Research* 66, no. 2: 118–137.

Rao, P. 2013. *Transformational Coaching: Shifting Mindsets for Sustainable Change.* Brooklyn, NY: True North Resources.

Stanier, Michael, B. 2016. *The Coaching Habit: Say Less, Ask More & Change the Way You Lead Forever.* Toronto: Box of Crayons Press.

# TRANSFORMATIONAL COACHING THEORIES, METHODOLOGIES, AND TRANSFORMATIONAL COACHES

Transformational coaching is embedded from a variety of disciplines, principles, concepts, and practices, including but not limited to athletic coaching, psychological theories, adult learning theories, modern education approaches, holistic and humanitarian psychology, management concepts, and the self-help approaches. Part III briefly explores some of these theoretical and abstract foundations of transformational coaching by investigating approaches, theories, practices, and disciplines.

## Chapter 7. Contributions to Implementation of Transformational Coaching

Chapter 7 provides brief explanations and descriptions of some of the most used theories, practices, and approaches by coaches who practice transformational coaching.

## Chapter 8. Transformational Coaching Integration Model

What is a coaching model? And what is the Transformational Coaching Integration Model? These topics are discussed in Chapter 8.

DOI: 10.4324/9781003304074-9

## Chapter 9. Transformational Coaching Methodologies

Chapter 9 covers the purpose of transformational coaching and participants' expectations of transformational coaching, including what transformational coaches must offer.

## Chapter 10. Transformational Coach

Mindset, principles, knowledge, skills, and competencies of transformational coaches, including their presence and agility, are addressed in Chapter 10.

# Chapter 7

# Contributions to Implementation of Transformational Coaching

Behnam Bakhshandeh

## Overview

As we mentioned at the beginning of this book, the concept of professional coaching for individuals and groups is rooted and evolved from a range of engrained disciplines, principles, concepts, and practices. Some of the primary coaching models originated from the concept of athletics coaching, different psychological theories and therapies, adult learning theories, modern education approaches, holistic and humanitarian psychology, several new management concepts, and the self-help approaches to personal and professional individuals and group development.

This chapter attempts to briefly explore some of the theoretical and abstract foundations of transformational coaching by exploring some approaches, theories, practices, and disciplines that influenced, contributed to, and added to the development and implementation of transformational coaching.

Even though the coaching approach is widespread around the world among personal and professional development professionals, coaching continues to be generally misconstrued. Professional coaches attribute this confusion to the fact that many people who developed coaching concepts have used and mixed many disciplines, techniques, practices, and approaches, which originate from various sources, making understanding what is coaching a little unsettling and difficult to understand.

Professional coaching is becoming one element of modern society and a growing phenomenon that entices different people from different layers of society and a variety of disciplines (Lasley et al. 2015). Brock (2008) predicted that the concept of coaching would become one of the elements and fabrics of modern society and people's interconnection through the enhancement of human relationships. Given this fundamental phenomenon, transformational coaching professionals greatly

DOI: 10.4324/9781003304074-10

prioritize partnership and collaboration between coaches and participants, which has helped to create leading ideas and results-oriented practices (Rogers 1995).

This chapter will cover brief explanations and descriptions of some of the most used theories, practices, and approaches by coaches practicing transformational coaching:

- Transformation theories
  - Cognitive transformational theory
  - Transformational leadership theory
  - Transtheoretical model of behavioral change
  - Conscious and competence theory
  - Transtheoretical model of self-change
- Ontological approach
- Educational theories and approach
  - Dewey's change theory
  - Adult learning theory
  - Experiential learning
  - Learning styles
  - Immunity to change
- Applied behavioral science
- Cognitive behavioral theory
- Psychological theories and approaches
  - Positive psychology
  - Humanistic psychology
  - Psychosynthesis
  - Existential therapy
  - Gestalt therapy
  - Awareness integration model
- Emotional intelligence
- Management theories and models
  - Process consulting
  - Managing transitions
  - Theory X and theory Y
  - The force field theory
  - Client-centered approach
- Nonviolent communication

## Transformation Theory

To distinguish between change and transformation, it will be beneficial to investigate Rorty's (1989) concept of "redescription." "Rorty conceptualizes transformation as a redescription of ourselves, our situation, and of our being in the world, similar to what Mezirow refers to as a perspective transformation" (Eschenbacher 2019, 255). Rorty's approach to changing vocabularies in the language used by individuals will provide a context that grants individuals clear characteristics and distinctions among the notion of change and transformation. "Rorty's vocabularies are more than just the way we describe ourselves and the world we live in; vocabularies are linguistic housings of certainty and clarity" (Eschenbacher 2019, 255). Rorty (1989) underlined "that the human self is created by the use of a vocabulary rather than being adequately or inadequately expressed in a vocabulary" (7). With our words, we are creating our world (Bakhshandeh 2009).

Wiltshire et al. (2014) pointed to many decades of research funding that supports the view that as individuals develop proficiency, they are inclined to obtain a profound theoretical understanding and awareness that aids them in focusing their attention on what they might see as meaningful signals and noticing particular patterns and some shifting patterns with somewhat of an understanding of their consequences. This understanding, or being present per se, allows individuals to predict what is coming and take preemptive action while evaluating the potential consequences of their choices. Being present to what is there is, in some shape or form, the beginning of personal transformation (Bakhshandeh 2015).

## *Cognitive Transformational Theory*

Klein and Baxter (2006) explained a propensity for individuals to perceive the concept of learning as the passive accretion of factual and objective knowledge and knowledge that accumulates from repeating routines and procedures, which in both cases becomes progressively flowing with practice.

> They imply that teaching and training practices that rely on this form of learning as their objective are inadequate because they do not focus on or adequately facilitate expertise acquisition. Rather, to the extent these teaching practices contribute to expertise, it is the routine form of expertise.
>
> (Wiltshire et al. 2014, 220)

With cognitive transformational theory, Klein and Baxter (2006) encouraged a different direction to accumulate expertise, and suggest teaching practices that support such an approach. According to the cognitive transformational theory, the pathway to accumulate expertise is learning factual, objective, and technical knowledge and one's capacity to identify recognizable patterns (Wiltshire et al. 2014). To support these plausible and useful changes, the cognitive transformational theory proposes four fundamental teaching practices:

1. Diagnostic evaluations that detect defects in learners' mental types
2. Learning purposes that underscore sense making and promote reflection of new learning approaches so greater mental types are developed and modified
3. Practice that integrates sense making to give learners experience and knowledge of figuring the relationship between information and its related contexts
4. Instant nondisruptive feedback encourages sense making and supports the learner to seek knowledge and interpret any negative self-feedback

(Wiltshire et al. 2014, 221)

## *Transformational Leadership Theory*

Leadership is one of the essential elements of organization development, motivating employees, and organizing an organization's resources to accomplish its vision and mission. Leadership is vital for growing innovation, improving employee engagement, enhancing performance, and increasing productivity. Different leadership models have been suggested as qualifications of leader effects with Bass's (1985) (1) transformational, (2) transactional, and (3) laissez-faire (or full-range) leadership theory, which is one of the most-researched modern-day leadership theories

(Antonakis and House 2014). Antonakis and House (2014) underline an important element of the leadership role in an organization: "Using precepts of functional (as well as pragmatic) leadership theory, we argue that beyond transformational and transactional-oriented influence, effective leaders must also ensure that organizations adapt to the external environment and use resources efficiently" (747).

However, successful organization leadership or management is not only about applying influence on employees'/organizations' interpersonal level but also on providing proficiency and knowledge on recognizing and executing solutions for many complex internal and external issues, such as the influence of social issues with the workforce and any related impact of workforce's work and jobs (Antonakis and House 2014). Managements' understanding of transformational coaching and its relevancy to employees' performance and productivity has a major role in their ability to be present to what is happening with their people, provide coaching and mentoring, and be able to recognize the root cause of the issues they are dealing with. Antonakis and House (2002) described this style of leadership as "instrumental leadership," a type of expert-based leadership power and influence (Day and Antonakis 2012).

Bass (1985) builds and develops further on Burns's (1978) conceptualization of distinguishing between transactional and transformational leaders. While this theory has been through several revisions during the last 30 years, its characteristics still continue to be relevant and informative for people who would like to learn more about leadership theories (Dobbs and Walker 2019).

### *Transactional Leaders*

According to Bass (1985),

> Transactional leaders are cognizant of what followers want to get from a particular relationship, and they try to ensure that followers get what they want, provided their performance contributes to what the leader wants from the relationship. This "responsiveness" to followers' self-interest is leveraged for performance.
>
> (11)

### *Transformational Leaders*

Bass (1985) described transformational leaders as those who

> achieve transformation by "raising [the] level of consciousness about the importance and value of designated outcomes," enabling followers "to transcend [their] own self-interest for the sake of the team, organization, or larger polity" by, amongst other things, "altering [their] need level . . . or expanding [their] portfolio of needs and wants."
>
> (20)

## *Conscious and Competence Theory*

According to W.C. Howell's (1982) conscious and competence learning theory, there are four categories of consciousness we might go through as we are learning something or attempting to transfer ourselves or a situation (Howell and Fleishman 1982).

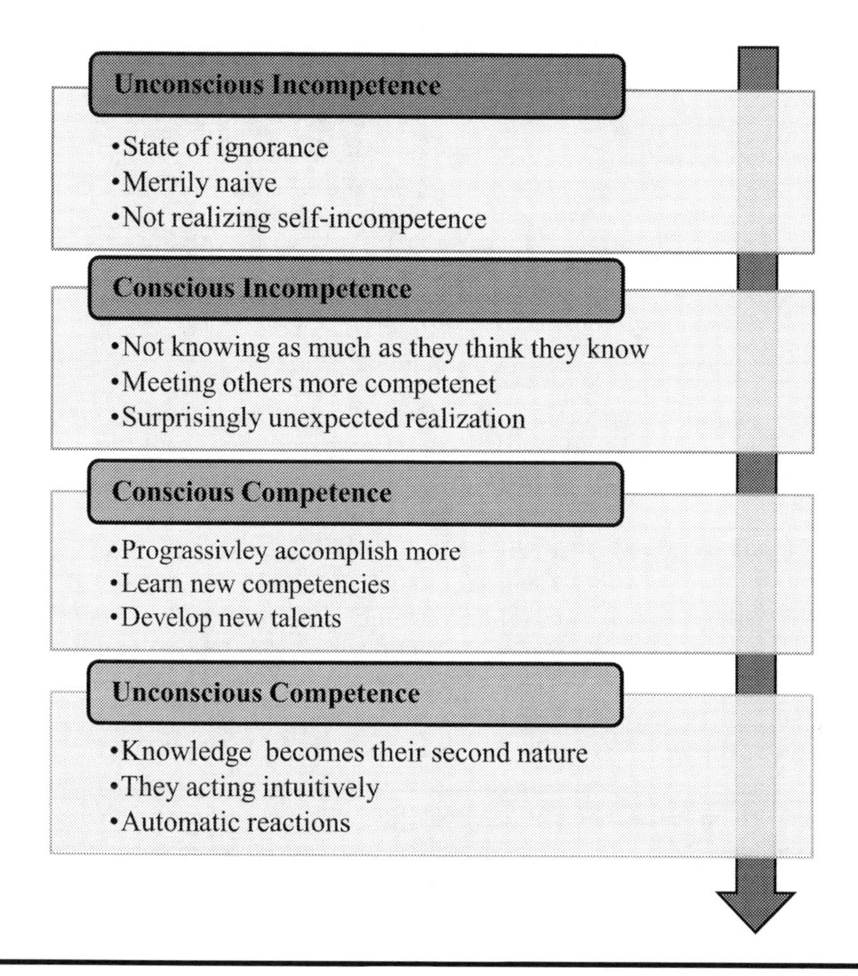


**Figure 7.1 Howell's Pathway to Learning a New Skill.**

*Source:* Adapted from Howell (1982); Howell and Fleishman (1982).

## *Howell's Four Stages to Learning*

Howell (1982) described the mentality of individuals in these four stages (see Figure 7.1):

**Unconscious incompetence:** At the state of being "unconsciously incompetent," people don't know what they don't know. They are missing knowledge and lack the skills to recognize questions in the concept at hand; ultimately, they are oblivious to their lack of knowledge and competency.

There is a possibility of people staying in this state for a long time because they are not sufficiently competent to realize: (1) they think they are incompetent, (2) they actually could be incompetent, and (3) there are more competent people than they.

In this state, individuals might be in one of these two places: (1) being oblivious to their situation, as people say, "ignorance is bliss," merrily naive, and not recognizing that they are incompetent; or (2) they may be pretending and acting as they are competent at their situation.

**Conscious incompetence:** At the state of conscious incompetence, people recognize that they are not as competent, knowledgeable, or skillful as they thought they were or as an expert they could be. The shift from unconscious incompetence to conscious incompetence can be a surprising and an unexpected realization when individuals meet someone who is undoubtedly more knowledgeable and competent than they are, or when a family member or a close and trusting friend "holds up a mirror" per se, to their unrealistic capability.

People can stay in this state for an extended period unless, because of their realization, they display acts of willpower to learn skills and show determination to move their level of incompetence to competence, which depends on their level of acceptance of their incompetence.

**Conscious competence:** Developing into the state of consciously competent usually is time-consuming, given that people progressively learning about the new skills and competencies, going through more formal learning opportunities, or accumulating experience. The fact in the matter is the length of this state depends on (1) the complexity of the concepts of new knowledge or skills, and (2) how much knowledge the individuals need and how talented they are in consuming the information and skills to become competent. This is when individual commitments and perseverance would make a difference.

**Unconscious competence:** This is when people finally get to a point where they no longer need to pay too much attention to what they are doing. Their knowledge becomes their second nature and they rely more on their intuition and automatic reaction.

## *Transtheoretical Model of Behavioral Change*

The transtheoretical model or TTM self-change model was developed by a psychologist named James Prochaska, PhD, during the 1990s to deal with smoking addictions. Prochaska et al. (1992) conducted a study that resulted in an integrated effect and influence of 18 varieties of psychotherapeutic and behavioral change models. Hence, the name of the model is transtheoretical, but it includes six stages of change (Prochaska and Bess 1994).

As we mentioned earlier, one of the primary structures of the transtheoretical model, or TTM, is its "stages of change," which is used to apply the behavioral change for developing individuals or groups. This model and its stages of change could apply while individuals or groups are going through the progress and facing what is occurring during each stage.

Table 7.1 depicts the six stages of change.

### *Processes of the Transtheoretical Model of Change*

Though the stages of the transtheoretical change model are useful in describing each stage, when and how the changes for individuals in areas of behavior, cognition, and emotion are taking place, the processes of such behavioral change assist readers or people with interest in

**Table 7.1 Six Stages of the Transtheoretical Model of Behavioral Change.**

| *Six Stages of the Transtheoretical Model of Behavioral Change* | | |
|---|---|---|
| *Stage* | *Name* | *Descriptions* |
| **One** | Precontemplation | At this stage, individuals are not present with the problems or thinking about the needed changes. They see no need for behavioral changes because they see no issue or probable risk about their actions and behaviors. Even if they try to implement changes, usually, they get discouraged and quit after several unsuccessful attempts and move back to the precontemplation state. |
| **Two** | Contemplation | As individuals learn of their risky and unworkable behavior, they move into the contemplation stage by expressing their want to change a certain behavior. During this stage, individuals examine the benefits or damages related to keeping the problematic behavior or changing such behavior. |
| **Three** | Preparation | At this stage, individuals realize their attempts to implement the behavioral changes to outweigh the dangers of not changing. Many people in this stage have tried to change their behavior but have failed, usually because they are not committed to the plan of action. Many existing and traditional action-oriented behavior change courses can be used at this stage. |
| **Four** | Action | At this stage, individuals show actual changes in their targeted behavior. Many other behavioral change programs start from an action plan, while TTM will be in its halfway place in the program. Relapsing and regressing to earlier stages are common in this stage. Keeping individuals on their action plan and consistency is challenging at this stage. |
| **Five** | Maintenance | As individuals accomplish their action plan, they are moving to this stage. The risk of relapse is lower, and people can continue with their commitment with fewer efforts while they are more engaged in change. |
| **Six** | Termination | This is the stage when individuals are completely taking over their attempt to behavioral change and "kick the habit" per se. There is still a risk of relapse, even at the last stage of change progress. |

*Sources:* Adapted from Prochaska, DiClemente, and Norcross (1992); Prochaska and Bess (1994); Prochaska (2020).

understanding how these changes transpire. According to Prochaska and Bess (1994), there are ten covert and overt processes (please see Table 7.2), which are divided into two categories of (1) cognitive and affective experiential process and (2) behavioral processes. These ten processes need to be employed to deliver successful progress of change and accomplish the desired individual and group behavioral change. Table 7.2 presents these ten processes under the two designated categories.

**Table 7.2 Processes of the Transtheoretical Model of Change.**

| *Processes of the Transtheoretical Model of Change* | | | |
|---|---|---|---|
| *Categories* | *#* | *Processes* | *Descriptions* |
| **Experiential Processes** | 1 | Consciousness Raising | Increasing understanding, information, knowledge, and awareness by the individual about their problematic behavior. |
| | 2 | Dramatic Relief | Individuals understand their emotions about their problematic behavior and availability of treatments and resolutions. |
| | 3 | Environmental Reevaluation | Assessment of individuals understanding and awareness about the impact of their problematic behavior on their environment. |
| | 4 | Self-Reevaluation | Increases individuals' self-assessment of their cognitions and emotions regarding themselves and problematic behavior. |
| | 5 | Social Liberation | Increases individuals' efforts to reduce their earlier problematic behavior in society. |
| **Behavioral Processes** | 1 | Reinforcement Management | Rewording and acknowledging individuals' positive behavioral changes. |
| | 2 | Helping Relationships | Individuals display trust and conduct open discussions about their problematic behavior with their supporting network. |
| | 3 | Counterconditioning | Individuals' problematic behavior is replaced by positive alternative behaviors. |
| | 4 | Stimulus Control | Individuals are in control of potential stimuli that would trigger relapse on the change progress, but they can avoid them. |
| | 5 | Self-Liberation | Individuals continue choosing the positive course of actions to alter the problematic behavior and commit to their choice. |

*Sources:* Adapted from Prochaska (2020); Prochaske and Bass (1994).

## Ontological Approach to Transformational Coaching

The ontological approach to coaching branches from the work and philosophies of Martin Heidegger, in combination with other works from J.L. Austin and John Searle with contributions of Humberto Maturana, Fernando Flores, and Rafael Echeverria. Martin Heidegger, especially in his groundbreaking book *Being and Time* (1953), studied the human condition and state of being regarding everyday living. In addition, Austin and then Searle established a philosophy of language, which regards language as not only descriptive but also performative and deeply action oriented (Sieler 2005).

The ontological approach to transformational coaching is generally centered on individuals' interpretation about and around four primary domains, (1) language, (2) emotions, (3) body, and (4) behavior (Sieler 2005). A transformational coach with competencies and skill in ontological coaching would be proficient at observing not only their coachees but also themselves in addition to other people in respect to these four domains, providing interventions in such domains to convey shifts in participants' state of being (Bakhshandeh 2009; Sieler 2007). We will discuss the ontological approach of coaching in much deeper detail in the next chapter.

## Observing

The internal link between observing our way of being forms our behaviors. As Sieler (2005) explained, individuals act and react based on how they observe circumstances around them, "Our Way of Being fluctuates daily, depending on our levels of energy, as well as our moods, and the impact of events and circumstances" (4). However, the experience and act/react varies among individuals, based on their deep ingrained way of being, because of life experiences, and learning, which are much invisible to others. That way of being operates underneath the cover of what they expose to the world around them (Bakhshandeh 2009). However, that way of being runs our day-to-day existence and has the strength to shape how we perceive reality and therefore respond to every situation in our lives, at home or at work. "Our Way of Being silently and invisibly informs us how to observe and engage with the world" (2005, 4). In a general sense, people have distinctive ways of being human observed by others. Human beings share many ways of being that are common among others. According to Sieler (2005), "Ontological Coaching is based on an interpretation that Way of Being is an interrelationship between language, emotions and physiology. This is the basic model of Ontological Coaching" (8). (See Figure 7.2).

## Emotions and Moods

The ontological approach to transformational coaching focuses on the fundamentals and significance of one's emotions. Our emotions and moods saturate most of our day-to-day lives. Our moods are constantly formed by our perception of what we are seeing, hearing, and acting on. Our mood helps create our perceived reality much differently from what is real. By understanding and being aware of our moods and emotions, their impact on our lives, the pros and cons of having them, and the prices we are paying or have paid for it because of our ways, we can disregard the existing mood and create a new one (2005).

## Language (Listening and Speaking)

The science of ontology has a distinct and much greater approach to language. Ontology works from the viewpoint and the assumption that human language is crucial to how our perceptive realities are being created. Humans are creatures of inventing what is mostly imagination of their minds, emotions, and moods by using language to create such a reality, when they are speaking as well as while they are listening. An ontological approach to transformational coaching supports participants in recognizing various ways of partaking in their language to produce more practical, positive, and workable realities in their day-to-day lives (2005).

## Body and Physicality

Another powerful and essential assumption on the ontological approach is that our body and physicality, such as our muscle tightness, postural placement, and our breathing, significantly play an impactful role in our awareness, perception, and learning and how we apply the change (2005).

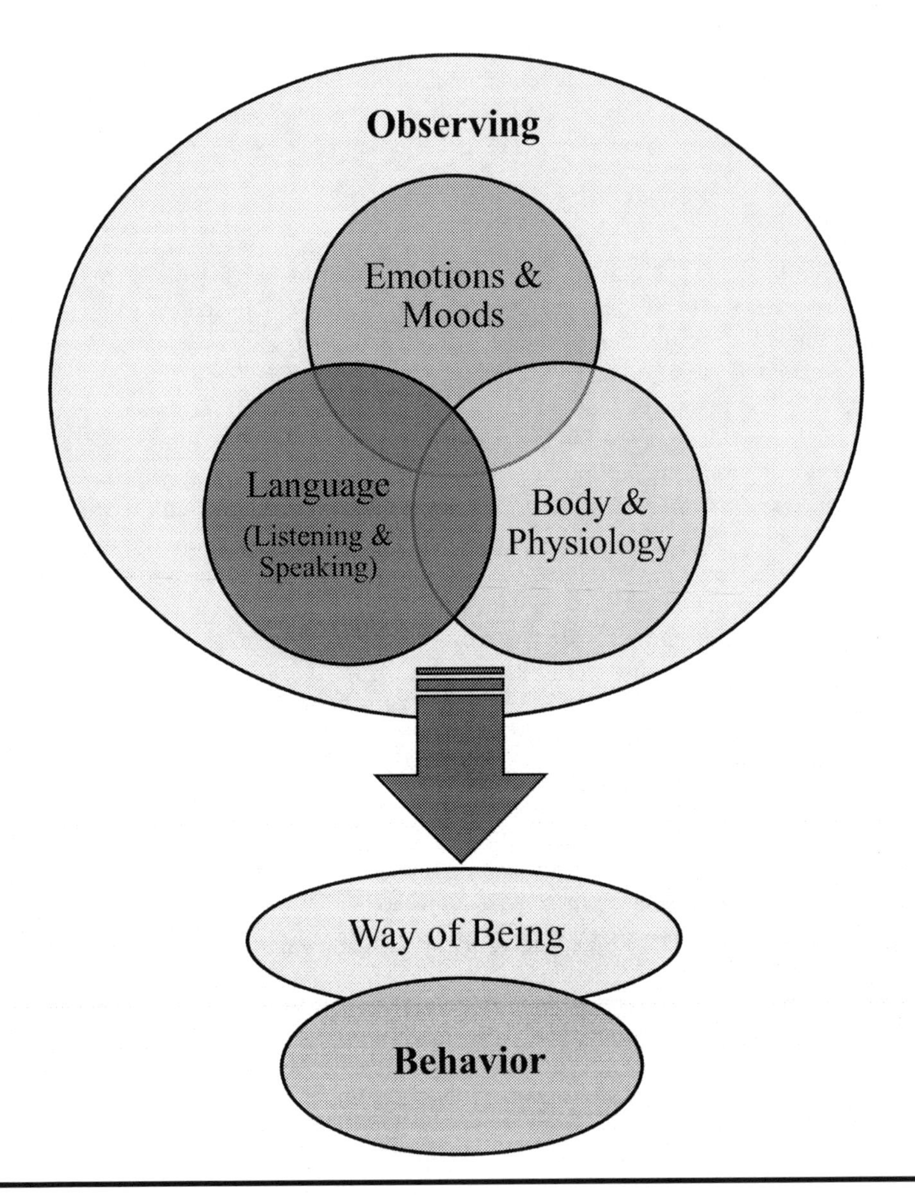


**Figure 7.2 The Five Areas of Observation in the Ontological Approach.**

*Source:* Adapted from Berto and Plebani (2015); Sieler (2005).

## *Way of Being*

Our behaviors reinforce and reveal our *way of being*. The expression *way of being* refers to how we perceive the world and how we either act or react to our perceived reality in time. How we experience the world is the byproduct and reflection of how we observe people, objects, events, and circumstances (2005). When we look closely, without judgment or attachment, a good deal of our relationship dysfunctions at work and at home are caused by our lack of ability to separate reality from interpretations and the act of adding or subtracting meanings to what is happening and what we are observing from not being able to act or behave in ways that produce the results we want (Bakhshandeh 2015; Bakhshandeh 2009).

### *Behavior*

According to Berto and Plebani (2015) and Sieler (2005), a result of mixing emotions, language, and bodily experiences causes people to be in a certain way and they therefore learn to behave in a certain way (see Figure 7.2). In transformational coaching, a professional coach will assist participants in distinguishing such experiences and decisions and guide participants to alter their ways of being and behaviors by pointing out their responsibilities and accountabilities for the outcomes of such ways of being and related behaviors.

#### *Difference between Feelings and Emotions*

Given that throughout this book we have mentioned *feelings* and *emotions*, it will be a good time to discuss the difference between feelings and emotions. Generally, the terms *feeling* and *emotion* are used synonymously; however, the fact is, according to professional psychologists, they are not interchangeable. While both *feelings* and *emotions* have comparable components, there is a noticeable distinction between them. According to Wake Forest University (2022): "A fundamental difference between feelings and emotions is that feelings are experienced consciously, while emotions are manifested either consciously or subconsciously. Some people may spend years, or even a lifetime, not understanding the depths of their emotions" (n.p.).

Allyn (2022) described the key differences among feelings and emotions:

- Even though the public uses them interchangeably, emotions and feelings are different.
- Emotions are triggered by sensations in people's bodies, therefore are real-time collectable data. While feelings could be subjective and influenced by mental misunderstandings.
- Emotional awareness can be developed, and ultimately can help avoid reactivity behavior caused by feelings because of false beliefs and perceived reality.

In the next chapter, we will discuss ontology and ontological approaches to coaching in much deeper levels.

## Educational Theories and Approach

Educational theories and models are other useful tools for implementing transformational coaching. Given that learning and application of new concepts are similar to process education and learning, transformational coaches use educational theories and models to transfer the knowledge to their participants.

In this section, we briefly cover some of the educational theories contributing to transformational coaching.

### *Dewey's Change Theory*

John Dewey was a notable contributor to educational theories and educational reform history. John Dewey's theory underlines that learners experience reality as it is; this means that students or adult learners must adjust themselves to their environments to learn (Dewey 1934). Dewey's view of the ideal learning environment is one of sharing experiences between students and the teacher together that produces additional value for both. This idea dramatically influences a positive, effective, and transformative relationship between managers and employees, which is the most central concept of Dewey's work experiences (Johnson 2010). The concept of one's experience relates to the transformation of learner and teacher's relationship, which is among subject (the learner) and environment (class, work, and the teacher, or manager), which happens because of dysfunction or breakdown caused by unworkable and disruptive behavior.

According to Petit and Ballet (2021), the unworkable behavior arises because either (1) the environment runs in conflict to the learner's needs, or (2) because the learner's needs conflict with the interests of the learning or working environment, or (3) because the learner's and environment's needs are communally mismatched. "This uncertainty indicates a desire for change on the part of the subject in the interest of restoring equilibrium: '[I]inner harmony is attained only when, by some means, terms are made with the environment' (Dewey 1934, p. 17)" (Petit and Ballet 2021, 659).

## Adult Learning Theory

The close similarities between adult learning theory and transformational coaching began in the 1960s when the concept of "life-catching" sparks from adult learning programs, and subsequently it was growing in societies (Chuang 2021). In the relationship between adult learning and transformational learning, Mezirow distinguishes transformative learning as "the process of learning through critical self-reflection, which results in the reformulation of a 'meaning perspective' to allow a more inclusive, discriminating, and integrative understanding of experience. Learning includes acting on these insights" (Cox 2015, xii).

Mezirow's (1990) theory underscored the position of experience in learning and particularly how it influences learning needs. According to Cox (2015), Mezirow claimed that "in transformative learning it is the need that creates a starting point for dialogue involving critical examination of assumptions, or meaning perspectives, underpinning deep-rooted value judgments and expectations" (27). In 1973, Malcolm Knowles created principles of adult learning to strengthen the layout of adult learners' classes. Many of these principles are aligned with modern coaching principles used in the coaching industry and transformational learning (Rachal 2002).

Knowles et al. (1988) adult learning principles are listed in Table 7.3. Others are listed in Rothwell (2020). Knowing these principles would assist transformational coaches and managers to pay attention to what would work for adult clients and participants in an individual or a group coaching.

## Experiential Learning

The basis for the experiential learning theory is learning from experience. Experiential learning concentrates on the notion and promotes actual experience as one of the best ways to learn things. Those learning and experiential experiences will be engraved in our minds and help us preserve information and remember the details (Kolb and Fry 1975).

### Kolb's Experiential Learning Theory

David Kolb published the experiential learning theory and its related model in 1985. Kolb credited his work to influences from John Dewey, Kurt Lewin, and Jean Piaget. The experiential learning

**Table 7.3 Knowles Principles of Adult Learning.**

| *Knowles Principles of Adult Learning* | | |
|---|---|---|
| # | *Principles* | *Descriptions* |
| 1 | Engagement | Adult learners want to be engaged when learning and discover the knowledge by themselves through inquiries. |
| 2 | Life Experiences | Adult learners desire to link their learning experience to their life and career experiences. This helps them to learn better from the new learning knowledge. |
| 3 | Goal Orientation | Adult learners are mostly goal oriented, and they are aware of what they want to accomplish and why. |
| 4 | Reasons | Adult learners want to see a reason or a purpose for the new learning and how it applies to their lives or relates to their jobs. |
| 5 | Qualities | Adult learners would rather focus on the qualities and attribution of the learning beneficial in their lives, personally or professionally. |
| 6 | Respect | Adult learners care about the display of respect and appreciation for their experience and what they are bringing to the learning process. |

*Sources:* Adapted from Knowles et al. (1988); Knowles (1984).

theory focuses on four learning stages (see Table 7.4): (1) concrete learning, (2) reflective observation, (3) abstract conceptualization, and (4) active experimentation.

> The first two stages of the cycle involve grasping an experience, and the second two focus on transforming an experience. Kolb argues that effective learning is seen as the learners go through the cycle and that they can enter into the cycle at any time.
>
> (WGU 2020, n.p.)

**Table 7.4 Stages of Kolb's Experiential Learning Theory**

| *Stages of Kolb's Experiential Learning Theory* | | |
|---|---|---|
| *Stages* | *Titles* | *Descriptions* |
| **One** | Concrete Learning | This occurs when a learner goes through a new experience or understands a previous experience in a new and fresh light. |
| **Two** | Reflective Observation | This is the next stage where the learners personally and independently reflect on their learning experience. They will view what they experience and their understanding of such experience to reflect on what such experience means to them. |
| **Three** | Abstract Conceptualization | This stage comes about when the learners construct new ideas or modifies their past thinking based on the new experience and their personal reflection on such experience. |
| **Four** | Active Experimentation | This stage occurs when the learner relates the new ideas to the actual world application around their lives or career and experiments if there are needs for any adjustments. |

*Source:* Adapted from WGU (2020).

Transformational coaches or managers attempting to use this approach to transform individual learning will encompass participants' experiential learning in their coaching process where participants will learn new coaching concepts through:

- Collecting knowledge by reading and listening to lectures or workshops
- Presenting and demonstrating new concepts by watching coaches or trainers demonstrate the new concept or process
- Practicing the concept by experimenting with the new concept's process or skills they learned
- Reflecting on their learning experience by capturing their insights and realizations about themselves and about the experience
- Applying new learning and potential modification of actions

## Learning Styles

Learning styles was developed by Rita Dunn and Kenneth Dunn around the 1970s and became one of the most used classifications of individual learning styles. According to Dunn et al. (1984), learning style categories are as follows:

### Visual Learners

Visual learners would rather watch the topic and learn by way of seeing. They learn better by visual imagery such as visual aids, videos, handouts, displays, pictures, diagrams, charts, and illustrations, and they love to take notes.

### Auditory Learners

Auditory learners prefer learning by listening. While they are listening, they are looking for the nuances of the lecturer's speech, which can include pitch, volume, tone, and pace of speaking. They enjoy listening to audiotapes, participating in discussions, or reading aloud.

### Kinesthetic Learners

Kinesthetic learners prefer learning by doing things, such as the experience of touching, moving items, and physically doing things. They mostly learn through experimenting, practicing, and role-playing. They just love to explore their environment through a hands-on tactic.

According to Honey and Mumford (1986), years later with the foundation of Dunn and Dunn work and the contributions of David Kolb and Peter Honey to the science of learning, Alan Mumford discovered four additional styles of learning:

### Activists

They enjoy new experiences, encounters, and concepts; however, they quickly get bored with the process of execution. Activists need to be engaged, involved with the idea, collaborate with others, enjoy the challenge, and want to lead.

### Reflectors

This learner likes to gather information and collect data. They enjoy examining the data carefully, considering different situations and various options and viewpoints. They love to study, analyze, and review the data and produce reports.

### *Theorists*

These learners like to observe and combine perspectives in complex but logical theories. They learn best when they put themselves in a complex situation and use their knowledge and abilities in defined conditions with clear intent.

### *Pragmatists*

These learners enjoy trying new things and experimenting with new ideas. They learn better when notions can be directly and practically utilized and when there is an opportunity for extensive discussions. They are looking for a clear connection between the subject and task they can try out with new procedures and receive feedback.

## *Immunity to Change*

Kegan and Lahey designed the immunity to change in 1984 by suggesting that individuals' development is sourced from their ability to make meaning of their experiences. Based on that assumption and theory, they created the immunity to change method for individuals to learn of their own behaviors and what is in the way of their desired change or from achieving their goals. To shed light on hidden obstacles to change, they established the immunity map (see Table 7.5), which investigates individuals' motivators behind commitments, their hidden competing commitments, and their damaging interpretations that push individuals' mindset, behaviors, and actions, limiting personal change and potentially blocking further personal and professional development (Lasley et al. 2015).

# Applied Behavioral Science

According to Regis College (2021), "The American Psychological Association defines behavioral science as a discipline that uses systematic observation and experimentation in the scientific study of human and nonhuman animal actions and reactions" (n.p.). The file of applied behavioral science is continuously developing and evolving with various applications in different areas such as sociology, education, and public health (Regis College 2021).

**Table 7.5 Kegan and Lahey's Immunity Map Worksheet.**

| *The Immunity Map Worksheet* | | | |
|---|---|---|---|
| *My Goal for Accomplishment or Improvement* | *My Behaviors That Work Contrary to My Goal* | *My Hidden Conflicting Commitments* | *My Damaging Interpretations* |
| | | | |
| **Actions I need to implement to achieve this goal** | | **What I am worried or concerned about** | |
| | | | |

*Source:* Adapted from Lasley et al. (2015).

One approach in practicing behavioral science is the application of the discipline of applied behavior analysis, or ABA, the employing set of behavioral principles in practical settings such as human behaviors associated with motivation or learning progress. Principles of ABA are beneficial to adults and children for managing the behaviors that influence several aspects of individuals' lives, such as interactions with others, relating to authority, working with peers, and with their family. ABA is frequently used to replace problematic behaviors of individuals or groups with appropriate, positive, and productive alternative behaviors (Regis College 2021).

In this section, we briefly cover some theories contributing to applied behavioral science.

## Cognitive Behavioral Theories

Cognitive behavioral theories are best explained as a group of theories developed from empirical psychological studies, academic writings, clinical research, therapy experiences, and observations from mental health practitioners. Cognitive behavioral theory is the mixture of cognitive procedures and behavioral approaches to attain cognitive and behavioral change(s) with individuals or teams (Kalodner 2011).

Given there are various theories and approaches credited to the cognitive-behavioral concept, there is no one specific description of the cognitive behavioral theory. However, all cognitive-behavioral theorists regard the part that cognitions play in developing and preserving human psychological difficulties (Salkovskis and Millar 2016).

### Cognitive Therapy

Cognitive therapy (CT) is a form of therapy developed by Aaron T. Beck around the 1960s. Cognitive therapy is understood to be the first psychotherapy that went under a clinical examination. This therapy would go under a larger canopy of cognitive behavioral therapy (CBT), which is a successful therapy to treat individuals. CT concentrates on individuals' immediate behavioral change by observing individuals' thoughts and related emotions. The CT approach is based on the therapist and participant working together to understand and correct the behavior(s) under question (Early and Grady 2016; Alford and Beck 1998). Considering all the psychological disciplines, theories, and practices, cognitive therapy is the theory and therapy that is most similar to the approach and process of transformational coaching. Figure 7.3 depicts the relationship between individuals' thoughts triggering their feelings and then their feelings triggering their behaviors, and finally it uses their behaviors to justify and support their original thoughts.

On one hand, the original emphasis of cognitive therapy was and continues to be on assisting individuals in understanding, being aware, and correcting their dysfunctional behaviors while learning to create new and more effective behaviors. But CT and related practices can also improve behaviors of functioning individuals to improve their existing behaviors or establish new behaviors that would support them in accomplishing their intentions and achieving their goals (Alford and Beck 1998). Like cognitive therapy, transformational coaching is centered on how individuals' thoughts impact their behaviors. In addition, transformational coaching works on transforming limiting beliefs, disempowering internal dialogues, and increasing individuals' views of what is possible for them in their personal and professional lives.

### Cognitive Behavioral Therapy

Cognitive behavioral therapy (CBT) has become one of the most widespread models for social workers' and mental health practitioners' interventions with their patients. CBT branches from

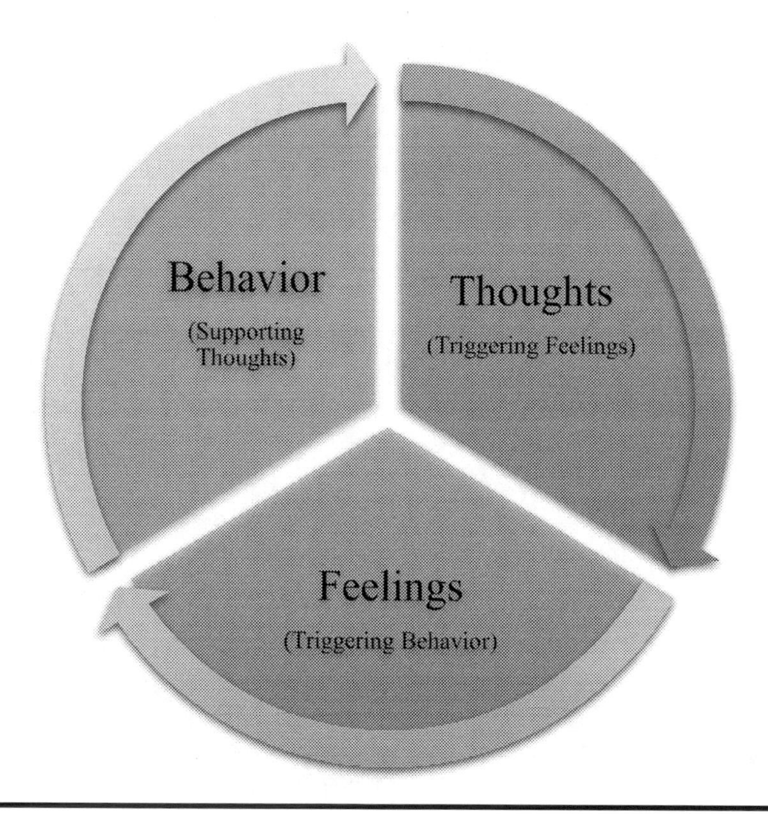


**Figure 7.3 Process of Cognitive Therapy.**

*Source:* Adapted from Early and Grady (2016); Alford and Beck (1998).

two very distinctive and exclusive theoretical paradigms with deep roots. However, in the domain of practicing these theories, the full potential of the CBT model is not understood, as behavioral theories are mostly credited and utilized as secondary to cognitive theories (CT) (Salkovskis and Millar 2016). Mental health professionals use the CBT approach for people dealing with anxiety, depression, phobias, and even addiction. However, transformational coaches also use it to create personal awareness for their clients. CBT allows individuals to become aware of how to deal with destructive behavioral issues positively as it broadens the individuals' understanding of themselves and the way they are operating.

Transformational coaching uses a form of combining the two CT and CBT therapies. This combined model helps individuals and teams to create new behavioral habits through awareness, thinking, and creating action plans during the coaching program. Considering this perspective, transformational coaching helps individuals and teams to conduct a brainstorming session to come up with new ways of thinking and to invent a new set of behaviors that matches their commitments and what they want to see in their lives and careers.

## *Alter Thinking Using Cognitive Behavioral Therapy*

According to the Mayo Clinic (2022), under the support of mental health professionals, individuals can alter their thinking and shift their thoughts in a positive and productive fashion by following the following process (see Figure 7.4):

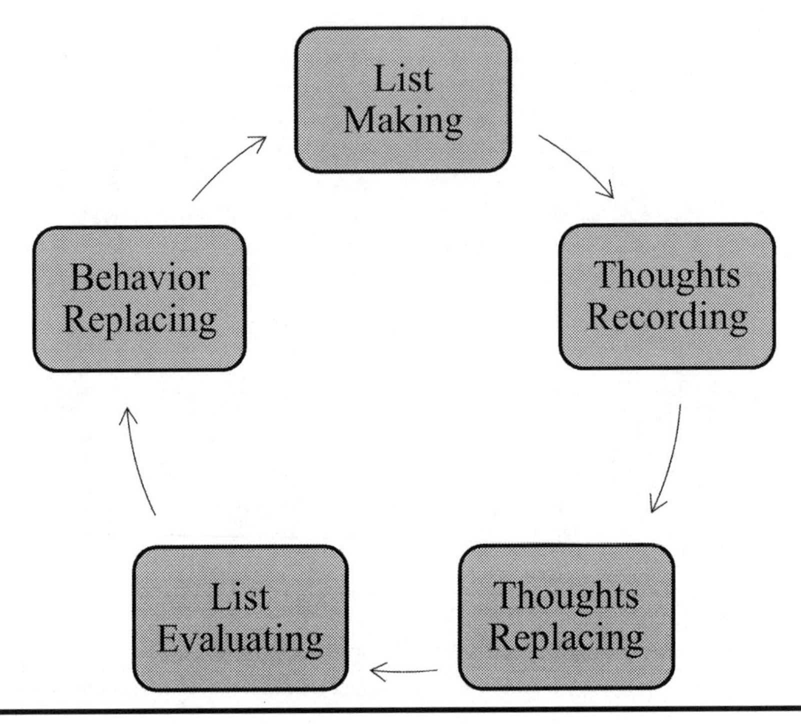


**Figure 7.4 Process of Alter Thinking Using Cognitive Behavioral Therapy.**

*Source:* Adapted from Mayo Clinic (2022).

- **List making:** Detect and distinguish disconcerting situations, events, or circumstances in your life (personally or professionally).
- **Thoughts recording:** Learn of your unproductive, negative, and destructive thoughts, emotions, and what you believe to be true about these situations, events, or circumstances.
- **Thoughts replacing:** After recognizing those negative, destructive, and inaccurate thoughts, replace them with more positive, constructive, and realistic thoughts.
- **List evaluating:** Keep reviewing your original list, your destructive thoughts, and what you have recently created. Get present to which one is empowering you and giving you access to better relationships, empowering life and happier situations.
- **Behavior replacing:** Replace your unpleasant and unwanted behaviors caused by the destructive thoughts with a new set of behaviors linked to the new thoughts you have generated.

## *Key Distinctions between Cognitive Therapy and Cognitive Behavioral Therapy*

- Cognitive therapy is a particular therapy employed by mental health professionals to understand one's behavior, thoughts, and emotions to treat them, while Cognitive Behavioral Therapy is a general term for a canopy of various therapies.
- Cognitive Therapy, Rational Emotive Behavior Therapy, and Multimodal Therapy are some therapies under the broader area of Cognitive-Behavioral Therapy.

- In the practice of Cognitive Therapy, the mental health practitioners use a cognitive model, context, or structure, while in Cognitive Behavioral Therapy, the mental health professionals use either a cognitive or a behavioral context and model.

(Difference Between 2015)

## The Iceberg Metaphor

We use the famous iceberg metaphor to display the importance of one's awareness and understanding of employing a change. For the behavior to change, there is a need for substantial change in one's mindset and attitude. If we take the iceberg metaphor (see Figure 7.5), the part of the iceberg under the waterline is the largest part of the iceberg's structure, something nobody can see or be aware of.

That is the part that transformational coaching will take under consideration and examine with individuals or teams, that is, their belief systems, their perceptions of themselves and others, the way they view the world around them, and the perceived realities they have invented for themselves

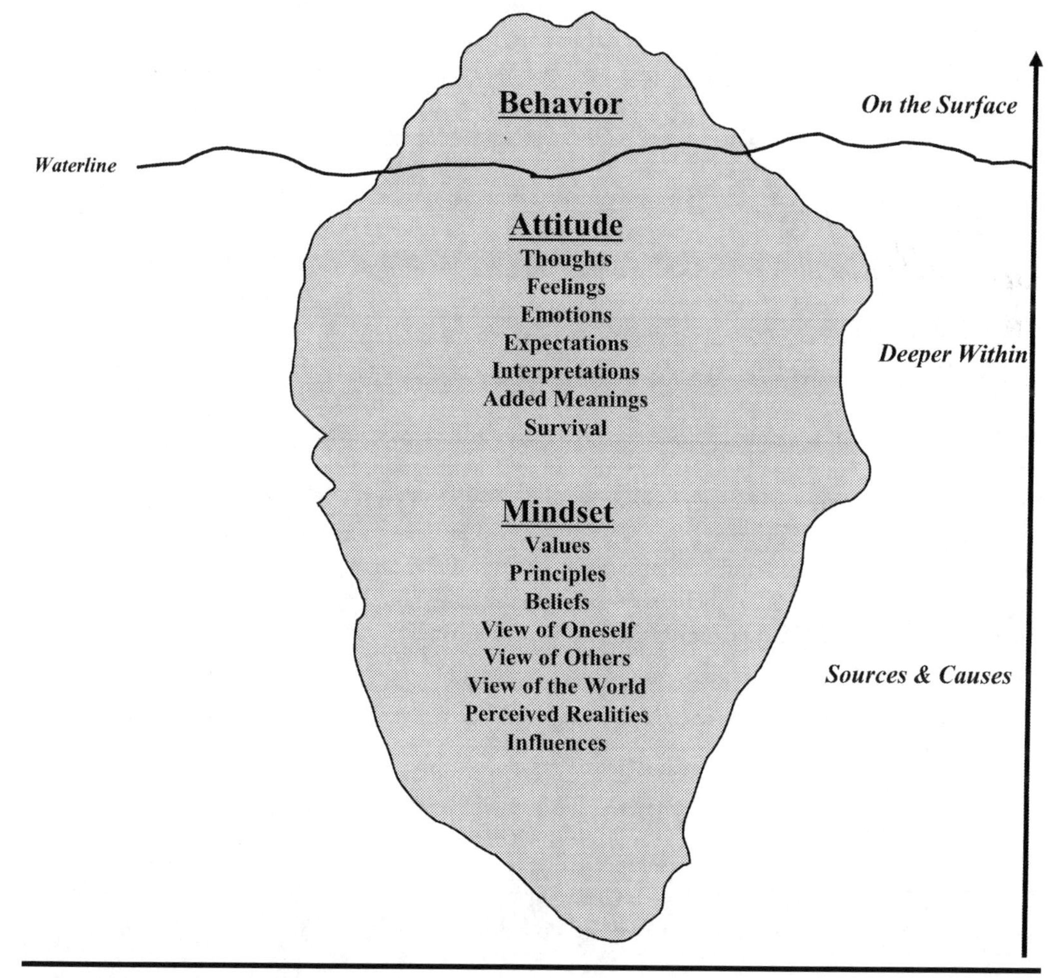


**Figure 7.5 Iceberg Metaphor for Modeling Relationship Between Mindset, Attitude and Behavior.**

*Source:* Author's Original Creation. Copyright 2022 by Behnam Bakhshandeh.

because of all aforementioned influences. Then they look at the source of their mindset, how it is created, and what was causing it. Finally, they consider what is deep inside the individuals causing their attitudes, their thoughts, feelings, emotions, expectations of themselves and others, the meanings they have to events around them, and all the interpretations they come with to justify their behavior. The behavior, the part above the waterline, where everyone observes it, is what causes a breakdown in relationships and productivity or allows open space for performance, success, and accomplishment.

For transformational coaching to work, coaches dig into individuals' thinking and help them design empowering thinking by digging into the beliefs, values, principles, and past experiences that determined their unproductive thinking and behavior.

## Psychological Theories and Approach

As we have mentioned in Chapters 1 and 2, psychology is one of the main fundamentals of transformation and has a substantial role in transformational coaching in general and in personal transformation. A psychological approach is defined as a viewpoint centered on specific assumptions about behavior. Each psychological approach possesses shared theories about explaining, defining, and predicting individuals' or groups' behaviors. In this section, we briefly discuss and introduce several psychological approaches to transformational coaching.

### *Positive Psychology*

Initially, positive psychology was created by Abraham Maslow in 1954 (Maslow 1970) and then progressed further by Martin Seligman, who has been credited as the father of the modern positive psychology movement. When the concept of positive psychology was created as a new academic field of study, it was facing asceticism and believed to be a passing trend among new waves of the psychological field (Seligman 2002).

Seligman attempted to shift the emphasis of traditional general psychology away from its predominant attention on mental illness, overall dysfunctions, and general unhappiness to nurturing competencies and individuals' abilities to improve their lives. The research done by positive psychologists primarily discovers the reasons for people's happiness or why they are not happy and what elements of life and modern societies are influencing and improving their happiness (Seligman 2002). In 1988, Dr. Seligman came up with the new Theory of well-being, or PERMA for short (Madeson 2022) (see Figure 7.6), and the five aspects of the model follow.

#### *Five Aspects of Seligman's PERMA Model*

1. **Positive Emotion.** As it means by its name, positive emotion is about individuals feeling good, which is an expressway to become happy. When they feel good, they feel fresh, happy, and positive. Smiling and talking positively is not equal to those who are really and

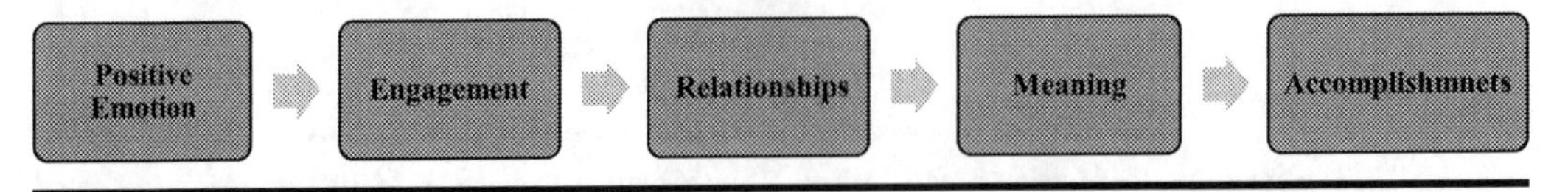


**Figure 7.6 PERMA Model and a New Theory of Well-Being by Martin Seligman.**

*Source:* Adapted from Madeson (2022).

authentically happy within; anyone can pretend and fake it. Positive emotion generated from freely accepting the bad and unpleasant past circumstances and hardships can experience and predict positively what the future might bring.

2. **Engagement.** Engagement implies something that interests individuals deep enough, so they get engrossed with or absorbed in it, like the experience of getting lost in a great book or getting involved with a project during which they forget about time because it is so engaging. Engagement causes positivity in people's emotions, intelligence, and skills, like a child who plays with a Lego set and builds a sky scrapper.
3. **Relationships.** It is a natural desire of humans to connect with others, be in a one-on-one relationship with someone special and be involved with teams and groups. Humans are hard-wired for wanting and needing interactions, affections, attention, and love which comes from immediate family, significant others, co-workers, and group members when things get tough, and we need emotional support and compassion.
4. **Meaning.** We need not go too far to see how important meaning is in our lives. Just review the news to see how many rich and famous people committed suicide because they feel empty and unhappy regardless of money, fame, luxury, and materialistic possessions. Research has proven that people need and want to have a meaning they can find in their personal and professional lives.
5. **Accomplishments.** People take pride and joy in something they have created, done, or accomplished. The feelings and sense of accomplishments strengthen people's self-esteem, sense of certainty, self-confidence, so they can feel as if they have done something worthy.

(Madeson 2022; CFI 2022)

The fundamental principle of positive psychology is that people are regularly fascinated by the perspective of the future much more than they are motivated by their past. Additionally, positive psychology indicates a mixture of people's positive experiences, feelings, and emotions regarding their past, their experience of the present, and the desire of the future, causing pleasant emotions and happy life in the present (Green and Palmer 2019).

In Chapter 8 we will further discuss the implications of positive psychology on transformational coaching.

## Humanistic Psychology

The humanistic psychology perspective posits individuals' ability and power for self-fulfillment and the significance of people's consciousness, self-awareness, and capability to make their own choices. According to this psychological perspective, human experiences are the key and crucial part of human psychology (Learning Theories for Educators 2022).

Humanistic psychology was developed in the 1950s by Abraham Maslow and Carl Rogers. Both psychologists rejected the negativism of old-fashioned psychology promoting the notion that individuals have no role in forming their destiny and that all people's actions were generated and caused by either (1) Sigmund Freud's theory of the unconscious mind that processes and is controlled by primitive sexual urges, or (2) by behavioral psychology, which was based on the premise that individuals' destinies are determined by their environment. Maslow and Rogers claimed that both psychological schools of thought failed to understand and underline the distinctive qualities that allowed individuals to make individual and objective choices that would give them complete control of their destiny (Waterman 2013).

Humanistic psychology focuses on the holistic development of individuals about these three key elements of attaining the peak level of self-understanding and personal development: (1) self-actualization, (2) self-fulfillment, and (3) self-realization (DeRobertis 2013).

Between 1943 and 1954, Maslow developed the hierarchy of needs, which is one psychological theory of motivation. This theory contains five levels of human needs to accomplish personal growth. According to Maslow (1987), people need to fulfill their lower needs in the hierarchy before getting to the higher needs, which would support them in their accomplishment and fulfillment. Maslow (1943) originally indicated that individuals must satisfy their lower-level needs before advancing on to meet their higher-level needs (see Figure 7.7 and Table 7.6). Later, he explained that people's satisfaction with a need is not an "all-or-none" fact. He admitted that his previous assertions might display "the false impression that a need must be satisfied 100 percent before the next need emerges" (Maslow 1987, 69).

According to Maslow, people's need to grow is not raised above current learning situations based on the background of lacking something, instead it is a wish and desire to grow as an individual. When these needs for growth have been relatively fulfilled, individuals have a better chance and ability to grow step-by-step and ultimately achieve the greatest level, known as self-actualization (Maslow 1987).

## *Psychosynthesis*

Psychosynthesis is considered a therapeutic method that concentrates on an individual's personal growth and development. Psychosynthesis specialists believe individuals combine several aspects of the self to develop and self-actualize (GoodTherapy 2017).

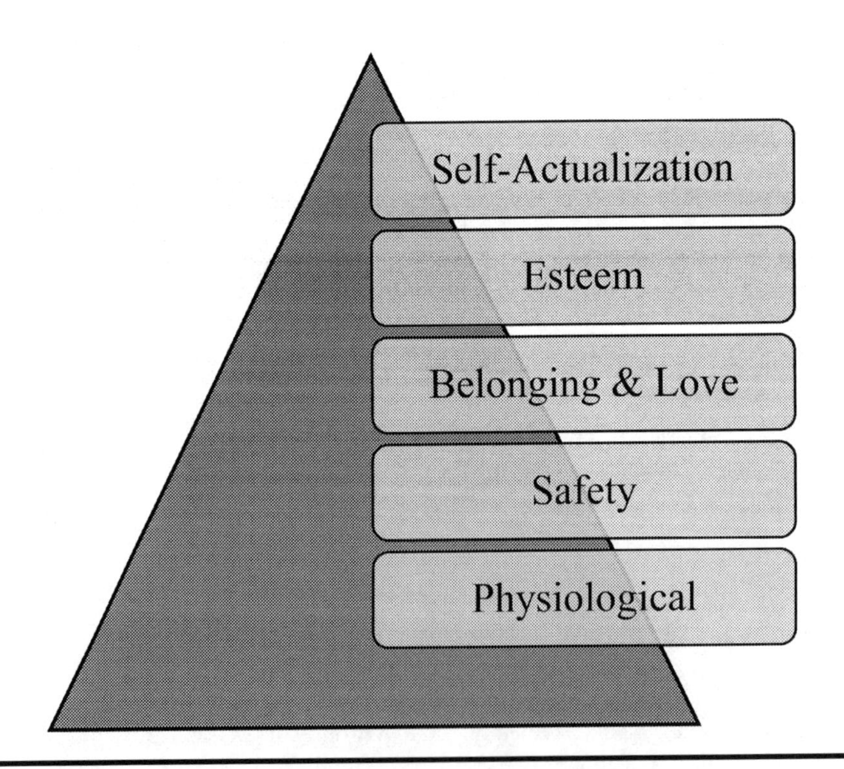


**Figure 7.7 Abraham Maslow's Hierarchy of Human Needs Pyramid.**

*Source:* Adapted from Maslow (1987).

**Table 7.6 Details of Abraham Maslow's Hierarchy of Human Needs.**

| *Maslow's Hierarchy of Human Needs* | | |
|---|---|---|
| *Levels* | *Needs* | *Attributions* |
| **Basic Level** | Physiological Needs | Food, water, shelter, clothing, warmth, rest |
| | Safety Needs | Security, safety |
| **Psychological Needs** | Belonging & Love Needs | Friendships, intimate relationships, human connections, societies, communities |
| | Esteem Needs | Prestige, the experience of achievement, accomplishment, personal growth |
| **Self-fulfillment Needs** | Self-Actualization Needs | Achieving full potential, creating activities, personal fulfillment |

*Source:* Adapted from Maslow (1987).

Initially, psychosynthesis was created by Italian psychiatrist Roberto Assagioli at the beginning of the 1900s. He was fascinated by Sigmund Freud's psychoanalysis but felt Freud disregarded essential elements of the human experience and their understanding. Because of such assumptions, he promoted a more inclusive, holistic standpoint on humanity. Additionally, Assagioli's development of psychosynthesis involved practicing yoga, dabbling in philosophy and theology, and Carl Jung's work (Lombard 2017). He was focusing on people's spiritual experience and how different elements of the individuals' "self" try to reach harmony. "Assagioli believed a person's primary task is to find a sense of completeness within the self and a connection to a larger whole, such as one's community or the world" (GoodTherapy 2017, n.p.).

## *Existential Therapy*

The practice and approach of existential therapy were developed based on the background and philosophies of Friedrich Nietzsche and Soren Kierkegaard. Kierkegaard was one of the first existential philosophers to speculate that individuals' dissatisfaction could be defeated only through their internal wisdom (Prochaska and Norcross 2003).

The primary assumption of existential therapy is that life is ambiguous and full of uncertainty, and people have a choice on how to react to their experiences (May 1999). According to Yalom (1980), people share the experience of confronting life's uncertainties and how that would affect them. Regardless of the issues people face in life, regardless of the uncertainty, everyone feels and experiences a sense of uneasiness, anxiety, and nervousness.

The transformational coaching process encompasses the discipline of existential coaching and pertaining its all-purpose methods to participants' specific experiences or issues they are facing by supporting them by investigating their beliefs, perceived reality, and views.

## *Gestalt Therapy*

Gestalt therapy was developed between 1940 and 1950 by Fritz Peris, Laura Peris, and Paul Goodman. It focuses on existential therapy and experiential psychology, with imperial emphasis on the present moment (Houston 2003).

Gestalt therapy mainly emphasizes individuals' personal responsibility in their relationship to their experience and the interpretations of reality. Beisser (1970) defined Gestalt's paradoxical concept of change as based on people's attempt to change, and the more they try to change and be who they are not in reality, the more they continue to be the same. But when individuals connect with their present and actual experience of themselves and who they are, and accept it as is without any attempt to change or alter the experience, or who they are, they will experience being whole and complete without lacking (Houston 2003).

### *Awareness Integration Model*

The awareness integration (AI) model is a new approach in psychotherapy developed by a psychotherapist, Foojan Zeine, around 2010. This model has been demonstrated to be influential in delivering a successful and accelerated direction to recuperation from a range of psychological and emotional issues with individuals (Zeine et al. 2017).

> Awareness Integration (AI) is a multi-modality psychotherapeutic model that enhances self-awareness, releases past traumas and psychological blocks, and promotes clarity and positive attitudes. The AI model incorporates various aspects of these treatments into one efficient, open-structured model that encompasses all aspects of the human experience in order to maximize its effectiveness and create enduring results.
>
> (Zeine 2014, 60)

As Siegel (1999) explained, interpersonal relationships are an essential and integral part of human culture, especially in Western societies, and are important to individuals, teams, and groups, as well as communities and societies on bigger scales. People's internal experience combined with their external environmental experiences affects their interpersonal relationships at home and at work. The AI model intends to harmonize individuals' internal thought processes with their external experiences to harmonize and integrate troublesome thoughts while substituting such thoughts with healthy and efficient cognitive procedures (Zeine 2014).

From the beginning of the intervention process, the intention of AI therapy is to gently introduce the participant to the process of change. At the beginning phase of the process, participants get access to their mindset and differentiate between their thinking, their emotions, and the related behaviors that have been generated from their mindset and feelings. That is the beginning of their understanding of how they have developed and adapted their mindset and become aware and conscious of their way of being related to their mindset (Zeine 2021).

Here is a simple example of this concept at work or at home. As Zeine (2021) explained, most individuals are aware of their emotions and how they feel when, at work, managers or supervisors, or, at home, spouses or significant others speak to them in a harsh tone of voice in an unpleasant way. Zeine (2021) continued,

> However, they are seldom as aware of how their own negative and demeaning thoughts, their feelings of anger, their tone, their words, and nonverbal body language affect the quality of their discussions and of the overall long-term quality of these relationships with their bosses or mates.
>
> (51)

## Emotional Intelligence

Emotions directly affect one's state of mind, and in some shape and form, they rule our day-to-day lives. We make decisions based on what we are feeling, for example sad, angry, happy, frustrated, or bored; therefore, subconsciously, we select activities correlated to the emotions we

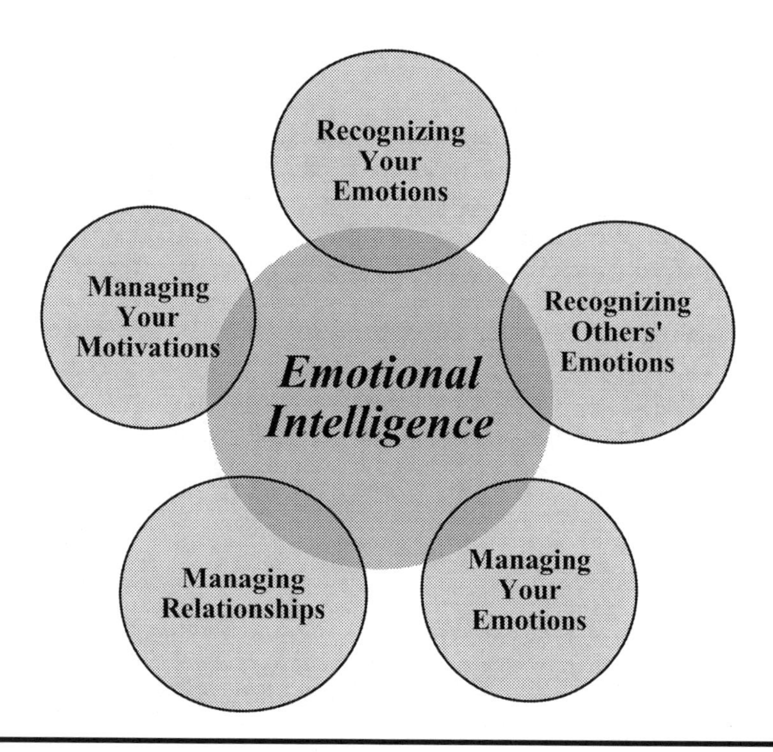


**Figure 7.8 The Five Domains of Emotional Intelligence.**

*Source:* Adapted from Salovey et al. (2004).

are inflaming (Hockenbury and Hockenbury 2007). "An emotion is a complex psychological state that involves three distinct components: a subjective experience, a physiological response, and behavioral or expressive response" (Hockenbury and Hockenbury 2007, n.p.).

Emotional intelligence, also known as EI or EQ, contains the individuals' capacity and capability to recognize, evaluate, and positively influence their own emotions and others around them. Emotional intelligence is considered a reasonably new behavioral recognition model, which rose to notoriety and reputation after Daniel Goleman's 1995 book *Emotional Intelligence*. Emotional intelligence has been characterized as the "ability to monitor one's own and others' feelings and emotions, to discriminate among them and to use this information to guide one's thinking and actions" (Salovey et al. 2004, n.p.). Originally, emotional intelligence developed around the 1970s and 1980s from the research and writings conducted by psychologists such as Howard Gardner, Peter Salovey, and John (Jack) Mayer.

Salovey et al. (2004) described the five domains of emotional intelligence as shown in Figure 7.8.

We will dig deeper into emotional intelligence, its elements, and its relevancy to transformational coaching in the next chapter.

## Management Theories and Models

There are many management and business operational distinctions and models that contribute to the process and use of transformational coaching used by coaches or managers. In this section we mention several such models, disciplines, and processes.

## Process Consultation

The process consultation was developed by Edgar Schein in 1969 when he published his first book about the process and viewpoint of process consultation. This process has been part of organization development activities, which strive for enhancing organizational and individual effectiveness and productivity (Schein 1988).

Process consultation assists clients (could be organizations, teams, groups, or departments) to find the solution to their problems by themselves without giving them answers or advice on how to fix the issues. Process consultation works best and is beneficial when there is no clear-cut understanding of the problem or an obvious solution (Schein 1999).

Transformational coaching is comparable to process consultation when coaches steer clear of giving clients or coachees their opinions or advice. Instead, they encourage their clients or coachees to obtain clarity on the problem(s) and discover their own solution(s); that way, they own both sides, what is not working, what they need to do, and how they need to do it (Rothwell et al. 2021).

## Managing Transitions

Another useful approach to realize and conduct a change is through the lens of transition. Managing transitions is part of the transition model process developed by William Bridges in 1991. According to Bridges (2003), transitions consist of a three-step process: (1) ending, (2) neutral zone, and (3) new beginning (see Figure 7.9).

Though change is considered an external occasion, such as new structure, new policies and procedures, or new management style, going through transition during the change happen to be an internal undertaking, such as facing the unknown, the fear of "what if," and letting go of what they know; it is all about their emotions and their experiences. The transition process by itself

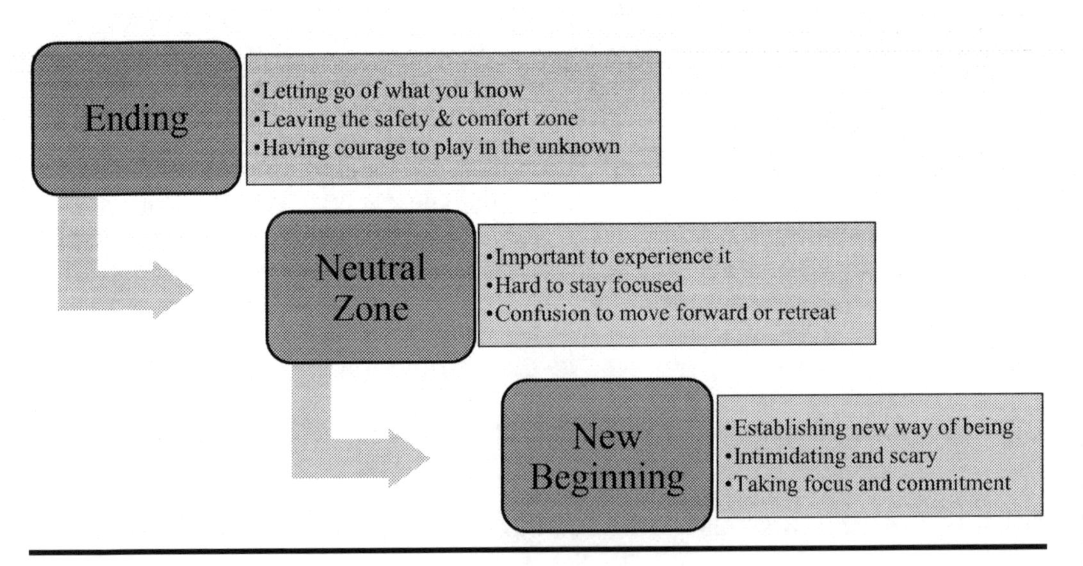


**Figure 7.9 Transitions Model Process.**

*Source:* Adapted from Bridges and Bridges (2019); Bridges (2003).

seems scary and hard; however, the change itself as an outcome that keeps individuals back is the fear, which is one of the biggest resistances to change and, in many cases, makes the change process unworkable (Bridges and Bridges 2019).

1. **Ending.** At this step, individuals feel there is a demand to give up in their minds what they believe about themselves, what they think is real, and their perspective of the world around them. People think what they know is their identity and asking them to let it go becomes terrifying. This step gives individuals feelings of being uncomfortable and leaving their safety zone but experiencing courage and power to imagine the future.
2. **The neutral zone.** This step is distinguished by ambiguity, uncertainty, and confusion. Individuals feel they are in limbo. Because of this mental space, this step takes huge amounts of motivation to stay on the course of change. This phase is uncomfortable and requires strong motivation to get through it. Some push through and some struggle to retreat to their past and what they were comfortable with.
3. **New beginnings.** On this last step, individuals must perform distinctly. It is difficult and intimidating for people to change their mindset and beliefs from an old way to new ways of being that require a new way of thinking. This happens when many people experience being consciously incompetent because of their difficulty operating in their new way of being. It takes a strong focus and a display of commitment not to lose the sense of competence in managing this phase.

## *Theory X and Theory Y*

Developed by Douglas McGregor in the early 1960s, theory X and theory Y explain the key difference between the assumptions about individuals' motivation, which draws the line between fundamentals of these two methodologies and styles of management: (1) theory X: authoritarian, and (2) theory Y: participative (Cummings and Worley 2015).

### *Theory X*

Theory X style managers have a pessimistic opinion of their employees. Their assumption is based on naturally unmotivated people who do not like to work hard or under a firm structure. Given that viewpoint, theory X managers think that individual employees need to be rewarded or punished regularly to complete their job and tasks. The usual working environment under this management is repetitive, and employees are constantly under the "carrot and stick" tactic. Employee performance appraisals and compensation are mostly based on quantifiable results, while management keeps tabs on their performance and productivity (Rothwell and Sredl 2014).

### *Theory Y*

Theory Y style managers are more positive and have an optimistic view of their employees while implementing a decentralized and participative management approach. From a theory Y viewpoint, this approach encourages individuals and teams to be more collaborative and welcome a trust-based connection with their managers and other team members. Under theory Y, the working environment is one of individual and team responsibility, while managers encourage employees to further develop their knowledge, skills, and abilities with suggestions for self and

**Table 7.7 Summary of Differences on Assumptions about Employees among Theory X and Theory Y.**

| *Differences in Assumptions about Employees among Theory X and Theory Y* | |
|---|---|
| *Theory X* | *Theory Y* |
| Workers do not like their work. | They are happy to work on their own. |
| Workers avoid responsibilities. | They are self-motivated to work. |
| Employees need constant directions. | They want to be involved in decision making. |
| They need to be controlled and forced to work. | They like to take more responsibilities. |
| They must be promoted or punished to make corrections. | They view work as challenging and a source of fulfillment. |
| They need to feel threatened or fear their managers. | They enjoy their work and display accountability and ownership. |
| They need to be supervised all the times. | They use creativity to solve problems. |

*Sources:* Adapted from Cummings and Worley (2015); Rothwell and Sredl (2014).

team improvements. Conducting performance appraisals for promotions is also common, but they are utilized to encourage people for open communication and teamwork versus controlling them (2014).

Table 7.7 summarizes differences in assumptions about employees among theory X and theory Y.

Theory Y has become the style of choice for management among modern organizations and is more popular among newer managers, which only reflects employees' growing desire for more meaningful professions that offer more than just compensation.

Transformational coaching shares the fundamentals of theory Y view of individuals and teams in organizations. As professional industries are learning more about individuals' mindsets, behaviors, and attitudes, the assumptions of theory Y performance overshadow management theories and their relationship to workers.

## Force Field Theory

Force field theory was developed by Kurt Lewin, a Gestalt therapy practitioner who was an expert in the group dynamic contrast and action research approach to conduct a change. From his viewpoint, for implementing a sustainable change, the system (individuals, teams, or organizations) needs to (1) either diminish and minimize the resisting forces to change or (2) maximize and strengthen driving forces to change. Force field theory foundation is based on assumptions that individual behaviors are affected by forces such as beliefs, perceived realities, invented expectations, and cultural norms. These influential forces can be positive, encouraging people toward behaviors, or can be negative, pushing people away from a set of behaviors (MBA Knowledge Base 2021; Lewin 2008).

Lewin used an ice block analogy and metaphor to explain the organizational change; however, this analogy also applies on individual and team levels. According to Lewin's (2008) force field theory, there are three steps to change: (1) unfreeze from the present state, (2) apply the desired

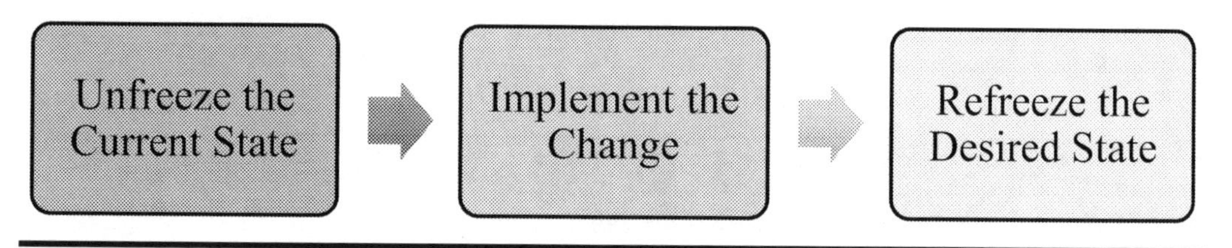


**Figure 7.10 Lewin's Ice Block Analogy to Explain Change.**

*Source:* Adapted from Lewin (2008).

change, and (3) refreeze to the new state. Please see Figure 7.10 and the following information for more clarity and understanding.

### *Unfreeze the Current State*

This first step is about recognizing inaction and disassembling the current mindset and the prevailing behaviors (Lewin 2008). In this phase, the responsible manager or a transformational coach needs to recognize and bypass individuals' and teams' protection mechanisms, such as what they know, how they do things, and what their already established mindset is. Unfortunately, this stage might take a little time because of potential resistance by participants because of fear of the unknown (Bakhshandeh 2009).

### *Implement the Change*

At this stage, participants are aware of their old ways of being, and their thinking mindset has been challenged; however, they don't clearly understand what is replacing it and how the change will be implemented. Given this lack of clarity, they might experience uncertainty and confusion (2008). Therefore, transformational coaches and managers need to be patient and provide necessary information to keep the participants on the damages of the old ways and the benefits of potential changes (2009).

### *Refreeze the Desired State*

This stage occurs when participants or the clients go back to a steady and secure state and understand where they are and how they got here. Refreezing activities could be included specifying new standards and procedures, designing new and relevant training and development, and implementing new policies (2008). At this stage, given the introduction of a new mindset and new habits and activities, the managers or the transformational coaches must check on participants to ensure they are not sliding back to earlier stages (2009).

## ***Client-Centered Approach***

The client-centered approach was developed by Carl Rogers around the 1940s and 1950s. Originally, he called it a "client-centered approach to psychotherapy" when he was developing humanistic psychology. During the early 1960s, Rogers introduced concepts of "empathy" and "unconditional positive regard" to the personal and professional development industry, when the traditional Freudian psychological approach depended on the therapist's viewpoints, opinions, and agendas (Rogers 1995).

Carl Rogers noticed his clients' need to be in a relationship in which they are accepted without prejudgment from their therapists. Therefore, he developed the client-centered approach and indicated various adequate conditions essential for the clients' approach to change (1995). Out of those conditions, three are used by transformational coaching:

- **Congruence or genuineness:** Coaches shall not act as an authority and shall forgo their own opinions based on their own experiences and discovery from their participants to expedite their relationship with their clients and the topic at hand.
- **Unconditional positive regard:** Coaches prevent judgment, approval, or disapproval of their clients or the clients' actions and accept them unconditionally. This approach will accelerate self-regard for the client.
- **Empathic understanding:** Coaches shall allow themselves to be empathetic and experience understanding of their clients' feelings, emotions, and inner experience. A correct understanding of the clients' internal status supports the clients' trust in their coaches' unconditional acceptance.

## Nonviolent Communication

Nonviolent communication, or NVC, also known as compassionate communication or collaboration communication, is the work of Dr. Marshall Rosenberg, who developed this technique in the 1960s as a means and technique in conversation science. The purpose of NVC is to provide a safe space for communication among people, with both sides understanding one another and delivering their messages and intentions without display of upset and potential violence (Williams et al. 2021).

The nonviolent communication method of communication is considered a two-sided approach: (1) as a spiritual practice that assists with people to get present to their common humanity on both sides of the isle, and (2) as a set of skills that assists people in generating greater human connections with one another, especially during communication (Rosenberg 2003). "Rosenberg seeks to foster interpersonal understanding and connections through the communication of judgment-free observations, recognition of people's feelings, needs and values and requests for specific actions to meet those needs" (Williams et al. 2021, 1).

Figure 7.11 presents the nonviolent communication's four-step model:

- **Observations:** How do I observe the situation free from judgment and evaluation?
- **Feelings:** How do I feel about the situation free from interpretation?
- **Needs:** What do I need from and value in this situation free from agendas and strategies?
- **Requests:** What requests do I have without manipulation or demand?

(Williams et al. 2021; Suarez et al. 2014; Rogers 2003)

For people to conduct the preceding inquiries, Rogers (2003) suggests that individuals practice these three ways of being to develop an effective connection with others:

- **Authentic self-expression:** Communicate issues and concerns in a way that inspires compassion within another person.
- **Empathy:** Listen to others' communication with compassion for what they are dealing with and how difficult it might be for them.

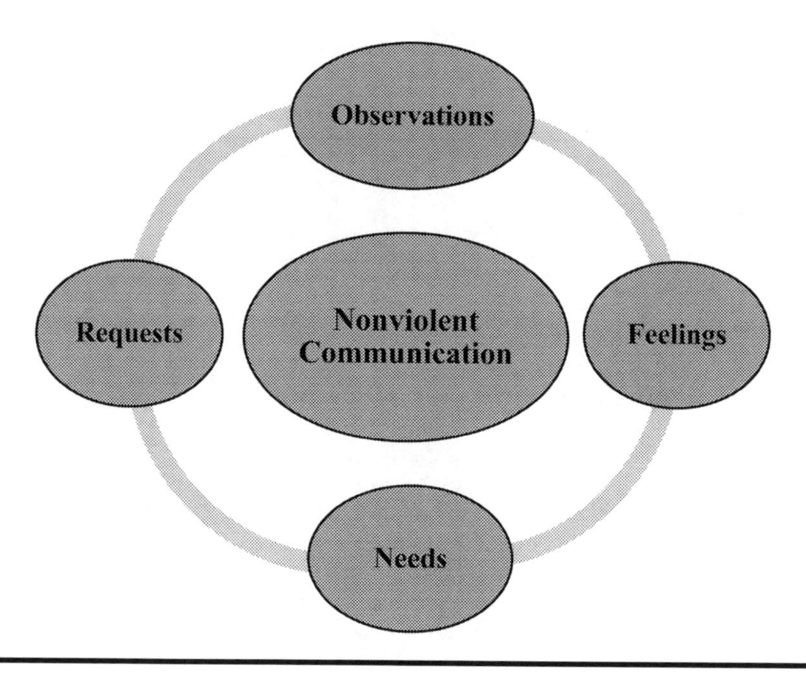


**Figure 7.11 The Four-Steps of Nonviolent Communication Model.**

*Source:* Adapted from Rogers (2003).

- **Self-empathy:** Practice developing compassion for yourself and how hard it is for you to communicate and deal with the issues you are facing.

## Key Takeaways

The following are important distinctions and key takeaways from this chapter:

1. Personal or group transformation is not a one-dimension undertaking.
2. Transformational coaching is not a one-size-fits-all kind of approach and has access to varieties of models and methods to support individuals, teams, and organizations to take on their transformations.
3. Transformational, educational, psychological, and management theories have made significant contributions to the developmental journey of transformational coaching.
4. Managers-as-coaches can educate and develop themselves by learning distinctions, processes, underlying dynamics, and practices of transformational coaching to make a difference with their workforces.

## Discussion Points and Coaching Questions

1. Are you clear about the contributions in the development of transformational coaching? If not, what are the areas in which you need further development?
2. What obstacle can you see in your way of developing competencies on learning and practicing these theories and disciplines to use as a coach for your people?

3. Have you developed an action plan to increase and develop more skills and competencies to deliver these models and methods?
4. Which theory, models, or methods were your favorite and you find easy to relate to and learn?
5. Which theory, models, or methods were your less favorite and you find hard or challenging to relate to and learn?

## References

Alford, B. A. and Beck, A. T. 1998. *The Integrative Power of Cognitive Therapy*. New York, NY: The Guilford Press.

Allyn, Rachel. 2022. "The important difference between emotions and feelings." *Psychology Today Website*. Retrieved from www.psychologytoday.com/us/blog/the-pleasure-is-all-yours/202202/the-important-difference-between-emotions-and-feelings.

Antonakis, John and Robert J. House. 2002. An Analysis of the Full-Range Leadership Theory: The Way Forward. In B. J. Avolio, and F. J. Yammarino (Eds.), *Transformational and Charismatic Leadership: The Road Ahead* (pp. 3–34). Amsterdam: JAI Press.

Antonakis, John and Robert J. House. 2014. "Instrumental Leadership: Measurement and Extension of Transformational—Transactional Leadership Theory." *The Leadership Quarterly* 25(4): 746–771.

Bakhshandeh, Behnam. 2009. *Conspiracy for Greatness; Mastery on Love Within*. San Diego, CA: Primeco Education, Inc.

Bakhshandeh, Behnam. 2015. *Anatomy of Upset: Restoring Harmony*. Carbondale, PA: Primeco Education, Inc.

Bass, B. M. 1985. *Leadership and Performance Beyond Expectations*. New York: The Free Press.

Beisser, Arnold. 1970. "The paradoxical theory of change." *Gestalt Therapy Now* 1, no. 1: 77–80. Retrieved from www.gestalt.org/arnie.htm

Berto, Francesco, and Matteo Plebani. 2015. *Ontology and Metaontology: A Contemporary Guide*. London: Bloomsbury Publishing.

Bridges, William. 2003. *Managing Transitions: Making the Most of Change*. New York, NY: Perseus Books Group.

Bridges, William, and Susan Bridges. 2019. *Transitions* (Special Ed.). New York, NY: Life Long Publishing.

Brock, Vikki. 2008. *Grounded Theory of the Roots and Emergence of Coaching*. Navi Mumbai: International University of Professional Studies.

Burns J. M. 1978. *Leadership*. New York, NY: Harper & Row.

"CFI" Website. 2022. Perma model. Retrieved from https://corporatefinanceinstitute.com/resources/careers/soft-skills/perma-model/

Chuang, Szufang. 2021. "The applications of constructivist learning theory and social learning theory on adult continuous development." *Performance Improvement (International Society for Performance Improvement)* 60(3): 6–14.

Cox, Elaine. 2015. "Coaching and adult learning: theory and practice." *New Directions for Adult and Continuing Education* 148: 27–38.

Cummings, Thomas. G. and Chistopher. G. Worley. 2015. *Organization Development & Change* (10th ed.) Stamford, CT. Cengage Learning.

Day, David, V. and John Antonakis. 2012. *The Nature of Leadership* (2nd ed.). Los Angeles, CA: Sage.

DeRobertis, Eugene M. 2013. "Humanistic psychology: alive in the 21st century?" *The Journal of Humanistic Psychology* 53(4): 419–437. Doi: 10.1177/0022167812473369

Dewey, J. 1934. *Art as Experience*. New York, NY: Minton, Balch & Company.

"Difference Between" website. 2015. "Difference between cognitive therapy and cognitive behavioral therapy." Retrieved from www.differencebetween.com/difference-between-cognitive-therapy-and-vs-cognitive-behavioral-therapy/

Dobbs, Randy and Paul Robert Walker. 2019. *Transformational Leadership: A Blueprint for Real Organizational Change*. Greenville, SC: Expert Leadership Performance.

Dunn, R., Dunn, K., and Price, G. E. 1984. *Learning Style Inventory*. Lawrence, KS: Price Systems.

Early, Barbara P. and Melissa D. Grady. 2016. "Embracing the Contribution of both Behavioral and Cognitive Theories to Cognitive Behavioral Therapy: Maximizing the Richness." *Clinical Social Work Journal* 45(1): 39–48.

Eschenbacher, Saskia. 2019. "Drawing Lines and Crossing Borders: Transformation Theory and Richard Rorty's Philosophy." *Journal of Transformative Education* 17(3): 251–268.

Goleman, Daniel. 1995. *Working with Emotional Intelligence.* New York, NY: Bantam Publishing.

"GoodTherapy" Website. 2017. Psychosynthesis. Retrieved from www.goodtherapy.org/learn-about-therapy/types/psychosynthesis

Green, Suzy and Stephen Palmer. 2019. *Positive Psychology Coaching in Practice.* New York, NY: Taylor & Francis, Routledge.

Heidegger, Martin. 1953. *Being and Time.* Translated by Joan Stambaugh. New York, NY: State University on New York Press.

Hockenbury, Don, H. and Sandra E. Hockenbury. 2007. *Discovering Psychology.* New York, NY: Worth Publishers.

Honey, P., and Mumford, A. 1986. *The Manual of Learning Styles.* Maidenhead: Peter Honey Publications.

Houston, G. 2003. *Brief Gestalt Therapy: Brief Therapy Series.* Newbury Park, CA: Sage Publications.

Howell, W. S. 1982. *The Empathic Communicator.* Belmont, CA: University of Minnesota and Wadsworth Publishing Company.

Howell, W. C. and E. A. Fleishman, eds. 1982. *Human Performance and Productivity. Vol. 2 Processing and Decision Making.* Hillsdale, NJ: Erlbaum.

Johnson, M. 2010. Cognitive science and Dewey's theory of mind, thought, and language, pp. 123–44. In Cochran, M. (ed.), *The Cambridge Companion to Dewey.* Cambridge, MA: Cambridge University Press.

Kalodner, Cynthia, R. 2011. "Cognitive-behavioral theories." In D. Capuzzi and D. R. Gross (Eds.), *Counseling and Psychotherapy* (pp. 193–213). American Counseling Association. Retrieved from https://psycnet.apa.org/record/2010-18469-009.

Klein, Gary, and Holly C. Baxter. 2006. "Cognitive transformation theory: Contrasting cognitive and behavioral learning." In *Interservice/Industry Training Systems and Education Conference, Orlando, Florida.*

Knowles, Malcom, S. 1984. *The Adult Learner: A Neglected Species* (3rd ed.). Houston, TX: Gulf.

Knowles, Malcolm, S., Elwood F. Holton, and Richard A. Swanson. 1988. *The Adult Learner; The Definitive Classic in Adult Education and Human Resource Development.* Houston, TX: Gulf pub.

Kolb, D. A. and Fry, R. 1975. Toward an applied theory of experiential learning. In C. Cooper (Ed.), *Theories of Group Process.* London: John Wiley.

Lasley, Martha, Virginia Kellogg, Richard Michaels and Sharon Brown. 2015. *Coaching for Transformation: Pathway to Ignite Personal & Social Change* (2nd ed.). New York. Discover Press.

Learning Theories for Educators. 2022. University of Wyoming. Retrieved from www.uwyo.edu/aded5050/5050unit9/intro.asp

Lewin, Kurt. 2008. *Organization Change: A Comprehensive Reader.* Vol. 155. Hoboken, NJ: John Wiley & Sons.

Lombard, Catherine Ann. 2017. "Psychosynthesis: A foundational bridge between psychology and spirituality." *Pastoral Psychology* 66, no. 4: 461–485.

Madeson, Melissa. 2022. Positive psychology.com website. Seligman's PERMA+Model explained: A theory of wellbeing. Retrieved from https://positivepsychology.com/perma-model/

Maslow, Abraham H. 1943. "A theory of human motivation." *Psychological Review* 50, no. 4: 370–396.

Maslow, Abraham H. 1970. *Motivation and Personality.* New York, NY: Harper & Row.

Maslow, Abraham, H. 1987. *Motivation and Personality* (3rd ed.). Delhi: Pearson Education.

May, Rollo. 1999. *Freedom and Destiny.* New York, NY: W. W. Norton & Company.

"Mayo Clinic" website. 2022. *Cognitive Behavioral Therapy.* Retrieved from www.mayoclinic.org/tests-procedures/cognitive-behavioral-therapy/about/pac-20384610

"MBA Knowledge Base" website. 2021. Modern management concepts. *Kurt Lewin's Force-Field Theory of Change.* Retrieved from www.mbaknol.com/modern-management-concepts/kurt-lewins-force-field-theory-of-change/

Mezirow, Jack. 1990. *Fostering Critical Reflection in Adulthood: A Guide to Transformative and Emancipatory Learning.* San Francisco, CA: Jossey-Bass.

Petit, Emmanuel and Jérôme Ballet. 2021. "Habit and emotion: John Dewey's contribution to the theory of change." *Cambridge Journal of Economics* 45, no. 4: 655–674.

Prochaska, James O. 2020. Transtheoretical model of behavior change. In *Encyclopedia of Behavioral Medicine* (pp. 2266–2270). New York, NY: Springer International Publishing.

Prochaska, James O., DiClemente, C. C., and Norcross, J. 1992. "In search of how people change: applications to addictive behaviors." *American Psychology* 47: 1102–1114.

Prochaska, James O., and Marcus H. Bess. 1994. The transtheoretical model: Applications to exercise. In R. K. Dishman (Ed.), *Advances in Exercise Adherence* (pp. 161–180). Champaign, IL. Human Kinetics Publishers.

Prochaska, James, O., and John C., Norcross. 2003. *Systems of Psychotherapy: A Transtheoretical Analysis* (5th ed.). Pacific Grove, CA: Brooks/Cole.

Rachal, John, R. 2002. Andragogy's detectives: A critique of the present and a proposal for the future. *Adult Education Quarterly* 52(3): 210–227.

"Regis College". 2021. What is Applied Behavior Science and Why is it Important? Retrieved from https://online.regiscollege.edu/blog/what-is-applied-behavioral-science

Rogers, Carl R. 1995. *On Becoming a Person: A Therapist's View of Psychotherapy.* Boston, MA: Houghton Mifflin.

Rogers, E. 2003. *Diffusion of Innovations* (5th ed.). New York, NY: Free Press.

Rorty, Richard and Richard Rorty. 1989. *Contingency, Irony, and Solidarity.* Cambridge: Cambridge University Press.

Rosenberg, Marshall B. and Riane Eisler. 2003. *Life-Enriching Education: Nonviolent Communication Helps Schools Improve Performance, Reduce Conflict, and Enhance Relationships.* PuddleDancer Press, Encinitas, CA.

Rothwell, William J. 2020. *Adult Learning Basics* (2nd ed.). Alexandria, VA: Association for Talent Development (ATD).

Rothwell, William J., Sohel M. Imroz and Behnam Bakhshandeh. 2021. *Organization Development Interventions.* New York, NY: Routledge.

Rothwell, William, J., and Henry J. Sredl. 2014. *Workplace Learning and Performance: Present and Future Roles and Competencies* (3rd ed., Vol. I). Amherst, MA: HR Press.

Salkovskis, Paul M. and Josie Fa Millar. 2016. "Still Cognitive after all these Years? Perspectives for a Cognitive Behavioural Theory of Obsessions and Where we are 30-Years Later." *Australian Psychologist* 51, no. 1: 3–13.

Salovey, Peter, Marc A. Brackett, and John D. Mayer 2004. *Emotional Intelligence: Key Readings on the Mayer and Salovey Model.* Port Chester, NY: Dude Publishing.

Schein, Edgar, H. 1988. *Process Consultation (Volume I): Its Role in Organization Development* (2nd ed.). Reading, MA: Addison-Wesley Publishing Company.

Schein, Edgar H. 1999. *Process Consultation Revised: Building the Helping Relationship.* Reading, MA: Addison-Wesley Publishing Company.

Seligman, Martin E.P. 2002. *Authentic Happiness: Using the New Positive Psychology to Realize Your Potential for Lasting Fulfillment.* New York, NY: Free Press.

Siegel Daniel J. 1999. *The Developing Mind: Toward a Neurobiology of Interpersonal Experience.* New York, NY: Guilford Press.

Sieler, Alan. 2005. *Coaching to the Human Soul Ontological Coaching and Deep Change, Volume I.* Melbourne: Newfield Network Inc.

Sieler, Alan. 2007. *Coaching to the Human Soul: Ontological Coaching and Deep Change: Volume II: Emotional Learning and Ontological Coaching.* Melbourne: Newfield Network Inc.

Suarez, Alejandra, Dug Y. Lee, Christopher Rowe, Alex Anthony Gomez, Elise Murowchick, and Patricia L. Linn. 2014. "Freedom project: Nonviolent communication and mindfulness training in prison." *Sage Open* 4, no. 1. doi:10.1177/2158244013516154.

Wake Forest University website. 2022. "The Differences Between Feelings and Emotions." https://counseling.online.wfu.edu/blog/difference-feelings-emotions/

Waterman, Alan S. 2013. "The humanistic psychology—positive psychology divide: contrasts in philosophical foundations." *American Psychologist* 68 (3): 124–133. doi:10.1037/a0032168.

WGU Website. 2020. Experiential learning theory. www.wgu.edu/blog/experiential-learning-theory2006.html#close

Williams, Brooke A., Alexander Simmons, Michelle Ward, Jutta Beher, Angela J. Dean, Tida Nou, Tania M. Kenyon et al. 2021. "The potential for applying "Nonviolent Communication" in conservation science." *Conservation Science and Practice* 3, no. 2: e540. Doi: 10.1111/csp2.540

Wiltshire, Travis J., Kelly J. Neville, Martin R. Lauth, Clyde Rinkinen, and Luis F. Ramirez. 2014. "Applications of cognitive transformation theory: examining the role of sensemaking in the instruction of air traffic control students." *Journal of Cognitive Engineering and Decision Making* 8, no. 3: 219–247.

Yalom, I. D. 1980. *Existential Psychotherapy.* New York: Basic Books.

Zeine, Foojan. 2014. "Awareness integration: a new therapeutic model." *International Journal of Emergency Mental Health and Human Resilience* 16: 60–65

Zeine, Foojan. 2021. *Awareness Integration Therapy. Clear the Past, Create a New Future, and Live a Fulfilled Life Now.* Newcastle: Cambridge Scholars Publishing.

Zeine, Foojan, Nicole Jafari and Fatemeh Haghighatjoo. 2017. Awareness integration: an alternative therapeutic methodology to reducing depression, anxiety, while improving low self-esteem and self-efficacy in separated or divorced individuals. *Mental Health in Family Medicine* 13: 451–458

# Chapter 8

# Transformational Coaching Integration Model

Behnam Bakhshandeh

## Overview

Someone can claim that transformational coaching is a model by itself. However, because it pulls on many disciplines and models (as we mentioned in Chapters 1 and 7) and is client-focused coaching, it does not restrict itself to a certain established model, as long as the focus is on the outcome, the transformation of individuals, teams, or organizations with sustainable outcomes. Because of that, different coachees would have different experiences of how transformational coaching works and how it has affected their lives.

As any professional coach will agree, the majority of coaching conversations are conceptual and abstract. Transformational coaches will support individuals with the freedom to express their thoughts, highlight their mindsets, talk about the emotions raised in the background of their mindsets, their values and principles, and what they envision for their lives, personally and professionally. The same concept is true for working with teams, departments, and organizations.

However, a coaching model provides the structure for the coaches and coachees to navigate through conceptual conversation, discuss theories, apply disciplines, and come up with actual and tangible action plans and structures that support such plans for coachees to produce results for which they are aiming.

This chapter will cover these concepts and topics:

- What is a coaching model?
- Transformational Coaching Integration Model
  - Positive psychology coaching
  - Ontological inquiries and approaches to coaching
  - Emotional intelligence coaching
  - Appreciative inquiry and coaching
  - Strength-based coaching

DOI: 10.4324/9781003304074-11

## What Is a Coaching Model?

A coaching model supports and serves both coaches and coachees as a conceptual structure and road map for how they will get to where they want to go by distinguishing where they are and how they will get to the desired destination. For this journey to succeed and be productive, both coaches and coachees will bring something to the table (see Figure 8.1). Transformational coaches will provide their knowledge, skills, and competencies on coaching concepts, other disciplines, and theories while bringing their professionalism and experiences in designing structures and supporting coachees in planning their action plans. The coachees will bring their hopes, desires to change, interest to learn, commitment to workability and being coachable, their values and principles, and their trust for the coach and the coaching process (see Figure 8.1).

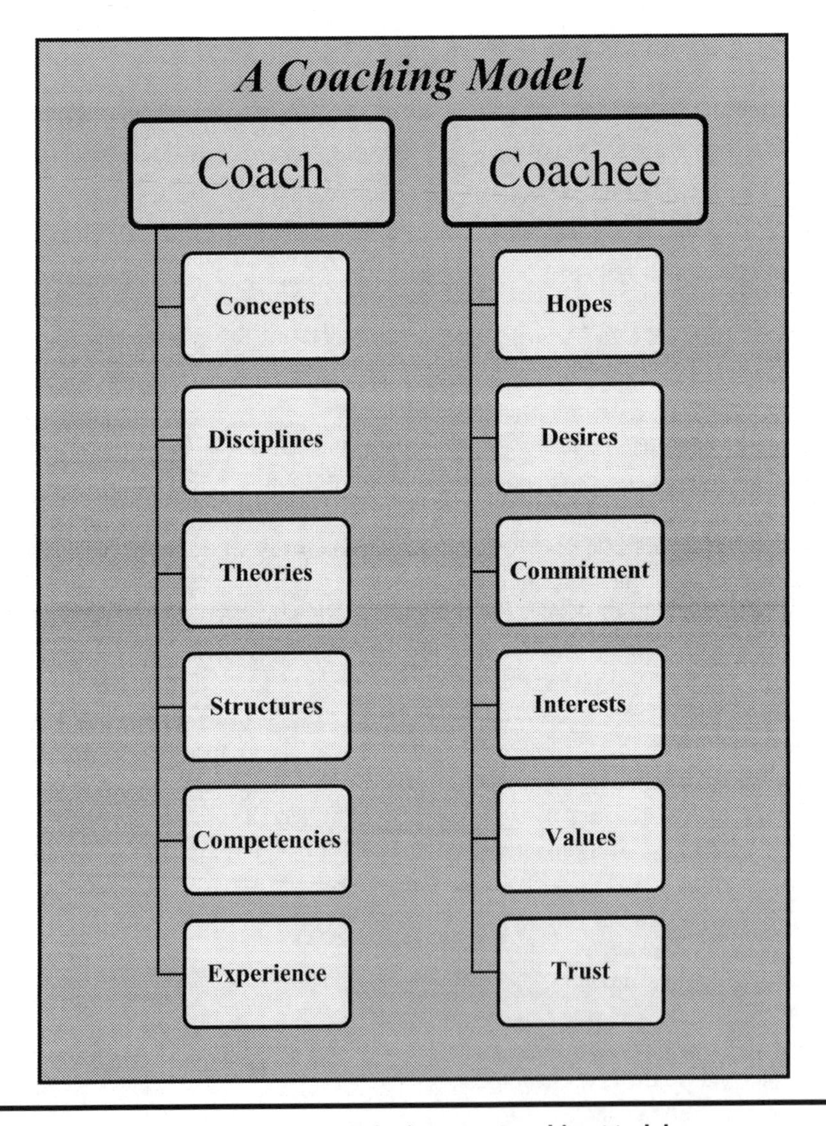


**Figure 8.1 What Coach and Coachee Are Bringing to a Coaching Model.**

*Source:* Author's Original Creation. Copyright 2022 by Behnam Bakhshandeh.

The transformational coaches' understanding of their coachees culture and background and listening to their life stories or personal and professional experiences (individually, as a team, or in departments) aids the coaching model to be stronger and more intimate and builds a strong and trusting bond between the coaches and coachees. A coaching model streamlines and explains the intricacies and structure of coaching, elements, and its progress.

### *Advantages of Following a Model in the Coaching Process*

Following a coaching model and applying elements of a coaching model improve participants in imagining their development and going through the coaching phases of the coaching process; however, mainly, the coaching model guides the coach to direct the coachees and walk them through stages of a coaching model to show them their progress, using conversations, figures, tables, and graphic or verbal displays. Overall, some benefits and advantages of following a coaching model for implementing transformational coaching are:

- Provides guidelines for coaching assessments and inquiries
- Acts as a proven tool for learning and practicing
- Gives coachees certainty about what they will learn from the process
- Organizes concepts, elements, and practices of a coaching approach
- Transfers theoretical concepts to a conceptual framework
- Uses distinct terminologies as the language of coaching to explain concepts
- Organizes and clarifies the coaching approach and steps for coaches
- Underlines the important fundamentals of coaching and its reasoning
- Emphasizes and focuses on what is important to the coachees
- Produces curious conversations and questions that would uncover challenges

## Transformational Coaching Integration Model

Many coaches are selecting and following a certain coaching model, receiving their training and getting certification from institutes or organizations training them to deliver their model and concepts of coaching.

The nature of a coaching model is to be a receptacle for a coaching process and procedures on a background of an idea or concept; however, it doesn't mean that professional and experienced coaches have strictly followed only one coaching discipline as a single designed model. But a combination of different and powerful coaching disciplines and models can support the coaches' and coachees' imagination and creativity and assist them in progressively going through the process.

This section briefly explains and defines a combination of powerful aspects of the Transformational Coaching Integration Model for personal and professional breakthroughs (please see Figure 8.2).

Using transformational coaching technology for organization development (OD) interventions or effective management (individuals, teams, departments, and organizations) is not a new approach and has been part of professional coaching for decades. Many OD practitioners and business consultants or trained managers use transformational coaching during their individual or team interventions, applying distinctions of philosophy, ontology, and psychology, such as *positive psychology* and *humanistic psychology*, in addition to elements of *appreciative inquiry*, *emotional intelligence*, *strength-based approach*, and *self-awareness* to help their coachees to better understand

and access their self-awareness, self-realization, and clarity between who they are *being* and how that has an impact on what they are *doing*, personally and professionally.

In this section, this chapter will explain and describe elements of coaching and inquiries that are the fabric of the Transformational Coaching Integration Model (see Figure 8.2) and will attempt to explain the use and effect of such disciplines, methods, and approaches, and when used to develop individuals, teams, and organizations.

## Presence of Transformation

Transformation is the display of a shift in an individual from one state of *being* to another (Seale 2011) that would influence their thought process, attitude, and behavior, which eventually would have the power to affect others around the transformed individuals such as a team or group (Bakhshandeh 2009). Related to the ontological state of *being* in an individual, Seale (2011) stated:

> In an individual, transformation means the whole of his or her being. Consciousness shifts to vibrate at a new frequency. In the same way, organizational or societal transformation means that the whole of the organization or society—its members, cultures, beliefs, and practices—is now sourced from a different vibrational frequency.
>
> (1)

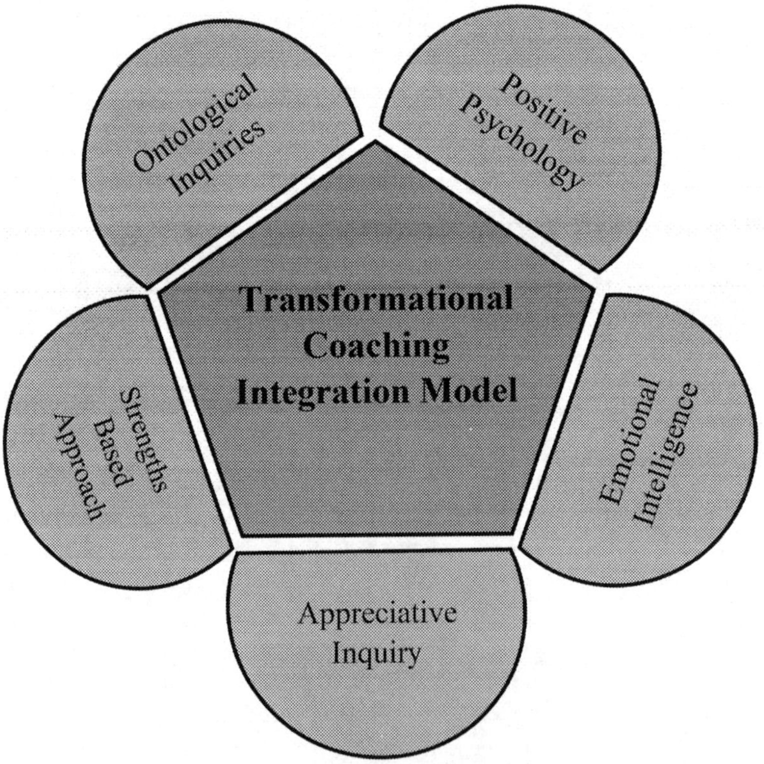

**Figure 8.2 Transformational Coaching Integration Model.**

*Source:* Author's Original Creation. Copyright 2022 by Behnam Bakhshandeh.

Seale (2011) attempted to describe and explain the definitions of *presence* and its relationship to "transformational presence" as follows:

## *Presence*

Presence is how an individual, a group, or an organization "shows up" and exists for others around their life, their work, and ultimately in the world. That would be their dynamics, their energy, and space, which are created and displayed by their *being* (2011). That is the energy and dynamics that such individuals bring to individual or group challenges and issues and opportunities to accomplish goals and fulfill dreams (2009).

## *Transformational Presence*

Transformational presence is a state of *being* in which individuals' relationships, directions, work, and engagements in their lives are generated from a place of significant and profound orientation and link to their souls, their committed life purpose, and the greater consciousness (2011). Transformational presence creates a partnership between individuals and groups for accomplishing visions and missions and causes success in all levels of OD interventions (2009). "This presence opens the door to the greater potential waiting to emerge at any moment, situation, or circumstance and becomes a steward for that potential to manifest" (2011, 2).

## *Use of Transformational Presence*

It is worth mentioning that transformational presence is not a method, success formula, or model to use at needed times, but a lifestyle, a way of living, a powerful and effective way of leading and serving oneself and others in both personal and professional settings. Transformational presence is an attitude and approach that delivers a compelling groundwork for conscious living and conscious leadership and governance (Seale 2017). A strong and powerful conscious lifestyle, the direction of transformation consciousness and awareness lifestyle, along with the progress of leadership, is becoming an emerging way in various elements of the world to form a larger conscious awareness, a general understanding of others, a much more effective perceptions of others, and transformational actions that make a difference in humanity (2017). Seale (2017) added, "It's built on the conviction that, in any initiative, all stakeholders can be served, all people and the environment can be honored and respected, and economic models can serve something more than just individual or organizational interests" (5).

Inside this transformational movement, there is also prevalent agreement that is moving the world forward in a successful, impactful, effective, and transformative way, which requires new competencies and skills and workable tools and much larger capacities for personal and group awareness and perceptions (2017, 2011). This need for new skills and capacities necessitates us to go beyond our familiar actions by including more analytical thinking and approaches that expand from those we are already familiar with. This is what the transformational coaching essence is about (2017, 2011; 2009). The combination of ontological inquiries, positive psychology, self-awareness, emotional intelligence, and appreciative inquiry can create an environment for the implication of transformational coaching that would create the space of conscious *being* that would have a transformational impact on conscious *doing*.

# Ontological Inquiries and Approach to Coaching

The *Merriam-Webster* dictionary defines ontology as "a branch of metaphysics concerned with the nature and relations of being. Ontology deals with abstract entities. A particular theory about the nature of being or the kinds of things that have existence" (Merriam-Webster 2022).

The *Oxford University Dictionary* defines ontology as "a branch of philosophy that deals with the nature of existence" and "that shows the relationships between all the concepts and categories in a subject area" (Oxford University Dictionary 2022a).

Wikipedia (2022) explains ontology as "the philosophical study of the nature of *being, becoming, existence*, or *reality*, as well as the basic categories of being and their relations." Customarily ontology is recognized as part of philosophy and identified as metaphysics, dealing with queries pertaining to "what entities exist or can be said to exist, and how such entities can be grouped, related within a hierarchy, and subdivided according to similarities and differences" (Wikipedia 2022).

Berto and Plebani (2015) tried to explain what ontology attempts to do:

> Biology studies living things. Psychology studies mental functions. Astronomy deals with celestial phenomena and mathematics deals with numbers. They all study something, of course, but none of them studies everything. They do not address the whole of reality or all that there is. Ontology does.
>
> (1)

In the analytic philosophy discipline, *Contemporary Ontology* deals primarily with queries about what things exist and what those things look, feel, and are experienced like (Effingham 2013). Certain philosophers, particularly the Platonic school philosophers, argue the point that all nouns, even conceptual nouns, describe the existents of individuals. Some philosophers argue the point that nouns do not constantly describe individuals or entities. For example, using "mind," as an alternative for referring to an individual describes an assortment of "mental occasions" that an individual was or is experiencing (2013).

The categorization of ontology can be linked back to Aristotle, who in Book Four of his *Metaphysics*, presented the concept of a science of "being qua *being*" or of "being as such" (Berto and Plebani 2015). According to Berto and Plebani (2015), after the "science of being" was rejected and ridiculed by considerably early analytical and neo-positivistic philosophers, the concept of *being* and ontology made a remarkable rebirth in the second half of the twentieth century.

This chapter provides examples and applications of ontology and state of being in further sections.

## *Ontological Approaches*

Modern ontology has found its place in psychology and social science, as many psychologists and social scientists have embraced the following main ontological approaches in their practices:

- **Realism:** The notion that facts exist independent of individuals and are waiting to be uncovered.
- **Empiricism:** The notion is that we are capable of observing and monitoring the world around us and assessing and comparing our interpretations of facts.
- **Positivism:** The notion we must concentrate on the evaluation and observations, considerate on the assertions about the facts rather than on the facts themselves.

## *Ontological Coaching*

Ontological coaching is an inquiry into human self-awareness, a reflection on humans' relationships to their *being*, and their relationship to reality. This coaching approach includes aspects of psychology, sociology, philosophy, linguistics, personal integrity, responsibility, and accountability. Ontological coaching concentrates on personal transformation through inquiry, reflections, self-observation, self-realization about one's state of *being*, and all related behaviors and attitudes caused by such a state. This model of coaching is aimed at personal and professional transformation developed by empowering participants to action through effective communication, emotional intelligence, creativity, leadership skills, and learning processes (D'Addario 2016; Effingham 2013; Bakhshandeh 2009; Sieler 2005). It is noteworthy to mention that Aristotle, Plato, Martin Heidegger, Friedrich Hegel, and Jean-Paul Sartre are some of the renowned ancient and modern ontologists (Berto and Plebani 2015; Wikipedia 2022). Alan Seale initiated further development in the role of the ontological approach to transformational coaching and extended the concept to be the ontology of human discussions and observation (Seale 2011; Sieler 2005).

## *The Pattern of Discussions*

The ontology of the human discussions and observation is constructed around individuals' interpretations, perceived reality, and understanding of the fundamental discussions and conversational patterns utilized with different successful undertakings by the majority of people and who they are during such discussions. This pattern of discussions is distinguished by three kinds of conversations (Seale 2017; Sieler 2007) (see Figure 8.3).

- **Explanatory Discussions**: This discussion is about distinguishing the problem(s). It is about what happened and how we got here. It is a discussion about patterns that happened in the past. Many transformational coaches and even management consultants use this approach, sometimes not knowing it is related to ontological approaches and inquiries. As you see from the meaning of its title it is about explaining what happened, how it happened, and how it became a problem. This is the time to come up with a problem statement.
- **Exploratory Discussions**: This discussion explores and identifies where we are and where we are going. What are we going to do about this problem? Or what should we do about it? This is about discussions that result in declaring clarity regarding the present situation(s) in the present time. This is the time to come up with an activity statement.
- **Activity Discussions**: This discussion is about coming up with ideas about how we will get there. We need to recognize where we need to go and then to generate activities to get there. This is living the future in the present time. This is about envisioning how things would turn out, what we have done, and what we have accomplished. This is the nature of the resolution statement.

## *Being and Doing*

The concept of individuals, teams, or organizations failing in their attempts at a change effort is not a new phenomenon. We have read about it, or we have seen it happen before. Research has shown that 75 percent of all change efforts in organizations fall under the desired expectations or plan (Rothwell 2015); the failure rate is high. Research also indicates that two-thirds of employees

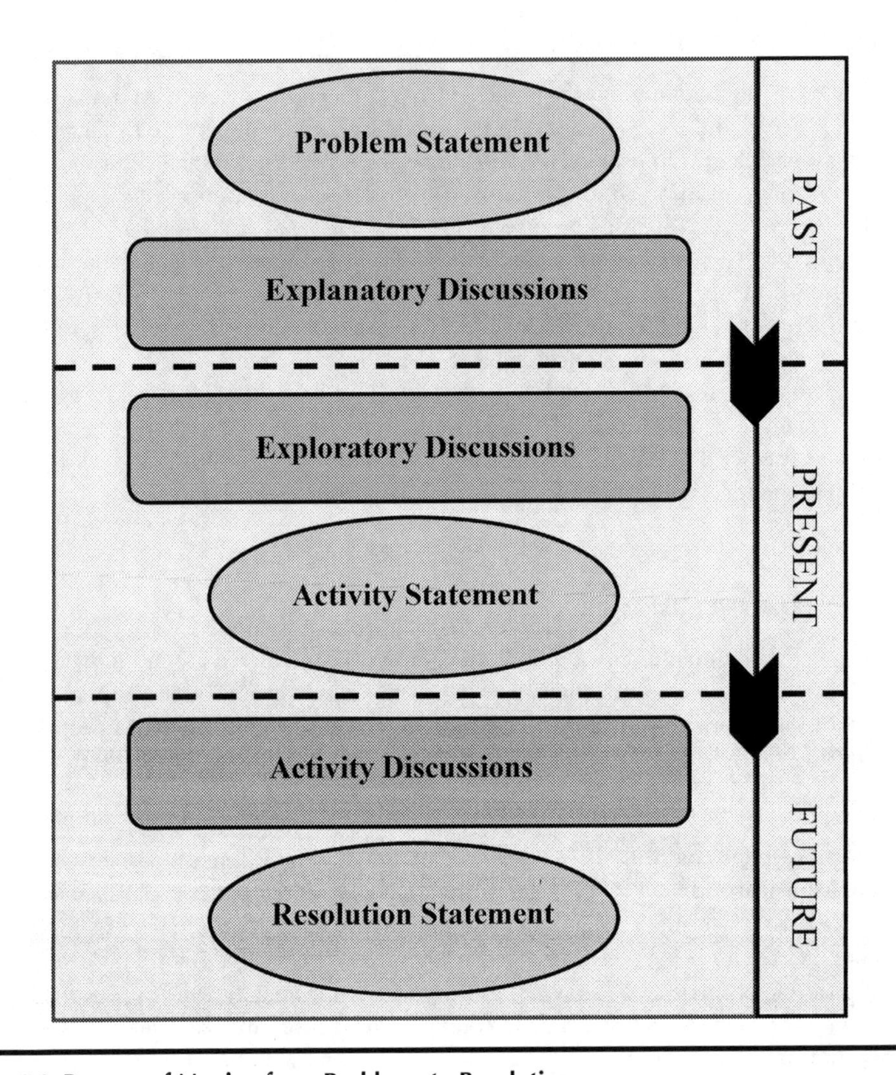


**Figure 8.3 Process of Moving from Problems to Resolutions.**

*Source:* Adapted from Seale 2017; Sieler 2007.

in organizations undergoing change activities would choose not to become involved at all (Levi 2016; Rothwell et al. 2016; Rothwell and Sredl 2014).

## Why Is This the Case?

Most people who go through change efforts come out of it unchanged or without having a deep impact because the trainers and consultants emphasize mostly the *doing* part of the change when what makes the biggest difference is the *being* part of a person. Most executives and managers in organizations plan their individual, team, and organizational successes on the doing and not on both being and doing. What gives an individual the ***doing*** is who he or she is ***being*** at that given moment and the way they are viewing themselves, others, and the world around them (Bakhshandeh 2009). There are two sides to any change, whether it is an individual change, a team-building change, or an organizational change. "The *Doing* side is about processes, measurement, tools, structures, and procedures. This side is about management. The *Being* side is about participation, commitment, attitude, creativity, overcoming resistance to change, and self-leadership. This side is about leadership" (Primeco Education 2022, n.p.). The ontological approach part of the Transformational Coaching Integration Model assists individuals and teams to dig into who they are being while they are doing what they are doing every day, regardless of being at home or at work.

## Human Being or Human Doing?

As human *beings*, most of the time spent is human *doing*. Regardless of age, gender, nationality, race, culture, or upbringing, people are aware that when others have some upsetting situation or when they are happy, they can identify their state of being even if they are not speaking or explaining their situation. They can recognize resentment, regret, unhappiness, and other ways of being in others. But they can also identify someone as *being* interested, engaged, committed, communicative, result-oriented, and being a leader. In the book *Being and Nothingness*, Jean-Paul Sartre, the French philosopher and ontologist, explained this phenomenon as "no being which is not the being of a certain mode of being, none which cannot be apprehended through the mode of being which manifests being and veils it at the same time" (Sartre 1943, 24–25). They need not do anything; even without their doing anything special, they can recognize those characteristics in them (Bakhshandeh 2009).

> State of being is what makes us all do what we do, or even feel what we feel. It makes us interested in what we do, and it allows us to relate to others or take ourselves away from them! It makes us succeed or fail, and it makes us love or hate ourselves and others!
>
> (22)

This approach to an organization's development, team-building efforts, or individual interventions with executives or managers reminds the management team that doing good management cannot generate sustainability and growth in the organization or in the team they are trying to restore and rebuild. Additionally, they need to adjust the *being* of an individual to ensure the sustainability and longevity of individuals because what they are *being* at any given moment (resentful, regretful, or disappointed) directly influences what they are *doing* (communication or productivity) (Bakhshandeh 2009). In one of his books, *Being and Time*, Martin Heidegger (1953), the German philosopher and ontologist, expressed his views on the transparency of being as "the self-evident concept. Being is used in all-knowing and predicting, in every relation to being, and in every relation to oneself, and the expression is understandable without further ado" (3).

One of the most important and influential elements of organization development is the role-modeling of organization leaders by displaying positive behavior aligned with desirable behavior for implementing individuals, teams, or organization development (Rothwell et al. 2016). This personal development and transformational effort by organizations is possible through transformational and behavioral coaching for individuals with a direct and impactful influence on a team or an organization's well-being. Behavioral coaching is not a new phenomenon in the application of OD, particularly in individual intervention. As part of behavioral coaching, professional and trained transformational coaches use the model of person-centered psychology, which is based on what is known as "holding up a mirror" (Rothwell 2015) for the individuals to get to know themselves on a much deeper level and get present to the history of their behavior and attitude development through the years. This is an effective approach to individuals' self-awareness and self-realization because by conducting an inquiry with the coaches' support, they will see through themselves. This way, they always remember their own process of self-realization because they find it and not something imposed on them by someone else.

You can see the connection and impact of *being* on *doing* through the *mindset* as it is displayed in Figure 8.4.

## *Impact of Who We Are* Being *on What We Are* Doing *and Quality of Life*

Transformational coaching uses an ontological approach and coaching to develop individuals to see the impact of who they are being on what they are doing and how learning effectiveness would open space for effectiveness and increase the quality of their lives (see Figure 8.5).

In the fast-paced life and work environment that constantly demands change, going on with a safe state of operation and leadership is not sufficient. That is a reason for organizations attempting to develop leadership qualities in their personnel so they can create strategies for essential elements of leadership and management, such as behavior, performance, productivity, and communication. To cause this environment, there is a need for a much richer learning approach and a much deeper understanding of one's behavior and what is causing their actions. Organizations need to provide transformational coaching that addresses deep elements of individuals *being* in a way that sheds light on the source of their behavior and assists them in realizing why they are behaving the way they do and be.

From the standpoint of the ontological approach to coaching, individuals' *state of being* is a persistent dynamic interaction between their emotions, their language, and their body that results in their behavior (as it was discussed in Chapter 7 and Figure 7.2), and individuals' behaviors would determine the quality of their communication and performance in a personal and professional environment (Sieler 2020). As you can see in Figure 8.5, the state of being holds the whole thing together and plays on the background of developing qualities in life. Without our

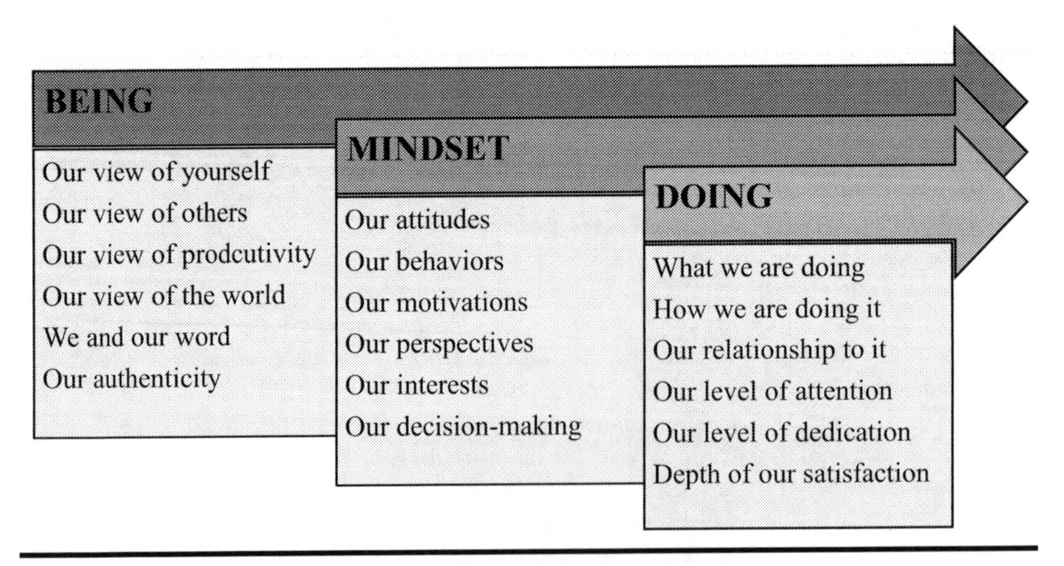


**Figure 8.4 Connection and Impact of Being on Doing Through the Mindset.**

*Source:* Author's Original Creation. Copyright 2022 by Behnam Bakhshandeh.

understanding of who we are *being* at the moment that we are doing something, we will be in the dark about why we have produced certain results in life. We can be resentful, regretful, reserved, closed, uncooperative, negative, scared, jealous, and keep ourselves away from others. But we can be happy, grateful, appreciative, cooperative, open, positive, and be in relationship with others. We have a choice. With ontological coaching, we can recognize our state of *being* that builds up the way we think, decide, and act (Bakhshandeh 2009).

### Role of Language

Human language is the ultimate human-invented technology. Without language, we could get nothing done and could not build up the world of technology and advancements the way humanity has done it until now. According to Sieler (2005), language is much more than explaining day-to-day life events; with our language we are inventing our own realities, and we would behave and act based on that perceived reality (Bakhshandeh 2009). The transformational coaches will work with individuals, using relevant tools and techniques that empower individuals to see the crucial role of language in their lives.

### Role of Feelings and Emotions

The transformational coach will assist individuals in reflecting on their feelings and emotions and their role in their mindset, behavior, and performance. Our feelings and emotions generate our moods, which will drive out our negative or positive behaviors and activities, including but not limited to communications and performances (Sieler 2020; Sieler 2005).

### Role of Body and Physicality

Our way of being is ingrained with many issues with a negative impact on our body and physicality. I am sure we all have heard the phrase "Old habits die hard." Ontological coaching invites individuals not to fight these engraved habits but to realize how slight and delicate changes in their body can have great positive effects on their moods and generate a better positive view of themselves, which would naturally affect their tendency to be more effective and productive (Sieler 2020; Sieler 2005).

## *Quality of Life, Experience, and Presence*

People's understanding of their way of being and their awareness of how their way of being impacts their language, emotions, and body will allow them to choose how they want to be in any moment of their lives. These choices directly affect the quality of discussion with others and the quality of relationships they have engaged in already or are building newly. These two major qualities directly affect people's effectiveness in generating a positive mindset and displaying positive behaviors. Quality of discussions and the quality of relationships have a direct influence on people's ability to relate and connect with others and effectively communicate with them (see Figure 8.5).

Recently, during the last several decades, researchers have shown an increase in an understanding of the vital role of communication and behavior in people's learning process, which is not separated from organizational learning and understanding of systems, structures, and processes. As you can see in Figure 8.5, under the umbrella of *state of being*, the quality of discussions and conversations increases the quality of relationships, which are the bloodlines of organizational effectiveness. This will naturally result in the quality of outcomes, including the organization's efficiency in activities and productivity, that will positively affect increasing performance and produce quality products and services.

However, we shall notice this sensitive fact, that as important and essential as the *state of being* is, without combining it with *state of doing*, nothing will happen in the real world and real results, personally or professionally. The state of being in the background holds the space and is the source of the entire operation, while what we are actually doing to produce the outcomes is happening in the state of doing (see Figure 8.5). The state of doing is as vital for producing results as the state of being. If we are planning for a successful organizational transformation, we shall pay attention to both sides.

> There are two sides to organizational change: I. The "Doing." This side is about processes, measurements, tools, structures, and procedures. This side is about Management. II. The "Being." This side is about participation, commitment, attitude, creativity, overcoming resistance to change, and self-leadership. This side is about Leadership. Good management (the Doing) is not enough to create lasting growth. The change also requires leadership. Our

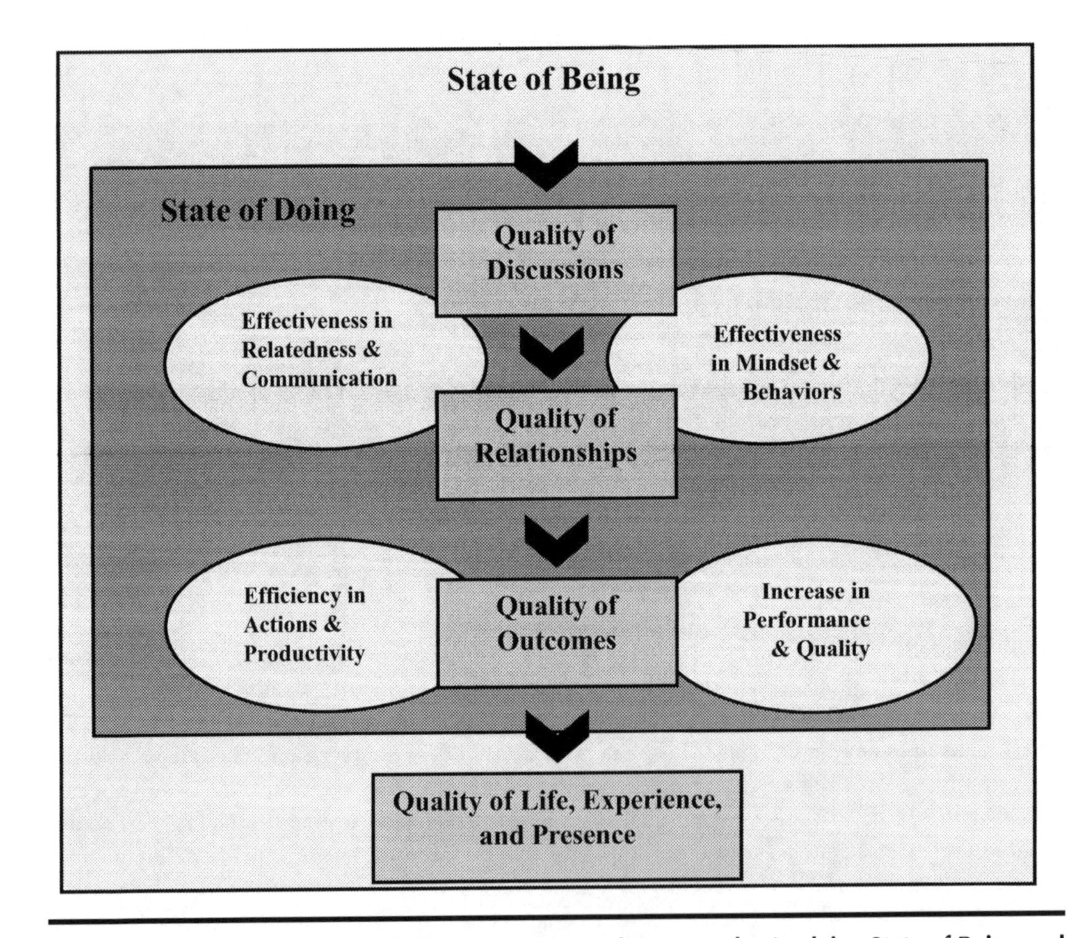


**Figure 8.5 Increasing Quality of Life, Experience, and Presence by Applying State of Being and Managing the State of Doing.**

*Source:* Author's Original Creation. Copyright 2022 by Behnam Bakhshandeh.

> powerful program is necessary to develop the Being side of businesses and organizations committed to sustainable change. By applying simple tools and concepts, desired changes in organizational performance occur through individual transformation.
>
> (Primeco Education 2022, n.p.)

### *Benefits of Ontological Approach to Coaching*

Some benefits of ontological coaching reported by individuals who went through transformational coaching are:

1. Increased individual velocity
2. Increased productivity and overall success
3. Recaptured interests and passions
4. Accomplished more in less time
5. Stretched imagination and self-expression
6. Invented a personal life vision and put it into practice
7. Communicated directly, clearly, and effectively
8. Increased overall efficiency and effectiveness
9. Developed relatedness and strong rapport with others
10. Fell in love with life again and lived it fully!

(Primeco Education 2022)

### *Ontological Approach to Transformational Coaching Questions*

Table 8.1 presents examples of questions that transformational coaches can ask to open inquiries for developing leadership qualities among participants.

## Positive Psychology Coaching

Throughout the history of humans, the subject of happiness and interest in being happy has been on top of people's interests. From ancient Greek philosophers to modem times, thinkers and psychologists have deliberated on matters associated with happiness and what it takes to be happy.

> St. Thomas Aquinas, John Stuart Mill, Gustave Flaubert, Charles, and Abraham Maslow are just a handful of the notable thinkers who turned their attention to the emotional Holy Grail—happiness. In modem times, happiness has, if anything, gained momentum in the popular imagination.
>
> (Biswas-Diener and Dean 2007, 28)

### *What Is Positive Psychology?*

Positive psychology is a branch of the science of psychology centered on individuals', teams', and groups' strengths, functionality, and improving well-being. The concept of positive psychology also applies to organizations and communities. The name *positive psychology* was originally

**Table 8.1 Examples of Ontological Approaches to Transformational Coaching Questions. Author's Original Creation.**

| *Examples of Ontological Approach to Transformational Coaching Questions* | | | |
|---|---|---|---|
| *Instructions*: Think of a situation that did not go well such as an upsetting one, an uncomfortable scenario, or a relationship you care for but is not going as well as you desire, at home or at the workplace. It could be an unworkable situation between you and your colleagues or manager. Relate these questions to the selected situation. | | | |
| *State of* | *Areas of Concern* | # | *Questions* |
| **BEING** | **Language: Speaking & Listening** | 1 | How do you see and relate to the speaker? |
| | | 2 | What is your interpretation of what they are saying? |
| | | 3 | What is your inner chatter saying about the speaker? |
| | | 4 | What is your interpretation of what you are hearing? |
| | | 5 | What are you observing about this interaction? |
| | **Emotions & Moods** | 1 | How do you feel about this situation? |
| | | 2 | What are the emotions while you are in the situation? |
| | | 3 | What are your moods when you are in a similar situation? |
| | | 4 | How do you describe your state of being in this situation? |
| | | 5 | Are you aware of who you have been being in this situation? |
| | **Body & Physiology** | 1 | What are your body sensations when being that way? |
| | | 2 | What is the link between your way of being and what you feel in your body? |
| | | 3 | What is your interpretation of your body sensation? |
| | | 4 | How are these sensations affecting your behaviors? |
| | | 5 | What happens to your body sensations when you alter your way of being? |
| **DOING** | **Quality of Discussions** | 1 | What way of being would help you to establish productive discussions? |
| | | 2 | What could you do differently to have a more quality discussion? |
| | | 3 | What elements of effective discussion should you work on? |
| | | 4 | What are your ineffective attitudes and behaviors that need to be altered? |
| | | 5 | What are you committed to producing in this situation? |
| | **Quality of Relationships** | 1 | What way of being would help you to establish effective relationships? |
| | | 2 | What could you do differently to have a more quality relationship? |
| | | 3 | What elements of being related should you work on? |
| | | 4 | What are your ineffective attitudes and behaviors that need to be altered? |
| | | 5 | What are your commitments to this relationship? |

created by Abraham Maslow, the therapeutic viewpoint of Carl Rogers, and other psychologists who encouraged the use of strengths in individuals (Foster and Auerbach 2015). Years later, Martin Seligman, a psychologist, established positive psychology as a psychological methodology based on scientific study and systematic concepts. This groundbreaking approach to the concept of happiness investigates why individuals want to be happy, why they are happy and what it would take to keep them happy and maintain such happiness in the main aspect of their lives and professions (Seligman 2002). The positive psychology approach comprises an accelerating combination of scientific and methodological research and positive psychology coaching approaches and techniques proven to improve individuals' chances to reach their goals in life (Green 2014).

## *Background of Positive Psychology*

When the concept of positive psychology was created as a new academic field of study, it was facing asceticism and was believed to be a passing trend among new waves in the field of psychology. However, Martin Seligman collaborated with many professionals and authorities in other fields, such as Mihaly Csikszentmihalyi, author of *Flow* (1990), one of the inflectional studies of its time, and Edward Diener, a prominent psychologist with many years of experience in research and study in happiness, and added solid credibility to the new concept of positive psychology (Rao 2013). By 1998, the mentioned researchers and scientists established the foundation for this new science in psychology, which was recognized by the academic and scientific communities. "Positive psychology is, indeed, a science, and it is profoundly significant in the coaching profession" (2013, 64).

When American psychologists published Seligman and Csikszentmihalyi (2010) and presented their innovative and pioneering argument on positive psychology, some pointed out that the science of psychology shouldn't only look for what is **not** working with people and their behaviors, but the field should also focus on generating a culture of positive well-being with the background of hope, personal development, growth, and prosperous mindsets (Green and Palmer 2019).

## *The Implication of "Positive" in Positive Psychology*

Under normal circumstances, people have reported the level of their positive feelings and emotions by self-evaluating levels of joy, happiness, satisfaction, or contentment in their lives, relationships, or professions. According to Foster and Auerbach (2015),

> Seligman tied positive emotions to what he termed the "pleasant life," in which a person experiences pleasures like a relaxing holiday interacting with others in ways that are pleasing and worth repeating. When the word positive is used to denote desirable ways of interacting, in referring to positive communication or positive relationships, the positive aspect is about contributing to the well-being of all the parties involved.
>
> (5)

Seligman (2002) concluded that people would find personal happiness in their lives within three dimensions that people can improve, nurture and encourage: (1) the Pleasant Life, (2) the Good Life, and (3) the Meaningful Life (see Figure 8.6).

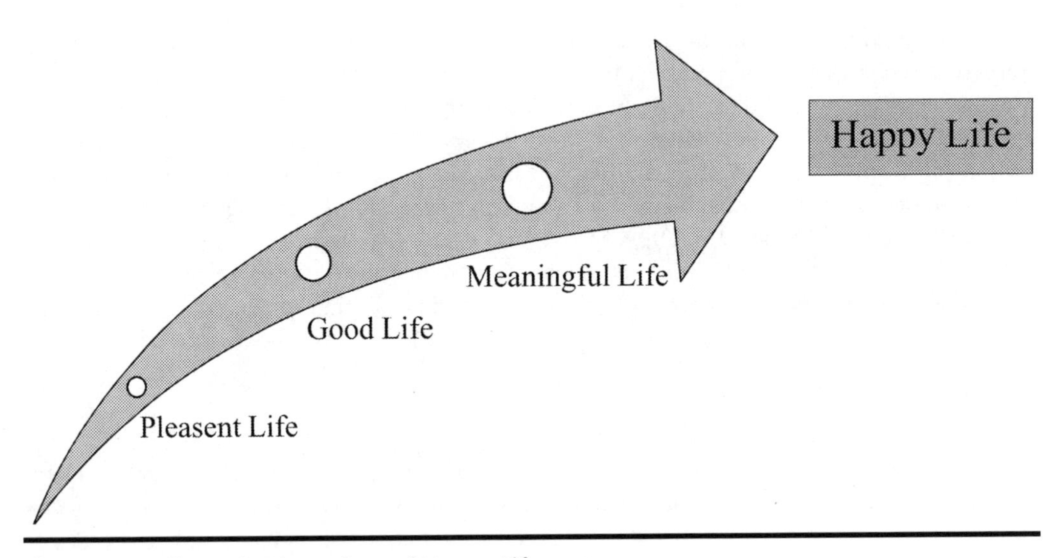


**Figure 8.6 Seligman's Dimensions of Happy Life.**

*Source:* Adapted from Seligman (2002).

## *Foundation of Positive Psychology Coaching*

Even though positive psychology and the field of coaching complement each other (Green 2014), there is limited scholarly research published on the results of blending these two disciplines (Green and Palmer 2019). However, as Biswas-Diener and Dean (2007) underlined,

> you do not need to be a trained research scholar to understand and use the literature on positive psychology. Unlike mathematical theories of light refraction or the cellular development of mycosis fungoid, psychology is a commonsense science that is easily accessible to all.
>
> (13)

The two fundamental foundations of positive psychology coaching according to Biswas-Diener and Dean (2007) are shown next:

### *One: Concept of Happiness and Positivity*

The first fundamental foundation of positive psychology coaching is the concept of happiness. Ultimate personal happiness and fulfillment is a matter and interest that affects everyone. However, knowledgeable transformational coaches realize that few coaching participants come to the coaching table intending to become happy and fulfilled.

> Perhaps this is because happiness is implicitly understood to be the single ultimate goal underscoring all other goals that grace the minutes of our coaching sessions. Perhaps it is because happiness is commonly seen as trivial, lighthearted emotional happenstance, which ought to take a back seat to weightier matters of work and family.
>
> (2007, 13)

However, it is worth mentioning that research indicates that happiness is much more than a goal. Happiness is one of the essential elements of people's healthy performance and functionality in their lives. The concept of happiness and positivity is most likely one of the most important personal resources that individual clients or teams and groups overlook (2007).

### *Two: Individuals' Character Strengths*

The second fundamental foundation of positive psychology coaching is people's character strength. Paying attention to individuals' characteristic strengths is not a new idea. Looking at human leadership, we can see many leaders who have inspired nations and the world with their characters and strengths. Mohandas Gandhi and Martin Luther King Jr. are examples of such concepts. Transformational coaches use positive psychology to underline individuals' strengths and positive attributes versus their weaknesses and shortcomings. That is the reason for the attraction of transformational coaching when participants take ownership of their power and personal strengths as a wonderful way to improve their self-confidence and build up more optimism and positivity (Biswas-Diener and Dean 2007).

## *Positive Thinking versus Positive Psychology*

Many people mistake positive psychology with positive thinking; however, there is a fundamental distinction between positive thinking and positive psychology. As Seligman (2002) explains, positive thinking is a mental and thought activity practiced by individuals thinking about positive things. Positive psychology is a psychological discipline supported by empirical research. Positive psychology is researched and supported by academic rigor, whereas positive thinking is mostly a pop culture practice.

Most would say that being a positive person and seeing the good in things and in people are desired characteristics. However, planning things, counting on just positive feelings, or believing what someone says to be positive is naive. It is important to have a positive outlook about life, events, and other things while still being responsible for doing our due diligence and researching their statements or declarations. After all those considerations, the choice becomes clearer about making a deal with someone, accepting someone's proposal, or starting projects. To be a positive person does not mean to judge and evaluate others at first sight but to benefit from the doubt by not mistrusting them or having some preconceived notion or inner chatter about them. Positivity is great as long as there is accountability for the reality of the situation in time, distance, and form.

Positive thinking, like positive psychology, has certain elements that would generate positive thinking in an individual. For people to participate in positive thinking, they need to participate and practice a set of positive mindsets and display positive behavior and a positive outlook about life and the environment around them. Figure 8.6 displays a combination of attribution to positive thinking from elements of positive psychology, mindfulness, and emotional intelligence (see Figure 8.7).

## *Benefits of Positive Psychology*

Research has proven many benefits of practicing positive psychology. The following are several of the most common results reported by positive psychology practitioners who have participated in such studies and have reported on individuals who underwent positive psychology practice:

1. They became much happier in their lives.
2. They established a deeper personal relationship.
3. They had a productive relationship at work.

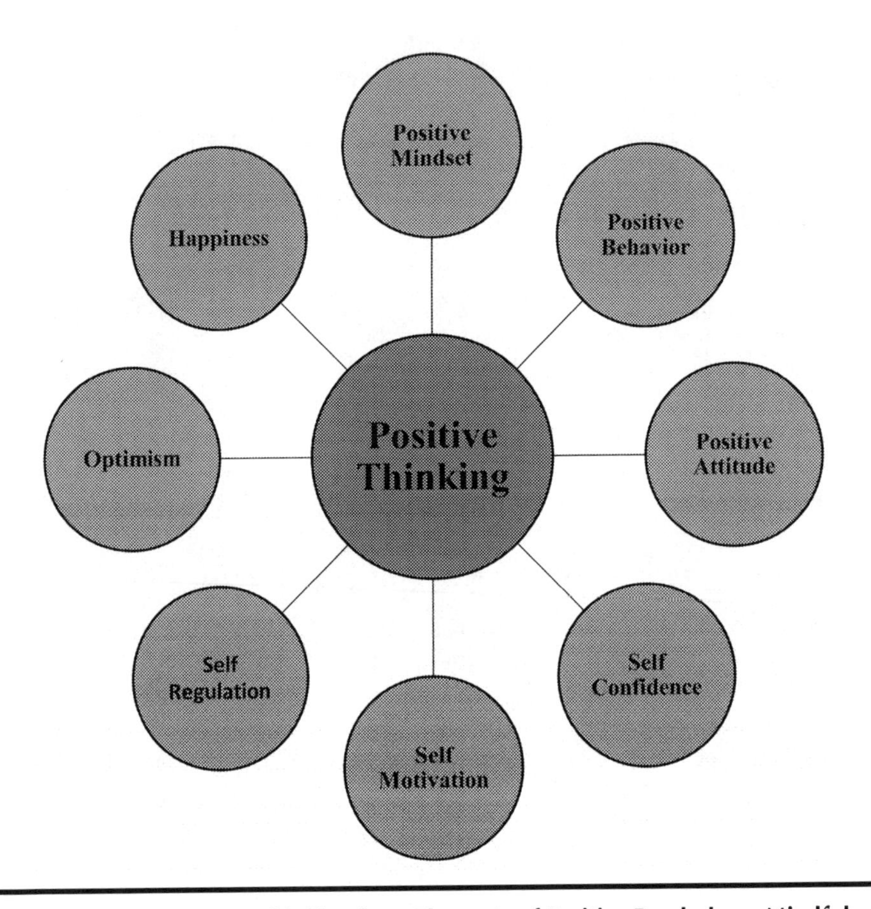


**Figure 8.7 Elements of Positive Thinking from Elements of Positive Psychology, Mindfulness and Emotional Intelligence.**

*Source:* Author's Original Creation. Copyright 2022 by Behnam Bakhshandeh.

4. They increased their self-confidence.
5. They were more effective and productive in their profession.
6. They positively affected their environment.
7. They took on their health and practiced a healthier lifestyle.
8. They were more influential in their communities.
9. Their positivity and happiness were contiguous.
10. They increased their vitality.

(Seligman and Csikszentmihalyi 2010; Green 2014; Diener et al. 2002)

## *Examples of Positive Psychology Coaching Questions*

Table 8.2 represents some of empowering and positive questions being used by transformational coaches during the implementation of positive psychology coaching. Please note the personal area questions and professional area questions could be used individually and intermixed with one another to produce results with the participants.

**Table 8.2 Questions by Transformational Coaches When Using Positive Psychology Coaching. Author's Original Creation.**

| *Some Examples of Positive Psychology Coaching Questions* | | |
|---|---|---|
| *Area* | # | *Questions* |
| **Personal** | 1 | What is going great for you? |
| | 2 | What are the things, people, or areas you are grateful for? |
| | 3 | What things, people, or areas do you feel so good about? |
| | 4 | Do you need more time to think about this desired change? |
| | 5 | Have you explored any other reasons or options for this discussion? |
| | 6 | What are the reasons for you to stop pursuing that change? |
| | 7 | Which one of your known strengths will help you in pursuing this change? |
| | 8 | What areas of your life are already going well for you? |
| | 9 | Which one of your strengths do you use for this change to go well? |
| | 10 | How can you apply the same strengths to succeed this time? |
| | 11 | What stimulates your curiosity? |
| | 12 | How do you rate your general positivity most times? |
| | 13 | What are you doing to increase or improve your positive mindset? |
| | 14 | What do you see as a possibility for increasing or improving your positivity? |
| | 15 | What do you see possible in your relationships by improving your positivity? |
| **Professional** | 1 | Have you listed your accomplishments? |
| | 2 | What are the top three things you like about your work? |
| | 3 | What are on your accomplishment goals list for this year? |
| | 4 | What do you use to measure your success? |
| | 5 | Have you investigated your motivations for making these changes? |
| | 6 | How do you rate your dedication to your success? |
| | 7 | In what degree of intensity are you willing to work on implementing this change? |
| | 8 | How will reaching your goals assist you in conveying your values? |
| | 9 | Which one of your principles will be fulfilled by reaching this change? |
| | 10 | Who else are benefiting from accomplishing this goal? |
| | 11 | What is your action plan to eliminate obstacles and remove challenges? |
| | 12 | Who can assist you in removing obstacles on your way to achieving your goals? |
| | 13 | Who are people you work reasonably well with? |
| | 14 | Who do you think has relevant strengths that can help you with this project? |
| | 15 | How could you enhance and improve your strengths? |

*Source:* Copyright 2022 by Behnam Bakhshandeh.

## Emotional Intelligence Coaching

This section briefly defines, explains, and touches on some key emotional intelligence and related skills and attributions. However, given the essential role of emotional intelligence in transformational coaching and its effect on effective leadership, we will explain this powerful concept and its influence on coaching in Chapter 13.

Emotional intelligence, also known as EI or EQ (Emotional Quotient), contains the individuals' capacity and capability to recognize, evaluate, and positively influence their own emotions as well as others around them. People who practice EI can relieve their stress in a healthy way, effectively communicate, overcome life challenges, and neutralize conflicts (Goleman 2007).

According to the *Oxford University Dictionary* (2022b), emotion is defined as

> any agitation or disturbance of mind, feeling, passion; any vehement or excited mental state.

It also defined emotional intelligence as:

> the ability to understand your emotions and those of other people and to behave appropriately in different situations.

Goleman (1995) shared his view of emotion as

> I take emotion to refer to a feeling and its distinctive thoughts, psychological and biological states, and range of propensities. There are hundreds of emotions, along with their blends, variations, mutations, and nuances. Indeed, there are many more subtleties of emotion than words for.
>
> (255)

### *Background of Emotional Intelligence*

Emotional intelligence is considered a reasonably new behavioral recognition model that rose to notoriety and reputation after Daniel Goleman's 1995 book *Emotional Intelligence*. Emotional intelligence has been characterized as the "ability to monitor one's own and others' feelings and emotions, discriminate among them, and use this information to guide ones thinking and actions" (Mayer, Brackett and Salovey 2004 n.p.). Originally emotional intelligence developed around the 1970s and 1980s through the research and writings conducted by psychologists such as Howard Gardner, Peter Salovey, and John (Jack) Mayer. Emotional intelligence is proven to be useful at both the team level and the organizational development level, given that the development of people in EQ doctrines provides a new perspective to observe, understand, and evaluate the individuals' mindsets, attitudes, behaviors, management styles, intrapersonal and interpersonal skills, and their potential for present and future personal and organizational endeavors (Rao 2013).

### *Levels of Emotional Intelligence*

Two different levels of emotional intelligence define individuals' abilities and behaviors (Goleman 2007; 1998).

## *Low Emotional Intelligence*

This level of emotional intelligence implies individuals' lack of ability to distinguish their emotions in themselves and others accurately. Individuals with low EI are not competent to use emotional experience to direct their thinking. Therefore, they cannot manage their actions and reactions to such emotions in all aspects of their lives (2007; 1998).

## *High Emotional Intelligence*

This level of emotional intelligence implies that individuals can control and manage their interactions with negative people with toxic mindsets. People with a high EI can keep their thoughts and moods in check. In case of the need to deal with toxic and negative people, they consider a rational approach and appropriate action. They can detect their own emotions, and they won't allow their hot and boiling emotions, such as anger or frustration, to add to already unworkable situations (2007; 1998).

Table 8.3 compares examples of individuals' abilities or lack of abilities to manage their emotions and actions in situations and in relation to themselves and others.

**Table 8.3 Comparisons of Abilities between Individuals with Low and High Emotional Intelligence.**

| *Some Examples for High & Low Levels of Emotional Intelligence* | | | |
|---|---|---|---|
| # | *Areas* | *Individuals with Low Emotional Intelligence* | *Individuals with High Emotional Intelligence* |
| 1 | Self-Awareness | Because of low self-awareness, they are not open to any new information and are opinionated because of low self-awareness. | Because of high self-awareness, they are aware of what they don't know and will collect information and make an informed discussion. |
| 2 | Empathy | Due to not having empathy, not relating to others, they are insensitive to others' emotions. | Due to a high level of empathy, they display understanding and relatedness with others. |
| 3 | Accountability | Because of no accountability, they will not take responsibility for their actions and always blame others. | Because of their strong relationship with accountability, they have no problem declining a project or saying no when they need. |
| 4 | Motivations | Given their low motivations, they are told to handle life's circumstances. | They are highly motivated, care about their performance and productivity, and deal with life circumstances speedily. |
| 5 | Interpersonal Skills | Due to the lack of social skills, they don't have strong and workable personal or professional relationships. | Due to their high social skills, they can resolve challenges with consideration for both sides. |

(*Continued*)

**Table 8.3 (Continued)**

| *Some Examples for High & Low Levels of Emotional Intelligence* | | | |
|---|---|---|---|
| # | *Areas* | *Individuals with Low Emotional Intelligence* | *Individuals with High Emotional Intelligence* |
| 6 | Self-Regulation | Because of their low self-regulation, they are emotionally unstable and unable to manage their emotional outbursts. | They have high self-regulation and can accept responsibility for their mistakes and move on to the next thing without drama. |
| 7 | Relationship Management | They are generally very self-serving and self-centered; everything is about them and their interests. | They are generous and participatory in projects that serve others and benefit the community or society. |
| 8 | Communication Skills | They are not aware of their lack of communication skills, and they cannot deliver their message effectively. They mostly interrupt and speak loud without clear directions. | They are good communicators and use elements of active listening that serve both sides of an issue and help resolve the issue at hand. |
| 9 | Self-Confidence | Because of their lack of self-confidence, they are not engaging in conversations or initiating an action. As a result, they do not receive criticism and ignore the input. | Because of their high self-confidence, they engage with others and conduct discussions well. They can receive criticism and responsibility. |
| 10 | Intrapersonal Skills | Given a lack of self-awareness and lack of confidence, they cannot share their emotions and feelings with others because they cannot distinguish them. | They can share their emotions and feelings with others responsibly and productively. |

*Sources:* Adapted from Goleman (2007); Bakhshandeh (2004); Goleman (1998).

## Emotional Intelligent Support in Leadership

Emotional intelligence is not just a good idea and a trend of fashionable dialogue. There is much valuable research conducted by many reputable researchers, authors, and academics behind this powerful approach to understanding the impact of emotions on people's psyche. Emotional intelligence is becoming the key elements of hiring managers and personnel in leadership positions by organizations that care about installing people with self-awareness and self-regulation in positions with constant interactions with employees.

Given that much research has been conducted in and about EL, there are also many perspectives about the elements of EI. They are all great, and they cover one another; for example, empathy, compassion, and relatedness can be all under the umbrella of social awareness. Integrity, responsibility, and accountability can go under one umbrella of self-regulation, which is also known as self-management. However, in this section, we are working on introducing four main elements of emotional intelligence as the four columns of EL. We dig deeper into the EI and these four pillars in Chapter 14 of this book.

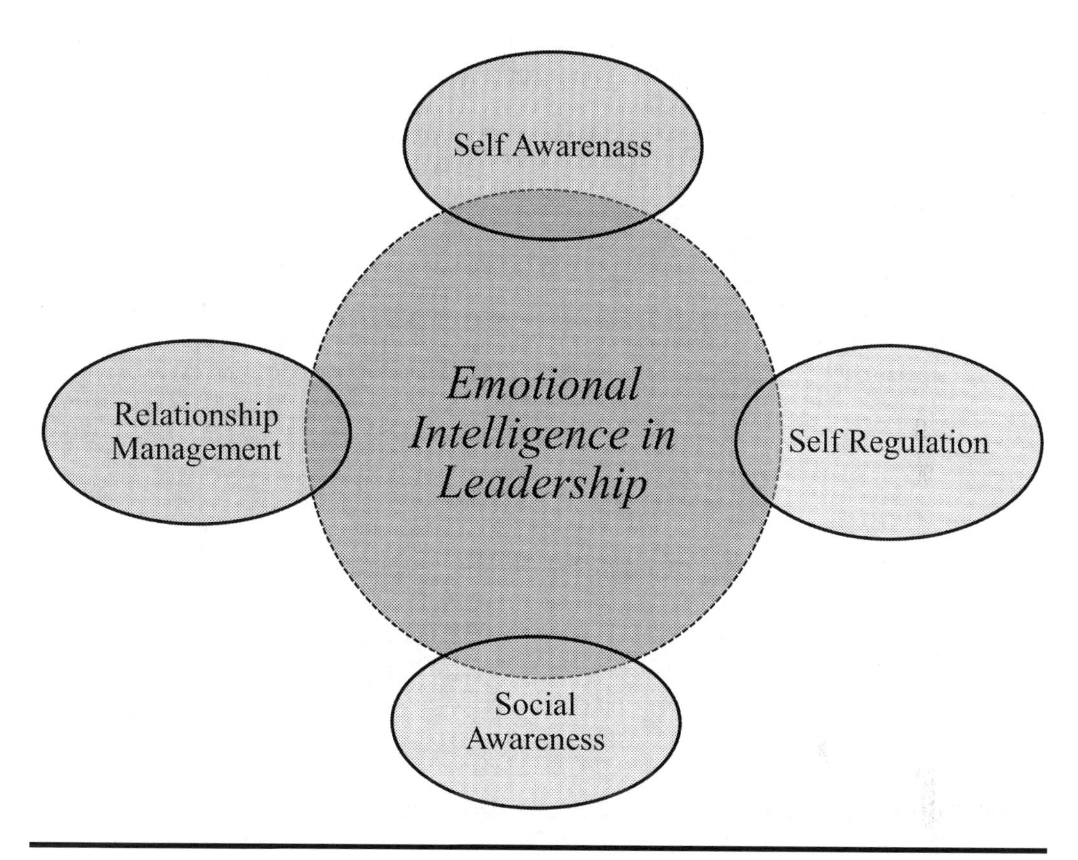


**Figure 8.8 Four Cornerstones of Emotional Intelligence for Supporting Leadership.**

*Source:* Author's Original Creation. Copyright 2022 by Behnam Bakhshandeh.

## *Four Cornerstones of Emotional Intelligence in Leadership*

As we mentioned earlier, according to researchers, there are many components of emotional intelligence; however, in this section, we are talking about the four cornerstones of EL, which encompass the emotions mostly related to leadership positions and used by transformational coaches to introduce to participants for developing them to become highly positive and influential in their leadership positions. These four cornerstones of EI are (1) self-awareness, (2) self-regulation (also known as self-management), (3) social awareness, and (4) relationship management (see Figure 8.8). As Connors (2020) also mentioned, the initial approach to being an emotionally intelligent leader is to understand the main elements of EI in leadership development and learning of your own emotions.

As we mentioned earlier, we briefly categorize these four EI cornerstones here, and then expand on them in Chapter 14.

### *Self-Awareness*

The EI cornerstones start with the individuals' self-awareness. That means the understanding of themselves and the emotional sources of their mindsets and behaviors, plus their understanding of where and how to use their understanding for their growth, development, and influences on others. Self-awareness has provided us with the ability to detect and understand our emotions, temperaments, dispositions, and motives and their influence on others. The qualities related to self-awareness include but are not limited to:

- **Emotional awareness:** An understanding and knowledge of the emotions they are experiencing.
- **Self-control:** The ability and capacity to channel their emotions to a healthy situation as an alternative to pushing them down or forcing them out.
- **Self-assessment:** The comprehension of a set of knowledge, skills, and competencies can provide them with insights into their understanding of their emotions.
- **Intrapersonal skills:** The ability to distinguish and realize their thoughts and related emotions.

(Bakhshandeh 2021; Connors 2020; Goleman 2015; Hockenbury and Hockenbury 2007)

## *Self-Regulation*

The second cornerstone is self-regulation, also known as self-management. This EI element is about people holding themselves accountable to their commitments and being adaptable to a variety of positive or negative situations and their related emotions. Self-regulation is our ability to recognize and redirect our disturbing inclinations and temperament with an inclination to concede immediate judgment and to apply considerations. The qualities called self-regulation include but are not limited to:

- **Emotional balance:** The state of being conscious of their emotions is sufficient to manage them reasonably and gently.
- **Adaptability:** The degree of severity on their ways, mindsets, and approaches in adapting to new ideas and situations.
- **Positivity:** The ability to positively affect their relationship with others, including peers, managers, organizations, and customers.
- **Accountability:** The state of being accountable, particularly on their willingness to take responsibility or to account for their actions.

(2021; 2020; 2015; 2007)

## *Social Awareness*

Social awareness indicates a continuum that runs from instantly sensing other's inner state, to being aware of their emotions and related thoughts, to recognizing complex social circumstances. This EI cornerstone necessitates social skills as much as having understood and controlled individuals' emotions. Their lifestyle or style of communicating and socializing or their popularity is not sufficient to have social awareness, and not enough to deal with contradictory and complicated situations from lack of social awareness and related emotions. The qualities related to social awareness include but are not limited to:

- **Empathy:** The ability to identify and understand others' emotions.
- **Compassion:** The ability to show kindness and understanding for others in the time of their suffering.
- **Diversity Awareness:** The ability to appreciate, understand, and relate to cultural diversity and overall general diversity and differences among people.

- **Active listening:** The ability to pay attention to the person talking and the content of the communication.

(2021; 2020; 2015; 2007)

## *Relationship Management*

The quality of life, both personally and professionally, depends on our relationships with others, both positively and negatively. However, that doesn't mean having relationships that are toxic or add nothing to our lives. Individuals with a deep understanding of EI are aware of this invaluable concept. To have a quality relationship, we must participate and invest in preserving the relationship and do our best to improve it.

- **Influence:** The ability to impact and influence others' mindsets, behaviors, and personal or professional developments. The ability to apply positive influence on people by specifying their strengths and virtues to empower and inspire them.
- **Trust building:** The ability to build trust with others. Establishing a base of trust is crucial to building an effective relationship at home or at the workplace.
- **Interpersonal skills:** The interest and ability to realize, relate, and effectively interact with others.
- **Communication:** The ability to act effectively and efficiently transmit information from and to others or places.

(2021; 2020; 2015; 2007)

A summary of the category of emotions and how it illustrates their qualities in shown in Table 8.4.

### EI Requirements for Delivering an Effective Transformational Coaching

For transformational coaches to use EI to influence people who they are coaching about ineffective leadership and to be effective, they must demonstrate these behaviors and develop a mastery of their own EI:

**Table 8.4 Qualities and Attributions of Cornerstones of Emotional Intelligence in Leadership.**

| *Qualities and Attributions of Cornerstones of Emotional Intelligence in Leadership* | | |
|---|---|---|
| *Types* | *Qualities* | *Attributions* |
| **Self-Awareness** | Emotional Awareness | • Concerning others' feelings<br>• Realizing misunderstandings<br>• Operating based on trust |
| | Self-Control | • Not making impulsive decisions<br>• Controlling their behaviors<br>• Possessing conscientiousness |
| | Self-Assessment | • Monitoring their learning<br>• Monitoring their goals' progress<br>• Conducting self-efficacy |
| | Intrapersonal Skills | • Appreciating oneself<br>• Being aware of self-motivation or agenda<br>• Displaying self-discipline |

*(Continued)*

**Table 8.4 (Continued)**

| *Qualities and Attributions of Cornerstones of Emotional Intelligence in Leadership* | | |
|---|---|---|
| *Types* | *Qualities* | *Attributions* |
| **Self-Regulation** | Emotional Balance | • Accurately identifying their emotions<br>• Being mindful of their emotions<br>• Managing impulse emotion |
| | Adaptability | • Being open to learning new things<br>• Adjusting quickly<br>• Embracing new ideas |
| | Accountability | • Taking responsibility for their actions<br>• Not blaming or pointing fingers<br>• Being transparent |
| | Positivity | • Being optimistic<br>• Being resilient<br>• Being grateful |
| **Social Awareness** | Empathy | • Being sensitive to cross cultures<br>• Understanding diversity<br>• Being at service to others |
| | Compassion | • Relating to others' issues,<br>• Looking for what is right<br>• Being at ease with others' failures |
| | Diversity Awareness | • Embracing uniqueness among people<br>• Having mutual respect for everyone<br>• Having universal treatment for everyone |
| | Active Listening | • Paying attention to the speaker<br>• Responding appropriately<br>• Providing feedback |
| **Relationship Management** | Influence | • Being charismatic<br>• Being humble<br>• Striving to help |
| | Trust Building | • Being friendly and approachable<br>• Being respectful of others' ideas<br>• Practicing integrity and accountability |
| | Interpersonal Skills | • Being sensitive to others' moods and temperaments<br>• Entertaining multiple perspectives on a situation<br>• Noticing differences among people |
| | Communication | • Being aware of nonverbal communication<br>• Delivering clear and concise messages<br>• Showing courtesy and listening keenly |

*Sources:* Adapted from Bakhshandeh (2021); Connors (2020); Goleman (2015); Hockenbury and Hockenbury (2007).

1. A mastery in understanding and ability to explain and give examples of cornerstones of EI for leadership development and their related qualities and attributions
2. Uninterrupted and continuous development and enhancement on their own emotional intelligence and related qualities and attributions
3. Their own vision and related to personal and professional values and principles as the foundation for their vision
4. Strong personal and professional relationships with your first circle of personal and professional people
5. The practice of integrity, responsibility, and accountability in their business practice as well as overall life
6. Participation in transformational coaching themselves and continue exercising practices that strengthen their abilities to deliver transformational coaching

## Some Benefits of Emotional Intelligence Coaching

Some benefits of emotional intelligence coaching reported by professional coaches who went through transformational coaching with individuals and teams are as follow:

1. Reduces stress caused by personal and professional responsibility
2. Prepares individuals to receive constructive criticism openly
3. Assists willing individuals in overcoming their insecurities and self-doubt
4. Improves communication and active listening skills
5. Enhances relationships, social awareness, and social skills
6. Helps establish a positive environment at both home and workplace

**Table 8.5 Questions Transformational Coaches Use When Emotional Intelligence Coaching. Author's Original Creation.**

| *Some Examples of Emotional Intelligence Coaching Questions* | | | |
|---|---|---|---|
| *#* | *Questions* | *Reasons Behind the Question* | *Benefits of Awareness* |
| 1 | Do you know how your feelings and emotions impact your behaviors? | Learning of how their emotions affect their behaviors. | Controlling negative decision makings based on experiencing emotions and increasing self-regulation. |
| 2 | Are you conscious of your disturbing emotional blind spots? | Learning of how their blind spots affect others. | Recognizing the gap and increasing the level of self-awareness. |
| 3 | Are you aware of what triggers your positive or negative emotions? | Knowing and acknowledging the range of emotions is vital to understanding how to control them. | Increasing how to control emotions and related potential behaviors and increasing relationship management. |

*(Continued)*

**Table 8.5 (Continued)**

| *Some Examples of Emotional Intelligence Coaching Questions* | | | |
|---|---|---|---|
| # | *Questions* | *Reasons Behind the Question* | *Benefits of Awareness* |
| 4 | Do you recognize your rising temper and when you are close to behaving negatively? | Understanding control over hot emotions and related temper tantrums. | Recognizing, reacting, and resisting hot emotions and preventing negative behaviors and increasing self-awareness. |
| 5 | Are you aware of others' emotions? | Understanding awareness about others' emotions. | Increasing on social-awareness and interpersonal relationships personally and professionally. |
| 6 | What are others' reactions to my emotions? | Becoming responsible for others' expression of who you are. | Assisting with self-regulation and social awareness. |
| 7 | What are your social signals when your emotions are about to explode? | Understanding social cues and signals to help control them. | Helping interpersonal relationships at home and at workplace. |
| 8 | Do you use body language and facial expressions to convey your emotions? | Learning of expressions that convey emotions and, therefore, a certain message. | Understanding and controlling our body language and facial expressions are attribution to an adult persona and help with social awareness and relationship management. |
| 9 | Are you practicing writing journals about your emotions? | Recording positive and negative emotions and understanding related expressions. | Recognizing patterns and consistency of emotions would allow for understanding how and when these emotions will get triggered. Helping with self-awareness and self-regulation. |
| 10 | Are you practicing using positive language? | Becoming aware of the type of language is being used regularly. | Helping with interpersonal relationships, relationship management, and social awareness. |

*Source:* Copyright 2022 by Behnam Bakhshandeh.

7. Improves level of patience for dissatisfaction
8. Assists individuals and teams in dealing with uncertainties caused by changes
9. Increases level of personal and professional responsibility and accountability
10. Reinforces inner teams' relationships and cohesiveness

(Bakhshandeh 2021; Connors 2020; Goleman 2015; Hockenbury and Hockenbury 2007)

## Emotional Intelligence Coaching Questions

Table 8.5 represents some of the empowering questions relevant to emotional intelligence coaching used by transformational coaches during their coaching sessions.

## Appreciative Inquiry and Appreciative Coaching

This section introduces appreciative inquiry (AI), appreciative coaching (AC), and their associated concepts, design, and principles. Many coaching models and professional coaches, including transformational coaches, use appreciative coaching for individual, team, and organization levels interventions. Appreciative inquiry is a process and approach for creating a positive change. This process applies to developing leadership qualities in individuals, such as managers, a particular department or a team and departments, or to an organization. Organizations have used AI for cultural transformation, strategic planning, staff training, vision building, and leadership development (Cooperrider et al. 2008).

### *History and Background*

AI is known as a strengths-based and collaborative undertaking to change by individuals, teams, and groups and at the organization level. Any systems involved require human participation. David Cooperrider is regarded as the creator of the Appreciative Inquiry Model. But the AI paradigm was developed around the mid-1980s by both Cooperrider and his mentor Suresh Srivastva, at the Weatherhead School of Management at Case Western Reserve University ("Appreciative Inquiry Commons" n.d.).

According to Cooperrider et al. (2003), the expression of Appreciative Inquiry is frequently referred as both:

- **The AI paradigm:** Conveys the notions, principles, and the underlining theory behind a strengths-based change method.
- **The AI methodology:** Conveys the particular operating techniques and processes being used to generate a positive shift in a system that runs with humans.

Essentially, AI procedures are consisted of open positive inquiries and of asking empowering questions that would increase the potential of possibilities in a nonaggressive environment. According to White (1996), "Appreciative Inquiry focuses us on the positive aspects of our lives and leverages them to correct the negative. It's the opposite of problem-solving" ("Appreciative Inquiry Commons" n.d.). According to Cooperrider et al. (2008), the AI paradigm is that people consistently explore ways to categorize their feelings, emotions, modes, thoughts, and beliefs into reasonable and easy-to-understand perspectives so they can better understand complex concepts and notions. Because when we gather and organize complex notions and ideas into a simple and easy-to-understand context, then we have formed a paradigm (Rothwell et al. 2021).

### *Stages of Appreciative Inquiry and Coaching*

"The Appreciative Inquiry, 4-D Cycle is a dynamic, iterative process of positive change" (Cooperrider et al. 2003, 101). Later, one new stage was added to the original 4-D stages, and that was the define stage as the first stage of the AI or AC approach and process, which is now known as the 5-D cycle (Watkins et al. 2011). Depending on working with an individual, a team, an organization, or a community, and the nature of what needs to be accomplished, this AI process can go from simple two-day coaching to even a year or longer process.

During the transformational coaching, the coaches will guide the participants through the five stages of AI by asking questions designed to support participants during the five designated stages. Coaches assist participants in becoming present to their dreams and preferred future from an inspiring standpoint instead of attempting to overcome a past failure. Coaches will direct participants to keep their minds on and inquire into "What is working?" as opposed to "What is wrong?"

**The phases of 5-D are as follows (see Figure 8.9):**

- **Define Stage**: This stage is about defining participants' interests and desired topics for the coaching undertaking and what they are focusing on. In this stage, with the guidance of the coach, participants will have inquired into "who else needs to be involved" or "what they need to bring to the game" to achieve the declared intention and the topic. The main inquiry in this stage is all about "what it is" and "who is involved" (Cooperrider et al. 2003; Cooperrider et al. 2008).
- **Discovery Stage**: This stage is about coaches establishing a positive relationship with the participants and leading them to an empowering viewpoint by validating the wisdom of "what is possible" and to have inquiries for the best attributes of "what it is" at this moment. This stage is about assisting the participants in discovering what the possibilities are and realizing opportunities for themselves and their desired future. The primary inquiry in this stage is around "why things are the way they are now" (2003, 2008).
- **Dream Stage**: This stage is about the coaches encouraging the participants to dream and create empowering images of possibilities by expressing and sharing their desired futures. The main inquiry in this stage is about "what could be," and envisioning "what is possible" for the participants and their lives. The transformational coaches will assist the participants in verbalizing their aspiring futures (2003, 2008).
- **Design Stage**: This stage is about transformational coaches supporting their participants in bringing their preferred dreams/futures into light and emphasis by affirming the realities of those dreams/futures. The main focus of this stage is on "how it could become" and describing the idyllic pictures of "what the future could be." While the coaches are supporting the participants in realizing their dreams/futures simultaneously, they are supporting the participants to design their action plans based on a realistic approach (2003, 2008).

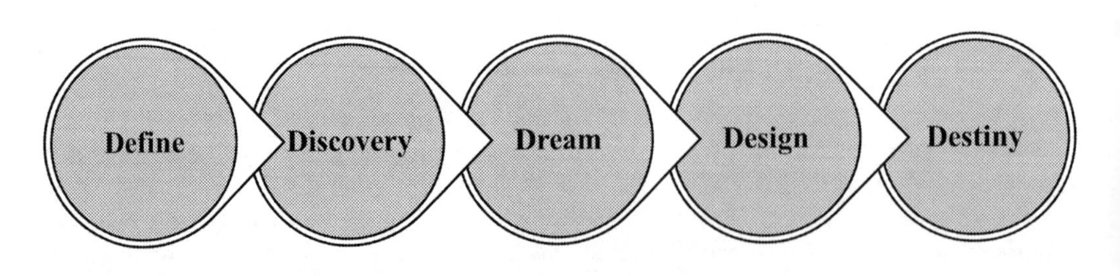


**Figure 8.9 Five Stages of Appreciative Inquiry and Coaching.**

*Source:* Adapted from Cooperrider et al. (2003).

- Destiny Stage: This stage is about focusing on "what will be" and for the participants to look into how to empower, learn, and adjust their action plans to realize their dreams/futures in the present time. This would be achieved by empowering participants to increase their capacity to generate the desired futures and being more and more inspired to hold on to their action plans. The primary inquiry at this stage is about "what it will be" (2003, 2008).

Table 8.6 summarizes the relevancy of these five stages, their central inquiries, and the descriptions of what would be included at each stage.

## The Primary Principles of Appreciative Coaching

The appreciative coaching process has five core fundamental principles and philosophies (Oren et al. 2007) as follows.

### The Constructionist Principle

During the coaching process, transformational coaches should look for declarations by the participants regarding their self-realizations and perception of their lives, families, and their careers. Throughout the coaching process, the coach should keep bringing the participants back into being clear of self-judgment

**Table 8.6 Summary of Five Stages of Appreciative Inquiry Coaching.**

| *Summary of Appreciate Inquiry Coaching Model* | | |
|---|---|---|
| *Stages* | *Central Focus* | *Descriptions* |
| **Define** | What it is? | • What is the topic of interest?<br>• What are you focusing on?<br>• Who else needs to be involved?<br>• What are they bringing to the game? |
| **Discovery** | Why it is? | • Establish a positive connection.<br>• Lead them to an enabling view.<br>• Create possibilities & opportunities.<br>• What is the aspiration? |
| **Dream** | What could it be? | • Encourage them to imagine the future.<br>• What does the future look like?<br>• Put that aspiring future in words.<br>• What is the inspiring future? |
| **Design** | How could it become? | • Bring focus to their intention.<br>• Confirm the reality of their dreams.<br>• Support relative and real activities.<br>• How are you going to do that? |
| **Destiny** | What will it be? | • Empower them to expand their capacity.<br>• Inspire them to stick to their plans.<br>• Keep their dreams alive for them.<br>• What is your action plan? |

*Sources:* Adapted from Cooperrider et al. (2003); Cooperrider et al. (2008); Cooperrider and Diana (n.d.).

and try to keep them whole and complete with no assessment of their past failures and shortcomings. Instead, coaches should keep pointing out participants strengths and abilities (2007).

### The Positive Principle

The transformational coaches ought to emphasize the participants' positive effects regarding their strengths and achievements. The coaches should keep altering the participants' language from a negative and problematic to a positive and resolution-related approach (2007).

### The Poetic Principle

The coaches shall pay attention to the participants' stories they have to keep repeating to themselves. In addition, coaches must utilize the situations to assist and encourage the participants to revise components of their stories by creating themselves in positive ways, recognizing new possibilities, and transforming their difficulties into strengths (2007).

### The Simultaneity Principle

The coaches shall consider maintaining their inquiry as to the participants source of awareness that guides their desired change. The suitable questions aid the participants in seeing their current challenges from a new viewpoint. Coaches should pay attention to the correlation between positive inquiry and where such inquiry could take the participants and their experiences (2007).

### The Anticipatory Principle

The transformational coaches could be influential in aiding the participants to generate positive pictures of themselves through self-declarations and visions for their future. Actually, it is an innate and natural trait of human beings to envision and look forward to their future (2007).

## Selection of the Topic and Language of Appreciative Coaching

Appreciative coaching's primary process starts with selecting the topic based on the clients' strengths. As Oren et al. (2007) stated: "Much of the language describing the appreciative approach is intentionally positive, or at the very least neutral" (17). This positive approach is evident in the first step of AC called *Topic* versus. Because, for example, when people set *Goals* there is always the possibility of failing in the process or not achieving the exact goal, which might come with some negative inclinations in the individuals' minds. *Topic* sounds more natural and safer for the participants.

Core questions in the AC process discover the client's strengths, personal and professional values, past successes and failures, and several aspects of life they desire to have or wish to be different. Inquiry into these answers will allow the clients to develop their own answers, which become the tools for further learning and possible changes (Oren et al. 2007).

## Practical Model for the Appreciative Inquiry Process

Many models have been proposed to define how the AI and coaching process works and what process to follow to ensure all the five stages of AI are implemented to provide a quality AI process for the participants. For example, the model illustrated in Figure 8.10 is a five-step practical model for implementing the AI process (Rothwell et al. 2016):

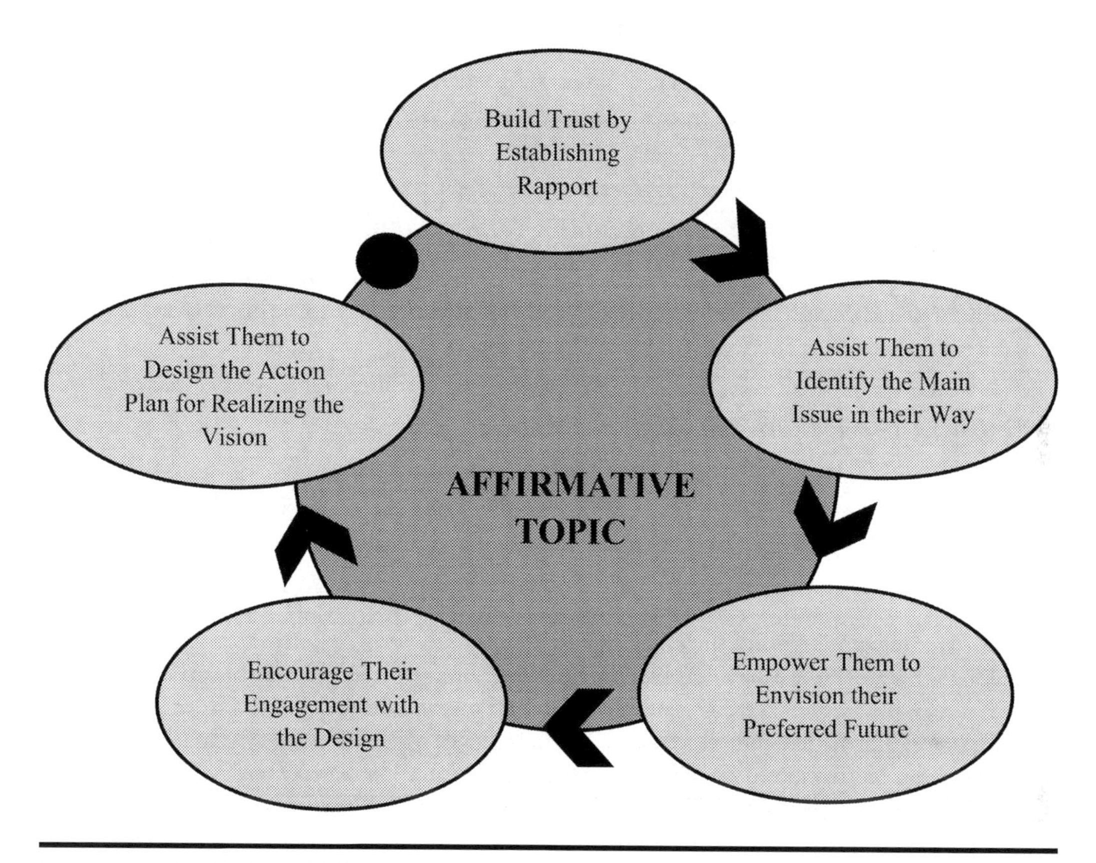


**Figure 8.10 Applied Model for Appreciative Inquiry Coaching Process.**

*Source:* Adapted from Rothwell et al. (2016).

## *Establish Rapport and Build Trust*

This part is the most critical element of building a successful coaching process with less resistance from the participants. Without establishing trust and building rapport, the coaching process will not work.

## *Assist the Participants in Identifying the Main Issues in Their Way*

It is the coaches' responsibility to aid the participants to get to the major problems in their way, and to design a compelling vision for their future which would include personal life and professional career.

## *Empower Participants to Envision Their Preferred Future*

Regardless of how hard this process might be, it is the coaches' dedication and responsibility to empower participants to find their exciting and foreseeable future built on what they imagine for themselves in their lives.

### *Encourage Participants' Engagement with the Design*

The transformational coaches must ensure that the participants are the ones focusing and working on constructing their desired future and ensuring they are encouraged during the process and acknowledged for their hard work.

### *Assist the Participants in Designing the Action Plan for Realizing the Vision*

This part is about the participants' action plans and managing the realistic steps to execute and fulfill their vision. The transformational coaches must assist participants in concentrating on creating their purposeful action plans and recognizing them.

### ***Benefits of Appreciative Inquiry Coaching***

As an imaginative approach to creating a refreshing personal awareness, individuals, teams, and organizations receive many personal and professional benefits going through the processes of AI coaching. The following are some of such benefits, according to Cooperrider et al. (2003; 2008):

1. Swift transformative and sustainable change
2. Changing direction from a problem-focused approach to possibility-focused
3. Refined and improved perception of oneself and individuality
4. Renewal of personal and professional commitments
5. Increased motivation to accomplish personal and professional goals
6. Built up positive energy
7. Increased empowering sense of hope for the future
8. Raised sense of curiosity, interest, and feeling of vitality
9. Advanced personal and professional relationships
10. Enhanced interest in conflict resolution approach

### ***Questions for Conducting Appreciative Inquiry Coaching***

Table 8.7 displays common questions used by transformational coaches when conducting appreciative inquiry and coaching during their coaching sessions with individuals or teams.

There are similarities in the sets of questions from positive psychology and appreciative inquiry, such as looking at individuals' intentions and strengths. However, simultaneously there are few differences in the focus of positivity and the direction of questions.

## Strengths-Based Coaching

The strengths-based approach to coaching centers on what individuals are doing well instead of trying to fix their weaknesses. This approach emphasizes who people are at their best. Individuals' strengths result from the natural talents they have built with knowledge, skills, and experiences (see Figure 8.11).

When people realize their strengths, they will relate to themselves from a compelling standpoint that can propel them in a forward motion regardless of their present circumstances (Rath

**Table 8.7 Common Questions for Conducting Appreciative Inquiry Coaching. Author's Original Creation.**

| *Common Questions for Conducting Appreciative Inquiry Coaching* | | |
|---|---|---|
| *Stage* | *#* | *Questions* |
| **Define** | **Questions that help define the interest in the project** | |
| | 1 | What are the areas you are concentrating on? |
| | 2 | Who needs to be involved with this? |
| | 3 | What should you bring to this project? |
| | 4 | What is the actual outcome of this project? |
| | 5 | Who else will benefit from this project? |
| | 6 | What makes you not feel the time passing? |
| | 7 | What other situations could enhance your actions when starting this project? |
| | 8 | What are the things you enjoy doing the most? |
| | 9 | Who could you join forces with during this project? |
| | 10 | What aspects of your life are meaningful to you? |
| **Discovery** | **Questions that inspire and encourage** | |
| | 1 | What is your aspiration for this project/goal? |
| | 2 | What else do you see possible out of this project/goal? |
| | 3 | What is expected out of this undertaking? |
| | 4 | Who are the people you are considering as role models? |
| | 5 | What are the characteristics of these role models that encourage you? |
| | 6 | What are you considering as your top three accomplishments? |
| | 7 | Can you remember a time that everything went smoothly on a project? |
| | 8 | What would be there if you didn't pay attention to your thoughts? |
| | 9 | Are there any strengths you wish for? |
| | 10 | What could you do to improve your positivity? |
| **Dream** | **Questions that lead the participants to see the desired future** | |
| | 1 | What does your desired future be like? |
| | 2 | Who would help you in making that future? |
| | 3 | Who do you think would benefit from that inspiring future? |
| | 4 | What are the top two areas of your life you are willing to change? |
| | 5 | From your perspective, what are the top four characteristics that describe you? |
| | 6 | What are the top two things you like to accomplish in the next year? |
| | 7 | What is the top thing you like to undertake in the next three months? |
| | 8 | What would you experience when you succeeded in your project/goal? |
| | 9 | What would be your legacy, and what would others know about you? |
| | 10 | How do you feel about yourself at your best and when everything goes well? |

*(Continued)*

**Table 8.7 (Continued)**

| *Common Questions for Conducting Appreciative Inquiry Coaching* | | |
|---|---|---|
| *Stage* | *#* | *Questions* |
| **Design** | **Questions that help establish activities and practices** | |
| | 1 | What is your plan for accomplishing this project/goal? |
| | 2 | What possibly stops you from implementing your plan? |
| | 3 | What would motivate and inspire you to move forward? |
| | 4 | What might undercut your action plan? |
| | 5 | What would be the top five actions you need to complete in this quarter? |
| | 6 | Who can partner up with you in supporting you in completing your action plan? |
| | 7 | Do you have any new practices you have not done before? |
| | 8 | What would you consider as meaningful activities for your plan? |
| | 9 | What would aid you in continuing to the end of the project? |
| | 10 | What would assist you to be more engaged with this project? |
| **Destiny** | **Questions that would keep participants focused** | |
| | 1 | In what area do you need further clarity? |
| | 2 | Are you doing anything not supporting your desired future? |
| | 3 | What would you change in your schedule that would support your action plan? |
| | 4 | What of your daily practices needs to alter to achieve your action plan? |
| | 5 | What new daily routine and activities would you consider to fulfill your intentions? |
| | 6 | How do you rate your discipline from 1 to 10 for following your plan? |
| | 7 | What would you do to help others who support you on this project? |
| | 8 | What is your maintenance plan after accomplishing your project/goal? |
| | 9 | How do you imagine your life after you accomplished your project/goal? |
| | 10 | How will other facets of your life be positively influenced by this process? |

*Source:* Copyright 2022 by Behnam Bakhshandeh.

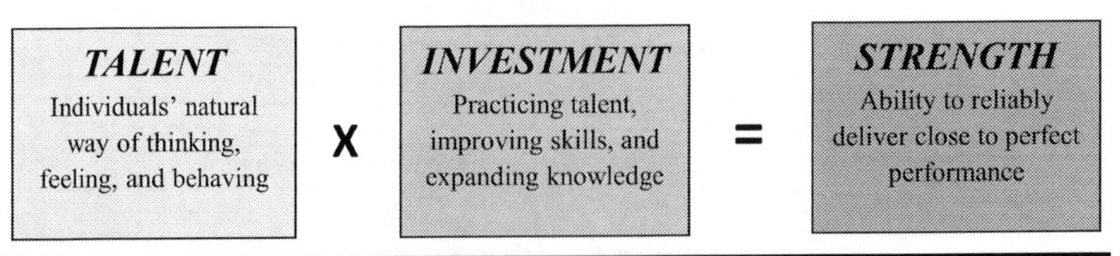


**Figure 8.11 Strength Formula According to Rath (2007).**

*Source:* Adapted from (Rath 2007, 20).

and Conchie 2008). Transformational coaching uses a strengths-based approach to naturally increase individuals' and teams' value of their strengths.

Transformational coaches will guide the participants to consciously recognize their strengths and use them more often and to enhance their success while not ignoring individual weaknesses that need to be worked on. In strengths-based coaching, the coaches and coachees look at the weaknesses together and come up with a plan to use their strengths to develop their weaknesses in a manageable state. The best part of strengths-based coaching time is invested in recognizing, being aware, improving, and applying participants strengths to accomplish their goals and intentions because their strengths are leveraging their top performance (MacKie 2016).

In strengths-based coaching, transformational coaches apply the same positive and empowering approach that positive psychology and appreciative inquiry coaching use to lift participants' spirits and get them to recognize their aspirations. That is one of the primary reasons we have added strengths-based coaching to the combination that developed the Transformational Coaching Integration Model (see Figure 8.2).

## History and Background

According to Saleebey (2008), the purposeful design of the strengths-based approach was developed in the early 1980s as an approach to social work at the University of Kansas' School of Social Welfare. Later, Weick et al. (1989) invented the term *strengths perspective* to explain a procedure in which social work practitioners understand the conviction and resources a client retains in the framework of their life story (Manthey et al. 2011). Initially, the strengths-based approach was a position to engage in opposing a mental health system, which excessively fixated on analysis, diagnosis, discrepancies, classification, and pointing at perspective issues. This approach was initially employed in case management, then moved into other fields of social work and occupations designed to help people (Manthey et al. 2011; Saleebey 1996).

Since then, the strengths-based approach has been used in a diversity of perspectives, including management, coaching, education, organizations, governmental agencies, and private practice. In addition, clients and participants vary from children, teenagers, individuals, couples, families, and teams (Saleebey 2008).

## Strength Roles

In his 2015 book *Standout 2.0*, Marcus Buckingham introduced nine strengths-based roles that individuals use in their personal lives and professional positions (see Table 8.8). Buckingham (2015) explained, "To create the StandOut strengths assessment, we combed through all the many hundreds of themes that are possible to measure and identified the most common and powerful theme combinations" (8). We must underline that the number of methods and techniques to calculate and determine the delicate individuals' distinctiveness is endless. However, Buckingham (2015) came up with nine general combinations as strength roles (see Table 8.8).

## Strengths-Based Coaching Process

Similar to any other coaching process, the strengths-based approach to coaching also has a process that transformational coaches follow. The order of steps does not necessarily have to be in sequence, as long as the coach and participants recognize their strengths, create a new set of values and mindset, and see the opportunities to be more productive and perform in a higher level.

**Table 8.8 Strength Roles Based on "StandOut" Strengths Assessment.**

| *Strength Roles Based on "StandOut" Strengths Assessment* | | |
|---|---|---|
| *#* | *Role* | *Descriptions* |
| 1 | Advisor | Pragmatic and solid thinkers are individuals at their most powerful space when responding to situations and attempting to solve them. |
| 2 | Connector | Catalytic individuals whose power lies in their appetite to bring people and concepts collectively to make a better situation for everyone. |
| 3 | Creator | Individuals who always try to make sense of the world around them. They are good at taking situations apart and coming up with a better arrangement. |
| 4 | Equalizer | Level-headed individuals powerful when attempting to keep the world around them in a workable, practical, and ethical balance. |
| 5 | Influencer | Engaging and persuasive individuals good at relating to others directly and encouraging them. |
| 6 | Pioneer | Viewing the world around them as a sociable place where good things will occur. They are optimistic when situations are uncertain. |
| 7 | Provider | Individuals who have the ability to sense others' feelings and are compelled to identify such feelings and are able to explain them. |
| 8 | Stimulator | Individuals who host others' emotions, taking responsibility for them, and attempting to turn them around. |
| 9 | Teacher | Thrilled by recognizing and observing the potential in others, their power lies in the power of learning how to release it. |

*Source:* Adapted from Buckingham (2015, 8–9).

The steps in the general process of a strengths-based approach to producing long-lasting changes are presented in Figure 8.12 and briefly explained as follows.

- **Establish rapport:** In any type of coaching, establishing rapport and creating a background of relatedness is the key to creating open and honest communication between a coach and participants.
- **Identify the needs:** Work closely with the participants to understand the need for the change and the necessity of such changes relevant to the need, either personally or professionally.
- **Declaring commitments:** This is the time to discuss their commitment to fulfill such needs and the process of strengths-based coaching. Their declaration of their commitment will be the foundation of this transformational coaching process.
- **Identify the strengths:** Using a series of questions (see Table 8.9) assists the participants to have inquiries about their potential strengths and what they are considered as their top three or four strengths that always caused their success.
- **Present opportunities:** Conduct inquiry into opportunities to use their strengths for getting closer to their desired needs. Provide empowering perspectives of what opportunity is and what they can do to take advantage of their strengths for such opportunities.

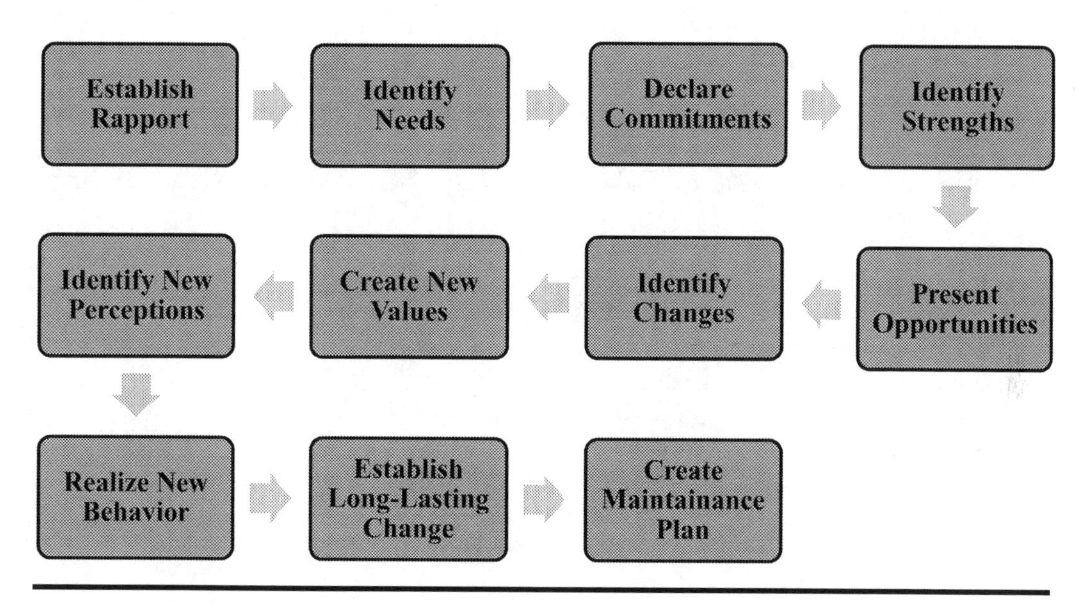


**Figure 8.12 The General Process of Strength-Based Approach to Long-lasting Change.**

*Source:* Author's Original Creation. Copyright 2022 by Behnam Bakhshandeh.

- **Identify changes:** Now that their strengths are identified and opportunities are presented, look at the changes in order. Make sure that they know making changes is their free choice. Distinguish for them that no choice is better than other choices; they only come with different consequences. Coach them in seeing the relevance between their choices and their needs.
- **Create new values:** What would be their new set of values and principles that would assist them in managing these new changes? Make sure they know there is nothing wrong with their previous values, and they don't necessarily need to disregard them, but they need to know for their success in managing new changes and using their strengths to do so, they need to come up with new values and the source of the changes.
- **Identify new perceptions:** Having perceptions and different points of view are just part of being human and nothing to be worried about. However, you need to coach them into seeing they have the power to generate a new perspective of themselves, others, productivity, and high-performance, using their new set of values and their desired changes in their approaches.
- **Realize new behavior:** Assist them in seeing how their new values and perspectives positively influence coming with new behaviors or adjusting their current behaviors to match their new values, principles, and views of themselves based on empowering their strengths and not paying attention to their weaknesses. See into them realizing their behavior.
- **Establish long-lasting change.** Have an open discussion and inquiry into the impact of their new mindset (based on their recognized strengths, new values, and perspectives) on their behavior and attitude that would only help them keep the new changes in their lives, personally and professionally.

- **Create maintenance plan:** Like any other change process, the maintenance of learning, process, and practices is vital to maintaining any change's positive effect. This is the time to establish a maintenance plan with the participants and assist them in coming up with a realistic maintenance plan.

### *Benefits of Strengths-Based Coaching*

The following are some benefits of conducting a strengths-based coaching approach as part of transformational coaching:

1. People see the best of themselves.
2. It increases individual and team motivation.
3. It increases personal and team productivity.
4. It uses strengths for a particular situation.
5. It is a great return on investment for the organization.
6. It encourages diversity and inclusion.
7. It assists in building up and developing skills and competencies to work on weaknesses.
8. It helps with creating stronger values and principles.
9. It builds stronger partnerships in teams and workplaces.
10. It enhances positive team and organization outcomes.

(Manthey et al. 2011; Saleebey 2008; Saleebey 1996)

### *Questions for Conducting Strength-Based Coaching*

Table 8.9 displays some of the common questions transformational coaches use when conducting strengths-based coaching sessions with individuals or teams.

There are similarities in the sets of questions from positive psychology and appreciative inquiry, such as looking at individuals' intentions and strengths. However, there are a few differences in the focus on strengths and direction of questions simultaneously.

## Key Takeaways

1. A coaching model supports and serves both coach and participants as a conceptual structure and road map to the desired outcome.
2. The nature of a coaching model is to be a receptacle for a coaching process and procedures on a background of an idea or concept; however, it doesn't mean that professional and experienced coaches have strictly followed only one coaching discipline as a single designed model.
3. Transformation is the display of a shift in an individual from one state of *being* to another (Seale 2011) that would influence their thought processes, attitudes, and behaviors, which eventually would have the power to affect others around the transformed individuals such as a team or group (Bakhshandeh 2009).
4. Ontological coaching is an inquiry into human self-awareness, a reflection on humans' relationships to their *being*, and their relationship to reality.
5. Positive psychology is a branch of the science of psychology centered on individuals, teams, and groups' strengths, functionality, and improving well-being.

**Table 8.9 Common Questions for Conducting a Strengths-Based Coaching Approach. Author's Original Creation.**

| *Some Common Questions for Conducting a Strengths-Based Coaching Approach* | | |
|---|---|---|
| *Areas* | # | *Questions* |
| **Identify Needs** | **Questions that help identify the needs** | |
| | 1 | What aspects of your productivity or performance are not working for you? |
| | 2 | From your viewpoint, what is missing in what you do or how you are doing it? |
| | 3 | From your perspective, what are the areas you need to work on? |
| | 4 | What do you see happening if you improve in these areas? |
| | 5 | What has been stopping you from working on these areas before? |
| **Identify Strengths** | **Questions that help identify strengths, skills, and abilities** | |
| | 1 | What are you good at? |
| | 2 | What are the areas you have always enjoyed doing? |
| | 3 | What characteristics do your family, close friends, or coworkers know you as? |
| | 4 | What are the areas that your manager or supervisor acknowledges you for? |
| | 5 | What are the things you are confident you can do well? |
| **Present Opportunities** | **Questions that help to get present to opportunities** | |
| | 1 | Do you see any opportunity to utilize your strengths? |
| | 2 | How could you use your strengths to achieve your personal and professional goals? |
| | 3 | Who could benefit from your strengths? |
| | 4 | How do you feel about yourself when using your strengths and things are getting done? |
| | 5 | How can your colleagues and team members benefit from your strengths? |
| **Identify Changes** | **Questions that help identify areas of change** | |
| | 1 | What would inspire you to implement changes? |
| | 2 | What possibly needs to change, and what would be the reasons? |
| | 3 | Who would benefit from these changes? |
| | 4 | How do you utilize your strengths for going through these changes? |
| | 5 | How could your strengths possibly be on your way to implementing these changes? |
| **New Values** | **Questions that would help create a new set of values** | |
| | 1 | What are you now valuing after you saw the need for change? |
| | 2 | What new principles could you follow to empower your strengths during this change? |
| | 3 | What would you change in your daily routine and work that supports you and your team? |
| | 4 | How could you share your values with your colleagues, such as being part of it? |
| | 5 | How could your values be helping to transform your weaknesses into new strengths? |

*(Continued)*

**Table 8.7 (Continued)**

| *Some Common Questions for Conducting a Strengths-Based Coaching Approach* | | |
|---|---|---|
| *Areas* | # | *Questions* |
| **New Perceptions** | **Questions that would help to create new and empowering perceptions** | |
| | 1 | How do you perceive your abilities and strengths now based on your new values? |
| | 2 | How do you view yourself and others around your workplace now? |
| | 3 | What would be new resources to support enhancing your strengths? |
| | 4 | What would be new resources to support you developing your weaknesses? |
| | 5 | Who can be involved to support you on your actions? |
| **New Behaviors** | **Questions that would help to establish new behaviors** | |
| | 1 | Do you see your present behavior match with your new values and perceptions? |
| | 2 | What are the old behaviors you would like to retire? |
| | 3 | What are the new and empowering behaviors that could support your strengths? |
| | 4 | What would enhance your positive behaviors around home and the workplace? |
| | 5 | What type of behaviors would cause deeper relationship between you and others? |

*Source:* Copyright 2022 by Behnam Bakhshandeh.

6. Emotional intelligence contains the individuals' capacity and capability to recognize, evaluate, and positively influence their own emotions and others around them.
7. Appreciative inquiry procedures consist of open positive inquiries and asking empowering questions that would increase the potential of possibilities in a nonaggressive environment.
8. The strengths-based approach to coaching centers on what individuals are doing well in contrast to trying to fix their weaknesses. This approach emphasizes who people are at their best.

## Discussion Points and Coaching Questions

1. From your perspective, what are the vital elements to build a strong bond between you and your coaching participants during a transformational coaching process?
2. Considering what you have learned from this chapter about the Transformational Coaching Integration Model; what else would you suggest adding to elements of transformational coaching? What was missing?
3. Do you think transformational coaching would make a difference in establishing strong and cohesive teams in organizations?
4. How do you rate yourself from 0 to 10 (0 being lowest and 10 being highest in this and all the questions that follow) on your ability to conduct positive psychology coaching?

- What is missing or in the way of your understanding of the process?
- Have you assessed your KSAs (knowledge, skills, and abilities) in this area?
- What is your action plan to increase your overall rate on this process?

5. How do you rate yourself from 0 to 10 on your ability to conduct an ontological approach to coaching?
   - What is missing or in the way of your understanding of the process?
   - Have you assessed your KSAs (knowledge, skills, and abilities) in this area?
   - What is your action plan to increase your overall rate on this process?
6. How do you rate yourself from 0 to 10 on your ability to conduct emotional intelligence coaching?
   - What is missing or in the way of your understanding of the process?
   - Have you assessed your KSAs (knowledge, skills, and abilities) in this area?
   - What is your action plan to increase your overall rate on this process?
7. How do you rate yourself from 0 to 10 on your ability to conduct appreciative inquiry coaching?
   - What is missing or in the way of your understanding of the process?
   - Have you assessed your KSAs (knowledge, skills, and abilities) in this area?
   - What is your action plan to increase your overall rate in this process?
8. How do you rate yourself from 0 to 10 on your ability to conduct strengths-based coaching?
   - What is missing or in the way of your understanding of the process?
   - Have you assessed your KSAs (knowledge, skills, and abilities) in this area?
   - What is your action plan to increase your overall rate in this process?

## References

Appreciative Inquiry Commons (n.d.). Definitions of Appreciative Inquiry. Retrieved from https://appreciativeinquiry.case.edu/intro/definition.cfm

Bakhshandeh, Behnam. 2004. *Effective Communication; Getting Present!* Audio Workshop. San Diego, CA: Primeco Education, Inc.

Bakhshandeh, Behnam. 2009. *Conspiracy for Greatness; Mastery on Love Within.* San Diego, CA: Primeco Education, Inc. Primeco Education, Inc.

Bakhshandeh, Behnam. 2021. *Perception Of21st Century 4cs (Critical Thinking, Communication, Creativity & Collaboration) Skill Gap in Private-Sector Employers in Lackawanna County, NEPA* (An unpublished dissertation in workforce education and development). State College, PA: The Pennsylvania State University.

Berto, Francesco, and Matteo Plebani. 2015. *Ontology and Metaontology: A contemporary guide.* London: Bloomsbury Publishing.

Biswas-Diener, Robert and Ben Dean. 2007. *Positive Psychology Coaching: Putting the Science of Happiness to Work for Your Clients.* Hoboken, NJ: John Wiley & Sons, Inc.

Buckingham, Marcus. 2015. *"Standout 2.0".* Boston, MA: Harvard Business Review Press.

Cooperrider, David, L. and Diana, Whitney. n.d. Appreciative inquiry: a positive revolution in change. In P. Holman and T. Devane (eds.), *The Change Handbook* (pp. 245–263). Berrett-Koehler Publishers, Inc.

Cooperrider, David, L., Diana Whitney and Jacqueline, M. Stavros. 2003. *Appreciative Inquiry Handbook: For Leaders of Change* (2nd ed.). Brunswick, OH: Crown Custom Publishing, Inc.

Cooperrider, David, L., Diana Whitney and Jacqueline, M. Stavros. 2008. *Appreciative Inquiry: For Leaders of Change* (2nd ed.). Brunswick, OH: Crown Custom Publishing, Inc.

Connors, Christopher, D. 2020. *Emotional Intelligence for the Modern Leader*. Emeryville, CA: Rockridge Press.

Csikszentmihalyi, Mihaly and Mihaly Csikzentmihaly. 1990. *Flow: The Psychology of Optimal Experience* (Vol. 1990). New York, NY: Harper & Row.

D'Addario, Miguel. 2016. *Ontological Coaching: Transformation and Development of Oneself* (2nd ed.) Translated by Sofia Navarro. San Bernardino, CA: European Community.

Diener, Ed, Carol Nickerson, Richard E. Lucas, and Ed Sandvik. 2002. "Dispositional affect and job outcomes." *Social Indicators Research* 59, no. 3: 229–259.

Effingham, Nikk. 2013. *An Introduction to Ontology*. Malden, MA: Polity Press.

Foster, Sandra, L. and Jeffrey E. Auerbach. 2015. *Positive Psychology in Coaching. Applying Science to Executive and Personal Coaching*. Pismo Beach, CA: Executive College Press.

Goleman, Daniel. 1995. *Emotional Intelligence: Why it Can Matter More Than IQ*. New York, NY: Bantam Books.

Goleman, Daniel. 1998. *Working with Emotional Intelligence*. New York, NY: Bantam Publishing.

Goleman, Daniel. 2007. *Social Intelligence*. New York, NY: Bantam Books.

Goleman, Daniel. 2015. *Emotional Intelligence; Why It Can Mater More Than IQ*. New York, NY: Bantam Books.

Green, Lucy, S. 2014. Positive education: An Australian perspective. In M.J. Furlong, R. Gilman, and E.S. Huebner (Eds.), *Handbook of Positive Psychology in Schools* (2nd ed., pp. 401–415). New York, NY: Taylor & Francis.

Green, Suzy and Stephen Palmer (Ed). 2019. *Positive Psychology Coaching in Practice*. New York, NY: Routledge; Taylor & Francis Group.

Heidegger, Martin. 1953. *Being and Time*. Translated by Joan Stambaugh. New York, NY: State University on New York Press.

Hockenbury, Don, H. and Sandra E. Hockenbury. 2007. *Discovering Psychology*. New York, NY: Worth Publishers.

Levi, Daniel. 2016. *Group Dynamics for Teams* (5th Ed.). Los Angeles, CA: Sage Publications.

MacKie, Doug. 2016. *Strength-Based Leadership Coaching in Organizations*. Philadelphia, PA: Kogan Page.

Manthey, Trevor Jay, Bryan Knowles, Dianne Asher, and Stephanie Wahab. 2011. "Strengths-based practice and motivational interviewing." *Advances in Social Work* 12, no. 2: 126–151.

Mayer, John D., Brackett, Mark A. and Salovey, Peter (2004). *Emotional Intelligence: Key Reading on the Mayer and Salovey Model*. Midrand: Dube Publishing.

Merriam-Webster Online Dictionary. 2022. Retrieved from www.merriam-webster.com/dictionary/ontology

Rao, Paulette. 2013. *Transformation Coaching: Shifting Mindset for Sustainable Change*. Brooklyn, NY: True North Resources.

Rath, Tom. 2007. *Strengths Finder 2.0*. New York, NY: Gallup Press.

Rath, Tom and Barry Conchie. 2008. *Strengths Based Leadership*. New York, NY: Gallup Press.

Oren, Sara, L., Jacqueline Binkert and Ann L. Clancy. 2007. *Appreciative Coaching: A Positive Process for Change*. San Francisco, CA: Jossey-Bass.

Oxford University Dictionary. 2022a. Ontology. www.oxfordlearnersdictionaries.com/us/definition/english/ontology?q=Ontology

Oxford University Dictionary. 2022b. Emotional intelligence. www.oxfordlearnersdictionaries.com/us/definition/english/emotional-intelligence?q=Emotional+Intelligence

"Primeco Education" website. 2022. Team and organizational training. www.primecoeducation.com/business-consulting

Rothwell, William J. 2015. *Beyond Training & Development (3rd ed.). Enhancing Human Performance through a Measurable Focus on Business Impact*. Amherst, MA: HRD Press, Inc.

Rothwell, William, J., and Henry J. Sredl. 2014. *Workplace Learning and Performance: Present and Future Roles and Competencies* (3rd ed., Vol. I). Amherst, MA: HR Press.

Rothwell, William, J., Jacqueline M. Stavros and Roland L. Sullivan. 2016. *Practicing Organization Development: Leading Transformation and Change* (4th ed.). Hoboken, NJ: John Wiley & Sons, Inc.

Rothwell, William J., Sohel M. Imroz and Behnam Bakhshandeh. 2021. *Organization-Development Interventions: Executing Effective Organizational Chang.* New York, NY: Taylor & Francis Group. CRC Press.

Saleebey, Dennis. 1996. "The strengths perspective in social work practice: Extensions and cautions." *Social Work* 41, no. 3: 296–305.

Saleebey, Dennis. 2008. The strengths perspective: Putting possibility and hope to work in our practice. In *Comprehensive Handbook of Social Work and Social Welfare: The Profession of Social Work* (Vol. 1; pp. 123–142). Hoboken, NJ: John Wiley & Sons, Inc.

Sartre, Jean-Paul. 1943. *Being and Nothingness: A Phenomenological Essay on Ontology.* Translated by Hazel E. Barnes. New York, NY: Washington Express Press.

Seale, Alan. 2011. *Create a World That Works: Toles for Personal & Global Transformation.* San Francisco, CA: Weiser Books.

Seale, Alan. 2017. *Transformational Presence: How to Make a Difference in a Rapidly Changing World.* Topsfield, MA: The Center for Transformational Presence.

Seligman, Martin E.P. 2002. *Authentic Happiness: Using the New Positive Psychology to Realize Your Potential for Lasting Fulfillment.* New York, NY: Free Press.

Seligman, Martin EP, and Mihaly Csikszentmihalyi. 2010. "Positive psychology: An introduction." In *Flow and the Foundations of Positive Psychology* (pp. 279–298). Dordrecht: Springer.

Sieler, Alan. 2005. *Coaching to the Human Soul Ontological Coaching and Deep Change, Volume I.* Melbourne: Newfield Network Inc.

Sieler, Alan. 2007. *Coaching to the Human Soul: Ontological Coaching and Deep Change: Volume II: Emotional Learning and Ontological Coaching.* Melbourne. Newfield Network Inc.

Sieler, Alan. 2020. *Why Coaching to the Soul is Good for Business.* Newfield Institute. Retrieved from www.newfieldinstitute.com.au/html/articles_OCCT_003.html

Watkins, Jane, M., Moher, Bernard and Kelly, Ralph Kell (2011). *Appreciative Inquiry: Change at the Speed of Imagination* (2nd ed.). San Francisco, CA: Pfeiffer.

Weick, Ann, Charles Rapp, W. Patrick Sullivan, and Walter Kisthardt. 1989. "A strengths perspective for social work practice." *Social Work* 34, no. 4: 350–354.

White, Thomas H. 1996. "Working in interesting times." *Vital Speeches of the Day* 62, no. 15: 472.

Wikipedia Online. 2022. Ontology. Retrieved from https://en.wikipedia.org/wiki/Ontology

# Chapter 9

# Transformational Coaching Methodologies

Farhan Sadique

## Overview

Coaching is often defined as a structured, focused, interaction-based combination of strategies, tools, and techniques to promote sustainable human development, performance improvement, and change, unlocking the long-term potential and success of the client or latent stakeholders (Cox et al. 2010; Ursillo 2020). Traditionally, the process is viewed as long term. Still, in today's fast-changing world, transformational learning may take from a few months to years, depending on the client's emotional attachment and life events (Barner and Ideus 2017).

Transformational coaching cannot be combined in the specifically structured diagram as it requires a profound level of personal engagement and deep self-reflective dialogues. However, the resources can guide transformational coaches to understand the process and develop their own customized approaches based on their capacity, personality, and traits. The systems remain highly flexible depending on the need of clients; in many cases, coaches adapt with their framework as they see the process as a systematic, structured behavioral pattern that works for them in the analytical process; others may find this problematic and would rather stay open to dialogue and gradually develop a framework as they ask questions and develop a rapport. Engaging in coaching requires a mutual space for self-reflection and awareness of beliefs, biases, and assumptions that shape clients' values and norms, how they react to a different situation, and visualize what they want to achieve. Transformational coaches must form a core identity to face challenges as clients open up about themselves.

This chapter attempts to underline the following:

- The purpose of transformational coaching
- Transformational coaching expectations
- What transformational coach must offer
- How the transformational leader creates a change

DOI: 10.4324/9781003304074-12

- Foundation of the transformational leadership framework
- The CLEAR model
- Characteristics of a transformational coach
- Transformational leading model

## Overview of Transformational Coaching Methodologies

Transformational coaching is the self-actualization process to grow as individuals, the way they envision themselves. Transformation takes time, but the impact is permanent. Transformational coaches take a passive role; instead of guiding the learner's activities, they analyze the mindset and impact of thoughts, beliefs, perceptions, and cultural influence. It means facilitating significant changes in people's life, going beyond their imagination and current reality through identifying their thoughts, emotions, and behavior toward an evolving vision. Transformational coaches ask powerful questions; the goal is not to find a solution for the clients; instead, it is a way of guiding them to think deeper, identify the reason they want to create a change, and how to see the result as the change emerges.

The questions are open-ended; the coaches start with a simple Why or How? And follow up with a broader perspective, "Tell me more . . ." or "If you had a magic wand . . . . " The whole course of action creates a fundamental shift and helps clients to interpret their philosophy better; a lot can happen between questions, in the silence, where the client is subconsciously developing their thought process. The role of a good coach is not to help, guide, lead, push or even pull; the coaches are there to ask good questions and listen carefully to build a relationship (Boyatzis et al. 2019). A particular coaching alliance based on trust and support is required to be a successful transformational leader. Changing is always tricky; anyone who wants to change something goes through some critical steps and always needs some support in the change process.

### *What a Transformational Coach Has to Offer*

It is imperative to ask what transformational coaches must offer that is different from other coaches or how transformational coaching is additional. Change may take on diverse levels, but a transformational change shifts the underlying assumption of specific values, expectations, and paradigms, unfolding their perception of the world. Transformational coaches must invest time to understand the client, their roles, goals, and challenges as transformation require dramatic change. It differs from transitional, goal-oriented, or situational coaching, which is a much shorter range and very specific to a few challenges.

The transformational coach must understand the client's vision and awareness of the path toward their vision. The transformational coach does not provide a specific goal but instead supports the journey to get there. Some coaches like to follow a structured analytical process with follow-up questionnaires to go through these steps of associating visions with reality. Some transformational coaches want to stay open and intuitive on each case as they dig deeper into the client's mindset. The coach leads by example and provides wisdom, skills, and competencies to develop strategies, but the client should produce his perspective of the future and the source of their desire. Some clients have a comparatively clear vision and a plan of action to undertake to make those changes. Unfolding what they want to do, the transformational coaches redirect the questions to identify challenges, particularly what stops them from consciously or subconsciously achieving their goal.

Transformational leaders focus on understanding the reality of the situation and provide hopes, dreams, and objectives to improve one step at a time. Transformational leaders observe closely and provide timely, specific, and meaningful feedback to contribute to learning and performance. Sometimes they let the silence take the space, as a deeper connection develops behind the moments of silence. The uplifting support makes clients feel empowered and helps them make their dream more vibrant.

### *How a Transformational Coach Makes a Difference*

The transformational coach must be passionate about the change; it requires plenty of time and effort above and beyond regular coaching. It is an operation for long-lasting change and requires a strong commitment from both leaders and participants. The coach needs to be a leader by choice and must listen to their own voice. It is a process to discover people's insights through meaningful conversation and universal truth. The coach must earn trust and reliability from the client and honor correct principles. As transformational leaders, the most indispensable components are intellectual stimulation to encourage clients, individualized consideration to support relationships, inspirational motivation to keep everyone motivated toward their goals, and idealized influence to manage followers (Cherry 2020). A transformational coach allows people to dive below the surface level to explore their beliefs, image, purpose, and place.

## Transformational Leadership Framework

Transformational leaders must understand the core values that will help them develop a robust trust-based relationship. The leaders explore the three most critical subconscious factors that direct an individual's intention: being, belief, and behavior. A transformational leader is not there to fix the problem; every person is complete and has the potential to choose their state of being. A leader needs to address and recognize the client's emotional state in consciousness, confidence, fear, and creativity. "Doing" encompasses the action; "being" is the underneath self-image, including values, thoughts, beliefs, and experiences—the moment of "being" influences the actions of an individual (Bakhshandeh 2009). The human mind needs to be in a state to engage in creative thinking and effective dialogues with transformational leaders. Humans have two forms of conscious awareness of "being": phenomenal consciousness engages in direct subjective experience, and access consciousness conceptualizes and reflects upon experience (Brendel et al. 2021). Emotional intelligence is an essential aspect of transformational leadership.

Transformational leaders adopt a wide range of mindfulness interventions, including cognitive, social, and emotional aspects, to observe the mind and body synchronizations of the client, experiencing moment to moment without judging. The leader provides intellectual stimulation, positive feedback, and meaningful examples to positively affect the client's well-being. It helps develop openness, patience, security, and trust. It is essential for the transformational leader to shift active consciousness, make clients aware of their awareness, and address them.

Belief addresses what the clients hold, which others might not be considered as fact. A negative belief can affect by dis-empowering the clients and create self-doubt. Beliefs directly affect the action of leadership, crisis response, the role of emotions, and communication. A positive, self-affirming belief system can change over time, influenced by the leaders through positive stimulations. Transformational leaders tap into the being and believe in fostering a positive behavior of the clients. The leader makes a difference in the client's psychological state by developing a relationship by sharing their belief and being and making a noticeable impact on their behaviors.

According to the theory of planned behavior, an individual's behavior variance is driven by attitude, subjective norms, and perceived control (Ajzen 1991). Transformational leaders develop four interconnected behavioral components known as the "Four I's": idealized influence, intellectual stimulation, inspirational motivation, and individualized consideration (Bass and Avolio 1994; Bass and Riggio 2005; Barbuto 2005; Farnsworth et al. 1969; Simic 1988). Please see Figure 9.1, which illustrates the Four I's of a transformational leader's behavioral component.

Transformational leaders maintain an identity that clients can emulate, admire, and follow. A transformational coach offers a combination of knowledge, skills, and attributes to work together to drive a transformational experience for clients. As the relationship is based on trust, leaders' behavior makes a massive difference in transformational coaching effectiveness and providing a role model (Simic 1988). The transformational leader must create a judgment-free zone for clients' mindfulness and well-being by redirecting and reframing the negative feelings without criticizing. The transformation is never easy and often takes a long period; the leaders motivate and inspire through enthusiasm and optimism around the client's vision. Each client is unique, and their challenges are different with the potential to grow, and the leader must pay attention to individual differences. There is no one-size-fits-all transformational coaching method; the leader must understand the client, earning their trust, and finding ways to delegate tasks to support clients.

## The CLEAR Method

The four levels of the CLEAR process are one of the most commonly used methods for transformational coaches created by Hawkins and Smith (2014), where transformational leaders shouldn't have a goal; instead, they focus on the time. The coaches allocate a general intent to flow in the coaching session, starting with a short introduction. The five phases of transformational leaders to address clients' needs, as explained by Hawkins and Smith, are contracting, listening, exploring, action, and review. Consider Figure 9.2, which shows the CLEAR model.

The CLEAR model also has four engagement levels: facts, behavioral patterns, reflex feelings, and assumptions. It is a combination approach of understating the client and taking actions based on the theory of planned behavior (Hawkins and Smith 2014). The contract starts with a conversation with a client, where the coach will try to understand what the coachee would like to get out

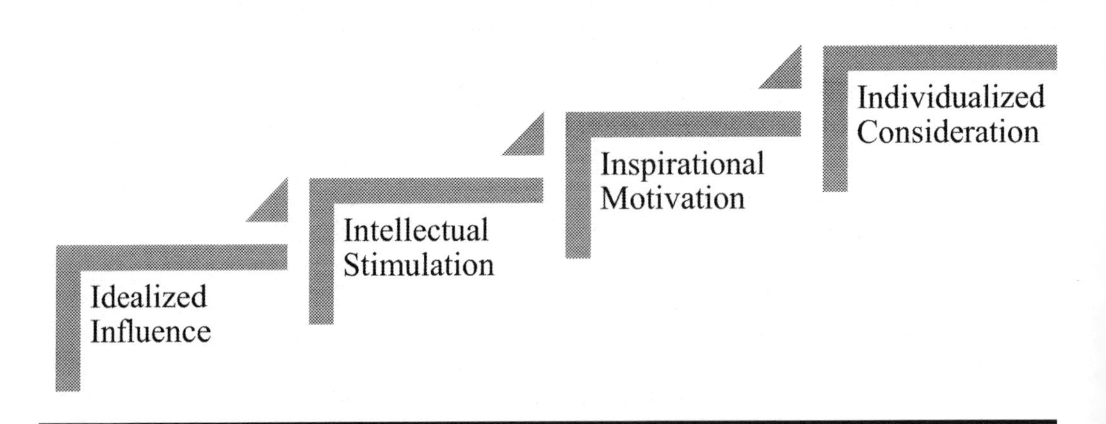


**Figure 9.1 Four I's of Transformational Leader.**

*Source:* Adapted from Simic (1998); Bass and Avolio (1994).

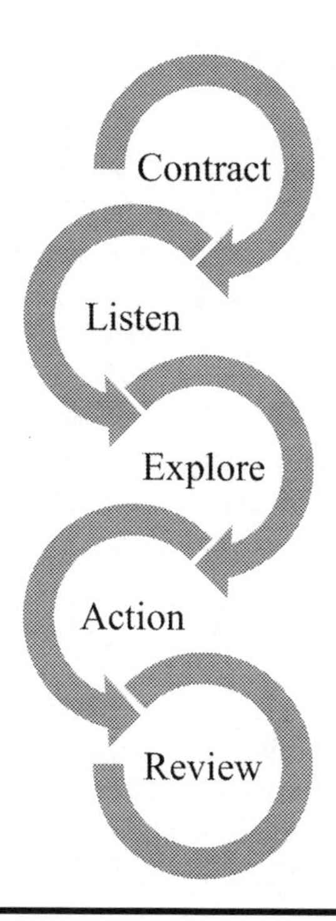


**Figure 9.2 Clear Method of Theory of Planned Behavior.**

*Source:* Hawkins and Smith (2014).

of the session, the goal, and the process. Listening helps understand the being and beliefs through reflex feelings, and assumptions and behavior through patterns and facts. It is the most crucial contribution of the coach, and a transformational coach must be a master of this skill. Coaches listen to a client's viewpoint carefully, take notes, and develop a spirit of cooperation by providing meaningful feedback. The transformational coach needs to be free from biases or judgment at any conversation stage. Besides listening, the transformational coach uses their profound observation to identify unspoken truths through choice of words or tone at this stage. One common error at this stage is trying to find a problem and offer a solution, but when coaches see a problem, they do not see the person anymore but rather focus on strategies to solve the problem, which triggers a stress response (Boyatzis et al. 2019).

The leaders identify actions and assumptions through contracting, listening, and exploring the facts from notes and observation. At the exploration stage, transformational leaders make the most important impact by asking deeper questions about the events and following up with investigative questions. The leaders act by providing a framework and timeline that helps the client prepare and plan for the future. At the review stage, the coach looks at the holistic output of the clients' results with no narrowed lens and with a broad open mind. The most important aspect of the review is identifying what worked and what did not work as expected. The CLEAR model is instrumental, with specific actions to take at each stage of discovering the client. Using planned behavior, the coaches can identify what they are looking for, such as facts, behavioral patterns, or reflex feelings. Each component carries a deeper route to understanding the client's source of concern and interpretation of their words, which coaches follow up with additional questions based on their assumptions.

## Transformational Leadership Model

Here is a small case brief before we proceed with the model:

Sheldon works for a company that supplies electrical products. He started as a sales representative and was promoted to sales manager. He loved to work for the company and felt very appreciated and recognized. He wanted to get into the corporate office and work as a senior buyer with lateral promotion; although he was a high performer, the company moved someone else from the team. He got frustrated, which affected his performance, connections, and family. He was not sure what to do at this point; what went wrong? What could he do better? Or should he just leave the organization as he felt he is not a good fit anymore? There were many negative thoughts around him, and he felt helpless. How does a transformational coach deal with this situation?

A transformational coach focuses on improving individuals' qualities and effectiveness by addressing their needs and potential. This leadership approach does not have a goal or outcome at the starting point; individuals feel a need for improvement to perform better in different capacities. The transformational coach must have the qualities to understand the need of clients better. Transformational leaders care about the people, support and encourage the client as a person, and utilize their interpersonal ability to understand the client: what motivates them? How do they accomplish goals? Or how that specific client will collaborate with the coach? The dialogues get deeper, and most transformational coaches follow a path to carry the conversation forward with attainable objectives. A transformational coach continuously challenges, inspires, influences, and motivates their clients; see Figure 9.3, which illustrates the transformational leadership model.

**Figure 9.3 Transformation Leadership Model.**

*Source:* Author's Original Creation. Copyright 2022 by Farhan Sadique.

### *Challenge*

The leaders listen and understand the client's consciousness and source of emotions before even starting the discussion. As there is no goal, the dialogues get priority, interpersonal communication stays in the core of the system. They invest time listening to the client's experiences and stories and creating an emotional bonding. As they listen and take ownership of the problem to provide a meaningful solution, they question with improvement goal. A transformational leader is self-aware and motivates an individual as a person. As they challenge clients with improvements, they are not afraid to take risks and admit mistakes.

### *Inspire*

The feedback is highly individualized, and leaders can adapt to different cases. The leader shows empathy for an adverse situation and encourages clients with an open mind. Transformational leaders are adaptable and innovative; at the same time, they lead with examples. They believe in continuous learning and improvement for themselves and the client; it is a cooperative system to develop as a team. The leaders influence their bonding, demonstrating high moral standards, values, and priorities toward the common good. It is essential to understand the value of communication, and the channel should always remain open.

### *Influence*

Transformational leaders influence followers through inspirational messages throughout their journey. The leaders look for motives, develop a common purpose, and provide feedback as needed. The most distinctive action of transformational leaders is that they are fantastic role models; they influence by example; walk the walk, not just talk the talk. The buy-in from the followers is essential in a demanding situation. The client plays something bigger than themselves; they need to play much harder and smarter to follow their sense of calling. A significant role of transformational leaders is to repeatedly remind the vision and meaningful model.

### *Motivate*

A transformational coach does not hold an iron grip to make a command; the only power is persuasion. Transformational leadership is where the coach is charged with identifying the needed change, creating a vision to guide the change through inspiration, and executing the change to enhance motivation, morale, and examples.

## Characteristics of a Transformational Coach

Emotional intelligence is often the key to developing an interpersonal relationship with the client, which helps to develop understanding and trust. Emotional intelligence comprises social intelligence, acting wisely, and pursuing others to do something; emotional intelligence combines self-awareness, managing emotion, motivating self and others, addressing others' emotions, and maintaining successful relationships (Goleman 1995). Transformational coaches might have a distinct set of emotional intelligence and continuously improve as coaches experience new challenges. Self-awareness is an important key, and the expected characteristics will be a meaningful tool for the transformational coach to evaluate and improve their emotional awareness and feelings by stepping back from experience. Interpersonal intelligence is essential for the transformational coach who helps them understand their client, their motivations, how motivating factors have influence, how they take actions, and ways to collaboratively work with clients. It is the inward capacity to respond appropriately to other people and guide the coach's behavior.

Again, transformational coaching is a way of being; it changes how we learn about ourselves as human beings in the world, and it requires a lot of engagement in learning and self-reflection. How do we practice being a good coach? Rather than telling what to do or how to do it, a transformational coach expands an individual's outlook, identifies self-limiting habits, and clarify beliefs and goals. Analyzing commonly available competencies, there are a few characteristics that help transformational coaches develop a better interpersonal relationship with the client based on trust and help create major changes. A successful transformational coach has common characteristics that demonstrate the next generation of transformational coach. Consider Figure 9.4, which illustrates the common characteristics observed in a transformational coach.

Each characteristic has a deeper connection to leadership style; Table 9.1 briefly describes how each characteristic makes a difference and provides a summary of typical characteristics of the transformational coach.

## Consciousness and Mindfulness Development of Transformational Leaders

As transformational leadership for coaching is investigated and discussed, the social and motivational factors need to be addressed. First, what is mindfulness? Renowned researcher and expert on mindfulness Kabat-Zinn (2015) describes mindfulness as:

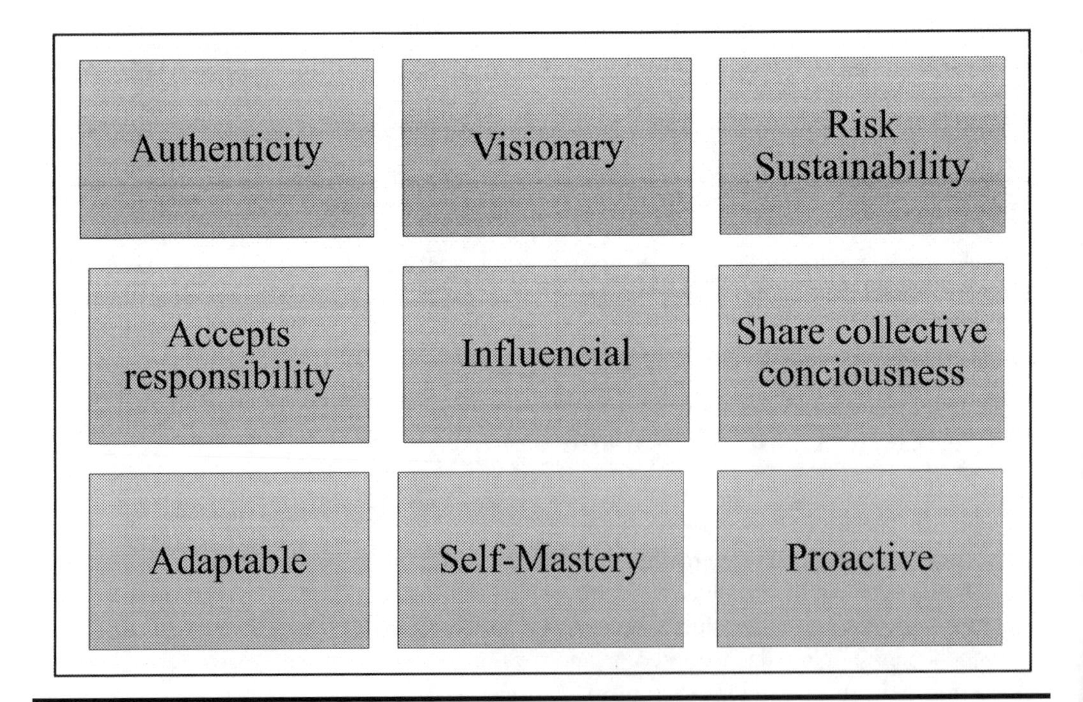


**Figure 9.4 Common Characteristics of Transformational Coach.**

*Source:* Authors' Original Creation. Copyright 2022 by Farhan Sadique.

**Table 9.1 Commonly Available Characteristics and Description of a Transformational Coach. Author's Original Creation.**

| *Typical Characteristics of a Transformational Coach* | |
|---|---|
| *Characteristics* | *Description* |
| **Authenticity** | Transformational coaches strive to stay authentic with their clients, keeping egos under control. They put the client's best interest and elicit trust to lead the best performance. |
| **Visionary** | Transformational coaches must nurture the vision for the future and cultivate the mind of clients to establish that through shifting consciousness from the present. |
| **Risk Suitability** | Depending on evaluating risk factors, transformational coaches will overcome irrational fears. Transformational coaches always take calculative intelligent risk-avoiding complacency and self-satisfaction. No transformation happens without some risk, and if the benefit outweighs the risk, coaches must pursue the goal. |
| **Accepts Responsibility** | Transformational coaches who venture into uncharted territory should be ready to accept the responsibility of the strategy does not work as anticipated. They assume some risk attached to each of their decision. |
| **Influential** | Transformational coaches have inspired others to rise to the occasion. They take the time to understand the best way to influence their client and motivate them toward the vision. A transformational coach must listen and inspire clients to think deeper and share ideas with an open mind. Words can be a powerful motivator to change people's mindsets, allowing transformational coaches to connect with their clients. According to Craig (2019), a transformational coach can take an audience and change their perspective on a particular topic with a fantastic way of communication. |
| **Share Collective Consciousness** | Transformational coaches have empathy and understands a detailed understanding of the clients. They must be free from any bias and share collective space to utilize dialogues effectively. The leader creates a positive and learning work culture promoting collective positivity and transparency. Constant meaningful communication and prioritized listening are the key factors to succeeding. |
| **Adaptability** | Adaptability helps transformational coaches to think differently and adjust their actions based on new possibilities reframing the strategy. They will make changes depending on the situation. Agile adaptability gives them the ability to stay open to innovation and creative ways of accomplishing their clients. Transformational coaches love what they do and always strive to be aligned with their values. |
| **Self-Mastery** | Self-awareness and mindfulness enable coaches to see their mindset in action and see the unconscious beliefs and assumptions without limiting themselves. Self-mastery and helping the coach to go deeper and work on personal healing and transforming core limiting beliefs seeing solutions and navigating through complexities (Anderson 2018). Transformational leaders are idealized role models who maintain high standards of moral and ethical behavior for their followers to provide a sense of vision and mission. Ego often comes on the way, preventing coaches from learning and growing, building better connections with clients, and self-mastery helps to keep it under control. |

*(Continued)*

**Table 9.1 (Continued)**

| *Typical Characteristics of a Transformational Coach* | |
|---|---|
| *Characteristics* | *Description* |
| **Initiative-Taking** | Being a proactive transformational coach can use the opportunity to detect the issue early and develop an innovative solution. Transformational coaches lead by example; any critical moments demand a response, bring unprecedented impact, and often come as an unordered surprise. Leaders' initiative-taking skills help them face the situation and sustain the moment. They are prepared to thrive, respond, and recover (LeHane 2020). |

*Source:* Copyright 2022 by Farhan Sadique.

> A moment-to-moment, non-judgmental awareness, cultivated by paying attention in a specific way, that is, in the present moment, and as non-reactively, as non-judgmentally, and as open-heartedly as possible. Mindfulness is an innate quality that we all have, but we simply need to cultivate it more through meditation practices.
>
> (1482)

Mindfulness is a state of mind that can be achieved through systematic practices or by cultivating our own stability of minds, breaking free of our persistent loss of sight and misunderstanding. Mindfulness develops nonjudgmental and non-reactive responses in leaders' minds and increases awareness of the moment. Without the right frame of mind, it's impossible to engage in effective dialogue with the client in transformational coaching, creative thinking, and eventually making the right decision while still being nonjudgmental (Brendel et al. 2021). Mindfulness practices also enable the expansion of our mind's conceptual states, which can help transformational leaders' empathy for their clients and decrease unconscious biases around age, race, health, and wealth (Brendel et al. 2021; Burgess et al. 2017; Kang et al. 2014; Krasner et al. 2009). Figure 9.5 shows the phases of conscious transformational coaching.

How does a transformational leader use consciousness? Transformational leadership is about influencing others' behaviors, understanding and relating to the followers, and developing a relationship based on trust and empathy (Bass and Riggio 2005; Stedham and Skaar 2019). To be transformed, a client needs to design what changes the client wants to see. Humans are often confined in the cage of their anticipated boundaries, and a shift in consciousness can bring the client and coach to a place where they can be engaged in effective dialogue. There are two general forms of consciousness: phenomenal consciousness orients us to the subjective form of direct experience and access consciousness orients us to conceptualization and reflection from our experience, and it is possible to use different psychological sources to help clients to guide, magnify, and concentrate on the conceptual and non-conceptual state of consciousness to bring the absolute dream without obstacles (Brendel et al. 2021).

Imagining the future might be impractical, but the challenge for leaders today is to look into a hopeless situation and build a bridge through consciousness, wisdom, and authentic leadership to surpass the human condition to reach the impractical and unattainable (Renesch 2010). Einstein warned us about the conscious mind; we cannot solve our problems with the same consciousness with which we created them, and shifting the consciousness is beneficial to take creative measures and initiate transformational practices. Mindfulness enables leaders' transformational behaviors and positively affects leaders' self-efficacy. Imagination has no boundary, and it unlocks endless possibilities for the future.

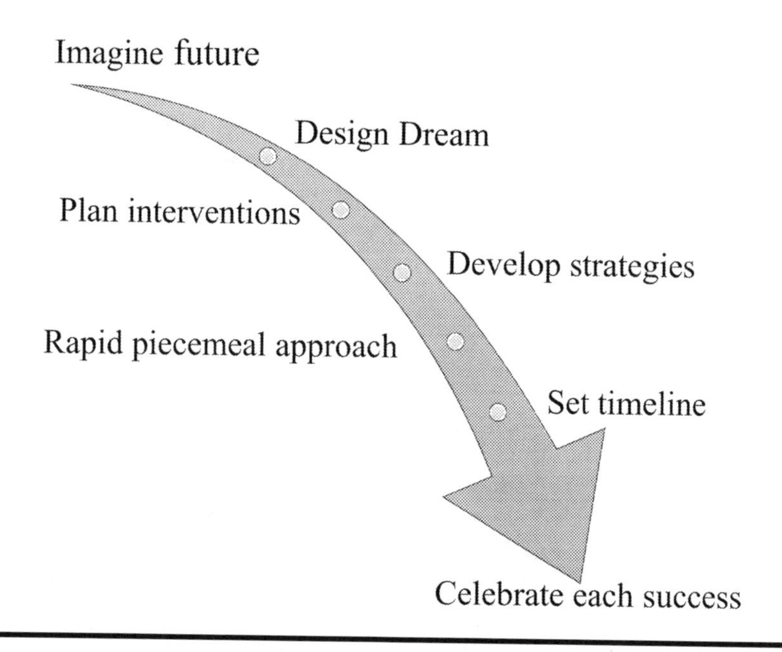


**Figure 9.5 Conscious Transformational Coaching Phases.**

*Source:* Author's Original Creation. Copyright 2022 by Farhan Sadique.

To envision the future and create something new, we need to rediscover ourselves, and that requires letting our egos go. Transformational coaches need to stay open and nonjudgmental. How do they ensure that they are in a space to unleash the potential of their clients without leading toward their own bias? It requires self-actualization, self-reflection, and crafting a body of knowledge, including values, theory, beliefs, methods, and skills. Transformational coaching requires presence at the moment to co-create the vision of the future, developing strategies to reach from present to envisioned future.

The conscious effort can bring a meaningful change in an individual's life. To free ourselves from the prison of our own minds, we need to shift our minds to a space with a magic wand and ask ourselves what we want to do with the magic wand? A powerful future vision can alone be a strong motivator for change. Being the changes you want your client to see; be an example of implementing change. You can change doing something at any time by doing things differently. Transformational leaders must examine themselves and be aware of their strengths and weaknesses with support from their clients, peers, or programs. They must have a compelling vision and strong stand for positive change.

According to Anderson (2018), even though we live in a volatile, uncertain, complex, and ambiguous time, the shift slowly leads to our dynamic paradigm of human evolution and conscious transformation. Transformational coaches must help clients to plan interventions and develop strategies. A piecemeal approach often helps them to move one step forward at a time. But those rapid actions must follow a timeline. Leaders always celebrate success at each step to keep the flow going and not only remind the client they are making progress but also remind clients about their dreams for the future. Transformational coaches help the client envision themselves with a passive role and support them on their journey to success. The coaches increase conceptual awareness by shifting consciousness and bringing out the true self.

## Tool to Understand Transformational Leadership Principles

It is essential to understand the leadership principles and values of transformational leaders. A set of questionnaires can help them understand how individuals fit in as transformational leaders. Although previous discussions provided good foundational information to define transformational leaders as people, the tools will clarify the need for improvement. It is crucial to hold some leadership positions to get a clear picture of their position. Table 9.2 provides a questionnaire that readers can use to understand self-transformational leadership principles.

## Key Takeaways

1. The expected period of transformational coaching can range from a few months to a couple of years; it requires significant time and dedication by both parties.
2. The transformational coach leads by example and uses wisdom, skills, and competencies; to develop a strategy, the client should produce his perspective of the future and the source of their desire.
3. Transformational coaching is all about making a change, and through shifting between two consciousnesses of the human mind, a transformational coach can be more inclusive and diverse.
4. It is important to understand one's own style and self-reflect to identify any bias on the one's process of change.

**Table 9.2 Questionnaire to Understand Transformational Leadership Principles. Author's Original Creation.**

| *Questionnaire to Understand Transformational Leadership Principles* | | |
|---|---|---|
| *Number* | *Questions* | *Comments* |
| 1 | What are some of your leadership beliefs? | |
| 2 | What is a metaphor or symbol that describes your leadership style | |
| 3 | What is your definition of a successful leader? | |
| 4 | What changes do you anticipate in your professional career? How do you plan for those changes? | |
| 5 | What elements of your behavior made you successful in your career? | |
| 6 | Do you work better independently or with others? | |
| 7 | What challenges have you faced in your leadership? How do you manage those challenges? | |
| 8 | What factors contributed most to your success in professional life? | |
| 9 | Who do you influence the most? How do you make an impact on that specific individual? | |
| 10 | Whom do you follow as a mentor? How do you describe their personality? | |

*Source:* Copyright 2022 by Farhan Sadique.

## Discussion Points and Coaching Questions

1. What are the steps of the transformational coaching model?
2. What characteristics must be practiced being successful as a transformational coach?
3. From your perspective, which element of transformational coaching requires the maximum time?
4. How do you rate yourself as a transformational coach or your ability to conduct the training?
5. How do you rate yourself based on the characteristics of a transformational coach?

## References


Ajzen, Icek. 1991. "The theory of planned behavior." *Organizational Behavior and Human Decision Processes, Theories of Cognitive Self-Regulation* 50, no. 2: 179–211. DOI: 10.1016/0749–5978(91)90020-T.

Anderson, Dean. 2018. "Accelerating transformation: The rise of conscious change leadership." *SOCAP Global* (blog). https://socapglobal.com/2018/12/accelerating-transformation-the-rise-of-conscious-change-leadership/

Bakhshandeh, Behnam. 2009. *Conspiracy for Greatness: Mastery of Love Within* (1st ed.). London: Primeco Education, Inc.

Barbuto, John E. 2005. "Motivation and transactional, charismatic, and transformational leadership: A test of antecedents." *Journal of Leadership & Organizational Studies* 11, no. 4: 26–40. DOI: 10.1177/107179190501100403.

Barner, Robert and Ken Ideus. 2017. *Working Deeply: Transforming Lives Through Transformational Coaching.* Emerald Group Publishing.

Bass, Bernard M., and Bruce J. Avolio. 1994. *Improving Organizational Effectiveness through Transformational Leadership.* London: SAGE.

Bass, Bernard M., and Ronald E. Riggio. 2005. *Transformational Leadership* (2nd ed.). Mahwah, NJ: Psychology Press.

Boyatzis, Richard E., Melvin Smith, and Ellen Van Oosten. 2019. "Coaching for change." *Harvard Business Review.* https://hbr.org/2019/09/coaching-for-change.

Brendel, William, Israa Samarin, and Farhan Sadique. 2021. "Open-source organization development: A platform for creating conscious of applications." *Organization Development Review* 53, no. 5: 18–31.

Burgess, Diana J., Mary Catherine Beach, and Somnath Saha. 2017. "Mindfulness practice: A promising approach to reducing the effects of clinician implicit bias on patients." *Patient Education and Counseling* 100, no. 2: 372–376. Doi: 10.1016/j.pec.2016.09.005.

Cherry, Kendra. 2020. "Effective problem-solving strategies and common obstacles." *Very well Mind.* Retrieved from https://www.verywellmind.com/problem-solving-2795008.

Cox, Elaine, David Ashley Clutterbuck and Tatiana Bachkirova. 2010. *The Complete Handbook of Coaching.* Thousand Oaks, CA: Sage Publishing.

Craig, William. 2019. "8 must-have transformational leadership qualities." *Forbes.* Retrieved from https://www.forbes.com/sites/williamcraig/2019/01/31/8-must-have-transformational-leadership-qualities/

Goleman, D. 1995. *Emotional Intelligence.* New York, NY: Bantam Books.

Hawkins, Peter and Peter Smith. 2014. Transformational coaching. In Elaine Cox, Tatiana Bachkirova, and David A. Clutterbuck (Eds.), *The Complete Handbook of Coaching.* New York: SAGE.

Kabat-Zinn, Jon. 2015. "Mindfulness." *Mindfulness* 6, no. 6: 1481–1483. DOI:10.1007/s12671–015–0456-x.

Kang, Gray Y., J. R. Gray, and J. F. Dovidio. 2014. "The nondiscriminating heart: Lovingkindness meditation training decreases implicit intergroup bias." *National Library of Medicine* 143, no: 3: 1306–1313.

Krasner, Michael S., Ronald M. Epstein, Howard Beckman, Anthony L. Suchman, Benjamin Chapman, Christopher J. Mooney, and Timothy E. Quill. 2009. "Association of an educational program in mindful communication with burnout, empathy, and attitudes among primary care physicians." *JAMA* 302, no. 12: 1284–1293. DOI: 10.1001/jama.2009.1384.

LeHane, Miles. 2020. "4 characteristics of transformational leadership." *Miles LeHane Employable Talent.* https://www.mileslehane.com/blog/4-characteristics-of-transformational-leadership

Renesch, John. 2010. "Conscious leadership: Transformational approaches to a sustainable future." *The Journal of Value Based Leadership* 3, no. 1: 1–6.

Simic, Ivana. 1988. "Transformational leadership—the key to successful management of transformational organizational changes." *The Scientific Jounral, Economics and Organization* 1, no. 6: 49–55.

Stedham, Y., and Skaar, T. B. 2019. Mindfulness, trust, and leader effectiveness: A conceptual framework. *Frontiers in Psychology* 10. www.frontiersin.org/article/10.3389/fpsyg.2019.01588

Ursillo, Dave. 2020. "What is coaching? Top 3 best definitions and common themes." https://daveursillo.com/what-is-coaching/.

# Chapter 10

# Transformational Coach

Sohel M. Imroz

## Overview

In the previous two chapters, we discussed various theories and methodologies of transformational coaching. This chapter focuses on the most critical component of transformational coaching—the transformational coach. To implement effective transformational coaching, transformational coaches must have certain mindsets and principles when working with the learners. Being knowledgeable about fundamental scientific studies and transformational coaching techniques is also useful for the transformational coaches. In addition, there are many skills and competencies required to be a successful transformational coach—coaching presence, agility, and assessment are just a few. Transformational coaches must be mindful of growing awareness of critical issues like diversity, equity, and inclusion. This chapter discusses these important aspects of transformational coaching.

**This chapter attempts to underline:**

- Mindset and principles of a transformational coach
- Knowledge of scientific studies and techniques
- Skills and competencies
- Coaching presence
- Coaching agility
- Diversity, equity, and inclusion
- Coaching assessment

## Mindset and Principles

While transformational coaching can be successful, transformational coaches must have certain mindsets and be aware of several fundamental principles when working with the learners. Jeftovic (2021) mentioned five such mindsets and principles: personalization, focusing on growth, keeping

DOI: 10.4324/9781003304074-13

course on goals, providing necessary resources, and continuity. According to Jeftovic (2021), one of the most important elements of transformational coaching is the coach's ability to provide the learners with personalized guidance, support, and encouragement. Benefits of personalization mindset and principles include receiving undivided attention and better feedback from the coach and customized learning and greater motivation for the learners (Tom Flick Leadership 2021). With personalization, a deeper level of trust is built between the coach and the learners, coach's feedback becomes more valuable and personal to the learners, and learners find themselves more engaged and motivated (Tom Flick Leadership 2021).

A growth mindset means that a person thrives on challenge and sees failure as an opportunity to leap forward for growth and development (Morin 2022). There are several ways transformational coaches can instill a growth mindset in the learners. For example, transformational coaches can encourage the learners to embrace challenges, see challenges as opportunities, reflect on failures and focus on lessons learned, welcome feedback, and view others' success as inspirational (The Peak Performance Center 2022). Transformational coaches and learners who foster a growth mindset don't give up easily, can deal with difficulties, overcome obstacles, and work harder to find success (Western Governors University 2022).

Successful transformational coaching can only take place if the goals and objectives set by the coach and the learners remain the primary focus throughout the coaching engagement (Jeftovic 2021). Ayodele (2017) offered several recommendations for setting goals and staying on course. One such recommendation is specifying the goals or objectives and prioritizing them. Many people often fail to achieve success because they establish goals that are too broad and not specific enough (Ayodele 2017). To overcome this challenge, setting SMART goals is a commonly used technique. SMART goals are **S**pecific, **M**easurable, **A**chievable, **R**elevant, and **T**ime-Bound. Figure 10.1 illustrates characteristics of a SMART goal.

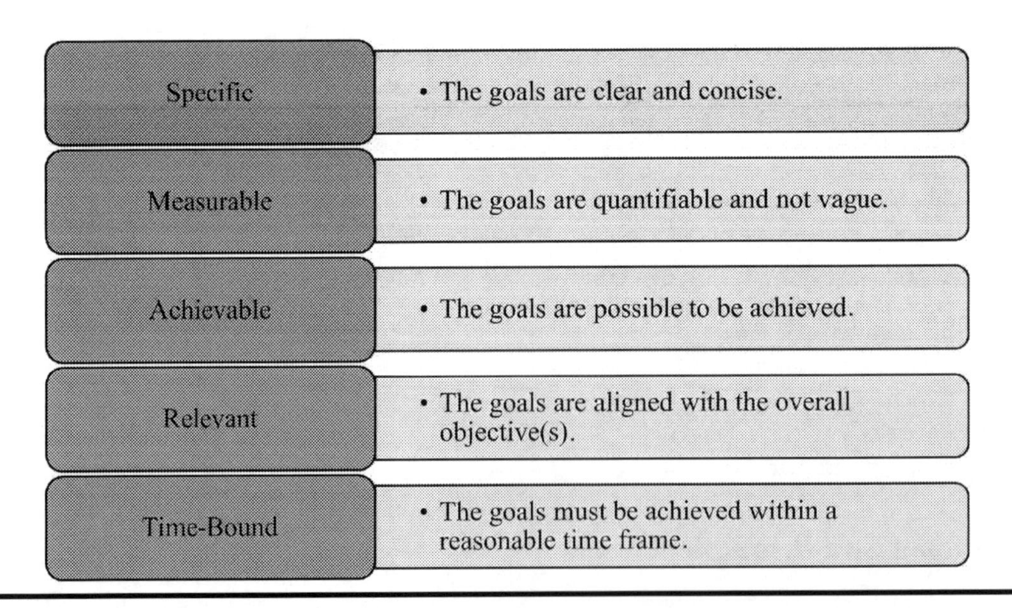


**Figure 10.1 Characteristics of a SMART goal.**

*Source:* Ayodele (2017).

Goal prioritization means identifying goals or objectives and ordering them based on their requirements, impact, urgency, value, or importance. Goal prioritization also requires us to appropriately allocate our resources such as time, effort, and attention; making sure that the most resources are utilized achieving the highest priority goals. Effectively prioritizing goals and objectives can help transformational coaches and learners reduce stress, increase productivity, create room for error checking, allow more time to relax, avoid procrastination, and keep motivated (Dalton 2021). Other recommendations offered by Ayodele (2017) for setting goals and staying on course include creating perspective and purpose, tracking progress, finding inspiration every day, and managing expectations.

Successful transformational coaching requires various tools and resources. It is the primary responsibility of the transformational coach to provide the learners with these tools and resources, or at least guide the learners and make them aware of these tools (Jeftovic 2021). Elsey (2022) provided examples of several tools and resources that may be useful for effective transformational coaching: powerful coaching questions, quizzes, journaling prompts (e.g., questions, lists, or dialoguing), metaphors or stories, personality and psychological assessments, coaching games, inspirational quotes, and so on. While these tools and resources can enhance the experience of the learners and help them get desired results more easily or faster, these tools and resources should be considered as supplementary, not replacement, to the actual transformational coaching relationship and conversation (Elsey 2022).

The last principle, according to Jeftovic (2021), is continuity. Continuity means that the learners should be able to continue in the path set out for them by the transformational coach once the transformational coaching relationship ends. If the process of transformation stops when the coaching relationship ends, then the learners are highly likely to fall back into the old habits, values, behaviors, and attitudes, thus, making the entire transformation process worthless.

## Knowledge of Scientific Studies and Techniques

To create a lasting change for the learners, Amatullah (2021) recommended transformational coaches to have knowledge on several scientific studies and transformational coaching techniques, including neuroscience, positive psychology, motivational interviewing (MI), cognitive behavioral therapy (CBT), and neuro-linguistic programming (NLP). The following section elaborates on these techniques.

- **Neuroscience** is the scientific study of the structure and function of human brain and nervous system (Amatullah 2021). Brains define who we are, what we do, store our memories, and allow us to learn (School of Neuroscience, Kings College London 2021). New thoughts and ideas are created by brain cells and brain circuits. According to Sinclair (2017), it is important for coaches to have at least the basic knowledge of how human brains work and their structure to "understand more about what could be happening inside the brain" of the learners (para. Brain basics). Sinclair (2017) listed these parts of human brains and the basic functions of each brain part:
  - Frontal lobe (thinking, memory, behavior, and movement)
  - Temporal lobe (hearing, learning, and feelings)
  - Brain stem (breathing, heart rate, and temperature)
  - Parietal lobe (language and touch)
  - Occipital lobe (sight)
  - Cerebellum (balance and coordination)

- **Positive psychology** is the scientific study of strengths with techniques to help individuals thrive at their highest (Amatullah 2021). It can also be defined as the study of what makes our life most worth living (Peterson 2006). There are several reasons transformational coaches should be familiar with positive psychology principles and values. For example, using positive psychology, coaches can better understand the learners' thoughts, feelings, and behaviors based on their strengths rather than weaknesses. Positive psychology can also encourage transformational coaches to build good lives for the learners rather than repairing bad ones. Last, using positive psychology, coaches can transform the lives of average learners to "great" instead of transforming their lives merely to "normal" (Ackerman 2022).
- **Motivational interviewing (MI)** is a learner-centered, directive method for encouraging the learners through the stages of change (Amatullah 2021). According to Miller and Rollnick (2013), motivational interviewing is
- . . . a collaborative, goal-oriented style of communication with particular attention to the language of change. It is designed to strengthen personal motivation for and commitment to a specific goal by eliciting and exploring the person's own reasons for change within an atmosphere of acceptance and compassion. (29)

Motivational interviewing can be useful to transformational coaches especially when the learners experience mixed feelings about the change (high ambivalence), are doubtful of their abilities to change (low confidence), are uncertain about whether they want to make the change (low desire), and are unclear about the disadvantages of their current situation or the advantages of the change (low importance) (Miller and Rollnick 2013).

Transformational coaches can use several key spirits of motivational interviewing during the coaching engagement with the learners: partnership, evocation, acceptance, and compassion. The partnership must be a collaborative process between the coach and the learners. Evocation is achieved when the coach draws out the learners' priorities and values to explore reasons for change and support the learners' success. Transformational coaches must accept a nonjudgmental stance with the learners and understand their perspectives and experiences. Coaches must also express empathy to the learners and highlight their strengths. Finally, coaches must respect the learners with compassion by selflessly promoting their welfare and well-being (Motivational Interviewing Network of Trainers 2019).

- **Cognitive Behavioral Therapy (CBT)** is a type of psychotherapy in which faulty or negative patterns of thought about the self and the world (e.g., depression, anxiety, eating disorder, panic disorders, etc.) are challenged to alter unwanted behavior patterns (Amatullah 2021; Stepko 2022). CBT can be useful for the learners with other types of emotional challenges, such as treating mental illness, coping with stressful life events, managing relationship conflicts, overcoming emotional trauma due to abuse or violence, and managing chronic physical symptoms (Mayo Clinic 2019).

Learners with these types of negative thinking and life experiences often manifest self-criticism or guilt or overestimate the likelihood of something harmful happening (Stepko 2022). Transformational coaches can use these four steps of CBT to help learners overcome these challenges and achieve their desired goals (Mayo Clinic 2019):

- Identify troubling situations or conditions in the learner's life.
- Learn the learner's thoughts, emotions, and beliefs about these problems.
- Identify negative or inaccurate thinking of the learner.

- Reshape negative or inaccurate thinking.
- **Neuro-linguistic programming (NLP)** is a field of study that attempts to build a set of transferable skills (e.g., communication, personal development, etc.) by programming the subconscious and unconscious mind (Amatullah 2021). While NLP is often considered pseudoscientific, transformational coaches may use various reframing techniques found in NLP to help the learners "changing the mind map to align with situational reality" (Ramanathan 2021, para. Reframing). Some of the reframing techniques are 6-steps reframing, timeline therapy, core transformation, change of state, perceptual positions, and visualization.

## Skills and Competencies

Animas Center for Coaching (2019) mentioned several skills and competencies necessary for transformational coaches: deep listening, holding space, observing and identifying, reflecting back, and challenge. The following section elaborates:

- **Deep listening** is the foundation of any effective transformational coaching. Deep listening means the transformational coach is aware of both what is being said and that what remains unsaid. Evans (2021) mentioned four valuable practices for transformational coaches to deepen their listening skill. These practices are:
  - Listen with whole self.
  - Pay attention to what is being said beyond the words—in the learner's tone of voice, choice of words, ideas, concepts, body language, etc.
  - Be mindful of any bodily reaction when communicating with the learner—such as muscle tightening, goosebumps on skin, shiver down the spine, increased heart rate, heavy breathing, etc.
  - Listen to intuition or "gut feeling".
  - Enter the learner's world of language and meaning.
  - Instead of assuming understanding of the true meaning of the learner's words or ideas, transformational coaches should inquire about their true definitions and meanings.
  - Watch out for the learner's underlying patterns of thoughts, values, and beliefs.
  - Create spaciousness in listening.
  - Practice silence to refrain from interrupting and talking over the learner to better understand what is being said and how.
  - Minimize inner chatter or self-talk and fragmented attention.
  - Connect with the learner.
  - Listen to the learner intently and intentionally.
  - Finally, believe in the learner.
- **Holding space:** A holding space refers to a safe learning environment created by transformational coaches where they are physically, mentally, and emotionally present for the learners. According to the Center for Transformational Coaching (2021), a holding space is a nonjudgmental learning environment full of compassion that offers the learners with more than a surface-level conversation; go deeper within; illuminate innate feelings, biases, or thoughts; and be able to express them for transformation. In such a learning environment, learners will make the journey from fear to acceptance, allowance, and trust, as they experience any situation, emotion, or belief (2021). The Gender and Sexuality Therapy Center (2020) offers a few tips for transformational coaches to create a holding space:

- Practice active listening—coaches should listen to the learners carefully with the genuine intention of understanding what they're saying and repeat what they've said to ensure proper understanding.
- Don't jump into problem-solving mode—transformational coaches should be nonjudgmental and must minimize the urge of offering solutions without understanding the learners.
- Don't center yourself—coaches should keep their own issues, biases, and experiences separate during their interaction with the learners and keep their focus solely on the learner.
- Reassure learners you believe them—coaches should affirm the learners that they trust them and believe their knowledge, intuition, and experiences.
- Be open to whatever emotions come up—learners can become vulnerable in a holding space and may display various ranges of emotions, even confusing and conflicting emotions. Therefore, coaches must be patient with the learners and reassure that they are with the learners no matter what emotions or feelings are displayed.

■ **Observing and identifying:** This competency refers to transformational coaches' ability to deeply see the learners' beliefs and patterns of behavior that are both readily apparent and hidden below the surface (Animas Center for Coaching 2019). The OBSERVE coaching model of Amit Soni, based on International Coaching Federation's framework and competencies, can be useful in practicing this competency (International Coach Academy 2022). The OBSERVE coaching model stands for Objective, Being, Support, Empower, Reflection, Vow, and Evaluation. Table 10.1 summarizes the phases of the OBSERVE coaching model, the purpose of each phase, and pertinent questions for the coaches to ask during each phase of the model (International Coach Academy 2022).

**Table 10.1 The OBSERVE Coaching Model: Phases, Purpose, and Questions.**

| *The OBSERVE Coaching Model* | |
|---|---|
| *Phase* | *Purpose and Questions* |
| **Objective** | Purpose: Establish the coaching agreement and set the goals or outcomes.<br>• What would you like to talk about today?<br>• What do you hope to gain from the sessions?<br>• What are the implications of this problem?<br>• How will you notice your problem has been resolved? |
| **Being** | Purpose: Build rapport to understand the real barriers, establish the coaching agreement.<br>• What does this mean to you?<br>• What is the significance of having this goal?<br>• What is the motivation for bringing this up?<br>• How will you know that you clearly understand the topic?<br>• What are you learning about yourself? |
| **Support** | Purpose: Help the learner to move forward.<br>• Where are you now?<br>• Where do you want to be?<br>• What's getting in the way?<br>• What else?<br>• What does it tell you? |

| *The OBSERVE Coaching Model* | |
|---|---|
| *Phase* | *Purpose and Questions* |
| **Empower** | Purpose: Enlighten, to illuminate; clarify; create awareness to clarify the gap.<br>• I hear the high spirit in your voice; your energy to me feels strong as you talk about your passion for this idea?<br>• I hear no excitement in your voice; your energy feels low when you speak about this idea?<br>• How does it feel to you?" |
| **Reflection** | Purpose: Reflect and acknowledge the wisdom inside.<br>• What have you accomplished since we started working together?<br>• What are you most proud of, beyond the accomplishments?<br>• Who/how did you have to be to accomplish those things? |
| **Vow** | Purpose: Enable personal commitment, motivation, identify and commit to action.<br>• What would be the smallest first step for you to move forward?<br>• With this realization what do you need to do next steps?<br>• What support mechanisms will you need to support this goal?<br>• What do you think you will need to do?<br>• How could you make the tasks/actions more enjoyable? |
| **Evaluation** | Purpose: Accelerate progress and closure the session. Check milestone, plan next steps with accountability.<br>• How successful was this session?<br>• What would you like to acknowledge yourself for today's session?<br>• What did you learn from this period?<br>• What's your next step after today?<br>• Is there another problem that should be discussed? |

*Source:* Adapted from International Coach Academy (2022).

- **Reflecting back:** This competency is demonstrated when transformational coaches give feedback to the learner and share valuable information they obtained during the coaching sessions. Reflecting back may be accomplished by providing three types of feedback: appreciation, coaching, and evaluation (Vrabie 2021). Appreciation feedback means recognizing and rewarding the learners for great work. Coaching feedback helps learners expand their knowledge, skills, and capabilities. Evaluation feedback assesses learners against a set of standards, aligning expectations and informing decision making (Vrabie 2021).
- **Challenge:** This competency is expressed when transformational coaches ask relevant, often difficult, questions of learners to elicit information, bias, assumption, or attitude change and guide the transformation. Examples of such questions are presented in Table 10.1 earlier in this section.

## Coaching Presence

Coaching presence can be described as when the coaches are present with the learners "moment-by-moment and, at times, in physical reference, too" (Bhattacharya 2018, 1). According to International Coaching Federation (2022), coaching presence refers to the coach's ability to be conscious and to create spontaneous relationship with the learners utilizing a style that is open, flexible, and confident. Exhibiting coaching presence helps create a safe space and a learning environment that allows the learners to dig out their inner feelings, biases, or thoughts for transformation (Bhattacharya 2018). Coaching presence is also important to support co-creation of the transformational coaching experience, to establish authenticity and trust in the coaching relationship, and, ultimately, to transcend from "doing" to "being" (Bhattacharya 2018).

To demonstrate effective coaching presence, transformational coaches should act on these behaviors (International Coaching Federation 2022):

1. Be present and flexible during the coaching process.
2. Access own intuition and trust their inner knowing.
3. Be willing to take risks and open to not knowing.
4. Explore different ways to work with the learners and understand what is most effective.
5. Use humor effectively to create energy and a relaxing and safe learning atmosphere.
6. Be able to confidently shift perspectives and experiment with new possibilities.
7. Self-manage and be confident in dealing with learners' strong emotions.

## Coaching Agility

Broadly speaking, coaching is about unlocking others' personal potential, helping them find different ways to do things, supporting them trying something new, and assisting them in developing themselves (Linders 2019). Agile coaches, or coaches having agility, help the learners transform and adopt new ways of working using agile practices and principles. According to the 2021 State of Agile Coaching Report,

> an agile coach helps organizations, teams, and individuals adopt agile practices and methods while embedding agile values and mindsets. The goal of an agile coach is to foster more effective, transparent, and cohesive teams, and to enable better outcomes, solutions, and products/services for customers.
>
> (State of Agile Coaching Report 2021, 3)

The concept of agility is based on the values and principles of the Manifesto for Agile Software Development (Linders 2019), and in transformational coaching, agility can be interpreted as a way of thinking that explains how learners can work together to deliver value. To incorporate agility in transformational coaching, Linders (2019, para. How I "coach" agility) often combines "teaching, facilitating, mentoring, coaching, and experience sharing to best serve people." Linders (2019) practices these behaviors, which may be useful for transformational coaches to reflect agility:

- Listen to the learners and help them explore what goals they want to accomplish and why those goals matter to them.
- Help the learners discover what they already know and the skills, strengths, and abilities they already have.
- Support the learners in visualizing and understanding how they think, work, and make decisions.
- Create and foster a learning environment where the learners can share their experiences and learn from each other.

- Help the learners reflect on how things are going and take action when necessary.
- Share knowledge and experience to guide the learners about possible solutions that might make them more valuable and productive.

## Diversity, Equity, and Inclusion (DEI)

To be effective and successful as a transformational coach, coaches must be mindful and respectful of the learners' diversity. According to DEI Extension (2022, para. What Is Diversity, Equity, and Inclusion?), "Diversity is the presence of differences that may include the learners' race, gender, religion, sexual orientation, ethnicity, nationality, socioeconomic status, language, (dis)ability, age, religious commitment, or political perspective." Transformational coaches should be especially attentive to those learners who are underrepresented in the classroom or in the broader society because they are more likely to experience alienation, marginalization, and loneliness (Rokach 2014).

Coaches should also maintain equity throughout the coaching relationship and provide an inclusive learning environment for the learners. Equity is promoting fair treatment, justice, equality of opportunity and advancement, and impartiality within the procedures, processes, and distribution of resources (Rosencrance 2021). The Society of Human Resource Management has described inclusion as the extent to which individuals feel welcomed, respected, supported, and valued as a team member, employee, or learner. Diverse and marginalized learners can enjoy the inclusion outcomes when the coaching relationship is inviting to all. Ladda (2016) illustrated several steps that can be followed by transformational coaches to create a more inclusive learning environment for all:

- **Step 1 (knowing):** Transformational coaches need to educate themselves on how to create an inclusive and respectful environment for classrooms and teams. Coaches should also know about regulatory laws that protect the learners. At first, coaches can learn about anti-discrimination and anti-bullying laws in their state using the internet. In addition, they should attend conferences on team-building and acquire resources (books, videos, etc.) about team-building and problem-solving activities promoting diversity, equity, and inclusion.
- **Step 2 (showing):** Coaches need to demonstrate practical ways of being respectful and inclusive. They can use signage in various places (e.g., lobby, locker room, conference room, etc.) of the learning center that reinforces the importance of inclusive and respectful behavior. Coaches should use language with learners that is inclusive and respectful regardless of their race, religion, culture, or sexual orientation. This can be done by implementing a formal policy prohibiting any racist, sexist, or homophobic language.
- **Step 3 (setting the tone):** Transformational coaches need to promote a culture of inclusion and respect among the learners. Coaches should provide the learners with activities to define respect and inclusive culture, celebrate learners' differences, and have learners develop rules and practices resulting in positive team culture.
- **Step 4 (stepping up and stepping in):** When learners' actions or behavior undermine the culture of inclusiveness, coaches must respond appropriately. For example, coaches must not tolerate when learners make a racist, sexist, or homophobic remark, and coaches should also guide the learners toward appropriate actions and behaviors that reflect inclusiveness.

Coaches can refer the learners to other resources, speakers, and professionals with expertise in promoting diversity and inclusion.

- **Step 5 (following up):** Coaches need to continue to promote plans, actions, and behaviors to maintain a positive team culture by reinforcing an inclusive and respectful culture. Various team-building activities such as position-appreciation practice day, peer-coaching, silence experiment (Freudenberg 2014), and so on, encourage inclusive collaboration culture. Coaches can also encourage learners to attend conferences and seminars that promote various issues related to diversity, equity, and inclusion.
- **Step 6 (building a legacy):** Finally, by reinforcing proper team culture and leading by example, transformational coaches can build a legacy that values learning and experience in a respectful and inclusive environment. Coaches can invite former learners to speak to the new learners and have them share their examples and experiences related to the importance of diversity, equity, and inclusion. Activities like this can be a great way to build and sustain the legacy of the transformational coaches and the learners.

## Coaching Assessment

Aguilar (2013) proposed a rubric for assessment of transformational coaches based on the following six categories.

1. **Knowledge base:** The coach understands and applies core coaching knowledge components. Knowledge base includes disciplines or subject areas (e.g., literacy, leadership, classroom management, etc.) on which the coach coaches, coaching approaches, adult learning theory, system thinking, emotional intelligence theory, and understanding of change management.
2. **Relationships:** The coach develops and maintains relationships based on trust and respect and demonstrates cultural competency to advance the work. The relationships category may also include how well the coach maintains confidentiality, cultural competence, and the ability to demonstrate empathy and compassion.
3. **Strategic design:** The coach develops strategic work plans based on data and a variety of assessments. The coach is continuously guided by the work plan, makes adjustments as necessary, and monitors progress along the way. Assessing this category should include how effectively the coach uses SMARTE (Specific, Measurable, Achievable, Relevant, Time-Bound, and Evaluable) goals with the learners as a part of the work plan. Besides the five components of the SMART goal-setting technique described earlier in this chapter (see Figure 10.1), many coaches use **E**valuable as an additional component. This additional component outlines the following (Aguilar 2013):

    a. What method will the coaches use to evaluate their goal setting process?
    b. Who will provide objective feedback?
    c. Did the coaches accomplish their goal? What worked? What didn't work? What did they learn?

Finally, strategic design should also assess how well the coaches break down the learning into chunks and identify coaching strategies for the learners.

4. **The Coaching Conversation:** The coach demonstrates a wide range of listening and questioning skills and effectively moves conversations in meeting the learner's goals. This category assesses the coaches' ability to effectively use a range of conversational coaching approaches and listen to the learners with empathy using nonjudgmental language.
5. **Strategic actions:** The coach implements high-leverage strategic actions that support learners' goals and uses a gradual release of responsibility model to develop their autonomy. This category assesses the coaches' ability to observe the learners in various contexts, guide them to develop reflective capacities when receiving feedback, and engage the learners in various coaching activities.
6. **Coach as learner:** The coach consistently reflects on his or her own learning and development and actively seeks ways to develop skill, knowledge, and capacity. Common elements assessed under this category may include how well the coach solicits feedback from the learners, seeks professional learning opportunities from other coaches, and stays informed of current research and best practices. Other elements for assessment may include the coach's ability to collaborate with other subject matter experts, to demonstrate emotional intelligence, and to be aware of their own personal transformation.

## Key Takeaways

The followings are the main takeaways from this chapter:

1. Transformational coaches must have a certain mindset and be aware of several fundamental principles when working with the learners: personalization, focusing on growth, keeping course on goals, providing necessary resources, and continuity.
2. Transformational coaches should be knowledgeable of several scientific studies and transformational coaching techniques, including neuroscience, positive psychology, motivational interviewing (MI), cognitive behavioral therapy (CBT), and neuro-linguistic programming (NLP).
3. There are several skills and competencies necessary for transformational coaches. Key skills and competencies include deep listening, holding space, observing and identifying, reflecting back, and challenge.
4. Transformational coaches should demonstrate coaching presence with the learners by being conscious and creating spontaneous relationships with the learners utilizing learning styles that are open, flexible, and confident.
5. Transformational coaches should behave in ways that reflect coaching agility.
6. Coaching assessment should include assessing the coaches' knowledge base, relationships, strategic design, coaching conversation, strategic actions, and their ability to reflect on their own learning and development.

## Discussion Points and Coaching Questions

1. This chapter provides several examples of mindsets and principles of a transformational coach. In your experience, what other mindset(s) and principle(s) could be useful for transformational coaches?
2. What other types of knowledge of scientific studies and techniques do you recommend for transformational coaches? Please explain.

3. What other skills and competencies should transformational coaches demonstrate?
4. Describe how you would demonstrate coaching presence and coaching agility as a transformational coach.
5. Explain the role of diversity, equity, and inclusion to become an effective transformational coach.
6. This chapter provides a list of coaching assessment categories. Are there other categories that should be included during coaching assessment? Please explain why.

## References

Ackerman, Courtney. 2022. "What is positive psychology & why is it important?" https://positivepsychology.com/what-is-positive-psychology-definition/#definition-positive-psychology

Aguilar, Elena. 2013. *The art of coaching: Effective strategies for school transformation*. San Francisco, CA: Jossey-Bass. https://brightmorningteam.com/wp-content/uploads/2017/09/Transformational-Coaching-Rubric.pdf

Animas Center for Coaching. 2019. "What is transformational coaching?" www.animascoaching.com/our-knowledge/faqs/what-is-transformational-coaching/

Amatullah, Ayisha. 2021. "Transformational coaching techniques you need to know." www.universal-coachinstitute.com/transformation-coaching-techniques-you-need-to-know/

Ayodele, Sade. 2017. "6 tips to set goals and stay the course." www.thebisforboss.com/blog/2017/10/16/4-tips-to-stay-the-course-achieve-your-goals

Bhattacharya, Sadhan. 2018. "The gift of coaching presence." https://coachingfederation.org/blog/gift-coaching-presence

Center for Transformational Coaching. 2021. "Holding space: A practice of presence, heart and leadership." www.centerfortransformationalcoaching.com/holding-space/

Dalton, Cynthia. 2021. "Prioritizing your life: The how, what, when, and why guide." www.calcoast.edu/news/prioritizing-your-life-how-what-when-why-guide

DEI Extension. 2022. "Defining DEI." https://dei.extension.org/extension-resource/defining-dei/

Elsey, Emma-Louise. 2022. "The complete guide to life coaching tools, forms and exercises (with examples)." www.thecoachingtoolscompany.com/life-coaching-tools-forms-exercises-complete-guide-with-examples/

Evans, Sarah. 2021. "Deep listening: Create a sacred & transformative space for your clients." www.thecoachingtoolscompany.com/deep-listening-create-sacred-transformative-space-for-clients-sarah-evans-mcc/

Freudenberg, Sallyann. 2014. "Inclusive collaboration and the silence experiment." www.infoq.com/articles/inclusive-collaboration-silence-experiment/

International Coach Academy. 2022. "The observe noticed or perceive". https://coachcampus.com/coach-portfolios/coaching-models/observe/

International Coaching Federation. 2022. "Current ICF core competencies." https://coachingfederation.org/credentials-and-standards/core-competencies

Jeftovic, Anja. 2021. "Transformational coaching: Complete guide." https://upcoach.com/group-coaching/transformational-coaching-complete-guide/

Ladda, Shawn. 2016. "Creating respectful and inclusive environments: The role of physical educators and coaches". *Journal of Physical Education, Recreation & Dance* 87(3): 3–4. www.tandfonline.com/doi/pdf/10.1080/07303084.2016.1131536?needAccess=true

Linders, Ben. 2019. "Coaching true agility." www.benlinders.com/2019/coaching-true-agility/

Mayo Clinic. 2019. "Cognitive behavioral therapy." www.mayoclinic.org/tests-procedures/cognitive-behavioral-therapy/about/pac-20384610

Miller, William and Rollnick, Stephen. 2013. *Motivational interviewing: Helping people to change* (3rd ed.). New York, NY: Guilford Press.

Morin, Amanda. 2022. "What is growth mindset?" www.understood.org/en/articles/growth-mindset

Motivational Interviewing Network of Trainers. 2019. "Understanding motivational interviewing." https://motivationalinterviewing.org/understanding-motivational-interviewing

Peterson, Christopher. 2006. *A Premier in Positive Psychology*. New York, NY: Oxford University Press.

Ramanathan, Ram. 2021. "5 NLP concepts that support coaching." https://coacharya.com/blog/neuro-linguistic-programming-nlp-techniques-benefit-coaching/

Rokach, Ami. 2014. "Loneliness of the Marginalized." *Open Journal of Depression* 3: 147–153.

Rosencrance, Linda. 2021. "Diversity, equity, and inclusion." www.techtarget.com/searchhrsoftware/definition/diversity-equity-and-inclusion-DEI

School of Neuroscience, Kings College London. 2021. "What is neuroscience?" www.kcl.ac.uk/neuroscience/about/what-is-neuroscience

Sinclair, Toby. 2017. "Neuroscience for coaches: How can it help you?" www.tobysinclair.com/post/neuroscience-for-coaches

State of Agile Coaching Report. 2021. https://f.hubspotusercontent40.net/hubfs/6606649/State-Of-Agile-Coaching-Report_February-2021.pdf

Stepko, Barbara. 2022. "How to find the right therapist." www.aarp.org/health/conditions-treatments/info-2020/find-mental-health-therapist.html

The Gender and Sexuality Therapy Center. 2020. "What 'holding space' means + 5 tips to practice." www.gstherapycenter.com/blog/2020/1/16/what-holding-space-means-5-tips-to-practice

The Peak Performance Center. 2022. "Fixed mindset vs. growth mindset." https://thepeakperformancecenter.com/development-series/mental-conditioning/mindsets/fixed-mindset-vs-growth-mindset/

Tom Flick Leadership. 2021. "The benefits of personalized coaching." https://tomflick.com/2021/06/23/the-benefits-of-personalized-coaching/

Vrabie, Evelina. 2021. "The three forms of feedback: Appreciation, coaching and evaluation." https://cto-craft.com/blog/the-three-forms-of-feedback-appreciation-coaching-and-evaluation/

Western Governors University. 2022. "What is a growth mindset? 8 steps to develop one." www.wgu.edu/blog/what-is-growth-mindset-8-steps-develop-one1904.html

# IV TRANSFORMATIONAL COACHING STRUCTURE, COMMUNICATION AND EFFECTIVENESS

Every structure is designed to support the learning, or enhance the skills and competencies, or teach participants how to get the maximum benefits from the structures and designed approaches. Transformational coaching is not different from any other such undertakings. Part IV is about these underlying structures and variety of elements that will make the transformational coaching a successful and long-lasting undertaking.

## Chapter 11. Workable Structure for Transformational Coaching

Chapter 11 addresses transformational coaching structure and effectiveness in coaching engagement, rapport, and workability.

## Chapter 12. Effective Communication and Active Listening Caused by Tranformational Coaching

Barriers to transformational coaching, and the role of inner chatter, effective communication, and active listening in transformational coaching effectiveness are covered in Chapter 12.

## Chapter 13. Personal Effectiveness

Chapter 13 discusses how we realize the way we relate to ourselves, to others, at work and in the world we have created around us.

DOI: 10.4324/9781003304074-14

# Chapter 11

# Workable Structure for Transformational Coaching

Behnam Bakhshandeh

## Overview

Everything that makes a difference for people, teams, and organizations has a structure designed to support the learning, enhance skills and competencies, and teach participants how to get the maximum benefits of their approach to learning. Transformational coaching is not different from any such undertakings.

This chapter covers main elements of a workable coaching structure for conducting transformational coaching, whether done on a one-on-one basis or in a team or group setting. This chapter will cover these elements of the transformational coaching approach:

- Transformational coaching structure
- Coaching engagement
- The gear wheels of coaching workability
- Rapport and background of relatedness
- Authenticity: expression of integrity, responsibility, and accountability

## Transformational Coaching Foundation

For the participants to benefit from coaching processes, they need to be committed, engaged, intentional, and have a clear purpose. They need to announce their intentions and commitment they are bringing to the coaching process. A transformational coach needs to direct and guide their participants to understand the coaching structure and what is expected of them during the coaching undertaking. It is a professional relationship.

DOI: 10.4324/9781003304074-15

## *Talking* about *Issues or Talking* for *Breakthroughs*

We all can *discuss* issues, or we can have a conversation *for* having a breakthrough regarding issues. During transformational coaching, conversations for having realizations, having awareness, understanding, and creating an action plan that would cause having a breakthrough on that issue is the topic of the coaching conversation. Conversations *about* issues and the topics that are not productive are to just talk about them with no commitment to alter the issues or take on any change efforts to have a breakthrough on change interventions. In talking *about* issues, the participants give all the reasons, justifications, and explanations why they can't do something about the issues, or the role others are playing in the persistency of the issues. Basically, they just point fingers outside of themselves not in their direction (Bakhshandeh 2015). Conversations for having breakthroughs regarding an issue is to have an introspective view about our role, our part, our responsibilities on what happened and why something has happened. What was or continue to be our expectations from the situations or our unrealistic needs from others involved with the issues? Conversations *for* something starts with us becoming accountable for what we created from our experiences in life and what unrealistic stories we came up with to cover our own lack of responsibility for or engagement with the issues (2015).

### *Influence of Our Words on Our Experience*

What we are saying to ourselves, internally or externally, to express our experiences is the basis of our surrounding environment. We are all adding together words and creating sentences that become the routine conversations we have with others. I am sure you can recognize some of your routine conversations and recognize them when others talk to you about their experience of dealing with life. We use disempowering words that directly create negative experiences in life, at work, and at home.

Conversations for having breakthroughs in issues are for individuals to see their part of their own experiences in life. People say things as they think like it is the truth, like "I am not good enough for . . .," or "I can't get this done . . .," or "It is so hard to . . .. " or "Nobody can do this . . .. " Many other sentences are generated from a lack of complete understanding of themselves and their abilities or lack of complete awareness of situations, but it is always much easier to express the first thing that comes to mind and display our opinions. The transformational coaching process brings the participants to the point of understanding what they have, such as opinions and viewpoints of themselves, others, and what they do. The human mind can make up many stories, day in and day out. However, our understanding of how we operate and the degree of how frequently we listen to our negative internal chatter about ourselves and others open doors to our personal awareness of our mindset and behaviors. "We are building our lives daily, hourly, moment-by-moment through our thoughts. With them, we are molding our futures" (Bakhshandeh 2015, 23).

Suppose we will use transformational coaching to resolve issues and have a breakthrough in handling situations. In that case, we shall think and speak *for* the breakthrough while ceasing to talk *about* it through nagging and complaining and gossiping. Commencing in irresponsible speaking or victimizing scenarios only adds to the weight of sticking to negativity and steering us away from causing any breakthrough in resolving issues or being effective in what we are doing (2015).

During the transformational coaching process, a coach will direct the participants to notice their negative conversations and the impact of the words they use of their overall personal experience, of others, and of what they do. Then, the coach will guide the participants to use more empowering words to express their expertise and describe their roles in such an experience.

## *Coaching Conversations: Focused Dialogues*

Transformational coaching is a constructive conversation based on the recognized participants' needs, the desired outcomes, and their commitment to learning something about themselves and their performance. In this focused conversation, the transformational coach assists the participants to dig into all facets of their *being*, while holding up a mirror for them to recognize their mindset, attitude, and behaviors around their personal or professional (as per the coaching intention and desired outcome) results.

A transformational coaching conversation is about opening participants' minds and eyes to the world around them and coaching them to see who they are in relation to this world created through the years. The best way that participants will benefit from transformational coaching is to bring their lives to the conversations and the practices, taking it personally and relating the elements of their learning to their lives versus going through the conversations and practices to collect information. I am sure you have heard people saying, "Knowledge is power." No, having the knowledge is not power! However, the implementation and application of that knowledge cause the power. "What you know makes no difference. What you do with what you know makes a difference" (Bakhshandeh 2015, 23).

Here is an example. Everyone knows how to lose weight, but how many actually lose weight? Probably few! Just pay attention to all the exercise equipment or weight loss commercials. You can get why there is so much emphasis on different weight loss approaches, because the marketing companies know people will not follow up on what they know! The simple fact is that unless an individual gets the barriers to their mindset and attitude around their relationship to themselves and weight, they will not break through these barriers to change their behaviors. We can use the same example for productivity, performance, and relationships.

Transformational coaching conversations assist participants to put their thoughts into actions by designing new practices that would alter their views of themselves and the issues they are focusing on. This intentionality happens during transformational coaching conversations. We can describe characteristics of coaching conversations as follows:

- Coaching is a highly effective tool for individuals, teams, and organizations.
- It happens with individuals committed to a different future than what is predictable.
- It is a nonlinear inquiry into the individuals' authenticity.
- It will assist and guide ambitious and open-minded individuals who strive for excellence.
- It is an empowering conversation that will expand the participants' perspectives and allows for viewing a whole new possibility.
- It helps to discover and identify what participants want from their personal and professional lifestyle.
- It assists participants in generating action plans and strategies to fulfill their desired outcomes.
- It will help individuals to identify the essence of who they are.
- It will generate awareness of people's patterns and will assist them in getting free from limiting beliefs, mindsets, and behaviors.
- It helps individuals invent their life vision, design their personal and professional goals, and create their future.

(Bakhshandeh 2015; Bakhshandeh 2009)

## Transformational Coaching Engagement

Transformational coaches use inquiries and dialogues, helping participants implement processes and action plans designed to empower them in pursuing their desired outcomes. Participants are coached to look directly at their fundamental beliefs and perceived realities about themselves and others that have determined the directions in their personal and professional lives. As participants become more aware of such fundamental beliefs and perceived realities, they will learn to understand the source of such beliefs and take responsibility for their mindset, attitudes, behaviors, and being accountable for their life choices. This awareness will assist them in breaking up barriers to their self-expression and allow them to create paths to personal and professional success and fulfillment.

Transformational coaching conversations give participants the directions they need to look at their lives and professions under different lights and get present to their challenges from a new perspective. Participants and their transformational coaches will develop approaches, actions, and practices that encourage a new and empowering way of looking at work and life in general. Many might ask if transformational coaching is a wise investment. The answer may lie in looking at the whole arena and asking ourselves if we are producing remarkable results in life personally and professionally, fulfilled and satisfied at home and at work, or if we have great excuses and reasons we are not.

### *Changing Thinking Patterns*

Consider this for a moment: if we take away your explanations, justifications, and reasonings about why you are not living a life you love or working on your dream job or having high performance and productivity, then you will have nothing to say! If we take away your options to have opinions or judgments, you will most probably have nothing to say about others' influences on your personal and professional history or outcomes! With certainty that as you are reading this, you probably have explanations, reasons, and justifications for why what we are suggesting is inaccurate because we don't know! You probably have some judgment and opinion about us, this book, what we are saying, and even about transformational coaching itself! However, we invite you to notice that your position, explanations, justifications, reasoning, and opinions make no difference in where you are in life and in your profession. What is the lesson here? If you want something different, you need to change your thinking patterns. You need to retire your good old thinking patterns, take to something new, and transform your mindset and the perspectives of yourself and others, ultimately the whole view of productivity and performance, personally and professionally.

Transformational coaching conversations and practices try to bring out participants' feelings, thoughts, hopes, notions, and desires about their life experiences at home or at work out on paper and to organize them in a systematic method that will assist participants in understanding how they operate the machinery they are, including perceptions, reactions, and practices they chose based on those reactions.

### *Transformational Coaching Sequence*

Table 11.1 represents general categories and elements of conducting transformational coaching and a common sequence of its approach. It depends on transformational coaching engagement with an individual, a team, or the whole organization. The length of these engagements varies on coaching and interventions and the size and responsibility of individuals, teams, or departments.

**Table 11.1 Common Sequence of Transformational Coaching Structure. Author's Original Creation.**

| *Common Sequence of Transformational Coaching Structure* | | | |
|---|---|---|---|
| *Phases* | *Categories* | *Elements* | *Descriptions* |
| **FOUNDATION** | **Initiation** | Sponsorship | • Who is the responsible party?<br>• Who is sponsoring the intervention and coaching?<br>• Who is paying the bills? |
| | | Agreement | • A contract is drawn and signed by both parties.<br>• The level of intervention<br>• Individuals, teams, groups, or the organization? |
| | | Introductions | • Executive & senior management.<br>• Middle & junior management.<br>• Organization-wide announcement. |
| | | Scheduling | • Schedule data collecting process with HR.<br>• List one-on-one interviews.<br>• List focus group interviews. |
| | **Engagement** | Establish rapport | • Set with all the senior managers before the data collecting process.<br>• Get related to individuals or focus group participants before the interview.<br>• Randomly introduce yourself to employees. |
| | | Create the context | • Explain coaching and intervention.<br>• Create a workable context for the coaching relationship. |
| | | Set up rules | • Set the rules of engagement and coaching.<br>• Explain the wisdom and workability of having rules in the coaching relationship. |
| | | Clarify expectations | • Ask their expectations.<br>• Express your expectations.<br>• Declare and share your commitments.<br>• Open an inquiry to their commitments. |

(*Continued*)

**Table 11.1 (Continued)**

| *Common Sequence of Transformational Coaching Structure* | | | |
|---|---|---|---|
| *Phases* | *Categories* | *Elements* | *Descriptions* |
| **LEARNING** | **Data Collection** | Observation | • Some team meetings<br>• Production meetings & planning<br>• Daily interactions, processes, & procedures |
| | | Document review | • Historical HR documents<br>• Hiring and onboarding documents<br>• Exit interviews<br>• Firing or resigning cases & history |
| | | Interviews | • Key senior managers<br>• Key middle or junior managers. |
| | | Focus groups | • Administration.<br>• Production teams.<br>• Couple of key teams or groups. |
| | **Needs Assessment** | Identify needs | • Look for the needs in interviews.<br>• Pay attention to what they are saying about what they need.<br>• Link what they say they need to their results. |
| | | Actual issues | • Try to pinpoint the actual problems.<br>• Keep digging deeper into the story and drama. |
| | | Symptoms | • Use described symptoms to find the actual issues.<br>• Explain the contrast between symptoms and the actual issue. |
| | | What is missing | • Keep asking what is missing for them.<br>• Locate what is missing between their expression of symptoms. |

| | | | |
|---|---|---|---|
| **DESIGNING** | **Design the Approach** | Models | • Select the model(s) you are using for the coaching process.<br>• Integrate models if necessary. |
| | | Elements | • Select additional elements for the coaching process.<br>• Integrate elements of other models if necessary. |
| | | Exercises | • Design necessary exercises for the coaching process.<br>• Link the purpose of the exercises to the presented needs and problems. |
| | | Tools | • Select tools and procedures to enhance the learning experience.<br>• Use additional tools to cause an increase in performance and productivity. |
| | **Implementation** | Executive coaching | • For senior managers and key individuals' coaching and interventions.<br>• Coach them on being the advocate for transformation. |
| | | Team coaching | • For teams and groups coaching and interventions.<br>• Emphasis on power of cohesive teams. |
| | | Inquiries | • Conduct inquiries to cause breakthroughs.<br>• Link inquiries to their needs and problems. |
| | | Practices | • Implement productive and empowering practices to continue the learning and implementing processes.<br>• Make sure practices are daily, weekly, and monthly. |

(*Continued*)

**Table 11.1 (Continued)**

| *Common Sequence of Transformational Coaching Structure* | | | |
|---|---|---|---|
| *Phases* | *Categories* | *Elements* | *Descriptions* |
| **FORWARDING** | **Action Plan** | Team leaders | • Help teams select a team leader to represent their team.<br>• Team leaders to be a partner with you in implementations. |
| | | Communication | • Create a communication charter with the help of all participants.<br>• Teach them about effective communication and active listening. |
| | | Check & Balances | • Helped by the team, leaders create a set of checks and balances for team practices.<br>• Ask for the weekly or monthly report of team progress. |
| | | Deadlines | • Helped by team leaders, set a deadline for processes delivery during implementation.<br>• Let them know the wisdom and necessity of deadlines. |
| | **Review & Evaluation** | Weekly tracks | • Helped by partnership with junior managers, review weekly progress.<br>• Helped by senior managers, design new and innovative processes. |
| | | Support sessions | • Schedule supporting sessions based on the results of progress reviews.<br>• Alter existing processes if you find it necessary. |
| | | Review action plans | • Train senior managers to review action plans.<br>• Schedule a quarterly meeting with key managers. |
| | | Evaluation forms | • Provide evaluation form for each working session with individuals or teams.<br>• Use the evaluation forms to implement corrective actions on your coaching. |

| **SEPARATING** | **Feedback** | Constructive inputs | • Provide constructive input after each review.<br>• Provide empowering and positive coaching. |
|---|---|---|---|
| | | Feedbacks | • Give positive feedback.<br>• Provide positive redirections for any corrections. |
| | | Ask for feedback | • Invite senior and middle management direct feedback.<br>• Share the result of the evaluation and feedback with teams and groups. |
| | | Acknowledgment | • Acknowledge their effort and undertaking.<br>• Show appreciation for what they are doing. |
| | **Maintaining** | Change Agent | • Helped by senior managers and HR, select a change agent.<br>• Provide coaching for the change agent. |
| | | Maintenance plan | • Design a maintenance visit and corrective coaching plan.<br>• The maintenance plan could be part of the original agreement. |
| | | Monthly checking | • Provide monthly or quarterly coaching sessions if you and the change agent find them necessary.<br>• These monthly or quarterly checkups could be done virtually. |
| | | Be available | • Make yourself available for any emergency meetings or coaching sessions.<br>• Be available to management and the change agents need. |

*Source:* Copyright 2022 by Behnam Bakhshandeh.

## Rapport, Relatedness, and Relationship for Workability

Establishing rapport and background of relatedness is necessary to build a strong and workable relationship with a participant or a team for transformational coaching. I am sure you have seen people, or you might know someone with the ability to connect with others with such ease it makes it seem so effortless. These people can get related and build rapport with others, no matter who they are or what industry they are from and create a sense of trust and comfort within a relatively short time.

By establishing rapport, relatedness, and relationships, we just support the foundation of workability (see Figure 11.1) and success for the process of transformational coaching. Establishing rapport and relationships with others especially our participants is building a partnership among the coaches, and the coaches are interested in the success of the coaching undertaking because they feel related and are comfortable with the coach.

### *What Is Rapport?*

"Rapport is one's capability to establish a background of relatedness and connect with others" (Bakhshandeh 2002, n.p.). Rapport is forming the base for a meaningful connection between two or more people.

The following are brief descriptions or definitions for rapport and establishing a positive connection with others.

- "Rapport is a positive connection with another person, one that involves caring and understanding" (Angelo 2012, 11).
- "I like to define rapport as a deep emotional connection and understanding between two people" (Gilmore 2019, 2).
- "Colloquially, rapport is the emotional experience of high-quality interactions. While the emotional experience of a high-quality interaction may often be associated with objective measures of high-quality interactions, this will not always be the case" (Baker et al. 2020, 330).

According to Tickle-Degnen and Rosenthal (1990), when establishing rapport with another individual, we are sharing in these ways:

- Attention: Both of us will focus on what the other person is doing while we are showing interest in what they are saying.
- Positivity: Both of us are friendly and content while displaying care and concern for each other.
- Coordination: Both experience synchronicity with the other person and experience of a shared understanding. Your energy levels, tone, and body language are also similar.

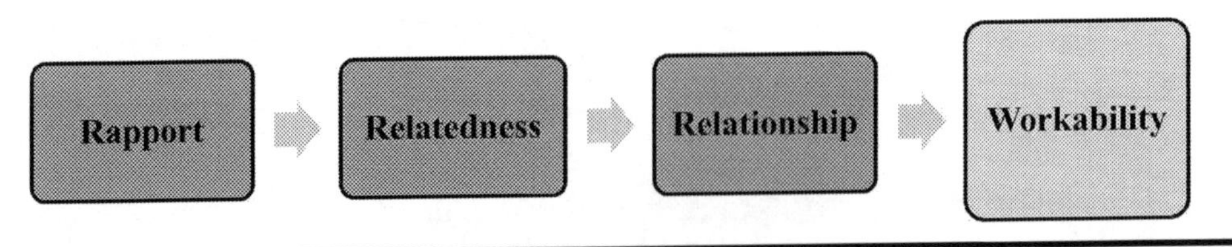


**Figure 11.1 Rapport, Relatedness, and Relationship to Workability.**

*Source:* Author's Original Creation. Copyright 2022 by Behnam Bakhshandeh.

We shall not relate to rapport as a tool for establishing relationships but as an effective practice and a path to success. As we establish rapport, we are setting up our connection and trust to another person and potential for positive influence and learning from one another. Rapport is being used for work opportunities, job interviews, social connections, or as an attempt to improve social skills (Tickle-Degnen and Rosenthal 1990).

Sometimes people establish rapport instantly, and sometimes it takes longer to develop the connection to establish trust necessary to saddle rapport. The effective performance of a manager or any other individual in a leadership position centers on the strong rapport and trust created between managers and their employees (Rothwell and Bakhshandeh 2022), and between transformational coaches and their participants.

Rapport is much more than a polite exhibit of social skills, friendship, or causal connection; establishing rapport involves displaying emotional awareness, such as compassion, empathy, and understanding of other's emotions (Rothwell and Bakhshandeh 2022; Gilmore 2019; Whitmore 2017). As Gilmore (2019) underlined, "It is a connection that puts those on the same page and opens the door for collaboration, communication, most importantly, deeper understanding" (2).

When rapport is established and grown, it is rooted deeply in both sides; it can persevere for a long time (Gilmore 2019; Angelo 2012; Rothwell and Bakhshandeh 2022). Travelbee (1963) mentioned,

> Rapport is a particular way in which we perceive and relate to our fellow human beings; it is composed of a cluster of inter-related thoughts and feelings, an interest in, and a concern for others, empathy, compassion, and sympathy, a nonjudgmental attitude, and respect for the individual as a unique human being.
>
> (70)

## *What Is Relatedness?*

The second step to establishing workability in a coaching relationship is to establish relatedness on the foundation created by establishing rapport. The following are definitions and descriptions of relatedness:

Lexico (2022) Dictionary of Oxford University defined relatedness as

- "The state or fact of being related or connected" (n.p.).

Keller (2016) depicted relatedness as

- "The social nature of human beings and the connectedness with others. Both can be considered as being part of the panhuman psychology, and both are intrinsically intertwined" (1).

Keller (2016) went further and proposed the mixture of relatedness and autonomy as two fundamental human needs:

> The definition of self and others can be regarded as embodying the two dimensions of autonomy and relatedness. Autonomy and relatedness are two basic human needs and cultural constructs simultaneously. They may be differently defined yet remain equally important. The respective understanding of autonomy and relatedness is socialized during the everyday experiences of daily life routines from birth on.
>
> (1)

The nature of relatedness and autonomy and their interrelation has been the topic of several points of view regarding conceptualizations over time (Triandis 1995; Hofstede 1980).

Aristotelous (2019) pointed at the compelling proof caused by literature review and research strongly suggesting that adopting relatedness between people through the development of greater human connections delivers more positivity in workplaces and organizations.

However, simultaneously, Aristotelous (2019) continued by underlining, "at the same time, preserving our humanity and our sense of relatedness with one another at such times of unprecedented technological development seems a daunting task" (53) (Rothwell and Bakhshandeh 2022).

### What Is a Relationship?

A relationship is an outcome of establishing rapport and having relatedness with another person or a group. A relationship is a way two people (or groups) feel and behave toward each other.

There are many ways people use to describe their good relationships with others. We all have heard them during casual conversations or when someone is describing their relationships (McMahon 2019):

- We understand one another.
- We have a good rapport.
- We have known each other for a long time.
- We are good friends.
- They are my buddy.
- We get along well.
- We have many shared values and interests.

For the transformational coaching with the participants to be workable, the coach needs to establish rapport and relatedness and build a relationship with the people.

## The Gear Wheels of Coaching Workability

The transformational coaching relationship is not different from any other coaching or mentoring relationship. As we mentioned in the preceding section, the first level of workability between the coaches and participants is establishing rapport and relatedness, which is the foundation of a workable relationship between both sides.

The second level of workability, which is what we call the gear wheels of coaching, are (1) respect, (2) trust, and (3) the context of the relationship (see Figure 11.2). In the next section, we will briefly explain what we mean by these three gears and their relevance to workability for an effective coaching relationship.

### Respect

The first gear is the gear of *respect*. Transformational coaches display their respect to their participants by giving them their **all**, swinging out, and not holding back. They will show their respect by not selling out when the going gets tough and not allowing participants to play small; they will continue to ask intrusive questions and demand that the participants dig deep. Committed

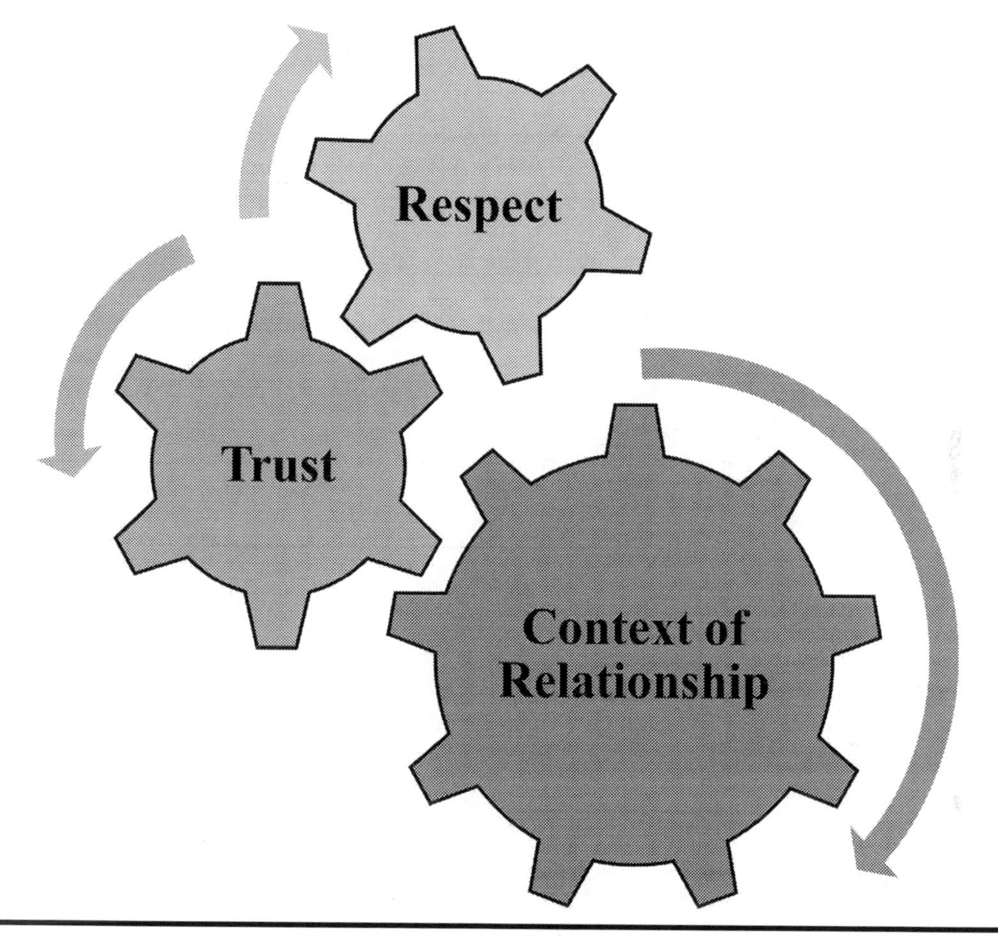


**Figure 11.2 The Gear Wheels of Coaching Workability.**

*Source:* Author's Original Creation. Copyright 2022 by Behnam Bakhshandeh.

coaches will display their respect for their participants' investments, such as time, effort, and monitory capital (either directly or indirectly from the clients or sponsors) by not giving up but pushing against resignation and despair caused by years of disappointment, not being understood, or not being listened to (Bakhshandeh 2015; Bakhshandeh 2009; Bakhshandeh 2002). (See Figure 11.2.)

Sometimes, participants will not like their coaches or the coaching process. They might feel like their coaches do not understand them, or they are too pushy or lacking compassion, and as result, they might have hurt feelings. Because the coach respects them, they push through all these feelings and emotions and keep digging deeper and harder. On the other side of this relationship is the respect of participants for the coaches. Respect is a two-way street. As participants, your display of respect for your coaches is for you not to take your coaches' teaching style and approach personally because it is not personal; it is the nature of transformational coaching that attempts to transform you to become more aware, effective, productive, and alive in every aspect of your lives, personally and professionally (2015; 2009; 2002). (See Figure 11.2.)

### *Trust*

The second gear is the gear of *trust*. It might sound unreasonable to ask participants to trust their coaches immediately, without knowing them or before establishing rapport and relationship. It is understandable to build trust within some time and interactions. What do the participants have to lose by starting the relationship by trusting their coaches unless they display evidence for mistrust. The transformational coach will start the relationship based on respect and trust with their participants, and request participants' trust for strengthening their relationship and come to workability sooner versus later (2015; 2009; 2002).

The coaches need to trust that participants will share their concerns, display their understanding, and tell the truth all the time. The coaches start by trusting that the participants will hide nothing during the coaching process and are truthful, honest, and authentic. The fact is this—if participants hide information and do not play full out, the coach cannot deliver the valuable coaching information, inquiry, and support to them. On the other side, the participants must trust that their coaches are on their side and committed to the best delivery of material and the process itself (2015; 2009; 2002). (See Figure 11.2.)

### *Context of Relationship*

The third and last gear is the gear of *context of relationship* between the coach and their participants. The only relationship here is the coach and coachee relationship, nothing else. We are not in any other relationship, such as spouse, siblings, family, or any other business partnership or a therapist and patient. This is because it is a natural human psyche to resist input from family and friends. The past experiences of potentially controlling and dominating behaviors by parents, siblings, and spouses or friends rushes to the surface when transformational coaches push deeper into designing and looking more closely at potential issues. Participants need to remember the context of this coaching relationship. Knowing this context is vital to establishing a workable and healthy coaching relationship with no expectations or misunderstanding (2015; 2009; 2002).

The coach cares more about the participants' learning, participation, actions, and how they manage their actions. Transformational coaches look at what you do and are not interested in your drama, stories, complaints, and excuses. They are more interested in what you are learning and how you are implementing what you learned as they create an action plan to do something about them. Now you can see, that if the coaching relationship is anything besides the context of coach and coachee, the relationship will not be workable or effective, given that in any other relationship, there will be many expectations and interpretations (2015; 2009; 2002). (See Figure 11.2.)

## Authenticity: An Expression of Integrity, Responsibility, and Accountability

Many people take pride in being honest, as they should. However, being honest is not necessarily equal to being authentic. Authenticity is a deeper level of honesty. We hope that you do not take this the wrong way; this conversation is not to put down honesty or honest people. It is for us to look at the differences between being honest and being authentic. To become effective during the processes of transformational coaching for effective leadership, we must become authentic with ourselves and with our coaches during inquiries into the topics related to understanding ourselves, our mindsets, attitudes, and behaviors. Topics may include:

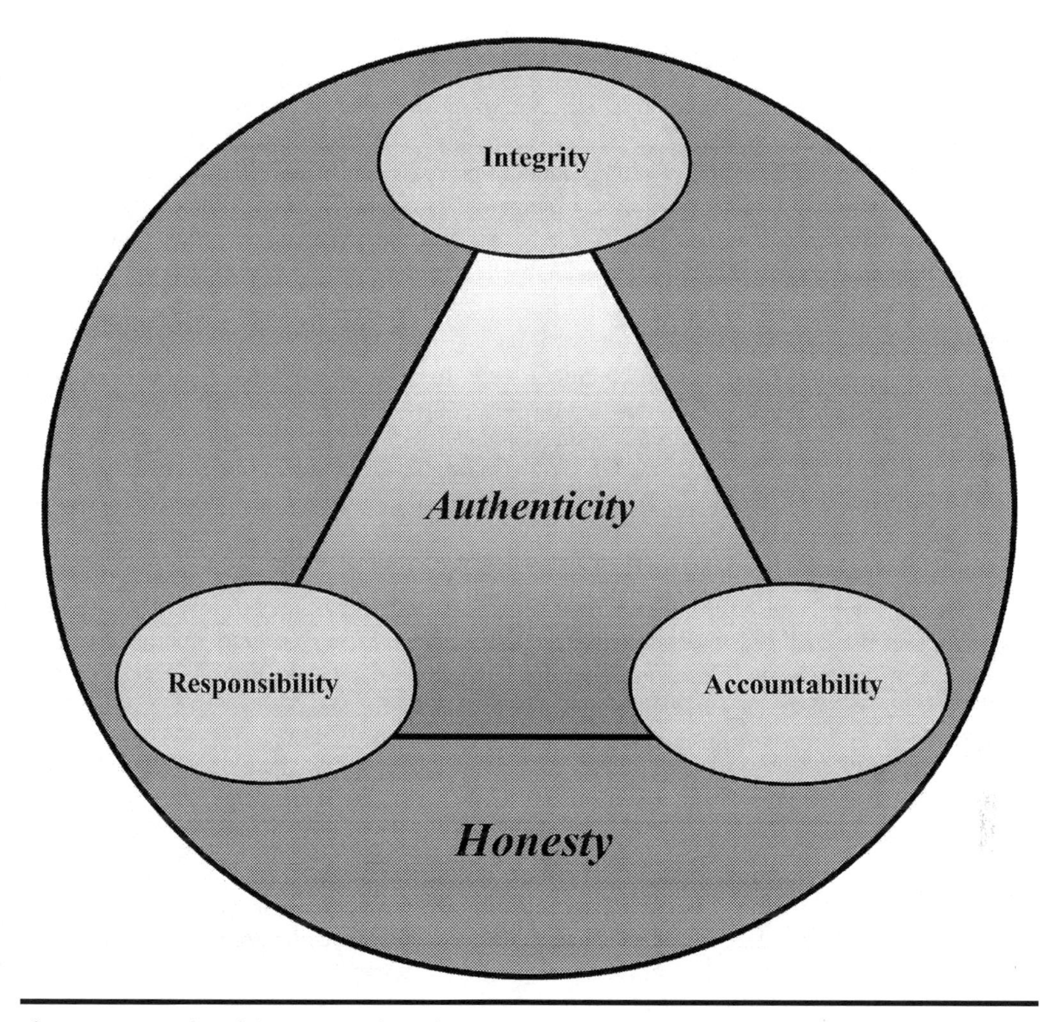


**Figure 11.3 Authenticity: Expression of Integrity, Responsibility and Accountability.**

*Source:* Bakhshandeh (2015, 37).

- Recognizing ourselves
- Distinguishing our mindset
- Understanding our behaviors around others
- Owning the patterns of our reactions to others' attitudes
- Recognizing the influence of our behavior on others, our lives, and ourselves
- Recognizing the negative impact of those behaviors
- Facing decisions we have made because of our mindsets

From a transformational coaching viewpoint, being an authentic individual is a much deeper level of being an honest person with a strong sense of personal ***integrity***, plus two side orders of ***responsibility*** and ***accountability***. Honesty is the foundation; it is the core of our being authentic while facing the issues in our lives. (See Figure 11.3.)

## Integrity

The first element of becoming authentic with others and ourselves is our personal integrity and how much we are practicing it.

Without integrity, responsibility and accountability mean nothing. You cannot be responsible or accountable for your actions if you have no integrity. This powerful force influences every part of our day-to-day lives and what we do. To change our lives, we must start practicing integrity in all we do with others and with our own personal affairs.

Who gives us the power and permission to judge others' integrity? What gives us the right to evaluate others' level of integrity on what integrity is or should be? We judge and evaluate others' decisions, their lifestyle or life choices, and anything else we can push our opinions on so we can impose our idea of integrity on them. When they do not accept our viewpoint, we become upset and resentful. We distance ourselves from them. When considering your idea of integrity, I invite you to separate your view of social law, religious beliefs and/or cultural beliefs from your idea of integrity at this moment. Look at integrity as a personal phenomenon.

Many historians and philosophers describe integrity as a lifelong yearning to follow values, moral and ethical principles, and "do the right thing" everywhere in all conditions and under any situations. Goleman (1998) described integrity as being real and true to yourself and not behaving in ways that would demean or disgrace you. This compelling distinction impacts every aspect of our lives, at home and at the workplace. Some characteristics of people with integrity are dependability, honesty, and trustworthiness (Rothwell and Bakhshandeh 2022).

For us to become authentic and have the ability to use our authenticity while facing our life problems, we shall bring our integrity to this game. It is a game of commitment to resolve our problematic issues and learn how to maintain a peaceful and fulfilling lifestyle. We need our integrity to become real and take advantage of learning about ourselves. We will use our integrity in this process by telling the truth, during a process of transformational coaching without mitigating justifications and pointing fingers at others. Consider integrity as the source of having power, magic, and miracles in life.

## Responsibility

The second element of becoming authentic with others and with us is personal responsibility.

When we are responsible, we show our willingness to own every thought we have and own up to every action we take—good or bad, right or wrong, happy or sad, enough or not enough. We did it, nobody else, just us. When we get this straight in our heads, we realize that we are the ones who make it or break it. Moreover, we must permit ourselves to do so, to own what we have done, what we have created, and become responsible for our creation. This allows us to live a great life with abundant peace of mind and fulfillment. This will allow us to bring transformation into our personal and professional life and make a difference in every aspect of our lives.

When we can look back on all the problematic events of our lives and see how we were responsible for the outcome of each event, we are free. I am not suggesting that problematic events did not happen in our lives on their own or at the hands of others. What makes the events more upsetting is when we drag them along behind us throughout our lives like a sack of pain. Our interpretation of these events and what we make of them reflect on ourselves, on others, and on life itself and allows the upset and anger to continue in our lives. A bad situation we lived through may not have been our fault, but the choice to rehash it repeatedly and allow it to affect us negatively is. This is where we need to take full responsibility. The most important things in life are continuing learning, thriving on challenges, and fighting ignorance.

How do we take responsibility? We do it by noticing what we have done in our lives and the messes we created during all our upsetting and problematic situations. Suppose we want to see a fundamental change in our lives. There, we need to know there are three steps to achieve it: (1) owning what we have done, (2) becoming responsible for the consequences of what we have done, and (3) moving forward on a plan of action to go in the opposite direction of what we have done! Therefore, we need to start by looking responsibly into what we have done.

Rothwell and Bakhshandeh (2022) pointed at Bivins (2006) who quoted Vincent E. Barry, a business historian, who depicted responsibility in business as "a sphere of duty or obligation assigned to a person by the nature of that person's position, function, or work" (Bivins 2006). In addition, some characteristics of responsible individuals are reliability, avoidance of complaining, and timeliness (Rothwell and Bakhshandeh 2022).

## Accountability

The third element of becoming authentic with others and with us is personal accountability. (See Figure 11.3.)

I do not know about you, but each time I hear *accountability* or *being accountable*, I think of something heavy and hard, like something I cannot do, something that is too far from reality, nearly unreachable. It is amazing that when we become present in our own lives, how we come to see how much we are not being accountable for! Accountability and responsibility go hand in hand. When you practice responsibility, you cannot help being accountable and having integrity. This is the essential component of the three-force combination.

Our power and presence are created and built on the foundation of our promises to ourselves and others. The well-being of our vision for our life, our hopes and desires, and our future depends on how we relate to our relationship with ourselves and how much we keep our promises. We have no idea how much our actions impact the world. That means that any action, broken promise, anything we do, and everything we say will influence our relationship with others. Our relationship with others will affect the quality of our lives. It is easy to be comfortable when we have no responsibility, no accountability, or no dreams. There is no difference between us and the tree in our backyard! However, that tree has no choice and no free will, but we do!

People who practice accountability are up to the blaming game to avoid their responsibilities. They are not pretending to be the victims of circumstances as a substitute for being responsible. Accountable people are not postponing their duties and what they are responsible for doing (Rothwell et al., 2016; Goleman 2015; Bakhshandeh 2015). Some qualities of people with accountability are (1) owning their actions, (2) not blaming, and (3) being transparent (Rothwell and Bakhshandeh 2022).

As you can see, these three powerful forces are vital elements of becoming authentic and ready to face what we have done. Using these elements is necessary for us to benefit from transformational coaching and to learn about how we operate in the face of problems, difficulties, and upset while telling the truth about ourselves and being real.

## Authenticity

What will lead us to become authentic is a combination of having the integrity and courage to own what we have done and with whom we have been in the face of an upsetting and difficult situation, then become responsible for what we have done and face the reality of how we have done it. Last, we must be accountable for the results in our lives and our relationships personally and professionally, and not point fingers at anybody or anything else but ourselves.

The hardest part of transformational coaching is to own the whole thing. That is where people give up on learning about themselves when they think owning one's results admits guilt. It is absolutely not like that! We experience one of the most powerful states of being any human can have in facing ourselves. It is powerful, it is solid, and it is fulfilling because it is authentic.

### The Flip Side of Authenticity Is Pretense

Naturally, when we are not authentic, we have no choice but to pretend. We do not suggest that pretense is bad; however, it is not good either. We can see how people pretend to be some way when they clearly are not that way. We can see and notice the pretense in society around us. As much as it is fascinating to investigate why humans protect themselves by pretending to be someone they are not, this is not a place or time to open that assortment of problems.

In upsetting, problematic, or difficult situations, people tend to withdraw and hold back their feelings about what is actually happening to them. We pretend everything is ok, and nothing is wrong. Meanwhile, we are eating our own hearts out. In that moment and in that relationship, we become inauthentic to our real selves. Authenticity and pretense are so closely related that it would be hard to recognize with untrained ears and eyes. Think of a fish in the water or a bird in the air. They do not recognize their own state of being by being involved and engaged with that way of being.

Pretending is much safer and more comfortable than being authentic and becoming true to one's real self. As much as almost everyone talks about or promotes being true to their real self, a genuinely real and authentic person is a rare breed. One must experience such pain and agony by not being real or experience such painful observations of un-real and in-authentic people we decide it is not the way we want to be because it is not a joyful expression of our real selves.

## Honesty

As you can see in Figure 11.3, we need honesty as the background and foundation of our authenticity. Without honesty, we will not practice integrity, responsibility, or accountability. Without honesty, we just have explanations, justifications, and reasoning for why we are upset or what our role was in the difficult and problematic situation.

You might ask what the difference is between being honest and being authentic. Many of us are honest. However, we are not aware that we are not being authentic. Here for example, in our marriages or our personal and intimate relationships, in normal and happy circumstances, we love our partners, care about them much, and are very committed to the well-being of our relationships, right? That is being honest, which is a great quality in any relationship, personally or professionally. However, we also have resentments, upsets, inner conversations, and negative and distractive inner chatter all over our minds. We have not expressed them or discussed them with our partners or spouses yet. The same exact scenario is happening at work too! Why?

Perhaps it is because we have concern or fear. Fear of upsetting our environment, concern they will not like the topic, or avoid an upsetting issue because we fear them leaving us or firing us. Can you see that? Can you feel it within you and all the upsetting and difficult issues you have not discussed with your family, friends, or employers? They are all over the place. That is when we are not authentic and real about what is going on in our lives. We are honest about being upset about something but inauthentic when we are not expressing it and seeking resolutions. We are not saying to just jump at any upsetting situation and start talking, screaming, and delivering your upset. What we are suggesting is this:

- Practice integrity by educating yourself about how **you** are operating.
- Become responsible, including holding back and not talking.
- Become accountable for how long you have held back your upset and, therefore, your affections and intimacy from your personal relationships and communication and workability in your professional relationships.

It is up to you to pinpoint where you have not been honest with yourself and others in your life. We also invite you to look at where you have been honest but not authentic with yourself and the people in your life. In this day and time, in the age of the internet and our massive access to information about personal development, psychology, ontology, and all other methodologies that would teach us about ourselves, there is no excuse not to learn about how we are operating and how our operation is affecting our lives and our relationships.

When we are responsible for our lives, circumstances do not determine the quality of our life. *We* do! Things are happening to us when we are alive, some hard, some sad, and some unplanned, while we are experiencing some great, some fun, and some joyful ones. All these events make up our lives to remind us we are alive!

[Content of the preceding segment is adapted from the book *Anatomy of Upset; Restoring Harmony* (Bakhshandeh 2015, pages 25–39) and used with express permission from Behnam Bakhshandeh and Primeco Education, Inc.]

## Key Takeaways

1. Transformational coaching is a constructive conversation based on the recognized participants' needs, desired outcomes, and commitments to learning something about themselves and their performance.
2. We can discuss issues or have a conversation for having breakthroughs. They are both raised in the domain of language and in a dialogue, but one of intentional commitment to causing something that would not happen by itself, a breakthrough on a persistence issue.
3. There is a workable sequence for delivering transformational coaching, (1) starting from establishing a foundation, (2) learning about the participants and the presented issues, (3) designing the coaching approach based on collected information and data, (4) implementing the coaching approaches, and (5) separating from the coaching approach and establishing a maintenance action plan (see Table 11.1).
4. To build a strong and workable *relationship* with a participant or a team for transformational coaching, the first level of workability is to establish *rapport* and background of *relatedness* (see Figure 11.1).

5. The second level of workability, which is what we call the gear wheels of coaching, are (1) respect, (2) trust, and (3) the context of the relationship (see Figure 11.2).
6. Authenticity is a deeper level of honesty, and it expresses integrity, responsibility, and accountability.

## List of Discussion Questions

1. From your perspective, or based on your experience, how do you define the *conversation about* something or *conversation for a breakthrough*?
2. How do you rate yourself from 0 to 10 (0 being the lowest and 10 being the highest in this and all the questions that follow) on your ability to conduct transformational coaching based on its sequence of coaching?
   - What is missing or in the way of your understanding of the process?
   - Have you assessed your KSAs (knowledge, skills, and abilities) in this area?
   - How do you evaluate your competencies to deliver the process?
   - What is your action plan to increase your overall rating on this process?
3. How do you rate yourself from 0 to 10 on your ability to conduct a conversation about trust, respect, and the context of a coaching relationship for conducting a transformational coaching approach?
   - What is missing or in the way of your understanding of the process?
   - How do you evaluate your competencies to deliver the process?
   - What is your action plan to increase your overall rate on this process?
4. How do you rate yourself from 0 to 10 on your ability to distinguish between *honesty* and *authenticity*?
   - What is missing or in the way of your understanding the differences?
   - How do you evaluate your competencies to deliver the distinctions?
   - What is your action plan to increase your overall rate on this process?

## References

Angelo, Gabriel, 2012. *Rapport; The Art of Connecting with People and Building Relationships.* Middletown: SN & NS Publications.

Aristotelous, Philppos. 2019. *The Marvel of Engagement.* Middletown, DE: Self-publishing.

Baker, Zachary G., Emily M. Watlington, and C. Raymond Knee. 2020. "The role of rapport in satisfying one's basic psychological needs." *Motivation and Emotion* 44, no. 2: 329–343.

Bakhshandeh, Behnam. 2002. *Business Coaching and Managers Training* (Unpublished workshop on coaching businesses and training managers). San Diego, CA: Primeco Education, Inc.

Bakhshandeh, Behnam. 2009. *Conspiracy for Greatness; Mastery on Love Within.* San Diego, CA: Primeco Education, Inc.

Bakhshandeh, Behnam. 2015. *Anatomy of Upset: Restoring Harmony.* Carbondale, PA: Primeco Education, Inc.

Bivins, Thomas. H. 2006. *Responsibility and Accountability. Ethics in Public Relations: Responsible Advocacy* (pp. 19–38). Thousand Oaks, CA: Sage Publishers.

Gilmore, Mike. 2019. *The Power of Rapport.* Middletown, DE: Partridge.

Goleman, Daniel. 1998. *Working with Emotional Intelligence.* New York, NY: Random House.

Goleman, Daniel. 2015. *Emotional Intelligence; Why It Can Matter More Than IQ.* New York, NY: Bantam Books.

Hofstede Geert. 1980. *Culture's Consequences. International Differences in Work Related Values.* Beverly Hills, CA: Sage.

Keller, Heidi. 2016. "Psychological autonomy and hierarchical relatedness as organizers of developmental pathways." *Philosophical Transactions of the Royal Society B: Biological Sciences* 371, no. 1686: 20150070.

Lexico.com 2022. "Relatedness". www.lexico.com/en/definition/relatedness.

McMahon, Lindsay. 2019. All Ears English website. "The English Adventure. How to Describe Relationships in English." www.allearsenglish.com/aee-1275 who-do-you-get-along-with-how-to-describe-relationships-in-english/

Rothwell, William, J., and Behnam Bakhshandeh. 2022. *High-Performance Coaching for Managers.* New York, NY: Routledge-Taylor and Francis.

Rothwell, William, J., Jacqueline M. Stavros, and Roland L. Sullivan. 2016. *Practicing Organization Development: Leading Transformation and Change* (4th ed.). Hoboken, NJ: John Wiley & Sons, Inc.

Tickle-Degnen, Linda and Robert Rosenthal. 1990. "The Nature of Rapport and Its Nonverbal Correlates". *Psychological Inquiry* 1, no. 4: 285–293.

Travelbee, Joyce. 1963. "What do we mean by rapport?" *The American Journal of Nursing* 63, no. 2: 70–72. doi:10.2307/3452595.

Triandis Harry, C. 1995. *Individualism and Collectivism*. Boulder, CO: Westview.

Whitmore, John. 2017. *Coaching for Performance; The Principle and Practice of Coaching and Leadership* (5th ed.). Boston, MA: Nicholas Brealey Publishing.

# Chapter 12

# Effective Communication and Active Listening Caused by Transformational Coaching

Behnam Bakhshandeh

## Overview

Most people are interested in having a good relationship with their family, friends, and colleagues at work, including their managers or supervisors. However, everyone will learn this the hard way; those good relationships are built on the background and foundation of good and effective communication and keen listening; good communication is an indispensable element of creating and sustaining workable relationships on personal and professional levels.

Understanding the importance of communication and its role in creating a working relationship is one thing, but developing communication skills and the ability to deliver the message without the other party misunderstanding what you are saying or meaning is a whole other ball game!

One of the main outcomes of transformational coaching is for participants to develop knowledge, skills, and abilities to deliver effective communication while providing active listening. These skills are part of leadership qualities displayed by managers and supervisors at the workplace and assist individuals in establishing personal and professional relationships. I am sure you have seen occasions, or even maybe have direct experience of it yourself, where the absence of effective communication skills has led to personal or professional arguments and even displays of disrespectful behaviors. This fact by itself is good evidence of the importance of having communication skills and the ability to provide active listening.

According to PMI (2013), the number one issue in inner-personal relationships is the lack of communication among people. The number one issue in organizations, among individuals, teams, and departments, is confusion in communication. Communication is divided into three types: (1) written, (2) verbal, and (3) Nonverbal, such as body language, facial expressions, and attitude. The last type covers over 55 percent of communication sent or received (PMI 2013; Bakhshandeh 2004).

DOI: 10.4324/9781003304074-16

In this chapter, we cover the following elements of effective communication and active listening:

- Inner chatter as a barrier to transformation and effectiveness
- The language of communication
- The ways out of chaotic inner chatter
- Effective communication through a transformed mind
- Active listening through a transformed mind and mindfulness
- Barriers to effective communication
- Communication charter, communication plan, and communication channel

## Inner Chatter; a Barrier to Transformation and Effectiveness

In this segment, we talk about conversations, not just any conventional conversation, but a distinctive type, because it is not a conversation we would have with someone else, and it is not communication! We might converse with different people with no objectives, which is normal, but it is not communication. Because communication is a dialogue among at least two individuals or teams and groups and has a purpose of accomplishing something, having an end goal, and getting somewhere with the individuals, teams, groups, or organizations with whom you are having the conversation. However, we have to underline that all communications are conversations, but not all conversations are communications. We use conversations to communicate (Bakhshandeh 2009).

This particular type of conversation, which is the point at this segment, is an internal conversation, which to distinguish it from intuition, we call *inner chatter* or internal chatter.

However, what we point to as what we call an *inner chatter* is distinct from the science of psychology that approaches this phenomenon from a scientific and psychological approach. "Hearing your own inner voice isn't in itself harmful. But some forms of internal monologue can cause auditory hallucinations when you may believe you're hearing voices that aren't actually there" (Brito 2020, n.p.). Brito (2020) explained the scientific and psychological definition of internal dialogue as [Also called "internal dialogue," "The voice inside your head," or an "Inner voice," your internal monologue results from certain brain mechanisms that cause you to **hear** yourself talk in your head without actually speaking and forming sounds] (n.p.).

The fact is that internal dialogue is part of being human and part of who we are as a species. Inner dialogue gives us our capacity to think, have reasons, and decide on situations (SkillsYouNeed 2022).

> Your internal dialogue is quite simply your thoughts. The little voice in your head comments on your life, whether it is what is going on around you or what you are thinking consciously or subconsciously. All of us have an internal dialogue, and it runs all the time.
>
> (SkillsYouNeed 2022, n.p.)

However, we need to reiterate the purpose of naming what we talk about as the "inner chatter" to separate the expected human psyche from the viewpoint of psychology, which underlines the healthy and expected existence of what they call "inner dialogue." What we do here is just suggesting that another side of this phenomenon exists that is holding us back; it is negative and not friendly and is what we call "inner chatter" for our ability to separate the two. Once we become more aware of our thinking, its process, the type of its designs and natures, and how it shapes and forms our thoughts and ultimately our actions, then we can do something about managing and altering them if we find it necessary and useful to our lives and relationships (Seligman 2010; Bakhshandeh 2009; Biswas-Diener and Dean 2007). This wisdom and ability to distinguish our thoughts from normal to something negative and destructive is why we call this pattern of thinking and internal conversation the inner chatter.

## *The Language of Communication*

The language that most of us use shows up in dialogue. Some individuals with special needs or disabilities use other forms of language, such as sign language for the deaf or the Braille system for the blind. Either way, all differ from languages, and they allow dialogue between people. However, another very common language is being used among everyone in the world, despite their nationality, age, education, religion, or profession! Body language! Body language is the most common language used by people. What is so common about that body language? Body language quickly displays the individuals' feelings and emotional status. We can tell if they are upset, distant, resentful, unengaged, or indifferent (Bakhshandeh 2009).

Our body language exposes things we may not want to say or expose. Our internal chatter causes our mindset, and our mindset determines our attitude, which leads to our behavior, such as body language and facial expressions. Usually, we can hear our inner chatter right before we say or do something. Sometimes the distance between hearing our inner chatter and what we say next or do next is so short we can't distinguish the outcome of listening to that inner chatter.

I am sure you can recognize the chatter in your head. This internal chatter or conversation or dialogue sounds like your negative perception, condescending opinions, belittling gossip, and sometimes it sounds like your complaints. The nature of inner chatter is negative, condescending, belittling, and justifying (Bakhshandeh 2015).

This chatter is not friendly, nor is it our friend. If we pay attention to it, each time we get ourselves in some trouble, at home, with our friends, or at work, we have heard it, and we have listened to it for split seconds before trouble starts! Regardless of who (ourselves, others, and society), where (in our privacy, at home, with friends, or at work), and how this inner chatter is generated and shows its ugly presence, there are common components to it. It could get nasty, sound condescending and belittling, and ultimately would justify our unproductive thoughts and damaging behaviors to ourselves and others around us (2015; 2009; 2004).

## *Be Aware and Block the Unproductive Inner Chatter*

To establish a certain level of mastery and understanding, similar to any other physical or mental exercise, we need to practice getting control of our thoughts and of our inner chatter. It takes more than what we might think to recognize it, separating it from expected internal dialogue and how to manage and control it. It will be difficult initially, but with consistency in practice, and awareness of its damages to you and your relationships, you can build some mastery around the issue (Goleman 2015; Bakhshandeh 2015).

Have you ever listened to your inner chatter and made a pre-judgment or decision about the outcome of a situation you are in or about to get engaged in before the situation played out, but the outcome was distinct from what you described in your head? Yes, we all have been in a similar situation because we listened to that negative, judgmental, and unfriendly inner chatter, and we did what it asked us to do. In many cases like this, we get embarrassed for making pre-judgment and making decisions about others and situations in advance, but we have no choice because we are not aware of inner chatter, and we cannot block or alter it.

> If you are present to what is going on around you, you will notice that each time you consulted with your inner chatter, you came out of that meeting being right about the topic of that consultation or the person about whom you were talking! You almost never come out of that inner chatter being in the wrong. Interesting, isn't it?
>
> (Bakhshandeh 2009, 120)

We have our inner chatter in our heads all the time, loud, judgmental, and unfriendly. We have this chatter about ourselves and everyone else around us, even about people or subjects far away from ourselves. Please look at Figure 12.1. Imagine we want to deliver a communication to someone or receive a communication from someone. Imagine the level of pre-notion, pre-decision and pre-judgment about us or others before, during, and after the communication. The people, subjects, or matters about which we are having inner chatters are one or mixtures of our inner chatters about personal, professional, or social matters (depending to whom we are delivering our communication, or from whom we are receiving communication), which may include any of the following:

- Ourselves
- Our relationships (spouse, significant others, partners)
- Our siblings and family members
- Other people (friends, neighbors, co-workers, managers, bosses)
- Work, job, or position (what we do and how we are doing it)
- Productivity and performance
- Education
- Finance and money
- Our body and health
- Nationality, race, or cultures
- Gender identity or sexual orientation
- Community, society, or neighborhood
- God, religion, and beliefs
- The economy
- Politics and politicians
- And more . . .

Look at Figure 12.1 again with all the chaos and confusion happening because of all our negative inner chatters. Suppose we want to communicate effectively with another person. In that case, the content of our communication must go through the dense and chaotic nature of what is happening in our heads, when the other party also has the same thing happening. What would be the chance for effective and workable communication?

## The Ways Out of Chaotic Inner Chatter

Figure 12.1 represents our heads and minds when we listen to our destructive inner chatter. We can see the effect of our chaotic inner chatter on our ability to communicate effectively or even be listened to what we are communicating.

We must generate some opening out of this dense of craziness and chaos. For us to be effective in our communication, giving or receiving, we must plow through the tight and unworkable nature of our negative and opinionated inner chatter in our heads! We must create opening

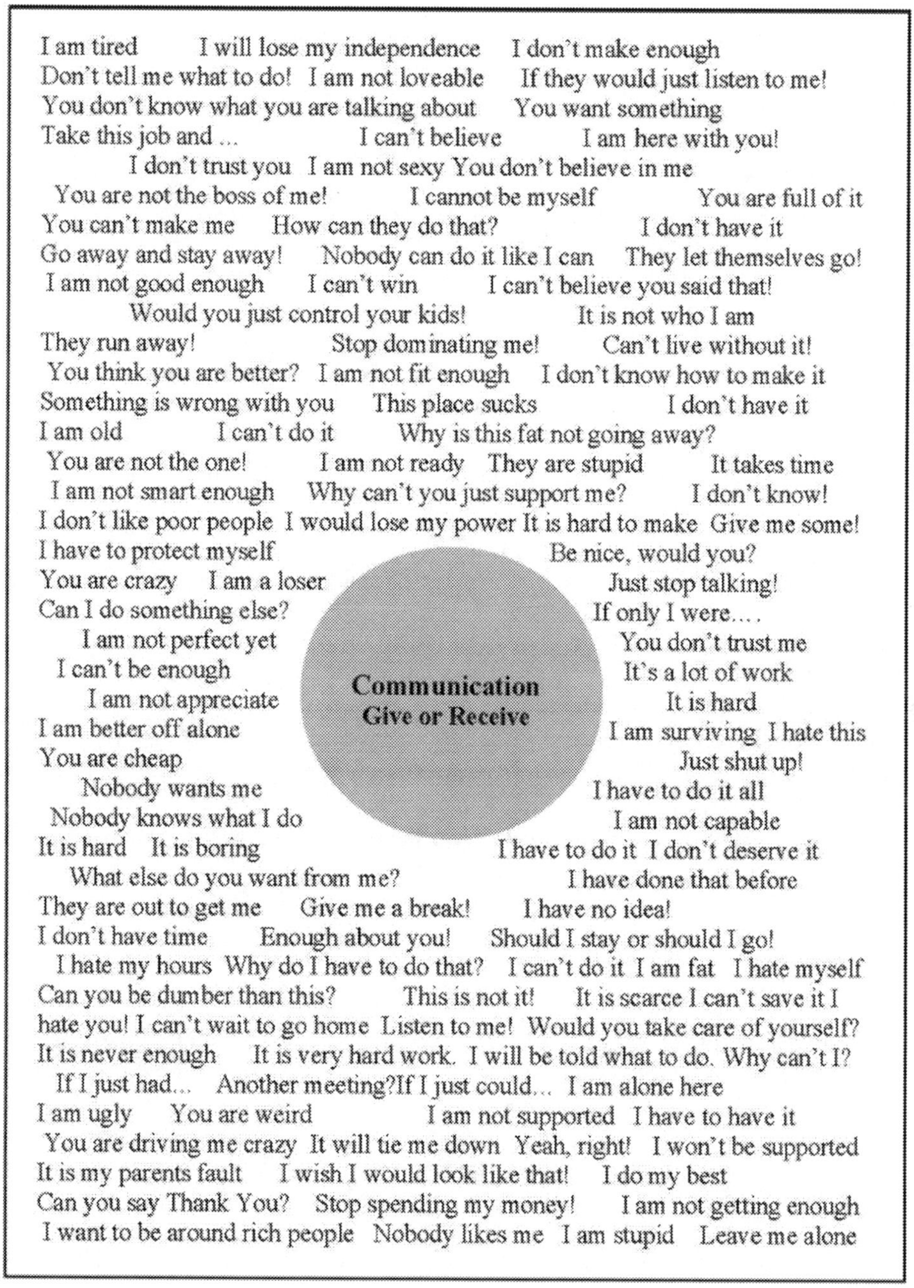

I am tired I will lose my independence I don't make enough
Don't tell me what to do! I am not loveable If they would just listen to me!
You don't know what you are talking about You want something
Take this job and ... I can't believe I am here with you!
I don't trust you I am not sexy You don't believe in me
You are not the boss of me! I cannot be myself You are full of it
You can't make me How can they do that? I don't have it
Go away and stay away! Nobody can do it like I can They let themselves go!
I am not good enough I can't win I can't believe you said that!
Would you just control your kids! It is not who I am
They run away! Stop dominating me! Can't live without it!
You think you are better? I am not fit enough I don't know how to make it
Something is wrong with you This place sucks I don't have it
I am old I can't do it Why is this fat not going away?
You are not the one! I am not ready They are stupid It takes time
I am not smart enough Why can't you just support me? I don't know!
I don't like poor people I would lose my power It is hard to make Give me some!
I have to protect myself Be nice, would you?
You are crazy I am a loser Just stop talking!
Can I do something else? If only I were....
I am not perfect yet You don't trust me
I can't be enough It's a lot of work
I am not appreciate **Communication Give or Receive** It is hard
I am better off alone I am surviving I hate this
You are cheap Just shut up!
Nobody wants me I have to do it all
Nobody knows what I do I am not capable
It is hard It is boring I have to do it I don't deserve it
What else do you want from me? I have done that before
They are out to get me Give me a break! I have no idea!
I don't have time Enough about you! Should I stay or should I go!
I hate my hours Why do I have to do that? I can't do it I am fat I hate myself
Can you be dumber than this? This is not it! It is scarce I can't save it I
hate you! I can't wait to go home Listen to me! Would you take care of yourself?
It is never enough It is very hard work. I will be told what to do. Why can't I?
If I just had... Another meeting?If I just could... I am alone here
I am ugly You are weird I am not supported I have to have it
You are driving me crazy It will tie me down Yeah, right! I won't be supported
It is my parents fault I wish I would look like that! I do my best
Can you say Thank You? Stop spending my money! I am not getting enough
I want to be around rich people Nobody likes me I am stupid Leave me alone

**Figure 12.1 The Complex of Our Internal Chatter and Our Communications.**

*Source:* Adapted from Bakhshandeh (2009, 129).

channels to the other side of this chaos! (see Figure 12.2). What is on the other side? Any communication we commit to delivering to someone. It may be something about an important subject matter or sensitive issues in our personal or professional lives directed to someone important to us about any of these important topics. We shall ask ourselves: What are we committed to creating in this situation? We can be positional and be in *the right* about what we think and take a firm, unwavering position about our view, which would result in us being more in *the right*, but more alone and more ineffective! (Bakhshandeh 2009; Seligman 2002).

However, if we want to be effective and productive, get to the other side of this mess where we can think without our one-sided opinions and baseless judgments or our yearnings to win at any cost, then we must create some access to the other side. You might ask, how can we do that? The answer is by self-reflection about any of these issues and by telling the truth to ourselves. It involves practicing self-awareness to recognize our agendas and not just wanting to win and having the last word (Green and Palmer 2019). Are we committed and attached to making our point, or are we committed to discovering the best resolution for everyone involved? "For any of us to go to that other side and to get to what we really want to say, which is deeply buried inside of what we are actually saying, we have to open some roadways. I call them *Roads to Purpose*" (Bakhshandeh 2009, 123). According to Bakhshandeh (2009), these roads are openings that will make a difference in our lives personally and professionally. These openings to the other side could be any of the following:

- **Our commitment to the result:** It always makes a difference to look into our commitment to any matter's end results and outcomes. Our choices in any communication could be a) a commitment to our agenda (presented or hidden) or b) a commitment to be a certain way and do something that would cause an opening that would produce productive results and satisfy both sides.
- **Where we are standing:** When we are standing to produce an outcome that would benefit both sides of a matter, the process of communication will work much better. Where we are standing in relationship to the matter makes the biggest difference! If we do not **stand** for something, we will **fall** for anything! When we are standing for workable and productive results, we will know unworkable agendas and unproductive conversations.
- **Practice integrity:** Without integrity, nothing will work. We shall look deeply within ourselves and see if we are generating or justifying inner chatter so as not to be responsible for what we can do and what we can produce. Are we lying and making things up? Are we justifying our approach to get what we want? Are we concealing the truth so we can control the situation? Are we wanting to win to come on top? We shall answer these questions to ourselves with complete integrity and self-awareness. That would help to produce effective communication.
- **Interest in workability:** With our commitment to workability and productive communication, we can plow through the congested negative and condescending inner chatter to open up workable communication channels. When we operate from our desire for workability, we can control our inner chatter and make things work with people who want to communicate with us and resolve issues. We must relate to a much bigger vision to source our actions rather than to win and be right for this to work.
- **Interest in effectiveness:** We will do things effectively when we show interest in being effective. When we review past scenarios in which we were ineffective, I am sure we can see who we have been being and what the inner chatter was that was holding us back from being effective in resolving those issues. We can recognize our very destructive mindset and behavior caused by listening to that negative inner chatter about the issues or people involved with them.

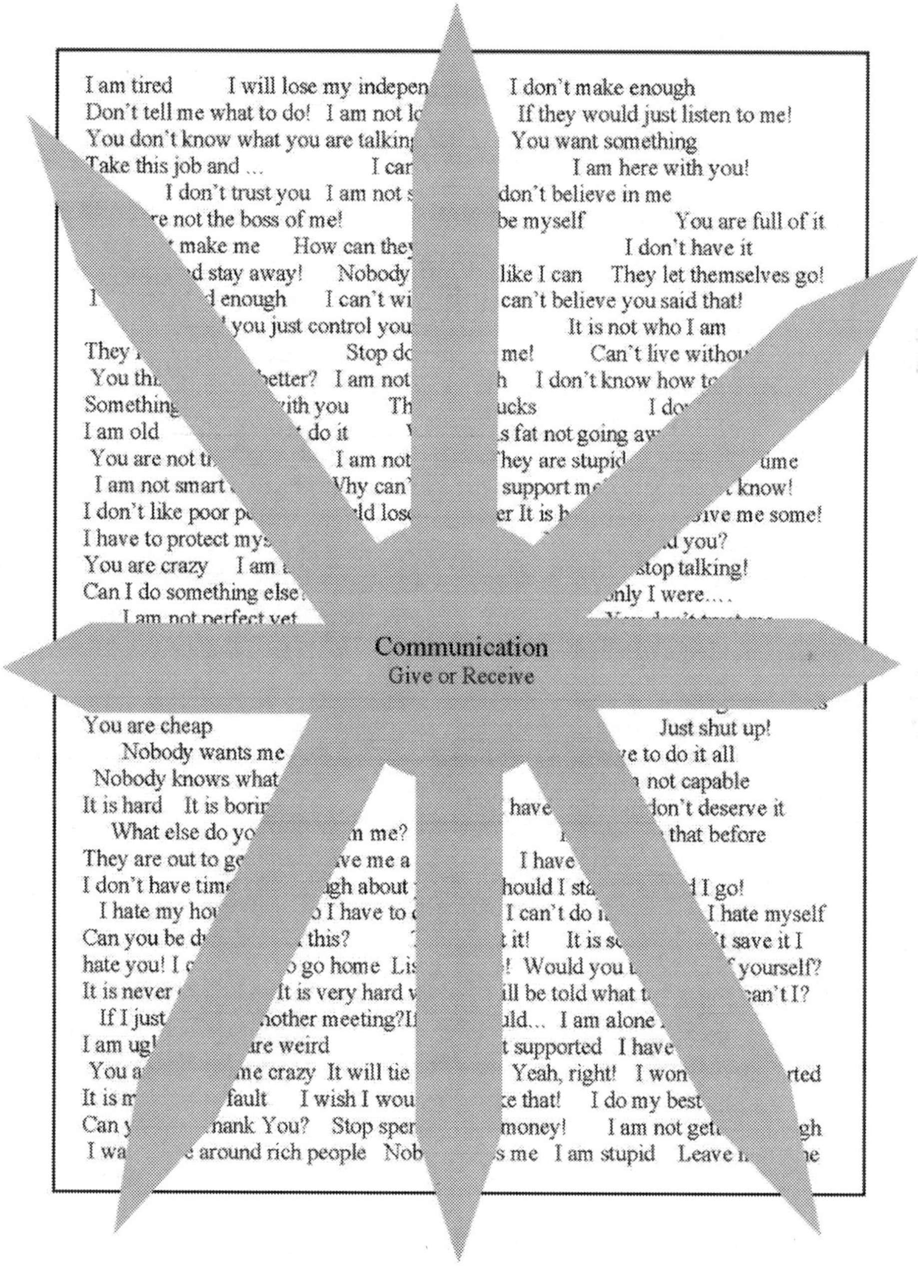

**Figure 12.2 Ways Out of Impressions of Internal Chatter.**

*Source:* Adapted from Bakhshandeh (2009, 132).

When we look at the issues resolved for both parties, we can notice commitment, integrity, workability, and effectiveness incorporated to make things resolved.

- **Applying the concept of teamwork:** Like it or not, notice it or not, there is the fact that we are working with different teams in our life (at home or work). We are in touch with different teams with our family or friends, with our spouses, at the workplace, or in our communities. If we apply the concept of teamwork to any communication issue, we can make things work among us. I know it is much easier to **say** versus to **do**, but the possibility of relating to others as team members always increases workability and effectiveness.

## Effective Communication through a Transformed Mind

Effective communication began with getting present to our ineffectiveness in communication! We shall get present to the degree of our ineffectiveness, so we can do something about getting effective, versus justifying and coming up with reasons about why we are ineffective in communication, and more often than not blaming others as the ones who are ineffective.

Without communication, there is no effectiveness and productivity, no workability or teamwork. Teams work synchronized when communicating effectively. We are all members of different teams, families, work, communities, and society. Harmony and fulfillment arise from communication; peace and love are functions of communication (Bakhshandeh 2004).

Table 12.1 displays fundamental contrasts between two mindsets, (1) an open mind sourced by desire and interest for personal and professional growth, and (2) a closed mind, which is fixated on what they know and sees no possibility for resolutions and workability.

**Table 12.1 Examples of Contrasting between Two Types of Mindsets in Communication. Author's Original Creation.**

| *Examples of Contrasts between Two Types of Mindsets in Communication* | |
|---|---|
| *Open Mind/Growth Mindset* | *Closed Mind/Fixed Mindset* |
| I want to learn more about communication. | I know how to communicate. |
| Learning more about communication will help me in my relationships. | There is nothing new I need to know about my relationships. |
| Learning about communication is a wise investment. | This is wasting my time. |
| I wonder how I appear to others when I am talking to them. | They should listen and follow my lead. |
| I want to make sure they understand what I am trying to relay in my communication. | They don't understand communication; they don't get it. |
| I recognize my shortcomings in communication skills. | There is nothing wrong with my communication skills. |
| I should ask them what they feel about my communication. | They just get offended so easily! |

| *Examples of Contrasts between Two Types of Mindsets in Communication* | |
|---|---|
| *Open Mind/Growth Mindset* | *Closed Mind/Fixed Mindset* |
| I shall change my approach to communicating with others if it is not effective. | I know I am good at communication, and there is no need to alter anything. |
| I have a lot to learn about effective communication. | I am good at communication. |
| I shall ask them if they are experiencing me listening to them. | I am sure they got what I am saying. |
| I repeat the context of what they are communicating. | They are wasting my time by babbling; where are you going with this? |
| I shall be patient and compassionate while they are communicating with me. | Come on, just get to the point. |
| Communication is of a vital source of rapport and relatedness. | I know they like me and want to learn from me. |

*Source:* Copyright 2022 by Behnam Bakhshandeh.

Table 12.2 displays a step-by-step action to produce and effectively communicate with others. To do this effectively, practice an open mind and get present to your ineffectiveness in communication. Remember that a transformed mind is an open mind with interest in personal growth, a positive view of others, and an interest in workability and producing positive results.

**Table 12.2 Step-by-Step Actions for Conducting an Effective Communication.**

| *Step-by-Step Actions for Conducting Effective Communication* | | |
|---|---|---|
| # | *Required Actions* | *Supportive Descriptions and Instructions* |
| 1 | Recognize your inner chatter | • You must hear it to believe it.<br>• It is there all the time, every day, and every night.<br>• You have no control over it; it has control over you.<br>• It is not your friend; it is what holds you back. |
| 2 | Get present to what you are doing | • Are you communicating or venting?<br>• Are you committed to a certain result, or do you want to be right?<br>• How important is it to you that everyone gets to communicate?<br>• Do you want to resolve the issue or just make your point? |
| 3 | Acknowledge ineffectiveness in communications | • Start from "I don't know how to be effective!"<br>• Look for yourself to discover what effectiveness is to you!<br>• Discover what effectiveness is to the other party.<br>• Create an outcome for the end result of your communication. |

*(Continued)*

**Table 12.2 (Continued)**

| *Step-by-Step Actions for Conducting Effective Communication* | | |
|---|---|---|
| # | *Required Actions* | *Supportive Descriptions and Instructions* |
| 4 | Tell the truth about your agendas and acknowledge them | • Ask yourself what your agenda is here.<br>• By telling the truth, you will have the freedom to communicate.<br>• Acknowledge it to others and let them know you are not committed to it.<br>• Keep noticing as your agenda keeps crawling in. |
| 5 | Give up your agenda to become effective | • By giving up your agenda, you will have freedom in being in communication.<br>• By having freedom, you have no attachment to the end results.<br>• By having no attachment, you become more effective.<br>• By being more effective, you have more of a chance to produce the outcome. |
| 6 | Understand who you are for yourself | • Acknowledge the way you are relating to yourself.<br>• Discover who you are for yourself.<br>• Recognize what you are gaining by pursuing your complaints about yourself.<br>• Acknowledge your attachments to your ways and the cost of it. |
| 7 | Distinguish who others are for you | • Own the way you relate to other people.<br>• Discover who they are for you.<br>• Discover what is in it for you by having so many opinions about others.<br>• Recognize how much you are losing by being this way to others. |
| 8 | Understand how you are relating to the world around you | • How do you relate to the world you have created around you?<br>• Have a deep look at yourself in this created world.<br>• Recognize your responsibilities in creating this world.<br>• Understand that your inner chatter keeps you in there. |
| 9 | Develop compassion and understanding of others | • Without an understanding of others, you can't communicate effectively with them.<br>• Understanding them comes from listening to them.<br>• Have compassion for what it takes to talk to you.<br>• Generate compassion for what it takes for them to communicate. |
| 10 | Come from your commitment to produce a result in that communication | • Without your absolute commitment to the result, there is no accomplishment.<br>• By getting committed to the results, you shall give up your position.<br>• Stand in a place of workability and commitment.<br>• Stay focused and continue being in communication. |

| *Step-by-Step Actions for Conducting Effective Communication* | | |
|---|---|---|
| # | *Required Actions* | *Supportive Descriptions and Instructions* |
| 11 | Get related to others' realities | • Give up that they "don't know what you are going through."<br>• Ask them about what they are experiencing now.<br>• Ask them if they need to say or give up anything before you talk.<br>• Understand there is only one world for them, their world! |
| 12 | Get related to others' realities in relationship to you | • Ask them who you are for them.<br>• Ask them if they need anything from you to produce the outcome.<br>• Ask them about what their experience is when talking to you.<br>• Ask them if they are comfortable or not. |
| 13 | Remember that they are not out to get you | • Bring your protection shield down to listen.<br>• If you are defending your point, you can't listen to theirs.<br>• Give up your attachment to how they should talk.<br>• Give up your attachment to what you must say. |
| 14 | Remember that they are not reacting to you | • If they are upset, it is not because of you.<br>• If you are upset, it is not because of them.<br>• Recognize where your past experiences are in play and let them go!<br>• When you are upset, it is because you have expectations. |
| 15 | Manage your facial expression and body language | • Recognize your attitude and give it up!<br>• Don't show your reactions with your body language.<br>• Don't act the way you don't want them to act.<br>• Understand that you are not a teenager anymore. |
| 16 | Know when to shut up and when to speak | • Stop your inner chatter about what they are saying.<br>• Stop thinking about what you need to say when they are talking.<br>• Don't keep talking because you are terrified by silence.<br>• Don't interrupt; ask them if they are finished talking. |
| 17 | Don't get invalidated or disempowered; stay present | • Don't react to what you heard; it is just what they are saying.<br>• Don't make it mean anything that it's not.<br>• If you are getting invalidated, it is because you are attached.<br>• You are getting disempowered because you are not present with the outcome. |

(*Continued*)

**Table 12.2 (Continued)**

| *Step-by-Step Actions for Conducting Effective Communication* | | |
|---|---|---|
| # | *Required Actions* | *Supportive Descriptions and Instructions* |
| 18 | Make sure an eighth grader can understand what you are saying | • Make your communication simple; simplicity is grace.<br>• Use common words and easy examples.<br>• Give up your ego by not using hard-to-understand lingo and jargon.<br>• Bring yourself down to where they can see you and touch you! |
| 19 | Notice when you become a six-year-old | • Recognize when throwing a tantrum.<br>• Notice your juvenile remarks before they leave your mouth!<br>• Don't act like a child when you don't get what you want!<br>• Acknowledge it for yourself and give it up before they point it out to you. |
| 20 | Notice when your shield is going up and bring it down fast | • When your shield is up, you are isolated.<br>• Bring your shield down before they notice it is up!<br>• There is no communication between two fully functioning shields!<br>• Keep your shield down; they will not hurt you! |
| 21 | Notice your agenda before starting any sentence | • Listen to what you are saying.<br>• Your agenda will justify itself minute to minute; notice it!<br>• Use your body language and facial expressions as a red flag for your agenda.<br>• Stay present and keep reminding yourself of your commitment to the result. |

*Source:* Adapted from Bakhshandeh (2004) with express permission from Behnam Bakhshandeh and Primeco Education, Inc.

Something worth remembering when leading people is this: "One of the things that makes you distinct from others is the way you leave people. The question worth asking is this: Are they left bigger or smaller than when you found them?" (Bakhshandeh 2004, n.p.).

## Active Listening through a Transformed Mind and Mindfulness

Given the vague meaning of active listening, different people have different definitions or meanings for active listening and use it in different frameworks (Leonardo 2020). In this segment, we attempt to explain the concept of active listening from the viewpoint of communication from a transformed mind, as we explained in Table 12.1 (examples of contrasting between two types of mindsets in the communication) and Table 12.2 (step-by-step actions for conducting an effective communication).

## *The Way for Effective and Mindful Listening*

In 1957, while developing a journal paper, two psychologists, Carl Rogers and Richard Evans Farson, established the concept of active listening and described the term as "a skill that requires a few actions: listening for the full meaning of a message, responding to emotions, and noticing nonverbal communications" (Leonard 2020, 5).

Many people think that just because they can **hear** the other person then they have listened to them and understood what they were saying and got the intent of the speaker's message. As you might recall, in the preceding session about our inner chatter, we explained its impact on our intentions and focused on the way we listen to communication.

There are several approaches to listening during communication; some of most researched approaches to listening are (1) critical listening, (2) reflective listening, and (3) passive listening (Leonardo 2020). In this segment, we look into these approaches to listening and see how they correlate to the concept of active listening in general.

### *Critical Listening*

Critical listening involves the most intention and effort from the listener. The listener stays focused on the message, processing the communication while separating opinions, perceptions, and bias from the facts in the message. This approach is useful when we are in a situation that needs evaluation of receiving information, such as with news or listening to someone's analysis of a situation or events (Leonardo 2020; Goulston 2010; Roberts 2005).

### *Reflective Listening*

Reflective listening involves utilizing our own words in communication when repeating back what the speaker has said and what we have heard in the message. In this approach, we need not evaluate, scrutinize, or judge the message versus informing and ensuring the speaker we have received and understood the intent of their message (2020; 2010; 2005).

### *Passive Listening*

Passive listening is all about the speaker. The listener needs to allow the speaker to deliver the content and the words they like to use with no interruptions or injecting words from the listener. "Unfortunately, this is the most common type of listening. Most people listen passively, merely waiting for their turn to speak" (Leonardo 2020, 4). In this listening approach, the listener is not paying attention to the speaker's content and the message (2020; 2010; 2005).

### *Active Listening*

Mindful, active listening includes a healthy dose of all the aforementioned approaches to listening (see Figure 12.3). People who practice mindful, active listening use critical listening to understand the message to form their judgments about the nonverbal cues and their related emotions from the speakers, while using reflective listening to make sure the speakers feel they are being heard and use passive listening to stay silent while the speakers are delivering their messages (2020; 2010; 2005).

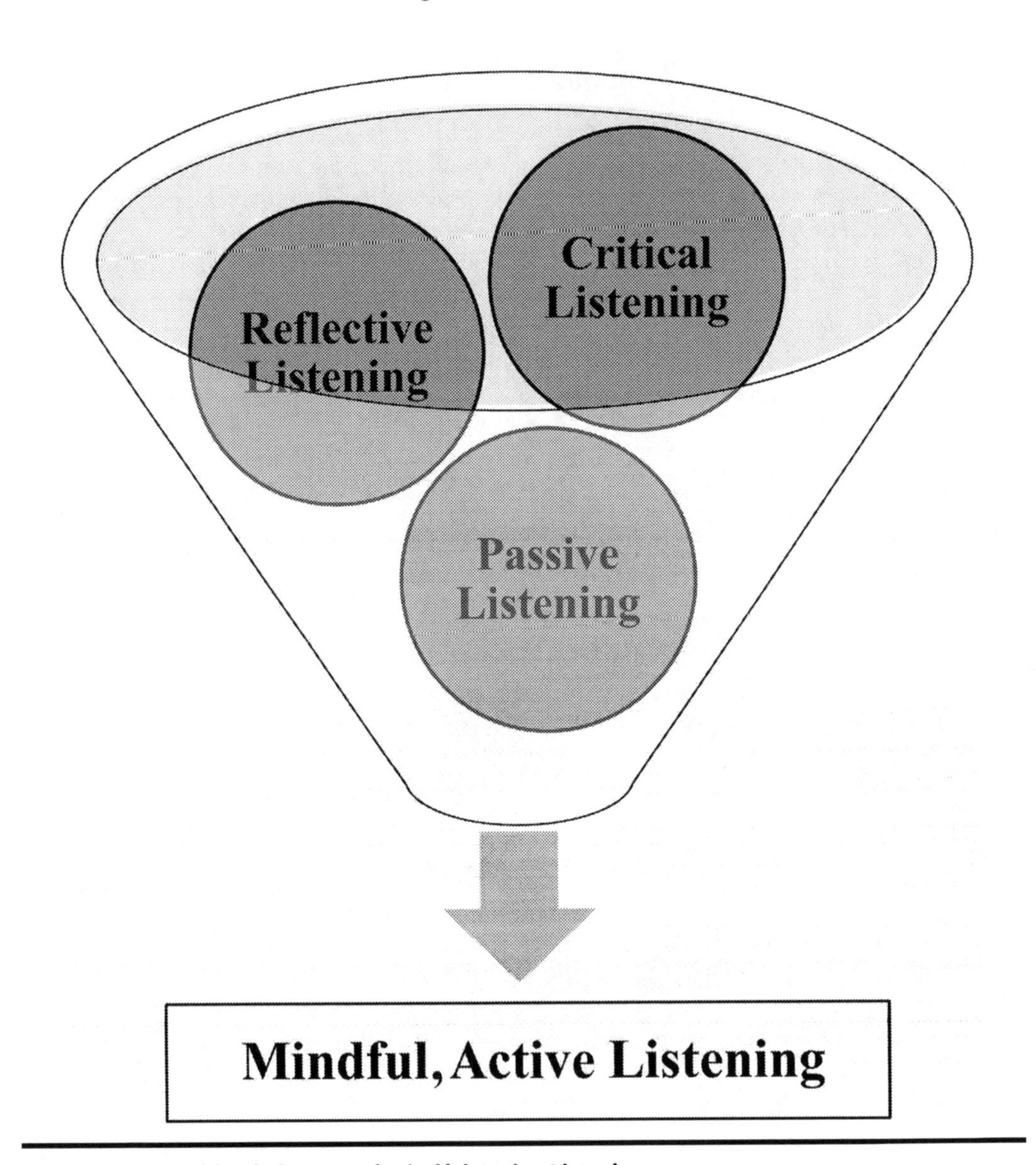


**Figure 12.3 Combined Element of Mindful Active Listening.**

*Source:* Author's Original Creation. Copyright 2022 by Behnam Bakhshandeh.

## *The Layers of Becoming a Mindful Listener*

Active listening is a compelling skill, otherwise known as one of the major elements of developing soft skills, which is desired by many organizations and businesses and among populations. The primary purpose of active listening is to understand the receiving communication and be able to decode the message accurately. However, as much as this main purpose is important, there are other benefits to the process of active listening. During the process of mindful, active listening, the speaker would develop the feeling of connectedness, relatedness, self-confidence, and respect.

It is not a mystery that many people in their personal relationships have a hard time receiving critical communication from their life partner, spouse, loved ones, family members, and friends. It is one of the natures of human beings that we are not open to what we might perceive as criticism and blame when people in our first circle of family and friends are communicating something sensitive with us. This issue also appears in the business world among managers, supervisors, and the workforces they manage, oversee, and direct.

There are four main layers to how someone will become a mindful listener (see Figure 12.4):

### *First Layer: Self-Realization*

The first layer is to realize what we feel about this communication. We shall ask ourselves *How do I feel about this*. Most people will become defensive when in their minds, someone is criticizing them, blaming them, and making them wrong. This feeling will arise as soon as we feel we are being attacked, and therefore, we raise a defensive shield to protect ourselves. When practicing mindful, active listening, we will stop and think about why we felt the way we did and what is behind our feelings. This self-realization act helps us to draw a line between the content of the message and our interpretation of the message generated from our defenses and concerns about ourselves. Self-realization is the beginning of understanding the content of the speaker's message (Bakhshandeh 2015; Bakhshandeh 2004).

### *Second Layer: Empathy*

The next layer is to develop empathy for the speaker by conducting an inquiry into *how they feel about this*. It would be a mindful act to turn our attention from ourselves to others and attempt to understand and feel what the other party feels and experiences during the communication; that is the basis of empathy for others. Self-realization and empathy bring us out of our self-concerns and what we feel and connect us to the world outside of ourselves (2015; 2004).

### *Third Layer: Self-Awareness*

Self-awareness is one of the main elements of emotional intelligence, which starts with individuals learning of their biases and hidden agendas. It is effective if we look into *what is the relevancy of how I feel about this issue*. This is a much deeper layer of self-realization. By realizing what we feel about the issue at hand, we can investigate what is the relevancy and connection between the two. What is the connection? What experience is boiling up? What is my attachment to this? (2015; 2004).

### *Fourth Layer: Leadership*

When we understand our bios, attachments, agendas, and what we feel about what we are hearing and then pushing them to the side, only at that point are we creating leadership by asking ourselves *how can I resolve this issue*. The last layer is not about us; it is about the speakers and the final outcomes. At this layer, we are looking for an effective way to resolve the communication issue and start creating a partnership with the speaker (2015; 2004).

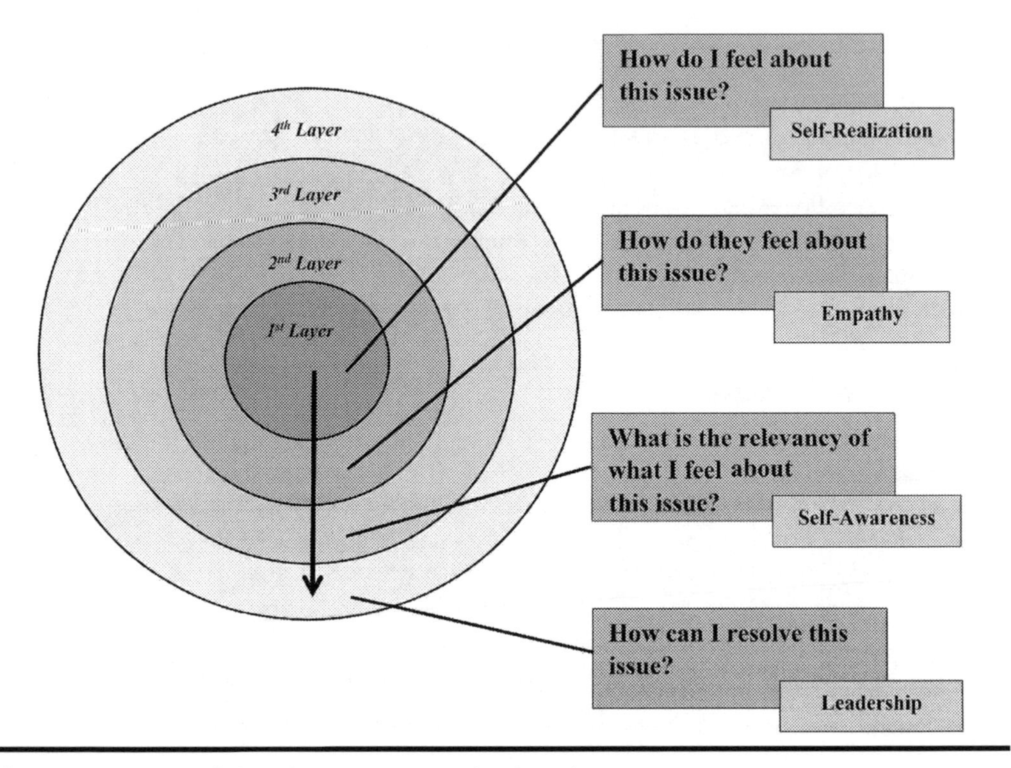


**Figure 12.4 Layers of Listening to a Communication About an Issue.**

*Source:* Author's Original Creation. Copyright 2022 by Behnam Bakhshandeh.

## Advantages of Practicing Mindful, Active Listening

There is a multitude of advantages of using mindful, active listening and becoming someone who is an expert in active listening through transformational coaching for effective leadership. Here are some of these advantages:

- **Receive agreement:** People are inclined to become more agreeable when they experience being listened to, understood, and respected.
- **Improve self-awareness:** When people learn how to communicate effectively, they learn more about themselves and improve their self-awareness.
- **Develop self-esteem:** As people become more skillful in their communication and build competencies, naturally, they increase their self-esteem and build stronger self-confidence.
- **Establish rules and boundaries:** Setting the rules and boundaries for communication is essential to communication effectiveness. For example, an active listener will acknowledge others' needs and listen to them intently and with respect without allowing the speaker to be out of line.
- **Build long-lasting relationships:** Displaying compassion and empathy results in closer relationships among individuals, personally and professionally.
- **Increase opportunities:** When people feel appreciated, understood, and respected, they are much more open to future opportunities and work with one another.

(Leonardo 2020; Goulston 2010; Roberts 2005)

## *Fundamental Practices of Mindful Active Listening*

In this segment, we review fundamental practices for developing mindful, active listening. It will be beneficial if we note that as useful and effective as these practices could be, they do not represent an act of active listening if they are conducted individually versus as a whole and through the process of mindful, active listening (Leonard 2020; Goulston 2010). These practices are not something new; many of us practice some every day which are not distinguished as active listening fundamental practices.

### *Rephrasing*

By rephrasing speakers' messages and repeating it for them, we are seeking clarification we have understood the speaker accurately. This way, if our rephrasing is inaccurate, the speaker can correct our understanding and make sure we got the message the way it was intended. According to Leonardo (2020), research has shown that when the speakers feel we understand them, the chances they become agreeable will be higher, and they will also have a positive impression of us as a listener, which will result in a satisfactory interaction.

### *Paralanguage*

Paralanguage, or nonverbal language, includes other types of communication like (1) body language, such as leaning toward the speaker; (2) facial expressions, such as smiling and eye contact; or (3) nonverbal cues or vocalizations like *ahh*, *humm*, or *mmu*. Use of paralanguage helps both speakers and listeners to feel comfortable, understood, and given attention to (Montague et al 2013). "When used in tandem, paraphrasing and nonverbal language leave speakers feeling more understood and connected to and therefore more satisfied with your interactions" (Leonardo 2020, 10).

### *Paralleling*

Also known as "mirroring," this occurs when the listener parallels the speaker's physical and behavioral poses and expressions, such as making natural eye contact, positioning their bodies similar to the speaker's, or adjusting their speaking volume and tone to match the speaker. This practice causes speakers to be much more comfortable with the progress of communication and delivery of their message. "According to a 2005 study in Psychological Science, speakers correlated mirroring with persuasiveness and likeability of a listener" (Leonard 2020, 12). This practice is more effective when done in a natural approach without exaggerating, which would seem fake and inauthentic.

### *Applying Silence*

Using silence is one of the masterful practices of mindful, active listening. Few people are comfortable with silence in communication and feel awkward when one part is silence and listening (Goulston 2010). Listeners' silence will give speakers room to deliver their message during an uninterrupted time, organize their thoughts, tap into their feelings, and recognize their emotions. This is also true for the listeners, who can gather their thoughts and recognize their emotions.

## *Responding to Emotions*

Our attention and response to speakers' emotions are as critical as our response to the speakers' verbal and nonverbal language. Responding to the speakers' emotions could be merely observing the emotions, acknowledging them, and naming them, so the speakers know we understand what they are feeling, which will give them confidence we are listening and we care about the communication (Roberts 2005; Bolton 1979). Responding to emotions will particularly work when there is a heated conversation or when one party is clearly upset or emotional. Examples of responding to emotions could be "I can see you are upset," "you seem unhappy or concerned now," or "I am sorry you are feeling disappointed."

## ***How Good Are Your Active Listening Behaviors?***

Table 12.3 can help you uncover your active listening behaviors and areas where you can improve. This rating system does not indicate your complete lack of communication or active listening competencies and skills but only directs you to pay attention to certain behaviors that would determine your presence with others during communication.

**Table 12.3 Active Listening Behaviors Self-Rating System. Author's Original Creation.**

| *Active Listening Behaviors Self-Rating System* | | | | | | |
|---|---|---|---|---|---|---|
| *Instructions*: Use this form to rate yourself on your active listening behaviors. Conduct this self-rating at least once a quarter and discuss your insights and realizations with your direct manager or supervisor. Always come up with what was missing and what are your next actions to bring up your rating level. | | | | | | |
| Date: | Participant: | | Team: | | | |
| Quarter: | Manager: | | Department: | | | |
| Rating Numbers | | 1 | 2 | 3 | 4 | 5 |
| Rating Descriptions | | Always | Frequently | Casually | Seldom | Never |
| # | Scenarios/Statements | | | | | |
| 1 | I pay attention to my mobile phone messages during conversations. | | | | | |
| 2 | I check my emails on my computer during conversations. | | | | | |
| 3 | I get annoyed with others who make ambiguous comments during a conversation. | | | | | |
| 4 | I easily get sidetracked during conversations with other people. | | | | | |
| 5 | I am not comfortable making eye contact with people during our conversation. | | | | | |

| *Active Listening Behaviors Self-Rating System* | | | | | | |
|---|---|---|---|---|---|---|
| 6 | I prefer email and text messages as means for communication more than video calls or face-to-face options. | | | | | |
| 7 | I evaluate and judge the style and the ways others communicate with me. | | | | | |
| 8 | I keep thinking about what the other person will say next versus listening to what they are saying. | | | | | |
| 9 | I ignore potential diversities with the people with whom I converse. | | | | | |
| 10 | I would immediately say what comes to my mind without sorting out my remarks for effectiveness. | | | | | |
| 11 | I am involuntarily rude to others during conversations. | | | | | |
| 12 | I can't read others' feelings by their body language. | | | | | |
| 13 | I can't understand people's communication by watching their facial expressions. | | | | | |
| 14 | People close to me complain about me not listening to them or not understanding them. | | | | | |
| 15 | I have the habit of getting into arguments with others. | | | | | |
| **Total score for each rating** | | | | | | |
| **Total of all above scores** | | | | | | |
| **Final average score (above total scores divided by 15)** | | | | | | |
| | | | | | | |
| What is missing for you to develop your competencies on active listening? | | | | | | |
| Missing 1: | | | | | | |
| Missing 2: | | | | | | |
| Two actions for this quarter that would bring up my two lowest scores by at least one scale on the next self-rating: | | | | | | |
| Action 1: | | | | | | |
| Action 2: | | | | | | |

## Filters on the Way of Our Active Listening

There are many filters in the way of mindful, active listening and our effectiveness in receiving the intent of the speakers' messages. These filters are somewhat hidden from us, and we do not notice them unless we become aware of our opinions, bios, judgment, stereotypes, and even prejudices. These filters have placed themselves in these categories:

- What we say
- What we see
- What we hear
- What we think

We have developed these filters through years of personal and professional experiences based on these labels:

- **Gender:** Male or female (stereotyping)
- **Age:** Young or old (experience)
- **Sexual orientation:** Gay, straight, bi, or transsexual (bias and prejudice)
- **Nationality:** Heritage or immigrants (opinion, bias, prejudice, and stereotyping)
- **Religion:** Ours and theirs (comparison, judgment)
- **Cultures:** Diversity (language, customs, traditions and interpretations)
- **Race:** Different skin colors (upbringing, prejudice, and racism)
- **Perceived knowledge:** What we have learned (others' opinions, readings, education)
- **Past experiences:** Parents, family, neighborhood, schools, workplaces (opinion, bias, prejudice, and stereotyping)
- **Opinions:** What we heard, believed, and thought we knew (bias, others' views, and upbringing)

These filters cause the following barriers to our effective and mindful active listening:

- **Pretending to listen:** Our judgments and biases keep us away from relating to the speakers and completely understanding their messages.
- **Distractions:** Our thoughts generated from our filters are distracting us from listening with the intent to understand. Our biases cause loud inner chatters that will distract us from connecting to the speakers.
- **Bias and closed-mindedness:** A closed mind will observe nothing. I remember seeing a bumper sticker that said, "Mind is like a parachute; it only works when it is open." That is so true about how we can understand the message and intent when our mind is open.
- **Impatience:** Because we do not listen, we get impatient and want to stop the conversation and move on to other things. The impression of impatience is shown in our body language and facial expressions.
- **Jumping to conclusions:** Making final decisions and conclusions about the speaker's messages' meanings and intent helps us close the conversation without any effective outcome, just because we are done listening.

## Barriers to Efficient and Effective Communication

Barriers to communication always are in the way of effectiveness and can lead to conflict among individuals, teams, or leadership within organizations. For our communication to become effective, we must understand the elements of communication and the potential barriers to its effectiveness so we can remove them.

Before we get to the barriers, let's get familiar with some terminology:

- **Noise:** Noise is called anything that disturbs and interferes with complete transmission and understanding of the message. Examples of noise have been mentioned earlier under barriers to active listening, such as biases, judgments, and stereotyping.
- **Efficient communication:** That is the communication without extras and unnecessary information that would confuse the message or the intent of the communication. It means delivering only information that is necessary and needed.
- **Effective communication:** That is the information and the content, which is presented in the communicative format, at the proper time, and with an intentional and productive impact.

(Levi 2017; Kold 2011)

### *Barriers to Communication Efficiency and Effectiveness*

- **Absence of communication channels:** One of the biggest sources of ambiguity and confusion among teams and organizations is the lack of clear and workable communication channels among employees and their management systems (see Table 12.5).
- **Lack of communication plan:** Another absence in communication is the lack of planning for communication. Good teamwork includes a good plan for communication (see Figure 12.6).
- **Lack of communication charter:** Any successful undertaking starts with a vision and mission for what is the purpose of a project and what the team will do to make it happen. Effective communication also needs a good solid vision, and that is when a communication charter helps the team or organization implement effective and efficient communication (see Table 12.4).
- **Physical distance:** Physical distance forces people to use communication technology such as audio and video platforms. On the one hand, the availability of communication technology helps the progress of business, but it takes away relatedness and rapport between sender and receiver. Time differences or availability of technology in different locations also adds to the ineffectiveness of communication.
- **Temporal distance:** History of communication and background of relatedness and comfort between the sender and receiver causes slow starts and some discomfort.
- **Language differences:** Given the fast expansion of globalization, almost everyone must deal with people from different cultures and, therefore, different languages, resulting in the presence of accents (pronunciation) and grammatical errors.
- **Disturbing environmental factors:** There are always some destructive environmental factors interfering with communication, especially in the workplace environment. Examples of

these distractions could be other people talking, office or cell phones ringing, other conversations in proximity, background noises such as email notifications, or just other people's interruptions.

- **Detrimental attitudes:** People's unprofessional conversations, inappropriate attitudes, or hostile behavior are harmful to any relationship and, therefore, to communication effectiveness.

(Bakhshandeh 2018; Levi 2017; Kold 2011)

## *Reviewing Elements of Effective Communication*

In this segment, we summarize and review important elements of effective communication, represented in Figure 12.5.

**A Sequence of Basic Communication:**

1. **Encoding:** The process of effective communication starts with the senders' choice of words, maybe some displays, figures, symbols, or images that support the intent of the message to the receiver, including the senders' ideas, thoughts, and requests.
2. **Transmitting:** This defines the transmission of communication as either of two ways, a one-way or direct and indirect process; the senders encode their messages and transmit it through their chosen channel to the receivers who will decode the message. This is where distracting environmental factors might affect the transmission of the message.

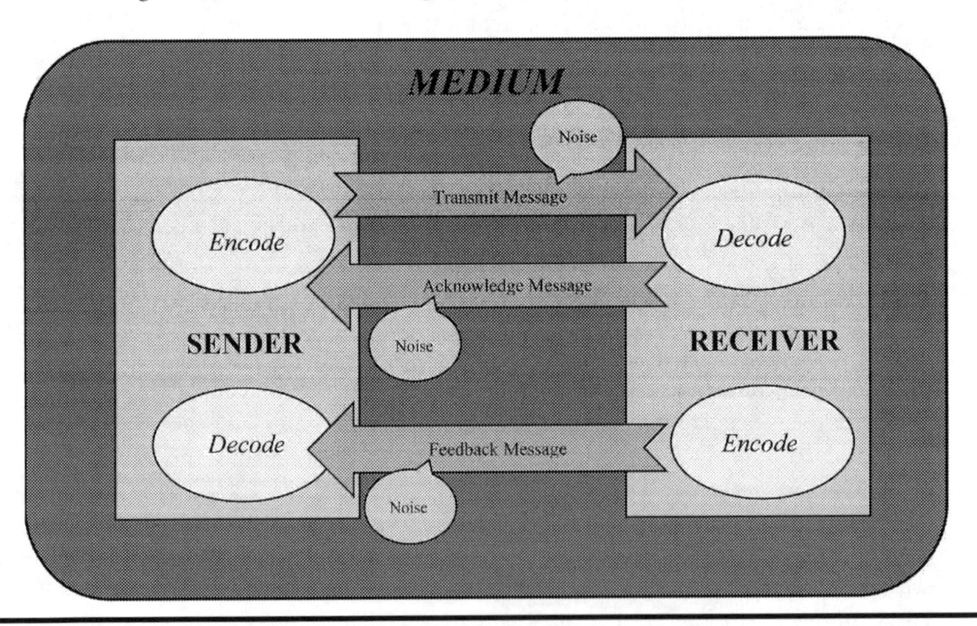


**Figure 12.5 Communication Medium, Process, and Influence of Noise.**

*Source:* Adapted from Bakhshandeh (2018); Levi (2017), and Kold (2011).

3. **Decoding:** Decoding a message is related to how the receiver understands and interprets the content of the senders' messages in a coherent form.
4. **Acknowledging:** This is about validating and confirming the senders' feelings. This differs from one of the active listening practices: repeating the message as a form of confirming that you received the message. This is about displaying empathy and understanding the senders' positions in communication.
5. **Feedback or response:** Feedback implies the receivers' responses that give the sender some idea of how their messages and their intentions have been received and understood or if further explanations or modifications are needed.

(2018; 2017; 2011)

**Some Things to Pay Attention to as a Sender:**

- As a sender, encode your message carefully, define what communication method you like to use, and verify that your message is easily understandable.
- As a sender, when encoding your message, you shall be aware of the following as some defining factors for the receiver:
  - **Nonverbal:** A big part of one-on-one or in-person communication is nonverbal language, based on your body language and facial expressions, and mannerisms.
  - **Paralingual:** Your pitch and tone of voice is helpful in conveying your message.
  - **Words:** Your choice of words and the way you phrase them are crucial elements of your message.
  - **Meanings:** The meanings that the receivers add to your messages depending on what words, nonverbal, and paralingual factors were included in the message, even in written communication.
- It is helpful to ask the receivers for responses or feedback to confirm the accuracy of the messages and the degrees to which the receivers understood the messages.
- You can receive your feedback if you ask questions at the end of the messages.
- Ultimately it is up to the receivers to make sure they have received the messages and understood the contents and intents of the messages.

(2018; 2017; 2011)

**Pay Attention to What Would Interfere with Communication:**

- Noise of any kind
- Distance, physically and temporal
- Ineffective coding of message
- Improper encoding of message
- Opinion, bias, and stereotyping
- Attitude and hostility
- Language differences
- Cultural differences

(2018; 2017; 2011)

## Communication Plan, Communication Charter, and Communication Channel

In this segment, we look at the benefits of the communication plan (Figure 12.6), communication charter (Table 12.4), and communication maintenance plan (Table 12.5).

### *Communication Plan*

Figure 12.6 depicts the three main aspects of creating a workable communication plan with all their related elements of organizational business operations: (1) the input, (2) the process, and (3) the output.

### *Communication Charter*

A communication charter works as the foundation for communication effectiveness among two individuals, team members, or managers and their employees. Table 12.4 is an example of a communication charter created by an organization to increase efficiency and effectiveness among their teams and internal teams and departments.

### *Communication Channel*

Organizing meetings to plan or review the production is always challenging and resisted by members of an organization due to what they find "ineffective" and what they call "waiting their time" (Levi 2017). Establishing a workable communication plan, using a communication charter, and

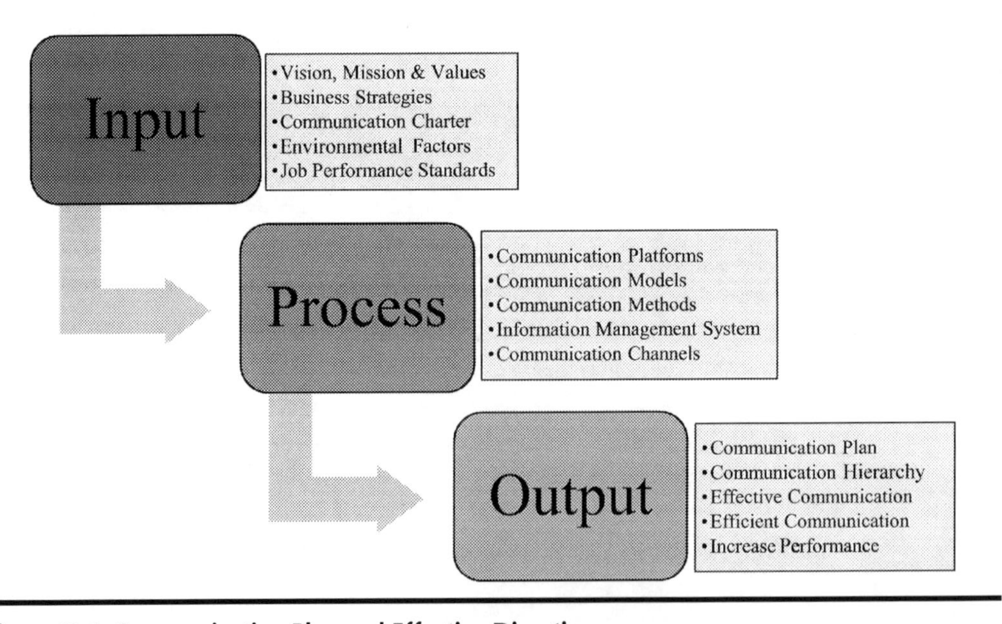


**Figure 12.6 Communication Plan and Effective Direction.**

*Source:* Author's Original Creation. Copyright 2022 by Behnam Bakhshandeh.

**Table 12.4 Example of a Communication Charter. Author's Original Creation.**

| *Communication Charter* | |
|---|---|
| *Areas* | *Descriptions* |
| **Upsets** | Go to the person you have an issue with within 24 hours to talk to them or to schedule a time to talk to them. |
| **Directive Coaching** | Directive coaching is delivered by higher supervisors or managers directly to employees or teams not conducting their processes and procedures in the way that their job and tasks are designed and expected to be complete. |
| **Indirective Coaching** | Indirective coaching or mentoring is done with permission only. Always give the other person the space to decline. |
| **Feedbacks** | Feedback is part of the process of progression and generating high performance, effectiveness, and productivity. Therefore, positive and constructive feedback is welcome and encouraged. |
| **Promises & Requests** | When making a promise or request, always use the X (what) by Y (date, time), with a condition for fulfillment formula (your required or desired outcome). Appropriate responses to requests are (1) accept, (2) decline, and (3) counteroffer (a promise to respond by a different day or time). |
| **Listening** | 1. Listen for the possibility or the unknown in what someone is saying.<br>2. Listen for **your** inner chatter and what filter you are using while you are listening.<br>3. Be responsible for who you are being and how you are listening. |
| **Being Your Word** | Communicate specifically to the person you gave your word to immediately if you are going to break it and make a new promise. |
| **Close the Cycle** | Always close the communication cycle. Don't let anyone follow you to get an answer you could give on any communication. Do not leave people hanging and waiting for your complete communication. |

*Source:* Copyright 2022 by Behnam Bakhshandeh.

organizing communication channels in organizations help management to produce efficient and effective meetings at all levels of management.

Table 12.5 is an example of planning channels of communication and how to maintain open and effective communication to keep everyone on the same page.

## Communication Skills for Managers and Leadership Positions

Leadership includes an act of inspiring others, providing positive directions, and being instrumental for change by empowering others around a common vision or cause to work toward achieving their objectives. Those in leadership positions (some managers and some not) must have powerful communication skills and competencies to effectively communicate with their followers or employees (Bakhshandeh 2002).

**Table 12.5 Example of Internal Communication Channel and Maintenance Plan. Author's Original Creation.**

| *Internal Communication Channel and Communication Maintenance Plan* | | | | |
|---|---|---|---|---|
| *Type* | *Participants* | *Method* | *Frequency* | *Purpose* |
| Executive Team Meeting | CEO, VP & CFO | In-person meeting | Once a month, on the 1st Monday of each month | Update, alignment & planning |
| Senior Managers' Meeting | CEO, VP, CFO, Director of HR & Plant Manager | In-person meeting | Bi-weekly on the 2nd & 4th Monday of each month | Update, alignment & planning |
| Project Team Feedback Report | Project managers | Email | Once a month, on the 1st Monday of the month | Giving and receiving feedback on projects |
| Team Meetings | Members of different teams | In-person meeting | Once a week, every Monday morning | Planning the weekly production |
| Department Head Meetings | VP, Heads of departments in the organization | In-person and video/ telephone conference | Once a month, on the 1st Tuesday of each month | Status update, giving and receiving feedback, planning, collaborations |
| Plant Manager Meetings | Plant manager, assistant plant managers (production & maintenance) | In-person meeting | Once a month, on 2nd Tuesday of each month | Exchange ideas, collaborate, internal planning, prevention |

*Source:* Copyright 2022 by Behnam Bakhshandeh.

Skills, abilities, and communication competencies are among the most important elements in leadership positions that connect leaders with their people and maintain their relationships. Table 12.6 represents some important communication skills for managers and people in leadership positions.

**Table 12.6 Important Communication Skills for Managers and People in Leadership Positions. Author's Original Creation.**

| *Important Communication Skills for Managers and People in Leadership Positions* | | | |
|---|---|---|---|
| *#* | *Skill* | *Wisdom/Reason* | *Actions* |
| 1 | **Listening** | Getting involved with the speaker actively and effectively | • Not interrupting<br>• Maintaining eye contact<br>• Paying attention to them<br>• Repeating their points |

| *Important Communication Skills for Managers and People in Leadership Positions* | | | |
|---|---|---|---|
| # | *Skill* | *Wisdom/Reason* | *Actions* |
| 2 | **Speaking** | Creating a safe space for communicating with others | • Speaking respectfully<br>• Maintaining eye contact<br>• Using non-threatening tone<br>• Managing body language |
| 3 | **Inquiring** | Designing ideas and managing others' understanding | • Creating a partnership inside questioning<br>• Empowering questions<br>• Asking tone versus accusing tone<br>• Giving credit away |
| 4 | **Educating** | Increasing others' knowledge and effectiveness | • Explaining context<br>• Giving information<br>• Promote unconventional education<br>• Engaging them in training |
| 5 | **Checking Reality** | Identifying or confirming information | • Distinguishing story from reality<br>• Promoting facts versus interpretations<br>• Enforcing fact collecting before communicating<br>• Encouraging factual speaking versus emotional outbursts |
| 6 | **Setting Expectations** | Managing listening and actions in advance | • Asking several preliminary questions<br>• Setting a couple of rules for communication<br>• Speaking firmly about your desired outcome<br>• Expressing your commitments for results |
| 7 | **Encouraging** | Supporting individual or team to perform | • Speaking from vision & mission<br>• Using "we" in communication versus "I"<br>• Supporting and implementing their ideas<br>• Getting into their projects with them |
| 8 | **Motivating** | Providing leadership | • Knowing them by name and acknowledging them<br>• Acknowledging their efforts and speaking about their future<br>• Taking away the failures and breakdowns<br>• Sharing their successes and triumphs |
| 9 | **Coaching** | Causing improving performance | • Being a mentor for their needs<br>• Sharing your success factors with them<br>• Directing their efforts in a productive direction<br>• Providing distinctions and contexts |
| 10 | **Negotiating** | Supporting mutually acceptable agreements | • Finding a happy middle for both parties<br>• Ensuring there will be no winners or losers<br>• Understanding their attachments<br>• Providing alternatives to their needs |

(*Continued*)

**Table 12.6 (Continued)**

| *Important Communication Skills for Managers and People in Leadership Positions* | | | |
|---|---|---|---|
| # | *Skill* | *Wisdom/Reason* | *Actions* |
| 11 | **Resolving Conflict** | Preventing disruptive effects | • Manage the emotions<br>• Speak in terms of equality and fairness<br>• Do not take sides, just facts<br>• Propose resolutions |
| 12 | **Summarizing** | Reviewing the process and main points | • Recap the main elements of communication<br>• Ask them if the summary matches their view<br>• Ask them if they need to add anything else<br>• Complete the process and acknowledge the effort |
| 13 | **Setting Up the Future** | Setting up the next actions and plans | • Ask what they think their next steps should be<br>• Offer potential next steps<br>• Open an inquiry into what might become challenging<br>• Point out potential obstacles |

*Source:* Copyright 2022 by Behnam Bakhshandeh.

## Key Takeaways

1. Once we become more aware of our thinking, its process, the type of its designs and natures, and how it shapes and forms our thoughts and ultimately our actions, then we can do something about managing and altering them if we find it necessary, and useful to our lives and relationships (Seligman 2010; Bakhshandeh 2009; Biswas-Diener and Dean 2007).
2. We have our inner chatter in our heads all the time—loud, judgmental, and unfriendly. We have this chatter about ourselves and everyone else around us, even about people or subjects far away from ourselves.
3. Without communication, there is no effectiveness and productivity, no workability or teamwork. Teams work synchronized when they are communicating effectively.
4. Many people think just because they can hear the speakers, then they have listened to them and understood what they were saying and got the intent of their messages. That is far from the truth.
5. Active listening is a compelling skill, otherwise known as one of the major elements of developing soft skills, which is desired by many organizations and businesses and among populations.
6. There are many filters in mindful, active listening and our effectiveness in receiving the intent of the speakers' messages.
7. Those in a leadership position must have powerful communication skills and competencies to communicate effectively with their followers or employees (Bakhshandeh 2002).

## List of Discussion Questions

1. How do you rate yourself from 0 to 10 on your understanding of elements of effective communication?
   - What is missing or in the way of your understanding it better?
   - How do you evaluate your competencies to deliver the process?
   - What is your action plan to increase your overall rate on this process?
2. How do you rate yourself from 0 to 10 on your understanding of elements of active listening?
   - What is missing or in the way of your understanding it better?
   - How do you evaluate your competencies to deliver the process?
   - What is your action plan to increase your overall rate on this process?
3. How do you rate yourself from 0 to 10 on your understanding of barriers to effective communication and active listening?
   - What is missing or in the way of your understanding it better?
   - How do you evaluate your competencies to deliver the process?
   - What is your action plan to increase your overall rate on this process?
4. How do you rate yourself from 0 to 10 on your skills and competencies of effective communication?
   - What is missing or in the way of your understanding it better?
   - How do you evaluate your competencies to deliver the process?
   - What is your action plan to increase your overall rate?

## References

Bakhshandeh, Behnam. 2002. *Business Coaching and Managers Training* (Unpublished workshop on coaching businesses and training managers). San Diego, CA: Primeco Education, Inc.

Bakhshandeh, Behnam 2004. *Effective Communication: Getting Present.* 2-Sets CD. San Diego, CA. Primeco Education, Inc.

Bakhshandeh, Behnam. 2009. *Conspiracy for Greatness; Mastery on Love Within.* San Diego, CA: Primeco Education, Inc.

Bakhshandeh, Behnam. 2015. *Anatomy of Upset: Restoring Harmony.* Carbondale, PA: Primeco Education, Inc.

Bakhshandeh, Behnam. 2018. *Team Building & Problem Solving* (Unpublished two-days' workshop on resolving team conflict and building a strong relationship among team members). Carbondale, PA: Primeco Education, Inc.

Biswas-Diener, Robert and Ben Dean. 2007. *Positive Psychology Coaching: Putting the Science of Happiness to Work for Your Clients.* Hoboken, NJ: John Wiley & Sons, Inc.

Bolton, Robert. 1979. *People Skills: How to Assert Yourself, Listen to Others, and Resolve Conflicts.* New York, NY: A Touchstone Book.

Brito, Janet. 2020. Healthline website. "Everything to know about your internal monologue." www.healthline.com/health/mental-health/internal-monologue

Goleman, Daniel. 2015. *Emotional Intelligence; Why It Can Mater More Than IQ.* New York, NY: Bantam Books.

Goulston, Mark. 2010. *Just Listen: Discover the Secret to Getting through to Absolutely Anyone.* New York, NY: AMACOM.

Green, Suzy and Stephen Palmer (Ed). 2019. *Positive Psychology Coaching in Practice.* New York, NY: Routledge. Taylor & Francis Group.

Kold, Judith, A. 2011. *Small Group Facilitation: Improving Process and Performance in Groups and Teams.* Amherst, MO: HRD Press.

Leonardo, Nixaly. 2020. *Active Listening Techniques*. Emeryville, CA: Rockridge Press.

Levi, Daniel. 2017. *Group Dynamics for Teams* (5th ed.). Thousand Oaks, CA: Sage Publications, Inc.

Montague, Enid, Ping-yu Chen, Jie Xu, Betty Chewning, and Bruce Barrett. 2013. "Nonverbal Interpersonal Interactions in Clinical Encounters and Patient Perceptions of Empathy" *Journal of Participatory Medicine* 5, no. 33. https://participatorymedicine.org/journal/evidence/research/20i3/o8/14/nonverbal-interpersonal-interactions-in-clinical-encounters-and-patient-perceptions-of-empathy/.

PMI (Project Management Institute, Inc.). 2013. *A Guide to the Project Management Body of Knowledge* (PMBOK guide-5th ed.). Newtown, PA: PMI, Global Standard.

Roberts, Deborah. 2005. *Everyday Communication Techniques for the Workplace*. Chicago, IL: Ragan's Management Resources.

Rogers, Carl R., and Richard Evans Farson. 1957. *Active Listening*. Mansfield Centre, CT: Martino Publishing.

Seligman, Martin E.P. 2002. *Authentic Happiness: Using the New Positive Psychology to Realize Your Potential for Lasting Fulfillment*. New York, NY: Free Press.

Seligman, Martin EP, and Mihaly Csikszentmihalyi. 2010. "Positive psychology: An introduction." In *Flow and the foundations of positive psychology*, pp. 279–298. Springer, Dordrecht.

SkillsYouNeed.com. 2022. "Managing Your Internal Dialogue (Self-Dialogue)." Retrieved from www.skillsyouneed.com/ps/managing-self-dialogue.html

# Chapter 13

# Personal Effectiveness

Behnam Bakhshandeh

## Overview

In this chapter, we look at how we see, relate to, and therefore perceive a world we have created around ourselves, which mostly causes suffering and ineffectiveness in our lives, at home or at work. Transformational coaching can cause awareness for individuals to see how they have created a certain relationship to the world around them and has caused a negative impact in their effectiveness (Seligman (2010).

This chapter will cover these elements of such an experience:

- How we realize the way we relate to ourselves
- How we realize the way we relate to others
- How we realize the way we relate to work and working
- How we have created our own world
- How we recognize differences between operating from opinion versus opportunities
- How we develop practices for inventing and empowering new opportunities

## Transforming Our Relationship to Ourselves, Others, and Productivity

In a position of leadership, not one of us can be effective and productive by having this negative image of ourselves, of others, of working, and of the environment in which we are living or working.

### *How Do We See and Relate to Ourselves?*

In the last chapter, we learned to recognize our inner chatter and how we create distractive inner chatter about ourselves, others, and almost every other area of our lives that affects our relationships at home, at work, and in society.

DOI: 10.4324/9781003304074-17

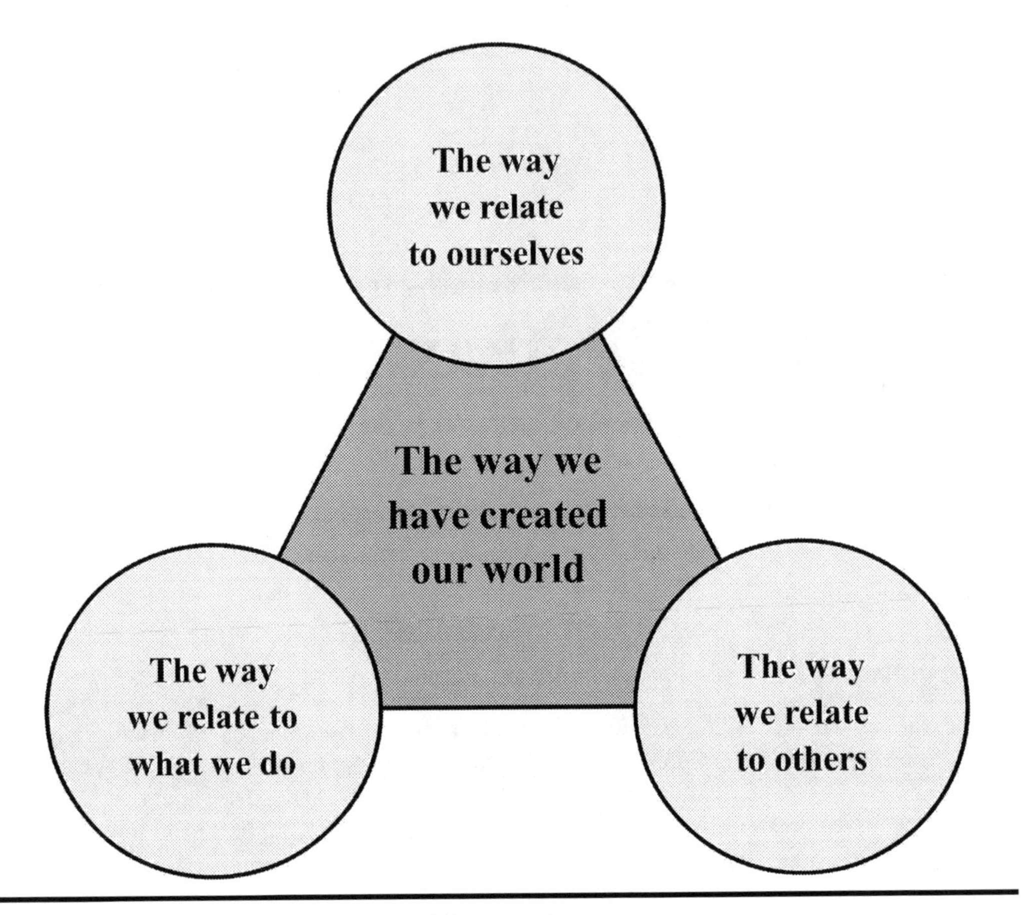


**Figure 13.1 The World We Have Created for Ourselves.**

*Source:* Bakhshandeh (2009, 181).

If you notice, **we** are always here, there, and anywhere that some upsetting situations related to us are found. We are always on one side of upsets, disagreements, arguments, fights, or breakdowns in our lives, in anything we do, or anywhere we go, or with any decision we make. We are one of the parties involved. The way we view and relate to ourselves is the primary factor.

Let's start from the first base, *ourselves*. The way we see ourselves. The following are examples of how people relate to themselves. These are the most common elements of self-relating that are at the source of ineffectiveness and suffering for many individuals (Bakhshandeh 2015; Bakhshandeh 2009) (see Figure 13.1).

## Enough—Not Enough

In many personal or professional situations or when opportunities arise, most of the time we are going to the "I am not . . ." faster than the "I am . . . !" Examples: "I am not good enough" or "I am not smart enough," just fill in the blank. "I am . . . enough." This way of viewing ourselves always holds us back from going after what we desire, such as events, jobs, or even a special relationship.

## Good—Bad

Some people always relate to themselves as bad or guilty of something. We cannot get them to see the good in themselves! To what degree are you *bad* in what you do or the way you talk or the way you think in your relationship to yourself? We always carry guilt, shame, and blame with ourselves because it is the way not to be responsible for the things we do or what we think.

## Worthy—Not Worthy

This is the other thing we do to ourselves. "I am worth it" or "I am not worthy of that!" It is the other thing we create from guilt, shame, and blame. The funny thing is that you can see the connection and relationship between these together when you say, "I am not enough of this so I am bad and not worthy of it." Can you see that? We invent them to keep ourselves away from what we *can* do and who we *can* become.

## Beautiful—Ugly

Do you wake up in the morning and see yourself in a mirror as an ugly person or as a beautiful person? Do you know that what you see in the mirror has nothing to do with your mind's perception of you in the mirror? I have seen so many beautiful, gorgeous, handsome, and attractive people who do not see themselves as fit, handsome, or beautiful.

## Smart—Dumb

"I am smart to do this" or "I am smart to do that." But we view ourselves as not smart enough to do something or complete a project. Do you know the percentage of high school dropouts? Do you know the number of people who do not complete their college education? Do you know people around you who do not complete their projects? Maybe because as soon as the going gets hard, they drop the ball because they are not relating to themselves as someone who can do it.

## Disciplined—Lazy

This has become a big problem for companies because people will not complete their work, and they always have something to say about why they have not completed their job. Do you see yourself as an organized and disciplined person or a lazy person? My only question is this. If you are organized and disciplined, why are your projects not getting completed on time?

Yes, you might be so happy and positive, read many positive-thinking books, and attended positive-being seminars, but you still relate to yourself in a certain way. That is the source of your ineffectiveness in life! That way of *being* is the source of your pain, and it is the conspiracy you have built to make sure that you continue to suffer. Access to the way of being that you have created *for* yourself is through the main criticism and complaint you have *about* yourself (Goleman 2015). This view is linked to so many things we have done, our experiences, and the ones we continue having. We are still dealing with it, maybe less than before, after having read so many books and attended so many self-realization seminars and classes! But we still deal with what we created—the way we see ourselves and the way we relate to ourselves.

Now, let's see how you have criticized yourself through the years. Be true to the decision and tell it the way it is from the viewpoint of a young person or a teenager who made that decision and just say it to yourself (Goleman 2015). When you make yourself wrong and judge yourself or when you are not generous and kind to yourself, what is the thing you are saying to yourself? What is that complaint you never let go of? That nasty and belittling comment you made about yourself and have been telling yourself? That fundamental criticism is the source of the way you see and relate to yourself.

As those committed to providing leadership in their positions, either at home or at work, it is vital to know how we relate to and view ourselves because this view influences how we relate and work with others.

## How Do You See and Relate to Others?

Now that we are done with ourselves, we move on to the second base, *others*.

But wherever we go there are also *others*! We cannot avoid them even if we try! They are at home, at work, on the freeways, on the streets, in restaurants, and every other place (Seligman (2010). Our peace of mind and our effectiveness in life and relationships correlate to how we relate to others. We are all in this world together; we cannot live—or even exist—without other people! So, since we are all in this together, we better get used to it! As soon as we understand this, the sooner we can minimize our suffering and drama about who those "others" are and the way they relate to us (see Figure 13.1).

Even when we keep ourselves away from people, it is because we are dealing with them in our heads and having a dialogue with them via our inner chatter. Staying with this concept and in the style of the same approach we did in the previous section (the way you relate to yourself), we are ready to look at the ways we relate to others. As I mentioned, I am not committed these ways are the only ways we see other people, but when we complain and criticize others, we will relate to one, two, or more of these elements (Bakhshandeh 2015; Bakhshandeh 2009).

### Enough—Not Enough

Do you see others as being enough of something? For example, are they smart enough for you, pretty enough for you, fast enough, or any other "enough"? As we all know, this is one of the most ineffective ways to deal with and view others.

### With Me—Against Me

Do you relate to others based on how you perceive their position regarding you? You can see it starting from an early age during our elementary school years when we were picking our friends based on our feelings about whether they were with us or against us. Lots of people still choose their relationships, friendships, and even business decisions based on this feeling into adulthood.

### Worthy—Not Worthy

Are these people worthy of you, your time, business, trust, or even your love? If the answer comes as a *no*, then they are gone, and we ignore who they are or what they say because they are not worthy of our time, attention, or anything else.

### *Reliable—Sloppy*

Can I rely on these people or not? Are they sloppy and unreliable in your view of them? This is another way we relate to other people and the ways we see them. Let's not forget this is one of the biggest ways we choose who we will hire to work for us.

### *Trustworthy—Crafty*

Can I trust them? Or are they crafty and shady? We look at others from this view also. You can see it in others' eyes in any business meeting or first dinner date. They can see it in your eyes, too. The one-million-dollar question is if I can trust them.

### *Generous—Selfish*

Are they generous? Are they giving? Are they practicing generosity with their time, love, money, attention, acknowledgment, and efforts? Or are they selfish with their attention, efforts, finance, intimacy, and sharing their thoughts or acknowledgments?

### *Safe—Not Safe*

Are they safe or are they unsafe to be open with? Do you view others on whether you can be safe with them or not? If you do not trust them and they are not worthy of your time, it is predictable for you not to feel safe with them as friends, family, or business associates!

These are the forces that cause us to see others in a limited and already framed view. It is limiting and disempowering to them and to ourselves, but that is not holding us back from doing that, or does it? Now, let's write down the way you view others, and the way you criticize or complain about them. Use a simple language, short and to the point. How do you criticize others?

As we have mentioned before, for those who will provide leadership in their positions, either at home or at work, it is vital to know how we relate to and view others because this view has an influence on how we relate and work with others, especially when we are at a position to manage and oversee their productivity.

## *How Do You View Working in General?*

The last piece is the way we relate to and see "working." I am not talking about the work you do as your career or your business. I am talking about the whole concept of working and doing what you do every day to earn a living. I know some of you love what you do. So do I. But for a long time, working was something I *had* to do. It was *difficult*, and I did it "in order to." Therefore, it is not about the work you do, but rather about how you relate to the work itself or the *working*. (Bakhshandeh 2015; Bakhshandeh 2009) (see Figure 13.1).

### *Hard—Easy*

Do you see working as an easy thing to do or as a hard thing to do? I am not talking about the time you got a raise, and you were happy for a week, but then you got back to your *hard* work. Overall how do you relate to working?

### *Hopeful—Resigned*

Do you go to work with strong hope and motivation, or are you resigned about your future in what you do? Do you see your work or job as a bright future or something you are doing to get paid?

### *Happy—Unfulfilled*

Do you go to work happy and excited, or are you going to your work, business, or job unhappy and unfulfilled, and you think there is no end to this?

### *Appreciated—Not Acknowledged*

Do you see your working situation as something others understand and appreciate who you are and what you do, or are you dealing with the black clouds of "Nobody understands what I do" and/or "Nobody appreciates the hard work I do"?

### *Productive—Getting By*

Are you being productive, and are you on time in what you do, or do you just get by every day and look forward to the weekends? Do you relate to your job or work as a way to be productive, or is it just another thing to do?

### *Love To—Have To*

Do you see the work you do as something you love to do or something you have to do?

### *Passionate—Just a Job*

Do you wake up in the morning and cannot wait to go to work because it is your passion, or is it just another job?

I promise you I am not trying to look at the negative part of working only, but in my long career of working, I have observed that about eight out of ten people are not happy and fulfilled with what they do for work! Look for yourself and tell the truth. You might love what you do now, but once, you were looking for a job you would have loved to do. Why? You were looking at what you did as something you did not like and made you unhappy. That way of being is still in you. You are still trying not to go back to what you did not like.

> You can live your life based on "Not failing," or you can live your life based on "Succeeding." You would be amazed to see that you can produce the same results but definitely have two different life experiences *while* you are doing it.
>
> (Bakhshandeh 2009, 168)

## ***How Do You See the World Around You?***

Now that you get how your criticisms of yourself, others, and what you do are affecting you, you can also see that you have perceived and created a particular "world" around you that does not support your potential, productivity, and effectiveness (Whitmore 2017). When I talk about a world, I am not talking about the world as a planet. I am talking about an environment, a created and invented space, in which you could continue complaining and eventually not being responsible for the quality of your life, your communications, and the relationships you could have personally and professionally.

Let's look at this perceived, invented, and created world:

## *Safe—Dangerous*

Is this world safe, or have you created an unsafe and dangerous world for yourself? Do you relate to the space around you as safe or unsafe?

## *Responsible—"It's Not My Fault"*

Do you relate to your life and the world you have created as your being responsible for the results of your life, or are you blaming other people or other circumstances for the results of your life?

## *Full of Joy—"Have to Make It"*

Do you enjoy the world you created, or do you have to make it in this world of yours? Do you wake up to a world of joy, or do you wake up to a world of suffering?

## *Contribution—"They Owe Me"*

Have you built a world in which you can contribute to others, and others are a contribution to you? Or have you created a world in which others owe you something because you are here?

## *"I Love What I Have"—"It Is Not Fair"*

Do you live in a world in which you love to live, you love what you do, and you enjoy what you have? Or in your world, are things or others not fair?

## *Accountable—"They Don't Know My Sorrow"*

Are you accountable for what you want, and are you getting what you want in your world? Or do you complain nobody knows what kind of life and trials you have gone through?

## *Opportunity—Resignation*

Finally, have you created and invented a world for yourself that is full of opportunities and joy? Or have you built a world in which nothing is attainable, nobody is good enough, no one understands you, and in which you are the victim?

Do you wake up in this world you created where anything is viable and where you plan your day, your month, or your year because you know you are the only one responsible for creating this world every day? Are you waking up to "What am I going to do now? It is hard, it is not fair," or are you waking up to "What am I going to do now? What am I going to build to bring me one step closer to my dream? How am I going to contribute to others around me today?" Write down the way you criticize the world around you.

## We Have a Choice

We become what we repeatedly do. We can choose excellence as a way of being and practice it as a way of living. If we do, it becomes a habit. However, we complain as a way of being and a way of living. When you stop complaining, you will have time and energy for anything! (Seligman 2002).

I had people around me who complained about everything and everyone. I know one person who could find no one or anything that would make her happy. She changed five offices in five locations in one company because the manager was "not fair, jealous, and did not understand her." Five in a row! Five jobs within seven or eight years! All these moves happened back-to-back, but each time I asked her to look at the problem, she brought it to my attention that the problem was not her but her manager. Finally, I told her, "I think that manager keeps following you and keeps quitting her job to keep bugging you!" This is a good example of someone creating her own world to be a certain way, and she keeps suffering in that created world. No manager will ever show up as understanding and fair. However, the person who suffers most is her. I call this phenomenon "drinking poison and wishing for others to die."

We walk around saying, "It should be this way" or "It should not be that way," or we say, "They should be this way" or "They should not be that way." "Should" and "shouldn't" are all over everything and everyone. We start from ourselves and apply it to everyone and everything. What do we get from doing that to ourselves and others? We get to justify our lack of happiness and satisfaction! I call it, "*Shoulding* all over ourselves!" There is nothing in these complaints, but they keep us away from having a life we love. Go after what you want and what you dream about; just do not complain about the process. Deal with the issues in the way they *are* or *are not*. Deal with them, resolve them, and move in a forward direction (Bakhshandeh 2009).

I put everything we talked about into Figure 13.2 so you can see it all together to help you to understand the relevance. As you can see, you and I have created this world for ourselves. We have

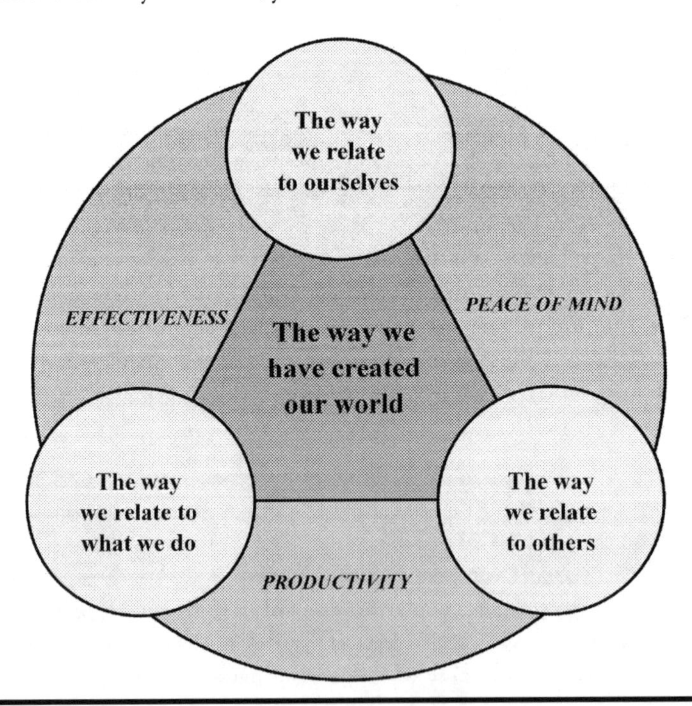


**Figure 13.2 What We Have Created is Affecting Our Productivity, Effectiveness, and Peace of Mind.**

*Source:* Bakhshandeh (2009, 185).

**Table 13.1 Self-Inquiry Questions for Maintaining Self-Realizations. Author's Original Creation.**

| *Self-Inquiry Questions for Maintaining Self-Realizations* | | |
|---|---|---|
| # | *Inquiries* | *Your Answers* |
| 1 | The ways I criticize and complain about myself are: | |
| 2 | The ways I criticize and complain about others are: | |
| 3 | The ways I criticize and complain about working are: | |
| 4 | The ways I criticize and complain about the words I have created for myself are: | |
| 5 | What I gain by holding on to these complaints and criticisms are: | |
| 6 | My excuses and reasons for holding on to these complaints and criticisms have been: | |
| 7 | How and where did I learn to use these excuses and reasons: | |
| 8 | What I lose by holding on to these complaints and criticisms are: | |
| 9 | What I have realized about myself out of this process are: | |
| 10 | What I promise myself about what I realized is: | |
| 11 | Who I am going to BE to keep my promises to myself are: | |
| 12 | What I am willing to DO to keep my promises to myself are: | |
| 13 | Who I will discuss my realizations with are: | |

*Source:* Copyright 2022 by Behnam Bakhshandeh.

invented this to protect ourselves, and then we forget that we have done that, and we blame others for our suffering and ineffectiveness! We are like liars who forget that we lied to ourselves. We continue to suffer and cause our own suffering and ineffectiveness.

This conspiracy of lying and believing our lies keeps us from being productive in our businesses, careers, jobs, or leadership positions. It keeps us from being productive in our home and our hobbies and life in general, while it takes away our peace of mind in relationship to ourselves, to others, and to life itself.

Take your time and answer the questions in Table 13.1. These questions assist your self-inquiry in maintaining an understanding of your self-realization pertaining to the preceding section on how you relating to and view yourself, others, what you do, and the perceived world you have created because of such mindsets and self-viewings.

## Opinion or Possibilities for Opportunity

The key inquiries in this section are these questions: How do you play in life? Opinion or Opportunity? Are you living your life based on what you know as your opinions collected over the years or are you forming possibilities around your life and relationships with others as you build opportunities? Do you understand the dynamics of how you play in life, including at work? Are you on the field of life and playing it fully, or are you watching from the stands? This is an ontological inquiry into one's nature of being (Bakhshandeh 2009).

> We participate in our lives in a certain way. We can also say there is a way that we *play* in life. The way you have played in the same way you participate in your personal life or your job and business.
>
> (Bakhshandeh 2009, 49)

In this section, you will see when and how you play or if it is *safe* to play or not. You can imagine when you and someone close to you, either at home or at work, like a teammate, are talking about various topics, particularly when the topic is sensitive like when pushing your side of the conversation, trying to make your points because you know you are right! (Bakhshandeh 2009). In this conversation, you need to put aside your knowledge, experiences, and evidence or your education to understand this unique experience. Start from "not knowing" and listen as you are open to a new way of being.

## *Opinion*

I want you to get present to the inner chatter you have with yourself all the time. You know what I am talking about! The voice speaking for you before you open your mouth to talk. That voice that most of the time is belittling, condescending, and, overall, a negative dialog with yourself. That is your inner chatter! That voice is deciding for you before you think. It makes judgments against everyone around you, at home, or at work, including judgments about yourself! I bet even as you are reading this, the same inner chatter is determining if you are receiving value from reading this part. Your inner chatter is doing the precise same process to your relationships with personal and professional people in your life, including your teammates. How? By dwelling and participating in these domains when others are talking to you, such as "I agree with it. . . . I disagree with it. . . ." or "I know all this. . . . I did not know this. . . ." or "This is right. . .. This is not right; it is wrong. . . ." or "This is bad; it is not good. . . . This is good. . . ."

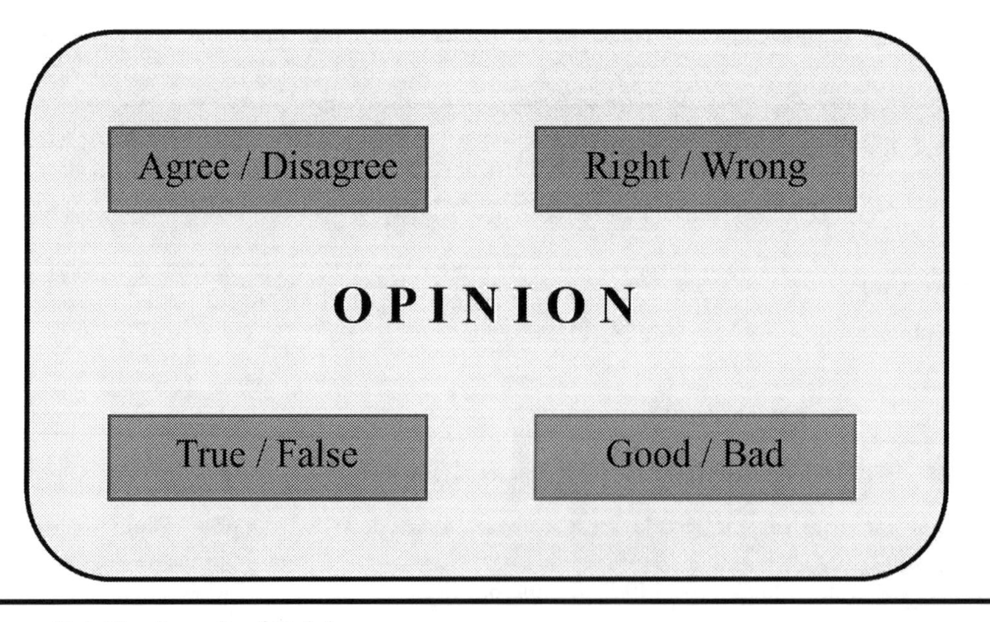


**Figure 13.3 The Domain of Opinion.**

*Source:* Adapted from Bakhshandeh (2009, 53).

This is what I call the domain of "opinion" with four cornerstones of (1) agree or disagree, (2) right or wrong, (3) true or false, and (4) good or bad (see Figure 13.3). In any moment, we listen to conversations from one, two, or all these opinionated areas, at home, at work, and when working as a team (Bakhshandeh 2009).

### *Red Flags of Opinion*

The time during which we run by our opinions and its expressions, we are not engaging the persons we are talking to or the topic at hand; we are involved in our opinions. What I call "red flags" are some states of *being* that we all have to be mindful of to help us identify when we are in the domain of opinion (Bakhshandeh 2009). Bakhshandeh (2009) explained,

> We are not aware of our *own* state of being! *Being* for a human is like water for fish or air for birds. Fish are not aware of their existence in water, nor do birds have any idea that they are flying in something called air! *Being* is the exact same way for us!
>
> (55)

We can recognize our state of *being* when we are in the domain of "opinion" by being aware of the following, either at home or at work with our colleagues and teammates:

- Talking about ideas and goals with no plan of action.
- Making fast decisions without considering other alternatives.
- Drawing immediate conclusions about situations.
- Not getting involved with correcting situations and complaining about it.
- Listening to your inner chatter and not being aware of surrounding conversations.
- Always being in a hurry for something without stopping to get organized.
- Not being constructive but having an opinion about how others should play!
- Knowing everything about everything and everyone without considering you might not know!

The preceding red flags indicate that you are playing at the sidelines while running your opinions about people and topics (Bakhshandeh 2009).

#### What Is "in" It for You?

In typical cases, we will do nothing in life or at work with no payoff, payback, or compensation. It could be as simple as feeling self-satisfaction and doing out of the goodness of our hearts or as official as a paycheck and payment. So, in this situation, there is something in it for us to keep playing in the domain of "opinion" and keeping ourselves on the sidelines of life and work. What is it? What is the attraction? Let's consider the following ontological and psychological payoffs to us running our opinions:

- Being right about our view, idea, or position (being right differs from being correct).
- Making others wrong because they do not agree with us.
- Taking a position and digging in our heels about being right.
- Justifying ourselves and our attitude or behavior because we were right.
- Invalidating others in conversations to justify our attitude and behavior.

- Sticking to our ways and not giving any consideration.
- Being closed and not being open to others' ideas and viewpoints.
- Nothing new! My way or the highway!

(Bakhshandeh 2009)

## Possibilities for Opportunities

What else is possible? Like anything in life, there are always alternatives. What alternative do we have for playing and participating in personal and professional aspects of our lives besides being on the sidelines? The other powerful option is the possibility of creating opportunities to recognize, be aware, manage and turn that destructive inner chatter around and direct your views to different but constructive, collaborative, and productive directions on the "opportunity" side, such as:

- Knowledge. Is it possible to learn something new from others?
- Contribution. Are we open to being contributed to, and allowing others to teach us something new?
- Consideration. Can we consider other ideas and viewpoints as valid as ours?
- Openness. Can we open the gates of our minds and allow possibilities to enter?
- Application. Can we apply new ways to see what would come out of it?
- Inquiry. Are we looking for short and speedy answers versus having open-minded inquiries?
- Values. Are we looking for new values or sticking to what we know already?
- Coachability. Are we coachable, or resisting and avoiding others' dominations?

The four main corners of the "opportunity" domain are (1) knowledge, (2) contribution, (3) consideration, and (4) inquiry (Bakhshandeh 2009) (see Figure 13.4).

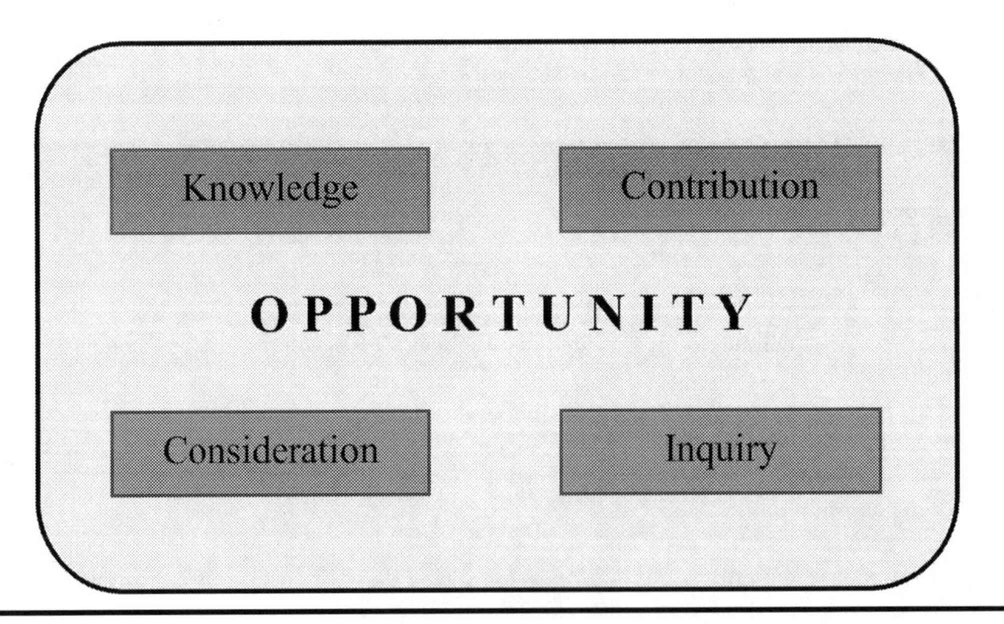


**Figure 13.4 The Domain of Opportunity.**

*Source:* Adapted from Bakhshandeh (2009, 81).

### *Evidence of Playing for Opportunity*

Now we have two options in the way we are playing in all aspects of our lives: opinions or opportunities. Neither domain is better than the other; they are just different domains with different consequences; one has us on the *sidelines* of our lives, and the other has us on the *field* of the game of life, personally and professionally. But how do we know we are in our lives? What signs and evidence indicate that we are on the *field*?

Let's look at these indications or actions that would be recognizable to us as we are playing on the *field* (Bakhshandeh 2009):

- Taking it on, whatever it is; however it is, we are playing and are engaged.
- Having compassion for people with whom we are engaging, their style of learning, and understanding.
- Having patience with people during conversations and inquiries.
- Getting involved where we can make a difference.
- Looking for resolutions and solutions for moving issues in a forward motion.
- Playing full out and playing as team members with no expectations.
- Looking at the bigger picture in all engagements, discussions, and conversations.
- Knowing we don't know everything about everything and everyone. Get to know others.

(Bakhshandeh 2009)

#### What Are We Gaining Playing on the Field?

There are again some benefits and payoffs for us to play on the field. What would we accomplish by playing this way on the field and the domain of opportunity? Where are the benefits of playing on the field of opportunity? We have these opportunities:

- Learn something new, even about something that we thought we knew.
- Be open to other views and how they see what we see, without resistance.
- Learn how to listen to others, without judgment and pre-notions.
- Learn how to speak to other viewpoints and be effective with them.
- Gain more respect for ourselves and for others.
- Build strong relationships, connections, and friendships.
- Develop a deeper understanding, compassion, and patience with others.
- Have peace of mind and freedom to be at ease with ourselves and others.

(Bakhshandeh 2009)

## The Domain of Opportunity versus Domain of Despair

Reading, applying, and practicing the preceding process assists us in understanding our mindset and potential of self-awareness and get present with others' mindsets and behaviors (Levi 2017). I hope some may feel inspired by seeing possibilities for opportunities and motivated to adopt this way of thinking and self-examination. That negative inner chatter should be in check so control of attitude and behavior is in check while interacting with others either at home or at work with colleagues and teammates.

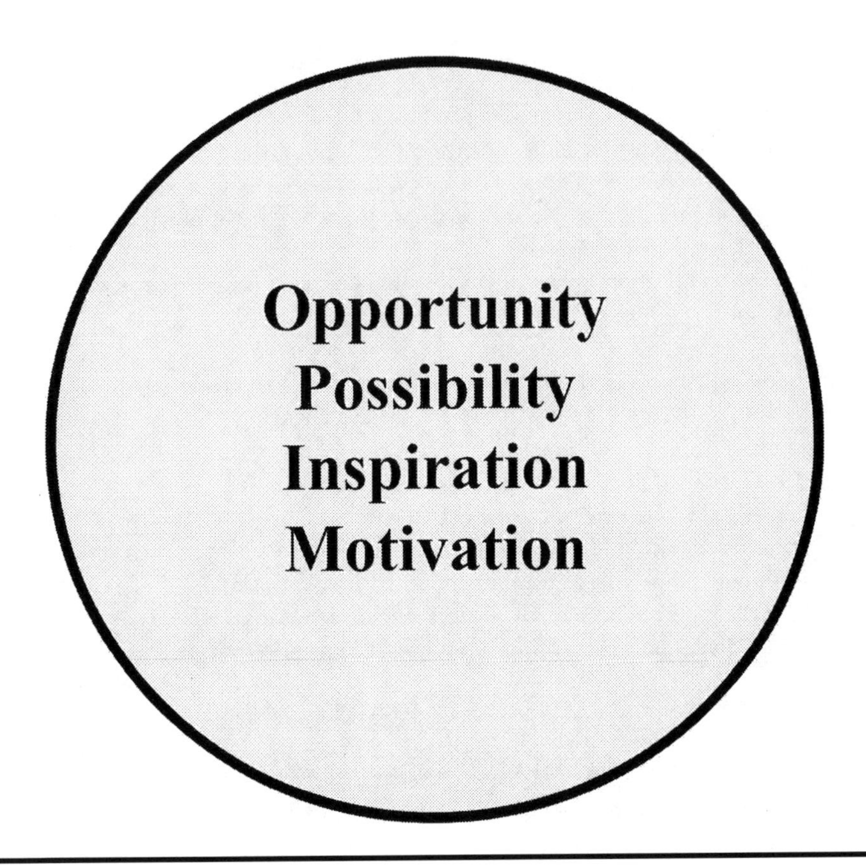


**Figure 13.5 The Domain of Opportunity.**

*Source:* Bakhshandeh (2009, 272).

That is one of the greatest characteristics of self-awareness and understanding of one's *being*, which can be called the domain of opportunity. As this new domain arises (see Figure 13.5) and people get present with it, they will feel the possibility of opportunities of being different and doing something new and powerful. It becomes something so inspiring that it scares them within, something that makes a difference for themselves and others, something that motivates them to do or to say because it is a part of who they are and motivates them into action (Bakhshandeh 2009).

Unfortunately, as soon as the domain of opportunity arises in the heart and mind, another domain immediately appears along with it and tries to cover it up. It is as powerful as the domain of opportunity itself. This is called the domain of despair (see Figure 13.6). As soon as opportunities arise, accompanied by inspiration and motivation, self-doubt and despair creep in, causing hesitation and resignation about any chances for success (Bakhshandeh 2009).

Many have seen and felt this domain during team meetings and decision-making processes. This domain has the power to take over the domain of opportunity and potentially suppress it.

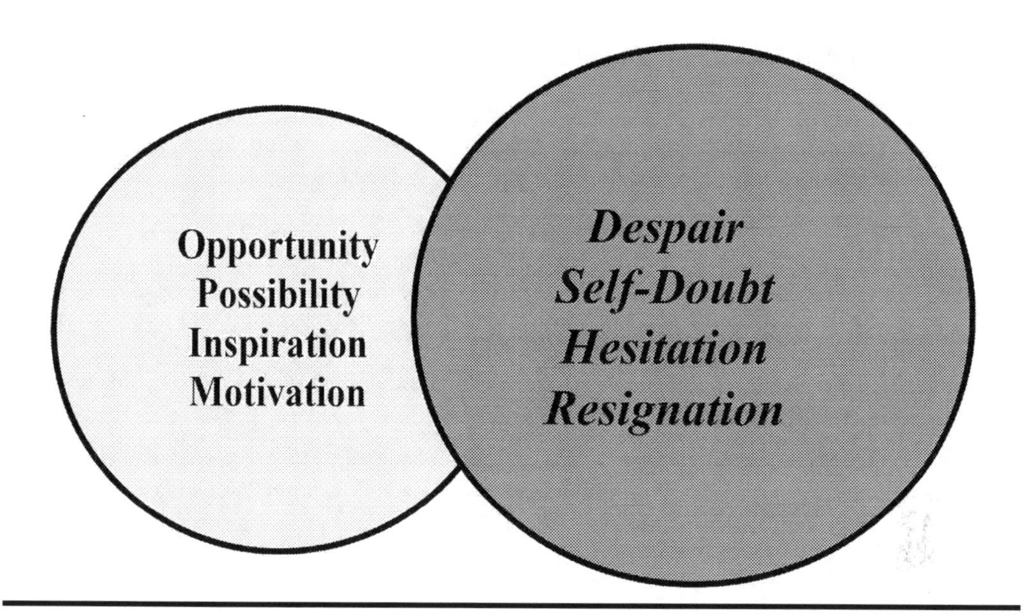


**Figure 13.6 The Domain of Despair.**

*Source:* Bakhshandeh (2009, 273).

This domain of despair is something to be aware of because it will crawl in and take over any possibilities and opportunities that would arise for the good of individuals and teams. It is essential to be aware of this phenomenon during any teambuilding processes or team collaboration and communication.

"Resignation and despair are so deep within us that possibility and inspiration have no chance to shine for long unless someone stands firm and commits to turning all those possibilities into realities" (Bakhshandeh 2009, 275). Daily awareness and inspiration are ways to protect any opportunities and invent new practices and ultimately make them real. It is proven that most individuals keep plugging their power into what they know from the past and their older practices. Basically, they continue to do something they are comfortable with and have done before, not something new, which is most uncomfortable (Bakhshandeh 2009).

Basically, coming up with new practices that would keep the domain of opportunity up front and center will eclipse the domain of despair, thus reinforcing new mindsets.

## *Inventing New Empowering Practices for New Opportunities*

Table 13.2 represents a strategy to invent new practices while eliminating old practices to empower the implementation of new opportunities. With your team or among individuals, look for what is in the way of being more effective, productive, cohesive, and communicative, or about any other issues in effectiveness and higher performance, individually or as a team (Rothwell et al. 2021; Kold 2011).

**Table 13.2 Practices for Inventing and Empowering New Opportunities.**

*Practices for Inventing and Empowering New Opportunities*

*Instructions*: Conduct a brainstorming session with your team (or any individual) and look at all potential opportunities in your productivity and effectiveness.

1. Name these opportunities and write them in the left column. Select a fun and relevant name.
2. Invent at least three new practices that would support the growth of these opportunities and guarantees the healthy implementation of such practices. Write them on the middle column.
3. Select elimination of at least three old practices that by doing, you can help the growth of new practices. Write them in the right column.

| Opportunities | Invented New Practices | Eliminated Old Practices |
|---|---|---|
| **1st** | 1. | 1. |
| | 2. | 2. |
| | 3. | 3. |
| | | |
| **2nd** | 1. | 1. |
| | 2. | 2. |
| | 3. | 3. |
| | | |
| **3rd** | 1. | 1. |
| | 2. | 2. |
| | 3. | 3. |
| | | |
| **4th** | 1. | 1. |
| | 2. | 2. |
| | 3. | 3. |

*Source:* Adapted from Rothwell et al. (2021, 169).

## Key Takeaways

1. By recognizing how we view and relate to ourselves, others, and the concept of working and productivity, we can transform our view of personal effectiveness and relationships.
2. The world and the environment we have created for ourselves result from how we relate to ourselves, others, and work. We have a choice to continue our limited and negative views or transform them into realistic and responsible ways to exist and perform in personal and professional aspects of our lives.
3. We always play in life from either our opinions or possibilities for creating new opportunities.
4. It is up to us to invent new and empowering practices for new opportunities in our lives, personally and professionally. This action becomes our personal responsibility for having effectiveness, productivity, and peace of mind.

## List of Discussion Questions

1. How do you rate yourself from 0 to 10 on your understanding of elements of personal effectiveness?
   - What is missing or in the way of your understanding it better?
   - How do you evaluate your competencies to deliver the process?
   - What is your action plan to increase your overall rate on this process?
2. How do you rate yourself from 0 to 10 on your answers to the self-inquiry questions for maintaining self-realizations?
   - What is missing or in the way of your understanding it better?
   - How do you evaluate your competencies to deliver the process?
   - What is your action plan to increase your overall rate on this process?
3. How do you rate yourself from 0 to 10 on your understanding of elements of opinion versus opportunities?
   - What is missing or in the way of your understanding it better?
   - How do you evaluate your competencies to deliver the process?
   - What is your action plan to increase your overall rate on this process?

## References

Bakhshandeh, Behnam. 2009. *Conspiracy for Greatness; Mastery on Love Within*. San Diego, CA: Primeco Education, Inc.

Bakhshandeh, Behnam. 2015. *Anatomy of Upset: Restoring Harmony*. Carbondale, PA: Primeco Education, Inc.

Goleman, Daniel. 2015. *Emotional Intelligence; Why It Can Mater More Than IQ*. New York, NY: Bantam Books.

Kold, Judith, A. 2011. *Small Group Facilitation: Improving Process and Performance in Groups and Teams*. Amherst, MO: HRD Press.

Levi, Daniel. 2017. *Group Dynamics for Teams* (5th ed.). Thousand Oaks, CA: Sage Publications, Inc.

Rothwell, William J., Sohel M. Imroz and Behnam Bakhshandeh. 2021. *Organization- Development Interventions: Executing Effective Organizational Chang*. New York, NY: Taylor & Francis Group. CRC Press.

Seligman, Martin E.P. 2002. *Authentic Happiness: Using the New Positive Psychology to Realize Your Potential for Lasting Fulfillment*. New York, NY: Free Press.

Seligman, Martin EP, and Mihaly Csikszentmihalyi. 2010. "Positive psychology: An introduction." In *Flow and the Foundations of Positive Psychology* (pp. 279–298). Dordrecht: Springer.

Whitmore, John. 2017. *Coaching for Performance; The Principle and Practice of Coaching and Leadership* (5th ed.). Boston, MA: Nicholas Brealey Publishing.

# V

# DEVELOPING EMOTIONAL INTELLIGENCE, ASSERTIVENESS, RESILIENCE, AND POWER OF INQUIRY FOR SHIFTING PARADIGMS IN LEADERSHIP

Training individuals and teams in emotional intelligence, assertiveness, and resilience are some of the proposed training and development elements that will support organizations on improving awareness among individuals and teams while working on their leadership competencies. Part V covers elements of developing individuals and teams on emotional intelligence, assertiveness, and resilience through the process of transformational coaching.

## Chapter 14. Emotional Intelligence Competencies and Effective Leadership Paradigm

Chapter 14 defines emotional intelligence, paradigms, paradigm shifts, and the role of emotional intelligence in paradigm shifts and effective leadership.

DOI: 10.4324/9781003304074-18

## Chapter 15. Developing Assertiveness and Resilience

What is assertiveness and assertive behavior? Developing assertiveness and resilience through transformational coaching—topics covered in Chapter 15.

## Chapter 16. Opening Powerful Inquiries

Chapter 16 discusses the characteristics of empowering questions, how to ask empowering questions, and how to turn inquiries to action plans.

*Chapter 14*

# Emotional Intelligence Competencies and Effective Leadership Paradigm

Behnam Bakhshandeh

## Overview

Based on reviewing the relevant themes in organizations and their managements' interest in training and developing their employees on effective leadership, we look at emotional intelligence (EI) as one of the proposed training modules that positively supports the organizations on developing awareness among their employees while training them in leadership competencies (Bakhshandeh 2021).

Emotional intelligence competencies' training and development cover many elements of leadership rooted in every aspect of emotional intelligence. Such a program can spur leadership development among employees and in all levels of management. It can also shift present paradigms by raising production levels on awareness, understanding, and implementation of effective leadership.

Competencies as a mixture of a measurable and observable assortment of knowledge, skills, attitudes, and behaviors (KSABs) can assist individuals in performing better at work while attaining their goals (Donahue 2018). Competency-based evaluations are becoming a common application among organizations for evaluating their employees' preparation and execution of their jobs and overall successes in their accountabilities. "Thus, the level at which a person can demonstrate specific competencies will impact how valuable the person will be to an employer" (Donahue 2018, 21).

However, using EI competency-based evaluation and implementing training associated with developing leadership skills is practical and relevant to improving the presence and use of such skills by the employees.

DOI: 10.4324/9781003304074-19

This chapter will cover these elements:

- What is paradigm and paradigm shift?
- Emotional intelligence and paradigm shift
- How do we define emotional intelligence?
- Emotional intelligence leadership
- Four emotional intelligence clusters and related competencies
- Self-examination and self-evaluation rating

## What Is a Paradigm?

Paradigms represent a set of rules and guidelines we have built based on patterns of thoughts, feelings, and behaviors we have constructed based on what we have learned or experienced. These patterns are used to determine personal and professional boundaries, make us come to conclusions about someone or something, and point us to resolutions on how to resolve problems.

Let's look at some definitions and descriptions of paradigms among people and businesses:

- "Accepted samples of practical method in science" (Kuhn 1962, n.p.).
- "Universally recognized scientific achievements that for a time provide model problems and solutions to a community of practitioners" (Kuhn 1974, n.p.).
- "A paradigm is a shared set of assumed facts. The paradigm is the way we perceive the world, water to the fish. The paradigm explains the world to us and helps us to predict its behavior. When we are in the middle of a paradigm, it is difficult to imagine any other paradigm" (Smith 1975, 20).

Someone's paradigm results from mental and emotional conditioning with deep roots in their family, social, and professional experiences. This rigid pattern of experiences impacts the way they think and feel, which directly influences how they are *being* and what they are *doing* (see Figures 14.1 and 14.2).

Figure 14.1 represents a good example of someone in a leadership position with a limited and fixed thinking pattern about the people under them. Yet, that is the paradigm they are in about their people.

## What Is a Paradigm Shift?

We can think of a paradigm shift as altering our way of thinking or feeling about someone or something, usually for a better or more effective or productive one. It is a transformation of a mindset and perspective that can have a revolutionary change on someone's behavior. However, it doesn't happen by itself, but rather is assisted by a change agent, such as a transformational coach.

*Merriam-Webster* dictionary defines Paradigm Shift as "An important change that happens when the usual way of thinking about or doing something is replaced by a new and different way. This discovery will bring about a *paradigm shift* in our understanding of evolution" (Merriam-Webster 2020). Thakkar (2020) describes a paradigm shift as "A fundamental change in approach or underlying assumptions" (13).

**Figure 14.1 Example of Fixed Paradigm.**

*Source:* Author's Original Creation. Copyright 2022 by Behnam Bakhshandeh.

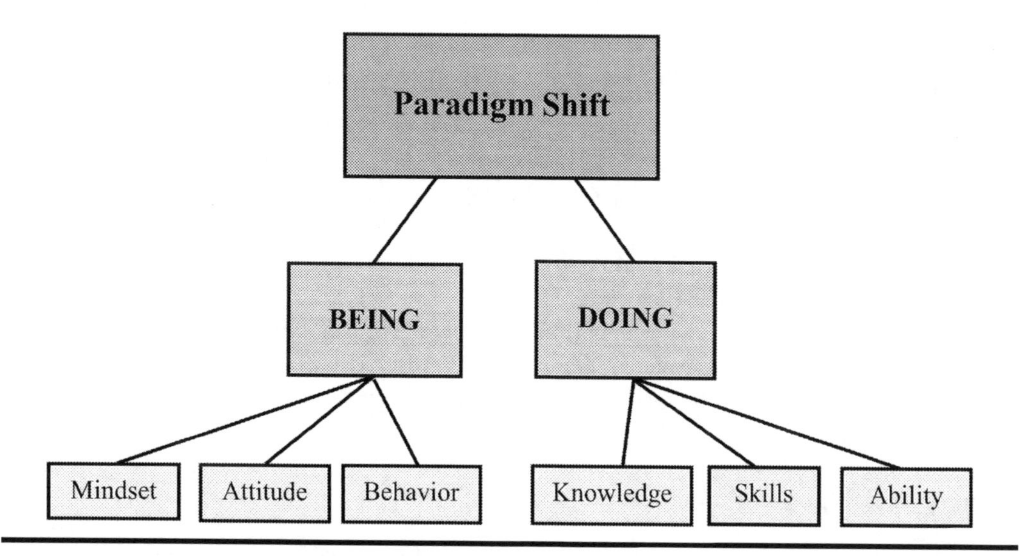


**Figure 14.2 Elements of a Paradigm Shift.**

*Source:* Author's Original Creation. Copyright 2022 by Behnam Bakhshandeh.

Figure 14.2 displays the positive impact of the paradigm shift of developing effective leadership among individuals in both personal and professional settings.

For the paradigm shift to be sustainable and effective, one needs to implement changes in both the *being* and *doing* domains. The primary change is in the domain of *being*, which positively affects the subjects' mindsets, thus reflecting on their attitudes and perceptions of their environments, which ultimately have a positive impact on their behaviors. These are important elements of effective leadership. People's mindsets can be influenced and polluted by their biases, opinions, and even prejudices.

The domain of *doing* comes next. This stage involves the interest in learning and adding to one's knowledge of what they are doing, developing skills on how to work with others and how to relate to different people, to understand diversity and differences among people, how to build up skills on effective communication and active listening and to develop abilities to be with upsetting or uncomfortable situations.

## Emotional Intelligence and Paradigm Shift

To increase our understanding of emotional intelligence, we must understand how paradigms affect our perceptions and our experience of the world, as well as the perceived world we have created. (We refer you back to Chapter 13 and Figures 13.1 and 13.2.)

As we have established, a paradigm is a mental and emotional screen beyond our life experiences and biases and our attachments to our views and opinions of people and the world and the meanings we add to people's behaviors and communications (Bakhshandeh 2009). Paradigms are created by our fundamental beliefs that influence our decision-making process and relationships (Grossman 2019). It is important to mention here we are not confined to only one type of paradigm. Depending on our situations, who we are with, or what we are doing, we might go from one paradigm to another at a different stage of our lives (Grossman 2019).

### *Presence of Emotional Intelligence in Organizations*

We have talked about emotional intelligence and its related meaning and definitions in Chapter 8, under Emotional Intelligence Coaching (please go back and review the main elements of Chapter 8). In this segment, we look at EI from different angles, particularly from competency-based leadership.

The concept of EI was actually raised at the beginning of the twentieth century. Emotional intelligence is crucial for developing a strong mindset, relationships, resilience, and communication that all individuals, teams, and organizations can benefit from and use. EI contains a set of soft skills that offer individuals some inner wisdom to adjust to life circumstances, either personal or professional, good or bad, expected or unexpected, and keeps us centered and focused on who we must be and what we have to do to resolve them.

### *Is EI Nature or Nurture?*

As human beings, we are all born with a brain supported by a system influenced by feelings and emotions, and we depend on the nature aspect of EI. However, at the same time, as we grow into adulthood and professional positions, we need to nurture our EI with training and development. On one hand, it is a nature's gift, and it is a nurture's skill (Connors 2020). We need to learn what to pay attention to, and what we need to get rid of, to be more effective and influential; that is how to develop skills and competencies.

Interestingly enough, both organization development literature (HBR 2017; Rothwell et al. 2016; Rothwell 2015; Cummings and Worley 2015) and emotional intelligence literature (Goleman 2015; Goleman 2014; Clarke 2006; Goleman 1998) suggested that EI is consumed by both nature and nurture. According to the HBR (2017), emotional intelligence is a mixture of several ingredients:

1. Genetic predisposition
2. Overall personality
3. Professional life experience
4. Some old-fashioned training

(Bakhshandeh 2021)

When consciously and intentionally utilizing and implementing EI, competency-based training and development encourage organizations, their management, and their employees to achieve exceptional performance (HBR 2017). In many shapes and forms, our emotions directly affect our mindset, which rules our daily lives. We all make fast decisions or draw immediate conclusions based on what we feel or emotions we experience at that time such as sadness, anger, happiness, frustration, or any other emotions; with that, unconsciously, we choose responses based on the emotions we are intensifying (Bakhshandeh 2015; Hockenbury and Hockenbury 2007). Developing our understanding of EI and its clusters and their competencies helps us to make a conscious decision and shifts our mental and emotional paradigms.

## Emotional Intelligence Leadership

The positive influence of emotional intelligence in creating effective leadership is neither a craze nor positive thinking but rather a researched and studied concept. The top organizations around the globe base their hiring for leadership positions on an emotional intelligence-based evaluation. "We'll delve into the pillars that comprise emotional intelligence and describe how you can use them to become a highly successful, influential leader" (Connors 2020, 13).

One of the primary steps to developing emotionally intelligent leadership is to identify with the main elements of EI leadership (see Figure 14.3):

1. Self-awareness
2. Social awareness
3. Self-regulation
4. Relationship management

In this segment, we categorize these four EI cornerstones and their related competencies, which we have briefly mentioned in Chapter 8.

According to Handley (2017), the topic and concept of emotional intelligence have been researched in two approaches:

1. The mental ability model, and
2. The mixed model, which includes many competencies such as motivation, traits, and skills.

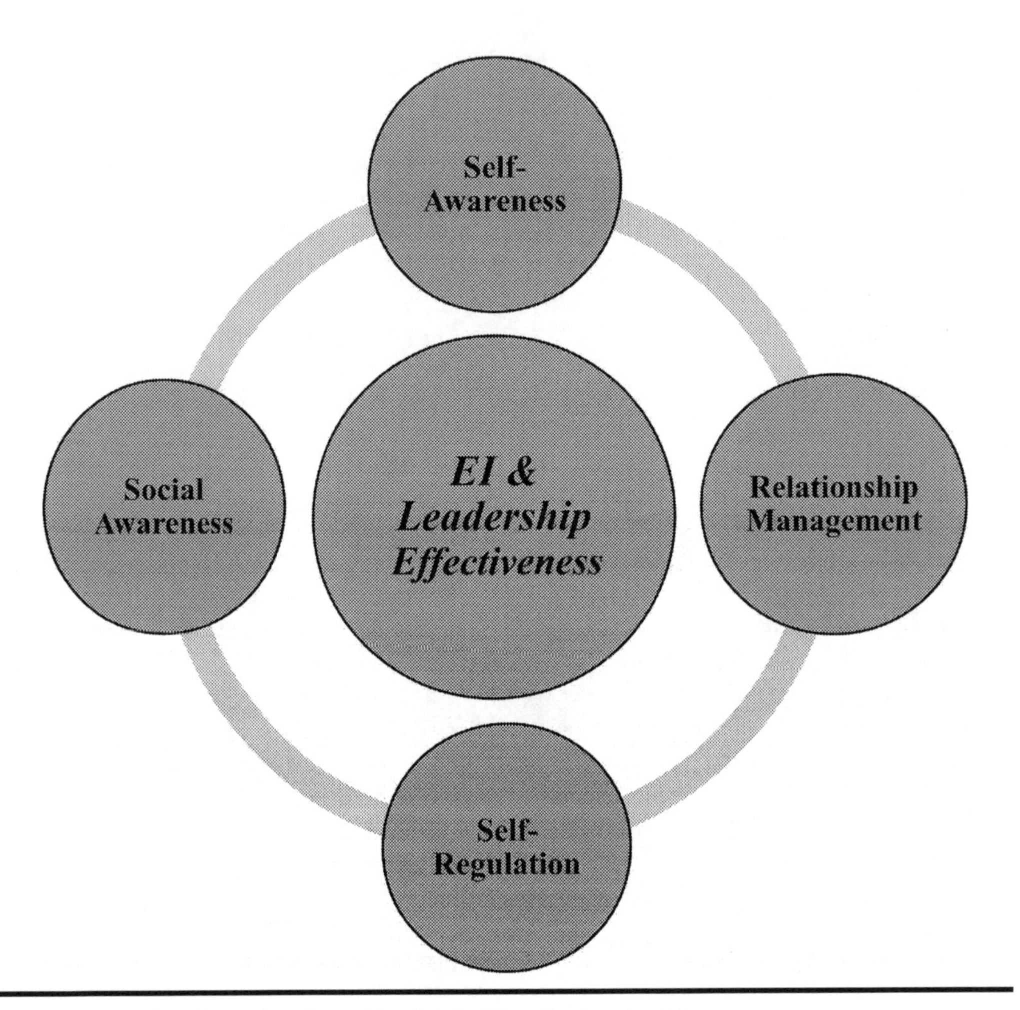


**Figure 14.3 Role of Emotional Intelligence in Effective Leadership.**

*Source:* Author's Original Creation. Copyright 2022 by Behnam Bakhshandeh.

In this chapter, we recommend the mixed model for training and developing employees for the EI skills. Handley (2017) Boyatzis and Sala (2004) analytically investigated EI competencies and determined the following four competency clusters: (1) self-awareness, (2) self-regulation, (3) social awareness, and (4) relationship management to be impactful on developing EI leadership (see Figure 14.4).

It is vital for business owners or organization leaders to offer their employees training and development in a mixed model of emotional intelligence knowledge, skills, and competencies that would contribute not only to their employees' development but also to their leadership and managerial skills. A variety of these qualities already exists in individuals who understand and practice these emotional intelligence clusters and competencies (Bakhshandeh 2021). In this segment, under Figure 14.4, we display at least four positive competencies under each of the four chosen EI clusters.

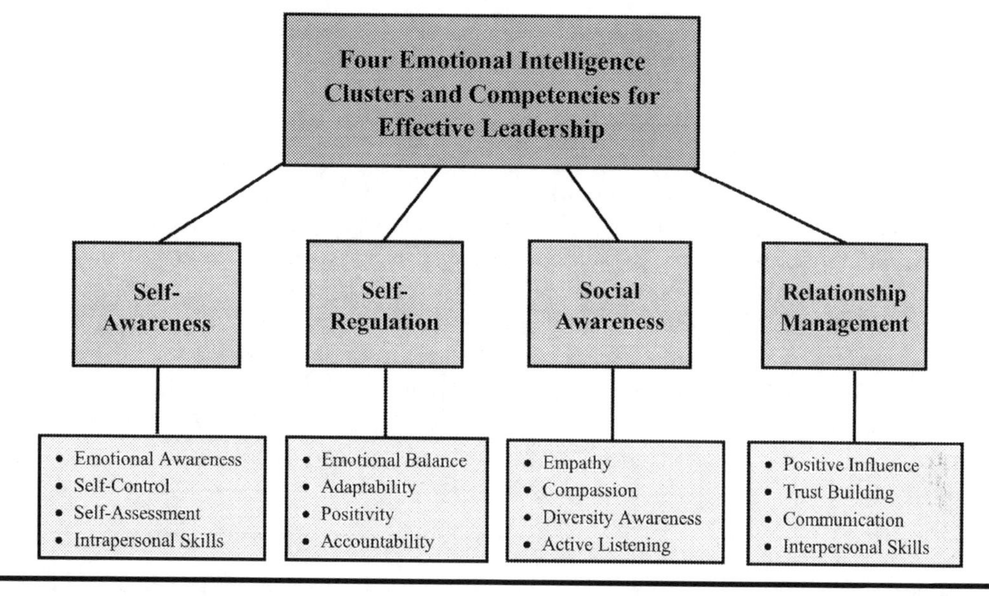


**Figure 14.4 Emotional Intelligence Clusters and Competencies and Their Relevancy to Effective Leadership.**

*Source:* Adapted from Bakhshandeh (2021, 337).

## Self-Awareness

The first element and key opening for Emotional intelligence is self-awareness. Self-awareness is the individuals' understanding of themselves and utilizing that understanding to learn and expand their mind to improve and grow, personally and professionally. This first step is the most challenging element of emotional intelligence to grasp since it is difficult to genuinely know ourselves and authentically own our motivations for why we are some way and doing something (Connors 2020).

We always rush to point others' shortcomings and somehow put their errors under a microscope and analyze what is wrong with them and how they should be fixed. However, it is much harder for us to look in the mirror to see and acknowledge our own shortcomings and errors in our mindsets, attitudes, and behaviors. "The most significant leadership work requires that we look inward at what we need to improve in ourselves and solicit feedback from people we trust and respect to inform us of how we lead, and how it impacts their lives" (Connors 2020, 15).

Self-awareness gives us access to mindful self-reflection to observe our thoughts and actions, toward ourselves and others. It would shed light on our impulsive thoughts and actions and reveal the consequences of such thoughts and actions (Bakhshandeh 2021).

Self-awareness is the capacity to identify and understand our emotions, temperaments, and motives and the awareness of our impact on other people. There are many valuable qualities and competencies referenced to self-awareness, but in this segment we review four of the many qualities and competencies of someone with self-awareness (see Figure 14.4) (Bakhshandeh 2021; Hockenbury and Hockenbury 2007).

### *Emotional Awareness*

This refers to the understanding and knowledge of the individuals' nature of their emotions and what emotions they feel. According to the Merriam-Webster Dictionary, emotion is "a conscious mental reaction (such as anger or fear) subjectively experienced as a strong feeling usually directed toward a specific object and typically accompanied by physiological and behavioral changes in the body." The Oxford Dictionary defines emotion as "a strong feeling deriving from one's circumstances, mood, or relationships with others." As it is displayed in both dictionary definitions, those notions are associated with one's feelings in a particular way. Some attributes of people with emotional awareness are (1) concerning others' feelings, (2) realizing misunderstandings, and (3) operating based on trust (Bakhshandeh 2021; Goleman 2015; Stevens 2009).

### *Self-Control*

One critical skill requisite for having and applying emotional intelligence is the individuals' capacity to channel their emotions instead of to push them down or to force them out (Wayne 2019). Emotions are a big part of the human psyche intended to notify us that there is something to pay attention to. How people react to the topic that their emotions point to in order to pay attention is to decide the level of importance of such subject matter and choose an appropriate and relevant course of action to address the topic (Goleman 1998). "There are no good or bad emotions; there are only good or bad responses to emotions" (Wayne 2019, 98). This way, people's reactions to their emotions are not impulsive. Stevens (2009) pointed out, "Self-control works to increase the process of rational thinking under pressure actively and is meant to encourage and boost productive actions" (45). Some attributes of people with self-control are (1) not making impulsive decisions, (2) controlling their behaviors, and (3) possessing conscientiousness (Bakhshandeh 2021; Wayne 2019; Goleman 2014).

### *Self-Assessment*

Self-assessment provides awareness into individuals' actual comprehension of a set of knowledge, skills, and competencies that can provide insights to detect gaps in their area of expertise and knowledge (Goleman 2015). In the same context, the University of Reading (2021) reflected on an important distinction regarding student self-assessment as "assessment methods [that] only measure students' ability to regurgitate knowledge, not how well they understand the topic. Self-assessment can provide insight into students' true comprehension and can help to identify gaps in students' knowledge" (The University of Reading 2021). As an important element of creating a feasible and comprehensive self-assessment, some organizations allow some degree of individual engagement in the design, redesign, and development of assessment criteria. This approach creates a more comprehensive and relevant self-assessment with a higher level of trustworthiness and relevancy. Some attributes of people who apply self-assessment are (1) monitoring their learning, (2) monitoring their goals' progress, and (3) conducting self-efficacy (Bakhshandeh 2021; Goleman 2015; Cummings and Worley 2015).

### *Intrapersonal Skills*

This is the ability of people to distinguish and understand their thoughts, emotions, and feelings. It is a skill for planning and directing their personal and professional lives (Rothwell 2015; Cummings and Worley 2015). Individuals with intrapersonal skills are proficient at looking within, inquiring inward, and sounding out their own feelings, emotions, motivations, and objectives. They are characteristically contemplative and thoughtful; by analyzing themselves, they seek self-understanding. Individuals with intrapersonal skills are intuitive and generally introverted. They mostly learn autonomously and through reflection (Shek and Lin 2015). "Intrapersonal competencies form the foundation of individuals' development, and they are fundamental qualities of leadership competencies" (Shek and Lin 2015, 255). Some attributes of people with intrapersonal skills are (1) appreciation for themselves, (2) awareness of their agenda, and (3) elimination of distractions (Bakhshandeh 2021; Shek and Lin 2015, Rothwell 2015; Cummings and Worley 2015).

## *Self-Regulation*

Self-regulation displays itself when people hold themselves accountable for their positive or negative emotions and understand how to manage them in a healthy way in private or public settings. These self-regulation mindsets and behaviors impact all aspects of their personal lives and professional work. "Excellent self-managers are flexible, organized, and adept at managing their time. They honor the plans they set forth for their day, knowing when to shift course and analyze changing information and emotions" (Connors 2020, 20).

Leaders who understand their emotional intelligence are aware of adjusting to adversity and being adaptive to different situations, such as a breakdown in production, employee turnover, different team dynamics, or even loss of market share. They face difficulties with confidence and audacity that inspire their people (Connors 2020).

Self-regulation is the ability to recognize and redirect our distracting impulses and temperaments with a tendency to defer immediate judgment and to apply considerations before acting against others (Bakhshandeh 2021; Hockenbury and Hockenbury 2007). The qualities and competencies referenced to self-regulation include but are not limited to the following (see Figure 14.4):

### *Emotional Balance*

Emotional balance is people's state of being mindful of their emotions and their ability to adequately handle them sensibly and gently. Being emotionally out of balance is caused by either not allowing themselves to experience their feelings when they arise and then discarding and suppressing them or being firmly attached to such feelings and being consumed by them (Goleman 2015; Goleman 1998). It arises when individuals permit themselves to feel the emotions that occur on the surface without feeling restrained or overwhelmed by them. Those who possess this balance learn about feelings and accept them with no judgment but act on them in responsible ways. Some attributes of people with emotional balance are (1) accurately identifying their emotions, (2) being mindful of their emotions, and (3) managing impulse emotions (Bakhshandeh 2021; Goleman 2015; Goleman 1998).

### *Adaptability*

Adaptability refers to the degree of strictness and harshness on individuals' ways, mindsets, and approaches and how they are efficient in adapting to new ideas, conditions, or environments. Stevens (2009) pointed to the importance of adaptability by stating, "Considering the only way to bolster teamwork is by putting together a cohesive team and showing a willingness to change their ways, which is something that any good leader should be on the lookout for" (50). Some attributes of people with emotional balance are (1) being open to learning new things, (2) adjusting quickly, and (3) embracing new ideas (Bakhshandeh 2021).

### *Positivity*

A good, positive attitude has a massive positive effect in the workplace. This positive impact influences people in how they relate to their peers, how managers lead, or how organizations deal with their clients and customers (HBR 2017). A positive temperament toward other people generates an environment for building relationships, trust, and loyalty among the workforce at every possible organizational level (HBR 2017). Conversely, when we do not display our care and commitment to workability and harmony, distrust will arise and cause massive dysfunction in relationships, in the home or at work, personally and professionally (Goleman 2015). Some attributes of people who practice positivity are (1) being optimistic, (2) being resilient, and (3) being grateful (Bakhshandeh 2021; Goleman 2015).

### *Accountability*

Merriam-Webster (2021) dictionary defined accountability as "the quality or state of being accountable especially an obligation or willingness to accept responsibility or to account for one's actions." One who practices accountability is not into the blame game, avoiding their responsibilities by pointing at and blaming others for what happens and how it happens. They do not act like the victims of circumstances as a replacement for being responsible. They do not procrastinate in their duties and what they are responsible for doing (Rothwell et al. 2016; Goleman 2015; Bakhshandeh 2015). "Accountability and responsibility go hand in hand. When you practice responsibility, you cannot help being accountable and having integrity. This is the essential component of the three-force combination" (Bakhshandeh 2015, 32). Some attributes of people who are accountable are (1) taking responsibility for their actions, (2) not blaming or pointing fingers, and (3) being transparent (Bakhshandeh 2021; Bakhshandeh 2015).

## ***Social Awareness***

Social awareness requires social skills. Even with business leaders' abilities to display understanding, empathy, compassion, and to control their emotions, it is not enough to deal with conflicting and difficult situations arising from lack of social awareness and related elements (Stevens 2009). This cluster of skills applies not only to employees but also to the organizations' customers and clients. "A person manages to do that by obtaining and maintaining a high degree of emotional intelligence, of course!" (Stevens 2009, 48). Additionally, those business leaders who understand social awareness elements, such as workplace diversity and differences at the workplace by disregarding stereotypes and generalizations of people can demonstrate social awareness results throughout the organization (Handley 2017). Handley (2017; as cited from Goleman 2014) stated that "Goleman describes this competency cluster with empathic listening, ability to grasp the others' perspective, political understanding, organizational awareness, and service to others" (146). Competencies referenced to self-regulation include but are not limited to the following (see Figure 14.4):

### *Empathy*

This is the ability to focus on others as the groundwork for empathy and the ability to develop relationships, personally, socially, and professionally. Business leaders able to effectively focus on others are the ones able to find common ground with others, and their opinions and input carry the most respect and acceptance among their people. They arise as natural leaders in society and in organizations despite their organizational hierarchy or social status (HBR 2017; Goleman 2015). Individuals' propensity to identify and appreciate others' emotional status is in dealing with others relating to the present state of their feelings and emotions (Goleman 2015). Some attributes of empathetic people are (1) recognizing talent, (2) understanding an other's emotional state, and (3) being helpful to others (Bakhshandeh 2021; HBR 2017; Goleman 2015).

### *Compassion*

The ability to demonstrate understanding, sympathy, and kindness for others in their time of sorrow, trouble, and hardship is displaying compassion. It is the consciousness of experiencing others' distress and grief and then interjecting interests and aspirations to ease their pain (HBR 2017; Goleman 2015). Compassion is taking empathy a little further and deeper. People with compassion feel hardship when witnessing other persons in hardship and distress and will act to assist them. Compassion is one element of social awareness that distinguishes between having understood someone and caring for them. Some attributes of compassionate people are (1) placing oneself in others' situations, (2) practicing active listening, and (3) being okay with others' failures (Bakhshandeh 2021; HBR 2017; Goleman 2015).

### *Diversity Awareness*

Organizations and individuals can attain diversity awareness when they appreciate and understand the advantages of cultural diversity and differences among people. A workforce with diversity awareness can establish an organizational culture built on the foundation of dignity, mutual respect and acceptance of the differences among people regardless of their cultural background, ethnicity, age, sexual orientation, gender, religion, socio-economic status, and physical abilities (Goleman 2015). Some attributes of people with diversity awareness are (1) embracing uniqueness among people, (2) having mutual respect for everyone, and (3) having universal treatment for everyone (Bakhshandeh 2021; Goleman 2015; Stevens 2009).

### *Active Listening*

As one of the most important elements of communication, active listening is a valuable skill that can be developed by practicing. Those with active listening concentrate completely on the persons talking and the content of the conversation instead of just passively hearing the speakers and their messages (Rothwell et al. 2016; Goleman 2015). Practicing active listening helps the listeners to gain the speakers' trust and respect by knowing that the listeners appreciate their situations. Active listening encompasses the listeners' desires to understand and extend support and empathy for the speakers. Active listening is a model of listening and replying to others that enhance mutual appreciation and understanding. It is an essential first step to neutralize a hard situation and pursue a workable solution to potential crises. Some attributes of people with active listening are (1) paying attention to the speaker, (2) responding appropriately, and (3) providing feedback (Bakhshandeh 2021; Rothwell et al. 2016; Cummings and Worley 2015).

## Relationship Management

The quality of life is connected and influenced by relationships that individuals have with other people, both positively and negatively. On a personal and professional level, there is no need to have relationships that add nothing and do not bring value to the relationship. People aware of emotional intelligence know this valuable concept (Bakhshandeh 2021). To have a quality relationship, besides looking for values and developing quality, people must also invest in maintaining the relationships and strive to improve them. "Emotional intelligence provides you the cognizance you need to maintain your valuable relationships and do away with the toxic ones" (Wayne 2019, 119). Similar to a personal relationship, in a professional relationship, a business leader needs to discover how to effectively employ their intelligence to let them realize and identify opportunities, effectively communicate, attempt to solve problems, and collaborate with their workforce and customers (Goleman 2015). "This ability to integrate is a crucial steppingstone to becoming a strong business leader. To be more specific, managerial positions have found that emotional intelligence is a critical part of relationship building and the development of dynamic leadership" (Stevens 2009, 31).

Competencies referenced to relationship management include but are not limited to the following (see Figure 14.4).

### Positive Influence

This capability and skill seek to impact and influence others' mindsets, behavior, character building, or personal and professional development. In relationship building, positive influence is the impression they can employ on themselves or on other individuals by indicating their strengths and underlining their qualities to empower and encourage them. Their influence becomes their nature; it will show who they are, what they do, and how they think (Longmore et al. 2018; Martz et al. 2016). Being used positively and for their good and others can be an effective tool to empower others, encourage them, and direct them to better results in life and profession. Some attributes of those with positive influence are (1) being charismatic, (2) being humble, and (3) striving to help (Bakhshandeh 2021; Longmore et al. 2018; Martz et al. 2016).

### Trust Building

This competency refers to the ability to build trust with others perhaps lining up with other personality traits and self-concept characteristics (Handley 2017). Forming a foundation of trust is critical to building an effective team because having trust among team members gives an impression of safety. Without trust among teams and groups, there will not be as much collaboration, expressions of creativity and innovation, and little productivity, while people devote their time to shielding themselves from others and protecting their interests (Handley 2017; Rothwell et al. 2016; Rothwell 2015). According to Rothwell (2015), the concept of team building is one of the most common forms of organization development. Business professionals consider the interpersonal relationships between team members to be an indispensable component of trust building, given that team cohesiveness and understanding of one another are vital to the success of the trust and team-building process. Some attributes of someone with the ability to build trust and teams are (1) being friendly and approachable, (2) being respectful to others' ideas, and (3) practicing integrity and accountability (Bakhshandeh 2021; Rothwell et al. 2016; Rothwell 2015).

### *Communication*

This is the ability to act on transferring information from one location, individual, or team to other people or places. All forms of communication include at least one message, one sender, and one receiver (Jones 2015). Steinfatt (2009) expressed his view of communication and its vital role in human connectedness: "The central thrust of human communication concerns mutually understood symbolic exchange" (295). Steinfatt's view of communication might not be accepted as a general definition of communication, but it sheds light on the importance of this essential skill. However, the term *communication* is commonly called transferring information from one person to another, in both personal and professional environments (Steinfatt 2009). Communication is one concept that has been and continues to be the topic of many theories and research about the human connection (Jones 2015). Without communication, there is no workability or teamwork. Teams are synchronized when they communicate effectively. Peace, harmony, and fulfillment arise in communication. Without effective communication, there will be no effective connection and productivity at home or at work (Bakhshandeh 2015). Some attributes of those with communication skills are (1) being aware of nonverbal communication, (2) delivering clear and concise messages, and (3) showing courtesy and listening keenly (Bakhshandeh 2021; Jones 2015; Goleman 2015; Steinfatt 2009).

### *Interpersonal Skills*

These skills refer to the ability to interact, relate, understand, and effectively co-operate with others, at home or in the workplace. Interpersonal skills are powerful aptitudes for building relationships and establishing cooperation with others (Spencer and Spencer 1993). While professional position hard skills are important to workers' ability to perform their work and job-related duties, effectively demonstrating abilities to work with others, delivering clear communication, and displaying self-confidence as interpersonal skills are as important as hard skills, and it can make a difference in the workers' professional advancement. Some attributes of someone with interpersonal skills are (1) being aware of themselves and others, (2) being collaborative, and (3) caring about relationships (Bakhshandeh 2021; Rothwell et al. 2016; Rothwell 2015).

## EI Self-Examination and Self-Evaluation

People who understand their emotional intelligence and are aware of their mindsets, attitudes, and behaviors can conduct a self-examination and self-evaluation of their thoughts, their actions, and the consequences of their actions.

Tables 14.1 and 14.2 are designed for individuals and organizations to conduct a self-rating on their understanding and level of their practices to use qualities and competencies of emotional intelligence.

Table 14.1 is designed for individuals to rate themselves on their understanding and practice of four EI clusters. As you can see, each cluster has four competencies with a total of

**Table 14.1 Use of Emotional Intelligence at Work Self-Rating System. Author's Original Creation.**

| *Use of Emotional Intelligence at Work Self-Rating* | | | | | | | | | |
|---|---|---|---|---|---|---|---|---|---|
| Date: | | Participant Name: | | | | | | | |
| Month: | | Direct Manager: | | | | | | | |
| Rating Scale<br>**1**=*Poor*, **2**=*Marginal*, **3**=*Acceptable*, **4**=*Good*, **5**=*Excellent* | | | | | | | | | |
| **Clusters** | | **Competencies** | | | **Rating Scale** | | | | |
| | | | | | **1** | **2** | **3** | **4** | **5** |
| **A** | **Self-Awareness** | *1* | 1 | Emotional Awareness | | | | | |
| | | *2* | 2 | Self-Control | | | | | |
| | | *3* | 3 | Self-Assessment | | | | | |
| | | *4* | 4 | Intrapersonal Skills | | | | | |
| **B** | **Self-Regulation** | *5* | 1 | Emotional Balance | | | | | |
| | | *6* | 2 | Adaptability | | | | | |
| | | *7* | 3 | Positivity | | | | | |
| | | *8* | 4 | Accountability | | | | | |
| **C** | **Social-Awareness** | *9* | 1 | Empathy | | | | | |
| | | *10* | 2 | Compassion | | | | | |
| | | *11* | 3 | Diversity Awareness | | | | | |
| | | *12* | 4 | Active Listening | | | | | |
| **D** | **Relationship Management** | *13* | 1 | Positive Influence | | | | | |
| | | *14* | 2 | Trust Building | | | | | |
| | | *15* | 3 | Communication | | | | | |
| | | *16* | 4 | Interpersonal Skills | | | | | |
| Sub-Total (total of each column) | | | | | | | | | |
| Total of above 5 rating scales | | | | | | | | | |
| Average (above total divided by 16) | | | | | | | | | |
| Two actions for this month that would bring up my two lowest emotional intelligence ratings by at least 1 scale on the next month rating: | | | | | | | | | |
| Action 1: | | | | | | | | | |
| Action 2: | | | | | | | | | |

*Source:* Copyright 2022 by Behnam Bakhshandeh.

16 competencies. Managers or supervisors can explain the process to participants and ask them to rate themselves on their understanding and practice of these competencies. The participants need to come up with at least two actions they are taking to improve their knowledge and practice of EI with their people or in their teams.

This self-rating could happen monthly until the managers or supervisors get confident in the participants' understanding of EI competencies.

Table 14.2 is designed for individuals at any management or supervisory level to conduct a self-evaluation and inquiry into their honest and authentic mindsets, attitudes, and behaviors related to their understanding and practices of EI or lack of such. Each of the four EI clusters contained six self-inquiry questions or statements, for a total of 24 such inquiries.

Participants should rate themselves with utmost honesty and authenticity in each cluster independently and as a whole at the end. Similar to Table 14.1, each participant should come with at least two actions they would do to bring their rating numbers higher for the next monthly or quarterly rating.

This is the time and place for managers to provide coaching and training to develop their employees with a higher level of understanding and practices of EI at work, which would directly increase the quality of performance and personal relationships.

**Table 14.2 Emotional Intelligence Self-Evaluation Inquiries and Rating System. Author's Original Creation.**

| *Emotional Intelligence Self-Evaluation Inquiries and Rating System* | | | | | | | | | |
|---|---|---|---|---|---|---|---|---|---|
| Day: | | Participant Name: | | Team: | | | | | |
| Month: | | Direct Manager: | | Department: | | | | | |
| *Rating Scale*<br>***1****=Never,* ***2****=Hardly,* ***3****=Occasionally,* ***4****=Generally,* ***5****=Constantly* | | | | | | | | | |
| **Clusters** | | # | | **Inquiries** | **Rating** | | | | |
| | | | | | **1** | **2** | **3** | **4** | **5** |
| **A** | **Self-Awareness** | *1* | 1 | I am conscious of my body language responses to others' communication. | | | | | |
| | | *2* | 2 | I am aware of my facial expressions when I am discussing matters at work. | | | | | |
| | | *3* | 3 | When evaluating a situation, I first check out my opinion and biases. | | | | | |
| | | *4* | 4 | Before making any important decisions, I take my emotional temperature into account. | | | | | |
| | | *5* | 5 | I can recognize my emotions before, during and after sensitive conversations. | | | | | |
| | | *6* | 6 | I think and consider the emotional reasoning behind what I say and what I do. | | | | | |
| | | | Sub-Total (total of each column) | | | | | | |
| | | | Total of above 5 rating scales | | | | | | |
| | | | Cluster "A" Average (above total divided by 6) | | | | | | |

*(Continued)*

**Table 14.2 (Continued)**

| *Emotional Intelligence Self-Evaluation Inquiries and Rating System* | | | | | | | | | |
|---|---|---|---|---|---|---|---|---|---|
| **B** | **Self-Regulation** | *7* | 1 | I can manage myself and keep my composure when I am angry. | | | | | |
| | | *8* | 2 | I can move forward and handle my responsibilities despite difficulties and obstructions. | | | | | |
| | | *9* | 3 | I do not act on a strong impulse to say something or do something. | | | | | |
| | | *10* | 4 | I reflect on my thoughts and feelings before any communications or actions. | | | | | |
| | | *11* | 5 | I can express what I feel authentically and responsibly without upsetting others. | | | | | |
| | | *12* | 6 | I can manage my attitudes and moods and not take them to work. | | | | | |
| | | | Sub-Total (total of each column) | | | | | | |
| | | | Total of above 5 rating scales | | | | | | |
| | | | Cluster "B" Average (above total divided by 6) | | | | | | |
| | | | | | | | | | |
| **C** | **Social Awareness** | *13* | 1 | I can recognize how others view me while interacting with them. | | | | | |
| | | *14* | 2 | I can recognize others' feelings and moods based on their non-verbal gestures. | | | | | |
| | | *15* | 3 | I can express empathy with others in a situation. | | | | | |
| | | *16* | 4 | I am aware of people's diversity and differences in cultures. | | | | | |
| | | *17* | 5 | I observe others' reactions to me to realize my behavior's effectiveness. | | | | | |
| | | *18* | 6 | I have compassion and understanding for why people are emotional. | | | | | |
| | | | Sub-Total (total of each column) | | | | | | |
| | | | Total of above 5 rating scales | | | | | | |
| | | | Cluster "C" Average (above total divided by 6) | | | | | | |

| *Emotional Intelligence Self-Evaluation Inquiries and Rating System* | | | | | | | | | |
|---|---|---|---|---|---|---|---|---|---|
| D | **Relationship Management** | *19* | 1 | I am quick to take responsibility for my mistakes and clean them up. | | | | | |
| | | *20* | 2 | I use encouraging language while talking to others about work issues. | | | | | |
| | | *21* | 3 | I try to empower others when they discuss issues with me. | | | | | |
| | | *22* | 4 | I deal with others' emotional behaviors with sensitivity and calm and collected manners | | | | | |
| | | *23* | 5 | I am liked and respected by others around me. | | | | | |
| | | *24* | 6 | I can convince and motivate others to consider my viewpoint. | | | | | |
| | | | Sub-Total (total of each column) | | | | | | |
| | | | Total of above 5 rating scales | | | | | | |
| | | | Cluster "D" Average (above total divided by 6) | | | | | | |
| **Final Sub-Total (total of all clusters averages)** | | | | | | | | | |
| **Final Average (above total divided by 4)** | | | | | | | | | |
| Two actions for this month that would bring up my three lowest ratings by at least one scale on the next month rating: | | | | | | | | | |
| Action 1: | | | | | | | | | |
| Action 2: | | | | | | | | | |
| Action 3: | | | | | | | | | |

*Source:* Copyright 2022 by Behnam Bakhshandeh.

## Key Takeaways

1. Emotional intelligence competencies' training and development cover many elements of leadership rooted in all aspects of emotional intelligence that would cause leadership development among employees.
2. Competencies are a mixture of a measurable and observable assortment of knowledge, skills, attitudes, and behaviors (KSABs) that assist individuals in performing better at their work while attaining their goals (Donahue 2018).
3. Paradigms represent a set of rules and guidelines we have built based on patterns of thoughts, feelings, and behaviors we have constructed based of what we have learned or experienced.
4. A paradigm shift is a transformation of a mindset and perspective that would have a revolutionary change on someone's behavior.
5. Emotional intelligence is a crucial skill for developing strong mindsets, relationships, resilience, and communication that all individuals, teams, and organizations can benefit from and use.

## List of Discussion Questions

1. How do you rate yourself from 0 to 10 on your understanding of the concept of paradigm and paradigm shift?
   - What is missing or in the way of your understanding it better?
   - How do you evaluate your competencies to deliver the process?
   - What is your action plan to increase your overall rate on this process?
2. How do you rate yourself from 0 to 10 on your understanding of emotional intelligence clusters?
   - What is missing or in the way of your understanding it better?
   - How do you evaluate your competencies to deliver the process?
   - What is your action plan to increase your overall rate on this process?
3. How do you rate yourself from 0 to 10 on your understanding of EI clusters' competencies?
   - What is missing or in the way of your understanding it better?
   - How do you evaluate your competencies to deliver the process?
   - What is your action plan to increase your overall rate on this process?
4. How do you rate yourself from 0 to 10 on your understanding of emotional intelligence self-evaluation and self-examination ratings?
   - What is missing or in the way of your understanding it better?
   - How do you evaluate your competencies to deliver the process?
   - What is your action plan to increase your overall rate on this process?

## References

Bakhshandeh, Behnam. 2009. *Conspiracy for Greatness; Mastery on Love Within.* San Diego, CA: Primeco Education, Inc.

Bakhshandeh, Behnam. 2015. *Anatomy of Upset: Restoring Harmony.* Carbondale, PA: Primeco Education, Inc.

Bakhshandeh, Behnam. 2021. *Perception of 21st Century 4cs (Critical Thinking, Communication, Creativity & Collaboration) Skill Gap in Private-Sector Employers in Lackawanna County, NEPA* (An unpublished dissertation in workforce education and development). State College, PA: The Pennsylvania State University.

Boyatzis, Richard. E., and Fabio Sala. 2004. "Assessing Emotional Intelligence Competencies." In Glenn Geher (Ed.), *The Measurement of Emotional Intelligence.* London: Nova Science Publishers. doi: 10.1016/S0160-2896(01)00084-8.

Clarke, N. 2006. "Emotional Intelligence Training: A Case of Caveat Emptor." *Human Resource Development Review* 5, no. 4: 422–441. doi: 10.1177/1534484306293844.

Connors, Christopher, D. 2020. *Emotional Intelligence for the Modern Leader.* Emeryville, CA: Rockridge Press.

Cummings, Thomas. G. and Christopher. G. Worley. 2015. *Organization Development & Change* (10th ed.) Stamford, CT. Cengage Learning.

Donahue, Wesley, E. 2018. *Building Leadership Competence. A Competency-Based Approach to Building Leadership Ability.* State College, PA: Centerstar Learning.

Goleman, Daniel. 1998. *Working with Emotional Intelligence.* New York, NY: Random House.

Goleman, Daniel. 2014. "What it Takes to Achieve Managerial Success." *TD: Talent Development* 68, no. 11: 48–52.

Goleman, Daniel. 2015. *Emotional Intelligence; Why It Can Mater More Than IQ.* New York, NY: Bantam Books.

Grossman, Robert. 2019. "How Paradigms Influence Your Emotional Intelligence." *LinkedIn*. www.linkedin.com/pulse/how-paradigms-influence-your-emotional-intelligence-robert-grossman/

Handley, Meredith. 2017. *An Interpersonal Behavioral Framework for Early-career Engineers Demonstrating Engineering Leadership Characteristics across Three Engineering Companies*. (Unpublished doctoral dissertation). Pennsylvania: The Pennsylvania State University.

HBR. 2017. *Harvard Business Review Guild to Emotional Intelligence*. Boston, MA: Harvard Business Review Press.

Hockenbury, Don. H. and Sandra E. Hockenbury. 2007. *Discovering Psychology*. New York, NY: Worth Publishers.

Jones, Virginia. R. 2015. "21st century skills: Communication." *Children's Technology and Engineering* 20, no. 2: 28–29. www.iteea.org/Publications/Journals/ESCJournal/CTEDecember2015.aspx?source

Kuhn, Thomas, S. 1962. "The structure of scientific revolutions." *International Encyclopedia of Unified Science* 2, no. 2.

Kuhn, Thomas S. 1974. "Second thoughts on paradigms." *The Structure of Scientific Theories* 2: 459–482. efaidnbmnnnibpcajpcglclefindmkaj/https://mail.uomustansiriyah.edu.iq/media/lectures/10/10_2019_02_17!07_45_06_PM.pdf

Longmore, Anne-Liisa, Ginger Grant and Golnaz Golnaraghi. 2018. "Closing the 21st-century knowledge gap: reconceptualizing teaching and learning to transform business education." *Journal of Transformative Education* 16, no. 3: 197–219. doi: 10.1177/1541344617738514

Martz, Ben., Jim Hughes, and Frank Braun. 2016. "Creativity and problem-solving: Closing the skills gap." *The Journal of Computer Information Systems* 57, no. 1: 39–48. doi: 10.1080/08874417.2016.118149

Merriam-Webster 2020. "Paradigm Shift." https://www.merriam-webster.com/dictionary/paradigm%20shift

Merriam-Webster 2021. "Accountability." https://www.merriam-webster.com/dictionary/accountability

Rothwell, William, J. 2015. *Organization Development Fundamentals: Managing Strategic Change*. Alexandria, WV: ATD Press.

Rothwell, William, J., Jacqueline M. Stavros and Roland L. Sullivan. 2016. *Practicing Organization Development: Leading Transformation and Change* (4th ed.). Hoboken, NJ: John Wiley & Sons, Inc.

Shek, Daniel T. and Lin, Le. 2015. "Intrapersonal Competencies and Service Leadership." *International Journal of Disability Human Development* 14, no. 3: 255–263. doi: 10.1515/ijdhd-2015-0406.

Smith, Adam. 1975. *Power of Mind*. New York, NY: Random House.

Spencer, Lyle. M., and Signe M. Spencer. 1993. *Competence at Work. Models for Superior Performance*. New York, NY: John Wiley and Sons, Ed.

Steinfatt, Tim. 2009. *Definitions of Communication*. In S. W. Littlejohn and K. A. Foss (Eds.), *Encyclopedia of Communication Theory* (pp. 295–299). Thousand Oaks, CA. Sage Publication, Inc. doi: 10.4135/9781412959384.n108

Stevens, Richard. 2009. *Emotional Intelligence in Business: EQ: The Essential Ingredient to Survive and Thrive as a Modern Workplace Leader*. Hoboken, NJ: John Wiley & Sons.

Thakkar, Bharat S. 2020. *Paradigm Shift in Management Philosophy: Future Challenges in Global Organizations* (1st ed.) Cham: Palgrave MacMillan-Springer International Publishing.

University of Reading. 2021. "Engage in Assessment." www.reading.ac.uk/engageinassessment/peer-and-self-assessment/self-assessment/eia-why-use-self-assessment.aspx.

Wayne, Jenny. 2019. *Emotional Intelligence 2.0. A Guide to Manage Anger, Overcome Negativity and Master Your Emotions*. Reading: University of Reading.

# Chapter 15

# Developing Assertiveness and Resilience

Sohel M. Imroz

## Overview

In the previous chapter, we learned about emotional intelligence and the role of self-awareness, self-regulation, social awareness, and relationship management on transformation. In this chapter, we will discuss another important component of transformation—developing assertiveness and resilience. Broadly speaking, being assertive shows that individuals respect themselves, stand up for their interests, and express their thoughts and feelings with honesty and confidence. On the other hand, resilience "is the process and outcome of successfully adapting to difficult or challenging life experiences, especially through mental, emotional, and behavioral flexibility and adjustment to external and internal demands" (American Psychological Association 2022, para. Resilience). To become successful in transformational coaching, both the coach and the learners should understand assertiveness and resilience, how to develop these skills, and implement appropriate behaviors.

**This chapter attempts to underline:**

- What is assertiveness and assertive behavior?
- Characteristics of assertive individuals
- Understanding passive, assertive, and aggressive communication styles and behaviors
- Developing assertiveness through transformational coaching
- What is resilience?
- Developing resilience through transformational coaching

DOI: 10.4324/9781003304074-20

## What Is Assertiveness and Assertive Behavior?

Assertiveness is the ability to honestly express one's opinions, feelings, beliefs, rights, and needs without anxiety and without violating the law or the rights of others (UC San Diego 2022). Alberti and Emmons (1974) stressed that assertive behaviors empower individuals to act in their own best interests, stand up for themselves without unnecessary stress or anxiety, express their honest feelings and opinions comfortably, and exercise their own rights without denying the rights of others. According to SkillsYouNeed (2022), few examples of assertive behavior include expressing one's opinions, wishes, thoughts and feelings; encouraging others to do likewise; accepting responsibilities; appreciating others for their work and effort; admitting to mistakes and apologizing when necessary; maintaining self-control; and behaving as an equal to others.

Borden (2022) highlighted various examples of assertive behavior. For instance, initiating conversations with others, making requests, asking for favors, ability to say "no," addressing issues that are bothersome, staying firm, and expressing both positive and negative emotions. Pipas and Jaradat (2010) and Bishop (2013) mentioned several verbal and nonverbal characteristics of assertive communication. Among the verbal characteristics, communication should have clarity (i.e., using language and words that clearly express the needs). In addition, communication should be non-threatening (i.e., not blaming or intimidating others) and positive (i.e., using constructive, effective, and supportive language). Lastly, communication should not be criticizing the recipient (Gatchpazian 2022). Nonverbal characteristics include direct eye contact, assertive body posture (i.e., a body posture that is upright and not hunched or bent), clear and confident tone of voice, positive facial expression (i.e., not expressing anger or anxiety), and proper timing (i.e., letting the other person finish without interrupting, pausing to give the other person time to understand) (2022).

## Characteristics of Assertive Individuals

Reyes (2015) described several characteristics of assertive individuals—high self-confidence, respect for other people's opinions, ability to validate the feelings of others, and being good listeners. The following section elaborates on these characteristics.

### *High Self-Confidence*

Assertive individuals have high self-confidence—a feeling of trust in their abilities, qualities, and judgment. Assertive individuals accept and trust themselves and have a sense of control in life. They are aware of their strengths and weakness and, in general, have a positive view of themselves. They also know what their boundaries are, what they do and don't like, are able to set realistic goals and objectives for themselves, and can handle criticism. Many individuals who struggle with assertiveness are self-critical, have low self-esteem, ignore positive qualities in themselves, and allow others to make decisions for them. To increase self-confidence, individuals should refrain from comparing themselves to others. Instead, they should start surrounding themselves with positive people; taking care of their physical and mental health by proper diet, exercise, meditation, and sleep; being kind to themselves; practicing positive self-thoughts; and facing their fears (Morin 2022).

## *Respect for Other People's Opinions*

Assertive individuals respect other people's opinions. Since they have self-confidence in their abilities, qualities, and judgment, they do not feel the necessity or urge to grandiose themselves or dis, insult, or degrade others. Some individuals insult others as a result of anger, insecurity, jealousy, lack of understanding, or simply by thinking that it is cool (Barber 2016). Assertive individuals can better handle this type of situation by regaining composure or staying calm, expressing how they exactly feel, using humor, or merely by ignoring it. Other useful behaviors they often show when dealing with insults are staying positive, stop making instant reactions, and not becoming too emotional when reacting (UP Journey 2021).

## *Ability to Validate Feelings of Others*

Assertive individuals can validate the feelings of others, which means, recognizing their emotions, experiences, and accepting their legitimacy. This process is also known as *emotional validation* (Draghici 2022). Emotional validation plays an important role in developing individuals' personality by confirming and strengthening their self-confidence (2022). Rather than trivializing other people's experience, assertive individuals may say that they understand what others have to say. Contrary to emotional validation, emotional invalidation is the process of denying, rejecting, or dismissing someone's feelings (2022). Table 15.1 provides few examples of emotionally validating and invalidating statements.

## *Being Good Listeners*

Assertive individuals are also good listeners who give others a lot of attention when they talk about something or about their problems and try to understand and support them. Being a good listener builds trust and strong relationships, helps resolve conflict, captures important information, identifies problems, and, ultimately, increases knowledge (In Professional Development 2021). Often people are so focused on responding to others that they stop listening to the message being communicated. Daniel (2020) listed several signs of poor listening—interrupting frequently, shifting every topic back to oneself, not asking relevant questions, nodding excessively, getting defensive, hinting for the speaker to hurry up, exhibiting unwelcoming body language, and avoiding eye

**Table 15.1 Examples of Emotionally Validating and Invalidating Statements.**

| *Examples of Emotionally Validating and Invalidating Statements* | |
|---|---|
| *Emotionally Validating* | *Emotionally Invalidating* |
| • I'm truly sorry to hear that.<br>• I understand what you must be going through.<br>• I am here to talk about it for as long as you want.<br>• I realize why you are feeling lost. | • You are too sensitive.<br>• I don't understand what you are going through.<br>• I don't want to talk about it right now.<br>• I think you are making too much of a big deal out of it.<br>• Stop making things up. |

*Sources:* Adapted from Draghici (2022) and Carrico (2021).

contact are few common ones. Assertive individuals strive to be effective listeners by avoiding these poor listening signs.

## Understanding Passive, Assertive, and Aggressive Communication Styles and Behaviors

Out of the three basic types of communication styles, being assertive is usually viewed as the healthier one (the other two styles are being *passive* and being *aggressive*) (Mayo Clinic 2022). A passive communication symbolizes when individuals prioritize other people's needs, wants, and feelings over their own; do not express their own needs, wants, or feelings; or do not stand up for themselves (TherapistAid 2017). With passive communication, individuals are often quiet or soft-spoken, and behave with poor eye contact and lack of confidence (2017).

Through aggressive communication, individuals express only their own needs, wants, or feelings, and they may end up bullying others if ignored (2017). Aggressive individuals can be easily frustrated, disrespectful to others, and unwilling to compromise. In addition, they may speak loudly, use criticism or humiliation, and frequently interrupt others (2017). Aggressive behaviors can be direct or indirect. While the behaviors just mentioned are examples of direct aggression, indirect aggression involves sarcasm, deception, manipulation, or insinuation. There's also another type of communication called *passive-aggressive*, when individuals appear to be passive on the surface, but they express resentment or anger in a subtle or indirect way (University of Kentucky Violence Intervention and Prevention Center 2022). They often mutter to themselves rather than confront others directly. An example of passive-aggressive behavior is when someone says "You did a great job. Hopefully no one will notice the mistake."

Behaving with assertiveness offers many benefits. It prevents people from taking unfair advantage of themselves. According to the Mayo Foundation for Medical Education and Research (MFMER), behaving with assertiveness can help individuals gain self-confidence, self-esteem, job satisfaction, and a sense of empowerment; understand and recognize other people's feelings and emotions; earn respect from others; improve communication and decision-making skills; and create honest relationships (Mayo Clinic 2022).

Some individuals may experience negative consequences if they consistently fail to behave with assertiveness. Few major consequences are depression, resentment, and frustration (Revelle College 2022). While there's no single cause of depression, it generally occurs when anger is turned inward and people feel helpless, hopeless, or a sense of having no control over their lives (2022). For some individuals, an upsetting or stressful life event (e.g., bereavement, divorce, illness, financial worries, job loss, etc.) can be the cause of depression (NHS-UK 2019). Individuals may be more vulnerable to depression due to certain personality traits (e.g., having low self-esteem or being overly self-critical) and even due to family history (2019).

Resentment happens when individuals have a feeling of anger or negative emotions (e.g., disappointment, bitterness, etc.) for being manipulated or mistreated by others (Revelle College 2022). Common symptoms of resentment are recurring aforementioned negative feelings; inability to stop thinking of the event causing the negative feelings; feelings of regret, remorse, or inadequacy; fear of avoidance; and a tense relationship (WebMD 2020). To overcome resentment, assertive individuals make a sincere effort to forgive others, use self-compassion (i.e., being kind and understanding toward themselves) and empathy, and practice gratitude (2020). Benefits of overcoming resentment include better health (e.g., reduced headache or chronic pain; improved insomnia;

lower risk of blood pressure, heart attack, and stroke), increased mental health and peace of mind, stronger relationships, and improved overall quality of life (Williamson 2022).

According to the Oxford dictionary, frustration happens when there's a feeling of being upset or annoyed, especially because of one's inability to change or achieve something (Lexico 2022). Left unresolved, frustration can lead to serious problems like aggression, depression, poor self-esteem, stress, and unhealthy behaviors (Scott 2022). Assertive individuals often use various strategies to increase their tolerance level of frustration and improve the way they respond. Some of the strategies are improving emotional intelligence, distracting themselves from the source of the frustration, practicing mindfulness, using helpful relaxation exercises and techniques, changing their attitude and lifestyle, and depending on social support (2022). Table 15.2 shows a comparison of passive, assertive, and aggressive communication styles and behaviors.

**Table 15.2 Passive, Assertive, and Aggressive Communication Styles and Behaviors.**

| *Comparison of Passive, Assertive, and Aggressive Communication Styles and Behaviors* | | |
|---|---|---|
| *Passive* | *Assertive* | *Aggressive* |
| Submissive form of expression | Positive form of expression | Negative form of aggression |
| Undervaluing yourself | Being aware of self-worth | Ignoring value of others |
| Give in/yield | Negotiate and compromise | Challenge and confront |
| Think your own needs, wants, or feelings don't matter | Recognize your own needs, wants, and feelings as well as others' | Think of only your needs, wants, and feelings matter |
| Don't talk or be heard | Talk and listen | Talk and not listen |
| Try to keep peace and not "rock the boat" | Try to achieve what is fair and rightful to you, and give others what is fair and rightful to them | Look out only for yourself disregarding others' concern |
| Allow yourself to be bullied | Stand up for yourself and not be bullied | Bully others |
| Damage your self-esteem and self-confidence | Build your self-esteem and self-confidence | Damage others' self-esteem and self-confidence |
| Damage relationships because others respect you less | Enhance relationships because others know where you stand and there's mutual respect | Damage relationships because you respect others less |
| Do not clearly express what you think or stand for | Express yourself confidently and clearly | Express yourself by shouting or speaking loudly |
| Minimum eye contact | Steady and appropriate eye contact | Stare aggressively |
| Be shy, scared, embarrassed, indecisive | Be direct, honest, responsible, accepting, smiling, staying calm | Be angry, bossy, frowning, shouting, yelling, intolerant, unbearable |

*Sources:* Williamson (2022); Scott (2022).

## Developing Assertiveness through Transformational Coaching

People develop different styles of communication based on their life experiences, culture, emotional intelligence, professional training, and gender (Mayo Clinic 2022; Williams 2017). Individuals can change their communication style or learn to communicate in healthier and more effective ways through transformational coaching.

Mayo Clinic (2022) shared these recommendations for individuals to become more assertive: assess their communication style, use "I" statements, practice saying "no" with proper explanation, rehearse what they want to say, use assertive body language, keep emotions in check, and start small. To assess their communication style, individuals should honestly answer these questions (2022): Do they voice their opinion or remain silent when participating in a conversation? Do they say "yes" to additional work even when their schedule is full? Are they quick to judge or blame others? Do others seem to dread or fear talking to them? Using "I" statements lets others know what they are thinking or feeling without sounding dismissive or accusatory. For example, when in disagreement, they should say, "I disagree" rather than "You're wrong." If they want to make a request, they should say "I would like you to help me with this" rather than "You need to do this for me." They should keep their requests simple, specific, and clear. If they are not able to accept a request, they should practice saying "No, I can't do that now" and offer an appropriate explanation that is simple and brief.

To increase assertiveness, individuals can write down what they want or think, and practice them by saying out loud to a friend, family member, or colleague. They should practice using assertive body language when communicating with others. For example, keeping an upright posture but leaning a bit forward, making regular eye contact, maintaining a neutral or positive facial expression, not crossing arms or legs, and so on. Practicing in front of a mirror or a friend or colleague can be highly beneficial in improving body language. They should remember that uncontrolled emotions and feelings can hinder conflict resolution or even make it impossible. If they feel too emotional going into a situation or participating in a conversation, they should wait, then breathe slowly and stay calm, and keep their voice even and firm when speaking. Lastly, they should understand that no change or improvement happens overnight, so it is recommended to start small and be patient. Individuals should practice the newly learned skills and behaviors in situations that have low risk, then gradually approach to handle more complex situations in personal and professional lives.

## What Is Resilience?

There is no single definition of resilience. In the beginning of this chapter, a definition of resilience from the American Psychological Association was presented. Ackerman (2018) referred to resilience as the quality of recovering quickly from a disappointment or failure and continuing to grow and advance one's personal development. To Cherry (2021), resilience means "understanding that life is full of challenges. While we cannot avoid many of these problems, we can remain open, flexible, and willing to adapt to change" (para. What does "resilient" mean?). According to the American Psychological Association (2022), three predominant factors that affect how well individuals adapt to adversities are the ways they view and engage with the world, availability and quality of social resources (e.g., support from family, friends, community, and organizations), and coping strategies (e.g., meditation, physical activity or exercise, engaging in spirituality, etc.). Other factors that can build resilience are self-esteem, communication skills, and emotional regulation (i.e., ability to control one's emotion) (Hurley 2022).

Cherry (2021) illustrated several characteristics of resilient individuals. They have a sense of control, problem-solving skills, strong social connections, survivor mentality, emotional regulation, and self-compassion (2021). The American Academy of Pediatrics summarized seven characteristics of resilience, knows as the 7-Cs: Competence, Confidence, Connection, Character, Contribution, Coping, and Control (Hurley 2022). According to Hurley (2022), the 7-Cs of resilience "illustrate the interplay between personal strengths and outside resources, regardless of age" (para. What are the 7-Cs of resilience?). These characteristics are essential in becoming more resilient.

## *Understanding Different Types of Resilience*

Wallace (2015) described four types of resilience: physical, mental, emotional, and social. Physical resilience refers "to the body's ability to adapt to challenges, maintain stamina and strength, and recover quickly and efficiently" (Hurley 2022, para. What is physical resilience?). In other words, physical resilience can be described as a person's ability to function and recover when faced with illness, accidents, trauma, or other physical demands. Regular exercise, healthy eating habits, stress management, getting a good night's sleep, and so on, are a few activities that can improve an individual's physical resilience.

Mental resilience, also known as psychological resilience, is an individual's ability and capacity to mentally cope with any uncertainty, hardship, adversity, challenge, or trauma (2022). Having a positive mindset, not getting stuck with self-limiting beliefs, taking control of one's life, making a commitment, accepting challenges to develop mental toughness, having self-confidence, and finding support from the loved ones can improve an individual's mental or psychological resilience (Kentucky Counseling Center 2022).

Emotional resilience can be defined as "the ability to adapt to challenges, the ability to keep calm during challenges, and the ability to bounce back and grow from challenges" (Billoni 2022, para. What is emotional resilience?). Qualities of emotionally resilient individuals are their emotional awareness, perseverance, optimism, social connections, and sense of control (2022). Other qualities may include their ability to learn from experience, ability to set and meet goals and objectives, empathy for others, persistence, and sense of humor (Well Clinic 2021). To improve emotional resilience, they should educate themselves and be aware about their emotions, build up support network, practice mindfulness, understand the limitation of personal abilities, and self-care (2021).

Hurley (2022) defined social resilience, also known as community resilience, as "the ability of groups of people to respond to and recover from adverse situations, such as natural disasters, acts of violence, economic hardship, and other challenges to the group as a whole" (para. What is community resilience?). It involves people connecting with others and working together to face adversities and solve problems that affect them individually and collectively (Cherry 2021). Social resilience can be developed by promoting access to public health, healthcare, and social services; disaster preparedness; expanding communication and collaboration among members of the society; engaging at-risk individuals and implementing programs to serve them; and creating social connectedness (Public Health Emergency 2015). Individual health and resilience is important for social resilience because healthy, socially connected, and prepared group of individuals make stronger communities that are better able to withstand, manage, and recover from adverse situations and disasters (2015).

## Developing Resilience through Transformational Coaching

Resilience is an increasingly essential competence. Individuals who are resilient are better able to cope with many adverse situations like unexpected change, setbacks and disappointments, high levels of stress, and excessive workload. Common signs of low resilience in individuals are inability to make decisions, frequent physical ailments, reduced self-confidence, feeling overwhelmed, lower tolerance, and short temper (Clutterbuck 2017). Through transformational coaching, coaches can help them in two major ways: by enhancing their ability to cope with current situations, and by improving their overall level of resilience. Sherlock-Storey (2012) and Clutterbuck (2017) proposed several targets on how to coach individuals for resilience. The following section elaborates on identifying their strengths and weaknesses, enhancing positive emotions, developing hope, and coaching for optimism.

### *Identifying Strengths and Weaknesses*

Knowing about individuals' strengths and weaknesses helps a coach determine how to best support them, help them transform, and achieve more favorable outcomes in needed areas. To identify their strengths and weaknesses, individuals can refer to performance reviews; 360-degree survey feedback (if available); awards and certifications; passion or things they enjoy doing; or results of assessment tests of their personality, behavior, preferences, or aptitude. They can use a variety of tests to identify strengths and weaknesses. A few popular assessment tests are Myers-Briggs Type Indicator (MBTI), DiSC Workplace Profile, Insights Discovery, Leadership Circle Profile, Hogan Assessments, Belbin Team Roles Assessment, Essentic's Point Positive, Cappfinity's Realize Strengths, Gallup's CliftonStrengths, Enneagram Personality Test, Blindspot Inventory Assessment System (BIAS), and 16Personalities from NERIS Analytics.

### *Enhancing Positive Emotions*

Positive emotions—such as joy, interest, contentment, love, happiness, and gratefulness—are moments in which individuals are not plagued by negative emotions—such as anxiety, sadness, anger, fear, and despair (Fredrickson and Fowler 2001). Positive emotions enable our brains to take in more information, store multiple ideas at once, and understand how different ideas relate to each other (Kids Health 2018). Thus, positive emotions increase our awareness, attention, and memory (2018). Individuals who have a high level of positive emotions in their lives are likely to be happier, healthier, better learners, and more sociable (2018).

There are several ways coaches can enhance positive emotions in their clients. Kids Health (2018) mentioned three ways to increase positive emotions in our lives: identifying and tracking positive emotions, focusing on a specific positive emotion and act on increasing it, and creating a positivity "treasure chest." A treasure chest can be described as a collection of positive experience reminders they have had (e.g., memorable photos, childhood mementos, favorite quotes or books, pictures they drew in the past, etc.). Houston (2019) provided a list of 19 positive psychology exercises (e.g., Self-Care Vision Board, Guest House Poem, Sensory Awareness, etc.) that coaches can use to enhance their clients' positive emotions.

### *Developing Hope*

Hope is a positive cognitive state of mind and individuals who have high hope generally have greater academic success and stronger friendships (Zakrzewski 2012). They also demonstrate more creativity and better problem-solving skills (2012). They can set clear and attainable goals, develop strategies to achieve those goals, and stay motivated even when they face adversity and challenges (2012). According to the hope theory, hopefulness is a human strength comprised of three distinct but related components—goal thinking, pathway thinking, and agency thinking (Snyder et al. 1991). Goal thinking means preferences about their future and a clear understanding of their goals and objectives (Zakrzewski 2012). Pathway thinking refers to their capacity of developing strategies and routes to achieve those goals and objectives (2012). Agency thinking is their level of intention, confidence, and motivation to follow strategies and routes to achieve the desired future (2012).

According to Houston (2019a), there are four types of hope—realistic, utopian, chosen, and transcendent. The outcome of a realistic hope is reasonable and probable (Wiles et al. 2008), for example, a couple hoping for a healthy baby. A utopian hope is "a collectively oriented hope that collaborative action can lead to a better future for all" (Houston 2019a, para. Utopian hope). Utopian hopes often show a belief that things can be improved much more than what is possible, therefore, they can be unrealistic. The hope for "achieving world peace" can be considered utopian in nature. Chosen hopes stand for life stance and they help individuals live with a challenging present in an uncertain future. An example of chosen hope is a person with cancer who resolutely believes that the treatment will be successful regardless of his or her current health condition. Transcendent hope, also known as existential hope, suggests that "goodness" will prevail and something good can happen (2019a). Viktor Frankl's experience in the concentration camps of World War II is a classic example of transcendent hope that shows, despite experiencing unimaginable personal suffering, despair, and dehumanization, it is possible to retain one's sense of self and reaffirm life's purpose (Ackerman 2018a).

Transformational coaches can use various tools to assess and measure level of hope in their clients. The Adult Hope Scale (AHS), also known as the Trait Hope Scale, is a 12-item questionnaire that measures hope for individuals over 15 years of age (Houston 2019a). The Adult State Hope Scale (ASHS), also known as the Goals Scale for the Present, is a six-item questionnaire that taps into the level of hope in adults at a single point in time and is based on their current situation (2019a). The Herth Hope Index (HHI) is a 12-item questionnaire that measures three dimensions of hope—temporality and future (i.e., presence of goals and positive outlook on life), positive readiness and expectancy (i.e., a sense of direction, seeing light at the end of the tunnel), and interconnectedness (i.e., feeling alone, faith that comforts, etc.) (2019a). Other useful tools to measure hope are the Children's Hope Scale (six-item questionnaire for children 8–16 years of age), the Herth Hope Scale (30-item questionnaire), and the Miller Hope Scale (40-item questionnaire).

To increase the level of hope in individuals, transformational coaches can conduct various hope interventions based on hope therapy. According to Lopez et al. (1991), hope therapy involves two significant stages: instilling hope and increasing hope. The first stage is about hope finding and hope bonding. The second stage involves hope enhancing and hope reminding. Sutton (2021) recommended few useful techniques that can be used by transformational coaches for hope therapy: conducting narrative sessions, developing a sense of agency, creating an internal movie, and preparing a pathway checklist. Other activities and exercises that can be used are creating a hope map, keeping a hope journal, and exploring individuals' beliefs about hope (Houston 2019a).

## Coaching for Optimism

Scott (2020, para. What is optimism?) defined optimism as "a mental attitude characterized by hope and confidence in success and a positive future." Lim (2020) mentioned several characteristics of optimist individuals—they are self-motivated, prefer surrounding themselves with other positive individuals, express gratitude, avoid cynics and naysayers, and like to stay happy and joyful. They view hardships as learning experiences or temporary setbacks, see the brighter side of things, experience more positive events in lives, better able to manage stress, and stay healthier (Scott 2020). Many empirical studies have found positive effects of optimism. A study by Dr. Martin Seligman from the University of Pennsylvania found that optimistic sales professionals outsell their pessimistic counterparts by 56 percent (Gielan 2019). Another study indicated that optimism is associated with a 50 percent reduction in cardiovascular disease risk (Boehm et al. 2012). Conversano et al. (2010) illustrated many studies finding positive impacts of optimism on physical and mental well-being. Coaches can transform individuals to be optimistic by helping them become more mindful, practice gratitude, enhance positive emotions, and exercise cognitive restructuring (Scott 2020). We already discussed enhancing positive emotions in the previous section. The following section discusses other aspects of being more optimistic.

According to the Greater Good Science Center at the University of California, "mindfulness means maintaining a moment-by-moment awareness of our thoughts, feelings, bodily sensations, and surrounding environment, through a gentle, nurturing lens" (Greater Good Science Center 2022, para. What is mindfulness?). Mindful breathing, mindful observation, mindful awareness, mindful listening, and mindful appreciation are few exercises that transformational coaches can use to increase individuals' optimism (Bee Well Living 2020). Mindful breathing is a type of meditation practice that focuses on individual's natural rhythm and flow of each inhale and exhale. Mindful observation is the mental process of noticing what is happening around individuals with consciousness and without distraction. Mindful awareness helps them to be aware of the thoughts and feelings most important to them. Mindful listening means paying full attention to others and listening to them consciously by overcoming distractions and without any judgment. Mindful appreciation is about being thankful, showing gratitude, and expressing appreciation for seemingly insignificant things or objects in life—things we often ignore or don't pay much attention to. Mindful appreciation can be practiced by writing a "gratitude journal"—recording and reflecting on things that individuals are grateful for on a regular basis. Transformational coaches should use effective tools, activities, and exercises to help them become more mindful, grateful, and ultimately, optimistic.

Cognitive restructuring, also known as cognitive reframing, is a process that changes individuals the way they think and replace stress-inducing thoughts with thoughts that are optimistic and do not produce stress (University of Concordia Health Services 2022). The American Psychological Association recommended this process to help individuals with eating disorders, depression, anxiety, PTSD, substance use disorder, mental illness, or marital problems (Healthline 2020). The cognitive restructuring process involves methods like thought recording, decatastrophizing, disputing, and guiding questioning to reduce stress and anxiety and have them replaced with practical and positive ones (Cuncic 2020). Transformational coaches can use these methods to restructure or reframe individuals' cognitive ability.

Thought recording is a technique used in cognitive-behavioral therapy (CBT) to help individuals recognize and change their unhelpful thoughts (2020). The term *decatastrophizing* was coined by Albert Ellis who introduced the Rational Emotive Behavior Therapy (REBT). Decatastrophizing is a cognitive restructuring technique that can be used to reduce or challenge the catastrophic thinking in individuals. Transformational coaches can ask them questions like "Realistically, what is the worst that could happen to you?" or "How would you cope if the worst did happen to you?" and based on the answers, guide them through the decatastrophizing process.

The next step of the cognitive restructuring process is disputing the thoughts—often irrational ones—to determine their validity and examining evidence. An example of irrational thought is when someone thinks "I failed to get an 'A' in the class, so I must be stupid and worthless." Transformational coaches should ask individuals several questions to determine the foundation of their thoughts and challenge the validity of those thoughts if necessary. Questions like "Are the thoughts accurate?" "Are the thoughts based on facts or feelings?" "What is the evidence?" "Could the evidence be misunderstood?" can help individuals justify their thoughts and make adjustments if needed. The last step is to replace their initial negative thoughts with accurate and positive affirmations by asking guiding questions. Transformational coaches should use this type of questions to explore a topic in greater depth and encourage them to elicit understanding by thinking deeply about the topic (Maria 2022). Table 15.3 provides a list of resources including tools, instruments, and courses that can be useful for transformational coaches to develop resilience.

**Table 15.3 Useful Resources for Developing Resilience through Transformational Coaching.**

| *Useful Resources for Developing Resilience through Transformational Coaching* | |
|---|---|
| *Subject* | *URL* |
| Master Resilience Training (MRT) in the US Army | https://www.armyresilience.army.mil/ard/R2/Master-Resilience-Training.html |
| Mental Resilience Training (MRT) in the British Army | https://www.army.mod.uk/people/join-well/mental-resilience/ |
| Penn Resilience Program (PRP) | https://ppc.sas.upenn.edu/services/penn-resilience-training |
| Institute of Coaching Masterclass on Resilience | https://instituteofcoaching.org/masterclasses/lessons-resilience |
| Coursera: Positive Psychology—Resilience Skills (Offered by UPenn) | https://www.coursera.org/learn/positive-psychology-resilience#about |
| Coursera: Foundations of Positive Psychology (Offered by UPenn) | https://www.coursera.org/specializations/positivepsychology |
| Coursera: Adaptability and Resiliency (Offered by UC Davis) | https://www.coursera.org/learn/adaptability-and-resiliency?= |
| Coursera: Build personal resilience (Offered by Macquarie University) | https://www.coursera.org/learn/build-personal-resilience |
| Coursera: Mindfulness and Well-being: Living with Balance and Ease (Offered by Rice University) | https://www.coursera.org/learn/foundations-of-mindfulness-ii-living-with-balance-and-ease |
| Coursera: Positive Psychology (Offered by UNC-Chapel Hill) | https://www.coursera.org/learn/positive-psychology |
| Udemy: The Complete Resilience Course - Master Emotional Resiliency | https://www.udemy.com/course/the-complete-resilience-course-master-emotional-resiliency/ |
| Udemy: Building Emotional Resilience | https://www.udemy.com/course/building-emotional-resilience/ |
| Udemy: Creating Resilient Teams | https://www.udemy.com/course/creating-resilient-teams/ |
| Udemy: How to Build Mental Resilience/Building Mental Resilience | https://www.udemy.com/course/building-mental-resilience/ |

(*Continued*)

**Table 15.3 (Continued)**

| *Useful Resources for Developing Resilience through Transformational Coaching* | |
|---|---|
| *Subject* | *URL* |
| Udemy: Resilience Skills—How to Handle Setbacks in Life | https://www.udemy.com/course/resilience-skills-how-to-handle-setbacks-in-life/ |
| Certificate in Resilience Coaching | https://www.wellnessprofessionalsatwork.com/certificate-in-resilience-coaching/ |
| LinkedIn's Developing Resilience and Grit learning path | https://www.linkedin.com/learning/paths/developing-resilience-and-grit |
| HeartMath Institute's stress test | https://www.heartmath.com/blog/health-and-wellness/stress-test/ |
| Resiliency quiz by Dr. Al Siebert | https://resiliencyquiz.com/index.shtml |
| Resiliency quiz by Dr. Nan Henderson | https://www.resiliency.com/free-articles-resources/the-resiliency-quiz/ |
| Resiliency quiz based on Cooper, Flint-Taylor, & Pearn (2013) | https://www.mindtools.com/pages/article/resilience-quiz.htm |

## Key Takeaways

1. Assertive individuals have high self-confidence, respect other people's opinions, validate the feelings of others, and are good listeners.
2. Three major types of communication style and behavior are passive, assertive, and aggressive. Individuals with passive-aggressive behavior appear to be passive on the surface but indirectly express resentment or anger.
3. Learners can develop assertiveness by assessing their style, using "I" statements, practicing saying "no," rehearsing what they want to say, using body language, keeping emotions in check, and starting small.
4. A lack of resilience can have a significant impact on motivation, performance, work engagement, job satisfaction, and overall well-being. Resilient individuals have a sense of control, problem-solving skills, strong social connections, survivor mentality, emotional regulation, and self-compassion.
5. Four types of resilience are physical, mental, emotional, and social.
6. Transformational coaches can develop individuals' resilience by identifying their strengths and weaknesses, enhancing positive emotions, developing hope, and coaching for optimism.

## List of Discussion Questions

1. This chapter provides several characteristics of people with assertiveness. In your opinion and experience, what other relevant characteristics do people with assertiveness have? Explain.
2. What other benefits, in addition to the ones mentioned in this chapter, have you experienced in your personal and professional lives for being assertive?

3. Have you experienced any negative consequences for being passive (not being assertive)? Explain what could you have done in those situations to be more assertive?
4. What other differences do you think there are when comparing passive, assertive, and aggressive behaviors?
5. In addition to the information provided in this chapter, what other recommendations do you think could be useful for individuals to be more assertive?
6. What resources (i.e., training programs, courses, assessment tools, or certificate programs), other than the ones listed in Table 15.3, have you found useful for transformational coaches to develop resilience? Why?

## References

Ackerman, Courtney. 2018. "How to build resilience with resilience training." https://positivepsychology.com/resilience-training-build-resilient-individuals-groups/

Ackerman, Courtney. 2018a. "What is self-transcendence? Definition and 6 examples." https://positivepsychology.com/self-transcendence/

Alberti, Robert E. and Michael L. Emmons. 1974. *Your Perfect Right: A Guide to Assertive Behavior.* Oakland, CA: Impact.

American Psychological Association. 2022. "Resilience." www.apa.org/topics/resilience

Barber, Nigel. 2016. "The psychology of insults." www.psychologytoday.com/us/blog/the-human-beast/201611/the-psychology-insults

Bee Well Living. 2020. "5 mindfulness exercises you can try today." https://beewell-living.com/5-mindfulness-exercises-you-can-try-today

Billoni, Bianca. 2022. "What is emotional intelligence?" https://projectbestlife.org/2022/07/what-is-emotional-resilience/

Bishop, Sue. 2013. *Develop Your Assertiveness.* London: Kogan Page Limited.

Boehm, Julia K., Kubzansky, Laura D., and Hinshaw, Stephen P. 2012. "The heart's content: The association between positive psychological well-being and cardiovascular health." *Psychological Bulletin* 138, no. 4: 655–691.

Borden, Margot. 2022. "Passive, aggressive, or assertive?" https://margotborden.com/assertive/

Carrico, Brittany. 2021. "What is emotional invalidation?" https://psychcentral.com/health/reasons-you-and-others-invalidate-your-emotional-experience

Cherry, Kendra. 2021. "What does it mean to be resilient?" www.verywellmind.com/characteristics-of-resilience-2795062#

Clutterbuck, David. 2017. "Helping your coachee or mentee develop resilience." https://artofmentoring.net/helping-coachee-mentee-develop-resilience/

Conversano, Ciro, Rotondo, Alessandro, Lensi, Elena, Vista, Olivia Della, Arpone, Francesca, and Reda, Mario Antonio. 2010. "Optimism and its impact on mental and physical well-being." *Clinical Practice & Epidemiology in Mental Health* 6: 25–29.

Cuncic, Arlin. 2020. "Understanding cognitive restructuring: How to reduce your stress by challenging your thinking." www.verywellmind.com/what-is-cognitive-restructuring-3024490

Daniel, Alex. 2020. "17 subtle signs you're a poor listener, according to experts." https://bestlifeonline.com/signs-of-poor-listening/

Draghici, Alexander. 2022. "4 steps to validate someone's feelings." www.happierhuman.com/validate-feelings/

Fredrickson, Barbara L. and Fowler, Raymond D. 2001. "The role of positive emotions in positive psychology: The broaden-and-build theory of positive emotions." *The American Psychologist* 56, no. 3: 218–226.

Gatchpazian, Arasteh. 2022. "Assertive communication: Definition, examples, & techniques." www.berkeleywellbeing.com/assertive-communication.html

Gielan, Michelle. 2019. "The financial upside of being an optimist." https://hbr.org/2019/03/the-financial-upside-of-being-an-optimist

Greater Good Science Center. 2022. "What is mindfulness?" https://greatergood.berkeley.edu/topic/mindfulness/definition

Healthline. 2020. "How to change negative thinking with cognitive restructuring." www.healthline.com/health/cognitive-restructuring

Houston, Elaine. 2019. "19 top positive psychology exercises for clients or students." https://positivepsychology.com/positive-psychology-exercises/

Houston, Elaine. 2019a. "What is hope in psychology + 7 exercises & worksheets." https://positivepsychology.com/hope-therapy/#hope

Hurley, Katie. 2022. "What is resilience? Your guide to facing life's challenges, adversities, and crises." www.everydayhealth.com/wellness/resilience/

In Professional Development. 2021. "What are the benefits of active listening?" www.inpd.co.uk/blog/benefits-of-active-listening

Kids Health. 2018. "The power of positive emotions." https://kidshealth.org/en/teens/power-positive.html

Kentucky Counseling Center. 2022. "How to build mental resilience." https://kentuckycounselingcenter.com/how-to-build-mental-resilience/

Lexico. 2022. "Definition of frustration in English." www.lexico.com/en/definition/frustration

Lim, Shawn. 2020. "5 qualities of optimistic people." https://everydaypower.com/qualities-of-optimistic-people/

Lopez, Shane J., Floyd, Keith R., Ulven, John C., and Snyder, C. R. 1991. "Hope therapy: Helping clients build a house of hope." In C. R. Snyder (Ed.), *Handbook of Hope: Theory, Measures, and Applications* (pp. 123–150). San Diego, CA: Academic Press.

Maria, Caitriona. 2022. "What are guiding questions? Examples + Tips." www.tprteaching.com/what-are-guiding-questions-examples/

Mayo Clinic. 2022. "Being assertive: Reduce stress, communicate better." www.mayoclinic.org/healthy-lifestyle/stress-management/in-depth/assertive/art-20044644

Morin, Amy. 2022. "How to be more confident: 9 tips that work." www.verywellmind.com/how-to-boost-your-self-confidence-4163098

NHS-UK. 2019. "Causes—clinical depression." www.nhs.uk/mental-health/conditions/clinical-depression/causes/

Pipas, Maria Daniela, and Jaradat, Mohammad. 2010. "Assertive communications." *Annales Universitatis Apulensis Series Oeconomica* 12(2): 649–656.

Public Health Emergency. 2015. "Community resilience." www.phe.gov/Preparedness/planning/abc/Pages/community-resilience.aspx

Revelle College. 2022. "Assertiveness." https://revelle.ucsd.edu/res-life/life-skills/assertiveness.html#How-to-be-effectively-assertive

Reyes, Zoe. 2015. "5 characteristics of an assertive person." https://thepeakcounselinggroup.org/5-characteristics-of-an-assertive-person/

Scott, Elizabeth. 2020. "What is optimism?" www.verywellmind.com/the-benefits-of-optimism-3144811#

Scott, Elizabeth. 2022. "How to deal with frustration." www.verywellmind.com/feel-less-frustrated-when-stressed-3145200

Sherlock-Storey, Mandi. 2012. "Coaching for resilience." www.leadershipacademy.nhs.uk/wp-content/uploads/2012/10/ NHSLeadership-TopLeaders-Coaching-CoachingForResilienceAndTransition-MandiSherlockStorey-2012.pdf

SkillsYouNeed. 2022. "Assertiveness—an introduction." www.skillsyouneed.com/ps/assertiveness.html

Snyder, C. R., Irving, Lori M., and Anderson, John R. 1991. "Hope and health." In C. R. Snyder and Donelson R. Forsyth (Eds.), *Handbook of Social and Clinical Psychology: The Health Perspective* (pp. 285–305). Elmsford, NY: Pergamon Press. https://scholarship.richmond.edu/bookshelf/157/.

Sutton, Jeremy. 2021. "How to perform hope therapy: 4 best techniques." https://positivepsychology.com/hope-therapy-techniques/

TherapistAid. 2017. "Passive, aggressive, and assertive communication." www.therapistaid.com/worksheets/passive-aggressive-and-assertive-communication

UC San Diego. 2022. "Assertiveness." https://revelle.ucsd.edu/res-life/life-skills/assertiveness.html

University of Concordia Health Services. 2022. "Examples of cognitive restructuring." www.concordia.ca/cunews/offices/provost/health/topics/stress-management/cognitive-restructuring-examples.html

University of Kentucky Violence Intervention and Prevention Center. 2022. "The four basic styles of communication." www.uky.edu/hr/sites/www.uky.edu.hr/files/wellness/images/Conf14_FourCommStyles.pdf

UP Journey. 2021. "What to do and what to say when someone insults you." https://upjourney.com/what-to-do-and-what-to-say-when-someone-insults-you

Wallace, Howe Q. 2015. "The four types of resilience." www.hqnotes.com/the-four-types-of-resilience/

WebMD. 2020. "Signs of resentment." www.webmd.com/mental-health/signs-resentment

Well Clinic. 2021. "What is emotional resilience and how to develop this important trait." www.wellsanfrancisco.com/what-is-emotional-resilience-and-how-to-develop-this-important-trait/

Wiles, Rose, Cott, Cheryl, and Gibson, Barbara E. 2008. "Hope, expectations and recovery from illness: A narrative synthesis of qualitative research." *Journal of Advanced Nursing* 64, no. 6: 564–573.

Williams, Oneil. 2017. "Factors that influence communication style." https://bizfluent.com/info-8169818-factors-influence-communication-style.html

Williamson, Tina. 2022. "7 reasons why you should let go of resentments." www.lifehack.org/articles/communication/7-reasons-why-you-should-let-resentments.html

Zakrzewski, Vicki. 2012. "How to help students develop hope." https://greatergood.berkeley.edu/article/item/how_to_help_students_develop_hope

# Chapter 16

# Opening Powerful Inquiries

Sohel M. Imroz

## Overview

In the previous two chapters, we talked about developing emotional intelligence, assertiveness, and resilience. In Chapter 14, we learned about the role of emotional intelligence, self-awareness, self-regulation, social awareness, and relationship management in transformational coaching. Chapter 15 discussed developing assertiveness and resilience through transformational coaching. In this chapter, we discuss using powerful inquiries and questions in coaching. Coaches should understand what kind of questions and inquiries are empowering, tips for asking powerful questions, and their characteristics. Results of powerful inquiries should also be reflected in an action plan and be followed by the coach and the learners.

This chapter attempts to underline:

- Asking empowering questions
- Characteristics of empowering questions
- Examples of empowering questions
- Turning inquiries into an action plan
- Action plan checklist

## Asking Empowering Questions

Coaching involves asking a lot of questions. The most important point to remember when asking questions is that the questions should engage the learners at a deeper level by opening themselves more fully about their experiences, perceptions, beliefs, or values. Empowering questions allow coaches to motivate and raise consciousness, energy, and passion of the learners (Jake and Gino 2021). Empowering questions are thought-provoking, open-ended, and challenging questions that allow the learners to look for answers, solutions, and new opportunities (2021). Polemis (2022) described several tips for asking empowering questions. The following section elaborates on a few.

DOI: 10.4324/9781003304074-21

## Use Open-Ended Questions

Open-ended questions cannot be answered with a simple "yes" or "no." Instead, open-ended questions require the leaners to further explore, explain, and elaborate on their points and thoughts. Coaches should ask open-ended questions when they want to develop a better understanding of the learners and their needs, get more context behind their actions, or investigate the reasons behind their feelings or opinions. To highlight the benefits and importance of open-ended questions, Woodward (2019, para 2) wrote, "Open-ended questions signal to the individual that they have the freedom to influence the conversation. With open-ended questions coaching, the conversation is dynamic, not directive." Closed-ended questions are valuable too as they seek specific, brief responses. These questions are helpful in finding facts and coaches can use closed-ended questions to gain the learners' commitment and to confirm what they have said.

## Avoid Asking Leading Questions

Unlike a simple (neutral) question, a leading question leads the respondents toward a premeditated response or suggests a particular answer that the questioner desires (Formplus Blog 2022). Table 16.1 provides few examples of simple (neutral) questions and corresponding leading questions.

Leading questions can be based on assumptions or interconnected statements. An assumption-based leading question communicates a preconceived notion. An example of a leading question based on assumption is "Which of our product features did you find most useful?" This question assumes that the respondents found the product useful and does not allow them to state if they did not find the product useful.

A leading question based on interconnected statements combines two closely related statements. This type of leading question often begins with a statement designed to elicit certain bias or predisposition in the respondent's mind, and then follow up with a question hoping that the respondent will agree with the statement (Mahmutovic 2021). An example of a leading question based on interconnected statements is "Many employees dislike wearing masks to work. How do you feel about this?" The statement in the first part of this question elicits a negative predisposition in the respondent's mind on wearing masks.

There is also a leading question with direct implications. The purpose of this type of question is to align respondents to the possibility of a future occurrence of an event (Formplus Blog 2022) or to consider the results of their possible reaction to something (Mahmutovic 2021). Questions such as "If you enjoy working for this company, will you recommend it to your family or friends?"

**Table 16.1 Examples of Simple (Neutral) Questions and Leading Questions.**

| *Examples of Simple (Neutral) Questions and Leading Questions* | |
|---|---|
| *Simple (Neutral) Questions* | *Leading Question* |
| Were you in Chicago last week? | You were in Chicago last week, weren't you? |
| Did you come home that night? | You never came home that night, right? |
| Had you been drinking? | Isn't it true that you had been drinking? |
| Did you see the stop light? | You didn't see the stop light, did you? |

*Source:* Adapted from Formplus Blog (2022).

is an example of a leading question with direct implication. Coaches should avoid asking this type of question because it sets the learners up for future action or behavior even if they weren't yet thinking that way.

### *Coercive Leading Questions*

This type of question usually forces respondents to provide a specific answer, usually in the affirmative (Mahmutovic 2021). The structure of these questions poses a statement followed by a question (2021). For example, "Our product satisfactorily met your needs, didn't it?" Coaches should avoid asking this type of question because they are usually framed in an aggressive or "extremely forceful" manner (2021, para. Coercive Leading Questions) and usually include explicit or implicit coercion.

### *Avoid Asking Defensive or Judgmental Questions*

Defensive or judgmental questions usually convey accusations, criticisms, or even anger, thus, resulting in defensive behavior or response from the respondents. Questions starting with "Why" can easily be interpreted as being judgmental and trigger defensiveness that could prevent effective conversation. For example, "*Why are you late?*" "*Why did you do this?*" or "*Why are you wearing that dress?*" can be interpreted as being accusatory. Wise (2018) suggested that rephrasing "why" questions as "how" or "what" is an effective way of avoiding judgmental tones. Another recommendation for avoiding a defensive or judgmental question offered by Wise (2018) is limiting the use of "you" from the question. By following these recommendations, the preceding examples of judgmental questions can be rephrased as follows to make them nonjudgmental: "What happened?" "How did this happen?" and "What is appealing about wearing that dress?"

Transformational coaches should ask empowering questions to build understanding with the learners, set direction, shape options, and define next actions (Soler 2014). To build understanding, coaches can ask the learners about what challenges they are facing, what matters to them the most, what's on their mind, what opportunities they are seeing, and what challenges they may encounter (2014). To set direction, the learners should explain what they think about the best outcome(s), what they are trying to achieve, what they want to happen next, what success looks like, and how they will know whether they have succeeded or not (2014). To shape options, coaches should help the learners generate ideas by discovering what they have tried until now, what options they have, the possibility of each option materialize, and pros and cons of each option (2014). Lastly, the learners should clarify what should happen next to define actions. For example, clearly understanding what information they need to make a decision, what action(s) can be taken now, what kind of resources/support they need and where to get those from, and so on, can help the learners define next actions (2014). In each case, coaches should offer observations and provide feedback, guidance, and advice based on their knowledge and experience.

## Characteristics of Empowering Questions

Empowering questions are powerful because they can change the learners' focus in an instant, transforming their state of mind from limiting to empowering (Tony Yuile Coaching 2022). Unlike disempowering questions that focus on blame, regret, excuse, and denial, empowering questions focus on possibilities and positive solutions that help the learners move forward (2022). According to Kee et al. (2010, 62),

> Powerful questions are a reflection of committed listening and understanding the other person's perspective that is confirmed through paraphrasing. This suggests a progression from listening, paraphrasing for understanding, and then asking powerful questions that yield clarity or mediation of thinking.

The Rhode Island Department of Education (n.d.) suggested that powerful questions are open-ended and have no hidden agenda. Kee et al. (2010) listed several important characteristics of powerful questions. For example, like paraphrasing, powerful questions demonstrate that the coach actively listens to and understands what the learners are saying. This type of question affirms the level of care, commitment, competence, effort, integrity, and skills of the coach. In addition, powerful questions give the learners an insight into their own assumptions or pattern of thinking and help them understand what holds them back. When faced with this type of question, learners are more likely to find greater clarity about their own learning, their own behavior, and motivation to look at something in a new way. Lastly, powerful questions can encourage the learners to move forward and learn how to act, set goals, and get the help they need.

## Examples of Empowering Questions

There are numerous empowering and powerful questions that transformational coaches can use to create possibilities for the learners and encourage discovery, deeper understanding, and new insights for them. The League of Women Voters of the United States (LWVUS) provided several situations when powerful questions can be asked to the learners. These situations may be during opening a conversation, understanding what's important, examining the current situation, exploring possibilities, going below the surface, probing for clarity, and closing the conversation. Table 16.2 illustrates a few sample questions for each situation (LWVUS 2018). These questions are nonjudgmental, and they seek to further the coaches' learning and strengthen the connection between the coach and the learners.

Apte (2009) proposed a framework for practice that considers transformational learning from the perspectives of the facilitator or coach and the learners. The framework outlines questions for reflection based on four components. The following section describes the reflection questions for each component focusing on the learners (2009, 173–174).

### Confirming and Interrupting Current Frames of Reference

- What is regarded as the "normal" behavior of the learners?
- What examples are used to describe their "good" and "bad" behavior?
- What ideas or stories claimed their attention and what is gripping about them?
- What are their expectations of themselves? Are any expectations impossible or contradictory? Are the expectations coherent with other learners' expectations?
- What information have the learners never contemplated before?
- What previous practices of the learners become lost along the way?

**Table 16.2 Examples of Situations and Sample Questions.**

| *Examples of Situations and Sample Questions* | |
|---|---|
| *Situation* | *Sample Questions* |
| **Opening a Conversation** | • What is on your mind?<br>• What are you hoping for?<br>• What do you make of it?<br>• What is the goal/issue/objective?<br>• What led/brought you here? |
| **Understanding What's Important** | • What do you want/need/feel?<br>• What is going on?<br>• What is important to you? Why?<br>• What will it get/prevent you?<br>• What does success/failure look like?<br>• What is at stake/risk? |
| **Examining the Current Situation** | • What is/is not working?<br>• What do you notice/see/think?<br>• What stands out?<br>• What strikes/bothers you?<br>• What drives/energizes you?<br>• Who drives/energizes you?<br>• Who/what drains you?<br>• What have you tried?<br>• What is it like? What is the reality?<br>• What do you think is best? |
| **Exploring Possibilities** | • What/what else is possible?<br>• What is different/new about this?<br>• What will work/change?<br>• What/How might you do?<br>• What will/might be next/different?<br>• What moves/resonates for you?<br>• What could you do more/less of?<br>• What if you could/could not? |
| **Going below the Surface** | • What/how do you wish/feel/want/love?<br>• What are you holding onto/letting go?<br>• What about it excites/scares you?<br>• What is good/bad about it?<br>• What/who are you tolerating/becoming?<br>• What is costing/stopping/encouraging you?<br>• How do you perceive me?<br>• How do I come across?<br>• What is the question/choice?<br>• What are you discovering/resisting?<br>• What are you learning from it?<br>**(to ask yourself)**<br>• What might I not see/understand?<br>• What pain am I experiencing/avoiding? |

(*Continued*)

**Table 16.2 (Continued)**

| *Examples of Situations and Sample Questions* | |
|---|---|
| *Situation* | *Sample Questions* |
| **Probing for Clarity** | • What/why do you mean/feel/like?<br>• What/who/how else?<br>• What now/then?<br>• With whom?<br>• By whom/when?<br>• What feels unclear/confusing/challenging?<br>• Would you?<br>• Like what?<br>• Say more. |
| **Closing the Conversation** | • What could you do/stop doing?<br>• What will you do next/commit to?<br>• How would you do/stop doing it?<br>• What should you do/stop doing?<br>• What one thing will you do/stop doing?<br>• What decisions/conclusions do you make?<br>• What is standing in your way?<br>• How are you going to overcome challenges?<br>• What is your back up plan?<br>• What can I do to help? |

*Source:* Adapted from LWVUS (2018).

## Working with Triggers for Transformational Learning

- What are the differences in perspective among the learners?
- What evoked their curiosity and anxiety?
- What were they surprised by?
- What specific dilemmas are they raising?
- What hopes do they express?
- Do the learners experience any contradiction between what they want to be and what they currently are?

## Acknowledging a Time of Retreat or Dormancy

- What indicates that the learners are having doubts about the change?
- Is there inertia around some things?
- What are the learners avoiding?
- What provokes their anger or defensive responses?
- What could the learners lose if their current assumptions are not confirmed?
- What aspects of their learning would require significant courage?
- Are there risks that might occur if the learners move forward with the transformational change?
- What do the learners say is impossible for them?

**Developing the New Perspective**

- What capabilities are emerging in the learners?
- How are their views shifting over time?
- What strategies are the learners interested in developing further and testing in their own lives?
- How can the learning be continued?
- What reactions do the learners expect from others?

## Turning Inquiries into an Action Plan

An effective action plan is the roadmap for successful transformational coaching. Information gathered after asking all the questions must result in creating an action plan to help the coach and the learners. An action plan is a checklist of steps, tasks, and resources needed to complete projects, achieve goals, or obtain desired results (Udoagwu 2022).

Bonilla (2019) mentioned several benefits of having an action plan. For example, an action plan can provide the coach and the learners with the clarity they need to prioritize their time and energy. An action plan is more than a simple "to-do" list. While a to-do list typically reminds us of what needs to be done, an action plan has goals and promotes action, momentum, and results (Gray 2018). For the coach and the learners, an action plan provides a systematic approach to managing their time most effectively. By taking the time to develop an effective and organized action plan, they can be more accountable and stay on track without forgetting tasks or missing critical steps needed to accomplish their goals (2018). In addition, following an action plan provides them a way to measure and track progress as they complete necessary tasks. Lastly, an action plan allows the coach and the learners to prioritize tasks based on criteria determined by them (2018). Athuraliya (2022) explained how to create an effective action plan in seven steps:

1. **Define end goals:** The first step for writing an action plan is identifying the goal(s). Failure to clearly identify what the coach and the learners want to achieve will result in an unsuccessful coaching engagement. Each goal identified in this step should be in SMART format—**Specific** (well-defined and clear), **Measurable** (include measurable indicators to track progress), **Attainable** (realistic and achievable using the resources available), **Relevant** (in line with other goals), and **Time-bound** (has a completion date).
2. **List the tasks to be completed:** These are the guidelines or step-by-step tasks that need to be completed to achieve the goals. Identifying necessary task should be a collaborative effort and jointly prepared by the coach and the learners so they are aware of their roles and responsibilities (Athuraliya 2022). Larger and more complex tasks should be broken down into smaller ones, so they are easier to execute and manage. Using a RACI (**Responsible**, **Accountable**, **Consulted**, and **Informed**) matrix can be beneficial in clarifying roles and responsibilities and planning for projects (2022).
3. **Prioritize the tasks and add deadlines:** The third step of creating an action plan involves prioritizing each task and assigning a realistic and reasonable completion date for each. Before setting up the completion date, consult with the person(s) responsible for carrying out the task and understand their capacity and competence. There are many ways of prioritizing tasks, for example, based on their *urgency* and *impact*. Urgency is a measure of how quickly a

**Table 16.3 The Eisenhower Priority Matrix.**

| *The Eisenhower Priority Matrix* | | |
|---|---|---|
| *Tasks* | *High Urgency* | *Low Urgency* |
| **High Impact** | Do first<br>(Highest priority) | Do later<br>(Moderate or low priority) |
| **Low Impact** | Delegate<br>(Moderate or low priority) | Eliminate<br>(Lowest or no priority) |

*Source:* Adapted from Victorino (2020).

task needs to be completed. Impact is the extent of potential negative consequences or damage caused by the task before it is completed. Table 16.3 illustrates the famous Eisenhower Matrix, also known as the Priority Matrix, which is a simple but powerful tool for action planning and strategic management.

4. **Set milestones:** A *project milestone* is a management tool used to delineate a point in a project schedule (e.g., start and finish of a significant task, mark the completion of a major phase, etc.) (Westland 2021). In a coaching relationship, a milestone can be defined as "an action or event marking a significant change or stage in development" (Seither 2017, para. Just what is a milestone exactly?). Regarding Jack Mezirow's ten phases of transformational learning, successful completion of each phase can be a milestone. By setting milestones, the coach and the learners look forward to something worthy to accomplish and celebrate in short term, which helps them stay motivated even though the ultimate goals can be achieved far later in the future.
5. **Identify the resources needed:** Project resources are components necessary for successful project implementation—people, equipment, money, time, knowledge, and so on. A lack of resources is a constraint on completing the project. According to Morgan (2021), an effective coaching relationship requires five essential resources: commitment, time, coachability, chemistry, and trust. Commitment requires a high level of motivation from the coach and the learners. Effective coaching takes time, which must be allotted, protected, and honored by everyone involved for the coaching process to work. Being coachable is one of the biggest prerequisites for transformational coaching success.

   Learners who are open to coaching and will engage earnestly in the process are more likely to be benefitted because of coaching. Like any relationship, there needs to be chemistry between the coach and the learners. The *chemistry* in a coaching relationship can be described as a connection among the participants rooted in mutual respect and admiration (Resnick 2021). Lastly, the learners cannot make progress in coaching if they don't believe in the commitment, competence, and expertise of the coach. The coach should also be diligent in building rapport and trust with the learners.
6. **Visualize the action plan:** This step presents and shares the action plan in a visual format so others can easily understand. Tools such as flow charts, Gantt charts, or simple tables can present the action plan and its core components such as tasks, task owners, deadlines, resources, and so on. By presenting the action plan using these tools, the coach and the learners can display a visual view of tasks against time. Other critical information such as

who is assigned to what tasks, duration of tasks, and overlapping activities can also be easily understood by visualizing the action plan (Kashyap 2022).

7. **Monitor, evaluate, and update the action plan:** The final step is to monitor, evaluate, and update the action plan after implementing it. Monitoring the plan helps the coach and the learners to ensure that the action plan is being implemented as expected. Several questions should be asked when monitoring the implementation: *Has each step been implemented correctly? Has each step been implemented on time? Has the expected outcome emerged by completing each step?* One or more corrective actions may be necessary based on the answers to these critical questions.

Once the action plan has been implemented, its results need to be evaluated. Evaluating the results allows the coach and the learners to determine the level of success in achieving the goals. Evaluating the results also helps them determine if the action plan should be updated as required. Regardless of the success or failure of implementation, evaluating the results allows the coach and the learners to understand lessons that can be utilized during future coaching partnerships. Based on the lessons learned, the action plan must be updated.

## Action Plan Quality Checklist

Based on the preceding discussion, major components of an action plan include goals, action steps, resources, and timeline. To assess the overall quality of an action plan, the quality of each component should be assessed. Table 16.4 illustrates a checklist of sample questions that can be asked to assess the quality of each action plan component (National Center for Pyramid Model Innovations—NCPMI 2020).

**Table 16.4 Action Plan Quality Checklist.**

| *Action Plan Quality Checklist* | |
|---|---|
| **Goals** | 1. Does the goal include one or more specific actions a learner will do?<br>2. Is the goal properly framed according to the SMART format?<br>3. Are there times of day, activities, routines, or transitions included to make it clear when the learner should implement the practice(s)?<br>4. Is the goal achievable within the next two to three coaching cycles?<br>5. Is it clear how the learner and coach will know when the goal is achieved? |
| **Action Steps** | 1. Are there two or more action steps to break down how the goal will be achieved?<br>2. Is there at least one action step that includes what support the coach will provide (e.g., modeling, side-by-side verbal/gestural support, videotaping, etc.)?<br>3. Are tasks, task owners, milestones, deadlines mentioned? |
| **Resources** | 1. Are materials or resources listed for all action steps?<br>2. Is there any contingency plan in place when resources are not adequate? |
| **Timeline** | 1. Is there a timeline of completion for each action step?<br>2. Are the timelines reasonable?<br>3. Have the timelines been agreed upon by the coach and the learners? |

*Source:* Adapted from NCPMI (2020).

## Key Takeaways

1. Tips for powerful inquiries and questions include asking open-ended questions, avoiding leading questions, and avoiding defensive or judgmental questions.
2. Situations in which powerful inquiries and questions are helpful include during opening a conversation, understanding what's important, examining the current situation, exploring possibilities, going below the surface, probing for clarity, and closing the conversation.
3. Creating an effective action plan requires seven steps: define the goals; list the tasks to be completed for each goal; prioritize the tasks and add deadlines; set milestones; identify the resources needed; visualize the action plan; and monitor, evaluate, and update the action plan as needed.
4. The quality of the overall action plan depends on assessing the quality of its goals, action steps, resources, and timeline.

## List of Discussion Questions

1. This chapter illustrates several tips for asking empowering questions. What other tips, in your opinion and experience, should be useful in asking empowering questions during transformational coaching?
2. This chapter also provides examples of various situations where empowering questions can be asked. What other situations you believe are appropriate? What empowering questions should be asked in those situations? Explain in detail.
3. Describe a project for which you created an action plan. How effectively did you implement each step of creating an action plan described in this chapter? What challenges were faced in each step? How did you overcome the obstacles?
4. How do you assess the quality of an overall action plan? Should other items be added to the quality assessment checklist? Explain why.

## References

Apte, Judi. 2009. "Facilitating transformative learning: a framework for practice." *Australian Journal of Adult Learning* 49, no. 1: 169–189. https://doi.org/10.3316/ielapa.860986056456275

Athuraliya, Amanda. 2022. "The easy guide to developing an effective action plan." https://creately.com/blog/diagrams/how-to-write-an-action-plan/

Bonilla, Natalia. 2019. "5 benefits of creating an action plan." https://nataliabonilla.org/2019/08/22/5-benefits-of-creating-an-action-plan/

Formplus Blog. 2022. "Leading questions: definitions, types, and examples." www.formpl.us/blog/leading-question

Gray, Athena Emert. 2018. "Action plan vs to-do list." www.linkedin.com/pulse/action-plan-vs-to-do-list-athena-emert-gray

Jake and Gino. 2021. "What is an empowering question and why you need to use them to connect with others." https://jakeandgino.com/what-is-an-empowering-question-and-why-you-need-to-use-them-to-connect-with-others/

Kashyap, Sandeep. 2022. "What is Gantt chart?—Definition, benefits & tools." www.proofhub.com/articles/gantt-charts

Kee, Kathryn, Anderson, Karen, Dearing, Vicky, Harris, Edna, and Shuster, Frances. 2010. *Results Coaching: The New Essential for School Leaders*. Thousand Oaks, CA: Corwin.

LWVUS. 2018. "Powerful questions." www.lwv.org/sites/default/files/2018-07/Powerful%20Questions.LWV%20DEI%20Training%20Resource.pdf

Mahmutovic, Jasko. 2021. "5 types of leading questions with examples + how they differ from loaded questions." www.surveylegend.com/survey-questions/leading-questions/

Morgan, Meg Myers. 2021. "5 essential ingredients for a successful coaching relationship." www.chieflearningofficer.com/2021/02/12/5-essential-ingredients-for-a-successful-coaching-relationship/

National Center for Pyramid Model Innovations—NCPMI. 2020. "Action plan quality checklist." https://challengingbehavior.cbcs.usf.edu/docs/ActionPlanQualityChecklist.pdf

Polemis, John. 2022. "Asking empowering questions." https://wp.nyu.edu/coaching/skills/empowering-questions/

Resnick, Ariane. 2021. "What to do when your relationship has no chemistry." www.verywellmind.com/what-to-do-when-your-relationship-has-no-chemistry-5186106

The Rhode Island Department of Education. n.d. "Asking powerful questions." www.ride.ri.gov/Portals/0/Uploads/Documents/Instruction-and-Assessment-World-Class-Standards/Instructional-Resources/Data-Use-PD/Turnkey_Data_Conversations_Day_10.pdf

Seither, Beth. 2017. "Staying on track: Building your coaching system through milestones and sprints." www.noomii.com/coach-blog/staying-on-track-building-your-coaching-system-through-milestones-and-sprints

Soler, Stephanie. 2014. "Coaching 101: Ask powerful questions." https://medium.com/@StephanieLSoler/to-be-a-great-coach-ask-powerful-questions-d6b18614fffb

Tony Yuile Coaching. 2022. "Ask yourself empowering questions." http://wellingtonlifecoaching.co.nz/wp-content/uploads/2020/03/TYCOACHING-ANXIETY-SOLUTIONS-GUIDE-EMPOWERING-QUESTIONS.pdf

Udoagwu, Kelechi. 2022. "What is an action plan? (with example)." www.wrike.com/blog/what-is-an-action-plan-with-example/#Action-plans-explained

Victorino, RC. 2020. "The eisenhower matrix: Prioritize your time on what matters most." https://slab.com/blog/eisenhower-matrix/

Westland, Jason. 2021. "What are milestones in project management?" www.projectmanager.com/blog/milestones-project-management

Wise, Will. 2018. "The power of how and what and the weakness of why questions." https://leadingwith-questions.com/leadership/the-power-of-how-and-what-and-the-weakness-of-why-questions/

Woodward, Jeanne. 2019. "Why open-ended questions drive effective coaching." www.richardson.com/blog/open-ended-questions-sales-coaching/

# ASSESSMENT, FEEDBACK, AND SELF-EVALUATION

Assessment, feedback, and self-evaluations are the hallmarks of committed leaders, managers, or transformational coaches. People committed to their development as professionals conduct the process of self-reflection and self-evaluation to better themselves. Part VI is about these valuable processes. In addition, this part is about reviewing how the readers learned and how they can use what they learned in their lives.

## Chapter 17. Assessment and Feedback

The importance of assessment and feedback in transformational coaching, including steps in how to carry them out, is covered in Chapter 17.

## Chapter 18. How to Use What You Learned

Chapter 18 covers how readers can utilize what they learned, and where and with whom they can use what they learned.

## Chapter 19. Transformational Coaches' Self-Reflection and Self-Evaluation through Self-Rating

Chapter 19 discusses Ttansformational coaches' opportunity for self-reflection and self-evaluation through self-rating systems.

DOI: 10.4324/9781003304074-22

# Chapter 17

# Assessment and Feedback

William J. Rothwell

## Overview

This chapter focuses on the important topics of assessment and feedback.

- What do those terms mean?
- Why are they so important?
- Who carries out assessment and feedback in transformational coaching?
- When and where are they carried out in the transformational coaching process?
- How can the steps of assessment and feedback be described?

What are different assessments—such as diagnostic assessments, formative assessments, summative assessments, ipsative assessments, confirmative assessments, norm-referenced assessments, and criterion-referenced assessments? What are different forms of feedback—such as diagnostic feedback, formative feedback, summative feedback, ipsative feedback, confirmative feedback, norm-referenced feedback, and criterion-referenced feedback?

This chapter addresses all these important questions.

## What Is Meant by Assessment and Feedback?

In the most general sense, *assessment* means discovering or exploring a person, object, and phenomenon. And, in the most general sense, feedback means returning information about a person, object, or phenomenon to the original source. Feedback is often associated with returning information about the output of a process to the input. There are 17 definitions of what feedback is (Yourdirectory 2022).

In organization development (OD), assessment is usually associated with gathering information from all important stakeholders about the status of their organization. That information can focus on existing problems (such as posing a question like "what seems to be the biggest problem facing your organization?"), existing strengths (such as posting a question like "what seems to be

DOI: 10.4324/9781003304074-23

the biggest strength of your organization?"), or both problems and strengths. Once that information is gathered, it is then fed back to all key stakeholders to gain some level of agreement on what are the problems or strengths of an organization (or other group such as department, team, or person). When that information is fed back to all stakeholders, it often creates *cognitive dissonance*, understood to mean a feeling in which descriptions of current conditions do not match among a group of people (Harmon-Jones 2019).

Cognitive dissonance can be an impetus for change, as all key stakeholders seek to bring their views into alignment. For some business observers, a key difference between organization development and other fields is that OD encourages stakeholders to take responsibility to do their own diagnosis of organizational conditions (rather than relying on an expert consultant), and the feedback process actually helps to build a readiness for change so important in preparing an organization for acting (Rothwell et al. 2017).

Assessing can be a change effort in its own right as it prompts people to reflect on present or future conditions—and differences between what is happening now and what should happen now or between what is at present and what should be in the future (Rothwell and Bakhshandeh 2022). Likewise, feedback can also be a powerful strategy to build readiness for change. When people know what other people think or feel, it can be a compelling engine for change. A classic work in organization development focused on giving and receiving feedback (Nadler 1977).

An important point to understand is that assessment and feedback in organization development often focus on the common elements identified across a group of people. That approach is familiar to those steeped in qualitative research methods in which interview transcripts are analyzed, coded, and common themes are identified (Bazely 2020). Finding common themes (viewpoints) across group members can be useful in surfacing shared understandings of problems, solutions, action plans, strengths, and ways to leverage strengths to future advantage. But it can also be important to identify, and flag for group consideration, issues pinpointed by vocal minorities when exploring issues affecting groups or organizations.

Assessment and feedback in coaching often involves gathering formation about individuals through informal means (such as interviews) or formal means (such as instruments) and then feeding that information back to the coachee to prompt self-reflection about problems, solutions, strengths, and actions. In transformational coaching, the coach usually tries to help the coachee move past initial, emotional reactions to data gathered and fed back and then to accept common themes for action.

## Why Are Assessment and Feedback So Important?

No individual or group will change unless a clear reason exists. It is a fundamental view of psychology that no individual or group can change unless the person or group is motivated to change (Burgett-Martell 2012). Assessment can prompt people to change by prompting self-reflection; feedback can prompt people to change by showing information gathered from other sources.

Assessment and feedback provide new insights for individuals and/or groups to prompt a willingness to change. The common threads identified in assessment will show common interpretations of problems—or of strengths. The common threads provided in feedback will prompt corrective action for weaknesses and opportunities for building on strengths.

## Who Carries Out Assessment and Feedback in Transformational Coaching?

Usually, assessment and feedback in transformational coaching is carried out by the coach. The coachee provides information. If other people are asked about the coachee, that information is also organized and fed back to the coachee as a starting point to begin the change process.

Assessment generally focuses on what needs to be changed and how that change should occur. But feedback generally focuses on the information gathered during the assessment from the coachee and from others. Insights of the coach are often provided, though care must be taken about making the coachee defensive.

Feedback itself should naturally lead into determining what actions should be taken to correct any gaps revealed through the assessment. In organization development, moving from providing feedback to setting plans for improvement is called *action planning.*

Coaching can be directive or nondirective. If it is carried out in a directive way, coaches typically assumes responsibility for identifying what the coachees should change and how the coachees should change. In nondirective coaching, coaches provide the coachees with the information gathered during the assessment—such as the results of a 360-degree assessment—and then guides the coachees through identifying areas for improvement and establishing action plans to bring about that improvement.

In transformational coaching, the goals of assessment and feedback transcend that of traditional directive or nondirective coaching in that transformation requires a quantum leap of perspective. Assessment and feedback are used to provide a baseline for improvement, but transformation requires going beyond obvious corrective solutions. Coaches bear the challenge of guiding coachees to see beyond immediate corrective actions to explore steps beyond those.

Perhaps a simple example will help to illustrate the difference between traditional coaching and transformational coaching.

Here is a situation. Jonna Henderson is a customer service manager. When the coach asks her workers about her, they complain that she lacks interpersonal skills. They willingly offer numerous examples of how she would berate workers publicly, ensuring their humiliation, or would scold workers publicly for what they did—or failed to do. When the coach fed back that assessment information to Jonna (the coachee), she rejected the feedback. She claimed that the workers did not like her because she was too direct, but she saw nothing wrong with being direct.

Often coaches find they must work through the stages in the Kübler-Ross stages of grief. Recall those stages are (Kübler-Ross 2011):

- ***Denial*:** When coachees initially hear feedback from others, they often deny what they hear. If specific examples are cited and the weight of evidence reaches a tipping point, coachees move to the next stage.
- ***Anger*:** As specific examples are cited, coachees may try express anger about those who offered the examples. They may try to diminish the value of what they hear by casting aspersions on those who provided the examples (for example, "that person never liked me").
- ***Bargaining*:** As a stage beyond anger—which may be reached if the evidence is substantial and the coachees have had time to reflect on that evidence, they may bargain. That can suggest easy ways to address the problem that do not address the root issues.
- ***Depression*:** When it becomes apparent that bargaining will probably not work, the coachees may grow depressed. That can be expressions like "I am [mention their age]. I am too old to change. I give up." That expresses depression.

**Table 17.1 Applying the Kübler-Ross Model to Transformational Coaching.**

| *Applying the Kübler-Ross Model to Transformational Coaching* | | |
|---|---|---|
| *Directions*: For each stage of the Kübler-Ross Model appearing in the left column, brainstorm in the right column what you—as transformational coach—should do to guide the coachee(s) through these steps. There are no absolute right or wrong answers, though some answers may be better than others. Add more space/paper if needed on this worksheet. | | |
| **Phases of Grieving in the Kübler-Ross Model** | | **What Should You (as Transformational Coach) Do to Facilitate the Coachee(s) to Move Past These Stages?** |
| 1 | **Denial:** The coachees reject what they were told. | |
| 2 | **Anger:** The coachees move from rejection of what they are told to anger about it. | |
| 3 | **Bargaining:** The coachees move from anger to efforts to negotiate what they heard or what they should do about what they hear. | |
| 4 | **Depression:** The coachees are depressed that they can never address the issues they heard about. | |
| 5 | **Acceptance:** The coachees accept what they have been told and move to a willingness to take corrective action. | |
| 6 | (*New and additional stage*)<br>**Transformation:** The coachees explore and investigate creative, innovative ways to address the results of assessment and the feedback they have been given about their behavior. | |

*Source:* Adapted from Kübler-Ross (2011).

- ***Acceptance*:** Given time, and prompting from coaches, coachees will overcome the depression stage. When they overcome depression, they will accept the need to change. At that point they are ready for effective coaching.

Table 17.1 as a tool for helping in applying these steps to transformational coaching.

In transformational coaching, coaches should facilitate coachees to move past acceptance and to get creative in their thinking about ways to overcome their problems (identified through the assessment) or to leverage their strengths (which can also be uncovered through assessment). Transformational coaching must facilitate a process by which coachees move past obvious solutions and actions to those that will lead to profound (quantum leap) change. Coaches may have to help coachees explore *double-loop learning* in which they reflect on how they learn to improve and move beyond that to creative, innovative solutions (Argyris 1976). Coaches who apply help coachees to explore double-loop learning may ask them to describe publicly why they behave as they do. That may reveal their motivations and the assumptions behind their actions. That process may prompt other people to offer alternative ways of thinking and behaving.

## When and Where Are Assessment and Feedback Carried Out in the Transformational Coaching Process?

Assessment and feedback is often carried out more than once during transformational coaching. Assessment and feedback can be first-order, second-order, third-order, or even fourth-order.

### *First-Order Assessment and Feedback*

Before coaches are invited to work with coachees, other people—whom we shall call the *change effort sponsors*—may observe the coachees, noting that they need to change their behavior. Perhaps the sponsors hear that from others—such as those who report directly to the coachee; perhaps the sponsors observe problematic behaviors with the coachees first-hand. In first-order assessment and feedback, the sponsors of the change effort may try to serve as coaches themselves.

### *Second-Order Assessment and Feedback*

If the first-order assessment and feedback effort proves ineffective, sponsors may call in other people to provide more professional coaching services. Those services would be carried out by transformational coaches, tasked with helping coachees improve their behavior and perhaps go beyond mere corrective actions to pursue new, and better, behaviors.

In second-order coaching, coaches may have to convince coachees of the need to change by gathering data. That data gathering effort is assessment. When data from several sources are collected and given back to coachees, it is the feedback phase. Assessment may also be carried out with instruments—such as the Myers-Briggs Type Indicator (MBTI), the Disc, and many other instruments. Feedback should motivate coachees to change.

### *Third-Order Assessment and Feedback*

In third-order assessment and feedback, coachees are encouraged to gather assessment information themselves. They then feed it back to their coaches and ask for help to make sense of it and to establish the most effective improvement actions. Coaches facilitate the assessment process carried out by the coachees themselves. Coaches also help coachees make sense of what they learned from the assessment.

### *Fourth-Order Assessment and Feedback*

In fourth-order assessment and feedback, coachees are encouraged to enlist other people beyond coaches and sponsors to help them assess their (the coachees') behavior and to interpret it. Fourth-order assessment and feedback is a sophisticated level, demonstrating self-awareness and mindfulness.

Figure 17.1 illustrates the four levels of assessment and feedback.

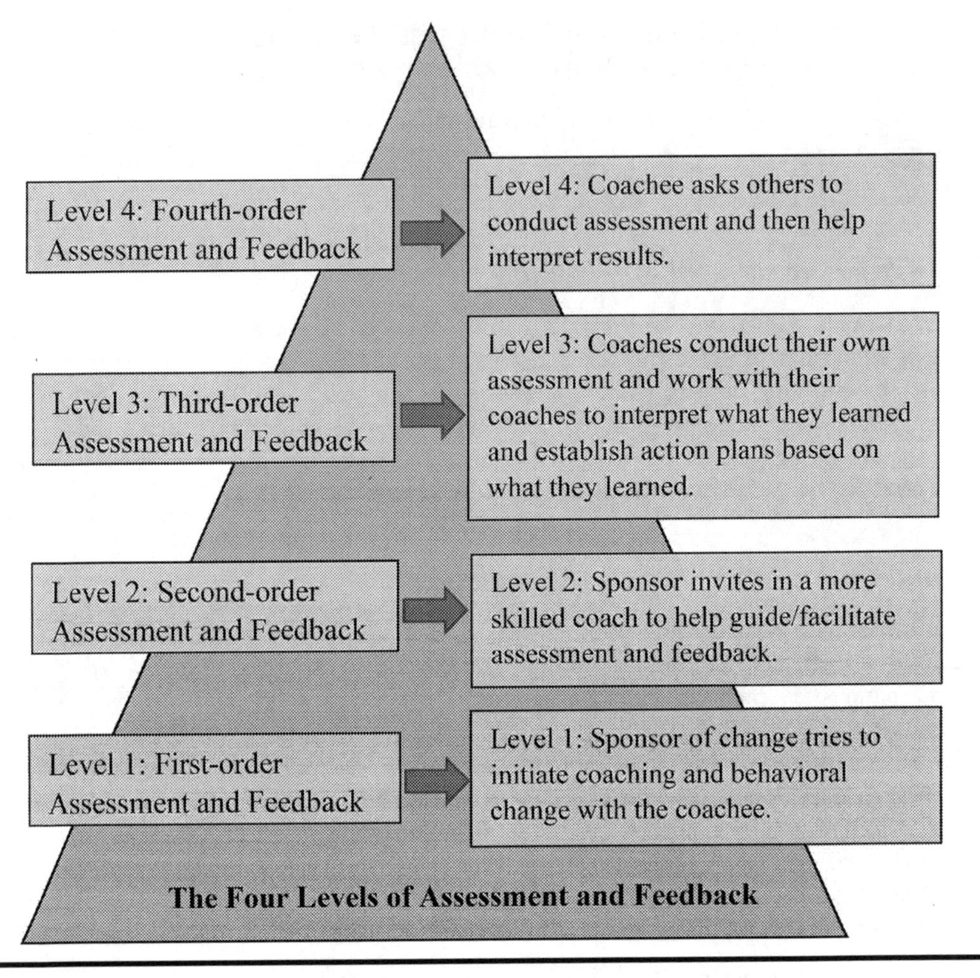


**Figure 17.1 The Four Levels of Assessment and Feedback.**

*Source:* Author's Original Creation. Copyright 2022 by William J. Rothwell.

## How Can the Steps of Assessment and Feedback Be Described?

Coaches organizing their coaching session—or sessions—may find it helpful to think of assessment and of feedback as a series of steps. By doing that, it becomes easier to structure assessment and feedback.

While variations can occur to accommodate specific client needs, a typical assessment protocol or sequence of steps might be:

1. Determine the purpose of the assessment.
2. Clarify the relative readiness of coachees to participate in assessment and secure support if needed.
3. Determine who should provide information.

**Table 17.2 A Worksheet for Conducting Assessment in Transformational Coaching. Author's Original Creation.**

| *A Worksheet for Conducting Assessment in Transformational Coaching* | | |
|---|---|---|
| *Directions*: For each step of assessment in coaching appearing in the left column, brainstorm in the right column what you—as transformational coach—should do to carry out the step. Try to list activities at the task level so you are clear what you will do before the session with coachee(s). There are no absolute right or wrong answers, though some answers may be better than others. Add more space/paper if needed on this worksheet. | | |
| **Steps in Assessment** | | **What Should You (as Transformational Coach) Do?** |
| 1 | Determine the purpose of the assessment. | |
| 2 | Clarify the relative readiness of coachees to participate in assessment and secure support if needed. | |
| 3 | Determine who should provide the information. | |
| 4 | Clarify what kind of information should be provided in keeping with the purpose. | |
| 5 | Select sources of data gathering by which to carry out the assessment. | |
| 6 | Organize the assessment results, pinpointing common themes. | |

*Source:* Copyright 2022 by William J. Rothwell.

4. Clarify what kind of information should be provided in keeping with the purpose.
5. Select sources of data gathering by which to carry out the assessment.
6. Organize the assessment results, pinpointing common themes.

Table 17.2 is a tool for help in applying these steps of assessment to transformational coaching.

The steps in feedback, which usually follow the assessment, are:

1. Analyze the relative readiness of coachees to receive feedback.
2. Ask coachees if they are prepared to receive the assessment results.
3. Organize the feedback in a way intended to garner results desired by the coach.
4. Select the best venue or medium by which to share assessment results.
5. Share the assessment results.
6. Listen to the coachees' reactions, paying attention to what is said and how the results are received.
7. Encourage the coachees to brainstorm on what actions to take because of the assessment and feedback.
8. Ask provocative questions to encourage the coachees to move beyond obvious solutions and actions to take and explore creative and innovative approaches to solutions and actions.

**Table 17.3 A Worksheet for Providing Feedback in Transformational Coaching. Author's Original Creation.**

| A Worksheet for Providing Feedback in Transformational Coaching | | |
|---|---|---|
| *Directions*: For each step of feedback in coaching appearing in the left column, brainstorm in the right column what you—as transformational coach—should do to carry out the step. Try to list activities at the task level so you are clear what you will do before the session with coachee(s). There are no absolute right or wrong answers, though some answers may be better than others. Add more space/paper if needed on this worksheet. | | |
| **Steps in Feedback** | | **What Should You (as Transformational Coach) Do?** |
| 1 | Analyze the relative readiness of coachees to receive feedback. | |
| 2 | Ask coachees if they are prepared to receive the assessment results. | |
| 3 | Organize the feedback in a way intended to garner results desired by the coach. | |
| 4 | Select the best venue or medium by which to share assessment results. | |
| 5 | Share the assessment results. | |
| 6 | Listen to the coachees' reactions, paying attention to what is said and how the results are received. | |
| 7 | Encourage the coachee to brainstorm on what actions to take because of the assessment and feedback. | |
| 8 | Ask provocative questions to encourage the coachees to move beyond obvious solutions and actions to take and explore creative and innovative approaches to solutions and actions | |

*Source:* Copyright 2022 by William J. Rothwell.

Table 17.3 is a tool for help in applying these steps of assessment to transformational coaching.

## What Are Different Types of Assessments?

### *Diagnostic Assessments*

*Diagnostic assessments*, as the phrase implies, helps diagnose what should be improved with coachees. Diagnosis implies that something is wrong and needs to be fixed. The term *diagnosis*, commonly used in medicine, suggests there are differences between signs and symptoms (the consequences of a problem) and the root cause(s) of the problems.

Diagnosis in coaching usually requires the gathering of information. There are many ways to do that. Diagnosis can proceed from data gathered through journals, assessment instruments, interviews, posters, focus groups, performance tests, surveys, diaries, and many more.

## Formative Assessments

*Formative assessments* are carried out to help coachees to learn and develop. They are assessments gathered "as you go along." Examples might include questions at the opening of the coaching session (such as "how do you think you are progressing in this coaching change effort?"), during the coaching session (such as "now that we taking a coffee break, how do you feel things are going?"), or at the end of one coaching session before others (such as "now that we have finished this session, how do you think things are going? What should we focus on in future sessions?").

## Summative Assessments

*Summative assessments* are carried out when the coaching intervention or change effort is winding to a close. Perhaps there have been many coaching sessions. When the coach and/or the coachees feel that the coaching effort is ready for conclusion, there may be need to summarize the progress made. As an example, the coach may ask the coachees "how do you feel things have gone since the beginning? How have you progressed? What more do you feel you should work on by yourself?").

## Ipsative Assessments

The word *ipsative* comes from the Latin term meaning "of the self." An ipsative assessment is thus an assessment carried out by coachees. They can do that in open-ended ways (such as keeping a diary or journal, or participating in discussions in which they ask questions about their progress), or they can do that in closed-ended ways using instruments.

Many instruments are popular to help people self-assess themselves. Among the most popular are the Myer-Briggs Type Indicator (MBTI) and the Disc. Many such instruments are described in the *Mental Measurements Yearbook*. The *Yearbook* can be found in most academic library reference rooms. Yearbooks list the complete statistical history of many instruments, indicating how valid and reliable they have been. Special topics can also be sourced among instruments. For instance, if coachees are concerned about proclivity to violence, the *Yearbook* lists instruments that predict the likelihood that individuals will commit violence in the workplace.

## Confirmative Assessments

A new way of thinking about assessment, *confirmative assessment* measures progress after a year or more. Important in continuous improvement efforts, confirmative assessment embeds assessment in every part of the coaching effort. Misanchuk (1978) originally introduced confirmative evaluation, but the same principle can be applied to coaching and not just learning or evaluation. Time distinguishes confirmative assessment from its formative and summative brethren. A common approach to this form of assessment is to rely not on one person but on a team of people to assess the coachees' performance.

## Norm-Referenced Assessments

A *norm* is an unspoken rule of behavior. Norms are the building blocks of corporate culture. When people work together for some time, they establish unspoken ways of interacting. At the small-group level those rules are called norms; at the corporate level, the rules are called culture.

*Norm-referenced assessments* compare an individual's behavior to that of other individuals. In colleges, students are familiar with tests graded "on a curve." The curve is a means of comparing student performance to other students in the same group.

When norm-reference assessments are carried out in coaching, individuals (coachees) are compared to other individuals. Workers may, for instance, be invited to compare the behavior of their supervisor to others—or else coachees will be invited to consider how they handle situations to how others carry out similar situations. That may offer perspectives that shed light on behavioral differences.

### Criterion-Referenced Assessments

*Criterion-referenced assessments* are based on established criteria ("what should be") standards of performance or behavior. Coachees may be compared to a pre-established yardstick of what behavior or job results should look like.

There are many ways to establish such criteria. Management in an organization may come up with a list of desired standards of behavior and/or performance. People are measured against those standards. The standards may be aspirational (meaning they are merely desired, but it is possible no one person actually aligns perfectly with the established standards) or research based. Research-based standards may be occupational (that is, behavior or performance established by a professional licensure or certifying body) or organizational (that is, behavior or performance established by studying those whose job performance is best-in-class or average).

Competency models provide an excellent way to think about criterion-referenced assessments. Experienced, and even top, performers are studied to discover what makes them so effective. A common way to develop competencies is to conduct behavioral event interviews (BEIs) with job performers. The results are then analyzed to find common themes using thematic analysis. The common themes are then turned into competencies, understood to mean the characteristics shared in common by performers. Competencies can be measured by behaviors or work outputs (see Rothwell et al. 2015). The behaviors linked to the competencies can be arrayed in order of preference—that is, some behaviors are more desirable or more linked to top productivity than to others.

The behaviors linked to competencies provide an excellent basis for assessment and feedback for use by coaches with coachees. Behaviors are observable, and it is easy to see them, count them, or measure their duration. Assessment carried out using competency-based approaches can be most helpful and can get away from purely subjective measures of performance or behavior.

## What Are Different Forms of Feedback?

### Diagnostic Feedback

*Diagnostic feedback* is offered to help coachees identify the root causes of issues identified through assessment. In directive coaching, the coach may simply declare what has been observed. In nondirective coaching, the coach may carefully summarize the assessment information gathered from one or many sources and then encourage the coachees to interpret what that information means to them.

### Formative Feedback

*Formative feedback* is offered as events occur. During the coaching process, for instance, coaches may comment about how they see coachees engaging in the change process. When coaches comment on the behavior of coachees during the coaching process, that is formative feedback. It can be powerful in changing behavior or affecting perceptions. Feedback is itself a change effort, as assessment is.

### *Summative Feedback*

*Summative feedback* is offered at the end of one or more events. For example, coaches may offer their thoughts on progress to date to coachees at the end of a coaching session or a chain of related coaching sessions. That would represent summative feedback.

### *Ipsative Feedback*

*Ipsative feedback* is conducted by coachees themselves. They may be asked to reflect on what they should change in the coaching experience, how they should change, why they should change, and what they should change. In ipsative feedback, coachees give themselves feedback on their own progress—and future change targets.

### *Confirmative Feedback*

*Confirmative feedback* is offered over time. Confirmative feedback is embedded in the change effort itself. It can occur minute-by-minute as social interaction occurs between coaches and coachees.

### *Norm-Referenced Feedback*

Normative-referenced feedback compares the progress of coachees to other people. If two people are in coaching to make similar changes comparing their progress and then telling them about it would be an example of normative-referenced feedback.

As a simple example, imagine that one coach is working with two managers to improve their active listening skills. The coach might make a statement like this to one manager: "Compared to Mary, you are progressing faster in improving your active listening skills." A statement, while normative-reference feedback, might be offered for numerous reasons. It could be an effort to compliment the coachee.

### *Criterion-Referenced Feedback*

*Criterion-referenced feedback* offers feedback to coachees based on standards of behavior or job performance. A simple example would be to prepare a survey instrument that invites raters to compare a coachee's behavior to that listed on a competency model for that individual's job category. When the rating is carried out, that is the assessment. When the results are fed back and used as the basis for identifying solutions, that is criterion-referenced feedback. When used in transformational coaching, coaches need to encourage thinking beyond the obvious solutions to breakthrough, quantum leap improvements that will require creative rumination.

## Key Takeaways

Important distinctions and major takeaways from this chapter are listed here. This chapter clarifies how assessment and feedback can be used in transformational coaching. What follows is a summary of the chapter's key points:

1. In the most general sense, *assessment* means discovering or exploring a person, object, and phenomenon. And, in the most general sense, *feedback* means returning information about a person, object, or phenomenon to the original source. Feedback is often associated with returning information about the output of a process to the input.
2. Assessing and providing feedback can be change efforts.
3. Assessment and feedback are important because they justify action.
4. Usually, assessment and feedback in transformational coaching is carried out by the coach. The coachee provides information. If other people are asked about the coachee, that information is also organized and fed back to the coachee as a starting point to begin the change process.
5. Coaching can be directive or nondirective. If it is carried out in a directive way, coaches typically assumes responsibility for identifying what the coachees should change and how the coachees should change. In nondirective coaching, coaches provide the coachees with the information gathered during the assessment—such as the results of a 360-degree assessment—and then guides the coachees through identifying areas for improvement and establishing action plans to bring about that improvement.
6. In transformational coaching, the goals of assessment and feedback transcend that of traditional directive or nondirective coaching in that transformation requires a quantum leap of perspective.
7. Often coaches find they must work through the stages in the Kübler-Ross stages of grief.
8. In transformational coaching, coaches should facilitate coachees to move past acceptance and to get creative in their thinking about ways to overcome their problems (identified through the assessment) or to leverage their strengths (which can also be uncovered through assessment).
9. Assessment and feedback can be first-order, second-order, third-order, or even fourth-order.
10. There are many steps in assessment. They include:
    - Determine the purpose of the assessment.
    - Clarify the relative readiness of coachees to participate in assessment and secure support if needed.
    - Determine who should provide information.
    - Clarify what kind of information should be provided in keeping with the purpose.
    - Select sources of data gathering by which to carry out the assessment.
    - Organize the assessment results, pinpointing common themes.
11. The steps in feedback, which usually follow the assessment, are:
    - Analyze the relative readiness of coachees to receive feedback.
    - Ask coachees if they are prepared to receive the assessment results.
    - Organize the feedback in a way intended to garner results desired by the coach.
    - Select the best venue or medium by which to share assessment results.
    - Share the assessment results.
    - Listen to the coachees' reactions, paying attention to what is said and how the results are received.
    - Encourage the coachees to brainstorm on what actions to take because of the assessment and feedback.
    - Ask provocative questions to encourage the coachees to move beyond obvious solutions and actions to take and explore creative and innovative approaches to solutions and actions.
12. There are many assessments and feedback types. The chapter reviewed them.

## Discussion Points and Coaching Questions

1. Sponsors do not always see the need for assessment. How can they be convinced that it may be necessary?
2. Coachees do not always accept the results they hear from assessment when fed back to them. How can they be helped to accept the results of assessment?
3. How should assessment and feedback in transformational coaching differ from the same approach used in other types of coaching?
4. When should assessment be carried out during coaching?
5. When should feedback be carried out during coaching?
6. What is your opinion about the best ways that coaches can learn to carry out assessment? Carry out feedback?
7. Although not discussed in this chapter, do you feel that assessment and feedback carried out using virtual methods might be different in quality than assessment and feedback carried out using other methods?
8. Should the coachee offer feedback to the coach? If so, how should that be done?
9. When should assessment stop?
10. What do you feel might be the future of assessment? Feedback? If you have time, do a quick browser search to see if you can find information on the future of assessment and/or feedback.

## References


Argyris, Chris. 1976. *Increasing Leadership Effectiveness.* San Francisco, CA: John Wiley & Sons, Inc.

Bazely, P. 2020. *Qualitative Data Analysis: Practical Strategies* (2nd ed.). Thousand Oaks, CA: Sage Publishing.

Burgett-Martell, Rita. 2012. *Change Ready: How to Transform Change Resistance to Change Readiness: A Manager's Guide to Managing and Sustaining Change in the 21st Century Workplace.* New York, NY: CreateSpace Independent Publishing Platform.

Feedback. 2022. "Yourdirectory" website. www.yourdictionary.com/feedback

Harmon-Jones, Eddie. (Ed.). 2019. *Cognitive Dissonance: Reexamining a Pivotal Theory in Psychology* (2nd ed.). Washington, DC: American Psychological Association.

Kübler-Ross, Elisabeth. 2011. *On Death and Dying: What the Dying Have to Teach Doctors, Nurses, Clergy, and Their Own Families.* Scribner, NE: Scribner Publishing.

Misanchuk, Earl. 1978. *Uses and Abuses of Evaluation in Continuing Education Programs: On the Frequent Futility of Formative, Summative, and Justificative Evaluation.* Tampa, FL: ERIC.

Nadler, D. 1977. *Feedback and Organization Development: Using Data-Based Methods.* Boston, MA: Addison-Wesley.

Rothwell, W., Graber, J., Dubois, D., Zabellero, A., Haynes, C., Alkhalaf, A., and Sager, S. 2015. *The Competency Toolkit* (2nd ed., 2 vols). Amherst, MA: HRD Press.

Rothwell, W., Stopper, A., and Myers, J. (Eds.) 2017. *Assessment and Diagnosis for Organization Development: Powerful Tools and Perspectives for the OD Practitioner.* London: CRC Press.

Rothwell, W. J. and Behnam Bakhshandeh. 2022. *High-Performance Coaching for Managers. Step-by-Step Approach to Increase Employees' Performance and Productivity.* New York, NY: Taylor & Francis Group. Routledge.

# Chapter 18

# How to Use What You Learned

Behnam Bakhshandeh

## Overview

Transformational coaching processes and approaches cover many professional and personal elements of participants' lives even if they participated in an individual format, as a team or group format, as a department, or even in the organization. As this book has covered many models, methods, and processes of implementing transformational coaching, you witnessed the depth of its engagement and how it would improve people bettering themselves in all aspects of their personal and professional lives by bringing about the compulsory changes, as they have developed their mindsets and actions. Unlike any superficial attempt to change or just try to act differently and hope for the best, people taking on transformational coaching work on changing their views of themselves, the way they view others, and their relationship to performance, productivity, and personal responsibility. They become accountable for their actions and try to make bone-deep changes in their lives.

In this chapter, you will look at these elements in the scope of the entire book, similar to an overall general review:

- How to use what I learned
- Where and with whom to use what I learned
- Transformation for effective leadership

## How to Use What I Learned

A transformational coaching process is a professional undertaking conducted by a skilled and trained professional coach who aids and guides participants through a series of most revealing and authentic self-realizations that result in those intimate moments of seeing the needed change. This is an act of leadership as an individual, team, or organization.

DOI: 10.4324/9781003304074-24

Throughout this book, we have pointed out so many great benefits of applying elements of transformational coaching and what is possible or predictable by participants engaging in what it takes to transform their *being*, and as a result transforming their *doing* (Bakhshandeh 2015). As a review of what you have learned from this book and how you can implement it to be effective leaders who can benefit yourselves and the people around you, we can mention these areas. However, at this point, we have to mention that the following results are applicable not only on a professional level but also on a personal level in any relationships.

- **Creating a new mindset:** Transformational coaching will shed light on participants' current mindset and show them the relationship between that mindset and their attitudes that cause their behaviors whether they are good, bad, or ugly. Then, as effective leaders, you can empower your people by showing them how they think and what would result from such thinking. This approach is key to establishing a rapport and having a safe space.
- **Focusing on present and future:** Transformational coaching does not rely on the past but emphasizes present and future potential. It's not like not knowing what happened in the past but that results in the present outcomes. Instead, it focuses on what can be done in the present and what in the future that is pulling us forward. This way, participants function with a clean-slate mindset, eliminating their attention on past negative experiences and their related negative feelings and emotions while working on envisioning what is possible and what they can do about creating a path to that future in their present time. As effective leaders, you can use these elements to empower your people to pay attention to their future versus dwelling on their past.
- **Realizing a greater level of learning:** Through transformational coaching, participants can learn more about themselves and how they are operating in life on a much deeper level and gain a greater awareness of their behavior and attitude. This is possible through implementing positive and solution-based questions and requiring those participants to create open access to learning and developing themselves. As an effective leader, you can use these elements to help your people to reveal their full potential.
- **Recognizing transformation is a process:** A transformational coach must remember that transformation is not just a goal and a destination but a journey through processes of self-realization, self-awareness, and constantly revealing what doesn't work and what can replace them. There is no finish line, just acquisition and application of skills. As effective leaders, knowing this will help you understand there is no need to push anyone to get somewhere they don't recognize.
- **Enhancing engagement:** Through transformational coaching, you can cause a higher level of engagement with your people because they will be more open to receiving your contributions and input, which naturally will have a positive effect on the team's effectiveness and productivity. As effective leaders, you can utilize this element because this higher level of engagement also aids in increasing job satisfaction among employees.
- **Recognizing emotions:** Transformational coaching teaches participants emotional intelligence. Through this understanding, participants learn to be responsible for the effect their feelings play on their emotions and how such emotions can make or break their relationships with others. As effective leaders, you want your people to understand their emotions so they can manage them responsibly before causing any damage to their relationships and productivity.
- **Improving relationships:** Transformational coaching helps participants to recognize their issues around personal or professional relationships with others and other issues regarding

their relationships with them. This recognition and awareness are the first steps to rebuilding or improving relationships with others. As effective leaders, you can use improving relationships among your people, which only results in improving cohesiveness and workability among teams and groups.

- **Increasing energy level:** Transformational coaching helps participants recognize the issues holding them back and as a result decreases their level of positive energy and their degree vitality. This awareness will help participants not to be so tired at work or home just because they just returned from work. As an effective leader, you want your people to have positive energy and display their level of energy so everyone on their team feels it.
- **Receiving common benefits:** During the process of transformational coaching, everyone benefits from the journey. The most obvious beneficiaries are the participants, individually or as a member of a team; the next is their family (in the case of personal transformation), their department (in the case of professional work), the organization itself, and the coaches themselves. The coaches are going through the same process each time they are conducting the transformational coaching process because they are seeing their processes while working with others. As effective leaders, you want to keep promoting transformational coaching as a vehicle for a win-win-win situation.
- **Dealing with reality:** Instead of resisting what is accurate, participants face the reality of what they have to do to accomplish what they were on the committee to do. Transformational coaching teaches participants to realize the reality of any situation and think about what needs to get done to alter the current situation instead of panicking.
- **Feeling free to express viewpoint:** Participation in transformational coaching allows for free expression of your perspectives and viewpoints, responsibly and respectfully, without concern about what others would think about you. As effective leaders, you want to create a safe space for your people to discuss sensitive or confidential personal and professional issues without fear of repercussions. This freedom benefits both sides of the aisle in any situation.
- **Communicating effectively:** Transformational coaching teaches participants open and honest communication and active listening, so participants deliver their messages accurately without additional meanings or interpretations. As effective leaders, you can use this element in every communication channel among your people.
- **Feeling empowered:** Transformational coaching allows participants to express their feelings and their experiences while knowing that the issues at hand are driving the coaching process. Participants will be empowered by visualizing their future, deciding the outcomes of their participation, and creating action plans to get to those results.
- **Not having a "one size fits all":** Regardless of the fact that there are certain principles and models that apply to the process of transformational coaching, an effective leader will remember this sensitive process is not a "one size fits all" approach. People have different perspectives, experiences, desires, and goals. Good transformational coaches will know this and will pay special attention to participants' conditions and differences.
- **Not being an authoritarian:** Transformational coaches are not authorities over participants' learning. Transformation is a process that will work only when there is a healthy relationship between the coaches and the participants based on established relationships, trust, and respect. As effective leaders, you want to pay attention to this fact, that you can force no one to recognize their state of being and alter their mindset just because you asked them to.
- **Being responsible:** Empowerment is the beginning of participants becoming responsible for their actions and the results of such actions. Transformational coaching teaches participants they are responsible for the outcome of their mindset, attitude, and behaviors affecting

the results in their lives and at the workplace, which are affecting others. As effective leaders, you want your people to take on personal responsibilities for their actions and behaviors.

- **Being accountable:** Transformational coaching teaches participants that accountability is being responsible before that fact, not after that fact. As effective leaders, you want to see your people holding themselves accountable for their results and actions without pointing fingers all around.
- **Improving health and vitality:** Participants taking on issues with their health is a common outcome of participating in a transformational coaching process. Because of self-awareness and recognizing their mindsets, participants take on vitality and self-care to assist them in producing the results they are committed to producing. As an effective leader, you want to exemplify such vitality and become a role model for your people.
- **Dropping bad habits:** As the natural outcome of taking on your health and vitality, transformational coaching gives you the perspective to objectively look at your habits and practices in life and recognize any negative effects, including dropping bad habits. In addition, as effective leaders, you and your team will benefit from having healthy and vibrant people in your team.
- **Recognizing and acknowledging:** Transformational coaches are their participant's biggest cheerleaders, encouraging their efforts, acknowledging their progress, and recognizing their greatness throughout their transformation journey. As effective leaders, you are those cheerleaders who keep your people empowered, engaged, and motivated.

Table 18.1 displays all the 20 elements found throughout this book and how and where to use them. Please use this table to rate these elements on your team or organization and simultaneously, look at what is missing and what you suggest for increasing the level of presence of such elements.

**Table 18.1 Assessing "How to Use What I learned" for Effective Leadership in Organization by a Transformational Coach. Author's Original Creation.**

| *Assessing "How to Use What I learned" for Effective Leadership in Organization by a Transformational Coach* | | | | | | | |
|---|---|---|---|---|---|---|---|
| *Name* | *Date* | | | | | *Organization* | *Team* |
| *Rating Scale: 1=Poor, 2=Marginal, 3=Acceptable, 4=Good, 5=Excellent* | | | | | | | |
| **Outcomes** | | **1** | **2** | **3** | **4** | **5** | **What is Missing?** |
| 1 | Creating a New Mindset | | | | | | |
| 2 | Focusing on Present and Future | | | | | | |
| 3 | Realizing a Greater Level of Learning | | | | | | |
| 4 | Recognizing Transformation is a Process | | | | | | |
| 5 | Enhancing Engagement | | | | | | |
| 6 | Recognizing Emotions | | | | | | |
| 7 | Improving Relationships | | | | | | |
| 8 | Increasing Energy Levels | | | | | | |
| 9 | Receiving Common Benefits | | | | | | |
| 10 | Dealing with Reality | | | | | | |
| 11 | Feeling Free to Express Viewpoints | | | | | | |

| *Assessing "How to Use What I learned" for Effective Leadership in Organization by a Transformational Coach* | | | | | | | |
|---|---|---|---|---|---|---|---|
| *Name* | *Date* | | | | *Organization* | | *Team* |
| 12 | Communicating Effectively | | | | | | |
| 13 | Feeling Empowered | | | | | | |
| 14 | Not Having a One size Fits All | | | | | | |
| 15 | Not Being an Authoritarian | | | | | | |
| 16 | Being Responsible | | | | | | |
| 17 | Being Accountable | | | | | | |
| 18 | Improving Health and Vitality | | | | | | |
| 19 | Dropping Bad Habits | | | | | | |
| 20 | Recognizing & Acknowledging | | | | | | |
| **Individual Columns' Totals** | | | | | | | Not For Use |
| **Total of Above Individual Columns** | | | | | | | |
| **Final Average (above total divided by 20)** | | | | | | | |
| Your suggestions for increasing the levels, or implementation of outcomes and their presence in the organization. | | | | | | | |
| Suggestion 1: | | | | | | | |
| Suggestion 2: | | | | | | | |
| Suggestion 3: | | | | | | | |

*Source:* Copyright 2022 by Behnam Bakhshandeh.

## *Where and with Whom to Use What I Learned*

Regardless of your position in life or the organization with which you are involved, the preceding elements of transformational coaching as an outcome can and will positively affect you and the people around you. The impacts and benefits of transformational coaching are wide, stretching from one side of life to the other side. These benefits leave a long-lasting and positive impact not only on your life and profession but also on people around you at home and at the workplace.

Transformational coaching has the power and influence to teach you a deeper, personal understanding. You have the potential to become great life partners, amazing and aware parents, productive and engaged members of society, and examples of model employees, supervisors, or managers of any organization leading your teams in high-performance and productive projects.

Working with a professional transformational coach and going through processes of transformational coaching can help you to develop yourselves as that individual at home or at the workplace while opening doors to self-realization, empowering perspectives, stronger self-confidence, good relationships, effective communication, and overall, a much more positive and healthier and productive life personally and professionally.

However, you can use elements of transformational coaching anywhere in your lives and careers as you wish. There are no limits on how and where you can utilize your transformation. The sky is the limit.

Like any other human behavior, you must work on developing a powerful mindset and an attitude you call positive, empowering or great. Why? Because many years of hot feelings and emotions, such as hurt, anger, upset, expectations, regret, and resentment, have covered our hearts and souls with a thick layer of resignation and cynicism. However, now you are also aware of your ability to forgive yourselves, correct your actions, complete issues, resolve problems, and move on in your lives. Through transformational coaching and personal development and your understanding of others and yourselves, the effects of your mindset on yourselves and on others, you can achieve that greatness and positive mindset and attitude to realize the desire of having a peaceful life and workable and productive professions.

As transformed people in positions of leadership, you can achieve many goals when you work on and develop yourselves as the people who are *being*:

- Peacemakers
- Critical thinkers
- Creative thinkers
- Teachers
- Learners
- Motivators
- Engagers
- Team players
- Resolution-oriented people
- Respectful people
- Inspired people
- Excited about life
- Positive about life
- Calm and collected people
- Loving people
- Leaders

During the development of great attitudes, you can compare your greatness to others' experiences of us. As effective leaders who practice transformational thinking and behavior, in your personal and professional lives, you will benefit while others receive benefits from being around us because you are aware of your greatness, and you are exerting that greatness on others. So, do you experience yourself, and do others experience you as someone who—

- Welcomes knowledge and opportunities to learn
- Doesn't give up on dreams and goals
- Believes in greatness and capabilities
- Experiences opportunities in life challenges
- Has self-respect and self-confidence
- Does not allow failures to derail future actions
- Expects hardships in life but knows how to work through them
- Is always present to possibilities available in life
- Sees life as a gift to be alive and happy

A great attitude benefits us and others. With it you gain respect among others and inspire them. It makes them believe that it is also possible for them to have a peaceful life. More positive people will get attracted to us, while negative people will take themselves away from you because you are not interested in their negativity and self-generated dramas. You will have more energy and be happier when you practice your great attitude. You will notice more beauty around you, and you will notice more smiles on others' faces.

Show your commitment to developing a great and positive attitude toward life itself and others around you by—

- Stopping negativity around your life
- Looking for what is working versus what is not working
- Making powerful choices in life
- Controlling your thoughts and actions
- Looking for reasons to be happy and providing happiness
- Reading autobiographies of inspiring characters in history
- Surrounding yourselves with positive and motivated people
- Keeping yourselves related to your life vision

## Transformation for Effective Leadership

As you might remember, throughout these chapters, you went through many aspects, models, methods, and practices of conducting a transformational coaching process. You also discovered many benefits as natural outcomes of participation and applying steps of transformational coaching for conducting effective leadership. However, you know it will be hard to remember all the results and all the related processes that will benefit you as effective leaders.

Because of this understanding, Figure 18.1, Transformation for Effective Leadership, illustrates the six main elements of your actions as effective leaders and the places you can stand for causing transformation for your team and organization. You can consider Figure 18.1 as a review of what matters the most for implementing transformational and effective leadership.

### *Vision-Based Foundation*

"Vision is an anchor for individuals to center their mindsets, attitudes, and behaviors in a productive way, both personally and professionally (Bakhshandeh 2009)" (Rothwell and Bakhshandeh 2022). The foundation of sustainable transformation is people's relationship to their individuals', teams', or organizations' visions. That is the source of their motivation and directly influences their performances and productivity in personal and professional settings. Regarding the positive role of visions on individuals and teams, Rothwell (2015) stated, "a clear, coherent view of how the future should appear. It is essential in providing a point of departure for what is happening" (106). A positive and empowering vision aids individuals in forming a team and working environment that promotes teamwork and points at directions of cohesiveness and productivity while providing access to improving ideas and causing a shared sense of camaraderie among employees (Rothwell et al. 2012).

To utilize the power of transformational coaching in effective leadership, you need to have a solid vision for the results you are standing to produce for individuals, teams, and organizations that will benefit everyone involved. To refresh your memory and read more about the importance of vision, review Chapters 1, 9, and 13.

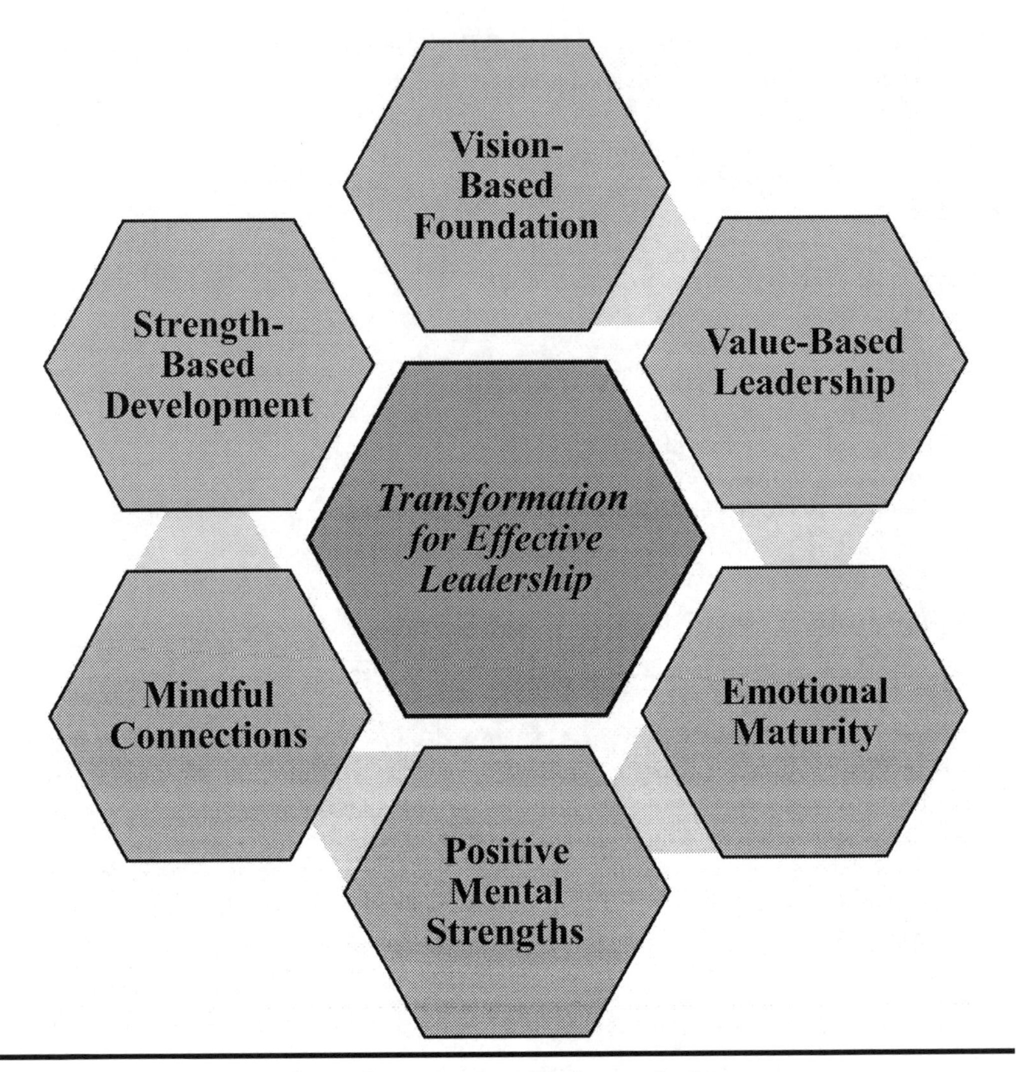


**Figure 18.1 The Elements of Transformation for Effective Leadership.**

*Source:* Author's Original Creation. Copyright 2022 by Behnam Bakhshandeh.

## *Value-Based Leadership*

What you value and what you stand for will make the biggest difference in the face of dealing with an issue on the way of transformation and effective leadership. This is regardless of what others think and pressure you to do. Relating to our principles is the essence of our character and is one of the most important elements of dealing with and facing what doesn't work. Your values and principles also keep you from being drawn into upsetting situations and getting involved with dramas. If you do not connect to your values and principles in a good way, you are connecting to your past, your wants, and your desires (Bakhshandeh 2006). These emotions are all subject to change based on what you feel at that moment. Relating to our emotions and feelings is just not a reliable source with which to build a case!

Values are qualities that define us and distinguish us from others. Values shape who you are and make us unique. They are the forces that give your lives meaning, purpose, and direction. Ultimately, your values determine our choices, guide your behavior, and direct your lives. You can define your values in four categories: (1) personal values, (2) social values, (3) cultural values, and (4) professional values (Rothwell and Bakhshandeh 2022).

As effective leaders, you want to investigate your own values and their relationship to your vision or their place in the organization's vision. These inquiries create an intimate connection with your individual or organization's vision that is the foundation of your leadership and positively influences your activities. To refresh your memory and read more about the importance of values and principles, review Chapters 1, 8, and 9.

## *Emotional Maturity*

Emotional maturity is your ability to deal with your emotional rollercoaster as functioning adults. Staying on the topic at hand and not becoming like a teenager with attitude is critical to resolving upsetting situations among individuals and teams. You can resolve emotional situations by dealing with any upsetting situations without extra interpretations and without adding hot emotion to an already difficult situation. Being aware of juvenile reactions and managing these reactions are the most appropriate qualities of being a functioning adult and an effective leader. Emotional maturity prepares us to bounce back from disappointment, frustration, and loss. It will bring us back to the solid ground of what is real and what needs to be done about the upsetting issue.

You know controlling one's emotions is one of the hardest things for you to do. However, by linking yourselves back to your principles, values, and vision, plus by understanding the ineffectiveness in your heated emotions, you can remind yourselves to stay focused on the issues at hand while trying to resolve them more effectively. As you have reviewed in earlier chapters, we divided emotional intelligence into these four clusters: (1) self-awareness, (2) self-regulation, (3) social awareness, and (4) relationship management (Linley et al. 2011).

As effective leaders, you want to be aware of your own level of awareness and recognition of emotional intelligence because that would affect your leadership among your people. For refreshing your memory and reading more about the importance of emotional maturity, emotional intelligence, and its related clusters, review Chapters 8, 10, and 14.

## *Positive Mental Strengths*

Positive mental strength is your capacity to sustain your focus and concentration over a long period, especially in tough and hard situations. You must develop your mental strength to respond to situations based on your visions, values, and emotional maturity regardless of pain, exhaustion, or inconvenience. Access to this strength comes from the belief you are responsible for what you do after you feel challenging emotions. This also includes how you act after observing another person's acts of upset and emotional outbursts. You cannot control what is happening to you, but you can control how to react to it. When you are responsible for your mental strength, you will own every thought you have and every action you take, whether good or bad, right or wrong, happy or sad, nobody else, just us! Remember your responsibility for your values, principles, and emotional maturity.

When you look back on all those upsetting, sad, dramatic events in your lives, at home or at work, and see how you were responsible for the events' outcomes, then you may be with the situation. We are not suggesting that upsetting events did not happen in your life, but what made the events more upsetting was when you dragged them throughout your lives in a sack of pain full of interpretations. Your interpretations of those events and what you made them mean to you, to others, and to life itself have caused the suffering, upset, and anger to continue in your lives. The situation may not have been your fault, but the choice to rehash it is, and that is where you need to take responsibility and rely on your positive mental strength.

As effective leaders, you need your positive mental strength to maintain your power to keep yourselves responsible and on the mark for staying away from your interpretations of updating situations and the emotional rollercoasters caused by such situations. To refresh your memory and read more about the importance of positive psychology and mental strength, review Chapters 7, 8, and 10.

## Mindful Connection

Mindful connection is a discipline to reflect on your own beliefs and commitment to your deepest values while practicing peacefulness and emotional maturity. You must develop the disciplines to continue relating to your beliefs, and what is important to you regarding your connecting to others, regardless of the circumstances you are facing in any life situation, at home or at work. For example, suppose you believe in peace and harmony. There, naturally, you try not to get engaged in upsetting conversations with others or at least actively listen to them without adding your interpretations and meanings to their communication. That does not mean you do not say what you need to say to whom you need to say it. It only means you stay away from including your interpretations and opinions about that person or the topic of discussion.

A mindful connection for you is different based on your beliefs in several domains: social beliefs, religious beliefs, spiritual beliefs, family upbringing, personal beliefs, peaceful disciplines, or just good old sets of values. Regardless of where this powerful connection originates, it is an important part of keeping you connected to your resources for generating a peaceful and content lifestyle and professional work connections. This powerful connection holds your values and emotional maturity together, and your mental strength helps to hold them to a place of serenity and the peaceful lifestyle you are designing at home or at the workplace.

As effective leaders, it is vital for you to maintain mindful spaces for creating positive coaction with people around you. To refresh your memory and read more about the importance of positive psychology and mental strength, review Chapters 1, 10, 11, and 12.

## Strength-Based Development

The strength-based approach to development is one element of effective leadership that centers on what individuals are good at compared to focusing on their weaknesses. Individuals' strengths result from their natural interests and talents they have developed through the years, plus the collection of their knowledge, skills, and experiences. Through transformational coaching, individuals consciously recognize their strengths and attempt to use them more often to improve their performance and productivity. However, that doesn't mean ignoring individual weaknesses that need development (Mackie 2016).

When individuals recognize their strengths, they view themselves from a powerful standpoint that would drive them forward with more interest and a higher level of engagement despite their situations (Rath and Conchie 2008). Effective leaders utilize a strength-based approach to increase individuals' and teams' performances and productivity naturally.

As effective leaders, you want to know your people's strengths, so you can use such strengths to develop them on needed skills or enhance their abilities and competencies. To refresh your memory and read more about the importance of strength-based development, review Chapters 6 and 8.

Use Table 18.2 to conduct a self-evaluation rating process. Consider your level of participation and competencies on the elements of transformation for effective leadership as a skilled transformational coach. Conduct this self-evaluation rating quarterly and adjust your efforts as needed.

**Table 18.2 Transformation for Effective Leadership Self-Evaluation by Transformational Coach. Author's Original Creation.**

| *Transformation for Effective Leadership Self-Evaluation by Transformational Coach* | | | | | | | | |
|---|---|---|---|---|---|---|---|---|
| *Name* | | *Date* | *Organization* | *Department* | | | | |
| *Rating Scale: Rating Scale: **1**=Poor, **2**=Marginal, **3**=Acceptable, **4**=Good, **5**=Excellent* | | | | | | | | |
| # | **Categories** | **Explaining Actions** | | **1** | **2** | **3** | **4** | **5** |
| 1 | **Vision-Based Foundation** | 1 | My personal life vision is the source of my life | | | | | |
| | | 2 | My life vision is positive and empowers me | | | | | |
| | | 3 | It Relates to my client's organization's vision | | | | | |
| | | 4 | Coach my employees based on their organization's vision | | | | | |
| | | 5 | Use vision to develop effective leadership in teams | | | | | |
| 2 | **Value-Based Leadership** | 6 | Have a set of values and principles for my life | | | | | |
| | | 7 | Use clients' values as the source of the outcome | | | | | |
| | | 8 | Be sensitive to people's source of their values | | | | | |
| | | 9 | Do not question the reasons for someone's values | | | | | |
| | | 10 | Develop effective leadership with their values in mind | | | | | |
| 3 | **Emotional Maturity** | 11 | Check the level of emotional intelligence with individuals | | | | | |
| | | 12 | Check emotional intelligence in teams' relationships | | | | | |
| | | 13 | Address social awareness with individuals and teams | | | | | |
| | | 14 | Address self-regulation with individuals and teams | | | | | |
| | | 15 | Address relationship management with individuals & teams | | | | | |

(*Continued*)

**Table 18.2 (Continued)**

| *Transformation for Effective Leadership Self-Evaluation by Transformational Coach* | | | | | | | | |
|---|---|---|---|---|---|---|---|---|
| *Name* | | *Date* | *Organization* | *Department* | | | | |
| 4 | **Positive Mental Strengths** | 16 | Be aware of my positive mental strength | | | | | |
| | | 17 | Recognize individuals' and teams' positive mental strengths | | | | | |
| | | 18 | Recognize individuals' and teams' short fuse for upsets | | | | | |
| | | 19 | Realize individuals' and teams' expectations of each other | | | | | |
| | | 20 | Recognize interpretations and perceptions instead of facts | | | | | |
| 5 | **Mindful Connections** | 21 | Be aware of my mindful connection with others | | | | | |
| | | 22 | Point out lack of mindfulness to individuals and teams | | | | | |
| | | 23 | Teach individuals and teams mindful connection | | | | | |
| | | 24 | Be patient with people who lack mindfulness | | | | | |
| | | 25 | Keep talking about peaceful and harmonious connections | | | | | |
| 6 | **Strength-Based Development** | 26 | I am aware of my strengths and weaknesses | | | | | |
| | | 27 | I help individuals and teams recognize their strengths | | | | | |
| | | 28 | Keep reminding weaknesses are opportunities for growth | | | | | |
| | | 29 | Remember that having strengths is not the end of learning | | | | | |
| | | 30 | Support individuals to plan their strength development | | | | | |
| **Individual Columns' Totals** | | | | | | | | |
| **Total of Above Individual Columns** | | | | | | | | |
| **Final Average (Above total divided by 30)** | | | | | | | | |
| Three actions I can take that will bring up my three lowest ratings by at least one scale on the next rating period: | | | | | | | | |
| Action 1: | | | | | | | | |
| Action 2: | | | | | | | | |
| Action 3: | | | | | | | | |

*Source:* Copyright 2022 by Behnam Bakhshandeh.

## Key Takeaways

1. A transformational coaching process is a professional undertaking conducted by a skilled and trained professional coach who aids and guides participants through most revealing and authentic self-realizations that result in those intimate moments of seeing the needed change. This is an act of leadership as an individual, a team, or an organization.
2. Regardless of your position in life or the organization you are involved with, the preceding elements of transformational coaching as an outcome can and will positively affect you and the people around you.
3. The impacts and benefits of transformational coaching are wide, stretching from one side of life to the other side, personally and professionally. These benefits leave a long-lasting and positive impact not only on your life and profession but also on people around you at home and at the workplace.
4. Like any other human behavior, you must work on developing a powerful mindset and an attitude you call positive, empowering, or great.

## List of Discussion Questions

1. How do you rate yourself from 0 to 10 on your understanding of the concept of self-rating on "How to Use What I Learned"? (Please look at the whole concept and all the related elements.)
   - What is missing or in the way of your understanding it better?
   - What is your action plan to increase your overall rate on this process?
2. How do you rate yourself from 0 to 10 on your understanding of the concept of self-rating on "Where and with Whom to Use What I Learned"? (Please look at the whole concept and all the related elements.)
   - What is missing or in the way of your understanding it better?
   - What is your action plan to increase your overall rate on this process?
3. How do you rate yourself from 0 to 10 on your understanding of the concept of self-rating on "Transformation for Effective Leadership"? (Please look at the whole concept and all the related elements.)
   - What is missing or in the way of your understanding it better?
   - What is your action plan to increase your overall rate on this process?

## References

Bakhshandeh, Behnam. 2006. *BraveHearts; Leadership Development Training*. Leadership Development Division (Unpublished training and developmental course on coaching executives and managers). San Diego, CA: Primeco Education, Inc.

Bakhshandeh, Behnam. 2009. *Conspiracy for Greatness; Mastery on Love Within*. San Diego, CA: Primeco Education, Inc.

Bakhshandeh, Behnam. 2015. *Anatomy of Upset: Restoring Harmony*. Carbondale, PA: Primeco Education, Inc.

Linley, P. Alex, Aimee Felus, Raphael Gillett, and Stephen Joseph. 2011. "Emotional Expression and Growth Following Adversity: Emotional Expression Mediates Subjective Distress and is Moderated by Emotional Intelligence." *Journal of Loss and Trauma* 16, no. 5: 387–401.

MacKie, Doug. 2016. *Strength-Based Leadership Coaching in Organizations*. Philadelphia, PA: Kogan Page.

Rath, Tom and Barry Conchie. 2008. *Strengths Based Leadership*. New York, NY: Gallup Press.

Rothwell, William J. 2015. *Beyond Training & Development (3rd ed.). Enhancing Human Performance through a Measurable Focus on Business Impact*. Amherst, MA: HRD Press, Inc.

Rothwell, William, J. and Behnam Bakhshandeh. 2022. *High-Performance Coaching for Managers*. New York, NY: Routledge-Taylor and Francis.

Rothwell, William J., Carolyn K. Hohne, and Stephen B. King. 2012. *Human Performance Improvement*. New Your, NY: Routledge.

# Chapter 19

# Transformational Coaches' Self-Reflection and Self-Evaluation through Self-Rating

Behnam Bakhshandeh

## Overview

As transformational coaches, we are involved with individuals, teams, groups, and organizations. Regardless of the intent for the engagement or the business purpose for the involvement to make a difference with people on their productivity or performance, we are engaging in a relationship with human beings.

Our participation in self-reflection and self-evaluation will enable us to authentically measure our strengths and weaknesses that need more attention to enhance the process and improve our coaching skills and competencies. In addition, this approach develops us as a more effective and competent coach that will allow us to have a much more positive and constructive evaluation of our participants and evaluation reports we submit to individuals, teams, and group supervisors or senior managers.

In this chapter, we will walk you through several self-reflections and self-evaluations as a transformational coach in these areas:

- What are self-reflection and self-evaluation?
- The purpose and importance of self-reflection and self-evaluation
- Role of self-evaluation on development
- Transformational coaches' self-evaluation in three general areas:
  - Organization environment related to coaching
  - Conversations about effective leadership
  - Organizations' coaching cultures
  - Coaching qualities
  - Emotional intelligence

DOI: 10.4324/9781003304074-25

- Leadership qualities
- Rapport
- Disciplines
- Skills and competencies
- The coaching process
- Coaching structure
- Coaching processes

All the self-reflection and self-evaluation approaches in this chapter are displayed in self-rating tables on two different fashions of ratings from scales of 1 (the lowest) to 5 (the highest) based on (1) **quality** or (2) **occurrence**, as you see here:

1. Quality Rating Scale: **1**=Poor, **2**=Marginal, **3**=Acceptable, **4**=Good, **5**=Excellent
2. Occurrence Rating Scale: **1**=Never, **2**=Hardly, **3**=Occasionally, **4**=Generally, **5**=Constantly

## What Are Self-Reflection and Self-Evaluation?

Self-reflection and self-evaluation (also known as self-assessment) are powerful means to learn about our strengths and weaknesses and to improve our learning, abilities, and practices (Bakhshandeh 2009). Therefore, these authentic reflections and honest evaluations play a significant role in coaching practice and in developing a transformational coach working with individuals and teams.

### *Self-Reflection*

Self-reflection allows us to use our experiences to have a deeper understanding of ourselves and our behaviors. Self-reflection fosters access to consciousness and self-awareness about our mindsets and behaviors that result in our actions and practices in life (Barbazette 2006). This self-awareness would empower us to distinguish areas about ourselves and our approaches that need to be discarded, enhanced, improved, or further developed.

Oxford Languages (2022) defines self-reflection as "meditation or serious thought about one's character, actions, and motives." According to the Merriam-Webster dictionary, synonyms for *self-reflection* are "introspection, self-contemplation, self-examination, self-observation, self-questioning, self-scrutiny, self-searching, soul-searching."

Performing self-reflection needs intentionality and a certain self-disciplined behavior that involves an interest in learning about ourselves and investigating what works and what doesn't work (Bakhshandeh 2018). In the case of transformational coaching for effective leadership, transformational coaches can use self-reflection to understand the level of their effectiveness in approaches with their participants and what they can do to improve their practices.

### *Self-Evaluation*

Self-evaluation is considered a self-review and assessment of our actions, practices, and performance at work or in other areas of our lives. Rothwell and Kazanas (2004) explained self-evaluation as an opportunity for employees to examine and record their own performance, activities, and their experience at work from their viewpoint. This approach is considered a self-diagnosis that employees can share with their supervisors or higher managers so together they can design a productive action plan to resolve issues or enhance performance.

Merriam-Webster dictionary provides these synonyms: "self-abnegation, self-revelation, self-examination, self-absorption."

**Note:** For this book and intentionality for this chapter, at this point we will use the term "self-evaluation" to represent these other terminologies: self-reflection, self-assessment.

### *The Primary Purpose of Self-Evaluation*

At the lowest level, the main purpose of self-evaluation in organizations is for employees to rate their own performance and productivity and then compare it with the evaluation from their supervisors during the annual performance review (Phillips and Pulliam Phillips 2011). At the higher level, self-evaluations aid employees in understanding their barriers to professional growth and development in their departments and organizations. Through self-evaluations, employees can align their personal and career goals with their managers (Thompson 2021). Self-evaluations give employees the freedom to express their perspectives and share their views with their employers, which would provide freedom for them and a path for a stronger relationship between employees and their higher managers.

In our book, transformational coaches' self-evaluation helps them develop a stronger and more effective approach to their coaching process and learn about the needed development.

### *Requirements for Self-Evaluation*

Self-evaluation requires individuals to review and assess their performance while reflecting on their mindsets, attitudes, and behaviors influencing such performances and productivities (Whitmore 2017). Ultimately this process enhances their learning progress and ownership of their result on both personal and professional levels. However, for self-evaluation to work, individuals need to do the following:

- Be honest and authentic and reflect truthfully.
- Give up being "right" about what is not working or damaging.
- Evaluate their performance in contrast to standards or criteria.
- Keep track of their progress in a timely fashion (weekly, monthly, quarterly, etc.).
- Recognize and distinguish their strengths and how they have developed them.
- Recognize and distinguish their weaknesses and what needs to be done about them.
- Set realistic, manageable, and measurable goals for what is not working.
- Design an action plan for working on their weaknesses and enhancing their strengths.
- Review their set of goals and action plans with their supervisors or higher managers.
- Request feedback from their supervisors or higher managers.
- Reflect on the feedback and adjust their action plan.
- Reflect and evaluate on their learning styles and models.
- Use outside resources (books, articles, webinars, etc.) to enhance their learning.

(Rothwell and Bakhshandeh 2022; Rothwell et al. 2021)

## How Effective Am I as a Transformational Coach?

Now we are getting to the nuts and bolts of evaluating and rating the levels of effectiveness and progress in developing individuals, teams, and groups on their leadership qualities, performance, and transformations by a transformational coach. We will break down this process into these three categories:

1. Organization environment
2. The coaches' self-evaluation
3. The coaching process

We need to get related to the power of numbers. Numbers on the tracking and rating columns on these self-rating tables represent the honest and real understanding of your performance and progress in your development as an effective transformational coach or any other coach regarding working with individuals, teams, and groups.

Every self-evaluation form and their self-rating tables contained these elements:

- **Name:** Add your name.
- **Date:** The date you conduct the evaluation. This will help you to manage the new rating on a weekly, monthly, quarterly, or annually and compare the progress.
- **Organization:** The name of the organization or business you are doing this evaluation for.
- **Department:** The department or group in the organization whose progress you are rating.
- **Rating scale:** Use quality of occurrence rating.
- **Categories, areas of interest or elements column:** Explain the elements, areas, and or categories you are rating.
- **Descriptions or explanations column:** Describe the areas of concern and or definitions of such areas.
- **Rating columns:** Log in the corresponding rates from 1 to 5.
- **Totals and average rows:** Total columns, and calculate weekly, monthly, or quarterly averages. These numbers help you to compare and track your progress.
- **Action rows:** Log the actions you are taking to improve your ratings.
- **Action column:** Log what is missing and or what needs to get done to improve the areas. (This element is not presented on all rating tables. Some tables use the action rows instead.)

## *Organizations' Environment Related to Coaching*

In this segment, we present the self-evaluation and rating of transformational coaches on these three categories related to the organizations' environment based on leadership and coaching:

- Conversations about effective leadership
- Organization culture
- Coaching culture

### *Conversations about Effective Leadership*

We divided the evaluation of conversation about effective leadership into two general sub-categories and frameworks:

1. Framework for Conversations about Effective Leadership in Organizations (Table 19.1)
2. Framework for Conversations about Effective Leadership with Individuals (Table 19.2)

The fundamental base for any coaching engagement is the conversations and inquiries started by the coaches and engaged by the participants (Bakhshandeh 2009). The general notion of the conversation about effective leadership is not separated from this fundamental base, which is the background of a framework that employs several conversations and dialogues on various topics

**Table 19.1 Transformational Coaches Performance Self-Rating Sheet in Framework for Conversations about Effective Leadership in Organizations. Author's Original Creation.**

| *Transformational Coaches Performance Self-Rating Sheet in Framework for Conversations about Effective Leadership in Organizations* | | | | | | | |
|---|---|---|---|---|---|---|---|
| *Name* | *Date* | *Organization* | *Department* | | | | |
| *Rating Scale: **1**=Poor, **2**=Marginal, **3**=Acceptable, **4**=Good, **5**=Excellent* | | | | | | | |
| **Area of Interest** | | **Purpose of Coaching Conversation** | **1** | **2** | **3** | **4** | **5** |
| 1 | **Establishing Rapport** | Form a mutual, respectful, and effective relationship between managers and employees resulting in a partnership. | | | | | |
| 2 | **Coaching Culture** | Ensure regularity in the application of coaching in departments and the whole organization. | | | | | |
| 3 | **Performance Enhancement** | Empower and promote individuals and teams' efforts to perform correctly and effectively. | | | | | |
| 4 | **Culture of Accountability** | Hold individuals and teams accountable for their levels of performance, progress, and results. | | | | | |
| 5 | **Constructive Feedback** | Provide positive and constructive feedback on individuals' and teams' performances and behaviors. | | | | | |
| 6 | **Environment of Inspirations** | Underline the possibilities of efforts and potential of individual or team transformations and performance improvements. | | | | | |
| 7 | **Talent Development & Retention** | Work on skills and competencies development programs and retaining talents. | | | | | |
| 8 | **Developing Strengths** | Develop individuals and teams' strengths to increase productivity and performance in departments. | | | | | |
| **Individual Columns' Totals** | | | | | | | |
| **Total of Above Individual Columns** | | | | | | | |
| **Final Average (Above total divided by 8)** | | | | | | | |
| Three actions I will take on for this rating period that will bring up my three lowest evaluation rates by at least one point: | | | | | | | |
| Action 1: | | | | | | | |
| Action 2: | | | | | | | |
| Action 3: | | | | | | | |

*Source:* Copyright 2022 by Behnam Bakhshandeh.

that encourage a thread of effective and productive outcomes in effective leadership in organizations as well as with individuals. This ultimately influences elements of leadership in team and group performances (Lee 2021; Cardy and Leonard 2011).

As transformational coaches, you want to evaluate your performance (by rating yourself from 1 to 5) by conducting conversations that will produce effective leadership in organizations, individuals, and teams. Table 19.1 displays the frameworks for effective organizational leadership.

**Table 19.2 Transformational Coaches Performance Self-Rating Sheet in Framework for Conversations about Effective Leadership with Individuals. Author's Original Creation.**

| *Transformational Coaches Performance Self-Rating Sheet in Framework for Conversations about Effective Leadership with Individuals* | | | | | | | |
|---|---|---|---|---|---|---|---|
| *Name* | *Date* | *Organization* | *Individual* | | | | |
| *Rating Scale: **1**=Poor, **2**=Marginal, **3**=Acceptable, **4**=Good, **5**=Excellent* | | | | | | | |
| **Area of Interest** | | **Purpose of Coaching Conversation** | **1** | **2** | **3** | **4** | **5** |
| 1 | **Career Advancement** | Discuss their future with the company or other future career development. | | | | | |
| 2 | **Assertion** | Confirm their correct career pathway and reflect on their progress. | | | | | |
| 3 | **Growth and Development** | Consider professional growth and the possibility of opportunities to learn more skills and competencies. | | | | | |
| 4 | **Promotability** | Define their interests and potential promotions and new positions. | | | | | |
| 5 | **Acknowledgment** | Acknowledge their progress, efforts, and performance. | | | | | |
| 6 | **Problem Solving** | Develop their problem-solving skills and remove obstacles in their performance. | | | | | |
| 7 | **Collaboration** | Provide a working environment that fosters partnership and creativity. | | | | | |
| 8 | **Feedback** | Give feedback and reflect on their performance and the coaching relationship. | | | | | |
| **Individual Columns' Totals** | | | | | | | |
| **Total of Above Individual Columns** | | | | | | | |
| **Final Average (Above total divided by 8)** | | | | | | | |
| Three actions I will take on for this rating period that will bring up my three lowest evaluation rates by at least one point: | | | | | | | |
| Action 1: | | | | | | | |
| Action 2: | | | | | | | |
| Action 3: | | | | | | | |

*Source:* Copyright 2022 by Behnam Bakhshandeh.

Table 19.2 displays the framework for effective leadership with individuals or teams.

## *Organization's Culture*

We invite you to conduct the self-evaluation into your effectiveness by assessing an organization's culture in these two areas:

1. Assessment of Team's Understanding of Organization's Values, Vision, and Mission
2. Assessing Organization's Coaching Culture

## Assessing Team's Understanding of Organization's Values, Vision, and Mission

It is important that individuals forming teams, groups, and departments in any organization be supportive and aligned with the organization's core values and principles and its vision and mission. This alignment is the backbone of an organization's performance and productivity, plus its positive influence on talent management and lowering employee turnover.

As a transformational coach, you want to know your participant's level of clarity in the understanding of their organization's values, vision, and mission. To do that, you can use Table 19.3 when talking to individuals or a team for collecting a focus group.

**Table 19.3 Transformational Coach's Assessment of Team's Understanding of Organization Values, Vision, and Mission. Author's Original Creation.**

| *Transformational Coach's Assessment of Team's Understanding of Organization's Values, Vision, and Mission* | | | | | | | |
|---|---|---|---|---|---|---|---|
| *Name* | *Date* | | *Organization* | | | | *Team* |
| *Rating Scale: **1**=Poor, **2**=Marginal, **3**=Acceptable, **4**=Good, **5**=Excellent* | | | | | | | |
| # | **Team's clarity on the organization's values, vision, and mission** | **1** | **2** | **3** | **4** | **5** | **What is missing for them? What actions are needed to increase the team's clarity?** |
| 1 | Members are aware of the organization's values and principles and their roles in its vision and mission. | | | | | | |
| 2 | They are aware of and support the organization's vision statement and its relevance to the team. | | | | | | |
| 3 | They understand and align with the organization's mission statement. | | | | | | |
| 4 | They recognize and align with why their team exists in their department. | | | | | | |
| 5 | They understand and align with the functionality of their team about the organization's vision and mission. | | | | | | |
| 6 | They have a shared view of how the team should get where it plans. | | | | | | |
| 7 | They know their job performance standards related to the organization's vision. | | | | | | |
| 8 | They understand and align on the progress plan and agree on the measurements. | | | | | | |

(*Continued*)

**Table 19.3 (Continued)**

| *Transformational Coach's Assessment of Team's Understanding of Organization's Values, Vision, and Mission* | | | | | | | |
|---|---|---|---|---|---|---|---|
| *Name* | *Date* | *Organization* | | | | | *Team* |
| 9 | They align with what is essential and not urgent in implementing a progress plan. | | | | | | |
| 10 | They have a shared view of what the organization or their team is doing best. | | | | | | |
| 11 | They are aware of and aligned with their team's strengths. | | | | | | |
| 12 | They are aware of and aligned with their team's weaknesses. | | | | | | |
| **Individual Columns' Totals** | | | | | | | Not For Use |
| **Total of Above Individual Columns** | | | | | | | |
| **Final Average (Above total divided by 12)** | | | | | | | |

*Source:* Copyright 2022 by Behnam Bakhshandeh.

## Assessing an Organization's Coaching Culture

Establishing a coaching culture in organizations is essential to the success and effectiveness of implementing coaching, especially the transformational coaching approach.

Coaching culture provides an opportunity for transformational coaches to implement coaching solutions for increasing performance and effectiveness with individuals and teams, with relatively less resistance and more welcoming of the processes and inquiries (Rothwell and Bakhshandeh 2022). A coaching culture that supports transformational coaching and effective leadership has distinct characteristics. Please use Table 19.4 to assess the organization's coaching culture's distinct quality. Then suggest new practices for improving the existing elements to establish a coaching culture in an organization.

**Table 19.4 Assessing Organization's Coaching Culture by a Transformational Coach. Author's Original Creation.**

| *Assessing Organization's Coaching Culture by a Transformational Coach* | | | | | | |
|---|---|---|---|---|---|---|
| *Name* | *Date* | *Organization* | | | | |
| *Rating Scale: 1=Poor, 2=Marginal, 3=Acceptable, 4=Good, 5=Excellent* | | | | | | |
| **Areas of Coaching Culture** | | **1** | **2** | **3** | **4** | **5** |
| 1 | The organization is built based on interpersonal trust and relationships. | | | | | |
| 2 | The organization encourages self-discovery and self-realization. | | | | | |
| 3 | The organization is built on openness and transparency. | | | | | |

| *Assessing Organization's Coaching Culture by a Transformational Coach* | | | | | | | |
|---|---|---|---|---|---|---|---|
| *Name* | *Date* | *Organization* | | | | | |
| 4 | Managers promote and enable self-awareness. | | | | | | |
| 5 | Managers promote and encourage learning and self-development. | | | | | | |
| 6 | It provides a safe space for employees to acknowledge their strengths and weaknesses. | | | | | | |
| 7 | It promotes and exhibits meaningful conversations to make a difference with people. | | | | | | |
| 8 | It inspires employees and promotes self-improvement. | | | | | | |
| 9 | The organization demonstrates the willingness to give and receive feedback for improvement. | | | | | | |
| 10 | Managers believe the potential for everyone's development and improvement. | | | | | | |
| 11 | Management believes in its leadership responsibility to develop its people. | | | | | | |
| 12 | It provides a safe and comfortable space for employees to challenge issues important to them. | | | | | | |
| 13 | Management demonstrates conviction and desire for having a coaching culture. | | | | | | |
| 14 | Managers demonstrate their interest in receiving coaching regardless of their ranks. | | | | | | |
| 15 | Managers encourage active listening and understanding. | | | | | | |
| 16 | Managers encourage employees to ask questions to uncover issues and find solutions. | | | | | | |
| 17 | The organization encourages and empowers teams and groups to practice team coaching. | | | | | | |
| 18 | It encourages using common coaching terminologies, concepts, and understanding of coaching processes. | | | | | | |
| 19 | The organization evaluates its people's performance in more than only one way. | | | | | | |
| 20 | Managers leverage on strengths for solving individuals' and teams' problems | | | | | | |
| **Individual Columns' Totals** | | | | | | | |
| **Total of Above Individual Columns** | | | | | | | |
| **Final Average (above total divided by 20)** | | | | | | | |
| Your suggestions to this organization's senior management for corrective actions or work on improving their coaching culture: | | | | | | | |
| Suggestion 1: | | | | | | | |
| Suggestion 2: | | | | | | | |
| Suggestion 3: | | | | | | | |

*Source:* Copyright 2022 by William J. Rothwell and Behnam Bakhshandeh.

## Transformational Coach Evaluating of Oneself

In this segment, we focus on the transformational coaches' skills, abilities, disciplines, and performances in the following five areas, which directly affect developing their participants in their effective leadership positions as individuals or teams:

- Emotional intelligence
- Leadership qualities
- Rapport
- Disciplines of success
- Skills and competencies

### Emotional Intelligence

In this section, we invite transformational coaches to evaluate and rate their understanding and practice elements of emotional intelligence. You can go back to Chapter 8 and read more about emotional intelligence and its role in transformational coaching.

Table 19.5 is designed for transformational coaches to rate their own level of understanding and use of emotional intelligence during practice with their participants. This will be their initial attempt and rating, which can be continued within the next six months or after a year, depending on whether the rating is high enough or too low.

**Table 19.5 Transformational Coaches' Emotional Intelligence Self-Evaluation. Author's Original Creation.**

| *Transformational Coaches' Emotional Intelligence Self-Evaluation* | | | | | | | |
|---|---|---|---|---|---|---|---|
| *Name* | | *Date* | *Organization* | | | | |
| *Rating Scale: **1**=Never, **2**=Hardly, **3**=Occasionally, **4**=Generally, **5**=Constantly* | | | | | | | |
| **Groups** | **Declarations** | | **1** | **2** | **3** | **4** | **5** |
| **Self-Awareness** | 1 | Be cognizant of body language reactions to others' communication. | | | | | |
| | 2 | Be aware of facial expressions during discussions. | | | | | |
| | 3 | Check out my opinions and biases when evaluating situations. | | | | | |
| | 4 | Realize emotions before, during, and after sensitive conversations. | | | | | |
| **Self-Regulation** | 5 | Manage oneself and keep composure when feeling anger. | | | | | |
| | 6 | Do not act on a strong impulse to say or do something. | | | | | |
| | 7 | Reflect on thoughts & feelings before any communications or actions. | | | | | |
| | 8 | Manage attitudes and moods and not take them to conversations. | | | | | |

| *Transformational Coaches' Emotional Intelligence Self-Evaluation* | | | | | | | |
|---|---|---|---|---|---|---|---|
| *Name* | *Date* | *Organization* | | | | | |
| **Social Awareness** | 9 | Recognize how others view me during interactions. | | | | | |
| | 10 | Recognize others' feelings and moods based on nonverbal gestures. | | | | | |
| | 11 | Express empathy and compassion with others in their situations. | | | | | |
| | 12 | Be aware of people's diversity and cultural differences. | | | | | |
| **Relationship Management** | 13 | Quickly take responsibility for mistakes and restore the situation. | | | | | |
| | 14 | Use encouraging language while talking to others. | | | | | |
| | 15 | Deal with emotional behaviors with sensitivity and calm manners | | | | | |
| | 16 | Convince & motivate others to consider new viewpoint. | | | | | |
| **Individual Columns' Totals** | | | | | | | |
| **Total of Above Individual Columns** | | | | | | | |
| **Final Average (above total divided by 16)** | | | | | | | |
| Three actions for this month that will bring up my three lowest ratings by at least one scale on the next month's rating: | | | | | | | |
| Action 1: | | | | | | | |
| Action 2: | | | | | | | |
| Action 3: | | | | | | | |

*Source:* Copyright 2022 by Behnam Bakhshandeh.

## *Leadership Qualities*

Transformational coaches directly influence building a learning environment for developing effective leadership with individuals and teams, directly influencing the same quality within organizations. To do so, transformational coaches need to develop a high level of leadership qualities within themselves (Bakhshandeh 2002; Bakhshandeh 2018). In this section, the transformational coaches evaluate their leadership qualities during interactions with individuals, teams, and organizations.

Table 19.6 represents a self-evaluation rating for some of these leadership qualities for a transformational coach.

**Table 19.6 Leadership Qualities of Transformational Coach Self-Evaluation. Author's Original Creation.**

| *Leadership Qualities of Transformational Coaches' Self-Evaluation* | | | | | | | |
|---|---|---|---|---|---|---|---|
| *Name* | | *Date* | *Organization* | | | | |
| *Rating Scale:* ***1****=Poor,* ***2****=Marginal,* ***3****=Acceptable,* ***4****=Good,* ***5****=Excellent* | | | | | | | |
| **Qualities** | | **Descriptions** | **1** | **2** | **3** | **4** | **5** |
| 1 | **Display Respectful Behavior** | Behave respectfully with everyone regardless of their position. | | | | | |
| 2 | **Exhibit Positivity** | Display positivity and influence others around them without creating resistance. | | | | | |
| 3 | **Share Victories** | Share the triumphs and celebrate victories as a team effort. | | | | | |
| 4 | **Ask Solution-Based Questions** | Ask solution-based questions to defuse problem-based behaviors in others. | | | | | |
| 5 | **Be Innovative** | Promote innovation and creativity by advocating learning and experimenting. | | | | | |
| 6 | **Have Open Communication** | Foster effective communication and active listening to create alliances for actions. | | | | | |
| 7 | **Be Engaged** | Engage with people and inspire them to express their passions and creativity. | | | | | |
| 8 | **Be Adaptable** | Adapt to volatile and changing circumstances with flexibility and agility. | | | | | |
| 9 | **Display Transparency** | Exhibit authenticity, encourage trust, and building up relationships with others. | | | | | |
| 10 | **Show Empathy** | Show empathy, compassion, and humility to boost morale. | | | | | |
| **Individual Columns' Totals** | | | | | | | |
| **Total of Above Individual Columns** | | | | | | | |
| **Final Average (above total divided by 10)** | | | | | | | |
| Three actions for this month that will bring up my three lowest leadership qualities ratings by at least one scale on the next month's rating: | | | | | | | |
| Action 1: | | | | | | | |
| Action 2: | | | | | | | |
| Action 3: | | | | | | | |

*Source:* Copyright 2022 by Behnam Bakhshandeh.

## *Establishing Rapport*

In today's business environment, too many managers fail to establish a workable and good rapport with their employees. Some organizations seek opportunities to form a more collaborative and meaningful work environment and connect on a deeper level with their employees

(Gilmore 2019). You can go back and read more about rapport and how to establish rapport in Chapter 11. In this section, we invite transformational coaches to self-evaluate their state of being to develop a connection with their participants.

Table 19.7 displays a self-evaluation system that transformational coaches can use to realize their level of fundamental state of being and related skills to establish rapport.

**Table 19.7 Underlying State of Being and Related Competencies of Transformational Coach for Establishing Rapport Self-Evaluation.**

| *Underlying State of Being and Related Competencies of The Transformational Coach for Establishing Rapport: Self-Evaluation* | | | | | | | |
|---|---|---|---|---|---|---|---|
| *Name* | | *Date* | *Organization* | | | | |
| *Rating Scale:* ***1****=Poor,* ***2****=Marginal,* ***3****=Acceptable,* ***4****=Good,* ***5****=Excellent* | | | | | | | |
| **State of Being & Competencies** | | **Descriptions of Qualities** | **1** | **2** | **3** | **4** | **5** |
| **Be Authentic** | A combination of being real, positive, approachable without concern of surrendering to something to please someone else. | | | | | | |
| | **Approachability** | • No presence of ego<br>• Humble<br>• Open and welcoming | | | | | |
| | **Positivity** | • Optimistic<br>• Resilient<br>• Grateful | | | | | |
| **Be Respectful** | Exhibit equal respect and regard for everyone regardless of their position, age, sex, gender, race, ethnicity, nationality, religion, or other differences. | | | | | | |
| | **Professionalism** | • Proper language<br>• No drama<br>• Ethical behavior | | | | | |
| | **Sensitivity** | • Uniqueness among people<br>• Mutual respect for everyone<br>• Universal treatment for everyone | | | | | |
| **Be Courteous** | Dedicated to courtesy to others regardless of past or present situations, with a display of empathy and compassion. | | | | | | |
| | **Empathy** | • Talent awareness<br>• Other's emotional state<br>• Helpful to others | | | | | |
| | **Compassion** | • Others' situations<br>• Active listening<br>• Okay with others' failures | | | | | |

(*Continued*)

**Table 19.7 (Continued)**

| *Underlying State of Being and Related Competencies of The Transformational Coach for Establishing Rapport: Self-Evaluation* | | | | | | | | |
|---|---|---|---|---|---|---|---|---|
| *Name* | | *Date* | *Organization* | | | | | |
| **Be Engaging** | Demonstrating desire in communication and understanding others' models of communication without pushing their agenda. | | | | | | | |
| | **Communication** | • Mindful of nonverbal communication<br>• Clear and concise messages<br>• Courtesy and keen listening | | | | | | |
| | **Interest** | • Attention to the speaker<br>• Appropriate responses<br>• Feedback | | | | | | |
| **Individual Columns' Totals** | | | | | | | | |
| **Total of Above Individual Columns** | | | | | | | | |
| **Final Average (Above total divided by 8)** | | | | | | | | |
| Three actions for this month that will bring up my three lowest states of being and competencies ratings by at least one scale on the next month's self-rating: | | | | | | | | |
| Action 1: | | | | | | | | |
| Action 2: | | | | | | | | |
| Action 3: | | | | | | | | |

*Source:* Adapted from Rothwell and Bakhshandeh (2022).

## *Transformational Coaches' Disciplines*

Like any other profession, transformational coaching or any other form of coaching must follow certain disciplines to develop as professional coaches and establish their successful practice. In this section, we look at what it takes for transformational coaches to succeed in their work.

Table 19.8 displays some of these fundamental disciplines that will help transformational coaches establish a successful practice.

**Table 19.8 Transformational Coach's Discipline of Success Self-Rating. Author's Original Creation.**

| *Transformational Coach's Disciplines of Success Self-Rating* | | | | | | | |
|---|---|---|---|---|---|---|---|
| *Name* | *Date* | *Organization* | | | | | *Department* |
| *Rating Scale: **1**=Never, **2**=Hardly, **3**=Occasionally, **4**=Generally, **5**=Constantly* | | | | | | | |
| # | **Disciplines** | **1** | **2** | **3** | **4** | **5** | **What is missing?** |
| 1 | Apply and practice elements of Critical Thinking during coaching sessions. | | | | | | |

| *Transformational Coach's Disciplines of Success Self-Rating* | | | | | | | |
|---|---|---|---|---|---|---|---|
| *Name* | *Date* | *Organization* | | | | | *Department* |
| 2 | Use the Solution-Based approach during their coaching sessions. | | | | | | |
| 3 | Practice precise and clear effective Communication with participants. | | | | | | |
| 4 | Practice elements of Active Listening during coaching sessions. | | | | | | |
| 5 | Display professional behavior and attitude with participants. | | | | | | |
| 6 | Be responsible for their performance during coaching sessions. | | | | | | |
| 7 | Be accountable for their actions and results of their coaching. | | | | | | |
| 8 | Clarify and distinguish the actual issues at hand with participants. | | | | | | |
| 9 | Maintain positive relationships with participants. | | | | | | |
| 10 | Learn from their success and failures and correct their approach. | | | | | | |
| 11 | Plan their approach and work with participants. | | | | | | |
| 12 | Schedule their work and communication and follow it. | | | | | | |
| 13 | Ask questions, conduct inquiries, and seek clarity. | | | | | | |
| 14 | Monitor and practice what works and what doesn't work. | | | | | | |
| 15 | Complete daily and weekly tasks and processes. | | | | | | |
| 16 | Stay in open and honest communication with participants. | | | | | | |
| 17 | Use and exhibit elements of Emotional Intelligence. | | | | | | |
| 18 | Empower both you and participants during coaching sessions. | | | | | | |
| 19 | Learn from the best active producers in their industry. | | | | | | |
| 20 | Have a clear career goal and vision. | | | | | | |
| **Individual Column's Totals** | | | | | | | Not For Use |
| **Total of Above Individual Columns** | | | | | | | |
| **Final Average (Above total divided by 20)** | | | | | | | |

(*Continued*)

**Table 19.8 (Continued)**

| *Transformational Coach's Disciplines of Success Self-Rating* | | | |
|---|---|---|---|
| *Name* | *Date* | *Organization* | *Department* |
| Three actions for this month that will bring up my three lowest rating disciplines by at least one point: | | | |
| Action 1: | | | |
| Action 2: | | | |
| Action 3: | | | |

*Source:* Copyright 2022 by Behnam Bakhshandeh.

## Coaches' Skills and Competencies

Skills and competencies are vital to any professional trade and work. The coaching profession is not different from any other profession that relies on its practitioners' skills and competencies. In this section, we ask transformational coaches to self-evaluate and rate their level of competence and mastery in their skills and competencies. The following rating system has two benefits for transformational coaches: (1) their understanding of their ability to perform general coaching with individuals, teams, and organizations, and (2) the significant impact of these skills on their enhancement as skilled and competent coaches.

Table 19.9 displays a list of such skills and competencies for transformational coaches' self-evaluation and rating.

**Table 19.9 Transformational Coaches Skills and Competencies Self-Evaluation Rating.**

| *Transformational Coaches' Skills and Competencies Self-Evaluation Rating* | | | | | | | |
|---|---|---|---|---|---|---|---|
| *Name* | *Date* | *Organization* | | | | | *Department* |
| | | | | | | | |
| *Rating Scale: **1**=Poor, **2**=Marginal, **3**=Acceptable, **4**=Good, **5**=Excellent* | | | | | | | |
| **Skills and Competencies** | | **1** | **2** | **3** | **4** | **5** | **What is Missing?** |
| 1 | Institute clear and specific expectations for both ends of the coaching relationship. | | | | | | |
| 2 | Apply new ideas and current coaching methods and models. | | | | | | |
| 3 | Adapt an effective coaching style for supplying the participants' distinctive needs. | | | | | | |
| 4 | Customize coaching conversations based on participants' vital needs for improvement. | | | | | | |
| 5 | Implement effective communication and active listening to realize participants' needs and viewpoints. | | | | | | |

| *Transformational Coaches' Skills and Competencies Self-Evaluation Rating* | | | | | | | |
|---|---|---|---|---|---|---|---|
| *Name* | *Date* | *Organization* | | | | | *Department* |
| 6 | Identify, and acknowledge participants' attempts to execute the coaching practices. | | | | | | |
| 7 | Identify and work on potential reasons for participants' low performance. | | | | | | |
| 8 | Give positive and constructive feedback to build participants' certainty in their performance. | | | | | | |
| 9 | Identify dysfunctions and sources of conflicts among teams and group members. | | | | | | |
| 10 | Recognize the source of participants' motivation for their current and future career work. | | | | | | |
| 11 | Give participants enough tasks and assignments before they feel overwhelmed. | | | | | | |
| 12 | Convey and distinguish the organization's values, vision, and mission. | | | | | | |
| 13 | Explain a bigger picture and break it into smaller goals for easier attainments. | | | | | | |
| 14 | Understand and characterize performance and objectives' potential risks. | | | | | | |
| 15 | Know the organization's compensation, benefits, incentives, and reward systems. | | | | | | |
| 16 | Describe the chain of command, their accountabilities, and management structure for workability. | | | | | | |
| 17 | Illustrate and clarify individuals' and teams' contributions to the organization's success. | | | | | | |
| 18 | Aid participants in setting their priorities, goals, and significance of their intentions. | | | | | | |
| 19 | Establish a safe environment for participation and encourage development. | | | | | | |

(*Continued*)

**Table 19.9 (Continued)**

| *Transformational Coaches' Skills and Competencies Self-Evaluation Rating* | | | | | | | |
|---|---|---|---|---|---|---|---|
| *Name* | *Date* | *Organization* | | | | | *Department* |
| 20 | Hold yourself accountable for the quality of your performance and transfer of coaching processes. | | | | | | |
| **Individual Columns' Totals** | | | | | | | Not For Use |
| **Total of Above Individual Columns** | | | | | | | |
| **Final Average (Above total divided by 20)** | | | | | | | |
| Three actions for this month that will bring up my three lowest ratings by at least one point: | | | | | | | |
| Action 1: | | | | | | | |
| Action 2: | | | | | | | |
| Action 3: | | | | | | | |

*Source:* Adapted from Rothwell and Bakhshandeh (2022).

## *Evaluating the Coaching Process*

In this segment, we examine the transformational coaches' understanding and abilities to go through the transformational coaching structure and processes. To accomplish this interest, we invite transformational coaches to review and self-evaluate in these two areas:

- Common Sequence of Transformational Coaching Structure
- Elements of Coaching Processes

### *Common Sequence of Transformational Coaching Structure*

As a part of the professional coaching concept, transformational coaching follows a certain structure and series of sequences for completing the coaching undertaking. Such structures and sequences vary based on the transformational coaching engagement with an individual, a team, or an organization. Also, the length of the sequence structure and order varies based on the nature of interventions and the responsibility of participants as an individual, a team, or a department.

Table 19.10 represents a list of common categories and elements for performing transformational coaching and its general sequence of elements.

**Table 19.10 Transformational Coach's Confident in Conducting the Common Sequence of Transformational Coaching Structure.**

| *Transformational Coaches' Confidence in Conducting the Common Sequence of Transformational Coaching Structure* | | | | | | | | | |
|---|---|---|---|---|---|---|---|---|---|
| *Name* | | *Date* | | *Organization* | | | *Department* | | |
| *Rating Scale: 1=Poor, 2=Marginal, 3=Acceptable, 4=Good, 5=Excellent* | | | | | | | | | |
| **Phases** | **Categories** | **#** | **Elements** | **1** | **2** | **3** | **4** | **5** | **What is Missing?** |
| **FOUNDATION** | **Initiation** | 1 | Sponsorship | | | | | | |
| | | 2 | Agreement | | | | | | |
| | | 3 | Introductions | | | | | | |
| | | 4 | Scheduling | | | | | | |
| | **Engagement** | 5 | Establish rapport | | | | | | |
| | | 6 | Create the context | | | | | | |
| | | 7 | Set up rules | | | | | | |
| | | 8 | Clarify expectations | | | | | | |
| **LEARNING** | **Data Collection** | 9 | Observation | | | | | | |
| | | 10 | Document review | | | | | | |
| | | 11 | Interviews | | | | | | |
| | | 12 | Focus groups | | | | | | |
| | **Needs Assessment** | 13 | Identify needs | | | | | | |
| | | 14 | Identify issues | | | | | | |
| | | 15 | Identify symptoms | | | | | | |
| | | 16 | What is missing | | | | | | |
| **DESIGNING** | **Approach Design** | 17 | Models | | | | | | |
| | | 18 | Elements | | | | | | |
| | | 19 | Exercises | | | | | | |
| | | 20 | Tools | | | | | | |
| | **Implementation** | 21 | Executive coaching | | | | | | |
| | | 22 | Team coaching | | | | | | |
| | | 23 | Inquiries | | | | | | |
| | | 24 | Practices | | | | | | |

(*Continued*)

**Table 19.10 (Continued)**

| *Transformational Coaches' Confidence in Conducting the Common Sequence of Transformational Coaching Structure* | | | | | | | | | |
|---|---|---|---|---|---|---|---|---|---|
| *Name* | | *Date* | | *Organization* | | | *Department* | | |
| **FORWARDING** | **Action plan** | 25 | Team leaders | | | | | | |
| | | 26 | Communication | | | | | | |
| | | 27 | Check & Balances | | | | | | |
| | | 28 | Deadlines | | | | | | |
| | **Review & Evaluation** | 29 | Weekly tracks | | | | | | |
| | | 30 | Support sessions | | | | | | |
| | | 31 | Action plans | | | | | | |
| | | 32 | Evaluation forms | | | | | | |
| **SEPARATING** | **Feedback** | 33 | Constructive inputs | | | | | | |
| | | 34 | Give feedback | | | | | | |
| | | 35 | Ask for feedback | | | | | | |
| | | 36 | Acknowledgment | | | | | | |
| | **Maintenance** | 37 | Change Agent | | | | | | |
| | | 38 | Maintenance plan | | | | | | |
| | | 39 | Monthly checking | | | | | | |
| | | 40 | Availability | | | | | | |
| **Individual Columns' Totals** | | | | | | | | | Not For Use |
| **Total of Above Individual Columns** | | | | | | | | | |
| **Final Average (Above total divided by 40)** | | | | | | | | | |
| My three actions for this month to increase and develop my abilities to conduct my lower rates on coaching structure: | | | | | | | | | |
| Action 1: | | | | | | | | | |
| Action 1: | | | | | | | | | |
| Action 1: | | | | | | | | | |

*Source:* Adapted from Rothwell and Bakhshandeh (2022).

## *Elements of Coaching Processes*

Transformational coaches can use these classifications and their related elements to perform a self-evaluation and rate themselves on their abilities, competencies, and skills as professional coaches. This is when the coaches' integrity, accountability, and honesty are important for conducting a valuable and real self-evaluation.

Table 19.11 displays a list of such classifications and their related elements. Transformational coaches can conduct this self-evaluation rating on a quarterly basis and adjust their approaches.

**Table 19.11 Coaching Processes Self-Evaluation for Transformational Coaches.**

| *Elements of Coaching Processes Self-Evaluation for Transformational Coaches* | | | | | | | |
|---|---|---|---|---|---|---|---|
| *Name* | *Date* | *Organization* | *Department* | | | | |
| *Rating Scale:* ***1****=Never,* ***2****=Hardly,* ***3****=Occasionally,* ***4****=Generally,* ***5****=Constantly* | | | | | | | |
| **Processes** | **Descriptions of Processes** | | **1** | **2** | **3** | **4** | **5** |
| **Desired Outcome** | 1 | My coaching methodology helps participants to be effective in their productivity. | | | | | |
| | 2 | My coaching approach causes improvement in participants' job performance. | | | | | |
| | 3 | My participants look forward to our coaching conversation and show gratitude. | | | | | |
| **Collaboration** | 4 | I demonstrate respect and courtesy to my participants during our coaching conversations. | | | | | |
| | 5 | I use supportive and encouraging language during coaching conversations with participants. | | | | | |
| | 6 | I create a positive environment for participants to safely discuss their issues or suggestions. | | | | | |
| **Empathy** | 7 | I make sure participants know I understand their points of view and situations. | | | | | |
| | 8 | During a sensitive conversation, I display empathy and understanding for participants' feelings and emotions. | | | | | |
| | 9 | I display patience and don't interrupt participants' dialogues or invalidate their problems. | | | | | |
| **Self-Awareness** | 10 | I make sure my mindset is in a positive and compassionate place before starting a coaching conversation. | | | | | |
| | 11 | I ask questions and use relevant examples that assist participants in discovering other options for problems. | | | | | |
| | 12 | I make sure by the end of a coaching conversation, participants have better clarity about their issues. | | | | | |

(*Continued*)

**Table 19.11 (Continued)**

| *Elements of Coaching Processes Self-Evaluation for Transformational Coaches* | | | | | | | | |
|---|---|---|---|---|---|---|---|---|
| *Name* | | *Date* / *Organization* | *Department* | | | | | |
| **Goal Setting** | 13 | I assist participants in setting relevant and valuable goals for their lives and professions. | | | | | | |
| | 14 | I ensure participants set realistic, specific, measurable, and attainable goals for their lives and professions. | | | | | | |
| | 15 | I encourage participants to review and adjust their goals quarterly for higher performance and accuracy. | | | | | | |
| **Action Planning** | 16 | I encourage participants to develop a simple, clear, attainable action plan to accomplish their goals. | | | | | | |
| | 17 | I assist participants to focus on achieving success through action planning. | | | | | | |
| | 18 | I review and check on participants' action plans and their progress. | | | | | | |
| **The Processes** | 19 | I ask participants to provide a brief report on the progress of their goals and action plans. | | | | | | |
| | 20 | I address any breakdowns and performance deficits directly with participants. | | | | | | |
| | 21 | I regularly acknowledge participants' progress and their positive efforts. | | | | | | |
| **Accountability** | 22 | I make sure participants know that accountability is being responsible before the fact, not after the fact. | | | | | | |
| | 23 | I hold participants accountable for their actions, behaviors, and attitudes. | | | | | | |
| | 24 | I hold participants accountable for presenting their action plans and their related details. | | | | | | |
| **Feedback** | 25 | I provide positive and constructive feedback on participants' productivity and performance. | | | | | | |
| | 26 | I stay away from harsh feedback in negative participation and performances. | | | | | | |
| | 27 | I explain the context of feedback to participants for their understanding and development. | | | | | | |

| *Elements of Coaching Processes Self-Evaluation for Transformational Coaches* | | | | | | | |
|---|---|---|---|---|---|---|---|
| *Name* | | *Date* / *Organization* | *Department* | | | | |
| **Ethics** | 28 | I follow all coaching industry ethical policies, rules, and approaches during my coaching conversations. | | | | | |
| | 29 | I keep all participants' information and conversations confidential. | | | | | |
| | 30 | I do not ask for any sensitive or uncomfortable personal and professional information or conversations. | | | | | |
| **Individual Columns' Totals** | | | | | | | |
| **Total of Above Individual Columns** | | | | | | | |
| **Final Average (Above total divided by 30)** | | | | | | | |
| Actions I will take to increase my three lowest ratings by at least one point on the next rating process: | | | | | | | |
| Action 1: | | | | | | | |
| Action 2: | | | | | | | |
| Action 3: | | | | | | | |

*Source:* Copyright 2022 by Behnam Bakhshandeh.

## Key Takeaways

1. Our participation in self-reflection and self-evaluation will enable us to authentically measure our strengths and weaknesses that need more attention to enhance the process and improve our coaching skills and competencies.
2. Self-reflection allows us to use our experiences to have a deeper understanding of ourselves and our behaviors. Self-reflection fosters access to consciousness and self-awareness about our mindsets and behaviors that result in our actions and practices in life (Barbazette 2006).
3. Self-evaluation is considered a self-review and assessment of our actions, practices, and performance at work or in other areas of our lives. Self-evaluation is an opportunity for employees to examine and record their performance, activities, and their experience at work from their viewpoint (Rothwell and Kazanas 2004).
4. At the lowest level, the primary purpose of self-evaluation in organizations is for employees to rate their performance and productivity and then compare it with the evaluation from their supervisors during the annual performance review (Phillips and Pulliam Phillips 2011).
5. At the higher level, self-evaluation aids employees in understanding their barriers to professional growth and development in their departments and organizations.

## List of Discussion Questions

Rate yourself from 0 to 10 on these concepts from this chapter.

1. How do you rate yourself on your understanding of the concept of self-rating on "Organization Environment Related to Coaching"? (Please look at the whole concept and all the related elements.)
   - What is missing or in the way of your understanding it better?
   - What is your action plan to increase your overall rate on this process?
2. How do you rate yourself on your understanding of the concept of self-rating on "Oneself as a Coach"? (Please look at the whole concept and all the related elements.)
   - What is missing or in the way of your understanding it better?
   - What is your action plan to increase your overall rate on this process?
3. How do you rate yourself on your understanding of the concept of self-rating on "The Coaching Process"? (Please look at the whole concept and all the related elements.)
   - What is missing or in the way of your understanding it better?
   - What is your action plan to increase your overall rate on this process?

## References


Bakhshandeh, Behnam. 2002. *Business Coaching and Managers Training* (Unpublished workshop on coaching businesses and training managers). San Diego, CA: Primeco Education, Inc.

Bakhshandeh, Behnam. 2009. *Conspiracy for Greatness; Mastery on Love within.* San Diego, CA: Primeco Education, Inc.

Bakhshandeh, Behnam. 2018. *Team Building & Problem Solving* (Unpublished two-days' workshop on resolving team conflict and building a strong relationship among team members). Carbondale, PA: Primeco Education, Inc.

Barbazette, Jane. 2006. *Training Needs Assessment: Methods, Tools and Techniques.* San Francisco, CA: Pfeiffer, an Imprint of Wiley.

Cardy, Robert L. and Brian Leonard. 2011. *Performance Management. Concepts, Skills and Exercises.* Armonk, NY: M. E. Sharp. Inc.

Gilmore, Mike. 2019. *The Power of Rapport.* Middletown, DE: Partridge.

Lee, Christopher, D. 2021. *Performance Conversations. How to Use Questions to Coach Employees, Improve Productivity & Boost Confidence.* Alexandria, VA: SHRM.

"Oxford Language" website. 2022. "Self-Reflection." https://languages.oup.com/google-dictionary-en

Phillips, Jack, J. and Pulliam Phillips, Patricia. 2011. *Handbook of Training Evaluation and Measurement Methods* (4th ed.). New York, NY: Routledge. Taylor & Francis Group.

Rothwell, William, J. and Behnam Bakhshandeh. 2022. *High-Performance Coaching for Managers.* New York, NY: Routledge-Taylor and Francis.

Rothwell, William, J. and Kazanas, H. C. 2004. *Improving on-The-Job Training.* San Francisco, CA: Pfeiffer, an Imprint of Wiley.

Rothwell, William J., Sohel M. Imroz, and Behnam Bakhshandeh. 2021. *Organization-Development Interventions: Executing Effective Organizational Chang.* New York, NY: Taylor & Francis Group. CRC Press.

Thompson, Megan. 2021. "Why is self-evaluation important for development." https://wethrive.net/performance-reviews-and-appraisals/self-evaluation-important-for-development/

Whitmore, John. 2017. *Coaching for Performance; The Principle and Practice of Coaching and Leadership* (5th ed.). Boston, MA: Nicholas Brealey Publishing.

# Appendix A

## By Farhan Sadique

As mentioned in Chapter 1, the purpose of this book was to introduce the concept of transformational coaching (TC) and to educate professional business coaches or mangers-as-coaches in organizations on the influential and relevant elements of *Transformational Coaching for Effective Leadership* for coaching individuals, teams, businesses or applying such elements.

This book must be helpful for readers to develop a deep understanding and clarity of transformational coaching, but the learning mustn't end here, rather, the enthusiastic learners can utilize the insight and seek supplementary resources on transformational coaching beyond the chapters and references. There are skills, techniques, and theories briefly mentioned in the book due to space and capacity, and they require additional materials for readers to apply the learnings into practice. *Appendix A* provides a list of recommended resources to develop a more comprehensive awareness of the critical topics and continue the deep learning process.

## Books


Anderson, Dianna, and Merrill Anderson. *Coaching That Counts: Harnessing the Power of Leadership Coaching to Deliver Strategic Value*. London: Routledge.

Bakhshandeh, Behnam. 2002. *Business Coaching and Managers Training (Unpublished workshop on coaching businesses and training managers)*. San Diego, CA: Primeco Education, Inc.

Bakhshandeh, Behnam. 2009. *Conspiracy for Greatness; Mastery on Love within*. San Diego, CA: Primeco Education, Inc.

Bakhshandeh, Behnam. 2018. *Team Building & Problem Solving (Unpublished two-days' workshop on resolving team conflict and building a strong relationship among team members)*. Carbondale, PA: Primeco Education, Inc.

Barling, Julian. 2014. *The Science of Leadership: Lessons from Research for Organizational Leaders*. Doi:10.1093/acprof:oso/9780199757015.001.0001.

Barner, Robert, and Ken Ideus. 2017. *Working Deeply: Transforming Lives Through Transformational Coaching*. London: Emerald Group Publishing.

Bass, Bernard M., and Ronald E. Riggio. 2005. *Transformational Leadership* (2nd ed.). Mahwah, NJ: Psychology Press.

Blane, Hugh. 2017. *7 Principles of Transformational Leadership: Create a Mindset of Passion, Innovation, and Growth* (1st ed.). Wayne, NJ: Weiser.

Brock, Annie, and Heather Hundley. 2016. *The Growth Mindset Coach: A Teacher's Month-by-Month Handbook for Empowering Students to Achieve*. Berkeley, CA: Ulysses Press.

Burke, W., 2008. *Organizational Change: Theory and Practice*. London: Sage Publications.

Hoggan, Chad, Soni Simpson, and Heather Stuckey. 2009. *Creative Expression in Transformative Learning: Tools and Techniques for Educators of Adults*. Malabar: Krieger Publishing Company.

Keizer, Wim A. J., and Sharda S. Nandram. 2010. Integral transformational coaching. In Sharda S. Nandram and Margot Esther Borden (eds.), *Spirituality and Business: Exploring Possibilities for a New Management Paradigm* (pp. 129–140). Berlin: Springer.

Lasley, Martha, Virginia Kellogg, Richard Michaels, and Sharon Brown. 2015. *Coaching for Transformation: Pathways to Ignite Personal & Social Change.* New York: Discover Press.

Levi, Daniel. 2017. *Group Dynamics for Teams* (5th ed.). Thousand Oaks, CA: Sage Publications, Inc.

Pershing, James A., ed. 2006. *Performance Technoloy.* London: Pfeiffer.

Rogers, Carl R., and Richard Evans Farson. 1957. *Active Listening.* Mansfield Centre, CT: Martino Publishing.

Rothwell, William, Jacqueline Stavros, and Roland Sullivan. 2016. Organization development, transformation, and change. In *Practicing Organization Development: Leading Transformation and Change.* Hoboken, NJ: Willey & Sons Inc.

Rothwell, William, J., and Behnam Bakhshandeh. 2022. *High-Performance Coaching for Managers.* New York, NY: Routledge-Taylor and Francis.

Rothwell, William J., Sohel M. Imroz, and Behnam Bakhshandeh. 2021. *Organization-Development Interventions: Executing Effective Organizational Change.* New York, NY: Taylor & Francis Group and CRC Press.

Rothwell, William, J., and Kazanas, H. C. 2004. *Improving on-The-Job Training.* San Francisco, CA: Pfeiffer, an Imprint of Wiley.

Ryback, David. 1997. *Putting Emotional Intelligence to Work.* London: Routledge.

Seale, Alan. 2001. *Intuitive Living: A Sacred Path* (Rev ed.). York Beach: Weiser Books.

Stout-Rostron, Sunny. 2019. *Transformational Coaching to Lead Culturally Diverse Teams.* London: Routledge.

Turnnidge, Jennifer, and Jean Côté. 2018. The theoretical underpinnings of transformational coaching in sport. In *Professional Advances in Sports Coaching.* London: Routledge.

Umidi, Joseph. 2005. *Transformational Coaching.* Place of publication not identified: Xulon Press.

Van der Pol, Leon. 2019. *A Shift in Being: The Art and Practices of Deep Transformational Coaching* (1st ed.). London: Imaginal Light Publishing.

Werner, Jon M. 2021. *Human Resource Development: Talent Development.* London: Cengage Learning.

Whitmore, John. 2017. *Coaching for Performance; The Principle and Practice of Coaching and Leadership* (5th ed.). Boston, MA: Nicholas Brealey Publishing.

Williams, Helen, and Stephen Palmer. Coaching in organizations. In Cary L. Cooper, James Campbell Quick, and Marc J. Schabracq (eds.), *International Handbook of Work and Health Psychology* (pp. 329–52). Oxford: Wiley-Blackwell.

## Articles

Allan, Veronica, Matthew Vierimaa, Heather L. Gainforth, and Jean Côté. 2018. "The use of behaviour change theories and techniques in research-informed coach development programmes: a systematic review." *International Review of Sport and Exercise Psychology* 11, no. 1: 47–69.

Allen, Stuart, this link will open in a new window Link to external site, and Louis W. Fry. 2019. "Spiritual development in executive coaching." *The Journal of Management Development* 38, no. 10: 796–811.

Anastácio, Zélia. 2016. "Self-esteem, assertiveness, and resilience in adolescents institutionalized." *International Journal of Developmental and Educational Psychology* 1, no. 1: 315–21. Retrieved from www.redalyc.org/journal/3498/349851776035/html/

Anderson Strachan, Peter. 1996. "Managing transformational change: The learning organization and teamworking." *Team Performance Management: An International Journal* 2, no. 2: 32–40. Doi:10.1108/13527599610114989.

Andressen, Panja, Udo Konradt, and Christopher P. Neck. 2012. "The relation between self-leadership and transformational leadership: competing models and the moderating role of virtuality." *Journal of Leadership & Organizational Studie* 19, no: 1: 68–82. Doi: 10.1177/1548051811425047.

Athanasopoulou, Andromachi, and Sue Dopson. 2018. "A systematic review of executive coaching outcomes: is it the journey or the destination that matters the most?" *Leadership Quarterly* 29, no. 1: 70. www.proquest.com/docview/2065253240/19BF7190F8004CA5PQ/2

Baca-Lonn, Lucyna. 2016. "Transformational-coaching-processes-with-application-of-the-graphological-analysis.pdf." *Graphology Consultation* 1–19. Retrieved from https://graphologysolutions.eu/wp-content/uploads/2020/09/Transformational-Coaching-Processes-with-Application-of-the-Graphological-Analysis.pdf

Bachkirova, Tatiana, and Simon Borrington. 2020. "Beautiful ideas that can make us ill: implications for coaching." Doi: 10.22316/poc/05.1.03.

Bass, Bernard M. 1997. "Personal selling and transactional/transformational leadership." *Journal of Personal Selling & Sales Management* 17, no. 3: 19–28. Doi: 10.1080/08853134.1997.10754097.

Bass, Bernard M. 1999. "Two decades of research and development in transformational leadership." *European Journal of Work and Organizational Psychology* 8, no. 1: 9–32. Doi: 10.1080/135943299398410.

Bozer, Gil, Marianna Delegach, and this link will open in a new window Link to external site. 2019. "Bringing context to workplace coaching: A theoretical framework based on uncertainty avoidance and regulatory focus." *Human Resource Development Review* 18, no. 3: 376–402. Doi:10.1177/1534484319853098.

Brendel, William, Israa Samarin, and Farhan Sadique. 2021. "Open-source organization development: A platform for creating conscious od applications." *Organization Development Review* 53, no. 5: 18–31. Retrieved from www.researchgate.net/publication/360931357_Open-Source_Organization_Development_A_Platform_for_Creating_Conscious_OD_Applications

Calleja, Colin. 2014. "Jack Mezirow's conceptualisation of adult transformative learning: a review." *Journal of Adult and Continuing Education* 20: 117–36. Doi:10.7227/JACE.20.1.8.

Callow, Nichola, Matthew J. Smith, Lew Hardy, Calum A. Arthur, and James Hardy. 2009. "Measurement of transformational leadership and its relationship with team cohesion and performance level." *Journal of Applied Sport Psychology* 21 no. 4: 395–412. Doi: 10.1080/10413200903204754.

Carter, Judith Corbett. 2009. "Transformational leadership and pastoral leader effectiveness." *Pastoral Psychology* 58, no. 3: 261–71. Doi: 10.1007/s11089-008-0182-6.

Carucci, Ron. 2021. "How leaders get in the way of organizational change." *Harvard Business Review.* Retrieved from https://hbr.org/2021/04/how-leaders-get-in-the-way-of-organizational-change

Chapman, Judith Ann. 2002. "A framework for transformational change in organisations." *Leadership & Organization Development Journal* 23 no. 1: 16–25. Doi:10.1108/01437730210414535.

Cranton, Patricia. 2002. "Teaching for transformation." *New Directions for Adult & Continuing Education* 93 no. 63: 64–71. Doi:10.1002/ace.50.

Deci, Edward L., and Richard M. Ryan. 2000. "The 'what' and 'why' of goal pursuits: human needs and the self-determination of behavior." *Psychological Inquiry* 11, no. 4: 227–68. Doi: 10.1207/S15327965PLI1104_01.

Dunphy, Dexter C., and Doug A. Stace. 1988. "Transformational and coercive strategies for planned organizational change: beyond the od model." *Organization Studies* 9, no. 3: 317–334. Doi:10.1177/017084068800900302.

Feldman, Nicola Feldman. 2018. Understanding experiences of the Bermuda government's youth-serving professionals in transformational coaching. Ph.D., United States—Minnesota: Walden University. Retrieved from www.proquest.com/docview/2085970039/abstract/9EFD05F9A69247BEPQ/1

Gass, Robert. 2015. "Transformational coaching #1: The ASPire Coaching Model," 25. Retrieved from https://atctools.org/wp-content/uploads/toolkit-files/transformational-coaching-toolkit.pdf

Georganta, Katerina, and Anthony Montgomery. 2022. "Workplace Fun Is Not Enough: The Role of Work Engagement and Trust." Edited by Daryl O'Connor. *Cogent Psychology* 9, no: 1: 2060603. Doi: 10.1080/23311908.2022.2060603.

Gilpin-Jackson, Yabome. 2017. "Participant experiences of transformational change in large-scale organization development interventions (LODIs)." *Leadership & Organization Development Journal* 38, no. 3: 419–32. Doi:10.1108/LODJ-12-2015-0284.

GivPlens, Roger J. 2008. "Transformational leadership: the impact on organizational and personal outcomes." *Journal: Emerging Leadership Journey* 1: 21.

Godard, John. 2001. "High performance and the transformation of work? The implications of alternative work practices for the experience and outcomes of work." *Industrial and Labor Relations Review* 54, no. 4: 776–805. Doi:10.2307/2696112.

Greenockle, Karen M. 2010. "The new face in leadership: emotional intelligence." *Quest* 62, no. 3: 260–67. Doi: 10.1080/00336297.2010.10483647.

Griffiths, Kerryn. 2015. "Personal Coaching: reflection on a model for effective learning." *Journal of Learning Design* 8, no. 3: 14–28. Doi: 10.5204/jld.v8i3.251.

Haan, Erik de, Joanna Molyn, and Viktor O. Nilsson, A. 2020. "New findings on the effectiveness of the coaching relationship: time to think differently about active ingredients?" *Consulting Psychology Journal: Practice and Research* 72, no. 3: 155–67. Doi:10.1037/cpb0000175.

Hague, Christopher. 2019. Assessing the effectiveness of a transformational coaching workshop on athlete outcomes. M.Sc., Canada: Queen's University (Canada). www.proquest.com/docview/2529979885/abstract/3527858A93C6444DPQ/1

Hummell, Caroline Elise. n.d. Examining the impact of the transformational coaching workshop on factors that influence behaviour change. M.Sc., Canada: Queen's University (Canada). www.proquest.com/docview/2524380515/abstract/8D308343EE3E4EBDPQ/1

Kabat-Zinn, Jon. 2015. "Mindfulness." *Mindfulness* 6, no. 6: 1481–1483. Doi:10.1007/s12671–015–0456-x.

Kemper, Jule. 2021. "Stimulating collective transformative learning experiences with an ESD whole-school assessment tool." *Glocality* 4, no. 1: 5. Doi:10.5334/glo.48.

Kevin Kelloway, E., and Julian Barling. 2000. "What we have learned about developing transformational leaders." *Leadership & Organization Development Journal* 21, no. 7: 355–62. Doi: 10.1108/01437730010377908.

Kincaid, David. 2020. "Research paper: Transformational coaching for organizational success." Retrieved from https://coachcampus.com/coach-portfolios/research-papers/david-kincaid-transformational-coaching-for-organizational-success/

Kindler, Herbert S. 1979. "Two planning strategies: Incremental change and transformational change." *Group & Organization Studies* 4, no. 4: 476–84. Doi: 10.1177/105960117900400409.

Kitchenham, Andrew. 2008. "The evolution of John Mezirow's transformative learning theory." *Journal of Transformative Education* 6, no. 2: 104–23. Doi:10.1177/1541344608322678.

Kotzé, Martina, and Ian Venter. 2011. "Differences in emotional intelligence between effective and ineffective leaders in the public sector: an empirical study." *International Review of Administrative Sciences* 77, no. 2: 397–427. Doi: 10.1177/0020852311399857.

Kowalski, Karren, and Colleen Casper. 2007. "The coaching process: an effective tool for professional development." *Nursing Administration Quarterly* 31, no. 2: 171–79. Doi: 10.1097/01.NAQ.0000264867.73873.1a.

Krishnan, Venkat R. 2012. "Transformational leadership and personal outcomes: empowerment as mediator." *Leadership & Organization Development Journal* 33, no. 6: 550–63. Doi: 10.1108/01437731211253019.

Lanigan, Tim. 2019. Transformational coaching and evangelism at the Calumet Halfway House in Manchester, New Hampshire. *ProQuest Dissertations and Theses*. D.Min., United States—Virginia: Regent University. Retrieved from www.proquest.com/docview/2203492117/abstract/15B0E875636 74308PQ/1

Lawrason, Sarah. 2018. Assessing the effectiveness of a transformational coaching workshop for changing youth sport coaches' Behaviours. Thesis. Retrieved from https://qspace.library.queensu.ca/handle/1974/24290

Lievens Pascal Van Geit Pol Coetsier, Filip. 1997. "Identification of transformational leadership qualities: an examination of potential biases." *European Journal of Work and Organizational Psychology* 6 no. 4: 415–30. Doi: 10.1080/135943297399015.

Lu, Hairong, and Feng Li. 2021. "The dual effect of transformational leadership on individual- and team-level performance: the mediational roles of motivational processes." *Frontiers in Psychology* 12. Retrieved from www.frontiersin.org/articles/10.3389/fpsyg.2021.606066

Macdonald, Stephen, and Justine Allen. 2019. "Coach-created talent development motivational climate in Canoe Slalom in the United Kingdom." *International Sport Coaching Journal* 6, no. 1: 74–87. Retrieved from http://ezaccess.libraries.psu.edu/login?url=Retrieved from https://search.ebscohost.com/login.aspx?direct=true&db=s3h&AN=134825342&site=ehost-live&scope=site

Martindale, Russell J., Dave Collins, and Jim Daubney. 2005. "Talent development: a guide for practice and research within sport." *Quest* 57, no. 4: 353–75. Doi:10.1080/00336297.2005.10491862.

Martz, Ben., Jim Hughes and Frank Braun. 2016. "Creativity and problem-solving: closing the skills gap." *The Journal of Computer Information Systems* 57, no. 1: 39–48. Doi: 10.1080/08874417.2016.118149

Mbokota, Dr Gloria, Prof Kerrin Myres, and Dr Sunny Stout-Rostron. 2022. "Exploring the process of transformative learning in executive coaching." *Advances in Developing Human Resources* 24, no. 2: 117–41. Doi:10.1177/15234223221079026.

McCleskey, Jim. 2014. "Emotional intelligence and leadership: A review of the progress, controversy, and criticism." *International Journal of Organizational Analysis* 22, no: 1: 76–93. Doi: 10.1108/IJOA-03–2012–0568.

Mcleod, Saul. 2007. "Jean Piaget's theory of cognitive development." Retrieved from www.simplypsychology.org/piaget.html

Mezirow, J., and E. Taylor. 2009. "Transformative learning in practice: Insights from community, workplace, and higher education." *Undefined*. Retrieved from www.semanticscholar.org/paper/Transformative-learning-in-practice-%3A-insights-from-Mezirow-Taylor/4e7ee9edf2d704410837f2618362f5cab373072d

Mezirow, Jack. 1997. "Transformative learning: theory to practice." *New Directions for Adult and Continuing Education* 74: 5–12. Doi:10.1002/ace.7401.

Mezirow, Jack. 1994. "Understanding transformation theory." *Adult Education Quarterly* 44, no. 4: 222–232. Doi:10.1177/074171369404400403.

Michie, Susan, Maartje M. van Stralen, and Robert West. 2011. "The behaviour change wheel: a new method for characterising and designing behaviour change interventions." *Implementation Science* 6, no: 1: 1–12. Doi: 10.1186/1748-5908-6-42.

Nerstrom, Norma. 2014. "An emerging model for transformative learning." In *Adult Education Research Conference* 7. Retrieved from https://newprairiepress.org/aerc/2014/papers/55

Nixon, William L. 2020. "LaVell Edwards: a transformational leader." *Strategies* 33, no. 5: 26–35. Doi:10.1080/08924562.2020.1781007.

Palmer, Benjamin, Melissa Walls, Zena Burgess, and Con Stough. 2001. "Emotional intelligence and effective leadership." *Leadership & Organization Development Journal* 22, no: 1: 5–10. Doi: 10.1108/01437730110380174.

Price, Melissa S., and Maureen R. Weiss. 2013. "Relationships among coach leadership, peer leadership, and adolescent athletes' psychosocial and team outcomes: a test of transformational leadership theory." *Journal of Applied Sport Psychology* 25, no. 2: 265–79. Doi: 10.1080/10413200.2012.725703.

Ramsey, Jase R., Raina M. Rutti, Melanie P. Lorenz, Livia L. Barakat, and Anderson S. Sant'anna. 2017. "Developing global transformational leaders." *Journal of World Business* 52, no. 4: 461–73. Doi: 10.1016/j.jwb.2016.06.002.

Rani, Mrs. M Suvarchala. 2015. "Emotional intelligence-a model for effective leadership, competency and career growth." *Indian Journal of Science and Technology* 8: 240. Doi: 10.17485/ijst/2015/v8iS4/67032.

Romano, Alessandra. 2018. "Transformative learning: a review of the assessment tools." *Journal of Transformative Learning* 5, no. 1. Retrieved from https://jotl.uco.edu/index.php/jotl/article/view/199

Rushton, Sharron, Allison A. Lewinski, Soohyun Hwang, Leah L. Zullig, Katharine A. Ball Ricks, Katherine Ramos, Adelaide Gordon, et al. n.d. "Barriers and facilitators to the implementation and adoption of improvement coaching: a qualitative evidence synthesis." *Journal of Clinical Nursing*. Doi:10.1111/jocn.16247.

Sammut, Kristina. 2014. "Transformative learning theory and coaching: application in practice." *International Journal of Evidence Based Coaching and Mentoring* 8: 39–53. Retrieved from https://radar.brookes.ac.uk/radar/items/5fd8c194-82e9-4353-a452-c08100cb8368/1/

Sivanathan, Niroshaan, and G. Cynthia Fekken. 2002. "Emotional intelligence, moral reasoning and transformational leadership." *Leadership & Organization Development Journal* 23 no. 4: 198–204. Doi: 10.1108/01437730210429061.

Strong, Scott R. 2015. "Measuring coaching effectiveness in the financial services industry." *Dissertation Abstracts International Section A: Humanities and Social Sciences*. ProQuest Information & Learning (US). Retrieved from www.proquest.com/docview/1715675561/19BF7190F8004CA5PQ/4

Turnnidge, Jennifer, and Jean Côté. 2017. "Transformational coaching workshop: applying a person-centred approach to coach development programs." *International Sport Coaching Journal* 4, no. 3: 314–25. Doi:10.1123/iscj.2017–0046.

Waal, André de. 2018. "Success factors of high performance organization transformations." *Measuring Business Excellence* 22, no. 4: 375–90. Doi:10.1108/MBE-08–2018–0055.

Yoon, Hyung Joon, Yu_Ling Chang, Farhan Sadique, and Issa Al Balushi. 2021. "Mechanisms for hopeful employee career development in COVID-19: a hope-action theory perspective." *Advances in Developing Human Resources* 23, no. 3: 203–21. https://doi.org/10.1177/15234223211017848.

Yukl, Gary. 1999. "An evaluation of conceptual weaknesses in transformational and charismatic leadership theories." *The Leadership Quarterly* 10, no. 2: 285–305. Doi:10.1016/S1048–9843(99)00013–2.

## Videos

Aguilar, Elena. 2020. "An introduction to transformational coaching." *Bright Morning.* Retrieved from https://brightmorningteam.com/2020/04/introduction-to-transformational-coaching/

Anderson, Dean. 2019. "Building a transformation strategy that achieves your vision." Retrieved from https://blog.beingfirst.com/building-a-transformation-strategy-that-achieves-your-company-vision

Animas Centre for Coaching, dir. 2018. What is transformational coaching—introduction to transformational coaching. Retrieved from Retrieved from www.youtube.com/watch?v=RL48e9921dw

Animas Centre for Coaching, dir. 2022. What is transformative coaching? Retrieved from www.youtube.com/watch?v=g2dGPzU0PDM

Brundage, Jeff. n.d. What is organizational transformation and when is it necessary. Retrieved from www.orginc.com/blog/what-is-organizational-transformation-and-when-is-it-necessary

Christine Jarvis, dir. 2015. Introducing transformative learning theory. Retrieved from www.youtube.com/watch?v=liU1zsi3X8w

Clarksville Vibe, dir. 2022. Ep 12: Transactional vs. Transformative coaching with Matt Sundstrom. Retrieved from www.youtube.com/watch?v=F8RyFarHGps

Coach Ajit x Evercoach, dir. 2019. *How To Deliver Transformational Coaching Sessions*. Retrieved from www.youtube.com/watch?v=q7VPSj8wQvM

Coach Ajit x Evercoach, dir. 2019. Michael Neill | how to become a transformational coach. Retrieved from www.youtube.com/watch?v=KZLQvRTnjs0

Coach Ajit x Evercoach, dir. 2021. 5 Proven principles to grow your life coaching business. Retrieved from www.youtube.com/watch?v=CwFI22FM_T0

Coach Ajit, dir. 2021. Life coaching model for transformation (FOR NEW COACHES). Retrieved from www.youtube.com/watch?v=7z836yB3nt8

Coach Transformation Academy, dir. 2021. Building foundation on trust & safety in a coaching conversation. www.youtube.com/watch?v=O8icM0VThKs

Coachology, dir. 2022. Transformational feedback—before the feedback with INSPIRE principles. Retrieved from www.youtube.com/watch?v=_xCyYg7MUL0

Coachseansmith, dir. 2013. The 6 STEP coaching framework For MAXIMUM client RESULT. *Coach Sean Smith.* Retrieved from www.youtube.com/watch?v=MGtU-Q5C3no

Coachseansmith, dir. 2018. *5* Steps to creating high impact transformational coaching packages. *Coach Sean Smith.* Retrieved from www.youtube.com/watch?v=QIqvil-K3LY

Coachseansmith, dir. 2020. Principles of coaching with confidence | life coaching certification module 1. *Coach Sean Smith.* Retrieved from www.youtube.com/watch?v=LakB3jkMnAc

Coachseansmith, dir. 2021. "11 DEEP coaching techniques to transform clients today!" | *Coach Sean Smith.* Retrieved from www.youtube.com/watch?v=XvctW_Cq4Es

Communication Coach Alex Lyon. 2020. Transformational leadership theory. Retrieved from www.youtube.com/watch?v=yOkqygQA6jY

Crane, Thomas G. 2012. *The Heart of Coaching: Using Transformational Coaching to Create a High-Performance Coaching Culture.* Edited by Lerissa Nancy Patrick (2nd ed.). San Diego, CA: F T A Press.

David Burkus, dir. 2020. Transformational leadership vs Transactional leadership. Retrieved from www.youtube.com/watch?v=l8s8lHVMhO8
Gavin Wedell. 2012. What is transformational leadership? Retrieved from www.youtube.com/watch?v=60O2OH7mHys
Gurthrie, Marisa. 2021. What does it mean to be resilient, and how can we build resilience in ourselves and in our businesses? *Marisa Guthrie Coaching*. Retrieved from https://marisaguthriecoaching.co.uk/blog/2018/11/14/what-does-it-mean-to-be-resilient-and-how-can-we-build-resilience-in-ourselves-and-in-our-businesses
Harvard Business Review, dir. 2022. A plan is not a strategy. Retrieved from www.youtube.com/watch?v=iuYlGRnC7J8
Heart Management, dir. 2020. Why transformational change. Retrieved from www.youtube.com/watch?v=FDMtwaaUslw
Hofstra University, dir. 2017. Self-assessment and coaching as a feedback model. Retrieved from www.youtube.com/watch?v=dHNvqr_7et0
How Communication Works, dir. 2018. Listen better: 5 essential phrases for active/reflective listening. Retrieved from www.youtube.com/watch?v=tgLfz3dh5UE
InstHealthSciences. n.d. What is transformational coaching? *YouTube*. Retrieved from www.youtube.com/watch?v=7zuajmcEqs4&t=3s
Jeff Dalto, dir. 2020. An intro to HPI/HPT with Guy Wallace. Retrieved from www.youtube.com/watch?v=WuV0gGZitzI
Krista Guerrero, dir. 2013. Transformational learning theory. Retrieved from www.youtube.com/watch?v=BpUukqlUAqE
LHH, dir. 2021. The 2021 coaching playbook: how to accelerate transformation through the power of coaching. Retrieved from www.youtube.com/watch?v=SHpggJQvPAI
Mary Grenchus, dir. 2022. The Grenchus foundation - transformational coaching! transformation time!! Retrieved from www.youtube.com/watch?v=0qrCHmMlANE
McKinsey & Company, dir. 2019. McKinsey transformation: tell a compelling change story to inspire your organization. Retrieved from www.youtube.com/watch?v=4FlP1-5WMyo
Michael Neill, dir. 2018. What is transformative coaching? Retrieved from www.youtube.com/watch?v=7PNfeKxHIi8
Michael Quinn Patton, dir. 2022. A theory of transformation. Retrieved from www.youtube.com/watch?v=76dsKpQn8LA
MindToolsVideos, dir. 2015. Improve your listening skills with active listening. Retrieved from www.youtube.com/watch?v=t2z9mdX1j4A
Nancee Bloom, dir. 2015. Conversation at home with Jack Mezirow. Retrieved from www.youtube.com/watch?v=iEuctPHsre4
Primeast US, dir. 2017. Transformational change management. Retrieved from www.youtube.com/watch?v=0gOcdpIe7N4
Pros, dir. n.d. The keys to driving transformational change. Retrieved from https://pros.com/learn/outperform-2020/the-keys-to-driving-transformational-change
RedleafPress, dir. 2019. Transformational coaching: promoting 'sticky' change. Retrieved from www.youtube.com/watch?v=PlsDyEngvZc
Robert White, dir. 2012. 8 elements of personal effectiveness. Retrieved from www.youtube.com/watch?v=3Fj4e1rE1NI
Sampson Coaching & Consulting, dir. 2020. The transformative self-coaching model. Retrieved from www.youtube.com/watch?v=D9x_pZyDOmg
Samuel Callan, dir. 2018. Jean Cote transformational coaching january. Retrieved from www.youtube.com/watch?v=i5cGo-xMSdo
Simple Academics. 2018. How to be a transformational leader (ANIMATED) | what is transformational leadership? Retrieved from www.youtube.com/watch?v=9u8_ctKso0Y
Skillsoft YouTube, dir. 2022. The road to transformative leadership: build, coach, reinforce. Retrieved from www.youtube.com/watch?v=64Ukbh8qcaI

Solutions For Resilience with Patricia Morgan, dir. 2021. Assertively think, speak, and act: assertiveness skills. Retrieved from www.youtube.com/watch?v=8cRtyoVwYeU

Sportsengine. 2018. "WEBINAR—what is transformational coaching?" *Ontario Soccer*. Retrieved from www.ontariosoccer.net/news_article/show/881355-webinar-what-is-transformational-coaching-

StaubLeadership, dir. 2012. Transaction vs transformation. Retrieved from www.youtube.com/watch?v=SqOjtO-g6QI

Talentrics, dir. 2013. Human performance improvement. Retrieved from www.youtube.com/watch?v=-FiLXoKGiIc

Teachers College, Columbia University, dir. 2015. Mezirow's legacy: The evolution and impact of transformative learning. Retrieved from www.youtube.com/watch?v=409Gu9M2Jsk

TEDx Talks, dir. 2013. Why do we ask questions? Michael "Vsauce" Stevens at TEDxVienna. Retrieved from www.youtube.com/watch?v=u9hauSrihYQ

Threefold consulting, dir. 2015. Otto Scharmer on the four levels of listening. Retrieved from www.youtube.com/watch?v=eLfXpRkVZaI

Transcend International, dir. 2020. Intro to transformational coaching. Retrieved from www.youtube.com/watch?v=_i5zJ7VzcVY

UCLA Ed & IS, dir. 2020. Critical conversations | transformative coaching and leadership. Retrieved from www.youtube.com/watch?v=iCfAvTDr9tk

UQ Institute for Teaching and Learning Innovation, dir. 2022. The top 10 myths of learning. Retrieved from www.youtube.com/watch?v=rj8uYPLUXIw

## Blog Posts

Abzhanov, Arkhat. 2018. "D'Arcy thompson's theory of transformation." *Serious Science*. Retrieved from https://serious-science.org/darcy-thompsons-theory-of-transformation-9290

Alsher, Paula. n.d. "Overcoming the challenges of transformational change." Retrieved from www.imaworldwide.com/blog/overcoming-the-challenges-of-transformational-change

Anderson, Linda A. 2020. "What works and what fails in transformation and organizational change." Retrieved from https://blog.beingfirst.com/what-works-and-what-fails-in-organizational-change-and-transformation

Arnott, Sherwin. 2018. "Making the leap: From independent contributor to people leader." *The Emotional Intelligence Training Company*. Retrieved from www.eitrainingcompany.com/2018/03/making-the-leap-from-independent-contributor-to-people-leader/

Baker, Dr Felicity. 2020. "How to use assertiveness to build resilience." *Ultimate Resilience* (blog). Retrieved from https://ultimateresilience.co.uk/assertiveness-skills-and-resilience

Booth, Brenda Ellington. 2020. "Emotional intelligence is key to strong leadership. Here's how to Sharpen yours." *Kellogg Insight*. Retrieved from https://insight.kellogg.northwestern.edu/article/emotional-intelligence-strong-leadership

Bosler, Shana. n.d. "Build the foundation for a transformative coaching culture—emergenetics." Retrieved from https://emergenetics.com/blog/build-the-foundation-for-a-transformative-coaching-culture/

Burkus, David. 2010. "Transformational leadership theory." *David Burkus* (blog). Retrieved from https://davidburkus.com/2010/03/transformational-leadership-theory/

Burns, James M. 2022. "Transformational leadership: characteristics, benefits, and uses." *Psych Central*. Retrieved from https://psychcentral.com/health/transformational-leadership

Chad, P. 2019. "Transformational coaching and effective feedback." Retrieved from www.linkedin.com/pulse/transformational-coaching-effective-feedback-chad-pfeifer/

Cherry, Kendra. 2022. "How do transformational leaders inspire and motivate followers?" *Verywell Mind* (blog). Retrieved from www.verywellmind.com/what-is-transformational-leadership-2795313

Creator. 2021. "What is transformational coaching and what can it help with?" *Greator*. Retrieved from https://greator.com/en/transformational-coaching/

Daly, Catherine. 2021. "How to manage transformational change in your organization." *Thought Exchange.* Retrieved from https://thoughtexchange.com/blog/how-to-manage-transformational-change-in-your-organization/

Engaged Sociology Editor. 2021. "Leadership coaching as transformative learning: how their core facets, processes, & paradigms align." *Engaged Sociology* (blog). Retrieved from https://engagedsociology.com/2021/01/04/leadership-coaching/

Guerrero, Moriarty. 2021. "Transformational coaching." *2Revolutions.* Retrieved from www.2revolutions.net/stories/transformational-coaching

Herman, Elyssa. 2015. "Coaching model: Transform." Retrieved from https://coachcampus.com/coach-portfolios/coaching-models/elyssa-herman-transform/

Ibarra, Herminia, and Anne Scoular. 2019. "The leader as coach." *Harvard Business Review.* Retrieved from https://hbr.org/2019/11/the-leader-as-coach

Juneja, Prachi. n.d. "Transformational change and change management." *Management Study Guide* (blog). Retrieved from www.managementstudyguide.com/transformational-change-and-change-management.htm

Kayadelen, Deniz. 2021. "Transactional vs transformational coaching." *Out of Comfort Zone.* Retrieved from www.outofourcomfortzone.com/post/transactional-vs-transformational-coaching

Kincaid, David. 2020. "Research paper: Transformational coaching for organizational success." Retrieved from https://coachcampus.com/coach-portfolios/research-papers/david-kincaid-transformational-coaching-for-organizational-success/

Krista Guerrero, dir. 2013. Transformational learning theory. Retrieved from www.youtube.com/watch?v=BpUukqlUAqE

Lauren. 2021. "My transformational coaching method | clarity, mindset & action." *Lauren on Location* (blog). Retrieved from https://laurenonlocation.com/transformational-coaching/

Lindley, Brooke. 2020. "Personal Transformation." *School of Positive Transformation* (blog). Retrieved from https://schoolofpositivetransformation.com/personal-transformation-through-positive-psychology/

Lisa, P. 2021. "What is transformational coaching and how can it help you?" Retrieved from https://lisaproshina.com/transformational-coaching-explained/

Lynch, Matthew. 2016. "Influence of Transformational Leadership on Behavior and Performance." *The Edvocate* (blog). Retrieved from www.theedadvocate.org/influence-of-transformational-leadership-on-behavior-and-performance/

McNab, Ali. 2019. "Reflections of a Transformational Coach". Retrieved from www.linkedin.com/pulse/reflections-transformational-coach-ali-mcnab/?articleId=6564510892942204928

Medcalf, Richard. 2017. "60 Personal Effectiveness Tips from World-Class Experts." *Xquadrant* (blog). Retrieved from https://xquadrant.com/personal-effectiveness-tips/

Michigan State University. 2021. "The 4 'I's' of Transformational Leadership." *Michigan State University* (blog). Retrieved from www.michiganstateuniversityonline.com/resources/leadership/4-is-of-transformational-leadership/

Mirzoyan, Vera. 2021. "What Is Transformative Learning?". Retrieved from https://uteach.io/articles/what-is-transformative-learning

Neill, Michael. 2016. "Transformation, Coaching, and the Three Principles." Michael Neill. Retrieved from www.michaelneill.org/cfts1042/

Oertli, Jennifer. 2022. "That Game-Time Feeling: High-Performing Teams in a Digital-First World." Retrieved from https://centricconsulting.com/blog/that-game-time-feeling-high-performing-teams-in-a-digital-first-world/

Open to Export. 2022. "7 Highly Effective Tips To Be A Transformational Leader." *Open to Export* (blog). 2022. Retrieved from https://opentoexport.com/article/7-highly-effective-tips-to-be-a-transformational-leader/

Powell, Gabriel. n.d. "Coaching from the Ground of Being." Coaches Rising. Retrieved from www.coaches-rising.com/podcast/coaching-from-the-ground-of-being/

Rankin, Ed. n.d. "Executive Coaching as a Transformative Learning Process." Retrieved from www.linkedin.com/pulse/executive-coaching-transformative-learning-process-rankin-sphr-pcc/

Rimbark, Marianne. 2022. "Transforming an Organization through High-Performing Teams." Retrieved from https://blog.iil.com/transforming-through-high-performing-teams/

Team Dream. 2020. "How Critical Self-Reflection Makes You A Better Coach." International Coach. Retrieved from www.internationalcoachguild.com/post/how-critical-self-reflection-makes-you-a-better-coach

Team Transformation. 2020. "The Art of Active Listening: How Teams Can Turn Chaos to Dialogue." *Team Transformation* (blog). Retrieved from https://teamtransformation.com/the-art-of-active-listening-how-teams-can-turn-chaos-to-dialogue/

Team Transformation. n.d. "Team Transformation Blog." *Team Transformation* (blog). Retrieved from https://teamtransformation.com/blog/

The Techeducator. 2018. "Successful Coaching Part 4: The Art of Listening—The Techducator." Retrieved from https://munshing.com/leadership/successful-coaching-part-4-the-art-of-listening

Transformation Coach—A Complete Guide. 2022. Retrieved from www.coaching-online.org/transformation-coach/

Upcoach. 2021. "Transformational Coaching: Complete Guide." Retrieved from https://upcoach.com/group-coaching/transformational-coaching-complete-guide/

Wilson, Victoria. 2020. "What Is Transformational Coaching?" *Exceptional Futures* (blog). Retrieved from www.exceptionalfutures.com/what-is-transformational-coaching/

Wonfor, Damion. 2022. "At the Heart of the Transformational Coach." *Catalyst 14*. Retrieved from www.catalyst14.co.uk/blog/at-the-heart-of-the-transformational-coach

Zbela, Stania. 2012. "Coaching Model: The Integral Coaching Process." Retrieved from https://coachcampus.com/coach-portfolios/coaching-models/stania-zbela-the-integral-coaching-process/

## Webpages

Active Listening: Hear What People Are Really Saying. n.d. www.mindtools.com/CommSkll/ActiveListening.htm

Agilemania. 2018. "Agile Transformation and High-Performance Teams." *Agilemania* (blog). Retrieved from https://agilemania.com/agile-transformation-and-high-performance-teams/

Aguilar, Elena. 2014. "Active Listening: The Key To Transforming Your Coaching." *Education Week*, April 28, 2014, sec. Education. Retrieved from www.edweek.org/education/opinion-active-listening-the-key-to-transforming-your-coaching/2014/04

Alsher, Paula. n.d. "Overcoming the Challenges of Transformational Change." Retrieved from www.imaworldwide.com/blog/overcoming-the-challenges-of-transformational-change

Amatullah, Ayisha. 2021. "Transformational Coaching Techniques You Need to Know." *Universal Coach Institute* (blog). Retrieved from www.universalcoachinstitute.com/transformation-coaching-techniques-you-need-to-know/

Avendaño, Daniela. 2022. "Transformational Coaching." *Toolshero*. Retrieved from www.toolshero.com/management/transformational-coaching/

Bickford, LesLee. 2021. "Evaluation, Feedback and Coaching: What You Need to Know." Bright Morning. May 3, 2021. Retrieved from https://brightmorningteam.com/2021/05/evaluation-feedback-and-coaching-what-you-need-to-know/

Celestine, Nicole. 2021. "Your Mindset Coaching Guide: Best Questions, Courses, & Tools." *PositivePsychology*. Retrieved from https://positivepsychology.com/mindset-coaching/

Chepur, Venugopal. 2021. "Preparing Talent for the Future of Work: A Transformational Approach." *Training Industry* (blog). Retrieved from https://trainingindustry.com/articles/strategy-alignment-and-planning/preparing-talent-for-the-future-of-work-a-transformational-approach/

Chron, Contributor. 2020. "Examples of Transformational Change." *Small Business—Chron.Com*. Retrieved from https://smallbusiness.chron.com/examples-transformational-change-18261.html

Coach Training World. n.d. "Whole Person Coaching." Coach Training World. Retrieved from https://coachtrainingworld.com/about-whole-person-coaching/

Conversational Leadership. n.d. "Dialogic Organization Development." Conversational Leadership. Retrieved from https://conversational-leadership.net/dialogic-organization-development/

Dadourian, Karmen. n.d. "Transformational Coaching Practicum." A Life Altering Event. Retrieved from www.artoftransformationalcoaching.com/tcp

Desimone, Rob. 2019. "What High-Performance Workplaces Do Differently." *Gallup.Com*. Retrieved from www.gallup.com/workplace/269405/high-performance-workplaces-differently.aspx

Friedman, Ron. 2021. "5 Things High-Performing Teams Do Differently." *Harvard Business Review*. Retrieved from https://hbr.org/2021/10/5-things-high-performing-teams-do-differently

Garvey, Joseph. n.d. "Positive Psychology for Coaching." Retrieved from www.peoplegoal.com/blog/positive-psychology-for-coaching

Gass, Robert. 2015. "Transformational Coaching Toolkit. Retrieved from http://stproject.org/wp-content/uploads/2016/05/transformational-coaching-toolkit.pdf

Gass, Robert. 2018. "A Transformational Approach," no. 18 no. 4. Retrieved from https://cdn.ymaws.com/www.associationforcoaching.com/resource/resmgr/Gass_and_Stockdale_-_How_tra.pdf

George, Mark O. 2010. "To Achieve High Performance, Think Transformation, Not Just Improvement." IndustryWeek. Retrieved from www.industryweek.com/leadership/companies-executives/article/21949973/to-achieve-high-performance-think-transformation-not-just-improvement

Goleman, Daniel. 2022. "Emotional Intelligence—Issues in Paradigm Building." 2022. Retrieved from www.eiconsortium.org/reprints/ei_issues_in_paradigm_building.html

Goncalves, Luis. 2020. "High Performing Teams: 14 Absolutely Mandatory Characteristics." *ADAPT METHODOLOGY®* (blog). Retrieved from https://adaptmethodology.com/high-performing-teams-characteristics/

Good Works Consulting. n.d. "Coaching." Good Works Consulting. Retrieved from www.goodworks.consulting/coaching

High Performance and the Transformation of Work? The Implications of Alternative Work Practices for the Experience and Outcomes of Work. Retrieved from https://journals-sagepub-com.ezaccess.libraries.psu.edu/doi/abs/10.1177/001979390105400402

Hine, Constant, and Robin Levy. 2019. "Transformational Coaching." *People Management*, Retrieved from https://dcf.wisconsin.gov/files/ccic/pdf/articles/transformational-coaching.pdf

Hoff, Kathryn. 2022. "Evolving Talent Management Tactics: Coaching for Leader Development and Organizational Change Agility." Retrieved from https://coachcampus.com/coach-portfolios/research-papers/talent-management/

Holloway, Julia. 2022. "Coaching Workshops-Transformational Coaching-Leadership Coaching." *Deep Transformation*. Retrieved from www.leadership-pathways.com/workshops

Kofman, Fred. 2016. "Transformational Learning: A Blueprint for Organizational Change." *The Systems Thinker*. Retrieved from https://thesystemsthinker.com/transformational-learning-a-blueprint-for-organizational-change/

Kotter. 2011. "Change Management vs. Change Leadership—What's the Difference?" Forbes. Retrieved from www.forbes.com/sites/johnkotter/2011/07/12/change-management-vs-change-leadership-whats-the-difference/

Lawton, George, and Mary K. Pratt. 2022. "What Is Change Management?—Definition from TechTarget. Com." *SearchCIO*. Retrieved from www.techtarget.com/searchcio/definition/change-management

Life Coach Directory. n.d. "Coaching Styles | Life Coaching Approaches. Retrieved from www.lifecoach-directory.org.uk/content/coaching-styles.html

Lindley, Brooke. 2020. "Personal Transformation." *School of Positive Transformation*. Retrieved from https://schoolofpositivetransformation.com/personal-transformation-through-positive-psychology/

Llopis, Glenn. 2018. "4 Things High-Performance Teams Must Have To Transform Their Organizations." *Forbes*. Retrieved from www.forbes.com/sites/glennllopis/2018/05/22/4-things-high-performance-teams-must-have-to-transform-their-organizations/

Martinez, Joynicole. n.d. "Council Post: To Become A Resilient Leader, Communicate Assertively." *Forbes*. Retrieved from www.forbes.com/sites/forbescoachescouncil/2019/11/06/to-become-a-resilient-leader-communicate-assertively/

McKinsey and Company. 2021. "The Science behind Successful Organizational Transformations | McKinsey." Retrieved from www.mckinsey.com/business-functions/people-and-organizational-performance/our-insights/successful-transformations

Miller, Lawrence M. 2013. "Transformational Change vs. Continuous Improvement." *IndustryWeek*. Retrieved from www.industryweek.com/leadership/change-management/article/21960254/transformational-change-vs-continuous-improvement

MITRE Corporation. 2013. "Transformation Planning and Organizational Change,". Retrieved from www.mitre.org/publications/systems-engineering-guide/enterprise-engineering/transformation-planning-and-organizational-change

NCDA. 2014. "The Heart of Coaching: Using Transformational Coaching to Create a High-Performance Coaching Culture." Retrieved from www.ncda.org/aws/NCDA/pt/sd/news_article/93488/_PARENT/CC_layout_details/false

Newman, James D. 2015. "What Is the Difference between HPE, HPT and HPI and Does It Matter?" *Human Performance Tools* (blog). Retrieved from www.humanperformancetools.com/difference-hpe-hpt-hpi-matter/

Nick. 2019. "What Is Transformational Coaching?". Retrieved from www.animascoaching.com/our-knowledge/faqs/what-is-transformational-coaching/

Profession. 2018. "Giving Feedback That Changes Behavior." December 2, 2018. Retrieved from https://rryshke.org/2018/12/02/giving-feedback-that-changes-behavior/

Quint. n.d. "Transforming into a High Performance Organization." Quint Wellington Redwood. Retrieved from www.quintgroup.com/en-us/global-challenges/transforming-into-a-high-performing-organization/

Red Hat. 2019. "Understanding Organizational Transformation." Retrieved from www.redhat.com/en/topics/organizational-transformation

Reilly, Al Kent, David Lancefield, and Kevin. n.d. "The Four Building Blocks of Transformation." Strategy+business. Retrieved from www.strategy-business.com/article/The-Four-Building-Blocks-of-Transformation

Scheele, Paul R. 2013. "Processes of Transformational Change and Transformative Learning | Scheele Learning Systems." Retrieved from https://scheelelearning.com/processes-of-transformational-change-and-transformative-learning/

Simplilearn. 2022. "The Secret Recipe to Building High Performing Teams in 2022." *Simplilearn.Com*. Retrieved from www.simplilearn.com/building-high-performing-teams-article

SMNash. n.d. "'Transformative Coach' &'3 Principles Practitioner' Explanation." The 3 Principles Understanding by Steve M Nash. Retrieved from www.smnash.com/transformative-coach/

Sutton, Jeremy. 2020. "12 Effective Coaching Models to Help Your Clients Grow." PositivePsychology.Com. Retrieved from https://positivepsychology.com/coaching-models/

Thrive with Strength. 2021. "High Performing Teams: How to Transform Your Team and Win!". Retrieved from www.thrivewithstrengths.com/blog/leadership-team-development

Transformational Change Leadership. 2021. "Transformational Change Leadership: Stories of Building a Just Future." *The Commons*. Retrieved from https://commonslibrary.org/transformational-change-leadership-stories-of-building-a-just-future/

Transformative Learning Theory by Jack Mezirow with Examples. n.d. *Valamis*. Retrieved from www.valamis.com/hub/transformative-learning

Vulpen, Erik van. 2019. "What Is Organizational Development? A Complete Guide." *AIHR*. Retrieved from www.aihr.com/blog/organizational-development/

## Webinars

Admin, W. I. 2020. "The Heart of Coaching." Lead Change. Retrieved from https://leadchangegroup.com/the-heart-of-coaching/

Arnott, Sherwin. 2017. "Emotional Intelligence and Leader Performance: Authenticity, Webinar Recap." The Emotional Intelligence Training Company. Retrieved from www.eitrainingcompany.com/2017/07/emotional-intelligence-and-leader-performance-authenticity-webinar-recap/

Bowman, Natasha, dir. n.d. *Cultivating Cultures of Mental Wellness through Coaching.* Retrieved from https://instituteofcoaching.org/conferences-events/webinars

Brooks, Mimi, dir. 2021. *Building the Sustainable, High Performance Organizations of Tomorrow.* Retrieved from www.lds.com/pov/building-sustainable-high-performance-organizations-tomorrow/

Catalyst-14, dir. 2021. *The Transformational Coach Framework—Free Coaching Webinar from Catalyst 14.* Retrieved from www.youtube.com/watch?v=CL3rW_R3e8k

Coach Ajit x Evercoach, dir. 2019. *How To Use Positive Psychology In Coaching | Niyc Pidgeon.* Retrieved from www.youtube.com/watch?v=JKPvpzPMT3E

Coach Ajit x Evercoach, dir. 2021. *How To Become A Successful Mindset Coach In 3 Simple Steps.* Retrieved from www.youtube.com/watch?v=4zfVQ4QF6dk

Coach Transformation Academy, dir. 2021. *Deeper Coaching Techniques: Shifting Focus on Person in Coaching Is the Key.* Retrieved from www.youtube.com/watch?v=Ic-w-AZCjJQ

Coach Transformation Academy, dir. 2021. *Essentials of Transformational Coaching by Dr. Haris Syed at Coach Transformational Tuesdays Webinar.* Retrieved from www.youtube.com/watch?v=TrrYDuXH308

Coach Transformation Academy, dir. n.d. *Coach Transformational Tuesdays.* Retrieved from www.facebook.com/watch/live/?ref=watch_permalink&v=2435155006779793

Coacharya, dir. 2019. *Transformational Presence: Building Bridges of Connection and Co-Creation | Coacharya.* Retrieved from www.youtube.com/watch?v=Y4T_tcta4us

*Core Energy Leadership.* n.d. Retrieved from https://coaching4good.com/resiliency-webinars-series/core-energy-leadership-video/

David Cory, dir. 2017. *Emotional Intelligence and Leader Performance: Coaching.* Retrieved from www.youtube.com/watch?v=24OXTf1OEwg

Dr. William Brendel, dir. 2016. *Transformative Learning Theory (Part 4).* Retrieved from www.youtube.com/watch?v=EYWb_GhHMVw

Eightfold, dir. 2020. *The Power of Skills: Empowering Talent Transformation in a Time of Disruption.* Retrieved from www.youtube.com/watch?v=R3oEwYToLPM

Eightfold. 2020 "Plan for the Next 10 Years: How to Transform Your Workforce for High Performance." Eightfold. Retrieved from https://eightfold.ai/resources/how-to-transform-your-workforce-for-high-performance/

Insight Coaching Community, dir. 2019. *Incredible Life Coaching Webinar On Creating You—Life Coach Training On How To Become A Life Coach.* Retrieved from www.youtube.com/watch?v=5QUmiWI5vmw

Learning In Action, dir. 2020. *Team Coaching: Applying Individual Coaching Techniques to Team Coaching | Heal The Divide Podinar.* Retrieved from www.youtube.com/watch?v=78YV-M-PsQk

MorganMcKinley, dir. 2016. *Webinar. 7 Simple Life Coaching Strategies to Banish Overwhelmedness and Be Happy | #SuccessSeries.* Retrieved from www.youtube.com/watch?v=waPZcHbbTpY

Performance Consultants, dir. 2021. *Webinar: Coaching at Its Most Transformational.* Retrieved from https://vimeo.com/647781722

Santander Global T&O, dir. 2021. *Architecting for Success: Building a High Performance DevOps Transformation Team: Sukhbir Jasuja GB.* Retrieved from www.youtube.com/watch?v=C5uj1S0TZT0

uExcelerate. n.d. "Reflective Practice of 'Coaching Super." Retrieved from https://uexcelerate.com/reflective-practice-of-coaching-super-vision/

World of Work Project. 2019. "The CLEAR Coaching Model: A Simple Summary." *The World of Work Project* (blog). Retrieved from https://worldofwork.io/2019/06/the-clear-coaching-model/

Zhou, Luisa. 2021. "How to Become a 6-Figure Mindset Coach in 2022." *Luisa Zhou.* Retrieved from www.luisazhou.com/blog/become-a-mindset-coach/

# Index

Note: Page numbers in *italics* indicate a figure, and page numbers in **bold** indicate a table on the corresponding page.

## G



## H



## I

## K



## L

## P

## Q



## R

## T

Printed in the United States
by Baker & Taylor Publisher Services